Essays and Correspondence, Chiefly On Scriptural Subjects, Collected and Prepared for the Press by W. Burton. [With] General Index

John Walker

ESSAYS

AND

CORRESPONDENCE.

ESSAYS

AND

CORRESPONDENCE,

CHIEFLY ON SCRIPTURAL SUBJECTS.

BY THE LATE

JOHN WALKER,

SOME TIME A FELLOW OF TRINITY COLLEGE, DUBLIN, AND A CLERGYMAN IN THE ESTABLISHMENT.

COLLECTED AND PREPARED FOR THE PRESS,

BY WILLIAM BURTON.

VOL. II.

LONDON:

SOLD BY LONGMAN, ORME, BROWN, GREEN, & LONGMAN'S;

E. MADDEN, & R. M. TIMS, DUBLIN; A. & C. BLACK, EDINBURGH.

1838.

TO

ROBERT LUCAS CHANCE, Esq.

THIS SECOND VOLUME

OF

MR. WALKER'S ESSAYS AND CORRESPONDENCE

IS INSCRIBED,

IN MEMORIAL OF HIS STEADFAST CHRISTIAN ATTACHMENT
TO THE AUTHOR,

AND AS

A TESTIMONY OF SINCERE ESTEEM,

FROM

HIS FRIEND AND BROTHER,

WILLIAM BURTON.

CONTENTS OF VOL. II.

Pages

The Petition of certain Christian People resident in London to the Honourable the House of Commons, praying for Relief in the Matter of Oaths. With Notes by one of the Petitioners .... 1—22

Statement of the Interruption of Christian Connexion between the Church in London and the Church in Dublin.................. 23—30

Some Remarks on H. M.'s Printed Letter .... 30—43

Some Observations on Mr. H.'s Pamphlet .... 43—46

Notes on the three preceding articles .... 46—53

Remarks corrective of occasional Mistranslations in the English Version of the Sacred Scriptures .... 54—122

I. On James v. 14—15.................... 56
II. — 1 Timothy v. 12.................... 60
III. — Mat. xvii. 24—27 62
IV. — Luke xvi. 9. 64
V. — John i. 9.......................... 66
VI. — Acts ii. 42........................ 68
VII. — Rom. viii. 17...................... 69
VIII. — Jerem. xxx. 21. 71
IX. — John v. 17, 18. 74
X. — —— i. 51. 77
XI. Instances of Ellipses inaccurately supplied,
on Luke xviii. 1. 80
— Heb. ii. 9. 81
— —— viii. 3. 84
— —— vii. 19. .... ib.
— 1 Cor. iii. 9. 85
— 2 Cor. vi. part of verse 1. 86
— Acts xix. 2............................ 87
XII. Instances of inaccuracy in the omission or insertion of the definite article,
on 1 Timothy ii. 8....................... 88
— 1 Tim. vi. 10......................... 89
— 2 Tim. iv. 7. .... ib.
— Acts xxi. 4.... 90
— Heb. iii. 13. .... ib.
— Rom. xv. 12, 13........................ 91
XIII. — Luke xviii. 20, 21................. 92
XIV. Instances of inaccuracy in the rendering of tenses—
on Luke i. 59.
— John xi. 11. } 96
— Heb. x. 37. 97
XV. — Ps. cxxx. 3, 4....................... 98
XVI. — 1 Thess. ii. 8. 103
XVII. — 1 Pet. ii. 7. 104
XVIII. — —— iii. 21. 106

Pages.
XIX. On Acts xvi. 25. 108
XX. — —— xvii. 22, 23. 110
XXI. — 1 Cor. vii. 21. .... ib.
XXII. — Heb. xiii. 10. 115
— 1 Cor. vii. 10, 11. 118
XXIII. — Ps. lx. 5. and cviii. 6. 119
— Rom. iv. 25. 121

Remarks expository of Texts of Scripture .... 123—142
I. on John xiv. 8. .... 123—128
II. — Pro. xiv. 9. .... 128—130
III. — Mat. vi. 9. .... 130—132
IV. — Rom. xii. 9. .... 132—134
V. — 1 Tim. ii. 9, 10. 1 Pet. iii. 3, 4. .. 134—135
VI. — Rom. iii. 3, 4. Eph. iv. 3. ...... ib.
VII. — Mat. xxv. 31—46. .... 136—137
VIII. — Mich. vi. 8. .... 138—139
IX. — Rom. iii. 25. .... 139—140
X. — 1 Sam. i. 17, 18. .... ib.
XI. — Gospel; or Glad Tidings. .... 141—142

Brief Animadversions on a Pamphlet by Doctor Richard Whately, entitled "Thoughts on the Sabbath, in reference to the Christian Festival of the Lord's Day". .... 143—151

Collection of Letters on Scriptural Subjects .... 152—523
I. To Alexander Knox, Esq. 152
II. — the Editor of the Evangelical Magazine 153
III. — the Rev. R. H. 157
IV. — Alexander Knox, Esq. 160
V. — Mr. P. N——. 161
VI. — the Rev. Mr. M—— 163
VII. — Mrs. N——. 165
VIII. — the Rev. H. M—— 166
IX. — Mr. W. T——. 171
X. — B. M—— 175
XI. — Mrs. S——. 178
XII. — Mr. O'B——. 181
XIII. From the Church in D—— to the Church in C—— 184
XIV. To the Editor of the Christian Advocate .. 186
XV. A detached Piece on the Office of Elders.. 189
XVI. To Miss M—— 190
XVII. — Mrs. S——. 191
XVIII. From the Church in D—— to the Church in R—— 193
XIX. To Miss Walker 195
XX. — the Same 197
XXI. — the Same 198
XXII. From the Church in D—— to M—— 199
XXIII. —————— to the same .. 202
XXIV. To ———— 203
XXV. — M. B—— 206
XXVI. — J. F. G——, Esq. 207
XXVII. — R. M'N—— 208
XXVIII. — B. B——. 210
XXIX. — B. M—— 211
XXX. — G. T——, Esq. 212
XXXI. — J. G. S——. 219
XXXII. — J. P—— 220
XXXIII. — J. G. S——. 223
XXXIV. — ———— 224
XXXV. — J. R. K——, Esq. 227

		Pages.
XXXVI.	To the Same	231
XXXVII.	— G. M——	234
XXXVIII.	— R. L. C——, Esq.	238
XXXIX.	— J. H——, Esq.	241
XL.	— R. L. C——, Esq.	244
XLI.	— the Same	246
XLII.	— M. B——, Esq.	249
XLIII.	— R. L. C——, Esq.	251
XLIV.	— the Same	253
XLV.	— the Same	254
XLVI.	— the Same	258
XLVII.	— the Same	260
XLVIII.	— the Same	262
XLIX.	— the Same	264
L.	— the Same	266
LI.	— J. B——	267
LII.	— the Same	272
LIII.	— the Same	273
LIV.	— J. A—— and T. D——	275
LV.	— J. L——	276
LVI.	— the People called Bereans, who addressed a Letter to the Church of Christ assembling in Stafford-street, Dublin	278
LVII.	— J. L——	282
LVIII.	— the Same	285
LIX.	— the Same	287
LX.	— the Same	288
LXI.	— Mr. J. C——	289
LXII.	— J. H——, Esq.	292
LXIII.	— the Church in C——	295
LXIV.	— J. L——	296
LXV.	— the Same	298
LXVI.	— the Same	300
LXVII.	— Messrs. D. K——, &c.	302
LXVIII.	— Mrs. L. S. G——	306
LXIX.	— the Church in C——	308
LXX.	— Mr. J. Haldane	311
LXXI.	— J. L——	312
LXXII.	— the Same	313
LXXIII.	— the Same	314
LXXIV.	— the Same	315
LXXV.	— the Same	316
LXXVI.	— the Same	317
LXXVII.	— the Church in London	320
LXXVIII.	— J. G. S——	323
LXXIX.	— the Same	324
LXXX.	— the Church in Dublin	326
LXXXI.	— T. M—— and T. P——	328
LXXXII.	— A. M'I——	337
LXXXIII.	— the Same	340
LXXXIV.	— T. A——, Esq.	343
LXXXV.	— Mrs. M——	345
LXXXVI.	— ————	347
LXXXVII.	— Mr. J. C. G——	348
LXXXVIII.	— the Same	349
LXXXIX.	— his brother, James Walker	352
XC.	— Dr. F——	354
XCI.	— J. L——	357
XCII.	— J. H——, Esq.	359
XCIII.	— Mr. B——	376
XCIV.	— S. W——	379
XCV.	— the Same	380
XCVI.	— Mr. P. C——	381

		Pages.
XCVII.	To J. R. K——, Esq.	387
XCVIII.	— the Same	388
XCIX.	— the Same	390
C.	— R. L. C——, Esq.	391
CI.	— the Same	395
CII.	— Mr. Y——	397
CIII.	— F. C——, Esq.	399
CIV.	— J. F——	401
CV.	— the Same	403
CVI.	— the Same	405
CVII.	— the Same	406
CVIII.	— J. L——	407
CIX.	— Mrs. C——	410
CX.	— Mrs. T——	413
CXI.	— the Same	417
CXII.	— the Same	418
CXIII.	— the Same	420
CXIV.	— Mrs. B——	421
CXV.	— J. L——	422
CXVI.	— Mr. J. H——	424
CXVII.	— P. H——	425
CXVIII.	— Mr. J. H——	426
CXIX.	— Mr. J. S——	428
CXX.	— Mrs. T——	430
CXXI.	— the Same	432
CXXII.	— Mr. J. G. S——	434
CXXIII.	— A. C——	435
CXXIV.	— W. C——, and J. M'G——	437
CXXV.	— J. H——	439
CXXVI.	— R. L. C——	440
CXXVII.	— Mr. J. H——	443
CXXVIII.	— J. L——	444
CXXIX.	— the Same	446
CXXX.	— the Same	447
CXXXI.	— the Same	448
CXXXII.	— Miss F——	449
————	Remarks on 1 Cor. v. ii. referred to in the preceding letter	450
CXXXIII.	To the Same	452
CXXXIV.	— the Same	453
CXXXV.	— Mr. W. C——	454
CXXXVI.	— R. L. C——	456
CXXXVII.	— the Church in London	460
CXXXVIII.	— Mrs. B——	462
————	Remarks on Acts xi. 19—21, referred to in the preceding letter	464
CXXXIX.	To J. L——	466
CXL.	— the Same	470
CXLI.	— the Same	473
CXLII.	— the Same	477
CXLIII.	— Miss J——	478
CXLIV.	— the Same	480
CXLV.	— Miss T——	483
CXLVI.	— R. L. C——, Esq.	485
CXLVII.	— D. L——, Esq.	487
CXLVIII.	— Mrs. B——	489
CXLIX.	— Miss Walker	491
CL.	— J. L——	492
CLI.	— R. L. C——, Esq.	493
CLII.	— ————	494
CLIII.	— the Same	495
CLIV.	— Mrs. B——	498
CLV.	— ————	502

	Pages.
CLVI. To ———	505
CLVII. — Mr. J——	508
CLVIII. — D. R. R——, Esq.	509
CLIX. — H. M——, Esq.	512
CLX. — the Same	514
[CLXI. — the Same	515
CLXII. — J. L——	517
CLXIII. — R. M. B——, Esq.	519
CLXIV. — A. B——	523

Letters on various Subjects .... 524—543

CLXV. To the Editor of the Literary Gazette	524
CLXVI. — the Editor of the Eclectic Review	525
CLXVII. — Sir W. C. S——	527
CLXVIII. — the Editor of the Times	528
CLXVIII. — the Editor of the Morning Herald	530
CLXIX. — the Same	531
CLXX. — one of the Public Papers	534
CLXXI. — one of the Public Papers	536
CLXXII. — the Editor of the Morning Chronicle	540
CLXXIII. — William Smith, Esq.	542

Review of "The Epistles of Paul the Apostle translated; with an Exposition and Notes. By the Rev. Thomas Belsham, Minister of Essex-street Chapel" .... 544—571

Review of "Thoughts on the Anglican and Anglo-American Churches. By John Bristed, Counsellor-at-Law" .... 572—595

Review of "A Greek and English Lexicon; in which are explained all the Words used by the best Greek Writers of Prose and Verse, &c. By John Jones, LL.D., Author of *the* Greek Grammar" .... 596—616

Observations on "An Answer to a Pseudo-Criticism of the Greek and English Lexicon, which appeared in the Second Number of the Westminster Review" .... 617—619

Review of "Lucian of Samosata; from the Greek, with the Comments and Illustrations of Wieland and others. By William Tooke, F.R.S., Member of the Imperial Academy of Sciences, &c." 620—634

Plain Truths; or a Speech which may be delivered in the approaching Session, by any Member who likes it, on a Motion for going into a Committee of the whole House upon the State of Ireland .. 635—647

An Essay on the following Prize Question proposed by the Royal Irish Academy, "Whether and how far the Cultivation of Science and that of Polite Literature assist or obstruct each other?" ...... 648—666

Letter to Editor of the Hibernian Evangelical Magazine 667

Remarks on Mat. vi. 22, 23 669

THE PETITION

OF

CERTAIN CHRISTIAN PEOPLE

RESIDENT IN LONDON,

TO

THE HONOURABLE THE HOUSE OF COMMONS,

PRAYING FOR RELIEF IN THE MATTER OF

OATHS.

WITH NOTES

BY ONE OF THE PETITIONERS.

Mihi, quanto plura recentium seu veterum revolvo, tanto magis ludibria rerum mortalium cunctis in negotiis obversantur. TACITUS.

[First Published 1822.]

ADVERTISEMENT.

For the NOTES, which are subjoined to the following PETITION, I am solely and individually responsible. I have been induced to draw them up, by the hope of exciting the attention of some of our Legislators to an application for relief, which seems to have hitherto failed of attracting any notice.

On the question of the expediency of the publication, different opinions may be entertained: and I have not had an opportunity of consulting many, to whose judgment on the occasion I should have been disposed to pay considerable deference. I think it therefore needful to exonerate them from all responsibility for the publication, by annexing to it my name.

The very grave complexion of some of the Notes, may perhaps deter many from looking at them. But I am more apprehensive of censure, from those whose censure I should most apprehend, for having ventured, in other passages, upon some topics which involve considerations of *legislative policy*. In this certainly I have departed from my own usual course: yet, I hope, with such temperance of remark, as will exempt me from the charge of having departed from the CHRISTIAN character.

JOHN WALKER.

Camden Street, Camden Town, London.

THE PETITION.

To the Honourable the House of COMMONS of The UNITED KINGDOM of GREAT BRITAIN and IRELAND, in Parliament assembled.

The PETITION of the undersigned CHRISTIAN people, resident in London, and sometimes distinguished by the name of SEPARATISTS,

Humbly Sheweth,

THAT Your Petitioners, as Christians,.(A.) are peaceable and well-affected subjects of the State; thankful for the many blessings which they enjoy under its mild and tolerant Government; and mindful of the divine authority which binds them to obey *the powers that be*, as ordained of GOD, and to suffer patiently whatever they may be called to suffer for conscience sake.

That they think it, however, consistent with this Christian duty, to renew their yearly appeal to the wisdom, justice, and humanity of Your Honourable House, for relief from the many trying losses and penalties to which they are subject, according to the existing laws of this country, in consequence of their obedience to the express command of CHRIST (B.) not to *swear at all by any oath*.

That Your Petitioners have long publicly maintained, and (as they are persuaded) sufficiently proved, that they act only according to the real meaning of that divine prohibition in refusing to take any oath: and that while the sincerity of their conviction is established by the severe forfeitures which many in their Churches have actually incurred (C.), and the still more severe sufferings to which they are all continually exposed;—the arguments by which they have publicly supported their sentiment have never yet, as far as they know, been even plausibly answered.

That Your Petitioners with all humility submit it to Your consideration, whether, in a country in which CHRISTIANITY professedly forms part of the law of the land (D.), it be not inconsistent that Christians should be subject to fines, imprisonment, forfeitures of various kinds, and general insecurity both of person and property, for obeying a plain Christian precept.

That, among many other sufferings and hardships, Your Petitioners are at present disqualified for acting as Executors to a Will; disqualified for answering any Bill which may be filed against them in Chancery, however false and iniquitous; disqualified for proving a debt under a commission of Bankruptcy; disqualified for obtaining a Certificate, if any of them should become Bankrupts, as well as for availing themselves of the Act for the relief of Insolvent Debtors; and in a great measure disqualified for acting either as Masters or Servants in importing, exporting, or manufacturing all articles connected with the Customs or Excise: and that from their inability to give legal evidence, they are continually liable to heavy penalties for apparent contempt of the Courts of Justice; although they are, from principle, among the most loyal subjects of the State, and dare not disobey its authorities—except when commanded to do that which the law of God forbids.

That Your Petitioners also beg leave humbly to represent to Your Honourable House, that no political inconvenience (E.) has been found to result from the indulgence, which the Legislature has long extended to the people called Quakers, of substituting a solemn affirmation for (F.) the imprecatory engagement of an oath:—that a participation in the same indulgence is the utmost to which Your Petitioners aspire:—and that if they obtain it, they must still remain subject to such civil privations and disadvantages, as may evidence the sincerity of their conscientious scruple; and may therefore afford a reasonable security that their solemn Affirmation is equally credible with an Oath.

That Your Petitioners therefore again humbly pray for (G.) such relief in the premises, as to Your legislative wisdom shall seem meet.

NOTES.

A. (page 2.)

Your Petitioners, as Christians, are peaceable and well-affected, &c. —On this topic I should wish to speak a plain language; though aware that, even here, the knowledge of our sentiments is little calculated to recommend us in the eyes of any party in the State.

We professedly belong to a kingdom, which *is not of this world*: and the principles of it debar us from intermeddling in the various political contests, which agitate the country.—For the peace and true prosperity of our country we pray: and to its Rulers, whoever they be, and whatever their measures, we find ourselves called by the word of God to yield implicit subjection. The unpopular principle of *passive obedience* and *non-resistance*, which that word binds us to adopt as disciples of Christ, we adopt—not politically, but religiously. Finding it plainly enforced on Christians in the Scriptures, we have nothing to do with the question, whether it accord or not with the principles of the British constitution; nor with the consideration, what the consequences might be, if all the inhabitants of the country were of the same mind with us. Indeed we are, and ever must be, a sect so small, that the world can suffer no loss from our declining to interfere in its contentions.

Yet, while we thus own ourselves bound to act as quiet and submissive subjects of *any* government, under which the providence of God may place us, we are by no means insensible to the many peculiar claims upon our grateful attachment, which bind us to the government of this favoured land. We reckon it one of them, that we can from time to time make such a temperate appeal to the Legislature, as the present, for obtaining relief from any hardships under which we lie: and that we are encouraged to look for that relief by the fact, that others have long ago obtained it.

B. (page 2.)

The express command of Christ, not to swear at all by any Oath.—Though we have no desire to obtrude on the attention of the world the views of Scripture, upon which our own practice in this and other matters is founded; yet it here seems to me not inexpedient to offer a few remarks on the divine command referred to, and on the glosses by which it is commonly set aside: and this, in order to clear us from the imputation of having, with inconsiderate levity or wild enthusiasm, taken up an interpretation of the passage inconsistent with its real meaning.

Matt. v. 33—37. "Again ye have heard that it hath been said by them of old time, Thou shalt not forswear thyself, but shalt perform unto the Lord thine oaths: But I say unto you, Swear not at all; neither by heaven; for it is God's throne: Nor by the earth; for it is his footstool: neither by Jerusalem; for it is the city of the great King. Neither shalt thou swear by thy head, because thou canst not make one hair white or black. But let your communication (λογος) be, Yea, yea; Nay, nay: for whatsoever is more than these cometh of evil."

I would remark, in the first place, that the words "I say unto you, Swear not at all,"—and the corresponding precept in Jam. v. 12;—"Swear not, neither by heaven, neither by the earth, neither by *any other oath*," appear at the first view so plain, so comprehensive, so absolutely definitive; that it should require very cogent arguments indeed to set aside their literal and obvious import. Perhaps I might say, that if it were the design of any speaker to prohibit all Oaths,—under whatever circumstances, and on whatever occasion,—it is hard to conceive what language could be employed for the purpose, more clear and more emphatic, than the language in these passages of sacred writ.

But I am free to admit, and forward to assert, that it is to the *real meaning* of the words of Scripture we are always to attend; and that, in estimating this, none of the aids of fair critical interpretation are to be rejected or undervalued. I also admit and assert, that it would be a most serious evil, for Christians to refuse obedience to any ordinance of earthly government, except where it *really* interferes with the subjection due to the paramount authority of the commands of God: and that we therefore need to be well assured, in this and all similar instances, that we do not put a false construction on the divine word.

In the next place, therefore, I look closer at the passage quoted. "Ye have heard that it hath been said by them of old time, *Thou shalt not forswear thyself, but shalt perform unto the Lord thine oaths.*" —Here I find a plain and indisputable reference to the direction given under the law of Moses, Numb. xxx. 2. et seqq. "If a man vow a vow unto the Lord, or *swear an oath to bind his soul with a bond;* he shall not break his word, he shall do according to all that proceedeth out of his mouth." It appears, then, that under the law of Moses the Jewish people were not prohibited from *swearing an oath, to bind their souls with a bond.* The only injunction was, that *if* a man had done so, he should not *forswear himself*, but should *perform unto the Lord his oath.* And now, after plainly referring to this, Christ adds, addressing his disciples, "*But* I say unto you, *Swear not at all.*" Words cannot more clearly mark, that the thing which was allowed or not prohibited to the Jews, under the Levitical dispensation, is absolutely forbidden to Christians, under that higher dispensation of "the kingdom of *heaven*," to which the former was but introductory.

But what was that thing, allowed by Moses, but forbidden by Christ? *The swearing of an oath to bind the soul with a bond:*—the religious engagement of the juror, with respect to some particular of his future conduct, under a *forfeiture*, to be divinely exacted, in case of his failure, or non-performance of his vow. Accordingly, Christ condescending to enforce his prohibition by shewing its reasonableness, goes on to mark, that, by whatsoever a man should attempt to swear, in order to bring himself under such a religious obligation, he must presumptuously pledge or stake that which is not properly his own, and over which he has really no power or control. If he should swear by heaven,—"it is God's throne;" if by the earth,—"it is God's footstool;" if by Jerusalem,—"it is the city of the Great King;" if even by his own head,*—he has no power to "make one hair white or black."

To the Christian, then, all *swearing of an oath to bind the soul with a bond* is absolutely forbidden; and is shewn to be unsuitable to the character of an altogether dependent creature. There ought to

* I have been assured by a gentleman long resident in the East Indies, that it is at this day no uncommon form of judicial swearing among the natives, for the juror to place his hand on the head of his child, wife, or some near connexion: and thus to stake a life so dear to him, for the veracity of the testimony which he is about to give.—Joseph's oath, "By the life of Pharaoh," was evidently of a similar import.

appear no room for any further inquiry; unless it be questioned whether the things, which are current throughout Christendom under the name of *Oaths*, be really of the same nature, as they are of the same name, with the thing divinely prohibited. This question, though it scarcely admits a serious doubt, I propose to meet in a subsequent Note (F.) But before I conclude the present Note, it is needful to add one or two remarks, for the purpose of exposing the manner in which this divine precept has been set aside by men, who, like the Scribes and Pharisees of old, " make the word of God of none effect by their tradition."

In general, they gravely tell us,—and pronounce it as if their assertion must of course be admitted upon its own authority,—that the thing forbidden is *voluntary* swearing, or swearing *lightly* upon *ordinary* occasions; but that it is assuredly very right to take an oath, when called to it at the requisition of a civil magistrate. One of the first effects of reverence for the word of GOD is, that it releases the mind from subjection to *human* authority in matters of religion. I must therefore be allowed to ask,—where is it that these gentlemen have found that the words " *Swear not at all*" mean, " Swear not, *unless* required to do so by a civil magistrate?" If Christians were commanded by a heathen potentate, under whose government they lived, to offer sacrifice to an idol; would the command of the civil magistrate render it lawful for them to comply? Assuredly not. In any matter not interfering with their allegiance to their heavenly King, they would be bound by that allegiance to comply with the ordinances even of a heathen government. But wherever the two authorities stand in opposition to each other, their course is equally plain,—to suffer patiently, even to death, whatever the laws of man may inflict upon them for adhering to the law of their GOD. Yet if the interests of men or the fashion of the country ran in that direction, commentators and divines might with equal reason tell us, that the authority of the civil magistrate could justify a Christian in direct idolatry, as they assert that it releases from the obligation *not to swear at all*.

But the passage of Scripture contains in itself an absolute refutation of all such glosses: and this, not merely from the universality of the terms in which the prohibition is couched, but from the nature of the following observations by which it is enforced. All these enforcements are derived—not from any consideration of the particular occasion or circumstances under which a man is supposed to swear,—not from any consideration of his swearing *voluntarily* or *lightly*,—but from grounds which, if they be allowed to be stable at any one time or occasion, must remain equally firm at all times and on all occasions. They are derived from the *intrinsic* nature of any oath, by which a man can swear *to bind his soul with a bond*. Does any one, for instance, admit the cogency of the argument—" neither shalt thou swear by thy head, *because* thou canst not make one hair white or black?" Then he must admit the intrinsic unlawfulness of such swearing, although all the rulers of the world should command it:—unless it be said that the interference of human authority can communicate to a Christian that power over his own head, which the word of Christ reminds him that he possesses not.

But it has been urged on the other hand, that swearing by heaven—by the earth—by Jerusalem—or by the head—were not forms of judicial oaths* among the Jews; and therefore that judicial oaths cannot be included in the prohibition.—I am ready to admit the premiss; but I deny the conclusion. Christ plainly shews, that *even* by the least of these oaths it is evil and presumptuous to swear. But instead of inferring that it is allowable to swear by a higher and more awful oath, the very opposite conclusion follows *à fortiori*. In the oaths prescribed by the Legislatures throughout Christendom, the juror certainly *binds his soul by a bond* the most solemn; pledging himself as to the conduct he will pursue even under the *forfeiture of the divine aid and mercy*. But no CHRISTIAN will say, that he has more power or control over that highest stake, which is thus sported with, than he has over *his own head*.

Again, it has been argued that Christ himself answered upon oath, when *adjured* by the High Priest. Matt. xxvi. 63. And thus do men attempt to set the example of Christ at variance with his own precept. But the vanity of this argument will at once appear, if we observe the import of the word *adjure* in other parts of the New Testament. In Acts xix. 13. we are informed that the exorcist Jews employed this language: "*We* adjure *you by Jesus whom Paul preacheth*." Here, certainly, all idea of an *oath* is excluded: and it is evident that the word means nothing more than, *We* charge *you by the authority of Jesus*. It is the very same word which is employed by Paul, in 1 Thess. v. 27. where our translators justly render it, *I* charge *you by the Lord*. And I would distinctly add, that I should have no scruple to answer, on any suitable occasion, thus solemnly *adjured* to declare the truth. But I fancy, that the lawyers would not consider me as therefore answering *upon oath*.

Equally futile is the argument, from the solemnity with which the apostle Paul on different occasions appeals to God, as the witness of the inward thoughts and motives which he declares. Rom. i. 9. 2 Cor. i. 23. The argument aims at confounding two things, which are essentially distinct. A simple affirmation, as contradistinguished from an oath, is not the less simple, for any degree of *solemnity* which accompanies it. However solemnly Paul, in the passages referred to, declares what God knew to be true; he does not confirm his declaration by any *oath*:—much less does he *swear an oath to bind his soul by a bond* with respect to his future conduct. And this, I repeat it, is the precise thing prohibited by the word of

* As to the ordinary judicial oaths among the Jews, I find no reason either from the Scriptures, or from any other documents, to think that they were at all of the same nature with the thing prohibited to Christians:—that they were either promissory or imprecatory. There was, in one case, an "*oath of cursing*" enjoined under the law of Moses: but it was a case, in which the miraculous interference of divine power was engaged to ratify the oath. Numb. v.—But in fact, Christians, not being under the law of Moses, need scarcely trouble themselves with any such inquiry. They are called to *hear* HIM, of whom Moses in the law and all the prophets testified.

Christ to his disciples. I may incidentally remark the dishonest inconsistency of the commentators in this matter. The same men, who interpret the precept of Christ as forbidding all oaths—EXCEPT *those required by the civil magistrate*, at another time refer to these passages in the writings of the apostle, as instances of his *swearing*—though not at the requisition of any magistrate.

Others have referred to the words of the apostle in Heb. vi. 16. as sanctioning the use of oaths. But they wrest the passage altogether contrary to the design of the writer. That design was evidently, not to express approbation or disapprobation of the practice among men, to which he incidentally refers; but to illustrate from it the manner in which God condescended to confirm his promise to Abraham. When HE is represented as swearing by himself for the confirmation of his promise, and thus as it were *pledging* his own being and glorious perfections to the heirs of promise for its accomplishment, He appears but in his rightful character of the sovereign and immutable JEHOVAH.

C. (page 2.)

The severe forfeitures which many in their Churches have actually incurred, &c.—A few instances of these it may be well to specify.—Some time ago no fewer than six* of our body, holding situations of trust and profit in the Bank of Ireland, and some of them with large families wholly dependent on them for support, were at once dismissed by the Directors, on account of their refusal to take the oaths annually administered in that establishment:—and this, although they offered to make any mere declaration, however solemn, of their acknowledgment of the duties prescribed, and of their serious purpose to fulfil them. The case of one of these persons, Mr. LAWRENCE, since dead, was marked with peculiar hardship. He had been for *thirty-four* years a clerk in the Bank; had grown grey in the faithful discharge of his duties; and at the age of *four-score* years was dismissed from his employment, without even any superannuated allowance.

One of our brethren, THOMAS LANE, M.D., has for some years forfeited his half-pay, as surgeon on the staff of the Wexford regiment of militia.—One has been imprisoned for refusing to give evidence upon oath: and others have escaped imprisonment only by the lenity of the civil authorities.

One is now lying in gaol from inability to avail himself of the act for the relief of insolvent debtors. Another remains, and is likely to remain all his life, an uncertified bankrupt; though his creditors make no opposition, and his failure in business many years ago was not attended with the least stigma on his character.

Others have been repeatedly subject to fines for non-attendance upon juries: and some have had considerable depredations committed on their properties, without the power of bringing the depredators to justice, even when they have been known.

* JOHN M'CAY, Assistant Secretary; and the five following clerks—JOHN LAWRENCE, THOMAS MORGAN, THOMAS MAUNSELL WHITE, EDWARD MADDEN, and ALEXANDER ENGLISH.

D. (page 2.)

In which Christianity professedly forms part of the law of the land, &c.—Blackstone's Comment. B. iv. C. 4. "Whither also may be referred—[i. e. to offences more immediately against God and religion] all profane scoffing at the Holy Scripture, or exposing it to contempt and ridicule. These are offences punishable at common law by fine and imprisonment, or other infamous corporal punishment; for *Christianity is part of the laws of England.*"

In any remarks which I venture to suggest on this topic, I hope that I shall not be suspected of being so foolish and presumptuous, as to think of controverting the legal principle. I am no lawyer: yet I am fully aware that the principle is incontrovertibly established, and statedly acted upon in the courts. But it may be allowed me—as a man—to consider its meaning; and as a Christian—to mark the *sense* in which it is *impossible* that CHRISTIANITY should form part of the law of any state.

In the Jewish nation, while the Mosaic dispensation lasted, their Church and State were completely identified by divine appointment. There was an absolute incorporation of their civil code with their religious, both having been alike delivered from heaven: and the violations of either were to be visited with the same temporal penalties. But that dispensation has passed way: and concerning the *heavenly* kingdom, which has succeeded the earthly, we have the express declaration of its great head—"My kingdom is *not of this world.*" John xviii. 36. Any attempt to incorporate this kingdom with the kingdoms of the world, is an attempt to change its nature. And any thing capable of being made part of the civil constitution of human governments, may indeed be called Christianity; but it neither is nor can be that thing, the name of which it assumes.

The laws of earthly kingdoms regulate the affairs of this world. The laws of CHRIST's kingdom have quite a different and a higher province: insomuch that if two Christians, walking together in the fellowship of the Gospel, have at any time, through the infirmity of the flesh, a controversy with each other about "things pertaining to this life," they cannot, according to the law of Christ's kingdom, even apply to the tribunals of earthly judicature for the decision of their controversy. (See 1 Cor. vi.) I know well that such divine regulations, as I refer to, are generally throughout Christendom considered quite obsolete* and out of date. But I know also, from the

* I have elsewhere noticed a very curious instance of the ease and *sang froid* with which the Commentators, miscalled Christian, set aside the word of the most High. When ROSENMULLER in his Scholia on the New Testament, comes to treat of that plain direction, which Christ gives to his disciples, in the case where one brother has trespassed against another, (Matt. xviii. 15—17.) he observes that this part of Christian discipline is *not suitable* at all to the Church in its *present* external and civil state; being adapted only to a smaller company governing itself absolutely by the commands of Christ, and not exhibiting even the shadow of civil authority. (Very true indeed). But he solves at once any difficulty which might hence arise, by telling us—that "the *learned* are agreed, and *he* agrees with them, that the direction was but TEMPORARY and LOCAL." "*Ceterum hanc admonitionem esse temporalem et localem, nostris institutis non accom-*

Scriptures, that this idea is an awful mistake, originating in real disbelief of the word of God. Christ's kingdom is *a kingdom which cannot be moved: not one of the stakes thereof shall ever be removed, neither shall any of the cords thereof be broken.* (Heb. xii. 28. Is. xxxiii. 20.) Of the forms of *nominal* and *professional* Christianity there is an endless variety. But real Christianity is ONE and UNCHANGEABLE: because "Jesus Christ is the same yesterday, to-day, and for ever;" and his word, like himself, "endureth for ever." (Heb. xiii. 8. 1 Pet. i. 25.)

Yet undoubtedly *Christianity is part of the laws of England.* But in what sense can I understand this acknowledged legal principle? Does it mean that every man in England must *profess* himself to be a Christian? or not avow that he disbelieves the Christian revelation? Certainly not. A JEW, though a native of England, is not subject (I believe) to any legal *penalty* for avowing himself a Jew; for avowing that he considers Jesus of Nazareth an impostor. Nor can it mean that the English law prohibits the *publication* of direct attacks on the English revelation. I have never heard of a prosecution commenced against any bookseller, for publishing or selling the writings of HOBBES, of SHAFTESBURY, of HUME, of GIBBON, or even of VOLTAIRE himself. And when I consider the free sale of the works of the last author, (which I should be very sorry to find legally prevented,) I confess myself puzzled to understand what class of infidel writings precisely is illegal in this country. I have heard it described as that in which Christianity is opposed, not by sober reasoning, but with scurrility and wanton ridicule. I own that I never found any more scurrilous ribaldry, or more destitute of any thing like calm and philosophic reasoning, in the writings of THOMAS PAINE, than in some of the pieces of the *philosopher* of FERNEY; and, (without thinking either of them a conjuror,) I do consider the former a more acute man than the latter, though not so witty.

However, I can understand *in general,* that the publication of such an infidel work as PAINE's Age of Reason is illegal. And I am far from questioning the *right* of any legislature, to make enactments against such a publication. But let me be pardoned for saying, that I question the policy and wisdom of such legislative interference. There was a period when Christians were subject to legal penalties for opposing the absurdities of Paganism, or for refusing to conform to its rites: and their sufferings for this are recorded under the name of *persecution.* It seems a strange thing, that those who bear the name of Christians should have long turned the tables upon the

modatam, recte ut opinor, monent eruditi. Nempe hæc publica admonitio non potest habere locum nisi in cœtu minore, ne speciem quidem auctoritatis civilis præ se ferente, seque ipsum e Christi præceptis liberrime gubernante. In statum ecclesiæ externum et civilem, qui apud nos est, hæc disciplinæ Christianæ pars parum convenit."—Was I not justified, when I formerly adduced this passage, in subjoining the following question? "Why do these men continue to have portions read to their congregations from the antiquated Bible? Is it not time to have a new one composed by the *new Apostles?* Or would it not be more suitable to read a section of the *ecclesiastical canons,* framed by clerical convocations for the government of the Church?"—*Thoughts on Religious Establishments, &c.*

infidels; and should now inflict civil penalties upon those who gainsay Christianity.

To protect the persons and properties of Christians, as well as of all other peaceable subjects, is certainly among the legitimate objects of human legislation and government. But I own, that I think there was sound wisdom in the remark of the politic TIBERIUS, when some wanted to draw down punishment on one who had violated the divinity of AUGUSTUS;—DEORUM *injurias* DIIS *curæ*. And I am so well assured of the stability of real CHRISTIANITY, and of the vanity of all assaults upon it either in the way of argument or ridicule, that I should wish the freest scope to be afforded to its assailants. Perhaps also the contrary course gives them an importance, which they do not intrinsically possess; and affords them too specious a pretext for representing—that the thing which they oppose needs to be screened from examination by human authority. However, it is only as a Christian, and not as a politician, that I express this opinion. To the latter character, I am not ambitious of making the least pretensions.

Well: I have arrived at *some* tangible meaning for the principle, that Christianity forms part of the law of the land. It is a violation of the law of the land, to speak or write against Christianity *in a certain way*; however difficult it may be to define what that way is. But is this the only meaning of the principle? I suspect that it is generally supposed to mean something more; but that there is no definite and precise idea of its further import.

Does it mean, that any one of the various forms of religion, current under the name of Christianity, is exclusively patronized and supported by the State? I should think that it cannot mean this. There is certainly in England, and in Ireland too, a form of religion, to the profession of which peculiar advantages are assigned by law. But, (not to urge that even there the profession of this is not *enjoined* by law, and that other forms have a legal toleration, which we cannot suppose would be conceded to violations of the law,) if we cross the Tweed, we shall find another form of nominal Christianity to be the one established, peculiarly favoured, and supported by the legislature: and if we go to his Majesty's dominions in North America, we shall find a third. I shall not argue the question,* whether Popery be or be not *established* by law in Canada. It is confessedly the religion supported by the state: and to its priests even the Protestant inhabitants are, or were, (for I will not go out of my proper sphere to examine whether any legislative change has been made in this respect,) bound by act of parliament to pay their *tithes*. His

* The reader may find some curious information on this subject in a pamphlet entitled, "An Account of the Proceedings of the British and other Protestant Inhabitants of Quebec," &c. 1775, by the present venerable Baron MASERES, formerly Attorney General of the Province.—In using the terms *Popery* and *Papists*, I really do not wish to give offence: nor can I understand why they should offend any, who acknowledge the wickedest Popes of Rome as Christ's Vicegerents upon earth. I should be very glad to think that they were becoming ashamed of that blasphemous absurdity. But I do not choose, either to sacrifice truth by calling them *Catholics*, or to violate the propriety of language by calling them *Roman Catholics*.

Majesty's Protestant subjects there are obliged by British law to contribute to the support of a religion which Protestants consider *Antichristian*.

I can understand the reason of that; though I more than doubt its policy. But, by parity of reason, I should look for Popery to be the favoured religion in Ireland also. Ireland, my unfortunate native country, has long been presenting a lesson to our legislators, which perhaps they will yet learn to read. One of its many pages is that, which exhibits the great mass of the people, amidst all their poverty, providing and supporting a *religion* for themselves; not only independent of any aid from the state, but in opposition to every political discouragement.—But I withdraw from the question, whether it be politically wise for the governors of a state to embarrass themselves with the care of providing religion for the people. It is a question, on which I cannot avoid having a decided opinion; but I desire not to obtrude it. I am not insensible also, that it is often much harder to correct a political evil which has long existed, than it would have been to avoid it originally. Yet, perhaps, it might be salutary, that legislators should have their eyes opened to the real nature even of those evils in the State, which admit not an immediate cure; in order to apply palliatives, if not gradual remedies.

I have been betrayed into these remarks, by considering the meaning of that legal principle,—that *Christianity forms part of the law of the land.* And I believe I must throw it back upon the lawyers. For the more I consider it, the more obscure and doubtful it becomes in my view.

E. (page 3.)

No political inconvenience has been found to result from the indulgence, &c.—That it is agreeable to the principles of the Constitution of this kingdom, to afford every indulgence consistent with the safety and good of the State to the conscientious scruples of all religious people, who demean themselves as sober, quiet, and industrious subjects,—we conceive it requires no argument to prove. And that we so demean ourselves, we can confidently appeal to all who know us: nor would the scriptural principles on which we act allow us to keep in our connexion any character known to be of an opposite description.

That the indulgence with respect to Oaths heretofore granted to the Quakers, and also to the United Brethren, is not injurious to the interests or welfare of the State, we humbly conceive may clearly be established; though we are aware that some think the statement controvertible. If it can be *justly* controverted,—if the indulgence afforded to the two other sects be found injurious to the public interests,—we freely admit that we could not without presumption look for an extension of it to us. The welfare of individuals, however grievously affected, must give way to the public good.

With respect to the United Brethren, or Moravians, I believe that they do not in general avail themselves of the Act: * and even when

* An Act passed in the twenty-second year of George II. for encouraging the people called Unitas Fratrum, or United Brethren, to settle in America.

the Act was passed in their favour, only *some individuals* among them had any scruples about swearing. It only remains therefore to show, that in the case of the Quakers, the admission of their solemn Affirmation, in place of an oath, has not been injurious to the welfare of the State.

And here I believe it will be allowed by all, that their evidence, wherever it is admissible by law, stands as unimpeached for truth and integrity, as if it had been confirmed by Oath. But it may be objected that the public weal is affected from time to time, and the ends of public justice defeated, by their refusal to give evidence upon Oath, in cases where this Affirmation is not received. *It is true*. but is this the consequence of the legislative *indulgence*, which receives their Affirmation in civil matters? Is it not rather the consequence of not extending that indulgence to criminal cases? Previous to the Act passed in favour of the Quakers, did they give evidence on Oath upon any occasion, on which they now refuse it? No: they only suffered more for their refusal; and the severity and publicity of their sufferings contributed, perhaps more than most other circumstances, to spread their principles.

We resemble the Quakers *in this respect*, that we could not retain in our religious connexion a person who would swear by any Oath; and that we feel ourselves called to suffer patiently whatever consequences may follow from this principle. Whether the principle be or be not detrimental to the public welfare, is a question which I think it here superfluous to discuss; though I shall meet that question also in the next Note, and prove that Oaths have none of that political utility which is commonly attributed to them. But the only real question in the present case seems to be, whether it be conducive to the public good that we should be exposed to much and continued suffering, for acting as we feel ourselves bound to do by the word of God.

We cannot apprehend that the British Legislature will participate in the narrow sentiment avowed by a magistrate of Dublin, (Alderman * *) that "Government ought to *exterminate from society* such principles" as ours. In fact, a principle seriously taken up from the Scriptures cannot be effectually opposed, or exterminated, but by showing that it has no real warrant in the Scriptures. *If* indeed it be judged politically expedient to try our steadfastness, by leaving us to still greater and longer sufferings than we have already sustained, in the expectation that we shall abandon our principles;—we have nothing to say, but that we hope to be strengthened for the trial by a power superior to our own.

Some have questioned the expediency of extending the desired indulgence to us, from an apprehension that among the various sects of Dissenters, others would desire to share the indulgence with us, or would prefer an equally strong claim to participate in it. In reply to this objection it may be sufficient to remark, that, even after obtaining from the Legislature the utmost indulgence for which we look, we should remain (like the Quakers) subject to numerous privations and disabilities, incapacitated for filling various situations, or exercising various professions, in which Oaths are required. And surely these remaining disadvantages would be sufficient to prevent any from professing an agreement in principle with us, unless they have the same conscientious conviction, and the same willingness to sacrifice worldly interests to that conviction of Christian duty. Any person, who at present either has no scruple about taking Oaths or who takes them in opposition to existing scruples, would still have abundant motives for continuing to act as he does; and for deprecating the idea of being put on a level with us, even though we had obtained all the legislative relief which we seek.

F. (page 3.)

Substituting a solemn affirmation for the imprecatory *engagement of an Oath.*—So little is *thought* about swearing in this country, that many who take oaths have never considered the precise nature of the act. I have found many, who assumed that there is no essential difference between an Oath and a *very solemn* Affirmation: and the language of some writers, who express themselves on the subject in vague generalities, may be thought, by those who wish to think so, to lend a kind of countenance to the opinion. But it is really indisputable, that the Legislature has contemplated an essential difference between the two things. For, while the law gives every latitude to the variety of *forms* in which Oaths shall be administered, according to the various principles or customs of the juror; it is only by a special Act of Parliament that the solemn Affirmation of some individuals is admitted, in place of an Oath; and even their most solemn Affirmation is not admitted, except in civil cases.

But the *imprecatory* import of our Oaths is indeed very obvious, from the express terms of the form, in which they are most statedly administered: and I have to own with shame how long I wilfully shut my eyes against this; and imposed on my own conscience the idea, that the words "So *help me God!*" might be understood as a prayer for the divine aid and assistance in fulfilling the engagement. Archdeacon Paley, (whom I quote, not as a divine, but as a civilian, and a man confessedly of a clear head and extensive information,) speaks honestly here—"The energy of the sentence resides in the particle *so; so,* i. e. *hac lege,* upon condition of my speaking the truth or performing this promise, may God help me, *and not otherwise.*" And thus, as the writers of the Encyclopædia state, every OATH is "accompanied by an imprecation of the vengeance of God, or a renunciation of his favour, if what we affirm be false, or what we promise be not performed."

The particular phrase—*So help me God!* has been borrowed from the old Romans; among whom we find the language, *Ita me Dii juvent,* &c.—in such a connection as decides its import. Nor is the imprecatory import of the English phrase less unequivocally established, when we observe how it is occasionally employed for the purpose of confirming by oath *the truth of an antecedent assertion:* as—"So help me God, it is true." But, in fact, Judges and lawyers are every year reminding the Jury or the witnesses, that they have '*pledged* their hope of eternal life, arising from Christianity, for the truth of their verdict or their testimony.'

I believe it is well known also, that when the court is examining whether a child be sufficiently acquainted with the nature of an Oath, to be admitted as a witness, the only answer which is considered satisfactory to the question—'What do you think will be the consequence, if you should not tell the truth after being sworn?'—is an answer, which conveys that the child considers he must in that case be *sent to hell*.

Indeed if the meaning of the phrase—*So help me God!* were what I so long strove to think it might be, a prayer for the divine help to keep the promise; (to say nothing of its being contradicted by the propriety of the English language) it would be very hard to say, in what consists the *peculiar* solemnity of obligation which all writers attribute to an Oath. According to this interpretation, a person taking the Oath of Allegiance, for instance, merely says—"I will bear true allegiance, &c. "and I pray God to help me to do so." A very suitable prayer certainly, after such a promise. But really I could suggest twenty other forms more solemn than this. Yet even those writers, who express themselves most loosely upon the subject, always describe a kind of mystic solemnity as attaching to the obligation of an *Oath*. And in what that peculiar mystery of solemnity consists, it is not very difficult to discern, if we are willing to see it.

And whatever be the *form* of an Oath, that its designed import is of the same *imprecatory* nature; that, as Plutarch observes, every oath terminates either explicitly or implicitly in a curse; (*πας ὁρκος εις καταραν τελευτᾳ της επιορκιας*) I scarcely think requires any argument to establish or illustrate.* I observed some time ago an account of a Japanese being sworn as a witness in one of our courts; and sworn, of course, according to the form of oath considered binding in his country. For this purpose he held up a porcelain bowl; and after pronouncing certain words, dashed the bowl with force against the ground, so that it was broken in pieces. What was the evident import of this, but an imprecation, that his idol-gods might similarly execute destruction upon him, if he should falsify?—Well; in this *Christian* country, in which Christianity forms part of the law of the land, the evidence of the Japanese cursing himself by his gods was legally established as credible; but the most solemn testimony of a Christian is not legally admissible evidence, unless he will, before giving it, violate the express command of Christ, by binding himself under a still more awful curse to declare the truth.

Yet let me now put it to the reader's candid consideration, whether it is possible that any such imprecatory engagement can constitute—in the view of a *Christian*—the obligation binding on his conscience not to falsify. That binding obligation is imposed on him by the word of God. Nothing which he or others may do or say, can either release him from it, or strengthen the validity of the obligation. And I confess that the man, who would solemnly and deliberately declare in evidence that which is false, must appear to me a very dubious witness, though he should confirm his testimony by a thou-

* Any reader, who wishes for more upon this subject, may consult the 34th vol. of the Monthly Review, for the year 1766; where there is a curious account of a work published by a M. Herrort, a citizen of Bern, for which he was put under arrest by the secret council.

sand oaths. I do not go so far as to deny, that some persons of this character may be restrained, by superstition, from falsifying upon oath. I admit, for instance, that there are multitudes in Ireland who will give false testimony without scruple, if they can contrive to kiss their thumb instead of the book, or if the book has not the sign of a cross imprinted on its cover: yet some of them will shrink from the same perjury, if they be sworn according to the form which they consider binding. But really *superstition* affords a very precarious security, and at least as frequently operates against the interests of society, as it promotes them. The same persons, to whom I have alluded, will conceive themselves under a moral obligation to cut your throat, if they have bound themselves to do so under the curse of an oath.

Having touched upon this subject, let me be pardoned for enlarging a little more, and examining what I am persuaded is a vulgar prejudice. There are many vulgar prejudices not confined to the *vulgar*.

Much of the language which I have met with upon Oaths, both in conversation and in reading, proceeds upon the assumption—that Oaths are the grand bond of civil society; that if they were abolished, society must be dissolved. Any principle founded in truth, the more it is examined, will be the more established and confirmed. Let not therefore the advocates of this sentiment be afraid to look at the following considerations.

Oaths are commonly divided into two kinds,—*promissory* oaths, and oaths of *testimony*. There is no real difference between them, as legally employed in this country. They are all *promissory* engagements, in which the juror binds himself under a curse as to his *future* conduct. The only shade of difference, which can be truly marked, is that some of these engagements have a prospective bearing to a very long period, perhaps to the whole life of the juror; but others to a much shorter period and a particular occasion. However, adopting the popular distinction, let us take a view of each kind of Oaths, to see if they really possess that political utility which is attributed to them.

And first, the *Oath* of *Allegiance:* which I find by a work already referred to (Mr. Herrort's) was not introduced in Christendom till the seventh century, and was then invented by the Clergy. I would put it to the consideration of my reader, whether he seriously believes that any man, disposed to engage in treasonable practices, was ever restrained from them by the consideration, that he had taken the Oath of Allegiance. It would be absurd to imagine it. Many may have been restrained by the fear of discovery, of failure, and of the gibbet: but really persons who have a taste for treason are not often distinguished for regarding the obligation of an oath.

Again; when the Directors of the Bank of Ireland dismissed from their service (and perhaps were obliged by charter to do so) six of my brethren, because they preferred the loss of their employments to the violation of Christ's precept against swearing; was it because the Directors apprehended that these persons would proceed to embezzle the property of the Bank, unless they annually bound themselves under a curse not to do so? Was it because they suspected that old

Mr. Lawrence, for instance, after thirty-four years' faithful discharge of his duty, aimed at becoming false to his employers, when he was just on the verge of the grave? No such thing. I may confidently appeal to the Directors themselves, whether they did not at the time consider these persons as among the most *confidential* servants in their employ. But they thought it necessary to uphold the practice of their annual Oaths, as importantly conducive to the interests of their Establishment. Yet do they really believe that it is by those annual oaths any of their servants are kept to the faithful discharge of their duties? They find from time to time, that persons in their employment commit depredations on the property of the Bank. Yet have not these persons taken the Oaths? And was there ever an instance in which one of them, forming a scheme of peculation, was restrained from putting it in practice by the recollection of his oath? The superabundance of securities, which our Banks require from their servants, is amusing. There is a district of Ireland in which, according to old tradition, every creditor used to require from his debtor a threefold security for payment, viz. a *pledge*, a *bond*, and an *oath*. The Bank Directors require all the same securities from their Clerks. They have their necks in *pledge*, forfeited to the law, if they should embezzle Bank property. They have also a *bond* from two solvent sureties, to the full amount of any possible loss which can be sustained. And one might imagine that these two securities (not to speak of regard to character, interest, &c.) were sufficient, so far as any securities can avail. But, no: they must also *bind their souls* with an *oath* of cursing. I cannot but say that in my view, the wickedness of the practice is only equalled by its absurdity.

I have myself had an opportunity formerly of observing, how little these promissory Oaths really influence men's conduct. There is plenty of such swearing in the University, of which I was long a member. Every lectureship or other collegiate office, to which a Fellow is appointed, brings its own Oath with it: for the first sweeping oath for the faithful discharge of his duties, which he has taken on his election to the fellowship, is considered insufficient; unless on each new change of office, however trifling, he again stake his soul's salvation for doing his duty. Well: (without intending to say any thing against that learned body, or any particular individuals composing it) it was a notorious fact, that some discharged their collegiate duties, and others—were not equally exemplary in the matter. But was it the Oath that influenced those who discharged them most carefully? For myself, I candidly avow that it was not; and that I am persuaded I should have been equally diligent and attentive as a lecturer, &c. though I had never bound myself by oath to be so. Indeed, any one, who rationally considers the real springs of human conduct, must be landed in the same conclusion.

Before we proceed to the Oath of testimony, let us look for a moment at the Oath by which a Jury, in this country, bind themselves to bring in a verdict according to the evidence laid before them, without favour or affection to either party.—(Any honest men in such circumstances will be on their guard against favour or affection to either side: but those, who are most aware of the danger and evil of such sinister bias on their judgments, will perhaps be most slow to put themselves under an awful imprecation in case it should influence their verdict. But waving this—) Is it to this Oath we are indebted for the honesty, which commonly marks the verdict of a British Jury? Some may be surprised at my answering that question confidently, with a decisive negative. But I think I can establish the truth of my reply by the evidence of incontrovertible fact. If it were by their *Oath* that a Jury were determined, in any case, to bring in an honest verdict; the same oath must similarly determine the same Jury in any other case. But it is notorious that there are cases, in which a Jury the most respectable will bring in a verdict contrary to the evidence laid before them, and contrary to their oath. Let one example suffice; though I might adduce others. On a trial for murder in a *duel*,—if the evidence which establishes the fact, satisfy the Jury that the murder was committed, as is called, *fairly*, according to the laws of honour,—where is the Jury who will not bring in a verdict of acquittal or at least of mere manslaughter? And is this because the Jury doubt the evidence? No. Or, because they conceive that the fact proved in evidence does not, according to the British Law, amount to murder? No: the Judge himself commonly informs them that it does; and probably they were all well aware of this before. But they think it a case, in which the law should not take its course; and without scruple assume to themselves the prerogative of the Executive; and without scruple, because the violation of their Oath in this instance is much more creditable in society than the observance of it;—because they leave the jury-box with characters unimpeached, and without even a reprimand from the Judge.

In holding so plain a language upon this subject, I really do not wish to give offence; and I regret the necessary offensiveness of truth. It is obvious, that the only consistent course for a jury in such a case would be, to find the accused guilty of murder, but to recommend to mercy. The other course is sanctioned by current practice: and I believe there is no instance known, in which their *Oath* forms any impediment to it.—Now can any one rationally come to the conclusion, that the verdicts of our Juries would not be as honest, as they confessedly are in general, if—instead of attempting to bind them under a curse to judge faithfully, they were solemnly reminded of their duty, and made a solemn declaration of their serious purpose to fulfil it?

But in our judicial trials, how should the truth be elicited from *witnesses*, unless they gave their evidence upon Oath? Just as effectually, under a solemn Affirmation, enforced by the same penalties on wilful and corrupt falsification, as are now annexed to perjury. Does the Oath prevent witnesses from concealing or disguising the truth? The conflicting testimonies, which are continually produced in our Courts of Judicature, prove the contrary. Yet I believe, that, in general, the truth is effectually elicited. But how? By the comparison of evidence, by estimating its internal characters, and especially by *cross-examination*. These form the security of the public against the known facility of obtaining any evidence, the most false, for money. And so far as the witnesses are persons of respectable character and integrity, their regard to character, their sense of shame, and their sense of right, form sufficient guards on the honesty of their testimony. Where a witness is of an opposite character, insensible to these considerations, and under strong inducements to suppress or disguise the truth; I believe the Oath is not found sufficient to restrain him.

Let me be pardoned for briefly suggesting what has often occurred to me, (perhaps very foolishly,) as likely to be an improvement in our judiciary proceedings. We know that if a person has been convicted of perjury, his evidence afterwards is not legally admissible. But the instances of prosecution for perjury are very rare, in comparison of the multitude of cases in which both Judge and Jury are convinced in their consciences that a witness has falsified or prevaricated. In such cases, might it not be useful that a record should be made, under the report of the Jury and sanctioned by the Judge, that the evidence given by N. M. has appeared to be not worthy of credit; and that this record should be legally considered as more or less affecting the credibility of his testimony on any future occasion?

As to the inutility, or rather pernicious mischievousness, of Oaths employed in the Custom-house and Excise, little needs to be said. Christians, (I mean those who are Christians indeed,) acknowledge the divine obligation imposed on them by the word of God—to "*render unto Cæsar the things that are Cæsar's*"—"*tribute to whom tribute is due, custom to whom custom*:" an obligation, which nothing can annul, and which no Oath can strengthen. And no doubt there are many others, who by various motives are influenced to a fairness of conduct in this matter. But as to *Custom-house* Oaths, are they not notoriously and proverbially considered an empty form by the majority of those who take them, and even by those who administer them?

If any of my readers think this language too strong, let them look at a pamphlet lately published in Edinburgh, by a person connected with the Excise, and addressed to the Chancellor of the Exchequer. It is there proved beyond contradiction, that there is a case—in which our exporters are made to swear that they *have paid* a duty, which they not only have not paid, but which the officer who takes the affidavit *knows* has not been paid, and will not be paid for many weeks!

Yet—*Christianity is part of the laws of England*.—In fact, there is more wilful and corrupt perjury committed in our Courts of Law and Custom-house in the course of a year, (perhaps I might say in the course of a week,) than there was for centuries in the republic of *heathen* Rome. I might make a similar remark on the crime of adultery, and some other crimes most deeply affecting the well-being of society. Some of the professed friends of Christianity, (who mistake the nature of the thing which they profess to patronize,) may be shocked at the plainness of this testimony; though I am sure they can never invalidate its truth. They will be apt to think that I concede some vantage-ground to the Deists; and rob the Divines of an argument, on which they are fond of expatiating, —that the mere profession of something under the *name* of Christianity has wonderfully improved the manners and the morals of society. I have no apprehension, that I give the Deists any advantage by avowing the truth. And I avow that I have read of very few forms of pagan idolatry, which exceeded in ridiculousness of absurdity, or in atrocious wickedness of principle and practice, some of the forms of religion long and widely current under the name of Christian. It is an acknowledged maxim, that the very *worst* thing is frequently produced by the corruption of the very *best*. And all the corruptions of Christianity, which have overspread the world in these "times of the Gentiles," so far from invalidating Scripture, do in fact authenticate it: just as in the times of the Jewish dispensation, the continued apostacies of that people from the God of Israel, and their various corruptions of the law of Moses, only verified what was declared in that law concerning their character.

And now I wish to mark distinctly, why I have been led, in this and some of the preceding Notes, to enter upon topics, which are not strictly within my department, either as a Scholar or as a Christian: topics, from which both myself, and those with whom I am in religious connexion, in general, studiously abstain. I have found that one of the prevailing prejudices, most unfavourable to our application for legislative relief, is connected with the sentiment, that civil society cannot subsist without Oaths; that we are therefore persons who do not merit any attention to our complaints, as our principle of refusing to swear (however conscientiously adopted) is hostile to the interests of the State. Am I not justified in endeavouring to remove a prejudice, which I am persuaded is groundless? This persuasion is intimately connected with my conviction of the divine command upon the subject: as I cannot admit the supposition, that Christ enjoins on his disciples any thing really hostile to the welfare of society. I have therefore been led, after stating the scriptural grounds of our practice in this matter, to look a little with the eye of reason, or common sense, at the current notion of the utility and importance of swearing:—not certainly with the vain expectation of inducing the Legislature to abolish the practice; but in the hope of influencing some of our Legislators to be more disposed to release a few Christians from heavy civil penalties for not complying with it.

Let not any thing of a political complexion, which I have offered on the subject, be so misunderstood, as to be considered the ground, in whole or in part, of our conduct as a religious body. That ground lies exclusively in the divine word; from the decision of which we have no appeal as Christians; and beyond which, in this or any similar case, we have no inquiry to make for the regulation of our conduct.

Here, however, I would add one remark. The more we look at the divine prohibition against *swearing*, the more we discern it in perfect harmony with all the fundamental principles of the Christian revelation. And though perhaps I should never have been led, except by that express prohibition, to perceive the unsuitableness of the thing to the Christian character, yet for myself I confess, that with my present views of it, I dare not swear by any oath, even if that particular prohibition were expunged, or if it could be proved, (what I am sure never can be proved,) that it has a different import from that which I have marked. A sinful creature, deriving all his hope towards God—and a sufficiency of good hope, from the revelation of MERCY made in the Gospel; an altogether dependent creature, "kept *by the power of* GOD unto salvation," (1 Pet. i. 5.) must awfully depart from the high character to which he is called, when he imprecates against himself the forfeiture of the divine favour, if he fail of keeping his engagements with respect to his future conduct.

G. (page 3.)

Again humbly pray for such relief, &c. We should consider it a relief quite adequate to all our wishes in this matter, if an Act were passed extending the legislative indulgence enjoyed by the Quakers, in the matter of Oaths, to any person, of whom two or more Quakers should certify, that to the best of their knowledge and belief he belongs to a religious society agreeing with the people called Quakers upon that subject.

This appears to be a suitable opportunity for presenting to the reader a short statement of the circumstances attending the preceding petition and the legislative enactment to which it led.

The severe forfeitures which the people, called Separatists, had endured, and the more severe sufferings to which they were exposed, through their refusal to swear, led them early to apply to the legislature for such relief as the Quakers had long enjoyed. A petition, similar to the preceding, was presented to both houses of Parliament, and continued to be for many years annually laid before them. In 1822, extensive circulation was given to printed copies of it, accompanied by Mr. Walker's notes, as they are now published. But though the petitioners' claims became thus more widely known, and the justice of them more generally admitted, no step was taken towards removing the grievance under which they laboured. A better prospect presented itself in 1830; and strong hopes were entertained that a still more comprehensive measure might be favourably received; one which should not be confined to the relief of a particular sect, but should embrace persons of all denominations who had a conscientious objection to Oaths. Petitions to this effect were framed by the Separatists; and to the printed copies which were then disseminated, Mr. W. added a summary of his Notes, in the form of uninterrupted observations. These differ so very little in substance from the Notes, that it has not beem deemed necessary to insert them in the present edition. The arguments by which he enforced the propriety, the superior facility, and the perfect safety of such an enlarged measure of relief, will be found in his correspondence. But on this occasion also the petitioners met with disappointment.

Their exertions to include others in the relief they sought, received no aid whatever from the many whom they supposed interested in an exemption from swearing; and a parliamentary investigation into the subject of Oaths terminated only in the abolition of a few hundreds of those imprecations which were hourly exacted in the Customs and Excise offices. The petitioners were decidedly averse from pressing their claims on the legislature without the sanction of the government; but this, neither their sufferings nor their patience nor the acknowledged justice of their demand succeeded in obtaining until 1833; when Lord John Russell, who had long been their advocate in Parliament, recommended their cause to the protection of the administration, of which he was then an influential member. On the 24th April, in that session, leave was given to Mr. Pryme, member for Cambridge, and Mr. Murray, member for Leith, to bring in a bill for allowing the people called Separatists to make a solemn affirmation instead of an Oath. It went through the different stages in the House of Commons, with the cordial support of ministry as well as of many other distinguished members, and with little opposition from any; and on the 24th June passed the third reading. On the 9th of August, Lord Gosford, who had shewn a warm interest about the bill, introduced it to the House of Lords, where it was strongly supported by Lord Suffield, Lord Plunket, and the Bishop of Chichester; and received a second reading. Owing to objections raised by some noble Lords in the Committee, an addition to the simple form of affirmation, proposed by the Separatists, was introduced, and submitted to on the ground of the essential difference between the most solemn affirmation and an oath. On the 19th of August, the bill, thus altered, came on for the third reading; when, after a sharp debate, in which Lords Gosford, Suffield, and Plunket, the Bishop of Chichester, and finally and conclusively Lord Grey, took part, it passed the House by a majority of nineteen—thirty-five being for and sixteen against it; and on the 28th of August it received the Royal Assent. This bill, drawn up by Henry Chance, Esq., of Stone-buildings, Lincoln's Inn, and containing but forty lines, attracted considerable attention by its strict legal precision, combined with a brevity not common in legal documents. The experience of its working, though short, has been sufficient to stamp it as a measure not less advantageous to society at large than to the parties more apparently benefited; and to remove the unfounded apprehension expressed by a late popular, though not always liberal member, 'that it was taking another screw out of the constitution.'—Ed.

STATEMENT

OF THE

INTERRUPTION OF CHRISTIAN CONNEXION

BETWEEN THE

CHURCH IN LONDON

AND THE

CHURCH IN DUBLIN.

SOME REMARKS ON H. M.'s PRINTED LETTER;

AND

Some Observations on a Pamphlet,

ENTITLED

AN EXPOSITION, &c. OF THE GOSPEL,

AND OF THE

DENUNCIATIONS AGAINST THOSE WHO REJECT IT.

London, June 2d, 1829.

As some disciples in Ireland, with whom we have been—and *ought* still to be—in acknowledged Christian connexion, may hear of the interruption of that connexion between us and those in Dublin, without hearing any distinct account of the circumstances which have led to it; for the sake of such it has been judged expedient to draw up the following Statement, and to print a few copies of it for private circulation among them.

For a long time, some of the brethren here have been pained by various reports which reached them of the course of the Church in Dublin, from which it appeared that their assembly had become the scene of strife and debate, and of all the evils necessarily consequent upon this. The last subject of protracted controversy among them has been the Apostolic precept given in 1 Cor. v. 11; to which we had all heretofore professed subjection. It is now more than five months, since one of their members was allowed, openly in their meeting, to disclaim subjection to that divine command: and—instead of his being immediately brought under the discipline of the house of God, and removed from among them if it failed of bringing him to repentance,—the precept has since continued a subject of disputation in their meetings, the ungodly rejection of it has spread wider and wider among them, and it lately appeared that the infection was communicated from them to some members of the Church in London.

Various private attempts had been made by individuals here, in their epistolary communications with individuals in Dublin, to admonish them of their evil course, and to recall them to those scriptural principles of Christian fellowship, from which it was plain they had awfully departed. These attempts were ineffectual. Authentic accounts were received very lately, that their disputation seemed as far as ever from any termination; and that all the evils connected with it, and the toleration of those evils by those who professed to maintain the command, continued. Indeed, it was manifest, that if they thought themselves at liberty to play this kind of game with the word for five months, they could have no good reason for not continuing to play it interminably;—unless perhaps that they were *tired*.

However, it was the appearance of the plague in a few of our own body that immediately occasioned our interference as a Church. Those individuals were taken into discipline without delay: and although some of the cases looked very dark at first, yet, through the mercy of God, they all ended happily. The subject was at large laid before the assembled brethren on the 26th of April; and on the 3d of May, the Church commissioned two of us to write in their name to the Church in Dublin a letter of admonition and reproof, for the evils that had so long existed among them. A copy of that letter follows. If there be any discrepancies between this copy and the letter despatched, they are very few, merely verbal, and purely accidental.

'*May* 6, 1829.

'To the Church of Christ assembling in * * * Dublin.

'Mercy and peace be multiplied!

'We have been deputed, dear Brethren, by the Church assembling in Portsmouth Street, LONDON, to address you in their name; and that in the way of admonition and scriptural reproof for evils, which exist among you, and the continuance of which would be inconsistent with the continuance of our connexion as Sister-Churches. We allude to the opposition which has been raised among you, and tolerated for months, against the Apostolic command in 1 Cor. v. 11.

'It is now some weeks, since a letter from one of the females in your body brought the melancholy intelligence that, *after a great deal of discussion in your Church, you were then pretty generally of one mind* for—(what we must term)—rejecting that command, as what could not be designed to regulate the conduct of the Corinthian disciples towards the wicked person spoken of, *after* he was put out from their body. That this is equivalent with the absolute setting aside of the precept, must be obvious to any disciple reading the whole chapter, unless his eyes be indeed holden. For the first injunction which the Apostle gives on this subject is, that the Church should forthwith—on their next coming together after the receipt of the epistle—put away from among them that fornicator: and as soon as that was done, some of you have discovered that it would be foolish in the Apostle to forbid their associating with him in civil life, as freely as with any fornicator of the heathen world! It is therefore plain, that according to this sentiment there was no room at all for the precept in the eleventh verse to be observed. As soon as such a character is found within a Christian Church, he is to be put out; and as soon as he is put out, (according to these interpreters) the disciples may hold all the same convivial intercourse with him as with a heathen!

'But we cannot be surprised, when we find disputers against the word of God taken in the craftiness of their own wisdom. We have no intention, Brethren, of maintaining any disputation with you on this precept. Ye have had more than enough of that. It would be hard to find any precept throughout the Scriptures more plain: and it is given us—not to be argued—but to be obeyed. However, we shall subjoin to this letter a brief statement of the view, which we maintain of the whole passage, in language the plainest we can employ, and substantially equivalent with the Apostle's.

'But we would now turn to those among you,—and we doubt not there are such,—who continue to assert with us the divine authority of that command, which the others gainsay and oppose. Brethren, we have to call *you* to repentance just as much as the latter;—to repentance for so long tolerating in the house of God rebellion against the authority of his word. Have ye forgotten, dear brethren, the principles in which heretofore we were professedly agreed?—that, if we surrender the sacredness of any one divine precept, we substantially surrender the sacredness of all, as they all rest on one common basis?—that he who is of God, heareth his Apostles? 1 John, iv. 6. —and that, if any man obey not their word, we are enjoined to note that man, and *have no company* with him? 2 Thess. iii. 14.—the selfsame course enjoined in 1 Cor. v. towards the fornicator that is called a brother.

'We are aware indeed that some have talked, as if the diversity of sentiment in your body upon this precept were of the less consequence, because your practice would be much the same, whether it be acknowledged or not; as a kind of taste—feeling—or private judgment—would restrain all from the familiarity of social intercourse with those who have been removed from your body. But, even supposing this were true,—what we are persuaded it is not,—the argument is utterly vain. What would you say, if one among you were found, denying the divine rule for our coming together on the first day of the week, to observe the Lord's Supper; and if he should plead that he ought to be borne with in this, because he joined you in the practice from thinking it useful and edifying? Is it of little consequence, whether our conduct spring from subjection to the Lord's command, or from our own fancy? And can it spring from subjection to his command, if that be not discerned and acknowledged?

'But we apprehend, brethren, that the main cause which has introduced all these evils into your body,—(after that common ungodliness of our hearts from which all evil springs)—is your having allowed the Church of God to be turned into a theatre for theological controversy and debate. Few things are more hardening to the conscience; few more contrary to the scriptural fear of God, and reverence of his word; few more calculated to stumble the weak, and to impede the real edification of all.

'Is every vain disputer to be allowed to start his crude novelty of some untaught question, or to throw up the ball of argument against a divine precept, under the name of discussion? We beseech you to consider, whether any such attempt ought not to be stopped, in the first instance, by those among you who are spiritual. If he think that he has discovered any part of divine truth or rule, which has hitherto escaped us, let it be submitted to the consideration of a few of sounder judgment; and not flung among you indiscriminately, as a doubtful question for debate. If to those few it can be shown to be founded on scriptural authority,—(and where real scriptural authority for any thing is clearly seen, it can in general be clearly and briefly pointed out)—let it be brought before the Church, recommended and enforced by a plain appeal to the word of God. But if it cannot be shown to be so enforced, ought not the introduction of the qnestion into the Church to be steadfastly resisted, even to the removal of the perverse disputer who would persist in pressing it, and of all who might be found taking part with him?

'But tho' we hold the subject to be of high importance, yet the space to which we are confined, as well as the immediate object of this letter, forbid us to pursue it at present. We commend it to your serious attention; and you, dear brethren, to that great Shepherd, who "feeds the flock of his heritage with his rod," (Mic. vii. 14.)—with that WORD OF HIS GRACE "which is able to build us up," —to *edify* us indeed; (Acts, xx. 32.) praying him that we may be given that "one heart and one way," (Jer. xxxii. 39.) which he only can give and maintain in us.'

'R. L. C.
'J. W.

'P. S.—[In the following, only one of us is responsible for any remarks which refer to the original Greek. They are very few and simple; and ye have among you some who will not hesitate to authenticate them.]

'After the Apostle has given the solemn injunction for putting away the offender from the Church, in verses 3, 4, 5, and enforced its suitableness in the three following verses; he appears very plainly to proceed as follows: *This is really such a case as I had in view, when I charged you in a* former (A.) *letter to* hold no society (B.) *with fornicators: a direction which some of you supposed to refer to heathen fornicators. But it did not: for what have I to do with the characters of those, who do not profess the faith of Christ? They are to be left to the judgment of God. And indeed, if ye were to hold* no *society with heathen fornicators, it would be necessary for you to quit the world alto-*

gether; as it is overspread with such. But now I tell you distinctly, that my direction referred to such wicked characters appearing among yourselves,—within *the household faith: and that these are to be so absolutely removed from your society and from all connexion with you, that you are not to hold with them* EVEN (C.) *that convivial intercourse which you may hold with heathens*; (1 Cor. x. 27.) much less *Christian fellowship. Accordingly, put away from among you altogether that wicked person.*'

A few additional remarks on the subject will be found subjoined at the close of these pages: but at present we shall pursue our narrative.

On the 10th of May, the receipt of an admonitory letter from the Church in London was announced to the body in Dublin; when *all parties* among them concurred in *refusing to allow the letter to be read.* It appears to have been considered an officious *interference*, a usurpation of *jurisdiction* over them: and one of those who professedly maintain the authority of the disputed precept is stated to have declared, that if *he* had received the letter, he would have thrown it into the fire. Strange ideas must such men have of the nature and principles of the Christian connexion! Strange ideas of that, which is the highest exercise of brotherly fidelity and love!

There were at this time three parties in their body: 1, the open and zealous opposers of the command; 2, the debaters, who professed that their minds were in a state of vacillation; 3, those who professedly acknowledged the divine authority of the precept. The two former classes indeed need not be distinguished; as it is obvious that the second class were not subject to its divine authority any more than the first. That the first of these parties should have been averse even to hear the words of reproof, was to be expected; but that the last should have concurred in refusing to hear them, and this even after they separated from the former,—(for on the following Sunday, May 17th, they did separate from the avowed opposers of the precept)—looks very much as if they were no more under the influence of scriptural principles, than those from whom they at length withdrew; and assuredly it at once closed the door against any further attempt on our side to communicate with them as with a Sister-Church.

Not that we by any means intend to assert, that *every* letter addressed to a Christian Church, in the name of a Sister-Church, either must or ought to be laid before the assembled brethren, or read in their meeting. Such a letter might possibly be very foolish, or very wicked. But to reject a letter of scriptural, and most needful, reproof and admonition, such as we are bold to say our letter was, evidently amounts to a virtual renunciation of Christian connexion with the Church, from whom the letter is sent: just as it would be inconsistent with the maintenance of Christian brotherhood between two individuals in the same Church, that one of them should refuse even to hear the other—attempting to reprove and admonish him *scripturally*.

However, on the 21st of May, one of us received a private letter from the person, to whom our letter had been transmitted, stating that on the 17th, he and others—(forming a minority of the whole body)—had withdrawn from the disputers *against* the precept, and held their meeting in another place. Now, the question may naturally occur to some who shall read these pages,—'Did not this in some degree indicate repentance on their side; and so far indicate that the end proposed by our letter of admonition was obtained without it?' We are sorry to say that this letter received from Dublin utterly forbade any such inference, as far as the individual writer was concerned. It contained not the slightest appearance of godly shame or sorrow for the evils, in which he had so long been walking, and had taken such a large share; and a few vague expressions, which might look like an admission that our admonition was just, were more than neutralized by a passage in which—(if words have any meaning)—he avows that, in a recurrence of similar circumstances, he would think himself justified in pursuing the same wicked course again.

It was therefore evident, that there remained for us but one course, that could be adopted consistently with Christian faithfulness. On the 24th of May, the two brethren commissioned by the Church to deal in the affair with those in Dublin, made a report to the body of the melancholy result: and the Church promptly came to a declaration, that our connexion with those in Dublin as a Sister-Church was dissolved. Deeply painful as this procedure had been, yet we are convinced that various evils, connected with their continued disputations, had come to such a head among them, that it affords a fairer prospect, under the divine blessing, of a closer and better reunion hereafter with some among them, than could otherwise be effected. But all consequences are to be submitted to the Lord.

There is no principle, which we would more strongly urge upon the attention of disciples reading these pages, than the utter unlawfulness of protracted debate and controversy in a Christian Church, under any circumstances. If the matter debated be among the things of Christian faith or practice decided by the word of God,—(and if it be not, it plainly comes under the class of "foolish and untaught questions" which we are to avoid, 2 Tim. ii. 23.)—the scriptural determination of it is to be simply pointed out, by those who see and acknowledge it: and it profanes the sacredness and divine authority of the word, if they afterwards allow *its* decision to be made a subject of controversy and debate. From the *perverse disputers*, who will *not consent to the wholesome words* of sound doctrine, disciples are called to *withdraw* themselves,—not—to go on disputing with them. 1 Tim. vi. 3—5. Rom. xvi. 17.—In cases of Christian discipline also, the word of God makes a similarly wise provision against their coming before the Church in any *disputable* form. All matters of fact connected with them are to be "established in the mouth of two or three witnesses." Matt. xviii. 16. Deut. xix. 15.—It is certain, therefore, that while disciples are kept adhering to the divine rule, there is not any case in which a Christian Church can become a school of disputation, such as long prevailed in Dublin. And it will be found, that where such perverse disputings prevail, it is because those who introduce and maintain them are not abiding in the truth of "the Gospel of God," however speciously they may talk about it. Kept abiding in that, we shall "dwell together in unity," and shall "be at peace among ourselves;" walking in that fear of the LORD, which is ever accompanied and manifested by a "trembling at his word."

The hardy fearlessness indeed, with which some of the Dublin disputers have set up what appears right in their own eyes, in opposition to the wisdom of God, is one of the most awful circumstances in their whole course. Some of their arguments against the precept in 1 Cor. v. 11, we have seen in a letter from one of them; and are assured by one of the opposite party, that all their arguments come to the same point. It is substantially this: 'all the same freedom of social intercourse, which the Corinthian disciples might lawfully hold with an heathen neighbour, the Apostle *could not consistently* debar them from holding with the incestuous person—*after he was put out from among them*; for he was *then no longer* called a brother, and therefore *could not* come under the rule given in the 11th verse, whatever be its meaning: he was THEN one of those *without*, and the Apostle tells us that he does not *judge them that are without*,' &c. &c.—Such a special-pleading argument is really more suitable to an Old-Bailey Solicitor than to a professing disciple of Christ. It rather becomes the Christian, to hear what the word of God does enjoin, than to conclude *a priori* what it can or cannot enjoin.

'But to restrain the freedom of social intercourse with him *after* he was put out of the Church, would be to *continue a course of discipline* towards those, who had to all intents returned to the world.' Just as reasonably might they reject the command given by the apostle John—"If there come any unto you, and bring not this doctrine, *receive him not into your house*."—(2 John, 10.) Such a false teacher was certainly one of those whom he had before described as having *gone out* from the pale of the apostolic communion, not continuing in it *because they were not truly* of it: (1 John ii. 19) and just as reasonably might those disputers charge this Apostle also with foolish inconsistency, in directing what they call *a course of discipline* to be *continued* towards a person that was *without*!

That the conduct enjoined on the Corinthian Church, towards the character mentioned in the other passage, was enjoined partly in the view of *mercy* towards him, and in the hope of its being blessed to his recovery from his wicked way, we are far from denying. That seems very plainly intimated in the 5th verse, and confirmed by the effect which, we find from the second Epistle, did actually result. And this indeed might check the letter-writer, to whose arguments we refer, from so boldly pronouncing that the person put away from the Church '*must be considered* a child of God or the contrary, there being *but two characters of men in Scripture*,' &c. Are there not many cases in which, while we cannot with any confidence regard a man as a child of God, we yet must shrink from pronouncing him a child of the devil?—unless we be ourselves in that mind high and lifted up, which goes before a fall; and the language of which is,

"Am *I* a dog, that *I* should do this thing?" But passing this; is it not obvious that the main purpose of the whole course, enjoined on the disciples towards that wicked person, was *their own* profit, to purge out from among themselves that leaven, a little of which leaveneth the whole lump? And are these wise disputers against the wisdom of God quite certain, that the *continued* restriction on the familiarity of social intercourse with that wicked person was not graciously and wisely adapted to keep the minds of the brethren awake to the due abhorrence of his wickedness? Truly, if any of them felt the same pleasure in his society, as they might feel in that of one who had never been in the Christian connexion, their minds must think very lightly of his ejection from the kingdom of God, and of that which had occasioned it.

But let us suppose that we were unable to discern any of the ends designed by the wisdom of God in giving this precept; is not the precept given, in language as plain and unequivocal as words can convey it? And does it not become those, who fear God, to *obey*, even though unable to discern *why* he commands? Such certainly was the obedience of believing Abraham. Now what is the letter-writer's answer to this simple appeal to the Scripture? We shall give it in his own words:—'*I admit an* INFERENCE *may be drawn from verses* 9, 10, and 11. *But* (in a matter so momentous) *we have a right to expect something in Scripture more explicit than an* INFERENCE?'

We shall make no remark on the presumptuousness of that sentiment and language, save this: that, if the person who has adopted them be ever "recovered out of the snare of the devil," (2 Tim. ii. 26.) he will look back on that language and sentiment with deep abhorrence.

SOME REMARKS ON H. M.'s PRINTED LETTER.

LONDON, August 28th, 1829.

OUR printed Statement, dated June 2d, ended with the fact of the Church assembling in Portsmouth Street having declared their connexion dissolved with the body in Dublin, as a Sister-Church. I would briefly remark on this step, that some have been led to mistake its nature by pursuing a fancied analogy between it and the last act of discipline, in a Church removing from among them one of its own members. The connexion between Sister-Churches is—not that either is an integral part of the other—but simply this: that they have such knowledge of each other, of the unity of their faith and walk, that a member of one visiting the other is ordinarily received into its fellowship upon the mere recognition of his being in fellowship with the acknowledged Sister-Church. In declaring that connexion dissolved we did but declare, that circumstances had occurred which interrupted that knowledge; (which cannot continue when either Church closes the door against scriptural communication from the other;)—and therefore interrupted the confidence, which could not scripturally continue without it. We simply declared that, if one of the Dublin body should visit London, and desire to join our fellowship, we could not receive him without *inquiry* whether he repented of the evils, which we knew all of them had so long tolerated, and in which therefore all had more or less share.

I have regretted that the printing of our Statement was not delayed a few days, in order that it might have contained the mention of an additional fact, which I gladly take the present opportunity of introducing. We had scarcely received the copies of that paper from the printer, when a letter the most satisfactory arrived from those in Dublin, who had withdrawn from the opposers of the precept in 1 Cor. v. 11. and now hold their meetings in Stafford Street. This letter was so full, unequivocal, and decisive in the evidences it afforded of genuine repentance, that it enabled us on our next assembling to confirm our love towards them, and to restore them joyfully to acknowledged union with us as a Sister-Church.

M.'s pamphlet bears the date of May 22. In this there is probably a mistake of a month. I did not obtain a copy of it till three weeks ago. The task of animadverting on it I have undertaken with great reluctance; and at first indeed rather yielding to the judgment of others than following my own. Never have I prosecuted any similar task with so deep pain. How painful is it in my last days to meet as an opponent one whom I have known so long, esteemed and loved so highly! to meet such a man in a character altogether new! to be obliged to expose the weakness of one of the ablest men, and the unfairness of one of the most ingenuous, I could formerly have named! But "what is man?"—M. has written in heat and in haste. His flesh revolts against the scriptural principle, which he has long taken a lead in opposing. He has taken up his pen to maintain that opposition, and to increase the party who strengthen each other in it. Against a truth, the evidence of which has been plainly exhibited, it is hard for an able man to write honestly; and it is impossible for the ablest to write conclusively.

With every thing that M. throws out against *human influence*, in the things of the kingdom of God, most heartily do I concur. Our continual tendency to be determined in conduct and practice by it, instead of by the word of God, is part of the common ungodliness of our hearts. But let some connected with M. recollect, that they are in at least as much danger from that temptation, as any can be with me. It ought to be a very sobering consideration to both of us, that —whatever colour or currency human ingenuity or human influence may for a time give to falsehood,—yet sooner or later that word of the Lord Jesus shall be made good, "Every plant, which my heavenly Father hath not planted, shall be rooted up." Matth. xv. 13.

It is with some art that M. (after awfully distributing the meed of his applause among some leaders in the rebellion) opens the subject by a discussion, extending through nearly three pages, on Matth. xviii. 17, in which he sets up men of straw to knock them down, puts upon us assertions that we have never made, and otherwise diverts the eye of his reader from the point really at issue between us. Whom he intends to oppose in a great part of that discussion, I really do not know. But he knows well, that it is not on the interpretation of this passage in the Evangelist we have separated, but on the precept in 1 Cor. v. 11. the command to disciples *not even to eat with* such a character as is there described. That precept is explicit. We assert, and they reject it, in the only obvious and proper sense of the words. *If* any, in the course of the disputes on the subject, which were continued in their meetings so long,—*if* any, argued from the words of the other passage, "let him be unto thee as an heathen man and a publican," that they also must be understood as *including* a similar injunction, to abstain even from social intercourse in eating with the person removed from the fellowship of the Church, —(because at the time these words were uttered by the Lord, the Jews were still debarred from such intercourse with *heathens*) ;—*if* any have urged this argument, it is one which M. certainly has not even attempted to refute, in all the words which he has multiplied upon that passage. Yet I think it injudicious in any to quote it, for the purpose of *establishing* the precept in Corinthians : because the latter is *express* upon the point contested, while the former bears upon it only by implication. In short, if we had not the express command *not even to eat* with such a person, I am not sure whether the attempt to infer it from Matth. xviii. 17, might not with some plausibility be opposed by the consideration, that we are now at liberty to eat with heathens, or with those who have never been in Christian fellowship with us. The attempt therefore to draw that inference afforded the adversaries a point of attack at least *comparatively* weak ; and M. has dexterously availed himself of it, by putting this forward in the first instance, as a passage on which we *found* our view of the precept in 1 Cor. v. 11.

But I am sorry to say that there is still more dishonest artifice manifested in the way he treats those words, "let him be unto thee as an heathen man and a publican :" and the artifice which he employs here is of a species that pervades almost every page of his pamphlet. It is that of attributing to us sentiments which he has abundant reason to know we do not hold ; and vehemently declaiming against those sentiments, as if he were in this refuting our errors. Thus, he employs more than two pages in contending that the terms *heathen man and publican*, 'designate those who are not of God, who are *without* ;' that the Lord uses the name of *publican*, as 'perfectly synonymous with the word *sinner*, or a *wicked* person :' and that when it is said *let him be unto thee as a publican*, it 'implies the same thing as the Apostle says, Put away from among yourselves that *wicked* person.' Now who denies any part of this ? Certainly we do not : nor is it conceivable to me, how M. can be ignorant that we do not. As to myself, my language upon the meaning to be generally attached to the word *publican* in the Gospels, my language that I am sure has met his eye in print, to say nothing of what he has heard times without number in our meetings, is (I think) as distinct and as strong as his. The following occurs in my remarks on the parable of the Pharisee and the Publican, p. 540. "The name of Publican was equivalent with that of a wicked profligate. This is evident, from our finding *publicans* and *harlots* classed together in the New Testament, where we see the publican ranking proverbially with sinners of the very vilest description upon earth. See Matt. xxi. 31, 32; ix. 10, 11; xi. 19; Luke xv. 1, 2." &c.—And if—as would appear to be the case—some in Dublin have (as I think, injudiciously) referred to Matt. xviii. 17, as confirmatory of the precept in 1 Cor. v. 11, because they conceived that the words of the Lord necessarily involved a direction identical with the Apostle's; did these very men deny, or think of denying, that the former *immediately* and *primarily* imported a direction to the disciples equivalent with that of putting away the wicked person from among them? No: I confidently answer that they did not. And *if* M. really conceived that they did, when he penned these extraordinary pages, it could only be because the exasperation of mind in which he has written, prevented the exercise of calm and honest judgment. Ajax *thought* that he was destroying the chiefs of the Greeks, while he was but slaughtering harmless sheep and oxen: and M. has been really fighting against shadows, while he—shall I say?—*imagined* that he was overthrowing us.

There is nothing else to be noticed in these pages but the arguments, which M. introduces by anticipation, that we adopt *a species of discipline* towards "one no longer subject to the discipline of the house of God, as having been put away from it." There was a species of wisdom in M.'s bringing forward this objection *here*; but I shall reserve the little that I have to say upon it for its proper place, and proceed to the consideration of the apostolic precept in 1 Cor. v. 11. This is the real matter at issue between us: and this being once established, all such objections against the wisdom of the divine command must be scattered into *thin air*, in the view of those who fear God and tremble at his word.

And here M. need not have laboured to prove, that throughout the chapter, "from first to last, the Apostle is speaking of the evil *existing* in the Church;" an evil which had *existed* awfully long, and which continued to *exist among them* at the time the Apostle wrote. This M. repeats over and over, and insists upon it vehemently, as if we denied it. But in insisting upon this, (which we would assert as strongly as himself) he takes care to involve this true assertion with an *assumption* of the falsehood which he maintains; namely—that throughout the chapter the Apostle gives no command to the Corinthian disciples, besides that of excluding the *wicked* person whom they had retained among them from all CHRISTIAN fellowship with them; leaving them at liberty to associate with him in all the civil intercourse of life, as freely as with those who had never been within the household of faith. This, I say, M. gratuitously assumes, and thus jumps to his conclusion without any trouble of argument, by the paltry sophism called a *petitio principii*. We have asserted, and we maintain that—besides removing the fornicator from the Church, and consequently from all Christian fellowship with them,—

the Apostle does, in the 11th verse, expressly restrict them from holding with him even that familiarity of worldly intercourse which (in the 10th verse) he remarks they were at liberty to hold with heathens. (D.) M. professedly writes to prove that no such restriction is imposed on the disciples in the 11th verse. And how does he pretend to prove it? By *assuming* it:—by asserting confidently, and repeating vehemently, that there is no command given throughout the chapter which was not fulfilled in the removal of the fornicator from the Church:—nay, even hardily asserting that the Apostle "tells them that he did not at all allude to worldly intercourse." (p. 10. see also p. 7.) But really no vehemence of declamation, or bold confidence of assertion, is equivalent with strength of argument or conclusiveness of proof:—though indeed too many writers substitute the one for the other, and the cheat passes upon too many readers. It is this alone that makes M.'s pamphlet dangerous.

Entering upon the subject, M. gives (pp. 4, 5.) what he appears to put forward as a summary view of the whole chapter. But I must say that he obscures it much, both by suppressing altogether the latter part of the 5th verse—"that the spirit may be saved," &c.—and by omitting the adversative conjunction "*But*" at the beginning of the 11th verse. Upon the first eight verses of the chapter it is not necessary that I should say much; as I am not aware of any disagreement between us as to their import. I should only wish to state distinctly, in order to supply M.'s omission, that the Apostle plainly marks a *twofold* object in the enjoined casting out of the wicked person from the Church:—the one object respecting the Church, that what defiled the temple of God, and was calculated to spread its defilement like leaven, might be purged out from among them;—the other object respecting the offender himself, "for the destruction of the flesh, that the spirit might be saved in the day of the Lord Jesus." According to the latter of these objects, we are warranted to regard the act of the Church in casting him out from among them into the world that lieth in the wicked one as an act of *mercy* to the offender, a step to be taken in the view and hope of its being blest for his recovery to repentance; as undoubtedly their having so long tolerated and retained him in their fellowship had been *calculated to harden him in his wickedness*. But it is the less necessary for me to insist that the Apostle does put forward this second object, as M. himself admits it in his 13th page. And *I* am quite ready to admit that, of the two objects presented to the view of a Church in such a case, the former—the purging out of the old leaven from among them—is the more immediate and primary, as that which is to be effected, even though the other object were never to be attained.

Well then; we are agreed that the Corinthian Church, in putting away from among them that wicked person, did (if they acted according to the mind of the Spirit in the Apostolic command) take that step in a *merciful* view towards him, and in the *hope* of his recovery from the snare of the devil. Would that I could engage H. M. to consider calmly the question, which I now press on the attention of disciples! *Did that merciful view and hope cease the same hour, in which his removal from the Christian body took place?* It is absurd to suppose that it should;—as absurd, in some respects, as it would be to say, that the hope of a patient's recovery to health should cease, the moment he is sent to an hospital for cure. (Now let not M. amuse himself and others by shewing that there are points of dissimilarity between the two cases. Who denies it?) Well then; if the merciful hope, under which the fornicator was put away from the fellowship of the Church, *continued* during the interval between that solemn act and his restoration to its fellowship; it follows—(I would say *undeniably*, but that M. has proved there is nothing which may not be denied—see his 10th page)—it follows that there was *without* the Church of God, and within the world—Satan's kingdom, a man whom the disciples were *taught* to view with a different eye, from that with which they regarded those who had never been within the household of faith.

And now, in asserting this, do I intimate, (as M. grossly misrepresents,) that the wicked person cast out from the Church is less wicked than those who have never been within it? Or that he is the less to me, *as* an heathen, for not being actually so? (M. knows, that ὥσπερ "*as, as if*" implies *similitude*; and that the idea of similitude not only does not imply *identity*, but excludes it.)—Or that he will less assuredly perish in his wickedness, except he repent? Nay truly: those who know me, know that I am not backward to assert that solemn principle declared in 1 Cor. vi. 9, 10, 11, and in Gal. v. 19, 20, 21. Why then, it may be asked, are they to be regarded *in any respect* with a different eye? I really feel no anxiety to answer that question. Having established even from the 5th v. of this disputed chapter that the wisdom of God has ordered it so, I do not feel myself at all bound to meet the bold questions, by which disputers attempt to impeach that wisdom. Yet I add, that I think disciples may easily perceive the reasonableness of the divine appointment, or rather, its consistency with the glorious nature of that faith, which this wicked person not only *had* confessed, but (we have every reason to believe) still continued to confess with the mouth.

And now, before proceeding to the latter part of the chapter in which stands that Apostolic direction which M. would set aside, I have no objection to concede to him,—if it may afford him any advantage,—that had the Apostle dismissed the subject at the end of the 8th verse, there might be some *plausible* ground for questioning, whether he designed to prohibit any intercourse with that wicked person, except what is intrinsically of a *religious* nature; whether his exclusion from all *Christian* fellowship with the disciples did not comprehend *all* that the Apostle designed. But let M. observe, that the concession which I speak of is only hypothetical—on the supposition that the Apostle had written no more on the subject than is contained in the first eight verses of the chapter. But the fact is, that he continues the subject through the five remaining verses: and M.'s *assumption*, or hardy *assertion*, that these contain no additional direction, no command to the disciples restricting them from the freedom of even social intercourse with that wicked person,—I say his bold assumption or confident assertion of this does not really weigh a feather against the plain command given us in the 11th verse. And here my main object is, to call the attention of disciples to the words of the Apostle, from the multitude of vain words in which M. has endeavoured to envelope the subject. That the passage, therefore, may be immediately under my reader's eye, I transcribe it at large; and I hope M. will not again be angry with me for having it printed in the Italic character, the better to distinguish the Apostle's words from mine.

9. *I wrote to you in an epistle not to keep company with fornicators:*
10. *Yet not altogether with the fornicators of this world, or with the*
covetous, or extortioners, or idolaters; for then must ye needs go out of
the world. 11. *But now I have written unto you not to keep company, if*
any man that is called a brother be a fornicator, or covetous, or a railer,
or a drunkard, or an extortioner; with such an one [no not] not even
to eat. 12. *For what have I to do to judge them also that are without?*
do not ye judge them that are within? 13. *But them that are without*
God judgeth. Therefore put away from among yourselves that wicked
person.

Now if any intelligent person—I care not whether believer or unbeliever—were to read those words for the first time, and were then asked, 'What direction did the Apostle give in the 11th verse about such characters, as he enumerates, when found within the Church? Was it only that they should be excluded from all *religious* fellowship with the Church? or did he also prohibit the disciples from holding with them *even* the familiarity of social intercourse?'—to such an inquiry what would be the reply of the person who should for the first time read the passage with intelligence? Would it not be expressive of wonder, how the question could be raised? Would he not be apt to say, 'Surely the Apostle expressly tells the Christians, that they are not *even to eat with* such characters: and surely eating or drinking with a man is an act not of religious fellowship, but of social intercourse.' Well: let me suppose one question more proposed to the same reader: 'Did the Apostle impose the same restriction on the Corinthian Christians towards similar characters of the world not professedly Christians?' Would not his reply be? 'No; he plainly tells them that he does not mean this, and assigns two reasons for it: one, that they could not abstain from social intercourse with such characters of the surrounding world without quitting the world, or human society, altogether;—and the other, that he as an Apostle, and they as Christians, had nothing to do with the characters and conduct of any except the members of the Church.'

Let the Christian reader, if necessary, read the words of the Apostle again; and then let him think whether the view of them which I have expressed be not that, which they must present—obviously and without any doubtfulness present—to every reader, whose judgment is not strangely blinded. And accordingly, as far as I know, there is not an interpreter or commentator, ancient or modern, that has ever assigned another meaning to the passage: in which certainly their judgment is the more impartial, because most of them never dream of obeying an Apostolic command, however they may interpret it. Yet M. has the hardihood to say (p. 6.)—"Had this chapter not been *distorted by human ingenuity*, ill-employed and ill-directed, its meaning had been plain, its purport obvious," &c.—(*i. e.* it would have been *plain* and *obvious* that the Christians were *not* restricted from eating ever so freely with the fornicator in the way of social intercourse!)—" but we have been for years *perverting* it—for years we have been acting imperfectly and miserably, upon a principle which it nowhere enjoins—we have been adopting toward people removed from the church a wretched partial system of non-intercourse, and this we have been *hypocritically calling a dealing of mercy,*" &c. &c. &c. Ah! M.—was not all this rattle of words and theological railing employed to drown the voice of conscience in your own breast, as well as to impose upon your readers? Wonderful, certainly, is the dexterity which we have in imposing on ourselves. And so you really assert—that but for human *ingenuity distorting* the Apostle's words, it would have been *plain* and *obvious* and *clear*, that by not even *eating with* that wicked person the Apostle meant not eating with him *in a religious way!* Does not a blush rise upon your cheek at the moment of reading this? Does not conscience whisper? 'I have been wrong in asserting it to be the *obvious* meaning of the words, even if I have been right in asserting it to be their true meaning.'

But how does M. make out the interpretation, which he contends for? Does he deny that the original words τῳ τοιουτῳ μηδε συνεσθιειν are accurately and literally rendered *not even to eat with such an one?* Does he assert that they admit any other correct version? No: he knows well that they do not. Does he assert that the Greek verb rendered *to eat with* includes, in its meaning, any thing of *religious* fellowship, any thing beyond the natural and social act—*convivial companionship?* No; he knows it does not: no more than the expressions—*to ride with*—*to sleep with*, &c. include, in their import, any thing religious. On what ground then does he find himself at liberty to foist in this idea, and thus daringly to interpolate the divine word? Simply on this ground; that he set off with the gratuitous *assumption*, and has continued it throughout his pamphlet, that the Apostle did not and could not enjoin on the disciples any different conduct or deportment towards the wicked person put away from among themselves, from that conduct and deportment which they maintained towards the rest of the surrounding world who professed not the Christian faith. He has assumed this, I say, and assumed it in the face of the Apostle's express command in this passage: and from this *assumption* he pretends to infer, that the Apostle did not mean what he says in the 11th verse; that he did not forbid *their even eating with* the wicked person mentioned, but only *their eating with him in a way of* religious *fellowship!*

I shall by and by glance at M.'s objections to the suitableness and propriety of the Apostle's command: but at present I say, that with those who fear God they ought to pass for absolutely nothing, or less than nothing, in the view of that command, explicit and unequivocal as it stands. I repeat it, therefore, that the whole of M.'s argument, if argument it can be called, is comprised in the following gross sophism:—'The Apostle could not forbid the freest intermixture of the disciples in *civil* life with that wicked person, after he was put out of the Church, because they were allowed it with those who had never been within the Church. Therefore in the 11th verse he does not forbid their eating with him in the way of convivial companionship, but only their eating with him in some way of Christian fellowship!'

In opposition to all this assertion, the disciple might well dismiss M. and his pamphlet with the following brief reply:—'But the Apostle actually does that, which you assume that he does not, and could not do. After having enjoined them to put him out of the Church, which certainly excluded him from *all* (E.) *Christian fellowship* with them,—he after this proceeds to enforce the prohibition against all intermixture with him, by expressly extending it to their *even eating with him*: and this not only without the slightest intimation that he intends any companionship in eating that was peculiar to *Christians*, but in such a connexion as proves (F.), that he means such a companionship in eating as they might hold with *heathens*.'—A few remarks, tending to explain and to establish the different parts of this brief reply, I throw into the form of notes.

Among the objections which M. brings against the Apostolic precept, he descends even to that which I noticed in our printed statement as really 'a special pleading argument, more suitable to an Old Bailey solicitor than to a professing disciple of Christ:' namely, That the wicked person—when removed from the Church—would then be one of those *without*; and that as the Apostle declares that he judges only those *within*, it would have been inconsistent to have forbidden them to eat with that man after his removal from the Church. I put as distinctly as I can the substance of the argument, which he reiterates in various forms and with tiresome verbosity throughout his pamphlet; while the obscurity with which he envelopes it looks much as if he were secretly ashamed of its being brought into the light. To this redoubtable objection I reply briefly, but decisively: Throughout this chapter the Apostle *pronounces judgment* on a wicked person *then within* the Church, and directs the disciples how they shall act towards him; that they shall remove him from the Church and all Christian fellowship, and that with *him* they shall not hold even that companionship in eating which they might with a heathen. When the Church accordingly put him from among them, he was certainly no longer *within*; but *did the judgment therefore cease*, which had been passed upon him when he was within, and for wickedness committed by him under the Christian name? No, truly: on the contrary, that part of the judgment, which debarred them from maintaining familiarity with him even in social life, *continued* in all its force, just as much as the sentence of his exclusion from their Christian fellowship *continued*.

But though I have now sufficiently exposed the weakness and unfairness of his objection, I confess that I doubt whether such cavils ought to receive any serious answer. When a writer on a scriptural subject resorts to them,—and especially a writer with such a clear head as M. possesses,—it only indicates that he is resolved at all hazards to maintain his opposition to the scriptural principle which he rejects: and having of course no really conclusive argument to advance, he does the best he can with the most disgusting sophisms, and depends on his reader's want of acuteness to detect them;—he makes a noise by firing blank cartridges, and hides himself in the smoke. Take away from M.'s pamphlet that poor sophism, in all the dresses in which it appears, and in all the inferences which he attempts to derive from it, and I scarcely know what would be left.

In note C. to our printed Statement a remark occurs, that the mere act of eating *at the same table* with the wicked person put away from the Church, does not necessarily constitute that companionship in eating, which is forbidden. Indeed it is very plain, that it would be as reasonable to suppose, that eating in the same house, or in the same street with him, were included in the prohibition. And it was added, that eating at the same table with him 'may be unavoidable, from the relations and duties of life.' The truth of the remark is obvious. Every one of scriptural judgment knows that positive institution gives way to moral duty;—that, however sacrifice be enjoined, mercy takes precedence of it; that David and those that were with him were guiltless in satisfying their hunger with the shew-bread, which none but the priests might lawfully eat, &c. Yet even this plain remark M. opposes. And why? Because among his objections to the Apostolic precept, he urges that our practice is inconsistent with the view of it which we assert. Were it so, this would really form no objection at all against the precept, or the correctness of our view. But how does he attempt to prove, that we cannot (according to our views) be vindicated in eating at the same table with the person put away, by the consideration of its being 'unavoidable from the relations and duties of life,' and that such eating is really no violation of the command? How does he refute this? I am ashamed for him, while I quote his argument. (p. 10.) "*Suppose we were to say that praying with a person put away may be unavoidable from the relations and duties of life!*" Suppose so, M. What then? The difference between the two cases is simply this. In the one case, we have said what is *true:* in the other case we should say what is *false*. Think you that a small difference?

But, says M. "the command is absolute; it no more admits of limitation or exception, than the command, *deliver such an one unto Satan*," &c. He might just as well tell us, that the command—*Submit yourselves to every ordinance of man for the Lord's sake*—is absolute; and infer that we ought to violate every command of Christ at the orders of an earthly magistrate. It is melancholy to be obliged to remind M. that the holy Scriptures are not written with the specialties of an Act of Parliament—'Provided always .... any thing in this Act notwithstanding:'—and that the opposite expectation would lead men to set scripture against scripture, and would open a door for every wildness and wickedness of interpretation. "Labour not for the meat which perisheth" is a very absolute precept in the form of expression; and probably the Thessalonian idlers availed themselves of it, to screen from censure their disobedience to Apostolic command. Ought not M. to be ashamed of holding a language, that would go to sanction such perversion of the word?

Connected with this is that wicked passage in his 11th page, artfully calculated to enlist on his side the feelings particularly of the weaker sex. "They mean, a man is not to show complacency in the society of his wife. What! she is to live in the same house—eat at the same table—she is one flesh with himself, and yet he is not to have complacency in her society! .... Let them, if they will be consistent, separate completely from a wife who is a wicked person. Nothing short of this is obedience to their view of the precept."—Let M. allow us to know our own views. It is very easy for him to say,—"let them separate completely from a wife," &c. According to our views,—(and we are not afraid that M.'s declamation will prove them incorrect)—there is *but one* ground on which a Christian man can ever be justified in putting away his wife, namely, for unfaithfulness to the marriage bed. And further, according to our views, while she remains with him as his wife, he is bound, under all circumstances, to shew her all possible kindness and tenderness and patience; and even when he cannot shew her the complacency of approbation, he is bound to feel—and therefore to manifest—compassion for her as the weaker vessel. I should never trouble myself about the inquiry, what complacency in her society he is—or is not—*to shew*. Let the feelings of his mind be scripturally regulated, and they will be scripturally manifested. But if M. mean,—(and if he does not, he is but beating the air)—that a Christian must and ought to feel, or to manifest, the same complacency even in his wife's society, after she has been removed for her wickedness from the Christian fellowship, as he did while they walked together in it; I tell him confidently that he is mistaken; and that the Christian, who feels undiminished complacency even in the wife of his bosom under such circumstances, is not regulated in his feelings either by true *kindness* for her, or by reverence for the word of God.

Would that I could make M. *ashamed*, for his profit! In this honest wish I add a consideration, which ought to bring conviction to his conscience that he has written dishonestly. If, instead of the amiable and most respectable partner in life whom he is blest with, he were married to a woman, who for some years walked with him in the fellowship of the Gospel, but was afterwards put away from the Church for one of those instances of wickedness specified in 1 Cor. v.—for *drunkenness*;—I ask him would he continue to feel the same *complacency* in her, and in her society, as he had before? No, indeed he would not. And if his conscience testify the truth of that assertion, I ask him again, what would he think of my dishonesty in such a case, if I should turn upon himself his own artillery of exclamations and invectives, and should call upon him to 'separate from her completely,' as the more consistent course? How is it then, that the change of feeling, and consequently of deportment, towards her, which he would think justifiable and necessary, *when the form of her wickedness was naturally disgusting and inconsistent with domestic comfort*, should become the object of his fearless abuse and indignation, when it springs from affectionate concern for her and from subjection of mind to the word of God?

There is a short passage in the last page of M.'s pamphlet, to which I should wish to recal his own attention, as well as direct that of my other readers. It is this. "Of the *suitability* of avoiding worldly social intercourse with those removed from the assembly of God's people, I shall say nothing. The question is not now, as to what is or is not suitable: the sole question is as to what God has or has not commanded." Very true, indeed. And yet the sole ground on which you reject and revile what God has plainly commanded on the subject, is your conception of its *unsuitableness*. You cannot deny, that the command is in the terms of it plain and explicit,—" not even to *eat with* such an one." You will not pretend that you can adduce any instance, in which that simple expression is employed for eating with a person *in a way of Christian fellowship*, as at a *Christian love feast*. And yet you would have us take for granted upon your bare assertion, that this is what the Apostle prohibits. And why? Because you think it would be *unsuitable* to forbid convivial intercourse of a ' worldly social ' character with the person put away. This is the substance of all your assertions, that it would be ' pursuing with a sort of Christian discipline one no longer subject to the discipline of the house of God ;' —that it would be, 'employing a system of temporal pains and penalties,' &c. All these objections resolve themselves into this, that you think the command given is unsuitable. Yet shall I indeed say, that you *really think* so? Nay, put the question to your own conscience. Can you honestly reconcile the style of invective against our view of the precept, with which you set off in the very first page, and in which your whole pamphlet is composed,—can you honestly reconcile this with the language which seems to have slipped from you in the last page? " *On the* suitability of *avoiding worldly social intercourse with*, &c. I shall say nothing." What! say nothing of the suitability of that, which you pronounce ' an *ungodly* practice' —a ' wretched partial system of non-intercourse,' 'hypocritically called a dealing of mercy,' &c. &c. You will say nothing of the *suitability* of this! Do not, M., do not add sin to sin, by denying that—at the moment you wrote that sentence—you were inwardly conscious of that *suitability*, about which you declined saying any thing. But let me shake your conscience a little upon that point.

Let us suppose, that—at Corinth—the day after the Apostle's letter had been received by the Church, and had been obeyed in the removal of that wicked person from among them, one of the disciples meeting him should have accosted him thus: ' Will you dine with me to-morrow? I expect a pleasant party, and among them two of my heathen neighbours, who have rendered me services, which make me wish to shew them civility: and I now find that I may do so, though they are addicted to the prevalent wickedness of the Corinthians. You are now, for the same wickedness, cast out from the Christian community into the world, to which they belong. Come and join our party.' Suppose this: and *suppose* also, if you choose, the words—' not even to eat with such an one'—did not form any express part of the Apostolic command. Would you really think the language and conduct of that Corinthian disciple *suitable* to the nature and spirit of that solemn act, in which he had taken part with his brethren the day before? Would you think it consistent with the due *abhorrence* of such wickedness in one bearing the Christian name,—with that *fear of* its contagious nature,—or even with that compassionate view of *mercy* to the offender, in which they had been called to put him out from among them? Indeed you would not. And yet, though inwardly convinced on the grounds of reason and consistency, that the Corinthian disciple could not *suitably* have adopted the same freedom of social intercourse with the wicked person put away, which he might with his heathen neighbours,—you think yourself at liberty to revile those who refrain from it on the ground of the Apostolic command, as hypocritically calling it a 'dealing of mercy,' &c. &c. Certainly we do hold, that any familiarity even in the intercourse of this life with that wicked person, which would tend to convey to him that we thought lightly of the wickedness for which he had been put away, and that we had the same complacency in him as before, would be contrary even to the principles of that *mercy towards him* in which the Church had been commanded to remove him: and this we must maintain, in spite of all the indignation and scorn which it appears to excite in M.'s mind. But M. knows that he misrepresents us in putting forward this consideration (as he does throughout in various distorted forms)—as the point which we insist on either *exclusively* or *principally*, in asserting the suitableness and wisdom of the Apostolic precept. To prove that he *knows* it is not so, I only quote the following words from the last paragraph but two of our printed Statement:—

"Is it not obvious, that the *main* purpose of the whole course, enjoined on the disciples towards that wicked person, was *their own profit*, to purge out from among themselves that leaven, a little of which leaveneth the whole lump? And are these disputers against the wisdom of God quite certain, that the *continued* restriction on the familiarity of social intercourse with that wicked person was not graciously and wisely adapted to keep the minds of the brethren awake to the due abhorrence of his wickedness? Truly, if any of them felt the same pleasure in his society, as they might feel in that of one who had never been in the Christian connexion, their minds must think very lightly of his ejection from the kingdom of God, and of that which had occasioned it."

In the 12th and two following pages of his pamphlet, M. professes to make observations on the precept in 2 Thess. iii. 6, 14: but appears to introduce it merely for the purpose of repeating the same invective, declamation, and misrepresentations, of which we have had abundance already. Upon that passage, therefore, I shall only notice the striking instance it affords of the deceitfulness, with which his false zeal leads him to handle the word of God. He writes thus: "Such [disorderly brethren] the Apostle commands and exhorts, with quietness to work and eat their own bread. *He commands the Church not to count these disorderly brethren as enemies, but admonish them as brethren. Should they, however, persist in their evil course,* he commands the Church (in verse 6) to withdraw themselves from such. In the 14th verse he repeats in other words the same direction."

Here M. evidently represents—and (I must say) with intentional artifice, represents—the Apostolic direction, *count him not as an enemy but admonish him as a brother*, as applying only while the disorderly brother was yet held in their fellowship by the Church, or *previous* to his removal from it. He found this necessary to maintain his system; and therefore boldly tears the 15th verse out of the position and connexion which it actually holds, and puts it *before* the 6th. To establish this charge, it is sufficient to quote the 14th and 15th verses.

14. *And if any man obey not our word by this epistle, note that man, and have no company with him, that he may be ashamed.*—15. *Yet count him not as an enemy, but admonish him as a brother.*

Alas! H. M., when we find ourselves involved in a system, which cannot be maintained without perverting Scripture so grossly, as you do here, we ought rather to suspect that our system is unscriptural; and instead of vainly striving to wrest the divine word into a seeming accordance with our system, we ought to rejoice that this should be corrected by that unerring standard. While I would press such suggestions upon you, and would beseech you not lightly to spurn them from you, I have to confess with shame of myself, that my own judgment was at one time led into a state of vacillation upon that direction in the 15th verse,—led into it (I believe) chiefly by the undue weight and influence, which I allowed the judgment of another to have upon mine. But, for a considerable time past, I have been made content to return to that simple view of the passage, which I long ago put forward, and which must at once present itself to every unbiassed reader.

SOME OBSERVATIONS ON MR. H.'S PAMPHLET, &c.

When the Exchange party discovered that the precept in 1 Cor. v. 11. which forbids us "*even* to eat with" the class of persons there described, is yet consistent with our maintaining the utmost freedom of *convivial intercourse* with them; I was certain, and avowed the certainty, that they would not stop there: that such of them as persisted in their opposition to that precept, after the plain exposure of it, would proceed yet further in their wickedness. What I predicted is abundantly verified in Mr. H.'s audacious production, and in the reception or toleration of it by the party. I have at length waded through his disgusting pages; and proceed to comply with your desire, in putting on paper the substance of the few remarks on the subject which I made to you in conversation, with a very little additional matter which the perusal of his pages has suggested.

The topic which he has selected to sport with—the final state of those who perish in their sins—is one, which a Christian in his right mind will approach with awe: and we certainly did not need Mr. H. to write a pamphlet to instruct us that some of the expressions by which that state is described are *figurative*. When we read such language as that in Mark ix. 44, 46. "Where their worm dieth not, and the fire is not quenched"—I believe none of us were accustomed to think of a literal *worm* or literal fire and brimstone.

But if the language of Scripture on the subject has *any meaning*, I may confidently assert that it imports a state of *miserable existence*, and not mere *non-existence*, or *annihilation*, as Mr. H. maintains. The condemned "shall go away into everlasting punishment," [εἰς κολασιν αἰωνιον] Matth. xxv. 46.—"shall be cast out into outer darkness, where shall be weeping (G.) and gnashing of teeth;" Matth. viii. 12. xiii. 42, 50. Luke xiii. 28. punished with everlasting destruction from the presence of the Lord." 2 Thess. 1, 9. &c. That all such language imports a *state of misery*, it would be a waste of words to set about proving: and the plainest believer of the Scriptures has abundant ground to reject Mr. H. as a teacher of lies, when he would persuade us that it imports no state of being at all, but the deprivation of all being, or *annihilation*—(you will find that he expressly employs this phrase several times in his pamphlet; as in pp. 24, 35, 40, 58, 63.)

As to argument in his pamphlet, in proof of what he maintains, there is really none, but a contemptible play on the expressions *destroy* and *destruction*. These he assumes to be equivalent with annihilation; though he must be well aware, that they commonly imply what we call *ruin*, the reduction of a thing or person to a state opposite to the state of *well-being*. If any one should throw some oil of vitriol on Mr. H.'s best coat, he would probably exclaim that it was *destroyed*; without at all intending to say that it was annihilated.

But perhaps I ought to consider as argument his daring insinuation of malignity and unrighteousness in God (p. 22.) if he should visit with everlasting punishment "*guilt contracted during a life* (H.) *of three score years and ten*;" and his appeals to our moral sense, in confirmation of this imputation against the most High. If this is to be considered argument, it is an argument which *I* will not undertake to answer. A day is at hand when it shall be refuted indeed, and its impious folly exposed to men and angels.

But I would here remark, that—next to the hardy fearlessness of his opposition to the divine word—there is no character in the pamphlet that strikes me more forcibly, throughout its pages, than its *dishonest artifice*. Among the instances of this, I reckon his arguing largely—or rather declaiming verbosely—against ideas, to which he knows that all scriptural disciples are as much opposed as he; as against the popish doctrine of purgatory,—against the notion of Christ having descended into Hell, the place of the condemned, to endure their torments, &c. Against this he seems to take pride in disporting himself, upon the notion of "an exchange of eternal for tridual torments,"—"of a three days' residence in flames being equivalent to a just and indispensable eternity of torture;" &c. p. 26, 27.—and appears so enamoured with the ingenuity of this redoubtable argument, (I.) that he repeats it three times in the space of less than two pages. Now all such parade of argument against sentiments professed by the most unscriptural, but wholly unconnected with the scriptural truth which he opposes, is really but a stalking horse to conceal that opposition, or an artful attempt to attach some imaginary force to it in the view of unreflecting readers: and such indeed are the generality. But under this head of dishonest artifice, I would mark particularly his constant style of language, in putting forward the grossest representations of Popery and Poetry concerning the state of the condemned, as necessarily coincident with the scriptural doctrine which he opposes; ringing perpetual changes on the idea of the wicked being made to endure "eternal *tortures*" in a "*Torture-House*,"—in which, "God had determined to torment them everlastingly;" p. 55.—the devil represented as "*forking* the wretched in flames;—while—benevolence itself hears, but regards not, the eternal shrieks of the malignant victims," p. 65. I almost shudder, while I transcribe his profane language: but it is well adapted to carry away many a reader. Now the dishonesty of artifice, which I notice in the whole of it, is this:—it insidiously represents us as holding, that the misery of the condemned is a misery superinduced on them by the infliction of torture, as by racks, wheels, &c.—and from which they would be exempt, if they were only *let alone* and *left to themselves*. So far from this being the case, I avow that I can conceive no more awful view of their misery, than that of their being *utterly abandoned to themselves*.

It is with sobriety I would think, or speak, upon the subject. The redeemed are told of their blessedness and coming glory: but we are told also that "we know not yet what we shall be;" and are restrained from idle speculation on the particular scene and circumstances of our future happiness. No marvel, therefore, that we are left equally in the dark concerning the particular scene and circumstances of the final misery of the condemned. We are furnished, however, with general conceptions of both, in the way of contrast. As we shall hear the joyful summons, "come ye blessed," and "shall be ever with the Lord," in whose "presence is the fulness of joy;" so they shall be banished from it, under the irrevocable sentence, "depart, ye cursed." As "the glory of God and the Lamb" shall be our *light* of enjoyment, (Rev. xx. 23.) so their utter exclusion from all this is aptly represented as a state of "outer *darkness*." As we "shall be like Him," so they shall be left under the bondage of that fallen nature, which is "enmity against God" and opposed to his image. Can imagination picture any thing more awful, than a number of such evil creatures *left to themselves*? to the fire of their own unsated passions, and the gnawings of remorse? Even in this world there are horrid scenes of human wretchedness arising from and essentially connected with human wickedness; of wretchedness so acute, that men often attempt (K.) a plunge into annihilation in order to escape it. But this world, as the stage on which God's wonderful work of mercy is going forward, has never yet exhibited human wretchedness or human wickedness, but accompanied with numberless circumstances mitigating the effects of both;

the restraints of civil government,—the connexions of social life imposing prudential control,—the sun of heaven shining, and the rain descending on the unjust, as well as on the just,—and God not leaving himself without a witness to the sons of men, in "doing them good" continually. This world would not otherwise be a fit stage for carrying on the divine purposes, for which it is as yet preserved.

But after those purposes shall have been accomplished, is Mr. H. prepared to arraign the Almighty, if he should not continue those manifestations of his goodness to the condemned? if he should not maintain a continuance of the same circumstances, to control their wickedness and mitigate its effects? Is he quite sure, that God is bound to terminate at once their wickedness and their misery, by annihilating them? that the righteous governor of the universe may not *leave them* to the continuance of both?—may not *leave them indeed to themselves*, a terrible memento to perhaps unnumbered worlds, and unnumbered ages, of the awful effects of a creature's apostacy from the Creator?

I might easily enforce and enlarge on the subject. But I gladly turn from it; and without noticing many other things in the pamphlet, which prove the writer to have plunged much deeper into systematic infidelity than he avows. I am glad of its *publication*: for none who fear God and tremble at his word can now be imposed on by Mr. H. or his party.

You remark, that H. must get rid of the resurrection of the unjust altogether; and no doubt the idea of their being *re-created* in order to be *re-annihilated* is *exquisitely* absurd. But how can he get rid of it, till he expunges such texts as Acts xxiv. 15. and Dan. xii. 2.? I should think it quite unsuitable for any of us to attempt any detailed reply to his pamphlet.

NOTES.

A. (page 26.)

A former letter. *Former* is not inserted in the text, but neither is it inserted 2 Cor. viii. 8, where we yet are sure that it is to be understood, as he there plainly refers to this first Epistle. We know also from 1 Cor. vii. 1, that previous to this letter there was an epistolary intercourse between the Corinthian Church and the Apostle.

B. (page 26.)

Hold no society. μη συναναμιγνυσθαι. That the Apostle employs this expression in the most comprehensive sense, as including both Christian fellowship and civil companionship, is plain from its use in the 9th verse, combined with his own explanation of his meaning in that injunction. And this establishes the meaning of the same word in 2 Thess. iii. 14.

C. (page 27.)

Not even. μηδε. Here our translators have expressed the emphasis of this negation by doubling the negative—"*no not*;" and in Eph. v. 3, by inserting *once*—"*let it not be once named among you*;" and of the equivalent ουδε, in the first verse of the present chapter, by inserting *so much as*—"*is not* so much as *named among the Gentiles*." (This however would be more accurately rendered—"*is not named even among the Gentiles*.")—The emphatic force of the negative—*not* EVEN *to eat*—at once exposes the worse than absurdity of those, who have interpreted the *eating* forbidden in verse 11, to mean eating the Lord's Supper!—That gloss indeed is abundantly refuted by the connexion of verse 11 with verse 10, from which it is undeniable, that when the Apostle says *not even to eat with such an one*, he intends an *eating* in which they were at liberty to partake with heathens.

We only add that, as the precept in v. 11, may evidently be violated in various ways besides *eating with* the person put away,—(as if we should call him to take a walk of pleasure with us, &c.)—so it may not be violated at all by the mere circumstance of our dining at the same table with him. This may be unavoidable from the relations and duties of life. It may occur, without our seeking, at a public table, or at the table of a friend with whom we have never been in Christian fellowship. And we protest against calling such cases *exceptions* to the Apostolic rule, as if there were any case in which obedience to his command might be dispensed with.

D. (Page 34.)

With heathens. M. in p. 9, of his pamphlet, quotes a passage from our statement, in which—in a kind of professed paraphrase—we endeavoured to set before our brethren a plain connected view of the last five verses of the chapter; and in quoting it indeed he chooses to make absolute nonsense of the passage, by omitting the words—"But it did not." This however is a trifle. But he is highly indignant with me, because in that paraphrase I substituted the expression—*heathen* fornicators—for that of "fornicators of this world." v. 10. For this he as usual rails at me as "perverting the right ways of the Lord," and "insidiously substituting" the one expression for the other, in order to make what he calls "a distinction between a professing fornicator of the world, and a non-professing fornicator of the world." When I knew H. M.—(but alas! it is quite another H. M. that I have now to do with)—he would have been ashamed even to intimate, that a paraphrase must or ought to consist of the *same words* as those paraphrased. It is indeed requisite that it should not. That the words which I so *insidiously* substituted convey exactly the meaning, which the Apostle intended to convey in the 10th verse by "fornicators of the world," is demonstrable. Corinth was a *heathen* city; though there were certainly in it Jewish inhabitants also, and a Jewish synagogue. With these, however, the Apostle could not have meant to say that the Christians might hold free worldly intercourse, because the principles of the Jew's religion would not allow *them* to hold it with Gentiles. When he therefore substantially tells them that they may lawfully hold such intercourse in eating, &c. with "fornicators *of this world*," he certainly did intend *heathen* fornicators.

And why is M. so angry at this paraphrase? Because he is determined to set aside the Apostle's plain command in the next verse, interdicting the Christians from holding even such intercourse with the fornicator appearing *among themselves*, and whom he calls them to put away from among them. M. is determined to maintain, against the express words of the Apostle, that he leaves them at the same liberty to eat with him as with fornicators of the world; and descends to maintain it even by that truly contemptible special-pleading, that this man—*when* put out of the Church—would be one of those *without*, a fornicator of this world!

Obliged, as I am, to pass over numerous things in his pamphlet which would call for exposure and reprehension, I should scarcely have taken any notice of this passage in his 9th page, did I not view it as closely connected with an error, which has been long working in Ireland among those with whom I was lately connected, and which distracted the Dublin Church for many months before the introduction of the disputes against the precept in 1 Cor. v. 11. The error to which I allude, has assumed various forms and dresses; for its partizans have been studious to disguise it; but it seems to have at bottom this principle:—that none are to be considered as even *professing* Christians, but those who are found in connexion with Churches of an apostolic character, following in faith and practice the first Churches "which in Judea were in Christ Jesus." From this erroneous principle evidently sprang the wicked efforts made, to impose on us a law against putting forward the Scriptures or scriptural truth to the attention of our fellow sinners around us, though for the purpose of exposing and refuting the Anti-christian errors which prevail throughout Christendom. The deep erroneousness of the principle referred to, I have long ago shewn at large in one of my pieces against the modern Baptism. Indeed it is sufficiently refuted by the Apostle's language in 2 Tim. iii. 1—5, where the awful characters of manifested wickedness which he enumerates are evidently described as what would appear in men *professing* the faith of Christ, though proving that they possessed it not, that they *were not what they professed to be*:—for it is only in contrast with the sacredness of that profession, that these characters of wickedness could be considered marvellous in any of the *human* race. The man who tells me, that he believes what the Evangelists and Apostles testify concerning Jesus of Nazareth, as the Messiah foretold in the Scriptures of the Old Testament; that he died, and that he rose again from the dead;—that man is in my view distinguished as a *professed* Christian, from heathens, and avowed infidels,—even when I find him under the deepest and most deadly errors, or walking in the foulest lusts of the flesh;—even when he is cast out from the household of faith for his wickedness, when he is to me "AS an heathen," and when his wickedness appears even more awful than that of heathens.

E. (page 38.)

Excluded him from all Christian fellowship, &c.—I would mark distinctly, that by *Christian fellowship* I mean all that fellowship which is peculiar to Christians one with another as Christians. I could wish that M. had employed as distinct a language to designate that companionship in eating, which he acknowledges the disciples are forbidden in the 11th verse to hold with the characters there described. But here he seems to labour for vague circumlocutions, such as indicate either indistinctness of ideas, or indisposition to express his meaning distinctly. He talks (p. 7.) of "Christian society *both religious and social;*" and of its being "as evil to retain a wicked person in *social Christian intercourse* as in *religious,*" &c. Now I confess that I am doubtful what he means by *social Christian society,* or intercourse, in opposition to *religious;* and I suspect that he has no clear or settled idea of it in his own mind. He does not mean the companionship in eating, &c. which Christians maintain indifferently with each other or with the world: for this he holds they are at liberty to maintain also with the wicked person put away from among them. Nor does he mean mutual intercourse in any things peculiarly Christian; for this would be of a *religious* character? What then is that *social* Christian intercourse, which is not of a *religious* character, but which he admits the Corinthian disciples could not lawfully maintain with that fornicator?

But let us try and feel our way. If there be a dinner-party or a tea-party, where all in the company happen to be members of the same Christian Church, will M. consider their companionship as necessarily constituting the "social Christian society," from which a wicked person must be excluded? I think I have witnessed such parties in Dublin, and that they would not have been at all defiled by the admission of a couple of the wickedest fiddlers, to aid the music or the dance: and this because the company were neither engaged, nor had been called together for the purpose of engaging, in any thing *distinctively Christian.* Eating together, or dancing together, or playing a piece of music together, may be all very good or harmless things in their place; but they are things not distinctively Christian, even in the circumstance I have supposed, where none but Christians happen to be engaged in them. Two Christians may have mercantile intercourse or dealings with each other; one may buy a horse of the other: but would M. call this "social Christian intercourse," because both buyer and seller are Christians? I think not. The intercourse is of a mercantile or worldly nature, just as much as if they were both heathens, or one a Christian and the other a heathen. Christians indeed are called, "whether they eat or drink, or whatever they do, to do all to the glory of God." But this does not debar them from eating and drinking with persons of the world, or engaging with them, as there may be occasion, in any acts not distinctively Christian. And thus, when I lately had the satisfaction of receiving in my house and at my table some of my brethren from Ireland,—while our intercourse proceeded on the ground of *Christian* brotherhood and *Christian* hospitality, it was not at all defiled by the entrance of an unbelieving friend or neighbour, (as happened more than once), and his eating and drinking with us.

I may seem to have dwelt needlessly long upon this topic; but I have found it necessary, from the ambiguity of M.'s language about *social Christian society*, &c., which was calculated to intangle the consciences of the weak. Perhaps however he puts forward something more distinct and specific, when he refers to Jude 12, as exemplifying that "*social* Christian intercourse," from which that wicked person was to be excluded, as much as from "religious Christian intercourse." There the Apostle mentions the *feasts of charity*, or *feasts of love*, customary in the first Churches, and called *Agapæ* from the Greek word expressing *love*. With respect to these, it is generally admitted, and the opinion is countenanced by what we read in 1 Cor. xi.—that they were a common meal, of which *the brethren* partook, in the place of their assembling on the first day of the week, either before or after their eating of *the Lord's Supper*; which meal was provided at the expense of the richer brethren. Now it is quite obvious, that this common meal of which members of the Church partook, and no others, and which it is plain was originally designed to express the *Christian* brotherhood and *Christian* affection of all who joined in it,—it is obvious (I say) that this was an act of *distinctively Christian fellowship*; and that it would indeed have been a profanation of that fellowship to have admitted to it any one not standing in connexion with the Church. Nor can I understand why M. conceives such a *Christian feast of love* not to participate in the *religious*, as well as *social* character. But amidst all the sharp rebuke, which the Apostle gives the Corinthian Christians for their gross abuse of this common meal,—(on account of which abuse he intimates that it would be better to lay aside the custom altogether), there is not the slightest intimation that they had ever thought of receiving any of those that were without to participate with them in it. Is it not evident therefore that the Corinthian disciples, when they found themselves enjoined to put that incestuous person out of their Church, must have understood that they were debarred from continuing to hold *any* Christian fellowship with him; and therefore from admitting him to that feast of love, which was peculiar to their Christian fellowship?

I must therefore say, that M.'s daring interpolation in the 11th verse would introduce a direction wholly superfluous, after the command given in the 5th and 7th verses. *I* should not dare to express myself thus, if the fact were, that the Apostle—after enjoining his removal from *all Christian fellowship* with them—had thought fit to specify in the 11th verse a particular exercise of that fellowship as the *smallest*. *But he has not.*

F. (Page 38.)

In such a connexion, &c.—In our printed Statement of June 2d (Note C. p. 47.) I had said, that from the connexion of v. 11 with v. 10, "it is *undeniable*, that when the Apostle says *not even to eat with such an one*, he intends an *eating*, in which they were at liberty to partake with heathens." M. by flatly denying it, proves that in one sense I was mistaken. However, gratuitous denials and gratuitous assertions are of very little weight. Let us examine the matter.

Probably M. *will not* deny that the two verses are closely connected, not merely in order of sequence, but in subject matter; though indeed he has concealed that connexion as much as he could, by the manner in which he has quoted them, as well as by his alteration of the word *altogether* into *at all.*—(Of either his meaning or his object in asserting that such ought to be the version of παντως, I confess myself ignorant.)—The connection is manifestly this. In the 9th and 10th verses he tells them that they had mistaken his meaning in a former letter, when they supposed that, by prohibiting all intermixture with fornicators, he had intended fornicators of this world: and he briefly marks to them, what might have prevented their mistake, that a command not to intermix at all with *them* would amount to a command that they should quit the world altogether.—(Now let it be noted that the intermixture with fornicators of this world, which he allows, and which they had mistakenly supposed he forbade, was certainly not of a *religious* character, not in any thing connected with Christian fellowship; but exclusively in the things of civil society and the ordinary intercourse of this life, as in eating together, &c.: just as in a subsequent chapter he says, 'If any of them that believe not bid you to a *feast*, and ye be *disposed to go*,' &c., 1 Cor. x. 97.) He proceeds in the 11th verse to mark what fornicators he really intended, and what their conduct towards them must be; and this, in manifest contrast with the mistaken sense in which they had before understood him. "But now:" But now I tell you that I intended not a fornicator of this world, but such a character appearing in the church—among yourselves; and that with such an one ye are indeed to have no intermixture, not even to eat with him, much less to retain him among you in Christian fellowship. Now when I say, that I am allowed to eat with a heathen fornicator, but am not allowed even to eat with a fornicator bearing the name of a brother; what reasonable and candid man could understand the expression—*eating with*—in two different senses, in the two clauses thus closely connected? or could question whether it is not *the same social act*, which is allowed me with the one, but forbidden me with the other? I almost blame myself for employing so many words, to prove what is really so plain on the very face of the Apostle's language in its connexion, that it is perhaps obscured in any attempt to prove it.

Hitherto I have marked only the connexion of the 11th verse with that immediately preceding, in proof that the Apostle means what he says, when he charges the Corinthian disciples *not even to eat with such an one*. But the same thing still more abundantly appears, from its connexion with the verse immediately following: "For *what have I to do to judge them also that are without? Do not ye judge them that are within?*" Now the conjunction—*For*, manifestly marks a connexion of this principle with the command *not even to eat with* such an one. As if the Apostle added—"I say with such a wicked person *among yourselves*. For why should ye suppose, as ye did, that I would extend that judgment to such characters of the unbelieving world? that I would command you not to eat with *them* ALSO? What have we to do with the characters or conduct of those that are without? Them God judgeth. We judge those that are within. Therefore put away *from among yourselves*, from all intermixture with you, not only in Christian fellowship, but *even* in social companionship, that wicked person who is among you under the name of a brother."—I ask the Christian reader, marking this connexion, whether the companionship in eating mentioned in the 11th verse can be considered as a different kind of eating, from that which is referred to in the 12th.—And here I believe I ought to close the subject, and to lay down my pen. The attempt is idle to force those to see who are determined to shut their eyes.

(G. Page 44.)

Honest Mr. H. partly quotes these words in p. 59. but with singular disingenuousness. His system, as any intelligent reader of his production must perceive, is that death is the *extinction* of *being* or *annihilation*; agreeing in this with all the French atheists; but differing from them in a point, which indeed only renders him much more extravagantly absurd. Unable to get over the declaration, that there shall be a resurrection of the *unjust*, as well as of the just, he holds that those who have died in their sins are to be restored to existence at the great day, but this only for the purpose of hearing the sentence pronounced on them, which shall consign them back to annihilation again! He declaims on the anguish they must feel—the *momentary* anguish in hearing their doom; and adds—"well might *the same* be described as a scene of wailing and gnashing of teeth." And so he gets rid of such passages. But any one who will be at the trouble of looking at the passages, where the expression does occur in the evangelists, will see that the Lord employs it—not to describe any momentary scene of anguish in the condemned, *previous to the execution of their sentence*, but the consequence of its execution; —not any *passing scene*, but a *permanent state*.

He attempts, with similar dexterity, to get rid of the plain words of Christ in Matt. xxv. 46. "We read" (says he, p. 52.) "of everlasting *punishment*: but never of everlasting *pain*, everlasting *misery*." It is truly a nice distinction between punishment and pain, between misery and a state described as that of outer darkness, with weeping and gnashing of teeth—(outer *darkness* may naturally be conceived to indicate the utter deprivation of enjoyment, as its opposite light is continually employed as the symbol of joy.)—But out of his own mouth the rash man shall be condemned. He tells us in a note, p. 9, "The term eternal or everlasting death is not in Scripture; *it would be a pleonasm*." Well, then, as we do read of *everlasting punishment*, this punishment cannot be the annihilation or extinction of being, which Mr. H. understands by *death*, and which he maintains to be the only denounced sentence against sin, and "the precise amount of penalty" due to it. But I am almost ashamed of attempting to expose such stuff.

H. (Page 44.)

It may appear to Mr. H. very wise and philosophical to estimate the amount of guilt by the *length of time* in which it has been contracted. But it is excessively absurd. We might as well make light of the wickedness of his pamphlet from the shortness of the time in which he penned it.

I. (Page 45.)

It might be curious to transfer a similar argument to his own idea of "the precise amount of penalty" (p. 65.) due to sin, and which he says the atonement paid, according to the view which he takes of *death* as the extinction of being. But it is not within my object to examine the tissue of absurd inconsistences in his pamphlet; and in which a much abler writer than Mr. H. would necessarily be involved, in maintaining his lie under a professed appeal to the word of truth.

K. (Page 45.)

In one passage (p. 59.) Mr. H. facetiously remarks "one good effect I will concede to the doctrine [of Hell torments :] it certainly has a tendency to keep men from hanging themselves. Yet he afterwards seems to retract this sportive concession: for he tells us (p. 63.) that annihilation is indeed the *most terrible* subject that a living being can contemplate." But he has himself some suspicion of a *more* terrible; for in p. 35. he guards the position with a *perhaps*;—"the apprehension of annihilation is *perhaps* more exquisitely dreadful than the expectation of eternal life, even in misery and torment!"—The phraseology of the whole sentence, if it were worth quoting at large, would shew a curious vacillation and misgiving of mind in the writer, when he indited it.

REMARKS,

CORRECTIVE OF

OCCASIONAL MISTRANSLATIONS

IN THE

ENGLISH VERSION

OF

THE SACRED SCRIPTURES.

[First Published 1831.]

TO WHICH ARE NOW ADDED

SEVERAL EXPOSITORY REMARKS,

NOT BEFORE PUBLISHED.

ADVERTISEMENT.

The following pages form a small part of a series of remarks which I have for some time wished to publish. The printing of these in a detached form is in compliance with the desire of a friend, to whom I happened to communicate the observations on the passage in the Epistle of James, and who conceived that they may be serviceable for checking some melancholy delusions, which have lately appeared in this city.

I cannot put out even these few corrections of our English Translation of the Bible, without distinctly stating, that I hold at a very high rate the general excellence of that translation. It was executed, with much pains and care, by men who were sound scholars, and (what is even of greater importance in this matter,) by men who were intentionally *faithful* in the work. In these respects it stands most favourably distinguished from the various *new* translations, put forward since, by persons deficient alike in learning and in honesty.

As men, however, our translators were fallible. They were also, in some degree, restrained from the free exercise of their own judgment, by the instructions of their royal employer; and their connexion with *state-religion* unavoidably produced some unfavorable bias on their minds. While I, therefore, deprecate the thought of displacing their version, to make room for any other which could now be substituted, I yet conceive that such occasional corrections of it, as are exemplified in the following pages, may be of use to the English reader for clearing the true meaning of particular passages.

No English readers need be deterred from perusing these Remarks by the Greek characters which occasionally occur in them. These may be altogether passed over, without any injury to the general meaning. In the few cases where I do quote the original, it is for the sake of those readers who are more or less capable of examining it, but who may not have any copy of the Greek Testament immediately at hand.

Let me add, that I have not in any instance thought it necessary to examine, whether I have been anticipated in my criticisms by any other writers. I am less solicitous about the originality of my remarks, than about their justice and utility. What has heretofore been done in the way of biblical criticism has generally been inaccessible to all, except the learned. It has been one of my objects to present what I offer in a form in which the Christian reader, who knows not any language but the English, shall be competent both to understand my remarks, and to estimate their truth.

REMARKS,

CORRECTIVE OF OCCASIONAL MISTRANSLATIONS

IN THE

ENGLISH VERSION OF THE SACRED SCRIPTURES.

I.

"Is any sick among you? Let him call for the elders of the church, and let them pray over him, anointing him with oil, in the name of the Lord; and the prayer of faith shall save the sick, and the Lord shall raise him up; and, if he have committed sins, they shall be forgiven him."—James v. 14, 15.

INSTEAD of the words, "*shall* save *the sick*," we should read "*shall* heal *the sick*," or restore him to health.

Nothing is more indubitable than this correction. The Greek word σωσει is applicable to deliverance from any danger or calamity, as preservation from drowning, (Matt. xiv. 30.) to escape in shipwreck, (Acts xxvii. 31, 44; xxviii. 1, 4.) &c. But in no fewer than eleven other passages of the New Testament, is the word applied to recovery from sickness, or deliverance from bodily infirmities, viz. Matt. ix. 21, 22; Mark v. 23, 28, 34; vi. 56; x. 52; Luke viii. 36, 50; John xi. 12; Acts iv. 9. In all these places our translators have rightly employed some English phrase denoting restoration to health, or bodily soundness; while, in all of them, the Greek word is precisely the same, as they have mistranslated *save*, in James v. 15. (The same verb also, only compounded with a preposition, occurs in the same sense in Matt. xiv. 36, and Luke vii. 3.)

That it is deliverance from disease that is here intended, appears indeed plainly from the words of the passage, "shall save *the sick*," and "the Lord shall *raise him up*." The latter expression is commonly applied to a person raised up from a sick bed, as in Matt. viii. 15; ix. 6, 7, 25; Mark i. 32. And as to the former words, no one capable of reading the original to any advantage, can doubt that the necessary import of the Greek σωσει τον KAMNONTA is,—"shall deliver him *from his sickness*." The man who does not feel this to be the decisive force of the words, at least when his attention is directed to it, may think that he knows Greek, because he has learned to spell it; but he really knows nothing of the language to any useful purpose.

Something of this may be felt even by the mere English reader, if for "*the sick*," we substitute the phrase "the *patient*." In marking the character or state of the person whose deliverance is spoken of, the nature of the deliverance intended is sufficiently intimated.

If one has fallen into the water, and I exclaim, "who will save that drowning man?" could any one doubt that the expression "*save*" in such a connexion, implied deliver him from drowning? Even so in the case of a sick person; if I speak of something as that which will save the patient, is it not manifest from the connexion, that, by his being saved, I mean simply delivered from his disease?

But some perhaps may urge, as an objection to this view, that it is written, "*if he have committed sins, they shall be forgiven him.*"— It is: and this leads me to mark one or two things for the further elucidation of the passage.

It is plain, that it could not have been the Apostle's design to give any directions by which a Christian should be exempted from the bodily infirmities, and ultimate mortality, which are the common allotment of all men in this world.

But beside such cases of sickness and of death as occur in what is called the ordinary course of nature, the Scriptures expressly teach, that there are other cases, which form part of the fatherly discipline which the Lord maintains over his children, for their profitable correction, and "that they should not be condemned with the world." Hebr. xii. 5, 7; Job v. 17, 18; xxxvi. 8, 10; Ps. lxxxix. 30, 33. Thus, when the Apostle Paul rebukes the Corinthian church for their gross abuse of the Lord's Supper, he declares to them, (1 Cor. xi. 30, 31.) "*for this cause many are weak and sickly among you, and many sleep,*" that is, have been visited with death. He recals their attention to the divine origin and nature of the ordinance which they had so much perverted, that it ceased with them to be the Lord's Supper, (v. 20,) and testifies that in this they were "eating and drinking judgment to themselves," (v. 29,) that is, bringing on themselves those judicial visitations of sickness, and death itself, by which the Lord mercifully rebuked their sin.

Now it is evidently *such* a case of sickness that is spoken of in the passage under consideration from the Epistle of James, when it is said, "*if he have committed sins, they shall be forgiven him:*" that is, if the sickness has been sent as a visitation of corrective discipline for sin. And, in such a view, the sick person appears to be represented as acknowledging it when he *calls for* the elders of the church, that he may be restored to health. His sin being forgiven, the rod of correction which it had occasioned shall be removed.

One word more on the *anointing with oil*, directed in the passage. As we have seen that the case of disease spoken of, was, in one sense, beside the ordinary course of nature, so also was its removal. The sick person was restored to health, through the intervention of the elders of the church, in the exercise of that supernatural "gift of healing," (1 Cor. xii. 9,) which existed in the Apostolic age, and for the confirmation of the Apostolic mission. Yet the cure, though superhuman, was preceded by an external application, and by prayer. And, in like manner, we find that the Lord Jesus, when about to confer sight on the man born blind, "*anointed his eyes*" with moistened clay, and directed him to "wash in the pool of Siloam," John ix. 6, 7. Many other examples might be adduced, but in Mark vi. 13, it is expressly related of the twelve Apostles, when first sent out by the Lord, and endowed with miraculous gifts, that, in healing the sick, they employed this very act of anointing with oil: "they cast out many devils, and *anointed with oil many that were sick*, and healed them."

I have treated this passage the more at large for two reasons: First, because it is by this text of Scripture alone that the Papists attempt to support their *extreme unction*, a rite which they employ, not with any view to the recovery of the sick person, (for they never administer it save when his recovery is hopeless, and he is considered "*in extremis*,") but as a kind of safe passport *out* of the *world*. The view of the passage which I have proposed, and which I defy all their priests to refute, affords a short and easy method of proving the corruption of that communion, and of refuting its arrogant pretensions to infallibility; when we find one of their so called seven sacraments, resting on the grossest mistake, about the meaning of the passage, by which they endeavour to support it. Perhaps it may please Him, who doeth great wonders, according to the counsel of his own will, to bring these pages under the eye of even some ecclesiastic of that most corrupt communion, and to bless to his conviction the plain remarks which I have offered; so that he may be no longer a blind leader of the blind, but may see and abhor the foulness of the imposture which he has been instrumental in palming on the people.

But, secondly, because I have known some who appeared really at a loss to account for it, that those who now maintain the obligation on disciples of returning fully to the enjoined practice of the Apostolic churches, do yet not think of acting in case of sickness according to the directions here given by James. Now, from the real meaning of it, which I have sufficiently established, it appears that there is, in these days, no room for putting that direction in practice, since the miraculous gift of healing no longer exists in the churches. We might as reasonably pretend to put in practice the Apostolic direction, in 1 Cor. xiv. 27, concerning the gift of tongues, although no such gift now exists, nor is ever likely to be renewed. Any attempt of the kind, in either case, would be found, on examination, to be not any conformity to Apostolic rule, but a farcical mimickry of what was practised in that day, under circumstances that no longer exist.

Having incidentally expressed my opinion that the miraculous gifts are never likely to be renewed in the churches, I would briefly state the grounds of that opinion. It is not that the Lord is less really, or less gloriously, with his people at this day than in the Apostolic age. It is not that his arm is shortened, or that their high privileges are diminished. O, no! He is the same yesterday, and to-day, and for ever; the same mighty God of Jacob, who wrought all the recorded wonders for Israel in Egypt, at the Red Sea, and in the wilderness; and believers of the Gospel are his true Israel, "a people saved by the LORD," a people for whom he has obtained eternal redemption, who are the "children of God, and as children are heirs, *heirs of God* and *joint heirs with Christ*," Rom. xviii. 17. Can any language express, or any imagination picture a height of privilege and blessedness superior to this?

Nor was the possession or exercise of miraculous gifts the greatest privilege of believers in the Apostolic days, nor any *peculiar part* of their privilege. They were possessed and exercised by some who were not disciples indeed, as they had been even by Judas Iscariot. The same folly and hardness of heart which Christ upbraided of old in that language, "except ye see signs and wonders, ye will not believe,"—it is the same that ever makes us think of the cessation of miraculous gifts as a diminution of our Christian privilege.

Of all these miraculous powers, as existing in the Apostolic Churches, I conceive that we may say what we are expressly taught of one of them, (1 Cor. xiv. 22.) that they were not designed to serve them that believe, but "were a sign to them that believed not." Now they were a sign simply of the divine authority, sanctioning the Apostolic ministry. They accredited that; were calculated to draw attention to that, and left without excuse those who rejected it; they did not communicate, and never were designed to communicate a knowledge of the truth. They did not enlighten the understanding of those who witnessed them, to discern the real import and glory of the Apostolic testimony. They answered, however, the temporary purpose for which they were designed. But could this revival in the churches answer the same purpose now? I think it could not. With respect to the great mass of Christendom, who verbally acknowledge the Apostolic mission, as of divine origin, there is not any need or occasion for that purpose to be answered to them. And, with respect to others, who avowedly reject their mission as a human imposture, (a small number comparatively, but an increasing number, and likely to increase much more, and rapidly,) the renewal of miraculous powers generally, among professing Christians, would seem to be calculated only for giving a kind of supernatural sanction, in the eyes of Deists, to all the corruptions and errors of the Anti-christian world; and, if we suppose them renewed only among those who are Christians indeed, (not to say that this would be directly opposite to what took place in the Apostolic age,) would it not be calculated to give such a supernatural sanction, as we have no reason either to expect or desire, to the Christian profession of certain individuals, or certain bodies, to the genuineness of their faith, and correctness of their practice? For such an end as this they certainly never were ordained of old.

For these reasons I look not for the renewal of miraculous gifts in the Church of God, nor regard their cessation as any want; while I am quite ready to admit that they shall be renewed, if any period or circumstances should return, when their renewal would be for His glory, and the good of His people.

Some may wonder that I have touched this subject. But I have been led to it from finding (what does not surprise me)—that parties and individuals are starting up in these countries who put forward, or insinuate, pretensions to the possession of miraculous gifts. This, and every other delusion, we may expect to be multiplied as the coming of the Lord draweth nigh.

II.

Having damnation *because they have cast off their first faith.*—1 Tim. v. 12.

Our translators seem to have been unfortunately fond of introducing this word *damnation*; and frequently, where the original conveys nothing at all like the import of that English expression. The present passage, for example, ought to be rendered "*having* censure," or "*incurring* censure, *because they have made light of their first faith*," that is, of the faith pledged to the first husband.

The second marriage of a female was generally considered *discreditable*. By contracting it she was conceived to throw a slight on the memory of her former husband, and so to violate a kind of *fidelity* still due to him, though dead. Thus Virgil represents the widowed Dido on Æneas's desertion of her, as bewailing her *breach of faith to the dead Sychæus. (Non servata fides, cineri promissa Sychæo!* Æn. iv. 552.)

The English expressions *damn* and *damnation* are immediately formed from the Latin *damnare*, and *damnatio*, which signify to *condemn—condemnation*; and in this general meaning the English derivatives were originally employed. But having long lost that *general* meaning, by the popular application of the terms exclusively to the future punishment of the ungodly, these expressions ought to be expunged from our English version, even where the Greek phrase does properly import *condemnation*.

But that is not the case in the passage under consideration. The word (κρίμα) which is there employed literally means *judgment*, or a *judicial sentence*, and is rightly rendered *judgment* in Matth. vii. 2; Acts xxiv. 25, and elsewhere. We know also that the Apostle, so far from considering the second marriage of a Christian female as necessarily involving apostacy from the faith, and final condemnation, expressly declares, in the 14th verse, that he would have "the younger widows to marry, and bear children," rather than incur the various evils to which they might otherwise be exposed. In that verse, indeed, our translators have given—"the younger *women*," without even printing the word "women" in the Italic character, to mark it as an ellipsis, which they have supplied. But it is evident from the whole context, that the ellipsis ought to be supplied with the word *widows*, which some Greek manuscripts indeed insert. The Apostle also expresses the same judgment in 1 Cor. vii. 8, 9.

We meet the same extraordinary mistranslation of the same word (κρίμα) in 1 Cor. xi. 29, "*he that eateth and drinketh unworthily, eateth and drinketh* damnation *to himself*," instead of "*eateth and drinketh* judgment *to himself*," that is, bringeth on himself those judicial visitations of bodily infirmities, sickness, and even death, by which the Lord marked his displeasure at their gross abuse of the ordinance of His Supper; and marked it thus (as the Apostle expressly teaches) "that they should *not* be *condemned* with the world." See v. 30, 31, 32, and the preceding article.

Again in Rom. xiii. 2, where we read, "*they that resist shall receive to themselves* damnation," we ought to read "*shall receive to themselves* judgment;" and the judgment immediately intended is that "wrath," spoken of in the 4th and 5th verses, which earthly rulers are designed to "execute upon him that doeth evil." At the same time it is to be admitted and maintained, that the Apostle enforces on Christians the obligation of quiet subjection to the civil government by a higher consideration than the mere avoidance of civil penalties.

That higher consideration is marked in the fifth verse, by the words, "*for conscience sake;*" "ye must needs be subject, not only for *wrath*, but for *conscience* sake;" not only to escape the human penalties annexed to resistance, but from regard to the appointment of God, considering civil government as *his ordinance*. In this the Apostle evidently does not regard the form of the government, or the character of the governors; whether the government be a monarchy, an aristocracy, or democracy; whether the governors execute their office well or ill. Christians are called to one course of quiet submission, and it is a course indeed suitable to those who belong to a kingdom "not of this world," while it is no wonder that others are disgusted with the rule, whose real infidelity is but ill concealed under a Christian *profession* merely verbal.

It may be remarked also, that the principles asserted by the Apostle have been as much abused and perverted by many worldly ecclesiastics, in professedly maintaining them, as they have been generally scouted by those who openly deny their obligation. Upon this passage in Romans, chiefly, the divines have rested their absurd doctrine of *the divine right of* KINGS; as if *kingly* government had more than any other the sanction of divine authority, or as if kings were, any more than consuls, the "ordinance and ministers of God." That *civil government* in general is a divine appointment, and mercifully calculated, even in its worst form, for the important good of man, Christians may well thankfully acknowledge; when they consider what consequences would follow from human wickedness, if the restraints thus imposed on it were removed. In fact, society would be so broken up, that it would be impossible to live in such a world.

In Rom. xiv. 23, we read, "*and he that doubteth is* damned, *if he eat.*" In this passage, the original verb is the compound κατακεκριται, and should be literally rendered, "is *condemned*;" that is, condemned in his own conscience. He who doubteth the lawfulness of that, in which he yet indulges, is brought in guilty at the bar of conscience for the indulgence, however intrinsically innocent.

III.

"*They that received* tribute-money *came to Peter, and said, Doth not your Master pay tribute? He saith, Yes. And when he was come into the house, Jesus prevented* [anticipated] *him, saying, What thinkest thou, Simon? Of whom do the kings of the earth take custom or tribute? of their own children, or of strangers? Peter saith unto him, Of strangers. Jesus saith unto him, then are the children free. Notwithstanding, lest we should offend* [stumble] *them, go thou to the sea, and take up the fish that first cometh up; and when thou hast opened his mouth, thou shalt find a* piece of money; *that take, and give unto them for me and thee.*"—Matth. xvii. 24—27.

The words rendered *tribute-money* and *tribute* in the first of these verses, and *a piece of money* in the last of them, are quite different from the words rendered "*tribute or custom*" in the 25th verse. They are Greek names of particular coins, equal in value to the *half-shekel* and *shekel* of the Hebrews. Accordingly, in the 24th verse we ought to read, "They that received *the half-shekels*,"—"doth not your Master pay *the half shekels?*" And in the 27th verse we ought to read, "thou shalt find *a shekel*." And we are thus at once led to note the justice of that reference to Exod. xxxviii. 16. which is made in the margin of our larger Bibles.

[I prefer the translation of "*half-shekels*" and "*shekel*," retaining the name of the Hebrew coins, to the Greek terms "*didrachms*" and "*stater*," which are employed by the Evangelists; because to many English readers the latter denominations of coin would be quite new, while they are well acquainted from the Old Testament with the equivalent Hebrew terms.]

I proceed to offer some remarks, which may shew the importance of this correction of our translation. According to the common version, it might be supposed that the occasion, to which this narrative relates, was the collection of some tax imposed on the Jews by the Roman government, under which they lived; such as the Lord was questioned about on another occasion, Matth. xxii. 17. But it really was not. The payment of such taxes was not in any sense *optional:* as the question put to Peter by the collectors intimated that the payment of this tribute was. It might seem also that the Lord, in his question to Peter and his inference from Peter's reply, designed only to assert his rightful claim to exemption from any tax imposed by "the kings of the earth," as ranking with them in dignity. But, in fact, it is an infinitely higher rank he claims; even one with the King of kings, with Jehovah, with the God of Israel.

The tribute-money really spoken of was that *divine* appointment of the Law, given through Moses, to the Jewish people, of which we read in the 30th chapter of Exodus, from the 11th verse, commencing with the words, "Jehovah spake unto Moses, saying, When thou takest the sum of the children of Israel," &c. Upon that *divine* authority it was enjoined that, when the people were numbered, every one of them from twenty years old should give *half a shekel*, neither more nor less, as "a ransom for his life unto the LORD, that there might be no plague among them." This is expressly called, "an offering unto the LORD,"—"the atonement money of the children of Israel;" and was appointed "for the service of the tabernacle of the congregation." See also 2 Chron. xxiv. 9.

It is now sufficiently evident that, when the Lord Jesus called the attention of Peter to the acknowledged principle—that any tribute imposed by *the kings of the earth* was imposed, not upon their own children, but on strangers, and that the children were therefore free from the payment of it,—he did not intend to claim a right of exemption merely from such *earthly tribute*; but to argue, by analogy, from it to that tribute enjoined by the immediate authority of the King of Heaven, the God of Israel, on his people, as an offering to HIM, and for the service of his sanctuary. And in the ground on which the Lord claimed a right of exemption from this, he plainly marks himself as THE SON OF THE MOST HIGH GOD, in that sense which imported perfect unity of rank with the FATHER. He humbled himself indeed to become the Son of Man, and was "made of the seed of David according to the flesh." But if this had been his only character, he would have been as much *bound* by every divine institution of the Mosaic Law, as any other Jew. Nay, the same *obligation* would have remained, if he had merely united with the human nature that of the highest angel, or the highest supra-angelic—but *created*—nature. Nothing could vindicate from blasphemous presumption his claim to liberty from a *divine* institution, but his being one with the Father, "God over all, blessed for evermore."

I would briefly add that, in some other passages where denominations of coin occur, our version might be improved; particularly where our translators employ the word *penny* to express an ancient coin, which was nearly of the value of eight pence. So, when we read in John vi. 7. "Two hundred pennyworth of bread is not sufficient for them, that every one of them may take a little;"—it would be more correctly rendered, "Six pounds worth of bread." In Matth. xx. 2. I would read, "for eight pence a-day." The common version of these passages is calculated to give a false view of the cheapness of bread and of day labour.

It would be superfluous to offer these corrections here, if readers attended duly to the marginal remarks and references in their English Bibles. But I apprehend that many do not. And indeed the fashionable liberality of the day has banished these important marginal aids from many of even the larger copies of the Scriptures, which are in circulation.

In Luke x. 35. we might perhaps best read generally, "he took out two pieces." The mention in the original of their particular amount is but to maintain, as usual, the dramatic character of the parable:—much as a painter, to give the air of natural truth to a scene which he represents on canvass, throws into it a tree of a particular character, or an individual animal, without at all intending that such a particular animal or tree should be considered essential to the general character of the scene. As for those who amuse themselves with drawing inferences from such incidental circumstances in the parables, and building doctrines upon them, aside from the main object which each parable is designed to illustrate,—it may be truly asserted that they open a wide door for the indulgence of the most delusive fancies.

IV.

"*Make to yourselves friends of the mammon of unrighteousness, that, when ye fail,* they may receive you *into everlasting habitations.*"—Luke, xvi. 9.

Some have indulged in very idle speculations upon the question, whom we are to understand by the expression—*they*; who they are, that are said to receive disciples into everlasting habitations? But all such questions are set aside by translating the passage correctly; "*ye may be received* into everlasting habitations." It is to be admitted, that the common version is the *literal*. But in every language there are idiomatic expressions, which would be very *falsely* rendered, if translated *literally*. The Greek expression in this passage is one of them,—an *idiom* borrowed from the Hebrew.

It is observable, that in another passage of this Evangelist, Luke xii. 20. our translators have rightly rendered the very same phrase;—"this night thy soul [life] *shall be required* of thee." Here the literal version, but not the more correct, would run,—"this night *they are about to require* thy life of thee." And I must confess, that in this instance we might observe something of the same idiom in the English language; as the pronoun *they* might denote some indefinite persons, without implying any thing that would particularly specify *who* they are. But the phrase is therefore justly rendered passively,—"thy life *is to be required* of thee."

So in Luke vi. 38. where it runs—"give, and it shall be given unto you: good measure, pressed down, *shall men give* into your bosom;"—we ought certainly to read, "shall be given into your bosom." The recompense, to which the Lord points his disciples throughout the passage, is one for which he refers them—not to their fellow-men—but to their heavenly Father. The word *men*, also, has been inserted by our translators, though not printed in the Italic character.

The same remark is to be made on that passage in John, iv. 38. "I have sent you to reap that whereon ye bestowed no labour: *other men laboured*, and ye are entered into their labours." The word *men* has been inserted without notice: and although the original is literally, "others have laboured,"—yet the just version would be, "*the labour has been another's*, into which ye have entered." I think it may not be unprofitable to add a few remarks, which may not only tend to establish the justice of this corrected version, but perhaps to throw some additional light upon the whole passage.

Let it be kept in mind that the occasion, on which the Lord spoke these words, was the memorable concourse to him of the people of Samaria, in consequence of the woman's report of him as the Messiah. The result of this, we are informed, was that not only many of the Samaritans believed on him for the woman's report, but many more from hearing his own words, during the two days of his abode with them; and declared their conviction that he was "indeed the Messiah, the Saviour of the world."

Now this was a kind of anticipation and earnest of the general gathering to him of sinners, of all nations and characters, Gentiles as well as Jews: for the Samaritans were as widely separated from all intercommunity with the Jews as any of the heathens. It was therefore an occasion, which naturally suggested (so to speak) to the mind of the Lord Jesus the glorious fruit of his coming into the world —the eternal redemption and salvation of the many sons given to him, out of every kindred, and tongue, and people. But it suggested at the same time, what was inseparably connected with this, the depth of suffering through which he had to pass in making a propitiation for their sin, by the one offering of himself—the just in place of the unjust. The hour of that his suffering upon the cross was now fast approaching: and so terrible was that hour, that in prospect of it, on another occasion, he is recorded to have exclaimed, "How am I straitened, until it be accomplished!"

Filled therefore with that "zeal of the house" of JEHOVAH (John ii. 17.) which consumed him, he replies to the desire expressed by his disciples that he would eat,—"I have meat to eat that ye know not of: my meat is to do the will of him that sent me, and to finish his work." But the Lord contemplates also the honour put upon his apostles, as employed by him to gather in that approaching harvest, of the nearness of which he calls them to observe an earnest in the gathering of the Samaritans to him;—that harvest, in which he was himself to "see of the travail of his soul and be satisfied," (Isa. liii. 11.) and in which they also were to rejoice with him. And while he broadly distinguishes himself as the *sower*, whose alone the *labour* was, from those whom he "sent to *reap* that whereon they bestowed no labour," he rejoices that in the harvest they were to be partakers of his joy.

Is it not now sufficiently manifest, that the real import of the latter clause of the 38th verse is, what I have offered as its just version,—"the labour has been another's, into which ye have entered?"

We have another instance in Luke xviii. 1. of the unwarrantable insertion of the word *men* by our translators, without even employing the Italic character to mark it as an insertion:—"And he spake a parable unto them, [to the purport] that *men* ought always to pray, and not to faint." We should read,—" he spake a parable unto them, that *they* ought always to pray."

The persons, to whom the Lord spake this parable, were *his disciples* ; as appears from the 22nd verse of the preceding chapter. The same thing is manifest from the Lord's application of this parable in the 7th verse :—" And shall not God avenge *his own elect*, which cry day and night unto him, though he bear long with them?" His *disciples* therefore are the persons whom he teaches, " that *they* ought to pray always." Indeed they alone *can* pray unto God, for they alone " believe that he is;" (Heb. xi. 6. Ps. xiv. 1.) they alone *know* God : and how can others call on him in whom they have not believed? (Rom. x. 14. John xvii. 3.) The divines, who talk of prayer as the *natural duty* of *all* men, have derived their theology from quite another source than the Scriptures of truth.

V.

" *That was the true light, which lighteth every man* that cometh *into the world.*"— John. i. 9.

That this version is incorrect, every Greek scholar must be convinced, on considering that there is no *article* prefixed to the participle; that the original is not παντα α. τον ερχομενον εις τον κοσμον, but π. α. ερχομενον. In the latter construction, if the particle be taken in connexion with "*every man*," the import of the words must necessarily be, "every man *at his coming* into the world."

But there is a degree of ambiguity in the structure of the original, which may in some measure be conveyed to the English reader by rendering the Greek words literally, and in the precise order in which they stand,—" the true light which lighteth every man *coming* into the world." And on such a literal translation the question may be raised,—what is it that is spoken of as *coming into the world?* is the participle " *coming*," to be connected with " *every man*," or with the word "*which?*"—" the true light, which coming into the world lighteth every man."—I maintain the latter, for reasons that I shall proceed to state :—only first repeating the remark that, if any will persist in maintaining the former connexion of the words, they yet must abandon the present version of them ; as the Greek cannot justly be rendered " every man *that cometh* into the world," but would then necessarily import—" every man *at his coming* into the world."

Now, that the words "coming into the world" are really to be referred to " the true light," the Messiah, is at once rendered exceedingly probable, if we observe that the Evangelist immediately subjoins in the very next verse, " *He was in the world*, and the world was made by him, and the world knew him not." The phrase also of *coming into the world*, and other similar phrases, are of the most frequent occurrence in the Scriptures of the New Testament, as applied to the Messiah. Nay, in John iii. 19. the expression is applied to him in the very same connexion, as "the light:" "this is the condemnation, that [the] light is come into the world, but," &c. And again in xii. 46, "I am come a light into the world."

But do we find the same phrase of *coming into the world* applied in like manner, to express the *birth* of men generally? No, truly. I believe that not a single instance of it in point can be adduced from Scripture. That which might seem to approach nearest to it is, perhaps, the Apostle's language in 1 Tim. vi. 7. "We brought nothing into the world:" but here, the mention immediately subjoined of our *leaving* the world,—"it is certain we can carry nothing out,"—at once accounts for the phraseology in the former clause. When the Messiah is said to *come into the world*, to be *sent into the* world, &c. there is evidently implied a reference to the *antecedent* glory, which he "had with the Father *before* the world was." (John xvii. 5.) But the Scriptures no where intimate any such antecedent existence of the human race in a former state, as would justify the same general expression for their being *born*.

On these grounds I conclude, without any hesitation or uncertainty, that the words, *coming into the world*, in John i. 9. refer to "the true light;" and that the passage ought therefore to be rendered,—"that was the true light, which coming into the world lighteth every man." Before the coming of Christ the revelation of the true God was confined (almost exclusively) to the posterity of Abraham, the Jewish people. "To them were committed the oracles of God." But when, in the fulness of the appointed time, "the sun of righteousness" arose, its light was *universally* diffused. The long foretold appearance of the Messiah introduced a dispensation, which extends to every kindred, and tribe, and tongue, and people, with a *universality* including Gentiles as well as Jews; and which, in this view, is continually contrasted with the Jewish dispensation, that was confined to the Hebrew nation; the whole code of Levitical observances forming a "middle wall of partition" between them and the rest of the world, till all the Levitical law passed away as a *shadow*, receiving its full accomplishment in Christ, and the things of his kingdom.

In establishing the correct translation of the passage, I have abstained from noticing those most unscriptural doctrines, which the common version has been often employed to countenance:—the doctrine, that the mind of the infant is at its birth in some mystic way *enlightened*, without the communication of any truth, human or divine;—and the doctrine, that Christ actually enlightens every individual in the world, although that individual live and die disbelieving the word of Christ, and therefore under the power of darkness; or without his having ever had even that *hearing* of the word of Christ, by which *faith* cometh. Rom. x. 14—17.

VI.

"And they continued steadfastly in the Apostles' doctrine and fellowship, *and in breaking of bread, and in prayers."*—Acts ii. 42.

This passage ought certainly to be rendered, "in the Apostles' doctrine, and *in the fellowship*," or "*contribution*." By the latter expression, the same Greek word (κοινωνια) is rightly translated in Rom. xv. 26.—"a certain *contribution* for the poor saints which are at Jerusalem." In 2 Cor. ix. 13. it occurs in the same sense; "for your liberal *distribution* unto them, and unto all:" which would literally run—"for *the liberality of your contribution*," *&c.* And again in Hebr. xiii. 16.—where our translators have rendered it verbally,—"to do good and *to communicate* forget not." And so the adjective κοινωνικος, formed from the substantive, is rendered *willing to communicate*, in 1 Tim. vi. 18. And in like manner the verb κοινωνεω, in Phil. iv. 15. Rom. xii. 13. and Gal. vi. 6.

These examples are more than sufficient to establish that the word recurring in Acts ii. 42. is employed in the Apostolic writings, for that communication of worldly goods to the necessities of their brethren, which the Christians were exhorted not to forget, and in which—as one of the *stated* ordinances—the Church at Jerusalem is declared to have "continued steadfastly." I say,—as one of the *stated* ordinances; for, in this view, the contribution here spoken of is to be distinguished from such an *occasional* collection for the necessities of distant saints, as the Apostle speaks of and regulates in 1 Cor. xvi. 1—3. See also Acts xi. 29, and 2 Cor. viii.

But why might we not retain the common version of that passage,—"in the Apostles' doctrine and *fellowship*"? understanding, *in fellowship with the Apostles*, or *in the Apostolic communion*. I reply, because the structure of the original will not properly admit this version. [To warrant it, the words should run τῃ των ἀποστολων διδαχῃ και κοινωνιᾳ, instead of τῃ διδαχῃ των ἀποστολων, και τῃ κοινωνιᾳ:]

I insist the more upon the corrected version of this passage, because it tends to prove that the communication of goods, which went on among the disciples in the first church at Jerusalem, was no other than that which the other Apostolic churches practised, and which the disciples *generally* were exhorted to maintain; nothing like that theological fiction of an absolute *community of goods* among the Jerusalem Christians, to the exclusion of all private property. That fiction would represent the thing which took place in the first Apostolic church, as an exempt case, not to be brought into precedent in other churches: for none but the wildest fanatics can hold, that Apostolic Christianity did away in general with the distinction between the two classes of *rich* brethren and *poor*. Now that fiction concerning the Jerusalem Church may, no doubt, be abundantly exposed from other considerations; as from its being related of Barnabas *particu-*

larly, that he sold a farm, and laid the price of it at the Apostles' feet, Acts, iv. 36, 37.—what all alike, who had any land, must have done, according to the popular hypothesis:—but especially from the following narrative concerning Ananias and Sapphira. There we have the express declaration of the Apostle, that the possession was *his own* before he sold it, and that after he had sold it, the price was *in his own power*; and this, so that he would have incurred no stigma, if he had kept either of them in his own hands.

These, and other considerations, do abundantly refute that supposed community of goods in the first church at Jerusalem: but so also, I repeat it, does the corrected version of the present passage; as it shews, in connexion with the other texts adduced, that the liberality of communication, in which the christians at Jerusalem continued steadfastly, was that which is recorded of the other churches also. And thus it appears, that none—in any age or place—who are followers of the Apostles, and of the Apostolic churches, can so count any thing they possess their own, (Acts iv. 32.) as to withhold, what they can spare themselves, from the real necessities of their brethren; even although this liberality of communication should oblige them at times to break in upon their *capital*. The reader may see the same subject treated in pages 366 and 367 of "*Seven Letters on Primitive Christianity*."

VII.

"*We are the children of God: and if children, the nheirs, heirs of God, and joint heirs with Christ;* if so be that *we suffer with him, that we may be also glorified together.*"
Rom. viii. 17.

[ειπερ συμπασχομεν, ινα και συνδοξασθωμεν.]

Instead of the translation, *if so be that*, &c. the words ought to be rendered—"*inasmuch as*"—"*since*"—or "*seeing that*:"—"*inasmuch as* we share in his sufferings, that we may also share in his glory."

In the connexion, in which the words stand, there is really nothing *conditional* or *uncertain* intimated. Having stated the high blessedness of which believers were made partakers, as *children* of God by adoption and grace, in Him who is the first-born among many brethren, and consequently "*heirs* of God and joint heirs with Christ;" the apostle meets an objection, which the flesh might raise against the reality of this their blessedness,—an objection derived from the tribulations in this life, to which *they* are even peculiarly called. It is as if he said,—Yes, we *are* heirs with Christ in all the blessedness included in having the everlasting God for our portion;

we *are* thus blessed, though we are "a poor and an afflicted people:" for in all our sufferings here we are but conformed to Him, who was "a man of sorrows and acquainted with grief," and this, that we may be conformed to Him in his glory. What a cheering assurance to the Christian in his deepest trials!

To the Greek scholar it would be superfluous to add a word for proving, that the conjunction *ἐπεὶ* has most frequently the force, which I have here assigned to it, of *since—inasmuch as*, &c. But in order to confirm the justice of the alteration to the mere English reader, it may be sufficient to remark, that it is the very same word which occurs in 2 Thess. i. 6. where our translators have rightly assigned to it this interpretation:—"*seeing* it is a righteous thing with God to recompense tribulation to them that trouble you," &c.

I would make the same alteration in Rom. viii. 9. "*inasmuch as* the Spirit of God dwelleth in you:" and in 1 Pet. ii. 3. "*inasmuch as* ye have tasted that the Lord is gracious." The Apostles, in their letters, address themselves to those whom they unequivocally consider as "saints in Christ Jesus,"—"appointed not unto wrath, but to obtain salvation," whom *as such* they call to a correspondent walk; and not in that language of uncertainty, which is very naturally employed by those who assume a kind of religious ministration over a mixed multitude, whom they pretend to manufacture into saints.

Many examples might be adduced of the same force in the simple conjunction *εἰ*, from which *ἐπεὶ* is formed. But I rather pass to notice one instance of it, in the cognate word *εἴγε*, as employed in 2 Cor. v. 3. In our English version the passage runs, "*if so be that, being clothed*, we shall not be found naked." I am quite satisfied that we ought to read—"*inasmuch as*, EVEN when *unclothed*, we shall not be found naked:"—that is, when divested of the earthly tabernacle, we shall be invested with an heavenly. [The biblical scholar will perceive, that I adopt the reading of several manuscripts—*ἐκδυσαμενοι* for *ἐνδυσαμενοι*,—the two words differing only by a single letter, or part of a letter, but the one importing *clothed*, the other *unclothed*. This reading is marked by GRIESBACH, as worthy of attention; but appears to me decisively recommended to our adoption as well by the plain and consistent sense which it affords, as by allowing its proper force of EVEN to the conjunction *και*:—*εἴγε* ΚΑΙ *ἐκδυσαμενοι οὐ γυμνοι εὑρεθησομεθα*.]

VIII.

"*And their* nobles *shall be of themselves, and their governor shall proceed from the midst of them; and I will cause him to draw near, and he shall approach unto me: for who is this that engaged his heart to approach unto me? saith the LORD.*"—Jerem. xxx. 21.

Instead of the plural expression—"their *nobles*," we ought indisputably to read it in the singular number,—"their *noble*," or "their *glorious one*." The original word is as decidedly singular as the following word, "their governor." Indeed, from the whole tenor of the rest of the verse, it is manifest, that one individual is spoken of, not several: and so little room was there for any mistake in the translation, that I have often suspected that it originated in the indistinctness of dictation, the first letter of the word, "shall" coalescing with the preceding word "noble." However this may be, there is no room at all to question the justice of the correction: and, small as it may appear, the remarks, which I am about to add, will perhaps convince the Christian reader of its importance.

The words stand in immediate connexion with the 18th verse: "Thus saith the Lord, Behold, I will bring again the captivity of Jacob's tents, and have mercy on his dwelling places," &c. Now if we receive the distinct interpretation of all such promises assigned by the Apostles, we shall be certain that it is to the times of the Messiah, they all point,—to *his* coming, and to *his* kingdom. Thus, the promise in Amos ix. 11. "In that day will I raise up the tabernacle of David that is fallen . . . . and I will build it as in the days of old;"—is obviously similar to this in Jer. xxx. 18—20. But we have the express authority of an Apostle, (Acts xv. 13—18.) that the promise in Amos pointed to what took place in the Messiah's kingdom and the Apostolic age; and we are therefore bound to interpret similarly the corresponding promise in Jeremiah.

We are therefore led at once to decide, that He who is marked in the 21st verse as *the noble*, or *glorious one*, of Israel,—as *their governor who shall proceed from the midst of them*,—is no other than the Messiah. We may leave it to the commentators and divines of the antichristian world to point to some earthly prince, or succession of earthly princes, raised up to the Jews after their return from the Babylonish captivity; as the unbelieving Jews still dream of such a prince to be yet raised up to them. The true Israel of God are called to "be joyful in their King," (Ps. cxlix. 2.); and to acknowledge with praise and thanksgiving to the Lord, that he "*hath* visited and redeemed his people;" that he "*hath* raised up an horn of salvation for us in the house of his servant David; to perform the mercy promised to our fathers, and to remember his holy covenant." Luke i. 68, &c.

But it is delightful to see various scriptures reflecting multiplied light upon each other. Must not the language—"their glorious one shall be *of themselves*, and their governor shall proceed *from the midst of them*," remind us of the promise uttered by the mouth of his servant Moses, and interpreted of the MESSIAH by the Apostle Peter? (Deut. xviii. 15. Acts iii. 22.) "The LORD thy God will raise up unto thee a Prophet *from the midst of thee, of thy brethren*, like unto me." [Rather "*as me*," *as* he hath raised up *me*. Gr. ὡς ἐμέ.] Every high priest, being "ordained for men in things pertaining to God," is "*taken from among men*," (Hebr. v. 1): and so our great High Priest, to be qualified for the office to which he was called, took part in flesh and blood with those whom he is not ashamed to call his brethren (Hebr. ii. 11—14), and was tempted in all things like unto them. They are bone of his bone, and flesh of his flesh, in a closeness of union, of which the marriage union is but a shadow. Eph. v. 25—32.

Again—does not the language, "I will cause *him* to draw near, and *he* shall approach unto me"—immediately refer us to that in Ps. lxv. 4. "Blessed is the man whom thou choosest, and causest to approach unto thee, that he may dwell in thy courts: we shall be satisfied with the goodness of thy house, even of thy holy temple." That *holy one* of JEHOVAH's choice has entered with his own blood into the holiest, as the great high Priest over his own house; is made most blessed for ever, crowned with glory and honour: and because He has drawn near with the offering for sin, which God has accepted, as taking it away, therefore *we* sinners are blessed in Him; and shall be satisfied with the goodness of the LORD's house, even of his holy temple, when we "shall see the King in his beauty," (Isa. xxxiii. 17.) and shall be with Him, where He is, for ever.

In perfect harmony with all these scriptures are the 15th and 24th Psalms; in which the character is given of THE MAN who shall abide in the tabernacle of JEHOVAH, and dwell in his holy hill;—some of the many Psalms perverted to their own destruction by unbelieving men, who apply the language to some imaginary excellence of character in sinners. And as, in the passage of the Prophet Jeremiah, we read of that *glorious one* "*engaging his heart* to approach" unto JEHOVAH; so, in these Psalms, He is described as "*swearing* to his own hurt, and changing not." He "sware not deceitfully:" he failed not in the awful engagement which he made, as the surety of his people, to take upon himself their sin, and be made a curse in their stead. He drew not back from this, great as was the cost of suffering, in which the fulfilment of his engagement stood him. [The Hebrew expression in the prophet for *engaging* his heart, is commonly applied to the engagement of a *surety*, or one who becomes bondsman for another.]

In connexion with the Scriptures already cited, I shall refer the Christian reader to but one more, the history of Korah's rebellion given in the 16th chapter of Numbers, and the language of Moses in the 5th and 10th verses. "Even to-morrow the LORD will shew who are his, and who is holy: even him whom he hath chosen will he cause to come near unto him. Seek ye the priesthood also?" In the whole of the narrative we may see with what divine jealousy the office of *high priest* was guarded under the law of Moses; and what signal vengeance fell upon any who attempted to intrude into it. Now all this was but a *shadow:* and I have heard of some who pretend that it shadowed forth the supposed sacredness and importance of the *clerical* character, and the great sin and danger of the so-called *laity* rejecting or encroaching on it. Little are those pious clergymen aware that in putting forward such a comment, they prove themselves to be among the characters that are described as perishing in the gainsaying of Core. Jude 11.

We are abundantly instructed in the epistle to the Hebrews, that the Aaronical priesthood and all the institutions connected with it were shadows of the MESSIAH,—of *his* priestly office and work: and are therefore assured that the destruction of those, who interfered with the divine establishment of the Levitical priesthood in Aaron and his sons, was but a type of the more awful judgment awaiting those who oppose the counsel of JEHOVAH, confirmed by an oath, establishing his anointed one a priest for ever after the order of Melchisedek. (Psalm cx. 4. Heb. vii. 21.) That decree of JEHOVAH (Psalm ii. 6, 7.) is as much and as really opposed by multitudes bearing the christian name, as it has ever been by avowed infidels. And it is opposed—not only by Socinians and others, who expressly deny the necessity or reality of Christ's propitiation for sin,—but by many devout and very serious persons, who would be shocked at their being supposed to deny it. If Christ has indeed *finished* that work, if he *has made peace* by his blood, if he *has put away sin* by the sacrifice of himself;—then every doctrine is antichristian, that would instruct sinners in some work which they have yet to do, in order to make peace or get peace with God, or to obtain the remission of their sins. And as grossly antichristian is the claim of any order of men, who now arrogate to themselves something of the *priestly* function; and who represent their exercise of this function, in the administration of what they profanely call *ordinances*, as necessary to convey the benefits of Christ's sacrifice to their fellow-sinners.

How few are there in this country, who do not think the doctrine I have intimated most dangerous and evil? While some others—(more cunning, as they suppose)—intimate in a *whisper* that they believe it to be true, but that it is not safe to tell it undisguisedly, or without great caution and many *guards:* to tell *wicked* sinners of the work which has taken away sin, and of the blessedness which is assured in consequence to every sinner without distinction or exception—believing the divine report of it! Yet all, who harbour such injurious thoughts against the Gospel of Christ, are of Antichrist. Whatever attachment they may feel to a false Christ of their own imagining, they are opposed to the true MESSIAH, and in their hearts "call Jesus accursed:"—as on the other hand, we have Apostolic authority for asserting, that "no man can say that Jesus is the Lord, but by the holy Spirit." 1 Cor. xii. 3.

IX.

"*Jesus answered them, My Father worketh hitherto, and I work. Therefore the Jews sought the more to kill him, because he not only had broken the Sabbath, but said also that God was* his *Father, making himself equal with God.*"—John v. 17, 18.

The expression of "*his* Father" altogether fails of conveying the force of the original, πατερα ιδιον, which imports "*his own*, his *special* Father;" so *peculiarly* his own, that no other could in the same sense claim the character of the Son of God.

The word ιδιος in this emphatic signification occurs most frequently in the New Testament, and is commonly rendered correctly by our translators, "his *own*," "their *own*," &c. nor do I recollect any instance of its mis-translation, beside the present. Out of the numerous examples of the word, one more may be sufficient to illustrate its import to the English reader. Luke vi. 44. "For every tree is known by *his own* fruit." Does not this manifestly mark the fruit *peculiar* to that species of tree, and which no other produces? And thus the Lord Jesus declared, not only that God was his Father, but that he was so in a *special* sense, exclusively *peculiar* to him, and not common to any other.

This remark removes all ground for wondering that his Jewish hearers understood him in this, as "making himself equal with God:" an inference, which they could not have drawn, if he had merely declared himself *a* Son of God, but not specially *the* Son; inasmuch as they were all accustomed to speak of God as their Father. Thus in John viii. 41. "We be not born of fornication, we have one father, even God."

But it is well to look at the passage a little more closely in its connexion, and at the occasion of it, as recorded by the Evangelist. That occasion was the healing of the impotent man at the word of the Lord—*rise, take up thy bed, and walk.* "And on the same day was the sabbath." The blind zeal of the Jews for that divine appointment was kindled. "They did persecute Jesus, and sought to slay him; because he had done these things on the sabbath day. But Jesus answered them, My Father worketh [hitherto] even until now, and I work. Therefore the Jews sought the more to kill him, because he not only had broken the sabbath, but said also that God was *his special* Father, making himself equal with God."

Now let us bear in mind the origin of the seventh-day sabbath; that the institution of it commemorated the completion of the heavens and the earth, when Jehovah ceased from that work of creation, which he so often claimed by the prophets as his own; in opposition to the idols, "that have not made the heavens and the earth." Jer. x. 11, 12. To this origin of the Mosaic sabbath the Lord Jesus evidently referred in the words, "My Father worketh hitherto, and I work." "Hitherto" ἑως αρτι. Rather *to the present hour—still*—or (as our translators very well render the same phrase in John ii. 9.) *even until now*. It is as if he had said,—the first creation of the heavens and the earth was indeed finished when God is declared to have ceased from that work, and to have sanctified (or set apart) the seventh day in commemoration of its completion. But know that there is another work of God, which is not yet finished, but is in progress to the present day; a work even greater and more glorious, in which I and my father are engaged, and which I have now come into the world to accomplish. In the finishing of *this* work, the true Israel shall know the real rest, or sabbath of the Lord; and shall indeed *keep his sabbath from polluting it, and take hold of his covenant*, (Isaiah lvi. 1—7.) in keeping the truth, in holding fast the faith of ME as *the beloved Son in whom God is well pleased*, and as *having finished that work*, which the Father hath given me to do.

Such appears plainly to have been the import, and in some respects, the *understood* import of the words "My Father worketh even until now, and I work." So far at least the Jews understood the words, as to perceive that the speaker made himself *equal with God*, and "Lord even of the sabbath-day:" (Matt. xii. 8.) although the veil still remained upon their hearts, so that they could not look to the end of that Levitical sabbath, which was about to be abolished. 2 Cor. iii. 13—16.

But have not these "times of the Gentiles" long afforded a more striking exemplification of the unbelieving mind, and of its ungodly adherence to false religion, under the profession of Christianity? The unbelieving Jews were right in considering the sabbath as one of the divine appointments of the law given by Moses; and they were but consistent in viewing as a blasphemer any one, who claimed lordship over the sabbath, while they did not acknowledge him as equal with God. But can the mass of those who bear the Christian name in these countries point to any divine institution of what they call the *Christian Sabbath?* Can they point to any word of Scripture, which commands them to pass the *first* day of each week, either in idleness, or in multiplied religious observances, by way of making it extraordinarily holy?

We do indeed find a Christian observance recorded as peculiar to the *first* day of the week: the coming together of the associated disciples of any place, as a church of Christ to eat the Lord's Supper, in commemoration of the work which he finished in his obedience unto death, and the divine acceptance of which, as the one perfect propitiation for sin, has been attested by his resurrection from the dead on the first day of the week. Yes; those who indeed believe that Christ has been raised from the dead by the power of the Father, may well hold sacred that observance of his Supper on the first day of the week, in which they at once commemorate his death and his resurrection from the dead.

But this observance, characteristic of every Christian church, is altogether set aside by the mass of professors bearing the christian name. The very idea of connexion with any body of disciples, at all resembling a scriptural CHURCH, they generally set aside as an antiquated and obsolete thing; while they apply the name of *church* to a worldly system of religious forms and ceremonies, overspreading a country, and incorporated with its political constitution. For the weekly commemoration of Christ's death, in the ordinance of his supper, they substitute—perhaps a monthly—perhaps a quarterly—receiving of what they call the Sacrament, preceded by a week's preparation for it: and profanely add a grand *annual* celebration of a crucifixion, and eat hot *cross-buns* on their Good Friday; following this by an equally grand celebration of a resurrection on the succeeding Sunday; and, finally, they conceive that they make more than amends, for rejecting altogether the only scriptural observance of the first day of the week, by transforming it nominally into a *sabbath-day*, which their divines call *the Christian sabbath*, but which is as little Christian as it is Jewish.

That it is not the Jewish sabbath is certain, for that was distinctly appointed to be observed on the *seventh* day of the week; and as to the notion that the sabbath was *changed*, by divine appointment, from the last day of the week to the first, it is one of those theological fictions which have not the shadow of foundation in the written word. Yet there are *divines* who unblushingly, and with grave countenance, assure us that *no doubt* such a change was communicated to the disciples during the interval between Christ's resurrection and ascension; and the besotted followers of those reverend impostors swallow this gratuitous assertion as indisputably true. But, indeed, they ought to employ their ecclesiastics to forge, at least, some more probable lie for the occasion; as we can prove indisputably, from Scripture, that in the Apostolic age no such change of the sabbath, from the last to the first day of the week, did take place.

I say, this admits of scriptural *demonstration* to those who understand the scriptures. It is certain that the Apostolic churches in heathen countries were generally composed of Jewish, as well as Gentile, converts to the Christian faith. See, for instance, Acts xviii. 8. It is equally certain, that at the same period the Jewish disciples continued to act as Jews, to observe circumcision, the distinction between meats clean and unclean, and all the other institutions of the Mosaic law. For the maintenance of this law, as still binding on the Jewish Christians, many of them were extremely zealous (Acts xxi. 20.); and some of them wished even to impose it upon the Gentile disciples. Nor have we any cause to wonder at this continued adherence to the Mosaic law, when we recollect that the Jew believing in Jesus of Nazareth, as the MESSIAH foretold by all the prophets, did not cease to be a Jew; that he continued to "worship the God of his *fathers*," (Acts xxiv. 14.) without any such change in his professed religion as took place in the converts from heathenism. The Apostles themselves were not, for a considerable time, fully acquainted with the absolute abolition of the Levitical law, contained in ordinances. Various things indeed had prepared them for that discovery: but it seems not to have been till the Epistle to the Hebrews, one of the latest, that the Jewish Christians were expressly instructed on this subject, and taught to consider all the Levitical institutions as shadows, that were "ready to vanish away." Hebr. viii. 13.—x. 1 Col. ii. 17. Perhaps they cannot be said to have actually vanished away, till the destruction of Jerusalem and the temple.

However this may be, it is certain that through the greater part of the Apostolic age, the Christian Jews continued to observe the law of Moses; and, among all its ordinances, there was none which they held more sacred than the *seventh day sabbath*. This, therefore, it is certain that they continued to observe, without any such change of it to the first day of the week, as is now pretended. It is certain, therefore, that on the first day of the week they laboured and did all manner of work; for to observe *it* also as a sabbath would have been as contrary to the fourth commandment of the law, as the non-observance of the seventh day. And thus, as I said, we have demonstrative evidence from the word *against* that fiction of the divines, which I had before only marked as destitute of all foundation in scripture.

And here we may incidentally remark, that a plain reason is discovered, why the disciples in the Apostolic age appear commonly to have come together in the *evening* of the first day (Acts xx. 7, 8.), simply because they had been previously employed, during the day-time, in their several lawful callings. In fact, the total intermission of these ordinary occupations of life, every seventh day, was an institution adapted only to *such a nation* as the Jews, forming among themselves an exclusive community, without intermixture with any others. And it is not wonderful, that the attempt to establish any such practice, in these countries, involves those who make it in a mass of inconsistencies and of hypocrisy.

I have taken the opportunity afforded by this article, of enlarging a little on a subject which I have not elsewhere treated; and on which I hold it is of high importance, that disciples should have their judgments scripturally regulated.

X.

"Hereafter *ye shall see heaven open, and the angels of God ascending and descending upon the Son of man.*"—John i. 51.

The expression rendered "*hereafter*" [ἀπ' ἄρτι] ought certainly to be translated "*henceforth*," as our translators have rightly given it in John xiv. 7. Matt. xxiii. 39, xxvi. 29, and elsewhere. "*Hereafter*" would seem to denote some indefinitely future period, but not so the original; it is literally *from now,—from this time*. I should scarcely notice the seemingly slight inaccuracy, but that it tends to obscure the glory of a most blessed declaration of the word. Let us examine the passage more closely, in its connexion with the preceding narrative.

Upon the commencement of Christ's public ministry, Philip—one of the first disciples called—speaks of him to Nathaniel, as their long-expected Messiah—"We have found him of whom Moses in the law, and the prophets, did write;" and on Nathaniel's expressing his doubt that "any good thing could come out of Nazareth," invites him to come and see for himself. The Lord, seeing Nathaniel approach, points him out as a true Israelite—"Behold an Israelite indeed, in whom is no guile." The words mark him, as not merely a descendant from Abraham according to the flesh, but a partaker of Abraham's faith, of "faith unfeigned." Nathaniel, expressing his surprise that Jesus should speak as knowing him,—"whence knowest thou me? Jesus answered and said unto him, Before that Philip called thee, when thou wast under the fig-tree, I saw thee."

I believe it has often been remarked, but the remark is not the less true and important, that Nathaniel—previous to Philip's finding him—had been engaged in secret communion with the God of Israel.* He had been *alone* under a fig-tree. No eye saw him, but the eyes of HIM from whom nothing is hid: and the language of the Lord Jesus, proving that HE had then been privy to and cognizant of the most secret aspirations of Nathaniel's soul, produces in this Israelite the suitable conviction, and the corresponding acknowledgment, "Rabbi, thou art the Son of God; thou art the King of Israel." All his doubts were now dispelled, whether Jesus of Nazareth could indeed be the MESSIAH, whose coming had been so long foretold, and was so ardently desired by the Jewish people.

But the Lord, in his reply, marks the grand design and effect of his coming in the flesh: and marks it as opposed and superior to any glory of an *earthly* kingdom, such as the Jews generally expected their MESSIAH to establish. "Because I said unto thee, I saw thee under the fig-tree, believest thou? Thou shalt see greater things than these. Henceforth ye shall see HEAVEN OPEN, and the angels of God ascending and descending upon the Son of man." In these words the reference is obvious to Jacob's dream at Bethel, as related in Gen. xxviii. when "he dreamed, and behold a ladder set up on the earth, and the top of it reached to heaven; and behold the angels of God ascending and descending on it. And, behold, the

* I happen to have no Annotator on the New Testament but ROSENMULLER; a man who exemplifies what a thin partition separates the modern German divine from the avowed deist. However, not wanting to get theology from him, or any man, I have kept him for the sake of a little sprinkling of *learning* in his Annotations. As I penned these remarks, I felt somewhat curious to ascertain whether R. admits the nature of Nathaniel's engagement under the fig-tree; and, if he does, how he could contrive to evade the conviction which forced itself upon the Israelite. Perhaps the reader may be a little amused, as I have been, at the learned German's annotation. After referring to the Talmud, to shew that the Jews were accustomed to select a station under fig-trees, for maintaining conversation with their friends, for meditation, for reading, for *prayer*, or study,—he adds, that Nathaniel seems to have been seated under a fig-tree *not far from Jesus; so that Jesus could see Nathaniel, and hear part of the conversation between him and Philip!* How fully is that word verified in these infidel divines—"he taketh the wise in their own craftiness." Professing themselves to be wise, they become fools indeed; and their folly is equalled only by their dishonesty. The avowed deist is at least more honest and more consistent.

LORD stood above it, and said, I am the LORD God of Abraham thy father, &c. . . . . and in thee, and in thy seed, shall all the families of the earth be blessed." Here the promise of the MESSIAH, given before unto Abraham, was now renewed to Jacob; and accompanied with a vision or dream, representing a medium of *free communication* established between heaven and earth, in that ladder upon which Jacob saw the angels of God ascending and descending.

And now the Lord declares to Nathaniel, that what was represented symbolically to Jacob in that dream should be realized, and have its full accomplishment in him, the Son of man, the promised seed. "Henceforth," from this period of my coming in the flesh to finish the work given me by the Father, ye shall see that fulfilled and verified, which was set forth in vision to Jacob at Bethel; "ye" believers in me "shall see *heaven open*," the way into the holiest of all, established and made manifest; the new and living way, by which sinners have free access unto God with acceptance, and are called to draw near to him continually with the sacrifices of praise; the way, in which JEHOVAH is seen at once just, and the justifier of the ungodly, glorifying alike his righteousness and his mercy, while he descends in continual blessing on his redeemed people, the people of his own inheritance.

All the blessedness brought unto sinners by the work of the MESSIAH was indeed testified of old; but it was in prophecy and type. We are taught, that "the way into the holiest of all was not yet *made manifest*, while the first tabernacle was yet standing" (Heb. ix. 8.); the gifts and sacrifices then offered being such as "could not make him that did the service perfect, as pertaining to the *conscience*." It was obviously impossible that "the blood of bulls and of goats, and the ashes of an heifer sprinkling the unclean," should take away sin, and so purge the *conscience;* however they produced that purification of the flesh, that outward and ceremonial cleanness, which was required under the Levitical law. But the MESSIAH having in the last age of the world appeared to put away sin by the sacrifice of himself (Heb. ix. 24, 26.), and having finished that work in his obedience unto death, as the substitute of his people, has now entered into the holiest of all, "into heaven itself, to appear in the presence of God for them." There the eye of faith sees him at the right hand of the Majesty on high, established and accepted as the great High Priest over that redeemed Church which is his house, established in this office even by the oath of Him who cannot lie.

In this work and office of the MESSIAH every sinner, believing the testimony of him, sees *heaven opened* indeed; is made perfect in things pertaining to the conscience; is thoroughly furnished with all that he needs for leading him to draw near with boldness to the throne of Grace, and to walk with the living God in peace and joy and filial confidence, with the assured prospect of speedily exchanging faith for sight, and of being ever with the Lord. To conceal the blessedness and glory of this view, is the great object of Satan and his agents, of all false teachers, in all their endless disguises, who would corrupt the Gospel of Christ. Indeed it is ever the ungodly tendency of that flesh, which in believers themselves is essentially and invariably contrary to the spirit, and lusteth against it. This is "*the* sin that doth so easily beset us," against which we are called to watch and fight in the strength of him whose the battle is, and who giveth power to the faint, and "increaseth strength to those that have *no* might." While we are kept "looking unto Jesus," we see *heaven open* indeed, and are "strong in the Lord and in the power of his might." Believers of the truth! Beware of dogs; beware of the concision; beware of Satan transforming himself into *an angel of light*.

In Luke xxii. 69. our translators have fallen into a similar inaccuracy, to that which I have remarked in John i. 51. Instead of "*Hereafter* shall the son of man," we should read "*Henceforth* shall the son of man sit on the right hand of the power of God." [Here the original is απο τȣ νυν, a phrase perfectly identical both in import and in structure with απ' αρτι.]

XI.

INSTANCES OF ELLIPSES INACCURATELY SUPPLIED.

"*And he spake a parable unto them . . . that* men *ought always to pray, and not to faint.*"—Luke xviii. 1.

IT ought to run—"that *they* ought always to pray." And it appears from the context, taken up from the 22nd verse of the preceding chapter, as well as from all the language of this parable, that the persons instructed by the Lord, "that they ought always to pray, and not to be discouraged," were *his disciples*, of whom he speaks as the "elect of God." v. 7.

"No man knoweth the Father, save the Son, and he to whomsoever the Son will reveal him," Matt. xi. 27.—literally—"is pleased to reveal him." Now those who know not "the only true God," cannot pray to HIM: for how *can* they "call on him in whom they have not believed?" Rom. x. 14. They may abound in the most fervent prayers and piety to the various gods which they have set up in their vain imaginations and unbelieving hearts; but on the name of the LORD no man ever calls, or can call, till he knows HIM, and therefore has that eternal life which is *his* gift. Rom. vi. 23. John xvii. 3.

Thus it is plain to every disciple, that this parable could not have been addressed to any but disciples. And it is in utter contempt of the word of God, that so many of the *divines* would inculcate the *natural duty* of prayer on all men, in recommending their idol of *natural religion*; which they represent indeed as *auxiliary* to revealed, while it is really set up in opposition to that "only true God," whom no man naturally knows, and none ever knew but those "to whomsoever the Son is pleased to reveal him."

"*That he by the grace of God should taste death for every* man."—Heb. ii. 9.

Here again the word "*man*" has been unwarrantably inserted. We should leave the ellipsis unsupplied, and read, "that he by the mercy of God should taste death for *all*." And who the "*all*" are, for whom he has tasted death, we may see distinctly marked in the words immediately following:—"for it became him, for whom are all things, and by whom are all things, in bringing *many sons* unto glory, to make the *captain of their salvation* perfect through sufferings. For both he that sanctifieth and *they who are sanctified* are all of one; for which cause he is not ashamed to call them brethren, saying, I will declare thy name unto *my brethren*; in the midst of *the church* will I sing praise unto thee."

Now what can be a more plain specification of the persons in whose behalf "Jesus was made for a little while lower than the angels for the suffering of death, that he by the mercy of God should taste death for all?" What can be more plain, than that the "*all*" here intended are all the *many sons*, of whose salvation he is the Captain; all whom it is the purpose of God to *bring unto glory* by him, and to whom he declares (or manifests) the name of the Lord; the whole of that *church*, or congregation, in the midst of which he sings praises to Jehovah? Ps. xxii. 22. And, in perfect accordance with this, Christ is declared to have "loved the church, and given himself for it:" Eph. v. 25—to have "laid down his life *for the sheep*," even those *his sheep* of whom he declares, "I give unto them eternal life; and they shall never perish, neither shall any pluck them out of my hand." John x. 15, 27, 28.

The notion that Christ has tasted death for any others, even for those who yet ultimately perish in their sins, is utterly inconsistent with the faith of the Gospel; and goes to pour utter contempt upon the cross of Christ. I am well aware that many who have spent their lives in maintaining the blasphemy, have at times—and particularly on their death-beds—spoken strongly of deriving all their hope towards God from the consideration that Christ died for them. But their strongest language to this effect, unaccompanied with any professed *change of mind*, must be considered by the disciple as "great swelling words of vanity." 2 Pet. ii. 18. For must it not be the most absurd inconsistency to maintain, at once, that any shall perish for whom Christ has died, and yet that *all* a sinner's hope of salvation is to be derived from Christ's having died for him? Assuredly, if Christ has tasted death for every individual of the human race, and if any such individual fails of salvation, those who are saved must owe their salvation to something else than to Christ's having died for them.

But as the holy Scriptures are the great storehouse, from which "the man of God is thoroughly furnished unto all good works," so Satan borrows from them his chief supply of weapons against the truth. Accordingly, the Arminian objector has often urged—Is it not said, that "Christ Jesus gave himself a ransom *for all?*" And is not this said in connexion with the declaration, that God "will have *all men* to be saved?" (1 Tim. ii. 4, 6.)—Yes; so it is written, and in such connexion. But if we read from the beginning of the chapter, we find this declaration connected with the Apostle's direction to Timothy, that "supplications, prayers, intercessions, and giving of thanks, be made *for all men*; for *Kings*, and for all that are in authority," &c.: which sufficiently marks that the expression "all men" imports men of *all* the various *ranks* and *conditions* in human society. But when I say *sufficiently*, do I mean that it will suffice to convince the Arminian objector? By no means. The Scriptures ever have been, and ever will be, "a gin and a snare to those who stumble at the word: and God is righteous in leaving any of them to strong delusion, that they should believe the lie which they love: while he yet magnifies his mercy in giving repentance, to the acknowledgment of the truth, to such of them as he has "ordained unto eternal life."

As I may probably have no opportunity more fair for introducing some remarks on a very important subject, I shall make no apology for the following additional observations:

I have distinctly asserted that Christ has not died for any—in the room or behalf of any—save those, whom he shall absolutely "bring unto glory." With those who deny this, or who shrink from asserting it undisguisedly, I can keep no terms, as if they and I were of one faith. So far, many would say of me—'this man is a *high Calvinist*:'—and so far I am. I look at *low*, or half-Calvinism, as combining great dishonesty with great folly.

Yet I must say, as plainly, that there is in this country a very numerous class of professors, and commonly designated as *high Calvinists*, from whom I yet differ essentially; and whom indeed I consider as no less opposed to the unadulterated truth, than the Arminians;—though they often employ a much more plausible and imposing language. I allude to those who hold, that justifying *faith* consists in a sinner's firm persuasion that Christ died for *him* specially; or in other words, that he is one of the elect.

Now this is not the faith of the Gospel; concerning which it is written, that "whosoever believeth shall be saved;" for a man may be filled with the most presumptuous confidence that he is a favourite of heaven, and yet be nothing nearer that favour of which he thinks himself the object. This is not the faith of the Gospel: for that faith has a divine *revelation* for its object and its basis, the *word* of the God of truth for its warrant and support; and assuredly that word no where testifies of any individual living, that he is one of Christ's sheep; though it does abundantly testify that it was *for his sheep* Christ laid down his life. And, accordingly, those who adopt the sentiment which I am now opposing commonly manufacture each for himself some *private revelation*, which they talk of as their *ex-*

perience; how they *heard a voice*, or felt a divine *impression*, assuring them that their sins were forgiven. And is it on such old wives' fables, on such delusive dreams, that a sinner's faith and hope towards God are to rest?

If I mistake not, it is related of CROMWELL, that on his death-bed, he questioned a *divine* attending him, whether he might be indubitably certain of the principle, *once in grace and always in grace:* and on his *reverence's* replying strongly in the affirmative, Well then, said the Protector, I am safe; for assuredly I was once in a state of grace, though I have been a sad backslider. Now, was the confidence, in which he thus bolstered up his mind, any thing like the confidence which the Gospel of Christ affords to him that believes it? No: it was essentially different. It was based upon the assumption that he *had been once* a real disciple; an assumption which any one may call in question, as his whole history seems that of a man, whose religion began in enthusiasm and ended in gross hypocrisy. But however that may be, it was on a gratuitous assumption that his confidence was based; and if that basis had been removed or shaken, his confidence must have given way with it. Not so the faith and hope of the believer in Christ. The ground of his confidence before God at any hour is not affected at all by the question what his state was the preceding hour, or during the whole of his antecedent life. The ground of *his* confidence is distinct from any thing in him or about him. It lies in that which is unchangeable and divine, in that "word of the LORD which *endureth for ever*," (1 Pet. i. 25.); in the revelation from heaven of the great *propitiation* for sin, which has been made by Christ's dying for the ungodly, and which his resurrection from the dead proves to have been divinely accepted; through which God is at once just and the justifier of the ungodly; and by which there is an open way of access to God for the chief of sinners, with assured acceptance in the Beloved. "THEREFORE let us draw near; let us come with boldness unto the throne of grace"—is the believer's joyful inference (Heb. iv. 16. x. 19, 22.): an inference warranted by the nature of that TRUTH from which it is derived; and equally warranted, whether the believer has been for years standing in the faith and hope of this Gospel, or whether he has been only this hour called to the knowledge of it.

But do I mean to say, that such a believer will then walk in uncertainty about his own election of God? Far be it! This would be utterly inconsistent with the confidence and assurance of hope, which the revealed testimony of God affords to all who believe it. But to confound the belief of it with any confidence about our own election, is calculated to harden men in fatal delusion; leading them to substitute a system of imaginary *favouritism* with heaven, in place of the Gospel of the grace (or mercy) of God, "reigning through righteousness by Jesus Christ unto eternal life," where sin had reigned unto death. Rom. v. 21. Yet, fatal as the error is, it often allows those who have imbibed it to talk a *language* so like the truth, that their unbelief is hard to be detected, except by the evidence in their *religious conduct*, that they utterly despise the word of the most High God.

"*For every high priest is ordained to offer gifts and sacrifices; wherefore it is of necessity that this* man [οὗτος] *have somewhat also to offer.*"—Heb. viii. 3.

Here the insertion of the word *man* is very injudicious. It is quite evident from the context, that the ellipsis ought to be supplied, "this *high priest*." A similar remark applies to Heb. vii. 24. and x. 12. in both of which passages we ought to read, "this *priest*," instead of "this *man*."

A similarly unwarrantable insertion of the word *men* may be noticed in Acts ii. 45. where the version ought to be, "and parted them to all, as any one had need." It is evident that we are to understand *all the brethren* that needed. The same remark applies to 2 Cor. ix. 13.

"*For the law made nothing perfect, but the bringing in of a better hope* did; *by the which we draw nigh unto God.*"—Heb. vii. 19.

The word "*did*," inserted by our translators, ought to be expunged; the *period* marked at the end of the 18th verse to be changed to a *semicolon*; and the words, "for the law made nothing perfect," to be inclosed in a parenthesis. Then the whole passage will run thus: "For there is verily a setting aside of the preceding commandment, on account of its weakness and unprofitableness; (for the law made nothing perfect) but an introduction in its place [ἐπεισαγωγη] of a better hope, by which we draw nigh unto God." *There* is a setting aside of the one, but an introduction of the other. (In this passage there is really no ellipsis. The punctuation alone needs to be regulated; and in that we may use all freedom, the most ancient Greek manuscripts being without any.)

And here again, as continually in the Apostolic letters, we find it marked as the distinguishing glory of the Gospel; that it reveals an *open* way of access for sinful man to the holy God; and reveals this, in the perfection of that sacrifice for sin which *has taken it away*,—what the sacrifices could not do, that were offered under the law. (Heb. x. 11.) But it is to be remembered, that the Gospel was before the law. We are expressly told that the Gospel was preached unto Abraham, four hundred and thirty years before the giving of the law. (Gal. iii. 8, 17.)—But the same Gospel, announcing that promised seed who should destroy the works of the devil, was divinely published immediately after the entrance of sin into the world. (Gen. iii. 15.)—The way also in which that seed of the woman should bruise the serpent's head by becoming the sacrifice for sin and dying in the place of the ungodly, was immediately set forth in shadow, and continually pointed to, in all the sacrifices of slain beasts: which never could have entered man's thoughts as a medium of his approach to God, had they not been divinely instituted; but which we may conclude were observed by the first guilty pair, from the coats of skins in which they were clothed. Through these sacrifices we find that believing Abel offered with acceptance. The same we can trace through Noah and the Patriarchs; till we find them incorporated with the Levitical law. These all pointed to "the Lamb of God that taketh away the sin of the world." It was through the unbelief of the Jewish people, that "their table became a snare before them; and, instead of welfare, a trap." Ps. lxix. 22. Rom. xi. 9.

In short, in every revelation of God from the beginning, one, and but one, way has been marked of a sinner's acceptance before God: —a way not of man's discovery, nor of man's provision, but of God's; and exhibiting in combined perfection *his* righteousnes and *his* mercy, while it brings blessedness to the sinner in its perfect adaptation to all his wants. That "gospel of the glory of the blessed God," (1 Tim. i. 11.) [το ευαγγελιον της δοξης του μακαριου Θεου]—which from the beginning was preached in promises and held forth in types, —is now sent unto all nations for the obedience of faith; proclaiming that Christ, the promised seed, has come in the flesh, and has finished the work which he undertook to accomplish. He that believeth it shall be saved; and he that believeth not shall be condemned.

"*For we are labourers* together with *God: ye are God's husbandry; ye are God's building.*"—1 Cor. iii. 9.

I do not stop to inquire, whether this passage might be more fitly brought under some other head: but at once remark that it certainly ought to be rendered "we are *fellow-labourers in the service of* God," or to that effect. Literally it runs, "we are God's fellow-labourers" [Θεου συνεργοι]: but the whole context proves indisputably that the Apostle's meaning is what I have expressed; and therefore that the passage affords no ground at all for the blasphemies, which Arminians have built upon it, of *man's co-operating with God* in a work belonging to both in common.

The Apostle, from almost the commencement of this Epistle, is sharply rebuking the Corinthian disciples for their carnal glorying in men; and for causing schisms in the church, by classing themselves under the different instruments employed in calling them to the knowledge of the Gospel. Some boasted that they had been called under the preaching of Paul; others of Apollos; others of Cephas, (or Peter); and some under Christ's personal ministry. i. 12. These vain-glorious divisions, Paul sets himself immediately to oppose: and continuing the same subject throughout this third chapter, he indignantly demands—"who then is Paul, and who is Apollos but ministers [διακονοι—servants, agents] by whom ye believed, even as the Lord gave to every man? I have planted, Apollos watered; but God gave the increase. For we are *fellow-labourers* in the employment of God."—The different Apostles and others commissioned to preach the Gospel, are fellow servants of one master, even God; and employedby him, as mere instruments, in one work: which is *his*, and not man's. For "neither is he that planteth *any thing*, neither he that watereth; but God that giveth the increase." v. 7.

Perhaps it would be difficult to find language more strongly opposed to all glorying in man. Yet upon this passage multitudes of religious professors justify their profane boast, of being "as Gods" to themselves,—*co-operating with God* in the matter of their salvation.

The reader may observe that I have incidentally suggested a correction in the translation of the 5th verse; substituting the word *servants* for *ministers*. Such indeed was originally the meaning of the word *minister*, borrowed from the Latin; but it has long passed into quite another acceptation, in common parlance, something of a *clergyman*; particularly in such a connexion as the phrase, "*ministers* of Christ:" and the cognate word *ministry*, in like manner, is too commonly understood as importing some exercise of what is called the *clerical* character or office.

That the word properly means a *servant*, or person *employed* by another, the mere English reader may satisfy himself by referring to Matth. xx. 26, 28. compared with Luke xxii. 26, 27. The expression rendered, "*he that serveth*," in the latter passage, is (I may say) identical with that rendered "*minister*" in the former. Also in Matth. xx. 13. xxiii. 11. and John ii. 5, 9. the original word rightly rendered *servant*, is the same which our translators have rendered *minister* in so many other places.

There is indeed anoth r word [δȣλος] which they frequently translate *servant*; as in Matth. xx. 27. This properly denotes the kind of servant, that is the absolute *property* of his master; or what we call a *slave:* and such are to be understood in all the Apostolic exhortations addressed to *masters* and *servants*. Yet I confess, that in many passages I should not wish to substitute the term *slave*: for to this the English ear commonly attaches the idea of *reluctant* servitude, a notion that is excluded from such applications of the term [δȣλος], as in Rom. i. 1. 1 Pet. ii. 16. The servants of Christ are indeed *not their own*, for they have been *bought with a price*. 1 Cor. vi. 19, 20. But in this consists their blessedness and their glory.

"*We then as workers together* with him *beseech, &c.*"—2 Cor. vi. part of verse 1.

THE common translation countenances an error with regard to these words exactly similar to that which I have just noticed. The original reads so: *We then working together beseech*, &c. i. e. obviously, *We* (to whom the ministry of reconciliation hath been given) *being engaged all of us in the same labour, and uniting our earnest endeavours, go on to execute that office to which God has called us, and in which He has joined us together as* ONE.

If any should object to the above remarks, and abide by the common version of these passages spoken of, it remains with such (putting the Greek text out of the question) to shew how an *instrument* can be said to *co-operate* with him that employs it, in any sense in which it will not be also absurd and impossible to suppose the contrary, and then to say so amounts to nothing. For my part, when it is gravely told me, that the axe *co-operates* with him that heweth therewith, I am not sensible of learning any thing more than that—an *instrument* is—an *instrument*.

"*And they said unto him, We have not so much as heard whether there be any Holy Ghost.*"—Acts xix. 2.

These words constitute the answer given by certain disciples at Ephesus to the Apostle Paul, when *he said unto them, Have ye received the Holy Ghost since ye believed?* and by some, they have been supposed to express ignorance with respect to the existence of the Third Person in the Sacred Trinity. It requires but little consideration, on the part of any who know what it is to be a DISCIPLE, to suspect the propriety of an interpretation, which represents these persons as ignorant of the first principles of that Gospel which an inspired writer declares they believed; in darkness with respect to Him by whose power they must have been enlightened; yea, totally destitute of the knowledge of that God, *whose they were and whom they served*. And as a suspicion of this nature will always lead them that love the word of God to a closer investigation, and a more accurate comparison of scripture with scripture; so the result will ever abound in satisfaction to the inquirer, and will repay the labour of his research with increased views of the excellence and consistency of the Sacred Writings. For such researches those who are acquainted with the original language are above others qualified, and they are, on that account, peculiarly called to make them, not only for their own information but for the instruction of such as possess not the same advantages. Having this object in view, I present my readers with a passage which has suffered much by misinterpretation, and propose to their acceptance what I deem a solution of such difficulty as appears to involve it. And,

1. We observe that our translators have been guilty of inconsistency in their version of this text, compared with their version of John vii. 39. *The Holy Ghost was not yet given.* They manifestly considered this last (as it occurs in the original) to be elliptical, for in it they have supplied (*given*) a word of their own: but, forgetting that analogy which unity of subject and coincidence of expression required, they have translated the other as if it were a complete sentence, merely introducing the word *any*, to express its supposed meaning more fully to the English reader.

2. In consequence of this inattention, the English version exhibits two different ideas, where the Greek text expresses but one; for, removing the supplied word from each, we read in John, *The Holy Ghost* WAS *not yet*; and in Acts, *Whether the Holy Ghost* BE: between which two clauses, *any* reader may discern an exact coincidence of expression, (allowing only for the change of tense) so that

the subject of negation in the former, and of doubt in the latter, must be acknowledged to be one and the same: whereas the common translation denies the *giving* of the Holy Ghost in the one, and in the other questions his *existence*.

3. The error will be corrected by applying the same rule of interpretation to both, and by looking for guidance to whichever of these passages may be more clearly determinable than the other.

4. Now that the passage in John is elliptical, is most obvious; because otherwise an Evangelist (for these are John's own words) must be supposed to deny the *existence* of the Holy Ghost previous to the glorification of Jesus. And not only so, but the context marks the propriety of that very word (*given*) which has been supplied; because it directs us to the long-promised descent of the Spirit of God, called elsewhere the *gift* of the Holy Ghost, which was not to take place till Jesus was glorified, being necessarily subsequent to that event which it was designed to attest. Accordingly, the first preaching of the resurrection, and the first descent of the Holy Ghost, took place on the same day, the day of Pentecost. The meaning of these words of the Evangelist being thus established,

5. We conclude that the passage under consideration is *also* elliptical, and is *also* to be supplied by the word *given*. It will then run so, *we have not so much as heard whether the Holy Ghost be given:* and thus the answer marks no ignorance of that spirit who dwelt in them, but merely intimates that they had not heard of the Holy Ghost's having yet been poured out; a circumstance which affected not their views of the only True God, involved no error in their faith of the gospel, and for which the place of their residence fully accounts.

XII.

INSTANCES OF INACCURACY IN THE OMISSION OR INSERTION OF THE DEFINITE ARTICLE.

"*I will therefore that* men *pray everywhere, lifting up holy hands, without wrath and doubting.*"—1 Tim. ii. 8.

We certainly ought to read—"that *the men* pray everywhere;" or literally, "in every place." *The men*, in contradistinction to *women*. The original is decisive—[τυς ανδρας]. Accordingly, the Apostle proceeds, in the next and following verses, to give his instructions about *the women*, the sobriety of their apparel, their silence in the church, &c.

It is therefore plain, that in the 8th verse, the expression *pray* imports leading in social prayer; as it is certain the Apostle never intended to debar Christian women from prayer, either from praying individually in private, or from joining in spirit with the social worship of the brethren. And the addition of the words, "in every place," marks, I think, that the Apostle extends his regulation beyond the meeting of the brethren on the first day of the week, to any other occasion in which several of them united in prayer: an instance of which we have in Acts xii. 12.—I make the observation, because, (if I mistake not) it was at one time maintained by Mr. WAKEFIELD, that all open engagement in social prayer is contrary to the direction which Christ gives his disciples in Matth. vi. 6. But that this direction related exclusively to private, or individual prayer,—and that the sentiment I have mentioned was utterly erroneous,—is proved decisively by the Apostle's language in this passage of his letter to Timothy.

"*For the love of money is the root of all evil.*"—1 Tim. vi. 10.

WE should read, "is *a* root of all evil." [ῥιζα γαρ—not ἡ ῥιζα.] —The common version would seem to imply, that the love of money is the *only* root of all evil.

"*I have fought a good fight.*"—2 Tim. iv. 7.

HERE we should read, "*the* good fight." The original is emphatic—[τον αγωνα τον καλον]—as if he said, "I have maintained the contest that is indeed *the* glorious one; I have finished the race; I have kept the faith."—The Apostle's language here and in the following verse obviously alludes to the public games, of running, &c. in which the Greeks especially delighted; and a prize in which they spoke of frequently as the highest honour attainable by mortals. We find the same allusion in 1 Cor. ix. 24—27. and elsewhere.

The Christian, while engaged in maintaining "the good fight of faith," (1 Tim. vi. 12.) must lay his account indeed to meet with the *contempt* and *scorn* of the world. But even in this he is enabled to glory, while kept looking unto the great forerunner. HE "endured the cross, despising the shame." HE was "*mocked*" and "*spit upon*." HE is "*despised*," as well as "*rejected*, by men." (Isa. liii. 3.) And the remembrance of HIM may well enable his followers even to "rejoice, when they are counted worthy to suffer shame for his name." (Acts v. 41.) But as yet "their life is hid with Christ in God." It is "when Christ, their life, shall be *manifested*,—[φανερωθῃ]—that they also shall be *manifested* with him in glory." (Col. iii. 3, 4.) And then it will appear to all, that the "fight of faith" which they have maintained, at whatever cost of suffering for his name, is indeed "the good fight,"—the honourable and *glorious* contest.

" *And* finding disciples, *we tarried there seven days.*"—Acts xxi. 4.

It should be—" And having *found out the disciples.*" [ανευροντες τους μαθητας.]

Here, besides the omission of the definite article, our translators have very imperfectly given the force of the preceding participle, which really implies that Paul and his Christian companions, on their arrival at Tyre, had inquired, or searched, for the disciples in that city. This is always the proper force of the compound verb [ανευρισκω]; of which we have another example in Luke ii. 16. The simple verb [ἑυρισκω] neither implies, nor necessarily excludes, the idea of such an antecedent search; and accordingly it is employed in the 2nd verse of this chapter; the finding of a ship sailing to Phenicia having been, perhaps, unlooked for.

Trifling as the correction which I have suggested may appear to some, it renders the narrative much more interesting to those, who are at all acquainted with the fellowship of Christian brethren. Paul, arriving at Tyre (as it would appear) on a Monday, sets about inquiring for the Christians of that city; and succeeds in finding them. Finding any one of them, he in effect found them all; for all were in one body most intimately associated. But the Apostle, anxious to meet with them all assembled on the first day of the week, and to join with them in shewing forth that which was the one foundation of their common hope towards God, tarries at Tyre for the purpose seven days. (We find him tarrying the same period at Troas for the same purpose, in the preceding chapter, v. 6 and 7.) Perhaps he had never before seen the face of one of these Tyrian disciples. Yet, O! what closeness of heart union, what endeared fellowship was there among them? And is not this intimated in that most striking, though most simple description, which is contained in the fifth and sixth verses?

Can we contemplate the whole narrative, without contrasting Apostolic Christianity with that which passes under the name, at this day and in this country? Shall we imagine a Christian stranger, of the Apostolic school, arriving in any city in Christendom for the first time; and proceeding to inquire for the disciples—for the Christians of that place? " The Christians! Sir: we are all Christians!"—Perhaps the inquirer has just passed by two of these *Christians*,—staunch upholders of Church and State—going out to the field of honour, deliberately to shoot one another. Perhaps—But I forbear. Too wide a field opens before me.

" *But exhort one another daily, while it is called to-day; lest any of you be hardened through the deceitfulness* of sin."—Heb. iii. 13.

It should be " of *the* sin" [της ἁμαρτιας]; namely, that sin of *unbelief*, against which the Apostle has warned the Hebrew Christians in the verse immediately preceding, and warns them throughout the Epistle.

Nor is it without reason, that in the 12th verse he connects the "evil heart of unbelief" with "departure from the living God." It is in the *doctrine* of Christ, that the *name*—or character and glory—of "the only true God" is declared. They who are turned from darkness unto light, from the false religious sentiments, which naturally possess the sinner's mind, to the *belief of the truth* as it is in Jesus,—they, and they alone, are turned to the only true God; are indeed *converted*, and have "repentance unto life." And, on the other hand, those who depart from the faith and uncorrupted truth of the Gospel, after having once professed it, do awfully "depart from the living God;" and are indeed apostates, for whom there remaineth a "fearful looking for of judgment and fiery indignation, which shall devour the adversaries." Heb. x. 27.

"*And again Esaias saith, There shall be a root of Jesse, and he that shall rise to reign over the Gentiles, in him shall the Gentiles* trust. [ἐλπιοῦσι.] *Now the God* of hope [τῆς ἐλπίδος] *fill you with all joy and peace in believing, that ye may abound* in hope, *through the power of the Holy Spirit.*"—Rom. xv. 12, 13.

We should read, "in him shall the Gentiles *have hope*. Now the God of *this hope*"—and—"that ye may abound in *this hope*." The Apostle speaks not of every hope, or of every religious hope, indiscriminately: but specially and exclusively of the hope of the Gospel; of that "good hope through grace," of which sinners believing in Christ are made partakers; which has the living God for its author, his faithful word for its warrant, his immutability and omnipotence for its guarantee.

The distinguishing character of *this hope* is marked in all the prophecies which the Apostle has quoted, and which declared that *the Gentiles* should be partakers of it: *the Gentiles*, whom the Jews were accustomed to consider as dogs, in comparison of themselves; and whose natural state is described as that of "aliens from the commonwealth of Israel, having *no hope* and *without God* in the world," "dead in trespasses and sins." (Eph. ii. 1, 12.) Herein "the hope of the Gospel" stands distinguished from all the vain hopes, which men derive from the consideration of some supposed worth, or wisdom, or power in themselves. It is for those that are *ungodly* and *without strength* (Rom. v. 6.); and it rests on the "sure foundation, which God has laid in Zion." In such Gentiles, the Apostle declares that "Christ is the hope of glory." (Col. i. 27.) And this is the hope that "maketh not ashamed."

XIII.

" *And when he was demanded of the Pharisees when the kingdom of God should come, he answered them, and said,—The kingdom of God cometh not with observation. Neither shall they say, lo here! or, lo there! for behold the kingdom of God is* within *you.*"—Luke xvii. 20, 21.

We certainly ought to read, " the kingdom of God is *in the midst* of you." And so the French version. The more closely we examine the context in the light of scriptural truth, the more will this correction appear indisputably just.

The Lord Jesus had not as yet publicly and avowedly put himself forward as the Messiah. On the contrary, he enjoined his disciples who acknowledged him in that character, not to tell any man that he was the Christ: and this, for the wisest reasons. The contrary course could at that time only have excited the people to revolt against their Roman governors; and so have countenanced the imputation that he was an enemy to Cæsar. Indeed we find on one occasion, that the people, excited by the miraculous feeding of the multitude, would have " come and taken him by force to make him a king." (John vi. 15.) How much more forward would they have been to engage in such attempts, had he not appeared in circumstances—and uniformly pursued a course—opposite to all the greatness and splendour of earthly kings?

The Pharisees, however, could not fail to understand the various intimations by which, from time to time, he left his hearers to conclude that he was the Christ; nor were they ignorant that his followers considered him as such. Accordingly they had agreed, " that if any man did confess that he was Christ, he should be put out of the synagogue." (John ix. 22.) And when the whole Sanhedrim condemned him to be guilty of death as a blasphemer, it was because he replied with an explicit affirmative, " *I am*," to the High Priest's question—" Art thou the Christ, the Son of the Blessed?" (Mark xiv. 61—64.) To ensnare him into such an avowal prematurely, and so to establish against him the charge of making himself a king in opposition to Cæsar, was the object of the Pharisees on many occasions, in which they endeavoured to entangle him in his talk: and it appears to have been their object in demanding of him, " When the kingdom of God should come?"

In the Lord's reply, we may admire that divine wisdom which ever flowed from his lips. Without either denying or asserting that he was the King of Israel, his reply strikes at the root of the false conceptions concerning the nature of the Messiah's kingdom, upon which the question of the Pharisees proceeded; and testifies against the blindness which possessed their minds. " The kingdom of God cometh not with observation,"—not with any outward display of greatness and power marking its arrival, so that men noticing it should say—" Lo here! or lo there! For behold the kingdom of God *is among* you." That kingdom, about which ye inquire when it *shall* come, IS here already—among you—in the midst of you—before your eyes. No wonder, if these Pharisees indignantly exclaimed, as on another occasion, " Are we *blind* also?" John ix. 40.

To disciples the subject rises in its interest, when we view it as exhibiting the contrariety of the ways and thoughts of God to the thoughts and ways—not of the Jews merely—but of man, fallen man, in every age and country. Indeed, in any other view, it would only tend to impress us with a notion of the extraordinary wickedness of the Jewish people and their leaders, above ourselves. But what have been all the attempts to incorporate Christianity with the various civil constitutions of Europe, but vain and ungodly attempts to transform the kingdom of Christ into a kingdom of this world? what, but attempts to take him (as it were) by force, and make him a king after the fashion of earthly kings, in opposition to his most express declaration, and, we may say, protestation against it?

While the Jewish dispensation lasted, there was indeed a real incorporation of *church and state*, of their religious and their civil code. They were, in fact, identified; and both emanated, not from man, but from the God of Israel. Yet even that dispensation, in which the institutions were shadows of better things then to come, and the peculiar sanctions of its law, temporal and earthly in their nature; even that dispensation is continually spoken of in the New Testament Scriptures as *worldly, and carnal, and passing away*; in contrast with the Messiah's kingdom which displaced it, and " which cannot be moved." (Heb. viii. 5, ix. 1—24, xii. 22.)

The Lord himself marks this contrast in his memorable confession before Pilate; while he declared himself a king, declaring as distinctly—" My kingdom is not of this world. If my kingdom were of this world, then would my servants fight, that I should not be delivered to the Jews: but NOW [νυν δε] is my kingdom not from hence." (John xviii. 36.) That word, " *now*," is emphatic; and plainly distinguishes the character of his kingdom from that of the Mosaic dispensation, which it superseded.

But just as the Jews, who " despised and rejected " Jesus of Nazareth, were most ardently attached to the false Messiah they had imagined, and were ready at any time to fight for *such* a king of Israel; even so, multitudes in anti-christian Europe burn with zeal for the false Christ, whom they have set up in their union of *church and state*, while they scorn and detest the only true Christ, the Christ of God, and manifest this by their contemptuous rejection of the word that testifies of him. The earthly splendour and pomp of the temples they have consecrated to their idol, the wealth of their endowments, the various orders of lordly priests, and various rituals of service they have appointed for his worship,—all these are things that of course have strong attractions for their earthly minds, and the stronger their attachment to these, and admiration of them, the more cordial is the disgust and hatred excited in them by that, which rejects them all.

Greatly, however, should I be mistaken, if I were understood to mark this Judaizing corruption of Christianity as peculiar to the religious establishment of the country. In various forms it just as much pervades the general mass of Dissenters. Hence all their efforts to attach some worldly *respectability* to their several synagogues and systems,—respectability from the number or rank of their adherents,—respectability from the paltry splendour of even *their* edifices,—respectability from the talents and eloquence of the *Reverend* gentleman, who apes the clergyman in his garb and style, and whose *ministrations* to a crowded audience of admiring pew-holders and hearers are substituted for the assembling of a few saints on the first day of the week, to break bread. But hence, above all, the various schemes of Churchmen and Dissenters conjointly to cover the offensiveness of the unadulterated GOSPEL, by concealing that heavenly truth which publishes salvation to the lost, justification to the ungodly, mercy higher than the heavens to the chief of sinners, and "reigning through righteousness by Jesus Christ unto eternal life;" concealing, I say, this heavenly and joyful truth, by substituting for it, the several counterfeit doctrines of men and lies of Satan, which are forged in opposition to that truth, but attired in its perverted phraseology.

And just as, among the Jews, the ringleaders of the opposition to Jesus of Nazareth, those who excited the populace to join in the cry —"crucify him, crucify him,"—were the persons most eminent in the nation for religious knowledge and zeal and strictness; as these were the persons most fired with indignation at Him, who avowed himself "the friend of publicans and sinners;" even so is it now. The Scribes and Pharisees would have borne with a great many other things which they disliked, and have been ready perhaps to acknowledge the Lord as a divine teacher and prophet; if he had only intimated that he came to favour persons so *good* and *respectable*, as they considered themselves, and had scowled upon the confessedly *wicked*. They would then have been ready, with the good young ruler, to admit his claim to the character of goodness, and, it may be, would have joined with that very *serious* inquirer in consulting him on the good question*—"what good thing shall we do that we may inherit eternal life?" So full of goodness and excellent moral dispositions were these "betrayers and murderers of that just One," whose coming they professed to expect most confidently, and to desire most earnestly.

Even so at this day the false teachers, hired by the people to feed them with the lies they love, hold out various false Christs, as in various degrees helping the *well-disposed*, those who have good desires, and much willingness to avail themselves of the *offered* aid.

* The commencement of Christ's reply to that inquirer is commonly read with an emphasis very falsely placed,—placed on the word *me*, instead of on the word *why*. "WHY callest thou me *good?* There is none *good* but One, that is God." The young ruler had complimented Jesus with the title, just as he thought that it belonged to himself. But he heard in reply a principle, which laid the axe to the very root of all his goodness, while it left the Lord's claim to the title of *good* neither affirmed nor denied.

And the doctrine that encourages *such*, that instructs and excites them to lay hold on the blessedness which is placed *within their reach* by the false Christ of the system, is termed *evangelical*. But to the absolutely bad and ill-disposed, who have no good desires, these teachers have no gospel, or none *till they become good*; and the Apostolic Gospel, which publishes a Saviour of such wicked, stubborn rebels against the Most High, is just as much an object of scorn and detestation and blasphemous reviling to these zealous champions of *goodness*, as ever it was in the Apostolic age.

We often find that the Pharisees expressed their desire, that the Lord would shew them "a sign *from heaven*," some display of sensible glory in the sky; having in view, no doubt, the prophecy concerning the Son of Man in Dan. vii. 13, 14. *That* sign of the Son of Man they demanded to see prematurely, that he might be authenticated to them as the Messiah; but he refused it to that generation, while he assured his disciples that they should see it in due season. (Matt. xxiv. 30.) On one of those occasions, the Lord rebuked the Pharisees and Sadducees for their blindness to the *signs of the times*, that were before their eyes. (Matt. xvi. 1—3.) At this day, in like manner, that second coming of Christ, which forms one of the articles of the national creed, much engages the thoughts and speculations of the religious world; they consider it to be at hand, and look anxiously for signs of its near approach. But I apprehend that the signs they mainly look for are connected with their false conceptions of Christianity; more *national conversions*, and an increased *flourishing* of their religion by an addition of numerous and respectable proselytes; while they see not the signs, which most distinctly mark to disciples the approach of "him that cometh."

Among these signs of the times, I especially regard that "consumption of the man of sin" (2 Thess. ii. 8.), which is quietly but progressively going on, "by the spirit of the Lord's mouth," by the word of truth, that "sword which proceedeth out of his mouth." This noiseless recalling of disciples to the purity of Apostolic doctrine and practice, from which they had been more or less borne aside by the wide flood of anti-christian corruption, this—so far as it excites the attention of the religious world at all—excites also their disgust and indignation. Yet this is among the most conclusive signs of the times, which indicate to disciples that the great day is at hand.

When the number of the elect is fulfilled, and the last of them gathered in out of Babylon, this world will then be as the lifeless carcase, upon which, wherever it is, the birds of prey fall, "the eagles are gathered together." (Luke xvii. 37.) It was so in the days of Noah. It was not till the day of Noah's entrance into the ark that the flood came. It was so in the days of Lot. It was so in the day of Jerusalem's judgment. And "even thus shall it be in the day when the Son of Man is revealed." And his coming shall be suddenly, in an instant—"as the lightning, that lighteneth out of the one part under heaven, shineth unto the other part under heaven;" —"in a moment, in the twinkling of an eye." (1 Cor. xv. 52.) How wisely and graciously is this ordered and revealed! All the vain speculations are thus put down, which would lead us to calculate the particular time of his appearing; and with them all that *agitation*, that *commotion* of mind, which the idea of its immediate arrival would necessarily occasion. This mental *perturbation* is the thing really imported by the expressions "shaken in mind" and "troubled," in 2 Thess. ii. 2. Our utter ignorance also of that day and that hour impresses on disciples, every day and every hour, that salutary monition—"Watch, as men who wait for their Lord, watch."

XIV.

INSTANCES OF INACCURACY IN THE RENDERING OF TENSES.

"*And they* called *him Zacharias, after the name of his father.*"—Luke i. 59.

It should be—"they *were calling* him Z." [εκαλουν.] They were about calling him after the name of his father; and would have done so, but for the interference of Elizabeth, to whom her husband had, no doubt, by writing communicated the name prescribed by the Angel.

"*Our friend Lazarus* sleepeth." John xi. 11.—It should be—"*hath fallen asleep.*" [κεκοιμηται.]

We are told that the Lord, after receiving the message from Martha and Mary announcing their brother's illness, "abode two days still in the same place where he was." And it is evident that he purposely waited so long, in order that the death and burial of Lazarus might take place before he should arrive at Bethany. With what anxious alternation of hopes and fears did the sisters, we may suppose, look out for his arrival, during the progress of their brother's illness! With what a sad sinking of the heart were their hopes apparently extinguished by his death! and not unaccompanied perhaps with some *chagrin*, when they heard that Jesus was coming. Little were they aware, that all which passed in their house of sorrow, had passed under his observant ken, and that he had *purposely* allowed it to take place, for the greater display of the glory of God.

Surely his followers may learn cheering and profitable lessons from the narrative, in seasons of their sorest affliction, and when the looked-for relief is longest delayed.

"For yet a little while, and he that shall come, *will come, and will not tarry."*
Heb. x. 37.

I should decidedly prefer to render this literally—"he that *cometh*," or, "he that *is coming*." ['ο ερχομενος] This more emphatically expresses our confidence that his arrival approaches, than the indefinitely future expression—"he that *shall come*." I would make the same alteration in Matt. xi. 3. and Luke vii. 19,—"Art thou *he that cometh*, or look we for another?"

From the latter passages we may collect, that the expression "*he that cometh*" was, with the Jews, a kind of title distinguishing the MESSIAH; for this was certainly the designed and understood import of the Baptist's inquiry.* And the phrase appears to have received this current acceptation from its use in Psalm cxviii. 26, "Blessed is *he that cometh* in the name of the LORD." In this language, the multitude of rejoicing disciples who attended the Lord on his last entrance into Jerusalem, acknowledged him as the MESSIAH; and in the same sense did the Lord apply the language to himself in his last lamentation over Jerusalem. Matt. xxiii. 39.

At this day indeed believers have to remember with joy, that the coming of Christ in the flesh has taken place; that coming which

* Some have conceived, that it was not for the satisfaction of his own mind the Baptist made this inquiry, but for the satisfaction of his disciples, through whom he proposed it. They think it impossible that any doubt upon the subject could have occurred to himself, after the divine information he had received, the evidence he had witnessed, and the testimony he had borne, identifying Jesus of Nazareth as the MESSIAH. But this idea proceeds upon a false estimate of what is in man. I am far indeed from conceiving that the Baptist was *allowed* to renounce that view of the Lord. But it is evident from the narrative, that he was *staggered* in his mind; and staggered, (it is more than probable) from finding that the Lord did not interfere at all to release him from prison. According to the generally prevalent misconceptions of the nature of the MESSIAH's kingdom, (prevalent, we know, at that time, among the most favoured disciples of the Lord, and no doubt affecting also the Baptist's mind,) he appears to have been quite unable to reconcile it with the greatness of that kingdom, that he himself should be left so long in the hands of his enemies. Perhaps also he designed, by making the inquiry, to put himself and his situation in the Lord's revived recollection.

Those who imagine, that so great a prophet could not have fallen into such a *halting* state, are puffed up with a vain admiration of him, and a vain conceit of themselves. Accordingly, the Lord, in his reply to the Baptist's inquiry, treats this manifestation of his fleshly mind with no more indulgence than he treated a similar manifestation in Peter, (Matt. xvi. 23.) Simply referring to the works of mercy in which he was engaged, he adds the declaration—"Blessed is he, *whosoever shall not stumble at me*:" words which plainly mark the mind that he rebukes in the Baptist, as the mind of unbelief; the tendency of which is to make men stumble at that stone, against which whosoever falls shall be broken. This mind "savours not the things that are of God, but the things that are of men:" and is of precisely the same ungodly character in those who are saved from its destructive tendency, as in those whom it destroys. When the iron (2 Kings vi. 6.) was miraculously made to ascend from the bottom of the water, and to float on the surface, *its own* tendency to sink to the bottom was just the same as before; and would have been at any moment manifested, if the supernatural power which raised it were but for a moment intermitted. Even such is every fancied *improvement of* our own nature by what the religious world miscall *Grace*.

"many prophets and righteous men desired to see," and to which they looked forward with eager expectation. This coming of Christ has taken place, and the work which he came to accomplish in the flesh is finished. He has been "made sin," or a sin-offering, for his church, and has put away sin by that one offering of himself in the place of the guilty, the just for the unjust. But still is he held out to the faith of his people as "*He that cometh*;" and still are they held out as a people who *love and look for* his appearing—who "look for and hasten unto the coming of the day of God." At that day, HE WHO COMETH shall appear the second time, WITHOUT SIN, unto salvation" (Heb. ix. 28); "to be glorified in his saints, and to be admired in all them that believe." (2 Thess. i. 10.) We are taught to "comfort one another with these words," which describe the glory of that day; and as we observe the signs of the times announcing its approach, it is cheering indeed to exclaim—"Behold, HE COMETH!" —Rev. i. 4, 8. iv. 8. xi. 17. xxii. 20.

Having been led to mention the second coming of the Lord, I may as well here introduce a corrected version of 2 Thess. ii. 1. That passage ought certainly to be read "Now *upon*," or "*concerning* the coming of our Lord Jesus Christ, and our gathering together unto him, we beseech "you brethren, that ye be not," &c. The common version—"We beseech you, *by* the coming.... and *by* our gathering," &c.—is, in every view, indefensible. The Greek preposition [ὑπὲρ] is employed, to indicate the subject *upon* which we speak, in Rom. ix. 27—2 Cor. i. 8, and elsewhere.

XV.

"*If thou*, LORD, *shouldest* mark *iniquities*, O Lord, *who shall stand? But there is* forgiveness *with thee, that thou mayest be feared*."—Ps. cxxx. 3, 4.

I believe this passage is generally quoted as intimating, that God is not extreme to notice what is evil in men; but that he overlooks, or winks at, such forms of it as are to be considered rather venial failings and infirmities, than sins. Such, at least, is commonly the imagination of the unbelieving mind, of "the fool who saith in his heart, *God is not*;" who denies the existence of the *only true* God, in denying his immutable holiness and perfect righteousness.

But, however the English expression, "*mark* iniquities," may seem to lend some countenance to that infidel imagination, the original lends not any; and the whole passage—rightly understood—presents at once the most awful view of sin, and the surest ground of hope to the chief of sinners. But who can understand it aright, except those to whom "the Son of God *hath given* an understanding to know the true God?" 1 John v. 20. It cannot be understood by any, who reject the principle so distinctly given in the New Testament for interpreting the Psalms, that they were uttered by David as a *Prophet*, speaking not from himself, but by the Holy Spirit; not of himself, but, as the Spirit of Christ that was in him did signify, of the sufferings of Christ and the following glories. Acts ii. 29—31. xiii. 33—37. Luke xxiv. 44. Mark xii. 36. 2 Pet. i. 21. 1 Pet. i. 10—12. It cannot be understood by those, who, in spite of this infallible interpretation of the Holy Spirit, persist in regarding the Psalms as the language of the sinner David about himself, his experiences, his joys and sorrows, his afflictions and deliverances, his conflicts and his triumphs.

But well is it for us, believers, that in hearkening to the voice which speaks in the 7th verse of this Psalm,—"Let Israel hope in Jehovah, for with Jehovah is mercy, and with him is plenteous redemption:"—well is it for us, that in hearkening to such a call we hearken not to the voice of a sinful man like ourselves, but to the voice of Him who indeed "was made of the seed of David *according to the flesh*," but yet is David's Lord; (Rom. i. 3. Mark xii. 35—37.) to the voice of Him, who, addressing his heavenly Father, said by the mouth of his servant David, "I will declare thy name unto my brethren: in the midst of the congregation will I praise thee." See Ps. xxii. 22. interpreted in Heb. ii. 10—12. and Ps. xl. 6—10. interpreted in Hebr. x. 5—10.

We are told in Hebr. v. 7. that Christ in the days of his flesh offered up prayers and supplications, with strong crying and tears, unto Him that was able to save him from death: and this short Psalm (the 130th) is one of those, in which we are admitted, as it were, to hear the Man of Sorrows pouring out his soul before God. In this view of it, and of him as at once the great High Priest and sacrifice for sin, let us take a survey of the Psalm: premising that the expression translated "*mark*" in the 3rd verse literally signifies to *keep or hold fast:* as the word rendered "*forgiveness*" in the following verse literally denotes *loosing, or relaxing*. The two words, as applied to *sin*, are nearly equivalent with the "*binding*" and "*loosing*"—"*retaining*" and "*remitting*", which occur in the New Testament. (Matth. xviii. 18. John xx. 23.)

Now *the iniquities of all* his people were *laid*, or made to meet, *upon him*, Isa. liii. 6. He was *made sin for them*. 2 Cor. v. 21. And as he took upon himself their iniquities, and endured the penalty of them, so he confessed them as his own. "*Mine* iniquities," saith he in the 40th Psalm, "are more than the hairs of mine head:" this Psalm is expressly interpreted of the Messiah in Heb. x. 5—9. And again in the 38th Ps. he saith, "*Mine* iniquities are gone over mine head: as an heavy burden they are too heavy for me." Under this heavy burden he groaned, and poured out his soul unto death; and whatever were the *instruments* of his sufferings, men or devils, they were but the *sword* of the Lord of hosts, called to "awake against his Shepherd, against the Man that is his fellow." (Zec. xiii. 7, compared with Matt. xxvi. 30.) It was under the righteous judgment of Jehovah against sin, that he suffered. Accordingly, he speaks in the Psalm last quoted, "*thine* arrows stick fast in me, and *thy* hand presseth me sore:" and again, in the 39th Psalm, "I wa dumb, I opened not my mouth, because *thou* didst it: remove *thy* stroke away from me; I am consumed by the blow of *thine* hand:" and again, in the 69th Psalm, "They persecute him whom *thou* hast smitten; and they talk to the grief of *thy* wounded one:"* and in the 42nd Psalm, "*All thy* waves and *thy* billows are gone over me."

"Out of these depths," awfully unfathomable, he "cried unto JEHOVAH:" and it was in the full assurance of faith, believing the *word* of the LORD with unshaken confidence, that he cried for the promised deliverance, and was heard. To him the divine word was passed, and confirmed by an oath, establishing him "a Priest *for ever.*" Heb. vii. 21. Of him JEHOVAH spoke, as in Psalm lxxxix. 18—35, "My covenant shall stand fast with Him: once have I sworn by my holiness, that I will not lie unto David,"—unto the *Beloved,*—for such is the import in Hebrew of the name *David;* and again, in Psalm xci. 15—16, "He shall call upon me, and I will answer him; I will be with him in trouble; I WILL DELIVER HIM, and honour him: with long life will I satisfy him, and shew him my salvation." (Compare this with Psalm xxi. 1—7.) Thus, our great *forerunner* had the word and oath of JEHOVAH for the basis of that confidence, with which he called upon God for deliverance.

With this his confidence he was taunted on the cross:—"*he trusted in God;* let him deliver him now, *if he will have him.*" (Matt. xxvii. 43.) And a glorious deliverance God did effect for him; and thereby proved that he had *accepted* his sacrifice. (Psalm xx. 3.) He that was by men adjudged worthy of death as a blas-

* So the passage ought certainly to be read; as it is in the Vulgate, the Septuagint, and the Syriac Versions. See Dathius. Led to name that German divine, I would say that I name him with respect, as honourably distinguished from many of his compeers, as both a scholar and an *honest* man. The prophetic character of *several* Psalms seems to have forced itself upon his mind; and he asserts it plainly against his theological brethren. Yet it is lamentable to observe how he commonly blunders and gropes his way in vain, like a blind man in broad daylight, from want of subjection to the *general* principle that David, inditing the Psalms as a prophet and by the Spirit of Christ, speaks throughout of Christ and of that Church, which is his body, one with him. A curious instance of this blundering has occurred to me, in drawing up the present article, and I would briefly mention it as exemplifying what I have said. Dathius prefaces his translation of the 20th Psalm with the observation, that it "contains pious vows, with which the people followed the king, as he was going *with his army* to a war; but that "*what war it was is altogether uncertain.*" The Psalm does indeed relate to the last great conflict, in which the King of Israel was engaged, but engaged "*alone,* and of the people there was none with him;" while his people are indeed represented as beholding and contemplating the conflict with awe, and with the deepest interest in the issue, praying for and anticipating the triumphant result. In the following Psalm, closely connected with the 20th, the same people are introduced, as celebrating and rejoicing in the triumph of their exalted Head. Many a poor old woman could have taught the Leipsic Professor of Hebrew and D. D. *what the war* was, which he pronounces to be *altogether uncertain.* The scriptural view of the book of Psalms may be seen copiously treated and maintained in the Preface to a metrical version of the Psalms by JOHN BARCLAY, of Scotland; a man reckoned mad, of course, by the devout and honourable of his country. But I have heard from some who knew him personally, that he used to say jocosely, tapping his forehead,—"Aye, folks say that I am *crack'd;* but that is the crack *the light* got in at." His Preface may be had separate from his metrical version.

phemer, or claiming to be the Son of God, was "declared to be the Son of God with power, according to the Spirit of holiness, by his resurrection from the dead." Rom. i. 4. Jehovah interposed to decide the controversy in his favour. He was "raised from the dead by the glory of the Father" (Rom. vi. 4); and exalted at the right hand of the majesty on high." (Heb. i. 4. viii. 1; Eph. i. 20—23.) From all the *burden* which had been laid upon him, he was *released*. He was "justified in the Spirit." 1 Tim. iii. 16. And then was his Church virtually "raised together with him, and made to sit together with him in heavenly places." Eph. ii. 6. Then were *all her sins*, that sore burden laid upon him, and from which he had cried for deliverance, "cast as a stone into the depths of the sea." Mic. vii. 19.

This justification, and consequent glory of his redeemed people, and the manifestation of the glory of his heavenly Father in this, had been "the joy set before him," in the assured prospect of which "he endured the cross." Heb. xii. 2. And in this 130th Psalm we hear him encouraging and comforting his heart with a view of it, in all the depth of his suffering, and under all the weight of sin that lay upon him. "If thou, Lord, shouldest *retain* iniquities, O Lord, who shall stand? But there is *forgiveness* with thee, that thou mayest be feared." As if he had said, 'If thou, Lord, shouldest not *loose* me from the burden of the iniquities laid upon me, and which "have taken hold upon me, so that I am not able to look up," (Psalm xl. 12.) would not all those whom "thou hast given me out of the world" sink with me for ever? and there would be no seed on earth to serve thee. But there is—assured in thy word of promise—that *loosing* of the burden, that release and justification of me, which brings redemption unto them, and which shall make thy name known and reverenced with godly fear by all my brethren, with whom I have taken part in flesh and blood, that I might bear and put away their sin.'

Continuing our survey of this Psalm, we read—"I wait for the Lord, my soul doth wait; and in *his word* do I hope. My soul waiteth for the Lord more than they that watch for the morning." It was in all the earnestness of thirsting desire, as well as in the full confidence of assured hope, that even in midnight darkness he looked for the coming day of his promised glory; looked for it to Him, *whose the night is*, and who, in the darkest hour, "hath *prepared* the light and the sun." (Psalm lxxiv. 16.) How emphatically does he express that earnestness of desire in the 42nd Psalm! "As the hart panteth after the waterbrooks, so panteth my soul after thee, O God. My soul thirsteth for God, for the living God; when shall I come and appear before God?"

It is with good reason, and on good and sufficient grounds, that he turns to his Israel, his ransomed Church, at the close of the Psalm, calling them to be followers of his faith and sharers in his hope, as they are joint heirs with him in his glory. "Let Israel hope in Jehovah: for with Jehovah is mercy, and with him is plenteous redemption. And he shall redeem Israel from all his iniquities." He that provided the lamb for a burnt-offering, that found the ransom, and has declared his acceptance of it as abundantly glorifying his law,—" He *will abundantly pardon*," and mightily deliver, all that " great congregation" of sinful men, in whose stead he was " pleased to bruise his Holy One."

Believers! let us look well at the characters of this MERCY which does " belong to Jehovah :" while the attribute commonly called *mercy* stands in direct opposition to his holiness and truth, and righteousness. Let us look well at the sure foundation, on which the MERCY of the LORD rests; at its exuberant riches, abounding where sin abounded; at its almighty efficacy, reigning unto eternal life " where sin had reigned unto death;" but " reigning through righteousness by Jesus Christ." (Rom. v. 21.) Say, is there in this MERCY any thing like that, which the world attribute under the same name to their false Gods? any thing like an *indulgence* of at least some sins as venial, an *overlooking* of them, and a *forbearing* to execute his denounced judgment against them? Rather, in the MERCY revealed as belonging to JEHOVAH is there not that which discovers " the only true God" as " glorious in *holiness*," " very greatly to be *feared* in the assembly of his saints, and to be had in reverence of all them that are round about him?" " Glory ye in his holy Name." " They who know that Name," or character,—who *believe* the heavenly testimony of Him who declares it, they " WILL put their trust in him." (Ps. ix. 10.) They, kept abiding in the truth, will be kept from the vain and ungodly labour of searching for some tokens of good about themselves, either naturally possessed or supernaturally bestowed; from searching for any thing to supply some supposed *deficiency* of hope afforded by that *one good* and glorious object, which the revelation of the glory of God in the face of his anointed *has discovered* to us from heaven. (Micah vi. 5, 8.) " Kept by the power of God," in the view of this, they will be kept " walking in the *light*, *as* children of the light and of the day :" they will be kept " walking in the *fear* of JEHOVAH, and in the *comfort* of the Holy Spirit." (Acts ix. 31.)

It affords the most abasing view of *ourselves*, of the unchangeable vileness of *our own* hearts, that nothing but the power of God can *keep* us thus walking in the truth, even after having " tasted that the LORD is gracious," after having been ever so long established in the faith. A " people bent to backsliding from HIM," is to the end our own character. (Hos. xi. 7.) But we may be assured that, if ever we be so far left to ourselves,—for shewing us " what is in our hearts," —(2 Chr. xxxii. 31.) as to walk in a mind contrary to the fear of his holy Name; he will not leave us altogether unchastised. Jer. xlvi. 28. However he may leave others to walk in their own ways, undisturbed by the visitations of affliction, he will not so deal with his children. Earthly parents may spoil their children by indulgence. But HE will make good that word of promise to his Holy One, (Ps. lxxxix. 30—32.) " I will visit their transgression with the rod, and their iniquity with stripes." " Whom the Lord loveth he chasteneth, and scourgeth every son whom he receiveth." Hebr. xii. 6. I do not mean to say, that the afflictions of his children, though always sent for their profit, are always sent in the way of *chastisement*. They may be " in heaviness through manifold trials," for the exercise and futherance of their faith, (1 Pet. i. 6.) and for otherwise glorifying God. But of this they may be assured, that, when they *turn* to any *way* contrary to the LORD, he will sooner or later make them *know and see* that it is an *evil thing and bitter they procure unto themselves*. He will mercifully but awfully make "their own wickedness to correct them, and their backslidings to reprove them." Jer. ii. 17—19.

XVI.

"*So, being affectionately desirous of you, we were willing to have imparted unto you, not the gospel of God only, but also our own* souls, [ψυχας] *because ye were dear unto us.*"—1 Thess. ii. 8.

WE ought certainly to read, "but also our own *lives*;" as the same word is rightly rendered in Acts xx. 24. and in numerous other passages: though I am far from denying that there are passages of the New Testament, in which the word does import the *soul*, in contradistinction to the body, and is so rightly translated.

In Matth. xvi. 25, 26. our translators, in the former verse, correctly render it *life*;—"whosoever will save his *life*—and whosoever will lose his *life*:" but erroneously turn to the other meaning in the verse immediately succeeding. This also ought to run—"For what is a man profited, if he shall gain the whole world, and lose his own *life*? Or what shall a man give in exchange for his *life*?" As a man's life is more to him than the whole world; so believers, looking forward to the coming of the Son of man in his glory (v. 27), have in view that "recompense of reward," which infinitely outweighs all that they can lose for his name; though they should suffer the loss of life itself.

Reverting to 1 Thess. ii. 8. it is obvious that the common version presents to the English ear an idea, which we cannot suppose to have been in the Apostle's contemplation. Yet some perhaps may think that it is countenanced by another passage, Rom. ix. 3. which in the English version runs thus: "For I could wish that myself were accursed from Christ for my brethren, my kinsmen according to the flesh." I believe the commentators have made various attempts to throw off the monstrous idea, which these words suggest, by a modified interpretation of them. But the fact is, that nothing more is needed to clear up the passage, than a corrected punctuation and literal version.

Removing the period at the end of the second verse, let it be read in continuation with the words "for my brethren, my kinsmen according to the flesh;" and let the intermediate clause, literally translated, be marked as a parenthesis. Then the whole will run thus:—"I have great heaviness and continual sorrow in my heart—

(for I *did myself* wish to be accursed from Christ)—for my brethren, my kinsmen, according to the flesh." The Apostle, expressing his affectionate concern for his Jewish brethren who remained in unbelief, reverts naturally to the period, when he was himself of the same mind, when he persecuted the Church of Christ, and abhorred the thought of any connexion with Jesus of Nazareth. It is as if he said, "I mourn (and well I may, for I remember what used to be my own mind) I mourn over my unbelieving countrymen."

For the clearing up of this passage I am indebted to a writer, who in many respects has rendered so much service to the Church of God, that it is no wonder his name is of very bad odour with "the devout and honourable" of the world; Robert Sandeman, M.D. of Scotland. Under the signature of Palæmon he published Letters to Mr. Hervey, on his Theron and Aspasio, and other pieces. I have not his work at hand, but am sure that I have given, substantially, the correction which he proposes in our translation of this passage. To me it seems indisputable.

On the substitution of "I did myself wish," for, "I could wish that myself were;" I am sensible that the Greek would admit the latter version; (ηυχομην being not inelegantly used for what is expressed in Acts xxvi. 29. by ευξαιμην αν). But it is undeniable that it equally admits the translation, "I *did*" or "*used*" to wish; and that this is the more literal. [Let me also suggest to the Greek scholar that, if the other were the meaning intended, we might rather expect a different construction of the following pronoun; εμαυτον, rather than αυτος εγω. I shall only add, that the proposed correction is supported by that ancient and valuable version, the Syriac.]

XVII.

"*Unto you therefore which believe*, he is precious."—1 Pet. ii. 7.

[ὑμιν ουν ἡ τιμη]

We ought certainly to read, "Unto you therefore which believe *is the preciousness*:" i. e. that preciousness of the corner-stone, spoken of by the Prophet. The Apostle has just quoted the word of the Lord concerning his Messiah from Isa. xxviii. 16. "Behold I lay in Zion for a foundation a stone, a *precious* corner-stone, a sure foundation: he that believeth shall not [make haste] be in trepidation." And this brings to his remembrance two other scriptures concerning the same corner-stone, Isa. viii. 14. and Ps. cxviii. 22. and leads him to contrast the *opposite results* of Christ's coming in those who believe and those who believe not: much as the Apostle Paul contrasts the effects of the Gospel in the two classes, when he says—"to the one we are the savour of death unto death; but to the other, the savour of life unto life." 2 Cor. ii. 15, 16. "Unto you therefore which believe is the *preciousness:* but unto them which *disbelieve* [ἀπειθοῦσι] the stone which the builders disallowed, the same is made the head of the corner, and a stone of stumbling, and a rock of offence, who stumble at the word, *disbelieving;* whereunto also they were appointed."

The first part of this quotation is obviously from Ps. cxviii. 22. a passage applied by the Lord to himself. (Matth. xxii. 42.) It is as obvious that the latter part is a quotation from Isa. viii. 14. a passage similarly applied to the Messiah by Paul (Rom. ix. 33.): and similarly quoted by him in combination with the other passage, Isa. xxviii. 16. It would appear therefore that any, who do not pretend to be wiser than the Apostles, or rather wiser than the Spirit of Christ in his Apostles, must acknowledge without hesitation, that in Isa. viii. 13, 14. there is a prediction of the Messiah; as "God the Saviour," a *sanctuary* and sure refuge to all that believe; but a *stone of stumbling*, at which those who disbelieve the word fall and are broken.

In this passage of Isaiah, He is distinctly characterized as "the Lord of hosts." Indeed, if the *Saviour* of his *people* were any other than Jehovah, the word that proclaims salvation to sinners would at the same time sanction *idolatry*. But is He not expressly marked by the same title in Ps. xxiv.? and this, combined with the description of his work of perfect righteousness as the Son of Man; in consequence of which He became "head over all things" to his ransomed Church; rightfully claimed those gates to be opened unto Him, into which nothing unclean could enter; and is set down as "the King of glory" at the right hand of the majesty on high. Compare Ps. cxviii. 19, 20.

The reader may have observed, that in both the 7th and 8th verses of 1 Pet. ii. I wish to substitute the expression *disbelieving*, or *unbelieving*, for *disobedient:* and this, because it more distinctly marks the contrast with those that *believe*, mentioned in the first clause of the passage. And in this sense the same word [ἀπειθειν] occurs, and is rendered by our translators, in John iii. 36. Acts xiv. 2. xvii. 5. xix. 9. and elsewhere. Indeed, when the Gospel is said (as in Rom. xvi. 26.) to be now "made known to all nations for the *obedience of faith;*" the expression simply marks the divine authority with which it is sent throughout the world, demanding the *credence* of those who hear it, "commanding all men everywhere to repent." Acts xvii. 30. This repentance, or change of mind,—the "repentance unto life," which is the gift of God, is repentance to the *acknowledging of the truth*. (2 Tim. ii. 25.) Those who disbelieve it are disobedient indeed, setting themselves in rebellious opposition to the authority of the most high God.

But on the proposed change in the version of 1 Pet. ii. 7. some perhaps may demand, "what matters it, whether we read the passage *unto you which believe he is precious*, or *unto you which believe is his preciousness?* Is not the meaning of each version identical?" I answer, No: not, at least according to the way in which the common version is ordinarily quoted and applied. I have known it ordinarily quoted as declaring the high *estimation*, in which believers hold the Messiah, his preciousness in their view—to their hearts. And often have I known it applied, in this sense, so as to minister rather to the self-conceit of religious professors, than to their profit. There is indeed no doubt that Christ is the "one pearl of great price" in the view of those who know him. But those who know most of his value have reason rather to acknowledge, that their highest thoughts of him fall infinitely below his intrinsic excellence, than to be engaged in contemplating how high they reach. What the Apostle asserts in the passage is, not any thing about the *believer's estimation* of Christ, but what Christ *is intrinsically* to his believing people. This his preciousness to them is infinite, unfathomable, past finding out, "the *unsearchable* riches of CHRIST." Eph. iii. 8. They may therefore understand something of that paradox, "having nothing, and yet possessing all things," and, though commonly "a poor and an afflicted people," may well glory in Him who "was rich, yet for their sakes became poor, that they through his poverty might be *rich*." 2 Cor. viii. 9.

XVIII.

"The like figure whereunto even baptism *doth also now save us, (not the putting away of the filth of the flesh, but the answer of a good conscience toward God,) by the resurrection of Jesus Christ.*"—1 Pet. iii. 21.

THE translation of this passage is, to say the least, very strange and obscure. It is a very harsh expression, to say that a *figure* saves: and, in the ordinary meaning attached to the term *baptism*, it is utterly false to say that *baptism saves* us.

The *literal* version of the original would be, "*the antitype baptism to which*," that is, the baptism answering to which as an antitype to its type. But the idiom of the English language scarcely admits this *literal* translation: and I would therefore substitute one a little different in construction, but perfectly equivalent in its import and much more intelligible: viz. "*which was a type* (or *figure*) *of the baptism that now saves us* also." To call one thing a *type* of another, and to call the latter an *antitype* of the former, are expressions obviously identical in their meaning.

In the preceding verse the Apostle has mentioned the preservation of Noah and his family in the ark; "wherein" (saith he) "*few*, that is, eight souls were saved by water:" and then follow the words that we have quoted, "which was a figure of the baptism (or washing) that now saves us also . . . . by the resurrection of Jesus Christ." But lest any should imagine for a moment that, in thus mentioning *baptism*, the Apostle intended that *rite* of baptism, or dipping in literal water, which marked the commencement of the Christian profession of the first proselytes, he immediately disclaims that meaning, and in language apparently indicating his abhorrence of such a mistake: "not the putting away of the filth of the flesh, but the answer of a good conscience toward God." The literal baptism, or washing with literal water, could but cleanse the body, or purify to the cleansing of the flesh. He therefore distinctly guards against the supposition, that this was the *baptism* he intended; and as distinctly marks that he speaks of that which *cleanseth our conscience* from guilt, "purging it from dead works to serve the living God," (Heb. ix. 14.) giving us peace with God, and leading us to walk with him as dear children.

Now we know, that it is the blood of Christ which thus *cleanseth the conscience*, that blood which has been "shed for many for the remission of sin," and the assurance given unto all by his resurrection from the dead of the divine acceptance of his one offering: we know (I say) that this is the baptism, or washing, which gives "the answer of a *good conscience* toward God." It therefore only remains to inquire, why the Apostle marks this as represented in figure by *the waters of the flood*, which preserved Noah and his family in the ark, but destroyed the rest of the world. It seems to me to intimate, that, as the flood of waters displayed the divine indignation, and executed the threatened vengeance against the wickedness of an ungodly world, while they yet bore up in safety the eight persons inclosed in the ark; so the death of Christ for sin, while it has effected the eternal redemption and salvation of all that are in Him, "a remnant according to the election of grace," is at the same time the most awful manifestation of the righteous judgment of God, as well as the surest pledge of its execution, against the "world that lieth in the wicked one."

Some perhaps may be surprised, that in the preceding remarks I have used the expressions—*baptism* and *washing*—indifferently, as equivalent. But that I have not done so unwarrantably, the mere English reader may satisfy himself by referring to Mark vii. 4, 8. Luke xi. 38. Heb. ix. 10. In all these passages, the words, justly rendered by our translators *wash* and *washings*, are the same with the Greek phrases *baptize* and *baptisms*: for these are but Greek words adopted into English. In fact, to *baptize* literally means, in Greek, to *wash by dipping*, or, in one word, to *bathe*. And thence it is sometimes applied to other forms of washing, as in Luke xi. 38.

I would incidentally remark, that there is a decided mistranslation in our common version of Acts xxii. 16. Instead of "arise, and *be baptized*," the Greek indisputably is "arise, and *bathe*." [*βαπτισαι*, the middle voice; not *βαπτισθητι*, the passive.] I do not introduce the observation with the least idea of applying it to what is called the *Baptist controversy*. The important questions, connected with that, are to be decided on much broader and stronger grounds.

XIX.

"*And at midnight Paul and Silas prayed, and sang praises to God: and the prisoners* heard *them*."—Acts xvi. 25. [ἐπηκροῶντο.]

It should be rendered—"and the prisoners *were listening* to them." The sacred historian marks the time, that it was the hour of midnight,—and the respective engagements of Paul and Silas on the one hand, and of their fellow-prisoners on the other; the former occupied in prayer and singing praises to that God, whose servants they were; the latter, in a separate part of the prison, *listening* to them: when "suddenly there was a great earthquake," &c. Amidst all the *simplicity* which distinguishes the grandest descriptions of the sacred volume from other writings, the scene represented in this passage claims the closest attention of disciples, and offers matter of reflection the most interesting and profitable.

Here were two men, led to the city of Philippi by the special guidance of their divine Master, yet apparently given over to the will of his enemies. Dragged before the rulers on a charge the most unfounded,—the whole population had risen up against them, as one man. The magistrates, without examining the cause, had rent off their clothes, and commanded them to be beaten with many stripes. Without any of that attention to their wounds which common humanity might have suggested, they had consigned them to prison, with a strict charge to the goaler to keep them safely; and the goaler—a stern and willing instrument of their cruelty—had "thrust them into the inner prison, and made their feet fast in the stocks."

There was indeed, sojourning in the city, a Jewess, to whom, and to her household, Paul and Silas had been made the instruments of communicating the Gospel of Christ; and how gladly would these, if they had been allowed, have ministered to the wants and soothed the affliction of the Apostles! But from any such service of love they were effectually shut out. Even the melancholy consolation was withheld—of the society of their fellow-prisoners.

Thus the darkness of the dungeon, and of the midnight hour, might seem but an image of the cheerless desolation of their circumstances. Yet in this thickest gloom of desolation, their voices are overheard—not bemoaning their situation—not venting the sounds of lamentation and despondency, but uttering the accents of prayer and *songs of praise* to God. Sounds so extraordinary have caught the ears of their fellow-prisoners; they are *listening* to the Apostles, and no doubt listening with surprise, wondering much what matter of rejoicing two men can find in such circumstances, and at such an hour.

Believers! we know what accounts for the marvellous fact. They had light with them in their dark dwelling, the light of "*heaven opened*." (See Remarks, No. X.) They had with them the presence of HIM, whom no prison walls or bars could exclude: of HIM, in whose "presence is the fulness of joy;" whose "favour is better than life:"—they had HIM with them, who is "our refuge and strength, a very present help in trouble;" and who suddenly interposed for their deliverance, and baffled in a moment all the power and precautions of his adversaries.

Without pursuing the particulars of the narrative further, let those, "who have obtained like precious faith" with the Apostles, learn this lesson from it among others:—that there are no circumstances in which we can be placed, so dark, so desolate, so grievous to flesh and blood, but that we *have* in the midst of them abundant matter for the joyful exercise of *praise*, as well as a gracious call to "pour out our hearts" in prayer before Him who "is a refuge for us," and "nigh unto all them that call upon Him." In the latter exercise, in prayer, we may almost say the believer *must* be engaged in the hour of affliction. But the more we are engaged in it aright, in the mind of faith, the more we shall be led to combine *praise* with our prayer; *praise* for the wonderful mercy that admits and calls *sinners* to the mercy-seat; *praise* for that divine word which warrants the full assurance of faith in our approaches to God, from the consideration of the great High Priest who addresses us in the cheering language just now referred to—"trust in him *at all times*; ye people, pour out your hearts before him: GOD is a *refuge* for us," (Psalm lxii. 8.);—*praise* for the infinite *blessedness* brought and secured to us in Him, with whom the covenant of JEHOVAH "standeth fast for ever," (Psalm lxxxix. 3, 28.) who was made a curse for us, to put away our sin, and who brings us with acceptance to his God, and our God—his Father, and our Father. Is there not here indeed abundant matter for combining *praise* with prayer; if it were even the first time the sinner ever called on the name of the LORD?

This combination is marked in what may be called the apostolic *recipe*, for keeping our hearts in perfect peace: "in every thing by prayer and supplication, *with thanksgiving*, let your request be made known unto God: and the peace of God.... shall keep your hearts and minds by Christ Jesus." Phil. iv. 6, 7. But it is in our great forerunner we see it perfectly exemplified. He, and He alone, could say—"*all thy* waves and *thy* billows have gone over me." (Ps. xlii. 7, 8.) But in these deepest waters he adds—"yet the Lord will command his loving kindness in the *day time*, and in the *night* his *song* shall be with me, and my prayer unto the God of my life."

The metaphorical sense is here obvious, in which the expressions *day* and *night* are to be understood. And the same is their high import in Psalm lxxiv. 16, "the *day* is thine; the *night* also is thine: thou hast *prepared the light and the sun*." Afflicted believer! in the darkest gloom of *midnight*, let *his song* be with you; in the assured prospect of that *light* which he has *prepared*, that *light* which "*is sown* for the righteous." Psalm xcvii. 11.

XX.

"*I perceive that in all things ye are* too superstitious. *For as I passed by, and beheld your devotions, I found an altar with this inscription,* TO THE UNKNOWN *God.* Whom therefore ye ignorantly worship, *him declare I unto you.*"—Acts xvii. 22, 23.

In this passage our translators have quite failed of preserving the dexterity of Paul's address. He did not at once offend his polished auditors, by telling them they were *superstitious.* He employed a word of *middle* signification, (to use the phrase of grammarians,) like our *religious*, or *devout*, [δεισιδαιμονεστερους.] "I perceive that ye are *extraordinarily religious.*"

But much less did the Apostle acknowledge them as worshippers of the God whom he was about to declare to them. The words falsely translated "*whom ye ignorantly worship*, [ὃν αγνοουντες ευσεβειτε.] would *literally* run "*not knowing whom ye are devout*;" but, to preserve the English idiom, ought to be translated "*whom ye know not amidst all your devotion.*" Yet upon this mistranslated verse I have known an opposer of scriptural truth raise a subtle distinction, between worshipping *a false God*, and *worshipping the true God ignorantly!*

[Every Greek scholar must be aware, that ευσεβειν also is a word that does not include in its signification either the good or the bad character of the devotion, to which it is applied; as well as that it never admits the construction, ευσεβειν θεον, as a verb transitive: so that ὃν certainly depends upon αγνοουντες, not upon ευσεβειτε. As to the expression in 1 Tim. v. 4, which some might think a solitary exception against the universality of this position, I am satisfied that it really is not; that the true reading there is περι τον, instead of πρωτον.]

XXI.

"*Art thou called, being a servant? care not for it; but* if thou mayest *be made free, use it rather.*"—1 Cor. vii. 21.

However strange the correction, which I propose, may appear at first view even to disciples, I am satisfied that the passage ought to be rendered;—"but *even* if thou canst be made free, rather lend thy service." [The Greek runs—αλλ ει και δυνασαι ελευθερος γενεσθαι, μαλλον χρησαι. Not ει δε δυνασαι.]

In the construction of the first clause, there is not the smallest ambiguity or difficulty. Every one, the most moderately acquainted with the original, must be aware when his attention is called to the words, that the version of them I have assigned,—"EVEN if"—conveys the only meaning, which they really admit. And here the translators and interpreters seem to have been led astray by their not conceiving it possible, that the Apostle should direct a Christian slave to continue in slavery, *even* if he *could* obtain his manumission. This indeed might be pronounced incredible, if we did not remember that the instruction is given to men not of this world, but whose "citizenship is in heaven." Phil. iii. 20. And I should hope, that the following remarks may be sufficient to satisfy the mere English reader, that I have given the true meaning of the original.

In the first place, then, that meaning is in perfect harmony with the entire context from the 17th verse to the 24th inclusive. That this may be more immediately under the view of the reader, let me quote the passage more largely. "As the Lord hath called each, so let him walk: has any man been called [to the Christian faith] in circumcision? let him not become uncircumcised. Has any man been called in uncircumcision? let him not be circumcised. *Let every man abide in the same calling wherein he was called.* Hast thou been called in slavery? care not for it; but *even if thou canst be made free*, rather afford thy service. For the slave that is called in the Lord, is the Lord's *freedman*: in like manner also the freeman that is called, is Christ's servant." [See No. xi. p. 86.] "Ye have been bought by a price; be not ye the servants of men." [Regard not any as your master, having property in you, beside Him who has purchased you with his own blood.] "In what state each has been called, brethren, therein let him abide with God." Now must not every candid and attentive reader acknowledge, that the direction to Christian slaves, here presented, harmonizes perfectly with all the rest of the passage?

But, in the second place, is the same harmonious consistency to be perceived in the common English version? I must acknowledge that, according to it, the direction to Christian slaves seems to me at absolute variance with that general rule,—which the Apostle evidently proposes to *illustrate* in the instance of slavery—if not to *contradict* it. Is it not inconsistent with the direction in the 20th verse—"let every man abide in the same calling wherein he was called,"—to subjoin immediately in the 21st verse a direction to the Christian slave—*not to continue* in the state of slavery, if he can obtain his freedom? Would it not completely nullify the former principle, if we should consider it as meaning—let every man abide in the same calling wherein he was called,—*unless he be able to change it for a better?* Surely the Christian slave, who *could not* obtain his freedom would necessarily remain a slave, if the Apostle had given no advice upon the subject.

I would add, in the third place, that the consideration by which the 22nd verse enforces his instruction given in the 21st verse, is deprived of all its force by the common translation of the latter. "*For* he that is called in the Lord, being a servant, IS *the Lord's freed-*

man."* What connexion is there between this consideration and the supposed advice to get manumission from his earthly master, if he can obtain it? But let the corrected version of the 21st verse be admitted, and the connexion of the 22nd at once appears with striking force: if thou wert in a state of slavery, when called to the faith of the Gospel, trouble not thyself about obtaining earthly freedom, even if thou canst; for thou *hast* an heavenly.

I confess myself somewhat uncertain of the precise meaning, which our translators intended to convey by the expression—"*use it rather*"—in the 21st verse. The version, which I have ventured to substitute—"rather afford thy service,"—seems to me sufficiently warranted [by the ordinary force of the middle voice in Greek, and the common use of the verb for *lending*, or affording to another the *use* of something which I might withhold or recall. Such would be the service rendered by the Christian slave, who might have his freedom, but rather remained with his master.]

It will probably surprise some, that I should take such pains to establish an interpretation, the accuracy of which they may still remain indisposed to admit; and indisposed, because they *dislike* it. Let disciples, however, in forming their judgment on the subject, beware of the influence of prejudice and disinclination.

I believe—(but have not examined the matter) that the interpretation I have offered is not only new, but in direct opposition to that which has been generally adopted hitherto.† And I readily admit that this—in itself and *prima facie*—forms a strong argument against the justice of my view; but IF that view be really correct, notwithstanding this *presumptive* argument, it only affords the stronger reason, with all who indeed reverence the Scriptures, to enforce the propriety and importance of asserting and defending the corrected version.

It was very slowly I adopted it myself, even after the construction of the original forced itself on my attention. I am now convinced, not only that it is indisputably the correct translation of the Greek, but that it harmonizes with the whole context, with which the common version is at variance. And I would beseech my Christian brethren to look attentively at the genius of Apostolic Christianity, as exhibited in this exhortation to persons *called in a state of slavery*. When Paul instructs such,—even if they *can* obtain their freedom,—rather to remain slaves, he does indeed give them an advice, against which all the principles of their earthly mind ever must revolt. Worldly wisdom will take fire, and will declaim earnestly on the propriety—nay, the duty—of trying to *better our condition* in life. And

* *Freedman*—not *freeman*—is the proper English expression for the Greek ἀπελεύθερος. It imports one who was formerly a slave, but has been manumitted: whereas the term *free-man*, ἐλεύθερος, applies to one who has never been in slavery.

† I find in a French edition of the Testament, 1724—1 Cor. vii. 21. translated thus—'Avez vous éte appellé à la foi etant ésclave? ne portez point cet etat avec peine; mais plutôt faites-en un bon usage, quand même vous pourriez devenir libre.'—

And in Antonio Martini's translation of the Bible, it runs thus—'Si tu stato chiamato, essendo servo? non prendertene affanno; ma potendo anchi diventar libero, piutosto eleggi di servire.'—ED.

perhaps this *is* wise for those who have their portion in this life. But I believe the children of God have often experienced the correction of our Heavenly Father for that very worldly wisdom; and have found the correcting rod formed out of its consequences.

However this be, *they* certainly are called to live for objects of infinitely higher consideration; even for glorifying Him, *whose they are*, in whatever station he is pleased to *employ* them. They are HIS servants; and are called to remember this character as their highest honour and blessedness;—*to live not unto themselves, but unto Him who has loved them and given himself for them.* 2 Cor. v. 15. Gal. ii. 20. And after all, is there any thing in this instruction given to Christian slaves, more extraordinary than in that general principle confessedly asserted by the same Apostle? 1 Tim. vi. 9. "They that will be rich [*that wish to be rich*, βουλομενοι πλουτειν] fall into temptation and a snare," or, than in the exhortation given in 1 Tim. vi. 8. Heb. xiii. 5.

It has also struck me, that this instruction to slaves is in harmony with another observable circumstance; namely, that while we are distinctly informed in the New Testament of persons *called* to the Christian faith *in the military profession*, than which there is perhaps none into which it would be more unsuitable or inexpedient for a disciple of Christ to *enter*,—yet there is not the slightest hint of a direction to those who became Christians after they were soldiers, to seek their discharge from that service.

I had written thus far, and conceived I had brought the article to a close; when an opportunity occurred of consulting the SYRIAC: and it gratified me to be able to say, that the interpretation of 1 Cor. vii. 21. which I have assigned, is decisively born out by that ancient and valuable version. It gratifies me—not as strengthening the conviction of my own judgment: I knew that the Greek could not admit the common translation of the passage; but I am glad that I can now produce an authority, which may lead some to pause before they reject an interpretation, against which I am aware that many will be disposed to revolt without consideration. It is only to believers of the Apostolic Gospel, that I have aimed at addressing myself throughout these remarks, but I know that the fleshly mind in them—their *own* mind—is as earthly, and as much opposed to the principles of the Kingdom of Heaven, as it can be in unbelievers.

It has also been my study all along, to keep back as much as possible the appearance of what is called *learning*: as I have wished to put forward nothing, upon which the plainest and most unlettered Christian may not judge, as well as the most literate. But, on the present occasion, I think it needful to offer a few observations for putting *scholars* on their guard, who may look at the passage in the Syriac; on their guard against the unfairness of the Editors.

In the folio edition by TREMELLIUS, the Syriac text will be found *apparently* countenancing, in some degree, the common interpretation: for though it plainly exhibits the Syriac for—"*even if* thou canst be made free," this is strangely followed by a direction to the slave to prefer freedom. The following is his Latin version of it in the opposite column:—"sed *etiam si* potes liberum fieri, elige tibi *potius quam* ut servias:"—that is,—" but *even if* thou canst be made free, let it be thy choice *rather than* to serve."—But if the reader cast his eye at the margin, he will there see a note by the Editor to the following effect:—" In the Syriac we do not read the particle signifying *rather than*. But the context shews that it must have escaped the copyist; as no sense can be extracted from the passage *unless it be restored*."

Let us try this, by omitting the words "*rather than*,"—which TREMELLIUS owns he has inserted on his own judgment, (or, as he expresses it, has *restored*)—without any corresponding expression in the Syriac copy. How then will it read without this interpolation? —" But *even if* thou canst be made free, *let it be thy choice to serve*."—Is there *no sense* in this? Nay: the meaning is very plain indeed, however it may be disliked.

But it is curious to observe that while TREMELLIUS rejects this plain meaning as nonsense, the spurious text and version which he fabricates of his own are really *nonsense*; from his retaining the Syriac word for "*even*," and yet foisting in the expression "*rather than*." EVEN *if thou canst be made free, accept thy freedom!* Is such language any thing short of nonsensical or absurd?

As to the Syriac conjunction, justly rendered by him—*etiamsi*—*even if*; it exactly corresponds, both in composition and in import, with the Latin *etiamsi*: and like the latter word is most frequently expressed in our English version of the N. T. by "*although*;" as it might be with perfect correctness in 1 Cor. vii. 21.

Looking at SCHAAF's edition in quarto I find him very inconsistent. He gives indeed the genuine SYRIAC text without the particle TREMELLIUS has interpolated; yet retains TREMELLIUS's latin version of it, inserting "*rather than*:" while it must be acknowledged that he does print the words "*potius quam*" in the Italic character.

On the whole, I am reminded of another instance of editorial unfairness, or presumption, connected with the Syriac version. The formerly disputed verse in the Apostle John's first Epistle appears in the text of SCHAAF's edition, in good SYRIAC, with a corresponding Latin translation: so that a scholar, consulting the volume on the subject, might very possibly close it under the impression, that the passage was supported by what would be indeed no contemptible argument for its authenticity. But in the short notes at the end of the volume, SCHAAF acknowledges that he has introduced that verse into the text from TREMELLIUS's edition!—where the latter, however, more modestly, had only offered it in the margin, as what *might be* a Syriac version of words, which he confessed did not exist in any Syriac copy, and which he therefore would not venture to insert.

The mere English reader, whose information exclusively I have generally aimed at in these remarks, will pardon me for having, in this one instance, added a little for scholars;—a little that I should probably have no other opportunity of bringing forward.

XXII.

"*We have an altar, whereof they have no right to eat which serve the tabernacle?*"—Heb. xiii. 10.

Instead of the words—"*have no right*"—I would prefer—"*are not allowed*"—or "*have no license;*" and I would make a similar change in Rev. xxii. 14.

That the phrase I propose to substitute coincides accurately with the proper import of the Greek, it would be superfluous to prove; every one at all acquainted with the language knowing, that the word strictly denotes a liberty *conceded* or *granted* by an authority, from which it has been derived. But I am sensible that, in proposing an alteration so very slight, I may incur the imputation of tampering *needlessly* with our received version; while I can honestly say that this is a mischievous vanity, which I have carefully endeavoured to avoid. But I do think that, small as the change is, it tends to present more clearly the real meaning of a very important, but much perverted, passage: and I candidly avow, that my principal object in this article is to set that true meaning before the reader. Mr. Parkhurst's Lexicon to the New Testament happens to lie before me at present. It is a work, that certainly contains much good and sound criticism: but its value is greatly lessened by the theological bias, which his clerical function and Arminian sentiments have given to many of his interpretations. I notice him here, for the purpose of marking and exposing his perversion of the passage at the head of this article. Quoting it under the word θυσιαστηριον, he gives the following extraordinary explanation. "*The Christian Altar,* that is *the table of the Lord,* considered as furnished with *the memorials of the sacrifice* of his death; of which memorials christians are to *partake* or *eat, but of which they have no right to eat who serve the tabernacle.*"

Assuredly such *divines,* still assuming an order of Priesthood, and professing to minister at an Altar in the exercise of that function, have been very inconsistent in ever abandoning the Popish sacrifice of the mass. But I may confidently assert, that in this passage the Apostle makes not the slightest allusion to the ordinances of the Lord's Supper, nor to the right of eating it, nor to the table at which disciples partake of it,—much less to that table as an Altar. And indeed, if Mr. Parkhurst's judgment had not been grossly warped by his clerical dignity and false theology, even the marginal reference in the following verse, in our common English Bibles, might have been sufficient to save him from such a blunder. That just and important reference is to Lev. vi. 30, where we read the following divine ordinance of the law. "*No sin offering whereof any of the blood is brought into the tabernacle of the congregation, to reconcile withal in the holy place, shall be eaten*; it shall be burnt in the fire." (See also Lev. iv. 11, 12, 21.) Thus, under the law, the greater sin offerings, whose blood was brought by the High Priest into the holy place to make atonement, were distinguished from peace offerings and others, of which the offerer was allowed to eat. (Lev. vii. 15. and seq. x. 18.) But as the Israelites were forbidden to eat of any thing unclean, and as, in the case of these sin offerings, the pollution of the offerer's guilt was ceremonially transferred to the victim, such a sacrifice was not to be used as food, but to be wholly consumed by fire on the altar of burnt offering. (Lev. i. 7—9.)

Now, in the passage under consideration, the Apostle calls the attention of the Hebrew disciples from the Levitical shadows which were "ready to vanish away," (Heb. ix. 13.) and directs it to the glorious accomplishment of all these types in the things of Christ and his heavenly kingdom: and let us recollect that he addresses persons who were not yet informed that the whole Levitical economy *had* passed away, but were still many of them exceedingly zealous for the law, though believing in Jesus of Nazareth as the promised Messiah.—"Jesus Christ," saith he, "is * the same yesterday and to-day and for ever. Be not carried about with divers and strange doctrines." And referring specially to the various questions concerning meats clean and unclean, raised by zealots for the law, and discussed with subtle minuteness even beyond the law,—the Apostle contrasts the uselessness and vanity of these questions with the glory and importance of that which is revealed in the Gospel, and is indeed worthy to occupy and fix our minds. "For it is a good thing that the heart be established with grace; not with meats, which have not profited them that have been occupied therein." *Established* with GRACE:—that is, (as the word continually imports) with the doctrine of that *divine mercy*, which reigns through righteousness unto eternal life by Jesus Christ our Lord. (Rom. v. 21.)

The glory of the Gospel as a revelation of this Mercy, and of the way in which it reigns where "*sin reigned unto death*," the Apostle goes on to mark in the words that follow; but still in contrast with the Jewish questions of meats. "We have an altar, of which those who serve the tabernacle [worshippers according to the law] *are not allowed to eat*. For [according to the law] the bodies of those beasts, whose blood is brought into the sanctuary by the high priest for sin, are [not eaten but] burnt without the camp. Wherefore [to fulfil this as the other Mosaic types] Jesus also, that he might sanctify the people with his own blood, suffered without the gate."

In connexion with this passage let disciples read the words of the same Apostle in Heb. ix. 7—14. and x. 19—22. "Into the second tabernacle the high priest goes every year, not without blood, which he offers for himself, and for the errors of the people. The Holy Spirit this signifying, that the way into the holiest of all has not yet

* The slightest inspection of the Greek is sufficient to shew that the eighth verse ought to be thus translated: and this, whether we take it in immediate connexion with the preceding verse, or, as I think preferable, with the following.

been made manifest, while the first tabernacle has still a place. But Christ having arrived, an high priest of *the* good things that *have*† come, by a greater and more perfect tabernacle, not made with hands, neither by the blood of goats and calves, but by his own blood, has entered in once for all into the holy place, having obtained eternal redemption." "Having therefore, brethren, boldness to enter into the holiest by the blood of Jesus, by a new and living way which he hath consecrated for us through the vail, that is to say, his flesh; and having an high priest over the house of God; LET US DRAW NEAR with a true heart, in full assurance of faith."

And now, believer, can we be at any loss to see the import of the Apostle's language, when he says in Heb. xiii. 10. "*We have an altar, of which those who serve the tabernacle are not allowed to eat?*" We have that *great sacrifice for sin*, typified by all those sin offerings, which were wholly consumed by fire on the altar, and of which the worshipper under the law was forbidden to eat.

These were shadows indeed of good things then to come, while their intrinsic inefficiency to cleanse the *conscience* by taking away sin was marked in their continual repetition. The shadows have passed away: the substance has come, in the one offering of our great High Priest, who has entered into the holiest of all—into heaven itself—by his own blood, "to appear in the presence of God for us." (Heb. ix. 24.) He by that one offering, which has taken away sin, has opened the way whereby the chief of sinners may draw nigh at all times to the mercy seat, with assured acceptance in the Beloved. And here indeed is abundant ground of glorying for a sinful creature, in himself ungodly and without strength. Here is that which is gloriously sufficient for *establishing our hearts with grace*, and for putting a new song continually into our lips, even praise and thanksgiving to Him who "is good to the unthankful and the evil" (Luke vi. 35.), whose *mercy* endureth for ever and is higher than the heavens.

And shall we hearken to those, who explain the *Altar* spoken of by the Apostle as importing what is called the Communion Table; and who interpret the language concerning it as a declaration, that adherents to the law of Moses had no right to partake of what is called the Sacrament?

One word more on the passage in Mr. Parkhurst's Lexicon. His application of the word *altar* to the communion table he attempts to justify, by showing that *Ignatius*, "the blessed martyr," applies the word in a similar view. I have no reason to impeach the faithfulness of the Greek quotation, which he adduces in confirmation of this; nor the *general* correctness of the interpretation he assigns to the Greek from Bishop Wake.

But from this specimen of the so-called *Fathers*, the simplest Christian may judge what weight is to be given to their authority.

† The reader who consults GRIESBACH's edition of the New Testament will see, in the various readings, that I have sufficient authority for adopting *γενομενων*, instead of *μελλοντων*, in the text of this passage; especially as the context really calls for the change. Some other slight alterations that I have introduced in the version are obviously supported by the Greek.

Ignatius was one of the earliest of them;—had seen some of the Apostles; and for this and his episcopal character, and his martyrdom, has been SAINTED, or made one of those demigods set up in the antichristian world under the name of *Saints*. Yet we find that IGNATIUS—the saint—the Bishop, "the blessed Martyr," does style the communion table an altar,—nay, the "*one altar*" of Christians! Indeed, in the selfsame sentence he gives the name of "*Eucharist*" to the Lord's Supper; and (almost expressly) contradicts the Apostles by denying the *Plurality* of Bishops (or overseers ἐπισκοποι) in a Christian Church. (Tit. i. 5, 6, 7. Acts xx. 17. 28. Phil. i. 1.)

Now, is not this a sufficient specimen for Christians of what is commonly called, but falsely called, *the primitive Church*?

The really primitive age of the Christian Church was the Apostolic: and even in it an Apostle teaches us that there were "many Antichrists" (1 John ii. 18.); that is, many, who under the christian name, opposed the purity and simplicity of christian truth. But the disciples were warned, that after the *removal* of the Apostles the adversary should come in as a flood. (Acts xx. 29, 30. 2 Pet. ii. 1, 3.) Can we then wonder that those who wish to counteract the promised consumption of the man of sin, that consumption, which has been, and is blessedly progressive, are so fond of appealing to the ages succeeding the Apostolic; and of quoting the authority of the *soi-disant* FATHERS in support of every antichristian corruption? it is a field, into which christians have no need to follow them.

"*Let not the wife* depart *from her husband;* but and if she depart, *let her remain unmarried or be reconciled to her husband.*"—1 Cor. vii. 10, 11.

To the attentive English reader there must appear something strange on the face of this passage. Would it not be strange if the Apostle should in one verse give a plain command to christian wives; and should subjoin in the next verse another command to the same persons, proceeding on the *supposition* that they would *disobey the former*? "Let her *not depart*, but and if she *depart*," &c.

The whole of this inconsistency disappears on a more accurate translation of the Greek. It ought to run thus: "Let not the wife *separate herself* from the husband:"—[the common reading χωρισθηναι is much inferior to that of some MSS. χωριζεσθαι, as in the 15th verse]—"but *even* if she *has been separated*, let her remain unmarried," &c. "*even* if she *has been separated*, [εαν δε και χωρισθη, pass.]—By the act perhaps of an unbelieving husband putting her away; or in consequence of a domestic disagreement previous to the receipt of this Epistle.

XXIII.

"*That thy* beloved *may be delivered, save with thy right hand, and hear me? (or answer me.)*"—Ps. lx. 5. and cviii. 6.

In order to convey the ***plural*** signification of the original word, we should read "***thy beloved ones.***" The Messiah pleads that He may be heard and delivered, in order that all the children given to him (Heb. ii. 13.) may be delivered; their life being wrapped up in his. And when he denominates them the ***beloved ones*** of his Father, we are reminded of the same designation of them by the Apostle Paul (Rom. i. 7.)—"to all that be in Rome, ***beloved of God.***"

In the gift of his own Son, whom he spared not, but delivered him up for us all, (Rom. viii. 32.) "God commendeth his love toward us." And thus estimated, it appears indeed to have been "***great love,*** wherewith he loved us, even when we were dead in sins." (Eph. ii. 4, 5.) And in every view of the greatness of the blessings bestowed on the rebellious,—the forgiveness of all iniquity, adoption into the family of God, the inheritance of an exceeding and eternal weight of Glory,—the love of our Heavenly Father toward us appears truly "marvellous loving kindness" (Ps. xvii. 7.); in the contemplation of which we can but exclaim, "O! the depths!"

But there is a view of the surpassing greatness of this love of God toward us afforded by a few words of Christ, as recorded in John xvii. 23, which pre-eminently discovers it as one of the unsearchable things of God; while the faintest and most imperfect glimpses of it may well fill our hearts with adoring wonder and praise. There the Redeemer praying to his Father, just before the closing scene of his sufferings on the cross, praying ***for all those who should believe on him*** through the Apostolic word,—declares that he had ***given them the glory which he had received of his Father,*** and adds these words—"that the world may know [or, have a decisive evidence] that thou hast sent me, AND HAST LOVED THEM, AS THOU HAST LOVED ME." [καθως εμε ηγαπησας.]

Be astonished, O heavens!—A sinful nation, a people by nature laden with iniquity, yet "***beloved of God,***" even as He is beloved of whom the voice from heaven pronounced—"this is my beloved Son." In Him, the righteous and Holy One, was no sin. He who humbled himself, to take upon him the likeness of sinful flesh, was ***one*** with the Father; and alone could say, "***I do always the things that please Him.***" John viii. 29. Yet it is He that says, addressing his Father,—"***Thou hast loved them, as thou hast loved me.***"

But in the very next verse the Redeemer is recorded to have said —"Thou lovedst me ***before the foundation of the world.***"—And can there in this respect be any parallelism between Him and his redeemed?—There is! Accordingly, they are declared to have been "chosen in Him *before the foundation* of the world," Eph i. 2. "Chosen IN HIM." Yes: HE is the "*firstborn* among many brethren." It is IN HIM—THE BELOVED—they are all "made accepted" (Eph. i. 6.): IN HIM they are sanctified (1 Cor. i. 2.)—justified—saved—and glorified, even with the glory given unto him;—"*Joint-heirs with Christ*," and therefore "heirs *of* GOD," is the wonderful account of that inheritance we are allotted in Him. (Eph. i. 11. Rom. viii. 17.) With good reason does the Apostle speak of the "riches of Christ as unsearchable." (Eph. iii. 8.) In exploring them, we explore the riches of our inheritance, and at the same time "the riches of the glory of his inheritance in the saints." (Eph. i. 18.) And in this wonderful salvation of sinners is the Glory of the only true God displayed in an effulgence, in which it could not otherwise have been discovered.

"GOD IS LOVE:" and herein is love, not that we loved him, but that he loved us, and sent his son to be the "propitiation for our sins." 1 John iv. 10. 16. According as "we know and believe the love that God hath to us," so do we "dwell in God, and God in us," ib. It is "by the Holy Spirit given to us," that this love of God, in the believing view of it, is "shed abroad in our hearts (Rom. v. 5.):" and that spirit in the highest exercise of this office, "fulfilling in us the work of faith with power," testifies of Christ alone; and *testifies none other things*, but what are "*written in the Scriptures* for our learning," and are declared to all alike wherever the Apostolic word is "sent among all nations for the obedience of faith."

In the following verses of the 60th Psalm, we are called to hear the same glorious speaker, exulting in the confidence of faith—in the full assurance that God would make good to him, what he had "spoken," or pronounced, by his holiness: that he should inherit the people given to him out of all the nations of the earth, not of the Jews only, but of the Gentiles also. The language indeed is figurative; that of a mighty conqueror glorying in the extent of his dominions and conquests. But the Apostolic interpretation of that prophecy in Amos ix. 11, 12.—concerning the raising up "of the tabernacle of David, so that they may possess the remnant of *Edom*, and of all the heathen that are called by my name, saith JEHOVAH,"—is the master key that opens the true import of such language, as we read in this Psalm, "over Edom will I cast out my shoe," as a token of his subjection; and the true import indeed of many other passages in the Psalms and other Scriptures.

We find in Acts xv. 13–17, that an Apostle expressly quotes the above prediction of Amos, as fulfilled in that wonderful work of God—the calling in of the Gentiles to be one body with the Jews, by the faith of the one MESSIAH. And if we receive this instruction of the Spirit by the Apostle, we can be at no loss to hear that MESSIAH, in the 6th and following verses of the Psalm, rejoicing in the contemplation of the "goodly heritage" given to him, surveying the number and extent of the conquests of his redeeming love.

Upon this let me only add, that in the 8th verse the words rendered—"Philistia, triumph thou, because of me"—ought to run "over Philistia is my shout of triumph." And without attempting to introduce here the critical reasons for this correction, (for which see

Dathius or Rosenmüller)—the English reader may be satisfied of its justice, not only by the context, but by referring to the perfectly parallel passage in Ps. cviii. 9. where he will read "over Philistia will I triumph." Having just now mentioned Rosenmüller, and having more than once referred to him, I think it needful to make a few observations for guarding the young scholar against him. It is one of the black characters which apply to all men by nature as haters of the only true God—that "they delight in lies," and "only consult to cast him down from his excellency whom God hath crowned with glory and honour." Ps. lxii. 4. Heb. ii. 7—9.

"*Who was delivered* for our offences, *and was raised again* for *our justification.*"
Rom. iv. 25.

Surely the literal rendering of the Greek preposition [διὰ] would be much more clear and emphatic:—who was delivered *on account* of our transgressions, and was raised again *on account* of our justification.

If any, contemplating the suffering and death of him, who was emphatically "a man of sorrows and acquainted with grief," over whom all the "waves and billows" of Jehovah passed,—and at the same time hearing the testimony of him, as the *righteous* servant of Jehovah, in whom was "no sin,"—should inquire on what account he was given up to be thus smitten and afflicted, on what account "it pleased the Lord to bruise him;"—the answer of the Lord is recorded, Is. liii. 8.—"*for the transgression of my people was he stricken.*" It was on account of sin that he suffered, the righteous one for the unrighteous;—on account of the sin of many, even of all that great congregation of the elect that were chosen in him out of an apostate world before its foundation, Eph. 1, 4. The awful penalty of their sin he stooped to bear in their place, "giving his life a ransom for many;" that they all might be fully released from that penalty, in the only way consistent with the glory of his Heavenly Father. And on what account was this their surety and substitute raised again from the dead? It was *on account* of their justification being completed,—their release effectually executed—in his obedience unto death;—because that work of righteousness was then finished, in which God is glorified and all the seed of Israel justified before him.

Undoubtedly, the common version—"*for* our justification"—may be understood in the same sense: but it is equivocal. For that expression might naturally be conceived to mean, that he was raised from the dead in order to obtain, or effect, our justification. Whereas the words "*on account* of our justification"—really import, that the work of our justification *was accomplished* by his death. He died, because we were sinners, who must else have borne our own sin: he rose from the dead because our sin was put away by his obedience unto death. When he with his expiring breath declared —"*it is finished*"—he pronounced the perfect removal of all the sin that had been laid upon him, and the consequent acquittal of all his ransomed people: his resurrection from the dead affixed the divine attestation confirming this joyful truth. Those who believe it are freed, of course, from the ungodly vain inquiry what they shall do to obtain justification in the sight of God: they have done with that question; and they glory in his holy name in whom they *are* justified; for his righteousness is unto and upon all them that believe, without difference and without exception.

My readers are aware, that the division into chapters and verses is altogether human and modern: also that the introduction of stops (or the punctuation) is posterior to the original text. These may therefore be altered without scruple, when the sense calls for it. Now I confess I think the last verse of the fourth chapter has been inexpediently disconnected from the first verse of the fifth; and that the comma in the latter should be placed after the word "justified," instead of after "faith." The whole passage will then run thus: "*Who was delivered on account of our transgressions, and was raised again on account of our justification. Therefore, being justified, by faith we have peace with God, through our Lord Jesus Christ.*" It seems to me, that the context recommends this change; as well as the tense employed in the original word for "being justified,"—or rather "having been justified"—[δικαιωθεντες not δικαιουμενοι.] In making this remark, however, I am well aware, the expression "justified by faith," &c. is of frequent occurrence in the writings of the Apostle; and that men hostile to the truth will continue to misinterpret such language, and to suppose that it countenances their idea of something meritorious in faith, as a godly *exercise* of the mind, which makes it the procuring cause of our acceptance or justification in the sight of God; while the believer knows that in this respect his *faith* has no more to do with his justification than his *works*. But the heart of man still seeks something "to cast Him down from his excellency," Ps. lxii. 4. upon whom God laid all the glory, and who alone shall "be glorified in his saints." 2 Thess. i. 10.—In Rom. iii. 24, the Apostle expresses the truth with admirable distinctness and accuracy, when he says—"being justified *freely* by his *grace, through the redemption* that is in Christ Jesus."

REMARKS EXPOSITORY OF TEXTS OF SCRIPTURE.

I.

"*Philip saith unto him, Lord, shew us the Father, and it sufficeth us.*"—John xiv. 8.

How very foolish, though very natural, was the desire expressed by Philip—"Lord, shew us the Father, and it sufficeth us!" "*Shew* us THE FATHER!" give us some visible manifestation of the invisible God. He evidently sought some wonderful impression on his corporeal organs; some discovery, of which his senses might take cognizance. Yet is it imaginable, that there should be any *colour—figure*, &c. or any combination of *figures—colours*, &c. of which it could be asserted without profaneness—'*that is God?*' And even if we should for a moment admit a supposition so monstrous, what benefit could a creature and a sinner derive from any such discovery of God? Of what imaginable use or service could it be?

But the absurdity of Philip's request—"Shew us the Father"—is still more strikingly marked by the consideration, that at the very moment he expressed it—he had before his eyes a manifestation of "the only true GOD," the most wonderful, the most indubitable, and the most sufficient to communicate blessedness everlasting and complete to every man discerning it. And of this the Lord's reply reminded him. "Have I been so long time with you, and yet hast thou not known me, Philip? He that hath seen me hath seen the Father; and how sayest thou then, shew us the Father?"

Greatly should we mistake, if we considered this discernment of the Lord Jesus as importing the sight of him with the natural eye. This would be but to "know Christ after the flesh." No; it imports that discernment of the glory of God in him, which we are given *in believing* the words of Christ;—that sight of him which is possessed at this day as really and efficiently by all who believe the divine testimony concerning him, as it could be enjoyed of old by any who ate and drank in his presence.

"No man hath seen God at any time: the only begotten Son, which is the bosom of the Father, he hath declared him." John 1, 18. Sent into the world by the Father to save sinners, by giving himself a ransom for them, he has discovered to us "the only true God," in a character which we could not naturally have conceived, and which it is now life eternal to know, as at once the just God and the justifier of the ungodly; has discovered him in the combined glory of perfect righteousness and holiness and truth, harmonizing with mercy higher than the heavens,—mercy abounding above all our abounding need of it,—mercy brought home to those who never could have advanced themselves to reach it,—mercy made sure to every one that believes the divine report, by its being established in him with whom the covenant standeth fast for ever, in Him who "is the head of his body the Church." Ps. lxxxix. 28. Is. lv. 3.

He has loved that Church, and given himself for it: and while we view this his love that passeth knowledge, we view the love of God; in the Son we behold the glory of the Father, kind indeed to the *evil* and the unthankful,—blessing apostate creatures and rebellious haters of him, blessing them effectively, eternally;—providing of his goodness, Ps. lxviii. 10.—his inexhaustible goodness—for the poor, for those who have nothing to render unto him—nothing but those sacrifices of praise with which He richly and continually furnishes them; while, left to themselves at any time, they would requite him with nothing but base ingratitude and evil.

Yes: it is very blessed to remember that, in viewing the mercy and compassion of the good Shepherd, we see exhibited in him the mind of the Father; that in hearkening to the good words and comfortable in which the Lord Jesus speaks to the guilty and the vile, testifying that he came to call such, and not the righteous; to seek and to save that which was lost, and that he will in no wise cast out any that come to him,—no, "in no wise," not on account of any extremity of unworthiness;—it is very blessed (I say) to remember that, in hearkening to these his gracious words, we have a declaration of the mind of the invisible God, "of his Father and our Father, of his God and our God;" to remember that saying which he spoke—"I and the Father are one." We there indeed come unto God by him. Our fellowship is with the Father and with his Son Jesus Christ. We have that discovery of the divine glory, of which we may say in the language of Philip—"*it sufficeth us.*" This wisdom cometh from above: and as the heavens are high above the earth, so superior is it—both in its origin and its effects—to all the systematic theories, whether orthodox or heterodox, which are taught in worldly schools of human theology.

I have intimated above that, so far as we are left to *ourselves* at any time, even to the last, we never fail to render to the LORD evil in return for all his goodness. It is a heavy charge against us, of the truth of which none but the children of God are convinced: and it is important indeed, brethren, that we should be so convinced of it, as to see in this an evidence of the unchanged and unchangeable ungodliness of our own hearts; that we may "have the sentence of death in ourselves" at all times, and may not trust in ourselves, but be kept, "looking for the MERCY of our Lord Jesus Christ unto eternal life." Jude 21. Some, who talk speciously about the Gospel, as glad tidings from heaven to the chief of sinners, are yet much shocked at the idea that it brings any glad tidings to sinners *as such.* They would allow that it speaks to believers good words and comfortable, as to those who *were* ungodly creatures: but they conceive that this is no longer their own character. And they cannot comprehend how we can be "walking in the fear of the Lord and the comfort of the Holy Ghost," while at the same time our own hearts are as utterly ungodly as they ever were in the days of our unbelief. It may perhaps be for the profit of disciples themselves, that we should consider this abasing truth a little more closely.

Where lay the root of our natural ungodliness? In our natural *atheism*; in our alienation from the life of God, "through the *ignorance* that was in us, because of the blindness of our hearts." Eph. iv. 18.—Many, no doubt, suppose that the vitiosity of our nature consists mainly in our *immoral* propensities; and many of the graver sort conceive that it lies in our want of *heart religion* and piety. But let us remember, brethren, that among unbelieving men, or those who yet remain in their natural state, there are several distinguished for what is called *morality*, amiable in their tempers, correct in their outward conduct, beneficial and useful members of society in their lives. And as to *religion*—many avowed haters of God and of his Christ—open blasphemers of the truth revealed from heaven,—abound in religion, in heart religion; and in their profession evince as much fervour, earnestness, and zeal, as any real Christian can in his. In all their unbelief and antipathy to "the Gospel of the glory of God," such false professors exemplify the principle that the carnal mind is *enmity against God*: and in this they but manifest the common character of *our own* hearts, our own *flesh*. They exemplify our own contrariety to the only true God and to the revelation of his distinguishing glory in the Gospel of his Son,—our own blindness to that light,—our own indisposition to admit it,—*our own* continued promptitude to turn from it.

When He who knows what is in man, and who knows us from the beginning (Is. xlviii. 3—8.) pronounced this word—"*my people are bent to backsliding from me*," it is plain that He pronounces their *continual* character, after they have been turned and brought near to Him. And may not this remind us of that divine aphorism laid down by the Apostle in 1 Cor. xii. 3.? "*No man can say that Jesus is the Lord but by the Holy Ghost.*" It is plain that the Apostle intends not hereby the mere utterance of these words, with the lips, but the owning of the truth imported by them from the heart,—that belief of the testimony concerning Jesus, which includes the understanding of it in its real meaning and the conviction of its divine certainty.

This is indeed "the work of God, that we believe on him whom he hath sent." And every believer knows that, had it been left to himself—to his own will or wisdom—whether he should believe the Gospel or not, he would be to this hour rejecting and opposing it, and—under some form or another of false profession—would be turning the truth of God into a lie. But blessed be the God of all grace, his arrows are sharp in the heart of the King's *enemies*, whereby the people are subdued unto him. (Ps. xlv. 5.) For wherefore is it, that none but He who spoke the world into existence,—who commanded the light to shine out of darkness,—wherefore is it that nothing short of HIS power can convince a sinner that Jesus is the Lord? that no man can own this truth but by the Holy Ghost? It is on account of the natural contrariety of the human mind—in all its principles and workings—to the glory of the only true God. It is therefore only a new creation that can bring us out of darkness into light, by discovering to us that glory as revealed in Christ: and this is a discovery that brings the chief of sinners to the footstool of the mercy-seat, in peace and thankfulness and joy. (Ps. xix. 7, 8.) That word—"the natural man receiveth not the things of the spirit of God, for they are foolishness to him,—neither can he know them,"—is a word which may well beat down the pride of human wisdom in the things of God.

But it is not alone in the first discernment of the truth, but in its *continued* indwelling, that this principle holds good,—"no man can say that Jesus is the Lord but by the Holy Ghost." And there are many, who professedly acknowledge the principle as applied to a sinner's original conversion, but are manifestly unacquainted with it in its application to his continued walk and standing in the faith:—many who seem to regard the faith of the Gospel as a kind of deposit put into *our* keeping; no otherwise than they look to the *use* and *improvement* we make of it as that, upon which the ultimate result must turn. And it is no wonder, that the father of lies furnishes them with one and another text of Scripture, which they hope countenances the proud delusion that they love. But let us remember, brethren, that it is not more true that "no man hath quickened his own soul," or brought himself into the life into which the sinner enters in believing on the Son of God, than it is true that the same Lord alone is he "who *holdeth our soul in life*, and suffereth not our feet to be moved." (Ps. lxvi. 9.) "He that *keepeth* Israel is He that *made* him" (Ps. cxxi. 3—5. c. 3.): and He keeps the feet of his saints, by "fulfilling in them that work of faith with power" (2 Thess. i. 2.) which is his from first to last, the one work of his Spirit in them, to which all their own hearts are from first to last opposed.

These views discover us to be continually dependent upon *mere mercy*;—as dependent at the last hour of our course as at the first. And to the natural mind this would appear very discouraging, and inconsistent with all "confidence and rejoicing of hope." Naturally men have no idea of hope, that is not ultimately founded in themselves: and to be absolutely destitute of all such hope, they conceive must of necessity be connected with absolute despair. Yet it is really to creatures so utterly destitute of righteousness and strength,—so totally and continually evil,—that the living God has revealed himself in the Gospel as the "God of hope"—of that hope with which he fills them in believing the testimony of his word. "They that know his Name (or revealed character) *will* put their trust in Him:" (Ps. ix. 10.) and blessed are they; for they "dwell in a peaceable habitation, in a sure dwelling, in a quiet resting place." (Is. xxxii. 18.) We indeed can no more at this hour "say that Jesus is the Lord, but by the Holy Ghost," than we could have done so at the first. But "the mercies of David"—of the beloved—are revealed as "sure mercies." (Is. lv.) And this is one of the "exceeding great and precious promises" in that covenant of JEHOVAH which "standeth fast with Him" (Ps. lxxxix. 2, 3, 28.); "my *spirit* that is upon thee, and *my words* which I have put in thy mouth, shall not depart out of thy mouth, nor out of the mouth of thy seed, nor out of the mouth of thy seed's seed, saith JEHOVAH, from henceforth and for ever." (Is. lix. 21.)

Now having maintained, that so far as a believer is at any time left to himself and to his own spirit—he brings forth no fruit but what is evil; it may perhaps be well to add one more remark, though it ought to be unnecessary. Let me not, then, be understood as asserting that, in such a case, he will of course turn to the indulgence of the flesh in the grossest forms of its lustings: although, in the view of the grossest of them, no Christian is warranted to say "am I a dog, that I should do this thing?" But even in the period of his acknowledged unbelief he may not have been addicted to these: and really from these either the animal constitution, or age, or worldly prudence, may be sufficient to restrain. But what I assert is, that—so far as we are left to ourselves at any time—we really forget God our Saviour, and like a broken bow start aside from him, and from the blessed hope in his revealed mercy, to some of those various forms of self, which are so many idols that we naturally serve. *Self* is the great ruling principle of our fallen nature; *self*-seeking, *self*-confidence, *our own* glory, *our own* wisdom, *our own* righteousness; *self* in one or another of the diversified forms it assumes. And to some of these, disguised perhaps under a specious form of very evangelical language—yea, of contention for the truth, we should at any time turn, unless the spirit of truth keep the words of truth in our remembrance, and thus the revealed glory of the only true God before our view.

We are sure that this his glory is not before the view of those, who are manifestly walking in the indulgence of their fleshly lusts, and therefore in a mind contrary to "the fear of the Lord." But let none of us deceive ourselves by inferring, that we must of course be holding fast the faith, because we are not walking in such fleshly indulgences, and talk a very correct language about the Gospel. It is perfectly consistent with all this to be at the same time going on in a course quite aside from the truth; neither working righteousness, nor loving mercy, nor walking humbly with our God.

The history recorded concerning *good* King Hezekiah, in 2 Chron. xxxii. 24, 25, 31, 32, may stand as an illustration of what I have said. Few among the kings of Judah are described as having done more of what was "right in the sight of the LORD," or having experienced more signal deliverances at his hands. Among these was his miraculous recovery from a mortal sickness; of which the LORD had condescended to assure him in answer to his prayer by a miraculous sign—the shadow receding on the sundial of Ahaz ten degrees. The King of Babylon, having heard of Hezekiah's sickness as the occasion of this wonderful phenomenon, sent ambassadors with letters and a present to inquire concerning it. (2 Kings xx. 12.) Well now, might we not expect that *good* king Hezekiah, so favoured of JEHOVAH, would gladly avail himself of this fair opportunity to set forth the glory of the true God, the God of Israel, in opposition to all the Babylonian idols? But it was quite otherwise. We are told,, that on this occasion "God left him to try him, that he might know—(or manifest)—all that was in his heart"—his own heart: and indeed it all proved to be very bad. "He rendered not again according to the benefit done unto him; and therefore there was wrath upon him and upon Judah and Jerusalem." But was it that he turned to commit adultery and murder, like his father David? or to such enormities of wickedness as distinguished his own son Manasseh? Not at all. His evil was indeed "naked and open to the eyes of Him with whom we have to do;" but would have been imperceptible to man. "HIS HEART WAS LIFTED UP:" and in the elation of his heart he shewed them all that was in his house; there was nothing among his treasures that he did not display to them (2 Kings xx. 13—15.)—thus diverting their admiration to *himself* and his kingly glory.

Such was Hezekiah, when left by God to manifest what was in his heart, and it was only the mercy of the Lord that made him—(as we are informed)—"*humble himself for the pride of his heart.*" What continual cause have we to be similarly humbled! In fact, the more we know of ourselves, the more shall we be convinced, that all the most awful descriptions given of Israel after the flesh—such as we may read in the 78th Psalm—are but a picture of *our own* hearts. Many, looking at a portrait so black, are disposed to thank God that *they* are not such. But believers in their right mind will rather say, with the Apostles,—"What, then, are we better than they? *No;—in no wise.*" Rom. iii. 9.

II.

"*Fools make a mock at sin.*"—Prov. xiv. 9.

THE following thoughts have been suggested by the perusal of a religious tract entitled "Sin, no Trifle."

Sin is indeed "no trifle." The greatness of that God, against whom all sin is rebellion, proves it. The hopeless misery of the angels that sinned, proves it. All the disorders, which sin has introduced into this lower world, prove it. Above all, the stupendous *propitiation for sin*, which is set forth in the Gospel, proves it. Yet *fools* do *make a mock at sin*, conceiving of it as a trifle: and this is one of the awful evidences of the blindness and hardened wickedness of the human heart: I say—of the *human* heart. For every man by nature is that *fool;* and continues so, till he is made *wise unto salvation* by the belief of the true doctrine concerning Jesus Christ.

Yet among those who believe not that doctrine there are many most sober and religious characters, who look with pity or indignation at the profane and irreligious; while they little imagine that they are themselves the very *fools*, who *make a mock at sin*. Is it no sin to deny the being of the only living and true God? The most religious professor who disbelieves the one unchangeable record which God hath given of his Son, walks in this sin and makes light of it: for in that record the true God testifies his name and character. Is it no sin to hate God? That professor rejects the true doctrine of Christ, because he dislikes it: and his dislike of it proves his aversion to the true Christ: and his hatred of the Son proves his hatred of the Father also. (John xv. 23.) That he may have the most raised and devout affections towards the false Christ in whom he trusts, and the false God whom he worships, I deny not. But he makes light of the sin of hating the true. Is it no sin to *make God a liar?* (1 John v. 10.) This is the sin of that professor. And of all these tremendous sins he is living—not in the occasional—but in the continued momentary commission: while he makes so light of them, that (amidst much disturbance of conscience on other accounts) he feels not the slightest remorse for these sins.

Nay, he goes a step beyond the irreligious fool. The latter makes a mock at sin, and regards it as a trifling thing: but the other admires it, and regards it as a good thing and acceptable to God. The system of false doctrine which he believes, and to which he attaches the name of Gospel,—he is zealous for, and often laborious in propagating,—sometimes even at the expense of life itself. The false Christ whom he represents to himself and trusts in, he serves with devotedness of affection. All his religious performances (or sacrifices) he engages in, as duties well-pleasing to Heaven: while the Scripture testifies that they are all an *abomination to the Lord.* (Prov. xv. 8.)

It is awful wickedness to *call evil good, and good evil;* to *put darkness for light, and light for darkness.* It is an awful woe that is pronounced against those who do so. Is. v. 20. This woe is more especially pointed against the religious world. The assertion of the truths of God against the infidelity of men—they call uncharitable bigotry and unchristian judging of others. The infidel hope, that those who hold various gospels may be alike accepted in the sight of God, if they be but pious votaries of their respective systems—to this they give the name of Christian charity and a catholic spirit. Preachers of lies, they call ministers—nay, even ambassadors, of Christ; and think it a religious duty to sit under their word, and a kind of sacrilege to arraign them as unbelieving men. The few witnesses of the truth as it is in Jesus—they term disturbers of the peace of the religious world; and commonly think they do God service, in propagating against them calumnies the most foul. The belief of what God declares in his word, they call by every contemptuous epithet—"the faith of devils," "a speculative notion," &c. To the unbelieving effort of the heart, by which they are taught to grasp at righteousness, they give the name of the precious faith of God's elect. Their anxious solicitude in making that effort, and their delusive joys in its imaginary success—they call Christian experience; and dare to ascribe to the Spirit of Truth that work of the father of lies.

The whole of the unbelieving world *lieth in the wicked one;* and is proved to be *not of God*, by not *hearing God's words*. (John viii. 47.) But the most religious part of it go into a still deeper malignity of wickedness; and (as far as they can) poison the very fountain of truth for others, by annexing false meanings to the words and phrases of Scripture, and thus applying the word of God to support and propagate the lies of Satan.

Me, said the Lord Jesus, *the world hateth, because I testify of it that the works thereof are evil.* Perhaps the world never hated any one for testifying that murder, and drunkenness, and adultery, and profane swearing, &c. are evil: for even they who walk in those things acknowledge that such works are wrong. But to testify (as Christ did, and as his disciples are called to do) that all its works—even those which it thinks most good, and performs as religious duties—are evil; that *the things highly esteemed amongst men are abomination in the sight of God;*—this has ever irritated the world, and most irritated those who abound most in these *highly-esteemed* works.

III.

"Hallowed be thy name."—Matt. vi. 9.

The children of God are called to sanctify him in their hearts and are taught to pray, "hallowed [or sanctified] be thy name." 1 Pet. iii. 15; Is. viii. 12, 13: and it is of high importance that we should have scriptural views of the thing intended by these expressions, holy—holiness—sanctification, &c.

The general idea of the original word is *separation*, and the recollection of this will afford a clue to the right interpretation of it in its various applications. Thus, in the highest application of the term "holy" to the only true God, it marks the infinite separation of character which distinguishes Him from every thing else that is called God, and worshipped; which forbids that He should be confounded with any of the gods of the world.

The Jews are charged with "*profaning* the holiness of Jehovah," in all the various idolatries which they attempted to combine with his professed worship. For this was the character of all their idolatries;—not an open and avowed renunciation of the God of Israel;—but an attempt to associate other gods with him;—as even in the case of the golden calf. Ex. xxxii. 5. Every such attempt must originate in forgetfulness of the *holiness* of his *name*, and of that glorious character, which exclusively belongs to him, and therefore *separates* Him infinitely from idols. The same idea of separation from ordinary purposes pervades all the applications of the term "holy" to places, garments, utensils made under the Levitical law, as the tabernacle, the temple and all its furniture, the vestments of the high priest, &c. The latter, for example, were not to be used as ordinary clothing; but were set apart appropriately for the occasions of his priestly functions. Thus again, when the Jews, as a nation, are called an *holy* nation, it is always in reference to their separation from the other nations of the earth, to be a peculiar people of the God of Abraham; as is expressly marked in Lev. xx. 26. "Ye shall be holy unto me, for I the LORD am holy, and have severed [separated] you from other people, that ye should be mine." The same is the true import of the sanctification or holiness attributed to believers under the Gospel. Our great High Priest who "sanctified himself;"—or was *set apart* to that office by the divine appointment, and has willingly undertaken it, prayed for his Church, "sanctify them through thy truth." John xvii. 17, 19. By that unadulterated truth of the Gospel in which the distinguishing glory of the only true God is manifested, by this truth declaring his holy name, they are all sanctified—separated from the world that lieth in wickedness, turned from idols to the living God as his peculiar people, set apart to be for Him and not for another; and suitably called to sanctify Him in *their hearts*, and to maintain sacred in their minds the holiness of His character, in contradistinction to them all; suitably taught to pray that, "His name may be hallowed;" its distinguishing glory asserted and manifested against all the gods of those who believe not the truth. Being thus "holy unto the Lord," "they have their fruit unto holiness;" though the fruits of holiness in them are no more their holiness or sanctification, than the fruits of righteousness are considered their righteousness. Of the holiness which I have attempted to mark, the religious world have no conception. Indeed, it stands in direct opposition to all that they reckon most excellent in religion, to all that liberality and false charity, which represent differences of doctrine (or mere opinions) as comparatively unimportant; and which in this represent it of little consequence what gods men acknowledge, if they but serve their gods with sincerity and fervent zeal, and cultivate piety. How many thousands are all their lives gabbling the words "Hallowed be thy name," while the whole course of their religion is a systematic profanation of its holiness.

As to the sentiment of different degrees of glory in heaven, regulated by the different degrees of fruitfulness and faithfulness here, it is one of those theological speculations, upon which I have very little to say: but I confess it smells to me strongly of fleshly pride and unbelief. "We know not yet what we shall be," 1 John iii. 2. but we know that a crown of righteousness is laid up, not only for the Apostles, but for all that love his appearing: 2 Tim. iv. 8. "in the world to come eternal life"—that is the enduring and satisfying portion of *all* the children. If an Apostle should ever have murmured at the thought of the thief upon the cross receiving as bright a crown as himself, I should confidently say, that the Apostle was not then in the mind of Christ, but was savouring the things that be of men: look at Matt. xx. 1—16, and look at it in connexion with the four last verses of the preceding chapter from which it has been injudiciously dissevered. Peter's flesh was on that occasion ready enough to put forward a kind of claim for extraordinary recompence for *extraordinary* sacrifices: and accordingly the Lord puts a great damper on the unloving pride of heart in which such a thought originates. Why should the labourers, who have borne the burden and heat of the day, murmur at finding that the fellow labourer, who had been but one hour in the vineyard, got the same payment with themselves? was their payment the less on that account? The idea springs from nothing but that vain affectation of pre-eminence above others, which men would carry with them even into the heavenly world.

But do I assert that all the heirs of glory shall be perfectly alike in their capacities, enjoyments, &c.? I say nothing for it or against it, for I know not any thing of the matter: but this I know, that it was truly said by one concerning the crown that is laid up for all the heirs of the kingdom, that "God crowns in his people the gift of his own mercy:" and assuredly the greatness of the gifts mercifully dispensed to any of them here cannot give such any *claim of right* to a brighter or richer crown hereafter.

IV.

"Abhor that which is evil; cleave to that which is good."—Rom. xii. 9.

The state of mind and sentiment, of which believers are here reminded by the Apostle as becoming the gospel of Christ, is that which nothing but the gospel of Christ, discerned in its unadulterated truth can produce and maintain in us. It is a sentiment and state of mind which, in its real nature, can be found only in those who know the joyful sound of that divine word which publishes salvation to the lost, bringing righteousness to the most guilty, and proclaims the name of the Lord God as the just God and the Saviour, just and justifying the ungodly. But this, like every other exhortation of the Apostles, is wholely misunderstood by the religious world, and (taken in the false meaning which they put upon it) becomes a part of that system of lies by which many of them are very earnest to regulate their hearts and conduct. One of these, for instance, devoutly thanking God (with the very religious character described by the Lord) that he is not as other men are, imagines that he abhors that which is evil, and cleaves to that which is good, while he looks with abhorrence at those gross forms of iniquity (extortion, adultery, drunkenness, &c.) from which he conceives himself exempt, and steadfastly adheres to that course of seriousness, and strictness, and piety, which he regards in himself, as the good work of, what he calls, the grace of God: looking with complacency at the characters in himself, which he conceives favourably distinguishing him from others his fellow sinners, he is filled with this (as he thinks) holy indignation against evil, and zealously affected (as he thinks) in a good thing. But all the time, so far from being of the sentiment to which the Apostle exhorts disciples, he is really cleaving to that which is evil, and abhorring that which is good; he hates and despises that one good thing in which Jehovah declares Himself alone well pleased, which He sets forth in his divine word as the propitiation for sin, in which the most wicked and ungodly, discovering it, find peace, righteousness, and salvation;—he cleaves to that which is evil, in maintaining that system of Antichristian religion and religious hope, which proceeds on the denial of the truth and holiness of God.—On the other hand, the chief of publicans, having his eyes mercifully opened to discern the propitiation for sin, which God has set forth, clings to that as all that is excellent, and glorious, and needed by a sinner—as divinely perfect: and so far as the word of truth abides in him, it will keep him cleaving to that which is good; it will discover to him the evil of all that is opposed to it, and therefore of all that is in himself, as well as of all the most specious forms in which the religious of the world would invade the sanctity, or obscure the glory, of the divine truth. But this *abhorrence* of evil, and this cleaving to that which is good, like every other part of the mind of faith in its genuine nature, is reckoned and must ever be reckoned by the world, a most evil and satanic mind. Their religion they think, of course, a good thing, and if we only were of another religion, but kept fair terms with theirs, they would naturally bear with us and judge that, among a variety of good things, we and they but differed in the taste of selection: and indeed there could not then be any essential difference between their religion and ours. But when they find that, which they reckon best, viewed by us with *abhorrence* as most evil and ungodly, we need not wonder if that be the natural expression of their feelings.—Away with such fellows from the earth—it is not fit that they should live! But let us remember that the servant is not above his Lord; if they have called the master of the house Beelzebub, how much more shall they call those of his household? The more we see of the genuine nature of the Gospel, the more we must be convinced that the friendship of the world is enmity with God.

V.

"*In like manner also that the women adorn themselves in modest apparel, with shamefacedness and sobriety; not with broidered hair, or gold, or pearls, or costly array; but (which becometh women professing godliness) with good works.*" 1 Tim. ii. 9, 10.

"*Whose adorning let it not be that outward adorning of plaiting the hair, and of wearing of gold, or of putting on of apparel. But let it be the hidden man of the heart, in that which is not corruptible, even the ornament of a meek and quiet spirit, which is in the sight of God of great price.*"—1 Pet. iii. 3, 4.

These two passages are of such perfectly similar import that what is said of one will immediately apply to the other. They both certainly enjoin on Christian females that sobriety and modesty of dress which corresponds with the heavenly mind: and in opposition to that fondness for finery of apparel, to which the sex have perhaps a natural tendency, the Apostles call them to have for their ornament "a meek and quiet spirit," with "good works," or works of kindness and beneficence, *rather than* any adorning of their persons—to recommend themselves by the former rather than by the latter. That the language "*whose adorning* let it be a meek and quiet spirit," *not* such and such *outward* ornaments, is really equivalent with, let it be the one rather than the other, might be shewn from various other passages: but one may suffice. In Hosea vi. 6, the clause "I desired mercy and *not* sacrifice" is immediately followed by—"and the knowledge of God *more than* burnt offerings." Now, the phraseology of the two clauses might be interchanged—("mercy *more than* sacrifice"—the knowledge of God and not burnt offerings,)—without making any alteration in their meaning. Certainly, sacrifices and burnt offerings were at that time enjoined under the law: and thus I think it appears that it is not any particular articles of dress or modes of dress which the Apostles forbid—but that they call the Christian female not to place *her ornament* in those, even in the finest of them. There is here something much higher than any regulation of the toilette.

A pretty Quaker, in all the nice simplicity of her apparel, may be in a mind directly opposed to that enjoined; and a Christian lady going in a court dress to the drawing-room at St. James's may be in a mind according with it. If it shall be said—But does not the Apostle forbid the Christian female to "*plait her hair or wear gold?*" I reply *certainly not*, for if the words of Peter were so to be interpreted, it would follow that he forbids her to put on apparel; for the former words are immediately followed by "or of putting on of apparel." Now we can be at no loss to interpret the words, "whose adorning let it not be the outward adorning of the *putting on of apparel.*" We are quite sure that the meaning is—not, that she should not wear some apparel, but that she should not make any apparel she wears her adorning in comparison of that which is inward. Must not then the preceding words be similarly interpreted?

VI.

"*Know ye not, that so many of us as were baptized into Jesus Christ were baptized unto his death? Therefore we are buried with him,*" &c.—Rom. iii. 3, 4.

"*One Lord, one faith, one baptism.*"—Eph. iv. 5.

In the former of these passages the apostle is simply shewing how inconsistent it would be for any who profess the faith of Christ to continue in sin; seeing that those who have professed to believe in him profess to have fellowship with him in his death, so as to be dead to sin, or to have their old man crucified with him; and to have fellowship with him in his resurrection, so as to be risen to newness of life in him. He expresses their conversion to the faith of Christ by the word *baptism*, in as much as that was the stated rite by which men, who had not before professed to believe what the Apostles taught, took upon them that profession. The Baptists often insist on the literal translation of the Greek word *Baptize*—namely, to *immerse*. Let them introduce it into this and similar passages; and to speak of, *as many as were immersed into Jesus Christ being immersed into his death*, will be something very like nonsense.

As to the latter passage, they take indeed a narrow view of the *one baptism* spoken of, who think it means one immersion in water. The words of the same Apostle in another passage are a sufficient comment on this—"By one spirit are all baptized into one body—and have been all made to drink into one spirit." 1 Cor. xii. 13.

VII.

"*When the Son of man shall come in his glory—then shall he sit on the throne of his glory: and before him shall be gathered all nations, &c.*"—Mat. xxv. 31—46.

There is in man a natural passion for prying into futurity: his vain mind is anxious for information which it cannot get, and which, if it could, would be unprofitable, if not pernicious; while he is at the same time neglectful of the information that *is* given about what shall happen, and what is most important: credulous and superstitiously prone to give in to foolish or uncertain predictions and vain prognostics, but incredulous of that declaration concerning futurity which rests upon the most indubitable authority, the authority of the God of truth.

These words contain what may be emphatically called "The great prediction." When every thing in this world, that now appears most great, shall sink into insignificance; when all that now most excites the hopes and fears, the joys and regrets of the children of the world, shall have passed away as a dream, then shall be known the great reality of the things set before us in this prophecy; then their enduring importance shall be acknowledged and felt by all. But we are assured in another part of Scripture, 2 Pet. iii. 3, 4. that previous to the appearance of "this great day of the Lord"—"there shall come in the last days scoffers, walking after their own lusts and saying, where is the promise of his coming?" and this declaration is at present progressively verified: increasing numbers openly throw off the profession of Christianity, and mock at its prediction of a coming judgment. Yet an event has taken place already, near two thousand years ago, that is a pledge of this, and that is as truly wonderful.—He, who shall come the second time, has come already the first: "God was manifest in the flesh." He came at first a man of sorrows, because he came to bear the sin of many—but he shall come the second time in his glory, because he shall come without sin. He shall then "appear"—be manifested—to be that which his disciples, whose eyes were opened, knew and testified him to be, even in the days of his flesh; what He, witnessing to the truth, declared himself to be—a king. Then every eye shall see him; for all nations shall be gathered before Him, the king of nations, the king of kings, the Creator and Judge of all, seated on the throne of his glory. A separation will be made, and made by Him, who knoweth those that are His, who cannot err; and there shall be but two classes, into one or other of which every individual shall be distributed. Numerous distinctions appear at present among men, civil, moral, and religious; but these cannot be of importance, for they shall not last; all shall be at that great day absorbed in this two-fold classification, which will be but bringing out to view the only great and important distinction which at present subsists among men, those who are the sheep of

Christ, and those who are not. He shall place the one at his right hand, separated from the rest, as *his sheep*. This is not any natural distinction: all are alike by nature sinners, children of wrath: that any should be acknowledged as his, and placed at his right hand, is of his redeeming work, not of themselves or their works; they were by nature even as others. The characters and marks of his sheep by which they come to be distinguished here are, that they hear his voice and they follow him; he brings them into his fold, brings them unto God: he speaks indeed of them as his sheep, even while they are dead in sins, "other sheep I have," &c.; but till he gathers them in, they are undistinguishable by men from those who perish, though they are known to Him. He laid down his life for them, and he has given to them eternal life. He addresses them, therefore, as the blessed of His Father, "Blessed art thou, Simon," &c. "Blessed is the people that know the joyful sound," "Happy art thou, O Israel," &c.: they are taught here to know and acknowledge the author and source of all their blessedness; they are taught to glory in the Lord, and to *begin* that song which they shall sing through eternity. He addresses them as *heirs* of the kingdom prepared for them. Who is an heir, but the son; and who among men are sons of God, but those "who are born not of blood, nor of the will of the flesh, nor of the will of man, but of God?" John i. 13. "If children, then heirs; heirs of God, and joint heirs with Christ." Rom. viii. 17.

But because many profess themselves to be Christians who are not, the Lord will produce the decisive evidence that proves those, whom he addresses as His, to be his disciples indeed; their works of *love*, shewed to his name; love to *his brethren*, for his name's sake; love not in word or in tongue, but in deed and in truth. These prove that they loved the Lord Jesus Christ in sincerity, that they believed from the heart the record of his love; "for we love him, because He loved us;" and "this is His commandment that ye love one another." These prove that they are what they are afterwards denominated, the *righteous*—justified in Him the Lord their righteousness; "created unto good works which God hath before ordained, that they should walk in them."

He addresses all others as wicked and accursed, and pronounces on them the awful sentence, "depart." Their hearts had long said that to Him. He addresses them as in their sins, and therefore vessels of wrath consigned to the same doom of the angels that sinned. And he produces the evidence of this in proving that they are none of his; and he proves that they are none of His—by what evidence? There are now appearing various evidences of this; all the works of the flesh, murder, adultery, &c.: "he that committeth sin is the servant of sin:" but then those outward fruits do not appear in many of the unbelieving world; many are sober, chaste, and religious. The Lord, therefore, omits all these, and produces one evidence comprehending all unbelievers within its application—their want of love to Him, and this evidenced by their want of love to his disciples, and this by their not having performed the acts of love.

VIII.

"He hath shewed thee, O man, what is good."—Mic. vi. 8.

This is an answer given through Balaam (a prophet, though an unrighteous man) to the question of Balack (stated in the preceding verses,) a carnal man, who, terrified at the displays of the power of the God of Israel in behalf of the Jewish people, anxiously inquired by what sacrifice he might propitiate his favour and engage the Lord on his side. The matter lay so near his heart that he was willing to make any sacrifice ever so costly to attain his object. It appears from the close of his question that the *sin* of his soul was that which made him apprehend the displeasure of Jehovah: he desired only to have it stated, what he should give for this, and he was ready to give it.—He was yet a carnal man; and this question was never proposed by any but a carnal man: its terms import ignorance of the object, ignorance of Jehovah, of sin, and of himself. It has more or less forced itself on the mind of every man in one form or another. It is a question that weighs with various degrees of solicitude upon various men, and upon the same man at various times: but there are times and occasions when all men are disturbed with the inquiry, and propose it with anxious uncertainty. Those who know God, or rather are known of him, cannot any longer ask it (except, as knowing the answer, to call the attention and admiration of themselves or others to the vanity of the question, and the glory of the answer.) Yet it has commonly been considered as one which, if only proposed with sufficient solicitude, argues the inquirer to be either in a gracious state, or approximating to it; in a state called *conviction of sin*. On the contrary, it proves him to be altogether ignorant of sin, and of the true God. Look at the question. Two beings are introduced in it—the inquirer a creature, and a sinful guilty creature—and Jehovah, the creator, glorious in holiness and righteousness and truth: the proud worm degrades the living God to a level with himself, and proposes to give Him something to bribe Him from his purpose against sin. A real knowledge of Him and of sin bars every such thought; and if it be supposed unaccompanied with the knowledge of the joyful answer, an acquaintance with which is inconsistent with the disquieting solicitude of the inquirer, can leave the sinner in no state short of absolute despair. No TRUE hope can spring in the sinner's mind but from a view of that which is the answer Jehovah is declared to have shewed. Till the sinner sees this he is *looking* out in vain for something to take away sin; and any hope derived in this way is the proud presumptuous vain hope of one under the power of darkness. HE hath *shewed* what is good—what He is well pleased with—what he has accepted as taking away sin. If HE had not exhibited it, (He against whom we have sinned) we could have no good hope. But He has, in the first promise, and in all the subsequent revelations of himself to the patriarchs—in all the types and sacrifices of the Levitical law—by all the prophets—by John the Baptist—by the Apostles: they all point to the Lamb of God that taketh away the sin of the world, and with one voice testify to him as the propitiation for sin.—And what doth he look for from us? not any thing to do that which he has already done—a work which all the angels would have trembled at the thought of laying their hand to; but that in the believing view of what he has revealed, in the happy enjoyment of the peace which he *has made*, we should have our conversation as becometh the Gospel—doing justice or bringing forth the fruits of righteousness, as accepted of God as dear children;—(an unrighteous man cannot work righteousness;)—loving mercy, the rich mercy whereby we have been saved,—delighting in every act of mercy towards our fellow sinners;—and walking humbly with our God. There can be no walking with God, but as our God;—How can two walk together unless they be agreed? nor except humbly; the proud he beholdeth afar off; walking by the faith of what he has shewed *in* Christ Jesus, as we have received Him.

IX.

"*Whom God hath set forth to be a propitiation through faith in his blood.*"—Rom. iii. 25.

THIS passage marks the nature and great object of all divine revelation, from the first to Adam to the last by the Apostles of Jesus Christ. How solemn is the thought that God hath made a revelation to man! yet man, generally acknowledging the fact, is commonly indifferent to the inquiry what the matter of this revelation is, and passes through life contented to borrow from it certain phrases and forms inherited by tradition. This indifference is partly to be accounted for by the apprehension with which the guilty conscience of a sinner regards the idea of a divine revelation: Adam hid himself. Yet, from the blessed nature of this revelation, the guiltiest sinner needs not be afraid to hear it: for it is a revelation of divine mercy to the guilty;—of that which every sinner needs; without which he is lost for ever, and with which he is blessed for ever.—Suppose but one sinful creature upon earth;—let us view him—fallen from God—a rebel against Him—What does he need? What can do him good? can all that is in the world—its riches, its honours, its pleasures? can these bring blessedness to a dying sinner? even if he possesses them all through this life, and goes on intoxicated by them, he but forgets his misery for a moment, but to awaken wretched and accursed: "Blessed is the man unto whom the Lord imputeth not iniquity." This then is what the sinner needs—to have his sin taken away; and all men more or less feel this want at times, and inquire anxiously, "what shall I give for the sin of my soul?" a vain inquiry—the sacrifice of the wicked is abomination.—But now God himself hath set forth the provision of his own mercy; a propitiation for sin; and this in his own son—one with Him—who alone could interpose in behalf of a guilty race, and who took upon Him the form of a servant to do this gracious will of his heavenly father.—He has appeared to put away sin by the sacrifice of himself, by bearing the sins of many. The perfect sufficiency of this atonement is marked in the words of the Apostle by the declaration that *God* has set him forth in that work, and for that purpose; and the faithfulness of the revelation is crowned by the truth, that this righteousness of God is unto and upon all them that believe, without difference.—All have sinned—all stand on one common level in the *divine sight:* all flesh is brought in guilty *before God;* that the glory of Jehovah may be revealed and all flesh see it together.

X.

"Then Eli answered and said, go in peace: and the god of Israel grant thy petition that thou hast asked of him."

"So she went her way, and did eat, and her countenance was no more sad."—1 Sam. i. 17, 18.

It is plain that she went her way, believing that she should have the petition which she had asked, and which the high priest had sanctioned, when he dismissed her with his blessing.

And in all our approaches unto God, when we pour out our hearts before him, have we not a great high priest sanctioning our requests, who has lifted up his hands and blessed us, and whose language is, peace unto you! "my peace I give unto you!" why should our countenance be any more sad?

XI.

THE GOSPEL; OR, GLAD TIDINGS.

That is a very brief, but very comprehensive, statement of the Gospel, which the Apostle gives in 1 Tim. i. 15, when he says, that "Christ Jesus came into the world to save sinners." Whoever understands and receives this saying, in the plain and only true meaning of it, is *wise unto salvation*.

Who is it that is here said to have come into the world?—*Christ Jesus*. The literal meaning of the Hebrew name *Jesus*—is Jehovah, *the Saviour*: and He who came into the world, who humbled himself to become the *Son of Man*, is declared to be the Son of God, "the brightness of his glory, and the express image of his person," *one* with the Father, yea "God blessed for evermore." He "took upon him the form of a servant," and appeared in the last age of the world as "a man of sorrows and acquainted with grief," to accomplish the merciful will of his Father, "to put away sin by the sacrifice of himself," dying the just, in place of the unjust. But though he "was numbered with transgressors," and crucified between two malefactors, he is now highly "exalted to be a Prince and a Saviour;" his resurrection from the dead, of which the Apostles were chosen witnesses, being the divine evidence that he is indeed the Christ, that God has accepted his sacrifice, and "is well pleased for his righteousness sake."

The name of Christ, or the Messiah, imports the *Anointed One*: and as under the Jewish law persons were set apart to various offices by anointing them with oil, so this "Anointed One of God" was consecrated by the fulness of the Spirit resting upon him to that office, which he sustains by the divine appointment. But what is this office?—That of *saving* sinners. Not (as so many doctors of lying divinity teach) of putting men into a way in which they may save themselves, in which they may make their peace with God, and may obtain eternal life by some good endeavour after it. No: his office is absolutely "to save unto the uttermost" those who have been "given to him out of the world;" to "give them eternal life;" to bring them unto glory, "as the Captain of their Salvation." In his character of the great High-Priest over his Church, he "gave himself for it," "offering himself through the eternal Spirit unto God;" and "has made peace" by his blood, and "obtained eternal redemption" for his people, by bearing their sins in his own body on the cross. Set as "King upon the holy hill of Zion," "head over all things to his Church," he has sent forth his word as the sceptre of his power out of Zion, and rules in the midst of his enemies, giving that word entrance into the minds of those who have been "ordained to eternal life," and calling whom he will to the belief of the truth; thus turning them from darkness unto light, and from the dominion of Satan into the kingdom of God; and keeping them through the power of the same word, unto the full enjoyment of that salvation, wherewith he *hath saved* them.

And what is the character of those, in whose behalf he came for this purpose into the world? Are they persons well-disposed and good? or half-good?—Quite the reverse. They are sinners, nothing but sinners; ungodly and without strength; whose sins had righteously earned that curse, the sentence of which was executed upon Him as their substitute, in order that they might be "blessed in him," in the only way consistent with the righteousness and truth of God.

And who are they that are partakers of this salvation, which is thus altogether of God?—Whosoever *believeth* the divine report of it, sent throughout the world in the Apostolic word. *Whosoever*; without distinction or exception: for God is no respecter of the persons of men. "It is not of him that willeth, nor of him that runneth; but of God that sheweth mercy:" and "therefore is it of *faith*, that it might be by *grace* (or mere mercy), that the promise might be sure to all the seed."

The Christ testified of in this word, revealing the glory of the only true God, "is despised and rejected by men," by all but those whom God calls to the knowledge of him by convincing them of its truth: and they are "a little flock," despised and "hated of all men" (as far as their sentiments are known) for the Son of Man's sake. But the day is approaching, when He, for whom they wait, "shall come the second time without sin unto salvation," to their joy, and to the confusion of those who hate him.

BRIEF ANIMADVERSIONS

ON

A PAMPHLET,

BY

DOCTOR RICHARD WHATELY,

ENTITLED

"THOUGHTS ON THE SABBATH, IN REFERENCE TO THE CHRISTIAN FESTIVAL OF THE LORD'S DAY."

[First Published 1833.]

BRIEF ANIMADVERSIONS, &c. &c.

ALTHOUGH the piece, on which I am about to animadvert, has been published two years ago, it is but very lately that I have seen and read it. Since its publication, the Author has been raised to the archiepiscopal See of Dublin; and it is not from any personal disrespect, that I prefer to designate him still as Dr. WHATLEY.

In a short advertisement prefixed to the edition from which I quote, (London: B. Fellowes, 1830,) the author speaks of "the Lord's Day," as "*precious* in the eyes of every right-minded Christian;" and of "its *proper observance*," as "of manifold utility." In what that *proper* observance consists, he has no where, as far as I can discover, informed us. If he suppose it to consist in the current attendance on multiplied *clerical ministrations*, in hearing many masses and many sermons, he may be assured that the "*right-minded* Christian" can take no part in such an observance of the day.

Dr. W. has very justly opposed the *sabbatical* observance of it; or any observance of it, which is rested on the fourth precept of the Decalogue as of continued authority. Yet, if I mistake not, he devoutly prays every Sunday, or professes to pray, that "his heart may be inclined to keep that law." He has not yet obtained permission from the king and parliament to lay aside that solemn mockery of the Most High. Such is *State-religion*.

But I must also assure Dr. W. that, to any "right-minded Christian," no religious observance of the first day of the week would be at all "*precious*," if it rested on the ground, on which alone he imagines it can be placed securely: namely, the same ground on which he observes "Christmas-Day, Good-Friday, Holy-Thursday, &c." (p. 21.) The Doctor thinks that he thus places the duty "on its *true* foundation." But it is a foundation, which the word of God sweeps away, along with every superstructure built upon it.

But what is this foundation, on which, according to Dr. W., the obligation rests of observing the Lord's-Day, Christmas-Day, Good-Friday, Holy-Thursday, &c? The authority of what he calls THE CHURCH: which CHURCH, he tells us (p. 23.) "has full power to SANCTIFY any day that may be thought most fitting."—Power to SANCTIFY! The assumptions of the man of sin can scarcely be carried higher than this. Here he appears indeed "as God, sitting in the temple of God." (2 Thess. ii. 4.) For who but the living God has power to *sanctify*, or constitute any thing *holy* to Himself? This necessarily includes in it the establishing of an *obligation* on all, who know his Name, to acknowledge the *holiness* of the thing thus *sanctified*, to regard it as holy unto the LORD; so that any profanation of it is a profaning of HIS holiness. Any men, therefore, who assume the power of sanctifying a day, assume the power of establishing *divine obligation*; and, in that, attempt to usurp the throne of God himself.

I shall by and by examine the grounds on which Dr. W. asserts, that what he calls THE CHURCH is "endued with ample powers to *enact*" such regulations as the sanctification of *Holy Thursday*, &c. (And in the catalogue let me not forget what he calls "OUR LADY'S DAY;" which, he tells us, "*Christians* annually *celebrate*." Among the number of such Christians *I am not*; nor are any, with whom I walk in religious fellowship.) But at present let us stop a little to inquire what the Doctor means by this same *Church*, to which he thinks God has transferred his authority.

Now, Dr. Whately is a logician; and has written, as I understand, upon Logic. He must therefore be aware, that in all close reasoning nothing is of more importance, than the distinct and definite use of words; especially of such as are immediately essential to the argument, or as have been currently employed in a variety of meanings: and that nothing can more absolutely vitiate any argument, than the use of any such term, without notice, in several different senses. Yet the Doctor in his short pamphlet, has fallen into all these vices of reasoning in his use of the word *Church*. When he rests so much of religious observance upon the authority of THE CHURCH, we might expect that he would have plainly stated what he means by that phrase; which, if I mistake not, is among those that Mr. LOCKE adduces, as exemplifying the mischievous ambiguity and uncertain signification of words in current use. But Dr. W. has not only left it enveloped in that mystical obscurity in which divines have involved it, but has increased the difficulty of ascertaining his meaning, by changing the sense in which he employs the term at least three times. However, I shall endeavour to trace him in all his applications of it; and, in each, to expose the invalidity of his arguments.

One sense in which I find him using the phrase "THE CHURCH," is, as equivalent with the men styled *Bishops* and *Arch-*

bishops, in the several states of Christendom. Now, common as it is with the benighted papists of Ireland to speak of their *Church* and of their *Clergy* as synonymous, yet it might seem almost incredible, that in the nineteenth century, the PRINCIPAL of ST. ALBAN'S HALL, OXFORD, should adopt any similar application of the word. But the fact is incontrovertible, as will appear from the following quotation of a passage already referred to, in the 21st page of his pamphlet. "And when it (the kingdom of Christ,) did come, his Apostles were, as I have said, not commissioned by Him to change the day, and perpetuate the obligation of the Jewish Sabbath; but they and THEIR SUCCESSORS, *even* THE CHURCH which He promised to be with 'always, even unto the end of the world,' were endued with ample power to *enact* regulations with a view to Christian edification; and among the rest to set apart festival days, such as the Lord's day, Christmas-day, Good-Friday, Holy-Thursday," &c.

Now what can be plainer, than that in this passage Dr. W. considers those whom he calls the "SUCCESSORS of the Apostles," as constituting what he calls "THE CHURCH?" Nor are we left at any loss to ascertain whom he intends by *the Successors of the Apostles*. For if we only look at the table of Ecclesiastical Officers, printed by authority, at the end of the English Bibles, we shall find the penultimate article running in these words:—"*Bishops*, successors of the Apostles in the government of the Church."

To expose the profane falsehood of this claim of the Hierarchy, I shall not insist upon the *line of succession*, through which those men professedly derive their successorship,—even through the vilest of the Roman Pontiffs:—nor shall I insist upon the *political intrigues*, by which in these countries they obtain an appointment to their function. No:—I abstain from these copious topics, that I may at once grapple with the subject more closely. And I tell Dr. W. that *there are not, and cannot be, any successors to the Apostles*; inasmuch as the Apostles still hold their office, and with respect to it are not *defunct*.

It was to the *word* of the Apostles, not to their *persons*, that the divine promise was given;—"Lo, I AM WITH YOU alway, even unto the end of the world:"—not, "with you and your *successors*." Nor was there a whit more of Christ's authority sanctioning their word *spoken*, than the same word *written*. Or will Dr. W. assert, that an authenticated letter from the apostle Paul, read in the Christian assembly at Corinth, carried with it less of divine authority, or of divine obligation on the disciples to obey the injunctions it contained, than if Paul had been personally present, and *spoken* the same things? To this day Christians have with them the word of the Apostles: and "*he that knoweth God heareth them*." (1 John iv. 6.)—But this is part of their language to the Churches of the saints:—"Let no man judge you in meat or in drink, or *in respect of an holiday*, or of the new moon, or of the sabbath days." (Col. ii. 16.)

Such was the apostolic language to a Gentile church, concerning the *holidays* that really had a divine origin, and were once of binding authority to the Jews; though but "shadows of good things" then to come, and shadows which, even to the Jews, were "ready to vanish away." (Heb. viii. 13, x. 1.) The Gentile Christians, therefore, were indeed enjoined "not to despise" their Jewish brethren for such Mosaic observances—(Rom. xiv. 3): but were as expressly enjoined to repel any attempt which false teachers might make, to impose these observances upon the Gentiles. And the adoption of such observances was, in the Gentiles, expressly marked as involving a departure from the Gospel. (Gal. iv. 9—11. v. 2.)

What then are we to say to a class of men, who pretend that the Apostles of Christ have been displaced from their office, and *succeeded* by themselves?—who, in perfect consistency with this arrogant assumption, have taken upon them to set aside the apostolic precept; and attempt to impose on disciples the observance of holidays and festival days, according to their own tradition; which they dare to represent as sanctioned by divine authority, and therefore binding on the conscience of a Christian. What are we to say to such men, but this?—"whether it be right in the sight of God to hearken unto you more than unto God, judge ye." Acts iv. 19.

Enough has been said to shew, that, while Dr. W. conceives that he places some religious observance of the Lord's day "on a rock," (p. 7.) by resting it on the asserted authority of the Bishops, as successors of the Apostles, to *sanctify* it, or what they call "our Lady's day," or any other day "that may be thought most fitting," (p. 23.) every "right-minded Christian" must feel himself bound, by divine authority, to resist the religious observance of any day resting on such a foundation:—and still more strongly bound to this, when the men who would impose that observance, embody in this attempt the claim to an office and character the most obviously Antichristian.

I pass to another meaning, in which Dr. W. employs the word CHURCH, as connected with the same subject. In page 28. he remarks, that "it is very useful to shew (to the strenuous advocates for the observance of the Lord's day) that an institution, which they would be very unwilling to see deprived of all *divine sanction*, can derive such sanction from no other source than from the power conferred by Christ on EVERY CHRISTIAN CHURCH:"—or, as he expresses the same idea in a few lines before, "a divinely-sanctioned power"—"vested in A CHRISTIAN COMMUNITY, and *binding on its* members."

Here the Bishops, successors of the Apostles, have disappeared; and, in their place, we are presented with an idea which is in itself perfectly scriptural; a *Church* of Christ in any place always importing in the New Testament the *community* of Christians in that place, coming together on the first day of the week, to shew forth their Lord's death in the ordinance of his supper. But is it true, that CHRIST has conferred on such a *community* of Christians the power of *sanctifying* such days, as "may be thought most fitting," and of imposing the observance of them as "binding on its members?" In other words, is it true that Christ has vested in each Christian Church the power to release its members from their allegiance to Him, to turn away their ear from his accredited ambassadors, and to assume to themselves the right of enacting laws and ordinances according to their several fancies? So far is this from being true, that every real Church of Christ has nothing at all to do with making any laws, or inventing any ordinances for their fancied edification. They are simply called to hear, and observe those promulgated by the King of Zion in the Apostolic word.

Accordingly, the Apostle Paul commends a Church, because they "remembered him in all things, *and kept the ordinances*, as he had delivered them," (1 Cor. xi. 2.):—and another Church, for being "followers of the Churches of God, which in Judea were in Christ Jesus," (1 Thess. ii. 14.); enjoining them to withdraw themselves from every brother "that walked disorderly, and *not after the tradition received* of the Apostles." (2 Thess. iii. 6.) They were charged in solemn language such as this:—"we beseech you, brethren, and exhort you by the Lord Jesus, that as ye have *received of us* how ye ought to walk and to please God, so ye would abound more and more."

In the way in which the Apostolic Churches were called to walk, there was no room for diversity of faith or of practice:—no room for any human contrivances in addition to the regulations of the Apostles. *Their* authoritative language was—"If any man think himself to be a prophet, or spiritual, let him acknowledge that the things that I write unto you are *the commandments of the Lord*." (1 Cor. xiv. 37.) "He that knoweth God heareth *us*:—he that is not of God heareth not us." (1 John iv. 6.) Thus it was of old; and thus it is at this day. That it is so, is a necessary result from the promise of HIM "whose words shall not pass away"—(Matt. xxiv. 35.)—"Lo, I am *with you* alway, even *unto the end of the world*." It was a promise made to the Apostles by their divine Master;—not to any pretended *successors* of the Apostles. The very terms of the promise involve the continuance of their function *unto the end of the world*; and therefore exclude all idea of any *successors* to them. I have known some indeed who wish to substitute for "the end of the world," in that promise, the version—"unto the end (or completion) of *the age*." And this translation is perfectly unobjectionable; but, understood aright, is perfectly equivalent with the common version. The "*last days*," (Heb. i. 2.) or *last age* of the world, had then commenced. The Kingdom of heaven was fully introduced, in opposition to the *earthly* kingdom of the Mosaic law. And as it was then the *last* age, the completion of that age *must* synchronize with the end of the world.

Many, I am aware, in order to make room for their traditions and human *enactments* in the Church of Christ, are accustomed to represent the Apostolic word, which Christians have with them at this day in the Scriptures, as *insufficient*, and not affording that fulness of regulation which the Churches of Christ require. They have never brought this to the test of experiment by obeying what *is* revealed. But none indeed can really be engaged in this attempt, but those who believe that *Apostolic* Gospel, which is "foolishness" and a "stumbling block" to the pride and ungodliness of man;—none but those who, being "ordained to eternal life," have been subdued to "the obedience of faith." (Acts xiii. 48.) To attempt to introduce the established laws of Christ's kingdom into the so-called Churches of the world, would be absurdly inconsistent, a vain and wicked profanation. They were adapted and designed for "saints in Christ Jesus," or (in other words) for *believers* of the unadulterated *truth* as it is in Christ; for they all are "sanctified through the truth." (John xvii. 17.) They were designed for such, and for no others. But I believe I may confidently assert, that all such, so far as they are engaged in the attempt to walk together by Apostolic rule, find that rule divinely full, and sufficient for the regulation of every thing in a Church which ought to be brought under rule. No doubt, in speaking of the Apostolic rule, I mean to include the recorded and approved *example* of the Apostolic Churches; and I am fully justified in doing so,—in regarding such recorded *example* as equivalent with express precept. I am justified in this, from the consideration, that it records *how the Apostles regulated* the Churches, which they planted; how they "taught always in every Church."

Under what head I should treat the following argument, I am quite uncertain; being quite uncertain in what sense Dr. W. employs the word *Church* in it. However, it seems as well to introduce the passage here, as in any other order. (p. 22.) "When our Lord 'appointed to his Apostles a kingdom,' and declared that 'whatsoever they bound on earth should be bound in heaven,' promising also to be 'with them always, even unto the end of the world,' HE MUST *surely* have conferred on HIS CHURCH a permanent power to ordain rites and ceremonies, and to institute and abrogate religious festivals, provided nothing be done contrary to God's word; and *must* have given the ratification of his authority to what should be thus ordained. For if his expressions have not this extent, *what* DO *they mean?*"

Upon this very extraordinary argument I would remark, in the first place,—that, as a mere *argumentum ad ignorantiam*, it has no degree of force whatever, for supporting the inference which Dr. W. draws from it. And of this he himself, as a logician, must be sensible.

But waving this; I say in the next place, that the argument is otherwise destitute of all *vis consequentiæ;* that there is not the slightest connexion between the conclusion drawn and the principle from which it is inferred. 'With the *Apostles* Christ is present, sanctioning their words, even unto the end of the world: *therefore*, the *Church* has power to *ordain* rites and ceremonies, and to institute and abrogate religious festivals!' Really, from the authority with which the *Apostles* were invested, to regulate all things in the Church of Christ, it would rather follow that the *Church* has no authority to regulate any thing.

But beside the promise in Matt. xxviii. 20. the Dr. also adduces the promise in Matt. xviii. 18. which does indeed apply to every Church of Christ, acting according to the Apostolic word; but is nevertheless as remote as the former from conferring any such power as the Dr. contends for. The words which we have now to consider, stand in immediate connexion with that grand law of the kingdom of heaven, for maintaining the free circulation of brotherly affection in a Christian Church, by directing the discipline to be exercised in the case of a brother trespassing against his brother, "Go and tell him his fault between thee and him alone. If he shall hear thee, thou hast *gained* thy brother. But if he will not hear thee, take with thee one or two more, that in the mouth of two or three witnesses every word may be established. And if he shall neglect to hear them, tell it unto THE CHURCH, (to the assembled disciples). But if he neglect to hear the Church, let him be unto thee as an heathen man and a publican:" (let him be removed from all Christian fellowship). Immediately after this injunction, the Lord adds the declaration,—"Verily, I say unto you, *whatsoever ye shall bind on earth shall be bound in heaven; and whatsoever ye shall loose on earth shall be loosed in heaven.*" These words, taken in their connexion, seem not obscurely to import, that his divine authority, as King of Zion, should ratify and sanction the act of that *Church*, however small and despised, acting in such a case according to this heavenly law; either in their putting away the offender, on his not hearing the Church, or in confirming their love towards him, on his manifesting repentance. Yet of this divine promise Dr. W. ventures to assert, that it MUST confer on the Church the power *to institute and abrogate religious festivals*, &c.! And he ventures to enforce this assertion, by demanding—if it confer not this power, "what *does* it mean?"—In return for Dr. W.'s question, let me be allowed just to suggest to him another question—*what is the authority which he conceives has abrogated that law of the Kingdom of Heaven, just now quoted?*

There remains yet a third sense, in which I find Dr. W. using the word CHURCH. It occurs in page 29, in the following extraordinary sentence:—"If we hold as indispensable the observance of the Lord's day, and that, on the CHURCH'S authority (which we must do, if it can be established, as a binding ordinance, by nothing else,) then, we must admit that OUR CHURCH'S claims to such a power (the power to *sanctify* any day that may be thought most fitting, p. 23,) are valid, and rest on the appointment of our Lord." Here it is evident that the Dr. employs the phrase "*our* Church," as equivalent with "*the* Church;" and that by "*our* CHURCH," he intends, what is called the united Church of England and Ireland.

Upon this application of the word, very little needs to be said here. The thing now introduced, as the Church of Christ, is a thing altogether of this world; one of the daughters of that "great whore," produced in the "fornications she has committed with the kings of the earth;" (Rev. xvii. 2.) and among them, with that good *Defender of the Faith*, our eighth HENRY. In the Mosaic economy, it may be said there was a real and perfect *incorporation* of *Church* and *State*, of the religious and the civil institutions delivered to that peculiar people; and delivered, both of them alike, from the GOD of ISRAEL. But that age has passed away, and *the kingdom of heaven* has taken place of it; a kingdom, which its divine Author has pronounced to be "*not of this world.*" Any attempt now to confound, or incorporate, his kingdom with the kingdoms of the world, is *virtually* a denial that "Christ has come in the flesh:" and in all such attempts the thing put forward, as Christ's Church, is always, and of necessity, a thing essentially different from it.

Indeed, if that great whore had not "made the inhabitants of the earth *drunk* with the wine of her fornication," they would have perceived indisputable evidence of this assertion in the very phrase, —the *Church* of England, of Scotland, &c. &c. The Scriptures afford no one instance of any such phraseology; but always use the word *Church*, or assembly, in its application to Christians,—either for the body of Christians *assembling* in a particular place,—or for the collective aggregate of all Christians, in every age and place; that "great *congregation*," in the midst of which Christ *declares*, (or manifests,) the name of the only true God to those whom "he is not ashamed to call his brethren." (Ps. xxii. 22. Hebr. ii. 11, 12.) Yet it is not surprising that those, who profanely attribute the title of Christ's *Church* to any of those politico-religious systems, which have been established by human enactments throughout Christendom, should maintain a *consistency* of profaneness by charging those with *heresy* and *schism*, who obey that solemn call, "come out of her, my people, that ye be not partakers of her sins, and that ye receive not of her plagues." (Rev. xviii. 4.)

But lest my meaning be mistaken, let me here remark, that I do not view the great mass of *Dissenters* in these countries with a more favourable eye, than those retaining their connexion with the Establishment. Both are equally remote from even the thoughts of returning to Apostolic Christianity in faith or practice. And if I were to be regulated at all in the concerns of religion by human traditions, I should certainly, as a matter of taste, prefer the regulations made by Acts of Parliament, to the inferior authority of one or more dissenting *Ministers*. The systems originating with the latter are no less Antichristian than the former; while they have much less of *worldly respectability and splendour*.

In the passage I have last quoted from Dr. W. he declares his opinion, that "the observance of the Lord's day can be established, as a *binding ordinance*, by nothing else than the Church's *Authority*," to *sanctify* any day that may be thought most fitting. *If* it were so, I have sufficiently proved, that "every right-minded Christian" would be *bound* to abandon its observance. But it really is not so. There is an observance obligatory on Christians upon the first day of the week; and the obligation rests indeed upon an immoveable rock, however weak and insufficient it may appear in the eyes of Dr. W. The recorded *example* of the Apostolic Churches, (Acts xx. 7. 1 Cor. xi. 17. 20.) and our certainty as to the source whence *they* received their regulations, to the end of the world must bind the Christians of any place, who professedly hear the Apostles, to come together on the first day of the week, as brethren, the redeemed of the Lord, for the purpose of shewing forth Christ's death in the ordinance of his Supper. (Some further observations on this head may be found in the "Remarks *corrective of Occasional Mistranslations*," &c. No. XII. on Acts xxi. 4. In No. IX. also, of the same publication, may be found a short exposure of the supposed *Sabbatical* character of the first day of the week.)

The observance of the Lord's Supper was so much the *leading* object of the weekly assembling of the Apostolic Christians, that this singly is selected to designate the object of that assembly; though we are taught that they came together for other exercises also of brotherly fellowship and mutual edification. But these were *subordinate* to the commemoration of that death and resurrection of the Lord, which formed the basis of all their hope toward God, and of all their heavenly union with each other.

I add only two more short remarks on the general subject. The first is—that the intimations given in the Scriptures of the way, in which the first Churches were directed by the Apostles to walk, were never designed to form such a systematic code of laws, as the vanity of gainsayers might require; though sufficient for the children of God, to mark out their course to the end of the world. The second is—that I have preferred the phrase of "*the first day of the week*," to that of "*the Lord's day*," by which Dr. W. designates it. The former continually occurs in the Scriptures of the New Testament:—the latter is to be found there only in the one passage, Rev. i. 10.; and it is more than doubtful, whether it be there employed to mark any particular day of the week; though I am aware that such an application of it is very common in ecclesiastical writers posterior to the Apostolic age. Certainly, "*the day of the Lord*" is used in very different applications, in other parts of Scripture, both of the Old Testament and of the New.

COLLECTION OF LETTERS

ON

SCRIPTURAL SUBJECTS.

I.

TO ALEX. KNOX, ESQ.

Nov. 4, 1802.

DEAR KNOX,—I thank you for the copy of your Remarks which you have sent me. I have read it this evening with attention, and not without a very serious engagement of mind before I opened it. It is written with your usual ability and in that gentlemanly manner which I expected; but I fear is too well calculated to counteract the good I hoped my little Address might produce in the Methodist society. However, so far as I am enabled to act with a single eye to the glory of God, I may with happy confidence leave all results to Him. I knew that my little piece would be very obnoxious to many in and out of that Society, and I know as well that yours will be very acceptable. Yet I confess to you that I would rather be the writer of mine than of yours. You give me more credit than is due to me for facility in composing. I mean, if life be spared, to answer your Remarks; but it will probably be the work of several months, i. e. of the horæ subsecivæ of several months. I desire not only to weigh my words well upon these subjects (and you will find I have done so more than you are aware in some of those passages where you think I am most open to attack,) but to have a close eye to the spirit in which I utter them: and all this is inconsistent with a hasty reply. But I shall probably without delay put to press a second edition of the Address (altering, however, the word "most" to "many," Vol. 1, p. 7.) as I see nothing in your remarks that ought to make me withdraw it from circulation, while I am glad that they will give me an opportunity of discussing some of the topics more at large in a reply.

And now, my good friend, will you pardon me for addressing a few words in this private letter, as a poor dying sinner addressing a fellow-sinner. My heart's desire for you is that you might be made a happy partaker of that simple faith in a glorious Saviour, against which I think in the latter part of your Remarks you at least covertly contend: except in the twentieth line, p. 50, when you assert what, rightly understood, *includes* the whole. If ever you be brought to Him, you will be brought to Him stripped of all your preliminary repentance and piety and doings of every kind—as a poor publican—

as nothing but a sinner to the Saviour of sinners: and you will find all in him that a poor ruined hell-deserving sinner can want for present and eternal salvation: and you will then see that the texts of scripture you have adduced are in no wise against the doctrine you oppose. Till then you will not find rest to your soul: till then any rest you take is a false peace. Before I begin to prepare a public answer to your work, I give you this simple testimony—not indeed as to me a matter of uncertain dispute. I testify that which I know; but I am right willing to have the testimony tried and proved by the word of God. That alone will abide for ever. May God give you the joy of simply believing his joyful word, and lead you into that rest into which you never will enter but by believing! But indeed, dear Knox, this is a joy and rest as open to the poor harlot that came into the Penitentiary to-day as to you, and as open to you as it was to Peter the Apostle. These things I know appear very strange—they ever have appeared so, and ever will—except to those who know their truth. The discussion of them—and not an *attack* upon the Methodists—which I never designed—is what you may expect in my reply. Your kindness (whatever you may think of those sentiments) will, I expect, excuse my freedom, which our former intercourse upon these subjects encourages me the more to take.

Believe me, &c.

II.

TO THE EDITOR OF THE EVANGELICAL MAGAZINE.

1802.

Mr. Editor,—You invited your correspondents to offer a concise and scriptural answer to the question which Simplex has proposed concerning the nature, object, and effects of justifying faith. All who are partakers of that faith must acknowledge the importance of the question: but it is awful to think that at the end of the eighteenth century since the promulgation of the Gospel, so many professors of the faith of the Gospel should be at a loss to reply, or disposed to give such various and contradictory answers. The following I can venture with confidence to offer as scriptural; and if it be not as concise as you desire, that must be imputed, not to any intrinsic perplexity in the subject, but to the various writers who have perplexed it by a heap of human lumber placed about the simplicity of divine truth. I say more than I may, to some readers, appear to say upon the subject, when I say that our gracious Lord, in commissioning his apostles to go through all the world and proclaim to every creature the glad tidings of salvation in his name, and in declaring that whosoever believeth their testimony should be saved—*really* and simply meant what he plainly uttered. Do any of your readers think that I say little towards the solution of Simplex's question in saying this?

I am sure that this is the substance of all that ever ought to be said, or can be said with truth upon the subject. There is no difficulty in the meaning of our Saviour's expression: every one knows what is meant by *believing* a testimony—the most illiterate old woman understands the term just as well as the most learned philosopher. But the difficulty lies in this, that men cannot think that our Lord meant what he says, because they really do not believe his declaration; and, at the same time professing to submit to his authority, they strive to get over the blessed force of his words by distorting them from their obvious meaning.

Here open infidels act much more consistently than many professing Christians. The open infidel understands the meaning of the expressions at once; and having no motive to conceal his infidelity, he avowedly opposes the truth of the declaration. 'How irrational!' he exclaims—'*Believe*, and thou shalt be saved! Is this a doctrine fit for wise or good men? No;—give us the religion of nature, which affords something on which to exercise our reason, and directs to the due exertion of our moral powers—and let the helpless, ignorant, and careless rabble adopt such an unphilosophical system.' Well, when we hear this language, we know whose language it is: but many a professor who is shocked at that infidel, is just as much an infidel himself, only less consistently. 'Oh, yes,' cries he, 'to be sure, whatever Christ says is true, and it is a terrible thing to be a deist. But then what Christ says—"he that *believeth* shall be saved"—he cannot mean literally what he seems to to say.' And then he proceeds to put the preceding truth into the crucible of his infidel fancy, and blows the furnace of his wit till he brings out a bit of something as different from the scripture which he put in as darkness from light, or dead earth from fine gold. Perhaps he brings out an eastern metaphor (like those divines whom a witty writer of this day so happily and justly exposes)—perhaps some mysterious and indescribable exertion of the sinner's mind—perhaps (as I have more than once heard from the pulpit) some mixture of good disposition and affection—some Corinthian brass that is neither gold, silver, nor copper, but composed of them all—something that he describes as faith, hope, and charity, all at once; while it is neither the charity, hope, nor faith which the scriptures plainly speak of. Alas! for poor sinners! If in calling them to believe the Gospel that they may be saved, we speak in an eastern metaphor, or called them to an exertion of mind difficult and inexplicable, or required them to attain every or any good disposition that they might become partakers of Christ,—would the Gospel, which we called them *thus to believe*, be a GOSPEL, i. e. glad tidings to lost sinners—dead in trespasses and sins? And when we attempt to bring these professors back to the joyful simplicity of our Lord's declaration and the declarations of his apostles after him, do they not betray their ignorance of Scripture and the infidelity of their hearts by crying out—'O! but, in that way, what will become of good works and morality?' Precious guardians of morality and good works! take your proper place with your brethren, the avowed deists,—(nay, do not despise them, for they are your brethren,)—

and employ yourselves in devising systems of morality, while the poor simple believer shall be saved—saved from his sins, from their guilt and from their power—and shall be led by his divine Saviour in the paths of righteousness for his name's sake, abounding in the fruits of righteousness, and rich in such good works as (if your eyes were opened) might put you to the blush for your immorality—yea, your immorality, even when you have your finest coat upon you of civil decency covered with the gold lace of self-devised religion.

Now, Mr. Editor, any of your readers that are made very *angry*, probably understand what the Scriptures mean by faith or believing the Gospel. May God give them repentance to the acknowledgment of the truth, that they may be saved; for they can never be saved in any way but by grace through faith—that precious simple faith which they so despise. Let them not go away indignant from the prophet's door, because he directs them to such a simple way of cure. It is of God's appointment: it is effectual, wise, and gracious; and there is no other. "He that believeth not shall be condemned." But as Simplex's question is proposed in such loose form, perhaps some of your readers may wish for a more methodical answer. I will endeavour to indulge them: but let them remember that in what follows I am not going to unsay what I have said hitherto. God forbid that the trumpet should give an uncertain sound! They will not understand what follows aright, if they understand it in any sense different from what has gone before. Simplex inquires—1st, the nature—2nd, the object—3rd, the effects of justifying faith. Then I say, first, its nature is this—it is *a divinely-wrought persuasion of things divinely revealed.* Secondly, its object is the Lord Jesus Christ—in that character and work of the Saviour of sinners, in which the Scriptures of truth reveal him. Thirdly, its effects are all the fruits of the Spirit, "love, joy, peace, long suffering, gentleness, goodness, faithfulness, meekness, temperance;"—in short, every good work—love to God and love to our neighbour. Allow me to add a few words by way of explanation upon each of these heads.

There must be a divine revelation for the basis and warrant and rule of the faith of which we speak: therefore, "faith cometh by hearing, and hearing by the word of God." They talk unscripturally who talk of any thing as the matter of faith, which is not revealed by God in his word—his revealed truth being now all comprised in the canon of Scripture, which is completed and closed. The things which he has revealed are things future or things invisible; and thus the Apostle divides them, Heb. xi. 1. into things "*expected*" (for so the word should be rendered,) as opposed to things present, and things "*not seen*" opposed to those which come under the observation of our senses. Faith is the "confidence of things expected and the conviction of things not seen;" or, in a word, the persuasion of those things divinely revealed: and the author of faith is God the Spirit, as a spirit of demonstration and of power. We are naturally creatures of sight and sense, and no man, whatever he professed, ever yet really believed or was persuaded of the things revealed in God's word, but by the Holy Ghost. And as this faith is originally of his operation, so we depend upon his continual influence for its maintenance and increase. By these two things, therefore, this faith or believing is distinguished from all other believing—that it has for its matter things divinely revealed, and for its author God; and though always necessarily combined with a perception, or view, or understanding of the truth (for we cannot believe what we do not understand), it is essentially distinct from the mere understanding of the propositions contained in the word of God; for it is one thing to *understand* a proposition, and another thing to be persuaded of its truth. Faith, therefore, will exist in various degrees, according as the spirit of wisdom and of revelation discovers to us the import, and persuades us of the truth of the divine testimony. But the Scriptures have been given "to make us wise *unto salvation*;" and both in the Old Testament and in the New, by Moses in the law, by the Prophets, and by the Apostles, bear one united testimony to the Lord Jesus Christ, as the only and the all-sufficient Saviour of lost sinners—God with us—manifest in the flesh—to make an end of sin and bring in everlasting righteousness—to bruise the head of the serpent—to destroy the works of the devil—to save his people from their sins—to be the Captain of our salvation, bringing many sons unto glory. In this—*his* person—*his* offices—*his* work—all the lines of divine truth meet as in the centre: for which reason (as well as others) he calls himself "*the truth*;" and intimates that his people shall be wise unto salvation by declaring, "I am known of mine;" and declares the great office of the Spirit in declaring—"He shall testify of ME"—"He shall glorify ME"—"He shall take of the things that are *mine* and shall shew them unto you." HE is therefore the great *object* of that faith which believes the record of God. "This is the record, that God hath given to us eternal life, and this life is in his Son." "He that hath the Son hath life, and he that hath not the Son of God hath not life." Lastly, this faith—both from the glorious matter which it believes, and from the divine Author which produces and maintains it in the sinner's mind, does and ever must work by love, purify the heart, and overcome the world. This faith is indeed *most holy faith*: the truth which it believes is indeed truth "according to godliness," and *through it* the great head of his church prays that his people may be sanctified. John xvii. Sinners, *believing* the record of the love of God that passes knowledge, are won to love him, are encouraged to draw nigh to him, are enabled to walk with him, are excited to serve him without fear in holiness and righteousness before him all the days of their life—are taught of him to love one another, and led by him as strangers and pilgrims upon earth—in Christ their living way, the way of holiness—to press toward the mark for the prize of their high calling, looking for and hasting unto the coming of the day of God. Triumphantly we may demand, Who is he that overcometh the world—who is he that is delivered from the bondage of corruption—who is he that possesses the glorious liberty of the sons of God, whereby they serve him with a willing service—but he that *believeth* that Jesus is the Christ? Neither my time nor the limits of this essay will allow me to treat more largely upon these effects of faith and their *necessary* connection with it, or the various workings of the fleshly mind—the evil mind of unbelief in opposition to it. I shall only say that, whatever garb he assumes, he is the enemy of holiness and of every good work who is the enemy of this precious simple scriptural faith of God's elect. May you, reader, be a happy partaker of it.

III.

TO THE REV. DR. H———.

——— 1803.

Reverend and much beloved sir,—I saw, with pleasure, your note on the cover of the Evangelical Magazine for March, intimating your kind acceptance of the letter I took the liberty of addressing to you. It is needless to detail the circumstances that have since prevented my writing: among them have been sickness and multiplicity of engagements. But indeed, now that I sit down to repeat the liberty I took before, (according to your permission) it is with a considerable mixture of wonder at the thought of having ever taken it, and with some feeling of shame (though unknown) at the recollection that I dropped a hint of wishing to make a few observations on different passages in the pieces you have published. That is all I can remember of my former letter,—and that I wrote under the constraining impulse of much brotherly affection towards you, for the truth's sake. And now, dear sir, as you encourage me to proceed, and as I trust I can appeal to the searcher of hearts that I have no allowed motive, in what I am about to offer, but the glory of that dear Lord, who, I believe, has called us both by his grace, and will soon take us to himself—bear with me while I offer the following remarks to your consideration. I think I see in your writings the manliness of a faithful soldier of Christ, desirous to advance his reproached cross in the face of all the opposition and contempt which the world throws upon it—not seeking to escape the reproach by hiding the object of it—or by dressing it up with some trappings which its enemies can like. Yet I think that you appear to have taken up unintentionally some of those views which many indeed, who are called evangelical, have long put forward, but which I am persuaded corrupt the glorious simplicity and obscure the characteristic offensiveness of the gospel. These views in *your* writings appear blessedly contradicted, from time to time, by plain testimonies which you bear to the unadulterated truth: and I cherish the persuasion that your testimony will progressively become more and more uniformly consistent with itself and with scripture. In proportion as it does, it will become more and more distinguished from that of many who bear the name of Christ's ministers, and from them you may expect a peculiar outcry. I shall select at present but two instances of what I mean. Examine, dear sir, the character and state of your "Zion's pilgrim" at the time when you represent him as first converted, regenerated, and entered on the road to Zion, (see from p. 5 to p. 8 of the third edition) and consider whether that great change can scripturally be said to have taken place in him at that period, or for some time after. He appears to have been then indeed deeply serious, and much concerned and engaged about divine and eternal things. But was he not still in wickedness—a stranger to the true character of God as a just God and the justifier of the ungodly? Could he be said to be in the way to Zion, when he knew not him who is the only way?—to be born of God, when he yet believed not that Jesus is the Christ, the anointed one of God for the office of saving sinners unto the uttermost and bringing many sons unto glory? to be converted, when—(though turning from *some forms* of the flesh which he before had served) he yet was not turned from himself nor brought to the Shepherd and Bishop of souls? I know it is common in the popular divinity to represent such very serious and religious characters—especially if inquiring with apparent candour about divine things—as at least fairly on the way *towards* salvation, if not already safe—though they believe not the gospel of God our Saviour. But does his word warrant any such representations? does it know any thing of what so many sermons and writings under evangelical titles are stuffed with—of half believers—a medley between—a state of nature and a state of grace? Does not the gospel, where it comes, find all alike dead in sin—and leave all as dead as it found them and more condemned, except those who are given to believe the record of him who is the resurrection and the life? That the mighty and gracious hand of God has been over those, even before they believed, leading them, controlling them, and variously working on them, I readily grant, and you have sweetly shewn; but I know not any stage of a sinner's course, till he is brought to the knowledge and belief of the truth as it is in Jesus, in which I have any warrant to address him, except as an alien from the life of God—an enemy against him—and willing captive of sin. If Satan be the father of *lies*, I can consider all false religion, even in its fairest form, but as among his devices:—and surely, the religion of Zion's pilgrim was false till he believed, and is described as false at p. 27. He might well acknowledge the rich grace of God in bringing him out of such false ways, but could not justly consider himself as entered on the road to Zion till brought out of them. The other instance which I would beg leave to mention, is from your paper against all despair. In various passages of it you give blessed testimonies to the sovereign riches and freedom of the grace of God—in opposition to all supposed *qualifications* in the object for receiving it. But have you not been led elsewhere to represent a previous awakening, and apprehension of having sinned beyond the possibility of forgiveness,—and a falling of the weapons of sin out of our hands, as that very qualification which, at other times, you deny? Why say, dear sir, that in any declaration of the gospel the unawakened, unhumbled, unconvinced sinner has no immediate interest? The Apostles declared it to thousands of such, and thousands of such, believing it, became new creatures. In one sense none but the *believer* of the gospel is interested in it,—in another sense, those who are most insensible to their need of forgiveness just as much as those who most despair of forgiveness—and it needs just the same divine power accompanying the word to reveal the grace of the gospel to the latter as to the former: and we are just as much warranted to declare to the former, that believing in the Lord Jesus Christ they shall be saved, as we are obliged to declare to the latter, that except they believe they shall be damned: the timidity to declare the rich grace of the gospel to sinners till they have had a previous work of supposed conviction under the law, I consider as one of the corruptions of the gospel, which the art of the devil, with the help of systematic divinity, has long introduced and widely diffused. You divide sinners into two classes—awakened to a sense of sin—and unawakened. Would it not be more scriptural to say believing and unbelieving? To the unawakened you observe there is not a promise in the whole Bible; no, nor to the awakened in any sense of the word, but that which includes the character of believing the gospel. The promises are all in Christ, and till we believe in him we are strangers to the covenant of promise. And if the most convinced and awakened sinners (so called—for I acknowledge no genuine—no gracious conviction or awakening, till we are given to believe) are led to suppose themselves interested in the promises of the gospel, by their being convinced and awakened, they will be led into a fatal error—while the declaration of our Lord shall continue to be fulfilled in the most unawakened, that the *dead* shall hear his voice, and they that hear shall live. Dear sir, I would not obtrude these plain remarks on you, did I not see that, when you get out of the systems of men, you so plainly declare the grace of God in truth, and justly state the being a sinner—not the being an awakened sinner—the only qualification for it. I trust you will not think the topics I have glanced at unimportant, or my observations hypercritical. But whatever you may think or conjecture of the writer, may the God of all grace bless to you, and through you to the church, what I have written. He can make use of the poorest instrument he has. Indeed, dear sir, while I have ventured this, (and shall not apologize for stating what I consider scriptural truth) I yet feel much more disposed to wash your feet as an honoured witness for our Lord, than to assume the office of censor. But we may communicate to one another for our mutual help and furtherance, without exalting ourselves above our dear brethren. Beside the warm affection with which my heart embraces you, I believe I have been led to those communications, by having been long pained at seeing the publications which come out under the name of Evangelical in England, in many of which the fundamental principles of the glorious gospel are insidiously undermined, and by having cherished the opinion since I saw your writings, that our Lord is progressively teaching and anointing you to oppose their prevailing errors. Look, for instance, at the Christian Observer for last March, p. 192, (and it happens to lie before me) where the Editors, opposing indeed an unscriptural opinion, talk of the " distinguishing circumstances of a hopeful nature in the case of penitents," who appear to be called at the eleventh hour,—of the Pharisees being far greater sinners than the publican—of the *probability* of repentance being proportioned to this and that;—and enumerate the circumstances of Mr. F.'s being the son of a clergyman—a professed believer—and a loyal man, as those *distinguishing* traits of character, which they intimate (though they will not speak out) induced God to have mercy on him, or contributed to render the means of grace effectual. Oh, dear sir, may the Lord enable you to lift up your voice as a trumpet against such earthly systems: may he establish, strengthen, and settle you more and more in the precious faith once delivered to the saints! Fear not, O man greatly beloved,—be strong, yea, be strong! and when enjoying boldness of access to the throne of grace, through the great high priest of our profession, and by that living way which he has consecrated for us, sometimes remember the least and unworthiest of your companions in the kingdom and patience of Jesus Christ in your unknown but most truly affectionate, &c.

IV.

TO ALEX. KNOX, ESQ.

Nov. 1803.

Dear Knox,—I send you my 7th and last letter, in which I have hurried over many of your concluding Remarks, in order not to have "more last words of Richard Baxter." I perceive that my letters have been becoming progressively offensive, from the nature of the subjects handled in them: and I am glad to learn from you that you are at length sensible that we see things in a very different light, because this affords me reason to hope that my meaning is now somewhat understood; while it must be with regret that I hear I have not excited in you the smallest doubt of the substantial truth of your own religious sentiments. The gospel is so unaccommodating and so repulsive to all our natural feelings, that it is indeed a miracle when any seriously accept it. Like its divine Author, though full of grace and truth, it exhibits no comeliness that can naturally allure either the irreligious or religious world. It will not bend to a coalescence with the prejudices of men—it cannot become an engine of state policy; it cannot become a step to influence or reputation. It is for the salvation of the lost, and answers no other purpose, except to display the justice of God in condemning those that perish. Its few professors must even be exposed to the most various and contradictory imputations—must be a sect every where spoken against. They can have nothing to support them in their testimony to the truth, but the preciousness of that truth and the good hope that it reveals. I can wish you no higher blessing than a participation in their sorrows and trials and their joys. I have lived to see taking place every thing that I had predicted as the probable effect of this controversy. Yet I reckon the day that I was led to commence it, one of the happiest of my life. I perceive an appearance of soreness in your last, under a veil of some jocoseness. In some respects I do not wonder at this, for though a man may at first bear without any emotion to have all his religious system opposed, yet a serious attack upon it must be wounding in proportion to the strength of his attachment to it, and the strength of argument by which it is invaded; the more religion he has, the less he can reckon this a trifle; here it would be unsuitable for us to be really jocose. But you seem to intimate some degree of doubt whether I have continued my endeavour not to wound your personal feelings needlessly; believe me I could remove that doubt by communicating to you some passages which I have altogether forborn to insert in my letters—one for instance upon the concluding sentence of the paragraph, p. 61, in your remarks. I would not repeat any assurance on this head, but for my anxious desire that you may be led to give a serious and candid consideration to my reply. I feel a good deal of solemnity in thus closing the controversy—perhaps finally—with you. We have thus far publicly asserted our respective tenets in religion. A solemn responsibility lies upon us both. But I forbear. Excuse the length of this—and believe me, dear Knox, with the best wishes, &c.

V.

TO MR. P—— N——.

May, 4, 1804.

My Dear N——.—The number of letters, along with other business that I have generally on my hands, has made me more dilatory than I could wish in replying to yours. I trust you will find me as ready as you can be, to meet a "quiet and friendly communication" upon the important subjects touched on in it; but I hope you will not think I depart from the spirit of *quietness* and of *love* in opposing you plainly where I think you wrong, nor shrink from the fair and candid discussion of differences as if it were controversy, and as if controversy on these matters were to be deprecated. That, indeed, is one of the principles in which I fear we differ, and in which I fear you are led to the sentiment you embrace, by your being insensible to the importance of divine truth. However that be—as long as you will bear with a faithful declaration and vindication of that truth, I rejoice to embrace any renewed opportunity of communicating with you upon it. But life is too short, and my master's business too urgent, to allow a correspondence on any other terms. You observe that you did believe I long considered you as taught of God. I did long cherish the hope that you were, although that hope was always weakened, by my never having any satisfactory evidence that you had been delivered from some errors, which I knew you had formerly adopted. But I did formerly maintain that hope more firmly of many others, of whom I now see every scriptural reason to think that they are under the power of darkness: because I see that Christ—the Christ whom the Scriptures testify—is a rock of offence to them—that they stumble at the word—and evidence every spirit of hostility against it and its witnesses. Now Christ declares that every one, who hath heard and hath learned of the Father, cometh unto Him—that he that is of God heareth God's words—that his sheep hear his voice and follow Him, and will not follow a stranger. I dare not, therefore, in fidelity to my Lord, pretend to consider those, who deny and oppose the Faith of the Gospel, as the children of God, or as lovers of God. They may love a false God ardently—but the glory of the only true God shines in the face of Jesus Christ: and he has said—"he that hateth me, hateth my Father also." Finding many religious professors of this stamp, whom I formerly did not know to be so, I am forced to change my view of their character—and in doing so and in declaring it—I know not that I transgress the law of love. Love to God demands adherence to the truths which declare his name—let who will be offended by them—love to man demands that I should not flatter any to their undoing. You ask, have my sentiments undergone no change? I am not conscious that my view of the saving truth has undergone any change for many years; except the change, which every believer of it may expect, and which I acknowledge with thankfulness to the Father of Lights—of increasing clearness in the knowledge of it—increasing firmness in the persuasion of it—increasing attachment to it—and increasing blessedness in the enjoyment of it. But, indeed, the question, how long have I known it? is a very unimportant one. As to the modes of expression, they are far from unimportant, as the truth is to be conveyed by *words*, and some are more likely than others to make its meaning understood. And that I have, for some time past, succeeded better in that than formerly is pretty obvious, from the offence and irritation felt by many, who formerly liked what they heard from me. And that many things in Sandeman have contributed to this better furnishing me for my work; and particularly contributed to it, by his plain exposure of the subtle evasions, by which many have corrupted the Gospel—and by his manly testimony against many writers of the greatest name, whose sentiments, though widely diffused through the religious world, were almost entirely unknown to me, till I found them laid open in Sandeman—this I freely and thankfully acknowledge. Except in this, he added nothing to me—for even the scriptural view, which he gives of the meaning of the word *Faith*, (although that—far indeed from unimportant, is yet altogether distinct from the truth believed) was nothing new to me; but what I had learned from Scripture, (Heb. xi. 1.) almost immediately after the publication of my sermon at St. John's. You ask me whether I can now ratify the whole of that sermon, and of my letters on Faith? I have scarcely read either of them, I believe, since they were published, and therefore cannot answer the question particularly: but it would surprise me very much, if two such early productions of my pen, (one of them, indeed, before I had come to manhood) did not contain many injudicious statements, and perhaps some false sentiments; though I believe they both contain, and am sure that one of them contains, all the essence of that truth which I am now so much more offensively, because more clearly witnessing. Nothing, however, from them, or from any thing else that I have ever written, will I allow to have the smallest force against the truth; nor would I turn aside from the declaration and vindication of that truth to discuss the question, whether it is opposed or not in this or that passage, adduced from my former publications, or how far back my knowledge of it may be traced in my writings. Nor can I wonder that, in the earlier productions of my pen, even after I knew the truth, my modes of expression are such as would now leave me doubtful about another whether he knew it. But at any period that I would have rejected the great truth clearly expressed, I am ready to admit that I was an unbeliever dead in sin. My paper is so nearly full, that I can only add, that I shall, as soon as possible, answer the remainder of your letter.

Affectionately yours, &c.

VI.

TO THE REV. MR. M.———

July, 29, 1804.

Rev. Sir,—I shall make no apology for addressing you on the sermon which I heard you deliver this day—it is one of the things which my hand "findeth to do," and which (according to the exhortation of your text) I would therefore "do with my might"—remembering that "there is no work nor device, nor knowledge, nor wisdom in the grave whither I am going." I heartily hope and pray that you may not be offended by the liberty I am about to use. But in a few years at most it will be of little consequence to me whether all the world has been offended at me as a disturber of its peace; while it will be a matter of eternal consequence to me, whether I am found "faithful unto death"—not ashamed to confess the faith of Christ crucified—and therefore to testify against those who deny that faith and corrupt his gospel.—I can truly declare that whatever desire I felt of having an opportunity to preach the gospel of Christ, this morning, in the church of S———, it would have given me tenfold more joy to have heard it faithfully preached by you. But it gave me proportional pain and grief to find that throughout your sermon there not only was not a syllable *like* the Gospel, but that its fundamental principles were directly contradicted—to hear the congregation told that sobriety, honesty, and diligence, in their respective callings, would "*entitle*" them to the favour of God and "*merit*" his rewards,—and this—not even followed by the poor salvo, with which such sentiments are usually accompanied, the complimentary mention of *Christ's merits* and the *Divine mercy*.

Too often have I heard the truths of God opposed from the pulpits of our churches; but seldom indeed have I heard them so unequivocally contradicted as this day.—O! sir, it is a solemn office that you undertake, when you undertake to be the guide of immortal souls; and awfully will the blood of those, who believe what I heard you declare to the people, be required at your hands, unless they and you receive repentance to the acknowledgment of the truth.—It would degrade the authority of those truths which you have contradicted, to refer you to the Articles and other formularies of the *Established Church* in which they are asserted. The truths which you have contradicted are the *Truths of God*. He has declared that "by the deeds of the law no flesh living shall be justified"—that those who are saved are saved by grace through faith, and that not of themselves, "not of works lest any man should boast;" that they are a people "saved by the Lord," and "justified in the Lord," "*his* workmanship created in Christ Jesus *unto* good works indeed, which God hath before ordained that they should walk in them—to the praise of the glory of his grace wherein *he has made them accepted in the beloved*."—But if you will address your congregation as those who may be *entitled* to eternal life by the works of the law, and may *merit* the rewards of God by something *they* can *do*; take heed how you substitute the meagre system of sobriety, honesty, and diligence, which I heard you describe, for the demands of that divine law which enjoins—"thou shalt *love* the Lord thy God with *all* thine heart, and mind and strength; and thou shalt *love* thy Neighbour *as thyself*." If they keep not this law, if they be sinners, take heed how you cherish their hope of escaping the curse that it denounces against every transgression of it, by any thing *they* can *do*. "Christ has redeemed his people, from the curse of the law, being made a curse for them,"—and is, "the end of the law for righteousness, to every one that *believeth*." "He hath received power over all flesh, that *He* should *give* eternal life to as many as the Father hath given him." "Neither is there salvation in any other." He is the only foundation laid in Zion; and is, at the same time, the great Rock of offence, to those who stumble at the word "which reveals him," to those especially who have most of that religion which leads men to "trust *in themselves* that they are righteous." "But whoso shall fall against that stone shall be broken, and on whomsoever it shall fall it shall grind him to powder."

May he have mercy upon you, and upon the poor blinded people to whom you have hitherto been a blind guide! If you yet become a preacher of the faith, which you are now destroying, it will be but one of those miracles of saving grace, of which (blessed be God) there are numerous instances.

Pardon, sir, the plain freedom of my testimony—indeed it is not designed to irritate or offend you; though I am well aware how offensive it is likely to prove, unless it be blessed for your profit. Were I to be another Sunday in S———, I should attend in the

Church for the worship of God, during our sound and scriptural Liturgy: but I should feel myself called on, not to wait longer in it to countenance by my presence, a system of doctrine from the pulpit, which I know must issue in the eternal ruin of those who believe it. —With every earnest wish, that you may be saved yourself, and be made the honoured instrument of declaring the Saviour's name to others,—

I remain—Rev. Sir,

Your faithful humble servant, &c.

VII.

TO MRS. N———.

Nov. 4th, 1804.

Very dear Friend,—I have been slow in answering your kind letter of the 27th ult., and, in fact, have been obliged to run in debt to all my correspondents. For much that I have to say on the subject of the late changes in my views and circumstances, I must refer them all to a printed address, which I have been busy drawing up, and is now at press. I suppose it will be published in about a week. I am to be congratulated, indeed, on the goodness of our dear Lord to me in rectifying my judgment, which was so long beclouded as to the rule by which his people are led to walk. May he graciously discover it to all the little flock, and give them one heart and *one way*, "that *his* glory may be *seen* upon them!" I share in your desire to have the disciples at C——, be they ever so few, gathered into one body, that they may walk together as a Church of Christ, according to the same rule with the Apostolic churches. And I trust this will be increasingly effected wherever there are disciples. But it is most important that, at the commencement of the attempt especially, those who join in it should be of one mind, have a clear view of the object which they propose, and pursue it with scriptural simplicity. If a visit from me may be subservient to this or any other part of the Lord's work among you, gladly will I visit you as soon as any opportunity may offer. For the present, however, my itinerancies must be greatly abridged, by the scantiness of my pecuniary means, and the necessity of staying for the most part in Dublin to earn my bread. I am under a promise also of visiting Scotland, as soon as my engagements at Bethesda shall terminate, which will probably be very shortly. Still I hope to see you before winter is over. I suppose you have heard that ——— has also come out and given up his curacy. I believe he is likely to reside for some time in Dublin to study medicine. Five disciples have united at P——— to walk together as a Church of Christ. They are labouring men, and I think I never saw the power of divine teaching more strikingly than in them. Thus, though ——— is about to be removed from P———, the standard of the cross will remain there. And surely it ought to be, in any place,—not with an individual preacher, but with the body of disciples. And so it will, when the disciples (wherever they are) walk in one body, by one rule (not any rule of man's invention, but those delivered by the apostles to the first churches)—and consequently separate from all who believe not. I pray that you, and all with you, who know the truth, may be kept *standing fast* in one mind and in one spirit, walking in the truth and holding it forth to the world. My love to all who love the Lord in sincerity. I long to speak with you face to face. Remember me to ———. The Lord be gracious to her, and make his name known to her! Then she will not let Mr. Fletcher or Mr. Anybody say a word against his truth. Whenever she knows the only true Gospel, she will not be afraid to adopt Paul's sentiment, Gal. i. 8. 9.

Your truly affectionate, &c.

VIII.

TO THE REV. H——— M———.

——— 1804.

My dear M———,—Your letter affords me great satisfaction, as it shews a readiness to give a fair and serious discussion to a subject which certainly demands it; and indicates a particular readiness to act according to the discovery of our Lord's will upon the subject from his word, whatever may be the issue of our discussion. May this mind be continued and encouraged in us throughout our communications, and then I do not fear but we shall ultimately agree both in judgment and in practice. As far as *I* know the spirit which is given me I can say, that it is not a zeal for proselyting to my own opinions that makes me forward to embrace every opportunity of calmly and patiently discussing it with every one that I consider a fellow disciple. No; I trust it is because I have been led to see our Lord's will plainly marked in his word, and to see also, in some degree, how much his glory is connected with his people's walking according to his will in this particular. But it is only so far as I have reason to think that others follow the same rule, from a discernment of it, and from subjection to its *divine authority*—it is only so far that I would feel any satisfaction in their acting as I have acted. Continue fairly to write all your objections, and to say every thing that you think is to be said against my views. But as we both appeal to the Scripture, and I trust heartily desire to be regulated by that rule, let us pray, and let us expect to be brought in the course of the discussion to a discernment of what the word commands, and to a consequent agreement in mind.

Your first argument for mixed communion.—But here, to prevent mistakes, let me precisely state what I mean by that mixed communion which I hold to be unlawful. I mean outward church fellowship with those who deny any of the essential principles of the Gospel of Christ, or with those who, confessing it with their mouths, manifest the insincerity of their profesed faith by walking after the flesh in any of its lusts (in either of which cases the Scriptures do not warrant my acknowledging them as brethren), or lastly with those whom I can scripturally acknowledge as brethren, but who will not, after admonition and instruction, walk with a church of Christ according to the rule of his word—or, in short, brethren that "walk disorderly." Except in these cases, the existence of mere professors in a church does not constitute its communion mixed in the sense that I hold unlawful. Other cases belong to the searcher of hearts alone.

Your first argument, then, in favour of mixed communion is drawn from our Lord's parable of the tares and the wheat growing together in the same field, and not to be separated till the harvest. You truly observe that this parable is explained by an infallible interpreter; and what does he tell us that the field is? A Christian church? nay —"the field is THE WORLD." And do I plead for the ministers of divine vengeance prematurely destroying the wicked from the earth? Nay—then indeed among those who now appear in that character many would be swept away who shall yet be found children of the kingdom. I believe I need say no more to convince one of your candour that this parable, so often applied to the defence of mixed communion, has nothing to do with the subject. Only let me add, that even if it had not been so decisively interpreted in a different way by our Lord, you might be certain that you mistake its meaning, because on the supposition of your application being just, not only would mixed communion be lawful, but any attempt at separating from a church, the most openly wicked, would be unlawful, and an inspired Apostle would be found expressly commanding a church to violate his Master's command. If our Lord's words, "let both grow together," bear the meaning you have supposed, what should we say of Paul's command—"put away from among yourselves that wicked person?"

Your next argument is borrowed from the visible mixture that confessedly existed in some of the apostolic churches. There were, as you say, in the Corinthian church particularly, very wicked persons. Well, but the question is, does the Apostle countenance your principle that they ought to be retained in the church? Does he not, on the contrary, solemnly and expressly enjoin the church to remove them? to purge out the old leaven that they might be a new lump, and not so much as to eat with any man called a brother who was a fornicator, or covetous, or an idolater, or a railer, or a drunkard, or an extortioner? nor is it the question whether the Corinthian church did fully act up to the apostolic injunction; but whether the apostolic injunction did not bind them to put away from among them all such? When you say that only the incestuous person was cut off from the communion of the rest, I only say that *if so*, and if others remained among them without repenting of their ungodliness, fornication, &c. (of which the Apostle expresses his apprehension) the Corinthian church did not in such cases comply with the apostolic injunction. But will their disobedience excuse ours? I cannot help observing how graciously it was permitted that such evils should have existed in the apostolic churches. Their existence gave occasion to the instructions and rules of discipline which the Apostles addressed to the churches, and of which we would otherwise have been destitute. And shall we quote the facts, that occasioned these instructions, as a reason for thinking that the instructions need not be observed? Or is the plain meaning to be set aside by a deduction from the symbolical language of probably a prophetic passage in the Apocalypse? This is your third argument. If it were necessary to bring such passages to the determination of the question, I would be much more warranted by the analogy of Scripture to infer that the few names in Sardis who had not *defiled their garments*, had come out from the dead church, and were separated, not touching the unclean thing, especially when I find them absolutely commended; while the Churches of Pergamus and Thyatira, otherwise praised, are sharply reproved for *having* IN THEM, and for SUFFERING those who held false doctrine. But in truth, however such obscurer parts of sacred writ may be illustrated from the plainer, we cannot safely proceed *vice versa*; much less can we safely build on them any doctrine opposed to the plainer.

Your fourth argument is taken from the fact, that under the Jewish law mere professors partook of the ordinances of circumcision and the passover. True, for they were all alike Jews, the natural descendants of Abraham; and to all such, by divine appointment, all these ordinances were to be administered; and their right to them was altogether unconnected with their character as persons carnal or spiritual. But what inference can you in your sober judgment draw from this? All Jews, without distinction, partook of Jewish rights, therefore the disciples of Christ may join in Christian ordinances with all men indiscriminately. Will the premises support this inference? Nay, but an opposite inference may be much more scripturally deduced from the Jews. They as a nation were typical of the spiritual seed of Abraham; and as the Jews would not and could not lawfully join in their Jewish rights with those who were not acknowledged by them as Jews, so neither can the true circumcision now join in Christian ordinances with those whom they do not acknowledge as brethren. And here is the thing that marks mixed communion in these ordinances inconsistent with their nature, that those who join together in the participation of them profess in them to have fellowship one with another—profess to be one bread and one body: and can you, dear M., in faithfulness to your Lord, or in faithfulness to the souls of your congregation, make this profession concerning those with whom you join.

In the fifth place you return to Judas. You mistake when you say that I have acknowledged that Judas partook of the supper;

nay, I believe it can be proved from a comparison of the narratives that he did not. But I shewed that, even admitting that he did, it would make nothing for mixed communion, as, although known to the Lord, he was not (upon this supposition) then known to the other disciples. And what is it you urge against this? You refer to Jno. vi. 70. as proving that he was long before pointed out by Christ as a false disciple; whereas our Lord there only declares that there was a traitor among them: but which of them it was, you know they remained uncertain till the sop was given. You refer to Mat. xxvi. 14. 16. to shew that Judas had before this covenanted to betray his master: very true, but was this known to his fellow disciples? How then should they appear so completely ignorant of it afterwards? and lastly you refer to Luke xxii. 21. to shew that our Lord pointed him out as a traitor at the time of the ordinance. But do you not know that *he* was not pointed out as a traitor till he had received the sop, and he then "*went immediately out*;" so that if you allow this, (for one part of your argument,) to have been before the supper, you are forced to give up your argument altogether, and to admit that Judas did not partake of the supper. Ah! indeed you would argue better if you had a better case. You observe it is in itself a very *striking* circumstance that our Lord should have taken Judas into the communion of the Apostles. Truly it is: and, among many other profitable inferences, it strikingly marks that in no church on earth, can the mere circumstance of outward church membership be rested in as ascertaining the character.

As to the Baptism of infants, which you think inconsistent with the Separation I contend for, no scriptural view of infant baptism will be found inconsistent with it. Supposing that in the apostolic churches the infant children of their members were baptized, yet surely neither the Apostles nor elders of those churches employed themselves in baptizing the infants of those who were not members of those churches: nor as the children of their members grew up would the circumstance of their having been baptized in infancy prevent the enforcement of the rules of apostolic discipline against them—if they denied the faith into which they had been baptized, or walked contrary to it. Any view of infant baptism that would tend to this is to be opposed as unscriptural.

You seem to question whether Christian communication be intended in 1 Cor. v. 11. But your idea that perhaps private intimacy and familiarity alone are forbidden with such offenders, while they are to be left in the church, is altogether opposed to the true nature of a Christian church—opposed to that close union as brethren, and sympathy which throughout scripture are represented as subsisting between its members. Now, I readily admit that even private familiarity is forbidden in that place with such persons; but this only marks yet more that excommunication is enjoined; for it is preposterous to say I will join with a man in the closest Christian fellowship, and will not join with him in the common intercourse of life; I will walk with him as a brother in the church—and stand aloof from him in the world, and not hold with him even such intercourse as I am allowed to hold with heathens. But you seem more than once (though reluctantly) to admit that those who are "guilty of *obstinate heresy* or of *gross sin*," ought to be excluded from a Christian church; and you say the Church of England "*admits* the same." Ah! M., how can you put this cheat on yourself? Christ orders a thing to be done in Christian churches: a nominal church admits or allows it to be done. But does she do it? or do you, in connexion with her, do it? or can you, connected with such a body, do it? I know that some clergymen have absurdly attempted in some instances to keep away certain individual offenders from the sacrament, as it is called, as if that ordinance were the only one in a Church, and as if the individuals thus marked out were a whit worse than the great mass of those who were admitted to it. With respect to heresy, how few are there in this country that do not expressly deny, when you come to speak with them, the most fundamental principles of the Christian faith? And with respect to gross sin, I suppose drunkenness and fornication may be reckoned so; and I know there are parts of the North where the communion in the Churches would be thin indeed, if only the known drunkards and fornicators were excluded. You say that an unmixed Church is desirable. I hold it only desirable in the sense which I have already stated, and in which a Church is *commanded* to be unmixed. I believe it would be very undesirable, if it were even practicable, that any Church on earth should be so constituted, that all who belong to it should be known to a certainty to be disciples *indeed*. There is degree of doubtfulness necessarily and profitably attaching itself to the characters of all men on earth. Yet this is not inconsistent with the brotherly confidence that ought to subsist between the members of a Christian church. In this confidence also there will be various degrees, according to the various degrees of evidence that we have of the sincerity of the faith of others. But while a Church walks according to the precept of the word, none will be in it but those whom the Scriptures warrant and command to walk together as brethren. Brotherly jealousy may be excited about many of them; and there we are to admonish, and reprove, and restore, and not let evil surmisings rankle in our minds. O! that you may see the divine glory of a Christian church holding fast the apostolic precepts, exhibiting to the surrounding world the truth of the Gospel and the influence of that truth! It is not in any national church (so called) that you can see this. It must be in a body of disciples, in some one place, that will join together to take the word of Christ for their only rule. The substance of your question about Diotrephes I have already answered; and does not the Apostle more than intimate that when he came, Diotrephes should not remain in that church, in which he usurped such unwarrantable authority. You will say that this is an extravagantly long letter, and I must not increase its length by adding more, than that I am yours in true affection.

IX.

TO MR. W—— T——.

—— 1805.

My Dear T——.—Let me now attempt to reply to your letter, and let me add what I had designed to write before I received your letter. To your too strong expressions of what you supposed you have received from me, I can only reply with an assurance that I never conceived myself as conferring any thing on you; that any kindness I have ever been able to shew has been but the natural expression of that true attachment which I felt, and has been more than repaid by the kindness which you returned. Upon the termination of our mutual intercourse, of which you speak, I must repeat what I have already observed, that it has not been, and shall not be my act; and from my heart I deprecate your taking that step: and consider, dear T., one of the many inconsistencies in which you are involving yourself by following this vague principle of common sense in opposition, I will say, to the word of God. You exclaim at the idea as awful and absurd, that I should think myself called by the word, not to company with one, whom I yet acknowledge as a brother, on account of an error in his judgment concerning scriptural rule; and at the same time you are about to break off all *intercourse* with one whom you acknowledge as a brother, for what you think an error of his judgment, trying it by the principles of common sense. This is only one of the instances in which, what is called common sense, (taken as our rule in place of Scripture) lands us in conclusions and practices the most inconsistent and irrational. Take another instance of it from yourself. You deny that the persons, about whom that precept in Thess. was given, were to be considered as brethren: you say that "admonish him as a brother," means only admonish him with kindness and tenderness—but not as a believing brother—for common sense tells you that an Apostolic church could not be called to withdraw from one whom they acknowledged as such. Well; consider, I beseech you, if so, what is that difference between him and those mentioned in 1 Cor. v. upon which, in your letter, you ground your different interpretation of the same word. The persons in the Cor. call themselves brethren, but shew by their works that they are not. Is not this, according to your position, precisely the character of those mentioned in the Thess. Yet, on the ground of a supposed great difference between the characters mentioned in the two passages, you now rest your opinion that a command expressed about them in precisely the same words is to be interpreted in two different meanings. While I am writing, my soul adores the wisdom of God in his word. It may truly bear the motto, "quocunque jeceris stabit:" and when all the wit of man is employed to overturn any part of it, all the wit of man will be only found foolishness. But let me acknowledge to you, dear T., that I find it very hard to persuade myself, that one, who has that acquaintance, which you have, with the text of the Greek testament, can seriously believe that, when the Apostle said νουθετειτε ως αδελφον, he intended that they should consider that person as an heathen man and a publican, or did not intend to say—consider him as a brother in Christ, and as such admonish him of the rule and order of Christ which he is transgressing. Indeed, if it were necessary, the matter admits of proof the most decisive, not only from the words as a brother, never once used throughout the apostolic writings in the sense which you put upon them, but from the precept, admonish him—or warn him, 1 Thess. v. 14.—never once given to the Churches about those that were not to be considered as believers; and even from the proper force of the expression ατακτοι and ατακτως—borrowed from the array of an army, in which soldiers do not cease to belong to the army, because they do not keep their ranks, or observe the prescribed order of march. But the truth is, that if your course now arose only from an error of judgment, my task would be easy: an explanation of such passages in Scripture, as you mistake the meaning of, might easily be given so conclusive and luminous, that as soon as it was fairly and fully proposed, your assent would follow, and your mistake be rectified. But here is the thing that pains me to the heart—pains and alarms me much more than any mere ignorance or mistake would—that you seem, where Scripture comes in your way, never to think seriously and candidly what its meaning is, but hardily to jump through it, assigning to it the first meaning that occurs to you as most for the purpose of your argument, however obviously preposterous and unwarranted the interpretation is. In the same way alone can I account for some of your assertions; as for your asserting it to be fully as probable that the Apostles actually held an open communion, as that they did not: nor in saying this do I mean to attribute to you intentional want of veracity: for I know something of the self-deceiving powers of the human heart; so that when we have prejudged a question, unwilling to have our opinion shaken, we rashly impose upon ourselves the belief of any thing which appears necessary to maintain that opinion; and avoid looking at the sentiments we express fairly in the face, because that alone would be sufficient to convince us of their absurdity or falsehood.

Thus we cheat ourselves sometimes, rather than intend to cheat others. This, however, is a state of mind very dangerous indeed: and when you consider the characters that we acknowledge as belonging to the human heart, can you be displeased with me, dear T., for intimating that either you or I am capable of falling into this state of mind, and for solemnly warning you of its awfulness, when I see so much reason to apprehend that you have fallen into it. Wherever you see, or think you see, occasion, discharge to me the same brotherly office of free and faithful admonition. If there should not be the occasion for it which you may imagine there is, I shall not be sore, nor think myself injured: if the admonition should be really needed, I trust it will be profitable: and now let me beseech you to consider the grounds on which you resolve to break off all personal intercourse with me. I have already called your attention to its inconsistency with the principles on which you object to my conduct. But examine the motive that influences you, examine how far pride operates in it, opposing natural spirit to the course of brotherly dealing, which you see I think myself called to hold towards you: examine also, dear T., how far a wish to avoid any discussion of a subject, which you would rather put to sleep, influences you. I confess the ground, that I seemed to gain in our last conversation, makes me peculiarly unwilling to drop the subject with you. Look to it, I beseech you, whether the same thing does not make you somewhat desirous that it should be dropped, and glad to avail yourself of a reason for declining interviews. I understand that you have since retracted one sentiment to which I seemed to have brought you—that you are bound not to continue to admit to the supper, persons who continue notoriously ungodly in their walk. I do not complain at all of your retracting this concession: it has been one part of our mutual agreement that you should have full liberty to retreat: nor am I at all doubtful of bringing you back to the same concession in continued communications on the subject. For I know that it can be *proved* to the conviction of any man of intelligence, that the Apostles did not, and could not, consistently with their principles, hold any open communion to which such characters were admitted. From persons of that class, I would proceed to the consideration of heretics, and by similar steps establish, incontrovertibly, against your opinion of their holding an open communion, that even admitting for a moment that heretics, who had been rejected by the apostolic church, were received for a few turns to the Apostle's open communion (on the ground of a supposed profession of the truth made in offering themselves to it) yet, continuing avowedly and notoriously heretical in their opinions, they would not, and could not, be admitted longer to that open communion. From them I would proceed, in like manner, to another class, those from whom the apostolic Churches withdrew, as walking disorderly; and would prove that they, continuing so to walk, would not, and could not, continue to be admitted to this same open communion of the Apostles. I would then prove the same thing of avowed heathens, continuing avowed heathens: and then shew, demonstrably, that the Apostles did not receive any to their open communion, but those with whom they joined in the communion of the Apostolic Church, that is, that they did not, and cannot, be supposed to have had any such open communion, as you think it not unlikely that they held: and that the supposition of their having held any such, under whatever regulations and restrictions you might chuse to introduce, cannot be maintained, but by maintaining that they violated their own most solemn injunctions to the churches, and taught the churches to violate the very precepts which they gave. I give you these outlines of the argument, which I mean to employ against your most extraordinary opinions; that you may throughout see the conclusion at which I drive: and I am not afraid of your being able to oppose my progress to that conclusion with any success. The denial of any of the steps, will only bring us back to some still plainer principle, with which that step is connected: so that feeling that my chain of posts is impregnable, I trust you will not find me impatient or uneasy at your assailing each of them with all your strength. The opinion which you advanced, and which has led me to this train of argument—(that it is not improbable that the Apostles actually did hold an open communion, nay, fully as probable as that they did not) is indeed a most extraordinary opinion, inconsistent with every scriptural view on the state of Christianity, and the course in which Christians walked in the apostolic days. But most extraordinary as the sentiment is, looking at it attentively, I perceive that it is necessarily involved in the vindication of the course you pursue. For if that sentiment must be given up; if it can be demonstrated, not only that the Apostles did no such thing, but that they could not be supposed to have done any such thing, consistently with the principles sanctioned by their own writings; then it will immediately follow that no such thing can be done now, without violating the same principles; and that on which you have formerly rested the vindication of it, that some other believers join with you in doing this thing, I am equally confident can be proved to be but an accumulation of evil. And now, dear T., I invite, I beseech you, to continue with me as a brother the personal discussion of this subject. You will say perhaps that I have expressed myself over confidently: but I feel that the strength of the ground on which I stand warrants this confidence: and I would undertake, with the help of God, to bring to the same conclusion any man of intelligence who, acknowledging the authority of scripture, would have patience to attend to the argument, let him oppose my progress with ever so much ability, and be ever so ignorant of the Gospel itself. Such a man might not know the nature of Christianity, nor the grounds of the Apostolic precepts to the christians of their time: yet I could prove to him the matter of fact, that the christians were commanded to walk in a way opposed to that which you suppose, and that the Apostles did no such thing as you think it likely they did. O! that without further fighting against the light you may yield to it, and spurn with holy indignation all those human traditions by which the word of God has been made of no effect. Bear with my plainness, and believe me, with the most affectionate solicitude, Ever yours, &c.

X.

TO B—— M——

January, 1805.

To B. M., the undersigned members of the Church of Christ, in Dublin, with which he is connected, wish grace and peace to be multiplied.

Beloved Brother.—When we associated together as a Church of Christ, we professed to be united each to the other by one great bond—our fellowship in the Gospel—our common participation of the same precious faith, and our consequent union in our one Lord. We also professed to aim at his word alone, as the rule by which we should be regulated in walking together as his disciples—and while we have to thank the Father of lights, and the God of all grace, for having thus put into our hearts to attempt what we are encouragingly persuaded is agreeable to his will, we have to thank him also for every increased discovery of the rule of his word, which he has afforded to any of us since the commencement of our attempt; and we desire to be kept waiting on him still for continued information from the scriptures, how we ought to walk and to please God in all things, that we may be filled with the knowledge of his will, and abound more and more to the praise of the glory of his grace.

In these sentiments we have confidence that we meet with your concurrence, brother; and that you will not charge us (as some have done) with departing from the true principles of our original union, because we avow that we have been led to discover certain great evils in which some of us too long ignorantly indulged, and certain important precepts of the word, which some of us too long treated with inattention and neglect. We allude particularly to that religious connection which we continued to maintain with individuals and sects, from whom we are now convinced the word calls us to be completely separated; such as the connection is, which you still hold with the religious Establishment of this country.

Suffer, beloved brother, the word of admonition which we would address to you, with an humbling recollection how long some of us walked in the same course, against which we now desire to testify, and with earnest solicitude that He, who has mercifully discovered the evil of it to us, may vouchsafe to own the attempt which we make in his name to point out its evil to you. And allow us to observe that the lateness with which any have been given to see a precept of the word, is no reason why they should not obey it as promptly, and urge it upon their Brethren as strongly, as if they had themselves seen it ever so long. We would urge no authority but the authority of God in his word, and that is not loosened by our tardiness to discern what he commands.

And now, brother, we would call your attention to a principle which we are persuaded you will acknowledge, that our Lord's kingdom is not of this world, and that every religious Establishment is.— The two things therefore are perfectly opposed in their nature: and the attempt to intermingle them, by any of the children of his kingdom standing in connexion with the purest religious Establishment that can be conceived, is an attempt to obscure and confound one of the essential characters of the kingdom of Christ, which it is one great object of a Christian Church to exhibit to the view of the world.

The kingdoms of the earth have long been enacting systems and laws of religion under the name of Christianity in their respective countries, according to their respective interests or fancies. They have been making Gods for their several nations, and putting them into their places by acts of parliament, and enacting the rites and ordinances by which they shall be served, and giving to these Gods and to their services of worship scriptural names; by which subtle snare of the father of lies even Christ's disciples have been long ensnared into an acknowledgment of those men-made Gods: while such of them as have been dressed up in a form most like to the God of the scriptures, are in this circumstance essentially distinguished from the Lord our God, in that their kingdom is of this world, that they are established in their respective countries by earthly Kings, and worshipped and served according to rites instituted by men.

That some of the ordinances of Christ's house (his Church) have been introduced into their service, disfigured and transformed into the ritual of their worship, this only marks the mystery of iniquity with more awful colours, and shews every established Church to be a descendant of that Babylon the Great, which is full of names of blasphemy, and is the mother of Harlots. We are confident indeed that whoever enters into the inspired description of Babylon as Her with whom "the Kings of the earth *have committed fornication*," will see the same feature in every one, even of the reformed Churches, as by law established; and if they be not the harlots of which she is the mother, what other bodies can answer to the title? Or was it without meaning that she is called in scripture, not only the great whore herself, but also "the mother of harlots."

But it may perhaps bring the matter in a plainer form to your conscience to observe, that while you are connected with the religious establishment of this country, you are living in the commission of acts positively prohibited by the word of God. There are no precepts more explicit in the apostolic traditions, than those which call the members of Christian churches to an outward separation, as to religious fellowship, from ungodly walkers, who call themselves brethren, from heretics, and even from real brethren who obey not the apostolic precepts, and walk not according to the apostolic rule. Even from the latter we are commanded to withdraw ourselves, that they may be ashamed, and this while we continue to admonish them as brethren. Now it needs no proof, that while you continue in the communion of the establishment, you are outwardly joining in the ordinances of Christ's worship with persons of all these classes; and that every open communion (as it is called) is professedly founded on a principle in direct contradiction to all those apostolic precepts.

We urge it again upon your attention, brother, that the first Christians were called not merely to a verbal testimony against such characters as we have enumerated, but to an outward separation from them as to religious fellowship. This you will acknowledge they were bound to in their respective churches: and can you believe they were left at liberty to engage with them in the same religious acts out of their church, in which they could not lawfully engage with them in their church?

Consider also the end for which they were called to put away such persons from among them, or to withdraw themselves from such persons. Was it not to bear a continued visible testimony to them, and to the world, for those principles of Christian truth or Christian practice which such men opposed?

Imagine to yourself, that at Corinth, for instance, a number of "fornicators, covetous persons, idolaters, railers, drunkards, and extortioners," were put away from the apostolic church according to the apostolic injunction; and yet, not choosing to lay aside the name of Christians, they should institute an open communion, in which they and disorderly walkers, and heretics, and persons who had been rejected by the apostolic church, or had never chosen to walk with it, should join promiscuously in the form of Christian ordinances: imagine to yourself this; and say, would the disciples, addressed in the apostolic epistles, be left at liberty to hold outward fellowship in this church, with those with whom they were debarred from holding outward fellowship in the "apostolic church?" No, surely: and yet in this you have a picture of the congregations connected with every religious establishment, which, so far from being sanctified by the presence and participation of ever so many real disciples, exhibit, on that account, the more awful appearance to an enlightened judgment.

When a Christian church is what it ought to be, it is a body which holds forth to the observation of the world the truth of the Gospel, and the conversation that becometh the Gospel. It is a body that stands unconnected with, and separate from, all other religious societies different from itself, and thus exhibits that separation from the world, which results from the belief of the truth—from being one in Christ Jesus. It is a body that walks by the same rule—the rule of his word—and thus manifests obedience to its precepts, as well as the reception of its doctrines. They both rest upon the same authority: and a Christian church is no more warranted to dispense with the one than the other—no more warranted to walk with those who transgress the precepts, than with those who deny the doctrines of the word of God. Nor is it possible that a church of Christ can, in its collective capacity, hold forth to the world any precept of the word, which some of its members are allowed to violate and reject, and yet continue in connection with that church. It behoves us, indeed, to look well to it, that, in every instance of preceptive rule which we propose, we have the decided authority of a scriptural command. But, wherever we see that authority, it is no longer optional whether we shall obey that command, and no more is it optional whether we shall walk with those who continue to disobey it, after means have been employed for laying it before them.

O, Brother! let us have joy in you, by your acknowledgment of the authority of God in this matter, rather than the authority of men of ever so great name. Let our bowels be refreshed, by finding you perfectly joined with us in one mind, and in one judgment; taking shame with us for an evil in which we so long have walked, but the malignity of which no length of usage can lessen, and from every appearance of which we henceforth desire to abstain. Viewing the subject, as we do, decided by the word of God, we dare not continue to stand in church connection with those who continue to walk contrary to this rule; and have to mourn over one who, on this account, has lately separated from us. We would still follow him with our prayers, and we pray that our solicitude about you, beloved brother, may be speedily exchanged for thankfulness and praise.

We wait in anxious expectation of a letter, that shall inform us of your mind, and commending this, our testimony, to the blessing of Him, who can clothe it with conviction to your conscience, we subscribe ourselves your affectionate brethren, in the gospel of the Lord Jesus Christ.

XI.

TO MRS. S——.

—— 1805.

VERY DEAR MADAM,—I believe I need not assure you of the deep concern with which I have heard of your withdrawing from our body and of the sentiments in which that step originates. Of the grief that we feel I shall say nothing, for my object is not by any means to work on your feelings, or overpersuade you (if I even could) to continue in outward union with a church with which you are not agreed. The only outward union that is worth any thing, is that which springs "from being perfectly joined together in the same mind and in the same judgment;" and it now appears that we have not been so, even while I thought we were; and wherever there is that diversity of sentiment, and the means of scriptural communication fail to remove it, I would much rather it should be avowed, though our numbers were to be lessened ever so much, than that it should remain latent. Still I cannot but feel an affectionate solicitude and earnest desire—yea, a sanguine hope also—that it may please our gracious Lord to restore you to our fellowship, by removing from your mind what I am convinced is a sentiment contrary to that word which alone can instruct us how we ought to walk and to please God. Suffer me, then, to call your attention to the subject as plainly and fully as the compass of a letter will admit. And, first, is there not that inconsistency in your conduct on the face of it, which should lead you to suspect that the principle which governs it is erroneous. You professedly shrink from the idea of withdrawing from Christian fellowship with those whom you consider as Christians; yet you withdraw from fellowship with a body that you consider as a church of Christ, and that you think conduct their Christian fellowship scripturally (except as far as relates to the principle we are now discussing), and this in order to maintain fellowship—with whom? with persons who, according to your own judgment—(I believe I may say so)—are walking in the habitual violation of some of the plainest rules of Scripture? Is not this strangely inconsistent? For illustration sake, I will suppose C—— or T——, and I will suppose them to be disciples indeed, though I confess the opposition they make to the plainest statements of the word, speaks little for the sincerity of their faith. But leaving that—I believe you are convinced that they are not walking in the footsteps of the apostolic Christians, or according to the precepts delivered by the apostles to the first churches of the saints: and I believe you acknowledge that both the recorded example of these churches (in which all things were regulated by the inspired and divinely-commissioned servants of the Lord Jesus), and the precepts given to them are at this day a rule of as binding authority as it was at first. By that rule, I believe you are sensible they do not walk, and we do walk, as far as it has been discovered to us. Yet you prefer fellowship with them to fellowship with us. But you will say, perhaps, you would rather hold fellowship with both, if we would agree to that. Yes—if we would surrender a *little* of the Scripture rule to the disobedience of professors, many would be content to walk with us. But do you seriously think we ought to turn out of that course which the word of God points out to us, in order to walk with these professors, who do not like that course? No, you will say; *in our church* we are right in adhering to the path marked for us in Scripture, and leaving them to come to us, but not going out of it to them. But private and occasional fellowship it is bigotted to withhold from them—and especially from those whom we regard as believers of the Gospel. Now, let me observe, we have no such certainty that they are believers of the Gospel, as we have that they are disobeying its precepts: and there was a time (but, to be sure, many ages ago) when the idea was quite strange of a person's receiving the truths that the Apostles declared from God, and at the same time rejecting the precepts which the same Apostles declared from the same God: there was a time when the doctrines they preached, and the precepts they delivered, were regarded as of the same divine authority. But leaving this for the present, if it be allowable to join with these persons occasionally in some exercises of Christian fellowship, what is there so different in any other exercises of Christian fellowship, that can make it unlawful for us to join with them statedly in all—to walk with them in our Church? And would you indeed think this allowable? But you will say—they are believers, and though mistaken in some particulars, yet they think themselves right. Be it so. Does this make them right, or lessen the evil of their error? If so, I know not what Turk or Socinian is wrong, as they also think themselves right

—and the argument will equally vindicate fellowship with them. In fact, the argument—current and plausible as it is—strikes at the basis of the authority and importance of all scriptural faith and practice. 'But we are not to judge our brethren.' Is this, then, what the word means, when it forbids us to judge one another? Does it mean, that we should hold the truths and precepts of the word so sceptically, so loosely, as not to venture to pronounce what is contrary to them, or not to testify against the evil? Nay—"Wo unto them that call evil good, or good evil." The believer discerning any principle of Scripture must discern the evil of all that contradicts it—and is called to maintain that principle against the whole world. 'But it is hard to refuse to worship with those whom we must love as brethren.' Nay, love itself commands us not to countenance their sin or encourage them in it, but to testify against it by withdrawing from them, and holding no fellowship with them, "*that they may be ashamed.*" 'But that precept in Thessalonians related only to those who led an idle life, working not at all.' I readily grant, that it was this instance of disobedience to the apostolic precepts which was the immediate occasion of Paul's giving that command to the Thessalonian church. But is not the command itself as general as words can make it—"that ye withdraw yourselves from every brother that walketh disorderly, and have no fellowship with him?" And lest we should be at any loss to know whom he means by walking disorderly, does he not himself immediately subjoin an explanation as general and express—namely, walking not after the tradition received of us—or precepts delivered to them by us: now, unless any one will say that the only precept delivered to the churches was that of labouring for their support; disorderly walking never can be confined to the solitary instance of an idle life, nor any more can the rule given to the Christian church for the treatment of disorderly brethren. Indeed, the objection that I am answering bears all the marks of an endeavour to get over a plain scriptural command, from indisposition to observe it: and once it comes to that point with any professor, I think the argument ought to be dropped, and a simple testimony left with him against his sin. But I have heard it said, that however right it may be to walk by apostolic rule, it cannot be so very important as the belief of the apostolic gospel, since it is freely acknowledged that disciples themselves have long lived and died in ignorance of that rule, and inattention to it, and yet have been saved; and I know few arguments that carry so much of the evidence of the carnal mind, as that argument. In the first place, when a professor talks of any command of God (for such are the commands of the Apostles) as unimportant, he plainly strikes at the whole authority of the word, and openly shakes off the fear of God, however he may talk of believing his word. Whatever ignorance of many things which the word contains has long covered the minds of disciples, yet their common character has been that they tremble at the word; and whatever they see declared or commanded in it, they would shudder at the thought of refusing it credence or obedience, of treating it as of small significance. The man who continues to talk or act contrary to this mind (whatever be his profession of the gospel) I am bound to consider as a carnal man, that needs more to be called to repentance than to be discoursed with on the scriptural rules of a Christian church. But in the next place, his argument manifests a mind as destitute of the love as of the fear of God. For what does he say? I may get to heaven without complying with such or such a divine precept, for others have got there who ignorantly walked contrary to it. I would only say to such a man, that unless God mercifully give him another mind, he will find himself awfully mistaken; that no one ever got to heaven who continued to the end in the mind expressed by his language. The believer desires to be filled with the knowledge of his Lord's will, that he may please and glorify him whom he loves in sincerity. This letter is already too long. I shall therefore only add, that I dare say you will be assailed with that argument also which C—— so strenuously put forward when in town—that those who profess to take all the Scriptures, and nothing else, for their rule, are yet disagreed upon some precepts—that there is therefore no certainty in tne matter, and we had better give up the attempt than involve ourselves in such doubtful and such novel inquiries. The argument comes with a very bad grace from a zealous protestant clergyman. Just so clamoured the papists at the time of the Reformation, urging against Protestants the doubtfulness of Scripture and the novelty of their religion. The only difference between the Papists and their successors now is, that the former referred to a guide which they said was infallible, in place of the word of God; but the latter, while they would equally take from us this guide, are, I believe, not yet willing to acknowledge the other; but would rather represent that Christ has left his house without any rule for its conduct, and that his disciples may walk according to their several fancies. The Lord extricate you and your dear children from the sleight and cunning craftiness of men who lie in wait to deceive! The Lord give us mutual joy in restoring you and them to our fellowship in one heart and one way! Excuse, dear madam, the plainness with which I have addressed you, and believe me, however much grieved, your still very affectionate,

---

XII.

TO MR. O'B———.

——— 1806.

My Dear O'B.,—I have just received your letter, and though my mind and body are both weary, yet I must try to write a few lines. I had intended it before, and upon this subject, for I deeply regretted that we were prevented from discussing it personally when you were in Dublin. My heart has long and often sunk within me and sickened at the prospect of those rending consequences which you foresee yourself from the want of agreement here. Nothing could support me under it but the consideration that the government is upon his shoulders who has loved his church and given himself for it—with some view and experience of that unspeakably precious invitation and promise, "cast thy burthen on Jehovah, and he will sustain thee." O let us strive together in prayer that he will do what he certainly can do, but he alone—that he will prevent those awful consequences by joining us perfectly in one mind and in one judgment, on this and every other part of his revealed will. Need I paint the stumbling of weak but dear brethren—the glorying of adversaries, &c.? Indeed, I sometimes think that the horror with which I have looked at the prospect, has made me unwarrantably timid in bringing the subject forward in the Church here.—Yet I have rejoiced in seeing what I am persuaded is the scriptural view of it gaining ground among us, and now know not any but D—— B—— who resists it. But I am wandering from the point. Consider then, dear O'B., that I by no means think of treating any young or old as *believers* who do not confess the truth: but if you and L—— have indeed instructed little A—— in the simple principles of that truth from the first opening dawn of his understanding, does he not confes, does he not acknowledge it? And why should you set aside that simple acknowledgment, because he is a mere child? Why should you not consider him a disciple or *learner* (as the word really imports) in the school of Christ, exactly on the same grounds on which the Apostles received any who acknowledged the truth of their testimony? Why should you, by presuming that he does not believe what he acknowledges to be true, make him an object of the most awful part of the discipline of Christ's house, to be employed against those who manifest reigning resistance to its master's doctrine or will? Why should you hesitate to employ with him the admonition of the Lord in the full sense of the word, *putting him in mind* of that doctrine of the Lord which he acknowledges, and from it deriving your warnings and your reproofs, with no other difference between him and the most adult disciple (or most grown child) but that which necessarily arises from his tender years? You think the form of expression in Eph. vi. 4. analogous to that in iv. 24. (By the bye, in the latter I conceive the literal rendering should be retained, holiness of the truth—i. e. the holiness produced by the truth in those *who are sanctified by it*. John xvii.) But allow it, and accordingly let us substitute for the admoni.ion of the Lord or of Christ—the terms *Christian admonition*, and consider whether it is not a most strained interpretation of the precept to say, that bringing up our children in Christian admonition means only that we should act in the spirit or manner of Christians while we admonished them.—But it may be said, that if you had instructed A—— diligently in the Koran instead of in the Gospel, he would now be a professed Mahomedan. I freely grant it; I freely grant, that children would acknowledge the truth of any facts or doctrines that their parents take pains to instil into them from the earliest age. But this is only saying that the Lord has not given us a precept impossible to be observed, but has so constituted our nature that a christian parent discharging his duty towards his offspring will find in them that acknowledgment of the doctrine of the Lord, which is the necessary ground of bringing them up in the admonition of the Lord. Nor does this view really trench at all upon the principles, that all are by nature children of wrath, and that Christians are the workmanship of God.—Every principle and tendency in A——'s nature (whether he acknowledges the truth or not) is opposed to that divine truth which I have supposed him to acknowledge, and if he really believe it, it is God that has given the increase to that seed which he employed men to sow. But that seed is *his word*, and we need not think it so strange that he should give it an increase where he has commanded it to be sown. Some appear to think that we cannot be children of wrath by nature, unless we grow up in a state of unbelief which we can afterwards recollect, so as to remember the time of our conversion. But, in fact, he that is declared to have been filled with the Holy Ghost from his mother's womb, was as much a child of wrath by nature as any who have persisted in their sins. And he must know little of himself who can find no evidence of the diabolical character of his flesh but by a retrospect to his unconverted state. As to difference between the children of believers and unbelievers, there is none, except that most important one, which the providence of God has made in their outward circumstances, and what springs from that. If the child of an heathen were transferred to my absolute care from its infancy, I conceive that I would be called on to bring it up as if it were my own. But we cannot wonder that the scriptures do not extend the precept to a case of such rare occurrence. If it be asked, why I would not have A—— taken into the fellowship of the church, I answer simply, because he is not of an age to join with *intelligence* in all the acts of the church. I can easily conceive a child of four years old believing that Christ Jesus came into the world to save sinners—that truth dwelling in him, and expanding with a progressive discovery of its glorious import and bearings, and bringing forth fruit in opposition to the flesh, and opposed by it: but to bring that child of four years old into the fellowship of the church, would be but to make a puppet of it, by calling it to concur outwardly in various acts, with the grounds of which it cannot be conceived acquainted, and indeed in various exercises with which its attention cannot be conceived adequate to keep pace. It must grow up under the parental admonition of the Lord, before it passes (if I may so speak) into the high school. Yet previous to this period it may manifest reigning resistance to the word of Christ, and so be to be dealt with according to the import of the precept in Deut. xxi. 18—21. I am well aware it may—for the human heart is capable of the earliest and the greatest wickedness: but I believe it a rare case where the parental duty is faithfully discharged. * * * * * * When you next write give me more explicit instructions about the paper.—Do you think, with the Baptists, that the *holiness* of the believer's children means only their legitimacy? do you think the first Christians found themselves released from the obligation of that treatment of their children which God had enjoined on them in the scriptures of the Old Testament, or indeed bound to treat them in a way directly contrary? What are B.'s sentiments? My heart is sick. But we have a gracious and mighty Lord, who shall keep us dwelling together in unity. Let us agree to implore this of Him.

XIII.

FROM THE CHURCH IN D—— TO THE CHURCH IN C——.

Nov. 1807.

Dear Brethren,—We received your letter, and had before heard with deep concern of the melancholy division which took place at C————,—we see in it much cause of mourning and of humiliation before the Lord—but would unite in prayer to him, with hope that he, who maketh men to be of one mind in a house—may graciously interfere to remove the stumbling-block which has been thrown in the way of weak brethren, and the occasion which has been afforded his adversaries to blaspheme. Our answer to your letter has been delayed, by our waiting to give the subject that close and serious discussion which its importance claims.

We shall not advert to the mistake concerning our principles under which you wrote, as we understand that mistake has been already removed; and that you are aware that we do not consider children as composing any part of the church, unless they have been proposed and received in the same manner as adults.

When parents are enjoined to bring up their children in the nurture (or instruction) and in the admonition of the Lord, we can be at no loss what we are to understand by the instruction of the Lord; and is it not as evident, that the admonition marks the kind of admonition the parents are to employ? Admonition derived from that doctrine of the Lord, in which they are instructing them.

We are well aware, at the same time, that this (as every other precept) must be used lawfully; and that, while parents are to instruct their children in the things of God, they are not to forget that it is written again, "That the natural man receiveth not the things of the spirit; neither can he know them, because they are spiritually discerned;" that it is written in the prophets, "And they shall be all taught of God," and that as many as believe on His name, are born not of blood, nor of the will of the flesh, nor of the will of man, but of God.—And in respect of that part of the precept, which relates to that admonition of the Lord—when we consider what other scriptures say of admonishing *one another* (addressed to the called of Jesus Christ, to saints and faithful brethren,) do not suppose that we hold, that the admonition of the Lord can be lawfully used to any child who does not acknowledge the truth.

But we find our view of the precept confirmed and illustrated by the repeated and solemn injunction on the same subject, given to the Israel of God, in the Scriptures of the Old Testament—we find it also harmonizing with the nature of the Gospel itself, that *binds* us to regard with hope, as heirs of salvation, all, whether children or adults, who acknowledge its truth, as long as that acknowledgment of it continues, and unless it is contradicted by avowed sentiments or conduct, inconsistent with the belief of the truth: this hope is not incompatible either with that general uncertainty which arises from inability to search the heart, or in some cases, with anxious solicitude, and jealous apprehension;—but if we refuse to cherish that hope, in the circumstances which we have stated, we conceive that we would refuse to give that honour to the truth of God, which he has put upon it.

We entreat you also, brethren, to consider, whether your refusal to treat as disciples of Christ your youngest children, whom you are instructing in the Gospel, and who acknowledge its truth, does not arise from some view of that glorious Gospel, contrary to its simplicity, or from some view of yourselves, contrary to that perfect equality in which you stand with the youngest child, with respect to the blessings of the kingdom of God. May we all be kept in memory of that maxim of his kingdom, that it is composed of such as little children, as utterly unable to advance themselves into it, and keep themselves in it, by any wisdom or power of their own; and that, except we receive his kingdom as little children, we shall not enter therein.

And now, brethren, suffer us to beseech you, by the mercies of God, to consider these things, and to receive as a proof of our affectionate concern this admonition, which we would offer you in meekness and fear, and to unite with us in imploring the Father of mercies that he may repair the breach which has been made, and join us together perfectly in one mind, and in one judgment, filling us all with the knowledge of his will, and giving us one heart and one way, for his glory and our good.—We send this to you by two brethren, whose personal intercourse with you we pray the Lord to bless.

Signed, in the name of the Church meeting in S——— S——.

XIV.

TO THE EDITOR OF THE CHRISTIAN ADVOCATE.

——— 1809.

Sir,—A few days ago, a friend put into my hand the 9th No. of your work for September, 1809, and directed my attention to the article in which you review Mr. Jackson's Pamphlet, and animadvert on a passage extracted from my Essay on the Apostolic Traditions, &c. It is far from my intention to reply to the personalities with which that article abounds. But it contains one misrepresentation of my sentiments so gross, another falsification of fact so extraordinary, and a challenge so confident, that I am led to address a few lines to you on each of these topics: and expect you will give them a place in your publication.

1. You quote the following sentence from my Essay: "They know not," &c. Vol. 1. p. 243, 244.; you then immediately introduce Mr. S. as indignantly replying—"has the King of Zion instituted an office in his kingdom—which that body can and ought to do very well without?—how dare any treat with lightness and disesteem the order of Christ's house," &c. In this, sir, you represent me as holding that a Christian church can and ought to *do very well without Elders*; whereas my assertion is, that before they have Elders, they can and ought to do without Elders, every thing which they are bound to do, after they receive that very important gift. The grossness of the misrepresentation is ill concealed by the trick of substituting the words, "*doing very well without Elders*," for—doing certain things, without having Elders. To you, sir, who are so nice a judge of language, I need scarcely observe, that *to do very well without a thing*, imports the uselessness or unimportance of the thing. Now, in the essay from which you have quoted that sentence, and in the paragraph immediately preceding—I find I have thus expressed myself—"A church destitute of Elders is lacking, &c."—(vol. 1. p. 243.) This, sir, is not the language of one "who dares to treat with lightness and disesteem" that part of the order of Christ's house.

2. After some of your observations on my *education*, &c., you add, —"*Hence the incessant changes which mark his conduct and writings.*" Here, sir, you state or intimate a fact which I would be far from controverting, were it true; but it is not. Great indeed is the change produced in any sinner, when he receives (what you call) "some glimmerings of the gospel ground of hope." And truly, compared with the intrinsic glory of that gospel, I know not how any believer can intimate that *he* has more than a glimmering view of it. But waving this:—It is now above five years, since I was mercifully convinced of the unlawfulness of my connection with the establishment; and this produced of course a great change in my conduct and writings: but since that period, I am not conscious of any change in either, though you speak of the changes in both as incessant. My

writings on scriptural subjects since have been, An Address to Believers, &c., An Essay on the Apostolic Traditions, Thoughts on Baptism, and Observations on a Reply to that piece; along with two short Tracts on the subject of the gospel, designed for indiscriminate circulation. I enumerate them, that you may search them all, if you think you can substantiate your assertion.

3. You close your philippic against me with the following words. "We call upon Mr. W. either to prove the thing he affirms, or to retract such daring assertions." I am not at all disposed to retract any of the assertions in that passage so offensive to you; nor would I think myself at all called on to take up the gauntlet you have thrown down, but that you thus afford me a fair opportunity of conveying an antidote, which may benefit some of your readers, through the same vehicle which conveyed the poison.

I proceed, then, sir, to prove the thing which I asserted, that churches, while yet without Elders, may and ought to partake of the Lord's Supper, and observe every other ordinance of his house, which they are bound to observe when they have Elders. You happen to have facilitated and shortened the proof for me, by strongly asserting the two principles, from which the conclusion inevitably follows. That there were apostolic churches without Elders, you not only acknowledge, but assert, is "a point that no one ever doubted." Again, in supposed opposition to the idea that two or three disciples may be a church of the living God, you assert what is indeed true beyond controversy, that "It is essential to the idea of a New Testament church that it consist of *an assembly* of believers, called to the knowledge of the truth, and meeting together in one place, for the worship of the true God. In their worship they must be competent to attend to the institutions of the Gospel; and they must be competent to go through the rules of discipline, which the Lord has instituted in his kingdom." Now, sir, if it be indubitable that there were apostolic churches without Elders, and if it be a conceded principle between us that it is *essential to the idea of a New Testament church* to be competent to attend to the institutions of the gospel,—then churches without Elders are competent to attend to the institutions of the gospel,—to all these institutions—and, among them, to the Lord's Supper. This inference is so necessary and evident, that you must either admit it, or retract one or other of the premises asserted by yourself. Your having happened to assert them, though for a very different purpose, has saved me the trouble of saying a word here to establish them. But, whether you assert or deny them, they are put beyond dispute by the word of God. One or two more brief remarks, and I have done. You mention a principle opposed by Mr. J., and mention it in a way, that shews you mean to support or countenance the principle—namely, that *a church cannot scripturally be organized by* PRIVATE *Christians*. I will make the most favourable supposition, that *private Christians* are opposed—not to the clergy—but to the Elders or office-bearers of a scriptural church. Now, if the principle, even thus explained, were just, there could be no such thing as scripturally organized churches, from the period when such churches first ceased to exist, to the end of the world.

The principle would, in fact, involve all the same wicked nonsense, as the pretended hereditary succession of the Roman pontiffs from the apostle Peter. A question occurs, which I dare say you, sir, can answer. Who originated the churches in connection with Mr. Glass? Did he carry with him into them some character superior to that of a private Christian? Let me here observe, that I introduce his name but for the sake of illustration, and would never wish to name him, or Mr. Sandeman, but with respect and affection for their memories for the truth's sake; while I must be excused, for not considering them as having come to the *ne plus ultra* of scriptural truth or practice.

You ask Mr. J., and me, what those things were, which the churches without elders wanted, if the Lord's Supper was not one of them? I answer your question in a word—Elders. But the whole of your argument upon this head proceeds upon the implied principle, that the great use of Elders in a church of Christ, is—to administer the Lord's Supper. Any who think so, know not—pardon me for repeating language that displeases you so much—their real use and importance: and it signifies little whether they call their Elders clergymen or not. The thing is evidently the same.

The highest churchman indeed could scarcely go further, than making such an application of the 16th chapter of Numbers, as you have made, for the purpose of proving that a church without Elders is "disqualified" for observing the Lord's Supper. I remember one who, at the time, held what you call, "that proud and elevated station of a priest in the temple of Antichrist," who yet, when preaching on the passage you refer to, protested against your application of it,—exposed the Anti-Christian presumption of any man on earth pretending to a character analogous to that of Aaron; —and applied the narrative in that chapter, as a solemn warning to those who attempted to set aside or intrude into the priestly office of the Lord Jesus Christ. This was many years ago: but to this day, I think his application of the passage more scriptural than yours. And now, sir, let me observe to your Christian readers, that the question at issue, between us, stands perfectly distinct from the many personal topics in which you have endeavoured to involve it. No matter what I am or have been, whether I affect to imitate the style of Mr. Sandeman, whether I write at random, whether I am dogmatical, dictatorial, &c. All these points should be put wholly out of consideration by the serious inquirer, in examining the scriptural question on which we differ. As to the tone of angry hauteur which you employ towards Mr. J. and myself, I confess I am not displeased to observe it. Anger is generally called in to supply a deficiency of strength, and conscious weakness sometimes assumes the air of haughty superiority, to conceal its apprehension of defeat.

I am, Sir, yours, &c.

[The following detached piece is inserted here as an appropriate supplement to the foregoing letter.—Ed.]

Against the views of this subject (Elders) contended for as scriptural, I have often known it objected that they quite set aside the necessity or use of Elders in a Christian church. "If," say the objectors "there may be a church without Elders, and if in that state they are competent, and called to do every thing in which they engage after they have Elders, what use in Elders at all?" Now, before I directly answer the objection, I would call the attention of the Christian reader to the sentiment avowed by those who urge it: do they not avow that the only use they conceive for Elders in a Christian church is to administer ordinances? and yet many of those men are at times ready to declaim against the clerical character as unscriptural, while they manifestly retain the same thing, under another name. When persons think of any class of men, as possessing peculiar qualifications to give validity to the ordinances of Christ, and to sanction their observance by his disciples, it is of very little consequence whether they *call* them Clergymen or Elders. But am I still pressed with the question—"What then is the use which you assign to real Elders?" I reply, that it is plainly intimated in their title of *Overseers*. They are persons charged with the special oversight of the flock, and acknowledged by the Church, as given them by the Lord for that gracious design. In this oversight much more is included, than any exercises in which they are engaged, merely, in the public meeting of the disciples on the first day of the week. There is included an habitual stated attention to the course and circumstances of each member, a watchful care maintained over every individual, a diligent labouring to apply the admonitions, reproofs, consolations, and instructions of the word to their several cases. Can this be considered as an unimportant task, when we think of the varied trials, afflictions, and dangers which are connected with the varying circumstances of the disciples? Or is its importance to be concealed by the ungodly fiction, that there are some of the institutions of Christ, which believers cannot lawfully observe, unless they are authorized to observe them by the presence and acts of Elders? This constant oversight of the flock, which I think forms the essential business of true Elders, does not indeed supersede the common duty of all to watch over each other in love. But as little does the latter set aside the importance of having some specially charged with it, and peculiarly called to give themselves to the work. And here I would remark, that the very circumstance of their being acknowledged by the Church as raised up among them, and given to them by the Lord, for the purpose of exercising this watchful care, is intimately connected with its inoffensive and profitable exercise. In a church, yet without Elders, some will commonly be found who take a more than ordinary lead in its concerns, and it may be impossible that they should avoid doing so, unless they held back from the service of their brethren, the gifts with which they are furnished by the Lord. But such must, from time to time, be exposed to the suspicions, however groundless, of attempting to thrust themselves forward unwarrantably, and to assume to themselves something above the other members. But let that church be furnished with scriptural Elders, and those, in taking the same lead, will be seen as but engaged in the very service to which it is acknowledged they are called. Yet then, also, while kept in the true spirit of their office, they will no more act as Lords over God's heritage, than they did before, when they rendered in a degree the same services to their brethren in an unofficial capacity.

XVI.

TO MISS M———.

Jan. 22, 1810.

Dear H———.—I could not, till now, sit down to reply to your letter of the 12th inst., and even now must reply much more briefly than I could wish. The main subject on which you inquire, is one which I never wish to discuss, except with those who confess the old faith once delivered to the saints; and it is so many years since I had any communication with you on that topic, and I was then myself so indistinct in my views, and unscriptural in much of my language and conduct, that I have no sufficient ground to proceed on with you. For those who have imbibed any of the popular gospels, any of the popular churches are much fitter than a scriptural connection. Some of your expressions, towards the close of your letter, lead me to fear, that what you call the gospel, is something which you conceive has a particular aspect, more joyful to you than to other sinners. You say, that the Lord "has shewn you, that all his perfections are engaged *for you*." Suffer me to ask how, or where, he has shewn you that? Is your faith something that is not testified in the Scriptures? In them I cannot find a word about H. M., or John Walker, particularly. The faith of many professors is little more than a good opinion of their own state; or a persuasion that Christ died *for them*, —that is, that they are of the number of the elect. You say the society you are connected with, hold the head. I more than doubt that. Christ abideth a king as well as a priest continually. Your society set him aside from the former character altogether, not only disobeying the laws of his kingdom themselves, but systematically maintaining that they are matters of mutual forbearance,—that is, matters intrinsically indifferent—matters which the weak, indeed, and over-scrupulous may observe, but which the strong well know have no binding obligation. That such are the matters in which forbearance is enjoined on Christians, appears at once from Rom. xiv.; nor do I think it seasonable at present to say more upon that subject. But if you wish for my sentiments on it more at large, you may see them in the little pamphlet I published on the Apostolic Traditions. I dare say Mr. M——— can shew it to you. But to return to your society as holding the head. I have observed that they are Antichristian in their opposition to him as king of Zion. As to his character of priest, I know your preacher, Mr. M., can speak a very fair and scriptural language: but I know, also, that there are held in your fellowship, those who deny and gainsay the simple doctrine of Scripture concerning the atonement, and that the great truth itself is thus made a matter of forbearance among you. He that speaks the truth ever so scripturally for himself, but holds that others, denying it, may yet be very safe and right, in that turns the truth of God into a lie. Can I talk of such persons holding the head? No—they may appear as angels of light to some, but they are of Antichrist, and manifested as such to those who are of the truth. If you ask me who are held in your fellowship that oppose the fundamental truth, I name one, ——,—another, ——, who has avowed to me a sentiment which no one can retain, (after it has been exposed) and hold the truth—a third, ——, (though he is one of those who can speak it very distinctly at times.) But I name also the whole mass of the most open adversaries of the Gospel, that form the congregation of the establishment. For you confessedly hold in your fellowship those, who hold fellowship with the whole mass of that Antichristian corruption: and what a farce is it to say that you do not hold fellowship with the establishment? If twelve men join hands in a ring, can any one of them say that he is not connected with every other? If I hold religious fellowship with a man who holds fellowship with a Turk, are not the three of us connected in religious fellowship? If you have seen two very short Tracts, one upon 1 Tim. i. 15., and the other upon Acts xiii. 38, 39, I would be glad to know what you think of them, particularly upon that paragraph of the first, beginning with the words, "Many are seeking earnestly," &c.—(vol. 1. p. 509.) I wish you seriously to consider the assertion there advanced, and indeed the whole Tract, and to say how far your opinions are expressed or contradicted. I must now conclude, but shall very readily write more if you choose, as long as there appears any profitable end likely to be answered.

Yours, dear H., with best wishes,

XVII.

LETTER TO MRS. S———.

1810.

I HOPE my dear Mrs. S., though *not of my mind,* will not refuse to read with patience and attention a few lines from me. Your note to Mrs. W. was communicated this day. To speak of the grief of heart it occasioned is useless. Every thing concurs to mark the justice of that exclamation, " Lord, what is man?" To the great Shepherd of Israel I look to glorify his own name by dispelling the thick cloud which envelopes your mind, to send his word and heal you. You had seemed to see the principles of his divine word: but how quickly do they become as if they never had been discerned, when he leaves us for a moment to our own hearts! Your note is really like that of one who never had heard or acknowledged the scriptural grounds of what you so lately professed. You say that I would not join with Mr. R. in prayer, because *I look upon all such men as deceivers.* And is it possible, after all you have heard, that you think that is my reason? Indeed, it is not. My reason is, that the word of God confines my Christian fellowship in any ordinance to those who walk with me in all, and commands me to withdraw from and have no company (or fellowship) with all—whatever they profess and whatever they be—who walk not after the precepts delivered to the disciples of Christ by his apostles:—and, *that they may be ashamed* of their sin. I refer not now to any one passage of the word exclusively, but to the whole of it. Of Mr. R. I know nothing personally. *If he* be a disciple of Christ (as I own I was while I was yet walking in his ungodly course), I am sure, that in declining all fellowship with him I pursue the course of true love to him, as well as the only course of obedience to my Lord. If any thing of human instability and wickedness were surprising, the ostensible occasion of your fall would be so. A pamphlet comes out from Mr. R., which you think contains the truth of the Gospel. Be it so. Was it now that you learned for the first time that men may speak the truth, who either are not of the truth, or who do not walk according to it? But because Mr. R., in his pamphlet, expresses himself according to the truth of the Gospel, all the principles you had professed upon the fellowship of believers are to be abandoned! Alas! the root of the evil must lie deeper. I am struck with appearances in your case most like that of Mr. D.'s. While outwardly with us, he had, as he avows, walked, and acted, and spoke in great pride of heart and contempt of others. Awakened, as he supposed, to see this evil (a most serious one), he at once returned to the religion of the world, and renounced all profession of attempting to walk as the first Christians were enjoined,—in this thinking that he was *humble.* If I understand your language in part of your note, you also seem to speak of " the church" (the political establishment of religion in this country) as if you were reconciled to it. Indeed, if you renounce the Scriptures as the one rule of Christian fellowship to the end of the world, it signifies little what rule of man's you substitute for it. Against your perversion of Rom. xiv. it might be well to consider in what different language the Apostle addresses Gentile Christians who were coming under the observances of the law in Gal. iv. 9—11. But I am as averse as you can be to enlarge in argument; I trust to prayer. May He who is rich in mercy restore you! so that I may be able still to subscribe myself, your affectionate brother.

XVIII.

FROM THE CHURCH IN D—— TO THE CHURCH IN B——.

March 11, 1812.

The church of Christ assembling in Stafford Street, having heard with much grief of the late change in your sentiments and conduct, have directed us to address you, in their name, with a solemn admonition, on what we consider an awful defection from the principles of the word of God; while we hope it is needless to remark, that in taking this step we only do what we conceive any of the other churches who have stood in connection with you would be equally called on to do, on receiving the same intelligence. As far as we understand the nature and progress of your late change, we apprehend that it has originated in that gradual departure from the *truth of the Gospel*, to which our common nature is continually prone; for to this we are obliged to trace the false estimate you appear to make of various religious characters, with whom you have connected yourselves as brethren. We earnestly beseech you to consider, on what scriptural ground you can regard with brotherly confidence those who persist in rejecting any of the commandments of God. The apostles of Jesus Christ received, in the first instance, as brethren all those who confessed with their mouth the truth of the Gospel; these gave all the evidence which they could then afford of believing the Gospel, and, therefore, of being among the vessels of mercy ordained unto glory. But if we inquire what is the scriptural evidence upon which alone it can be proved that *a man really believes* that Gospel which he has professed, we find his works appealed to by the apostles. They tell us, he that is of God heareth them: and they speak of themselves as in *readiness to revenge all disobedience* against that word which they delivered as the commissioned ambassadors of Jesus Christ. The Lord also, who gave them their commission, expressly states the *keeping of his commandments* as the evidence of that love to him which characterises those who know his name. While we adhere, therefore, to these plain principles of the word of God, we find ourselves bound on the one hand to reject all who deny the truth as it is in Jesus; to reject them as persons who avow their unbelief: and, on the other hand, equally bound to reject all who (under a verbal profession of that truth) refuse to hear and obey any of the apostolic precepts; to reject these as persons who do not afford the only scriptural evidence of their really believing what they confess. When you, on the contrary, receive such as brethren, it appears to be on some favourable judgment of their religious character formed *independently* of the word of God, and in opposition to the authority of Jesus Christ: you appear to have received the infection of that ungodly sentiment which puts forward an indefinite sincerity and conscientiousness in the place of the only standard by which characters are estimated in the Scriptures; and in this you appear to have departed from the *fear* of the *Lord*, who has made known in the Scriptures his character and will. We find a further evidence of the same evil mind in your palpable abuse of those passages of Scripture by which you attempt to vindicate the laxity of your fellowship:—we allude to the passages in which weak brethren are mentioned, and the stronger admonished to bear their infirmities. Upon all such passages (so commonly urged by the present advocates of popular forbearance) we entreat you to consider,—whether it be not plain, that the weak brethren are spoken of as discovering their weakness in an *overscrupulous conscience*: and whether the cases there marked as of mutual forbearance, be not matters of intrinsic *indifference*, in which neither side *sinned*, however they differed in conduct. We appeal, therefore, to your consciences in the fear of God, whether such passages be not *wickedly perverted* when applied to characters who *do not* scruple to disobey the precepts of the Lord, and to matters which are enjoined by the authority of his word. To what extent you may at present carry your principles of forbearance in speculation or practice, we are uncertain; nor does it much signify. For when it is once allowed that *any* precept of Christ is to be treated as a matter of mutual forbearance, the only ground upon which obedience to ALL of them can rest is abandoned: and with the divine *authority* of his word, the basis of *the truth* is abandoned also. It must be from some other teaching than the Scriptures that you can learn to distinguish among the precepts of God, which of them may be set aside; and we would remind you, that they are some of the apparently minuter directions to Timothy which are closed by the Apostle with the solemn charge—"I charge thee before God, and the Lord Jesus Christ, and the elect angels, that thou observe these things." (1 Timothy v. 21.) In what a different view from yours are these things presented in the apostolic word! Finally, brethren, we call on you to consider (what you have been accustomed to acknowledge with us) that he that endureth to the end, the same shall be saved—that the church of Christ is still his kingdom, that he is still king in Zion, and that the writings of his apostles still declare to us his truths and precepts. If, indeed, you still acknowledge this, with what consistency can you set aside any thing which they declare as not still binding, or as that which may be rejected and disobeyed without invalidating the Christian profession of him who disobeys it? Have you indeed gone so far from the truth as to urge the *sincerity* of the *disobedience* and the fairness of the transgressor's character before men, in vindication or extenuation of his sin? We commend this our admonition to the blessing of Him who can make it effectual for calling you back to the mind of steadfastness in maintaining the truth, and patience in keeping the commandments of Jesus; and would still cherish the hope of having our affectionate concern for you succeeded by rejoicing in you, and thankfulness to God on your account.

(Signed in the name of the church.)

XIX.

TO MISS WALKER.

April 5, 1813.

My Dear Child,—Let me put on paper some observations and suggestions, against we resume the subject of yesterday's conversation. Agitated as you were, it is awfully striking how you at once put forward, and continued to express, the very sentiments and objections most current among the religious adversaries of Christ's kingdom. All the reasons you assigned for declining connexion with the church in Stafford Street—(the only Christian connexion I acknowledge in Dublin)—come under one or other of these heads:—1st. We are not as *good* as we ought to be:—2dly. We do not pray with others, whom *you say* we must acknowledge as believers, or else must profess that there *are* no believers in Dublin but ourselves. 3dly. We find differences appearing from time to time among ourselves. As to the *first*, I hope we shall never be employed in vindicating ourselves against the charge: and I am indeed well aware that those who lay themselves out to "make a fair shew in the flesh," will quite distance Christians in the exhibition of piety and zeal, and demure strictness. But while I see their zeal and strictness running in the old direction of making light of the commandments of God, and setting up as important the traditions of men,—I hope I shall ever view them, and testify against them, as descendants of those to whom the Lord said of old—"Ye are they who justify yourselves before men; but God knoweth your hearts." That they make light of the precepts of God, is abundantly proved by the religious friendship which they maintain towards those who do not obey what even *they* profess to receive as divine precepts. But if there were no other manifestation of this mind in them, it would be sufficiently manifested to any of spiritual discernment, by their attempt to impose on disciples the *traditions of men*—"thou shalt not go see a balloon"—"thou shalt not sing a song"—"when ye drink tea together of an evening, ye must not part without a hymn and social prayer," &c. Wherever such a mind appears, there is decisive evidence of a mind opposite to the fear and knowledge of the true God—though the professor may assume the garb of an angel of light.

As to the *second* head of objection, it proceeds on a radical error as to the standard, by which disciples are bound to be regulated in acknowledging any as brethren. It proceeds upon the ungodly sentiment, that a plausible profession of the lips, joined with some general strictness of religious conduct, affords evidence of discipleship—while the authority of Christ is disacknowledged, and set aside by disobedience to the laws of his kingdom. Any church, professing to be scriptural, professes to be regulated by the word of Christ: and if they do not regard as disobedient to that word those who walk not with them, or who walk by any other rule,—they only avow that they are not themselves following any rule which they consider of divine authority. If they say of professors not joined with them, that they are indeed walking contrary to the word of the Lord, *but* that they are so sincere, &c., in their disobedience, that their Christianity cannot be called in question;—in this language they profanely set up the sincerity of man, in opposition to the authority of Christ. Nor is my avowal, that there may yet be disciples scattered in the most Antichristian connexions, at all inconsistent with my assertion, that I am forbidden by the word to *receive* any individual as a disciple, who continues in that wickedness. It is one thing, what may be known to God; and quite another thing, what is scripturally manifested to his people. But I confess, that I think it much more probable, that there are such scattered disciples in any of the most *openly* antichristian connections of the world, than that they should be found in such a connection as that which you have been led to look at with complacence. Those joined with the latter, have all, more or less, had the principles of Scripture presented to them, and pressed on their attention,—even by the very notoriety of the differences between them and us:—and when, after this, I find them "loving darkness rather than light," and only embittered in their minds and tongues against the followers of Christ,—though I would not dare to pronounce, that even they *are not* disciples who shall be brought to glory,—yet I confidently say that they present to view some of the most striking features of the subjects of Antichrist; and that I hold their ways only in the greater abhorrence, on account of the plausible mask of evangelical profession which they assume. Connected with this head is the opinion you expressed, that there may be two different churches *of Christ* in the same place:—an opinion which you must abandon, or else assert that the nature of Christ's kingdom is totally altered since the apostolic days.

On the *third* head, I know well the representations current among—alas! that I should say—your religious friends. But until you adduce some other instance of these supposed differences, than that which appeared for a time in Mr. F——, I believe I may dismiss the topic. Only let me call your attention to the readiness with which you seemed to admit, that we should have been bound to remove Mr. F——, if he had continued after admonition to maintain that diversity of sentiment. Now suppose that had taken place; should we have been warranted in worshipping with him the next day in *private?* But it would be endless to press such inconsistencies.

Let me entreat you, my dear child, seriously to consider what I have offered: and when we renew the subject in conversation, I hope you will be able to speak your mind coolly and collectedly. I was going to request that Miss F——, the Misses B———, &c., might not be taken into your council on the present occasion: but, on second thoughts, I retract the desire, as they cannot instil more of their poison. Oh, that divine mercy may interfere for you, to snatch you from the evils of the worst part of the world; and for me, to spare me one of the keenest trials I could encounter! To Him, with whom there is boundless mercy and boundless power, I look in your behalf.

XX.

TO THE SAME.

April 16, 1813.

My Dear Child,—As our next conversation may possibly be final on the subject, I am anxious to put you fully in possession, previous to it, of all I wish you to consider.

Last Sunday I expressed considerable satisfaction at your admission of some principles, which seemed scarcely to leave room for ultimate difference. But I confess that satisfaction was considerably abated, if not wholly done away, by your parting expressions. I do not recollect the words: but they briefly intimated that your mind was made up upon one point, and your resolution taken with respect to joining in worship with others, beside those who walk together scripturally in the fellowship of the Gospel. When Christians are merely under *error* about any part of the revealed will of God, *instruction* from the Word may be expected to remove the error. But when we are under a carnal bias, determining our minds to one side of a question, the clearest exposure of our error is unavailing. "The man convinced *against his will*—is of the same opinion still." It is not instruction we want in this case; but that subjection of mind to the divine authority, which nothing can produce, but the revealed truth of God clearly discovered, and powerfully swaying our consciences. That more than nine-tenths of the *erroneous sentiments*, prevalent in the religious world, are of the latter description,—that they are intimately connected with *indisposition* to what the Scriptures reveal,—I have long been convinced. Indeed the Word obliges me to conclude that this is the case, wherever its admonition fails of producing its proper effect, after it has been clearly and fully laid before the mind. Upon that determination, therefore, which you seemed to express, I shall only solemnly refer you to the words of Christ in Matth. x. 37.

I shall say little more, also, upon the vanity of the pretext, which you principally urged in our last conversation—that the various classes of professors, with whom you would pray, are *examining*—sincerely examining—the Scriptures, upon the points in which they are yet disobedient to the word. As I observed, I know not any religious professors, who do not profess to be habitually examining the Scriptures. But when the principles of Scripture are pointed out to them plainly, and laid before them repeatedly, and they reject them—(*reject*, in the sense in which we agreed the term is to be used)—it is too wickedly ludicrous to talk of their sincere examination of the word in extenuation of their sin. One of the pious churchmen, or presbyterians, or moravians, &c., with whom Mr. Kelly would bow the knee, (very consistently in him)—is living all his life in disobedience to the plainest principles of the word of God: but he tells me with a grave face, that, indeed, if he saw these principles in

Scripture, he would submit to them, and that he is very sincerely *examining* the Scriptures on the subject. And, therefore, you say he is to be received into the fellowship of Christ's ordinances, or *some* of them;—though you admit that the brother, who has been walking with me in the full fellowship of the Gospel, is to be removed, if disobedience to any of Christ's precepts appear in *him*, and is persisted in after admonition. If this be not setting up man's sincerity against the truth and authority of God, I know not what is. Yet I well know what use is made of that argument.

I have only to add the melancholy acknowledgment, that if your mind should ultimately fix on that side, to which it appears too much inclined, I am too conscious of my great shortcoming in the duty of a Christian parent—(peculiarly difficult as my circumstances have been)—not to feel the trial deeply embittered by that sad and humbling consideration. I still, however, look to Him with whom *is Mercy*.

XXI.

TO THE SAME.

April, 1813.

My dear Child,—A few words more and I have done,—very few are now needed: and I prefer this mode of communicating them, on account of the state of animal agitation which is produced by conversation.—After shifting your ground in each of our interviews, you have terminated in a principle *undisguisedly* profane. You say that we cannot be charged with *disobeying* a divine command which we do not *see*. It may be plainly in the scripture: it may be laid before us from the scripture:—but if we do not *see* it, if we be not *conscious* of our disobedience,—we cannot be said to disobey.

On this I observe—That it at once sets aside the word of God, as the one regulating standard and authoritative rule for his people's conduct; and substitutes in its place, their varying *opinions* of what is right or wrong; thus "establishing iniquity by a law:"—that the language of the Apostles is, "He that is of God, *heareth us*," and "If any man be spiritual let him *acknowledge* that the things which we write unto you, are the commandments of the Lord:" but the language of this principle is, that a man may be evidenced to be of God and spiritual, though he remain deaf to the apostolic word, and does not acknowledge as the commandments of the Lord the things written in it.—I repeat it, also—that the very same principle equally goes to sanction all the false Gospels which those embrace, who are left to "strong delusion, that they should believe a lie," and goes to say that the stronger their delusion, the more harmless it is, and the more justifiable. If we cannot be said to disobey the divine commands unless we *see* their authority, neither can men be said to reject the divine testimony, unless they *see* its truth.—I am taught, however, that it is the distinguishing character of the people of God, that they are given to *discern* that which is hidden from the world, and that the word (which carries no weight to the children of disobedience) sways their conscience. Certainly, none can obey it really, but those who *discern* it.

The intimations you throw out of the supposed ambiguity and obscurity of the scriptures on these matters, are but of a piece with the ungodliness of the principles you now avow. However, they have been given as the one revelation of the Divine mind and will, for enlightening and regulating the church of God: and take heed how you set up any *other rule* of faith or practice, or how you impeach *their sufficiency* for the end for which they were designed by God. This is at the bottom of the illustration you employed—"could you be said to disobey *me* in a matter in which you merely had not *understood* what I desired?" This is, in short, saying that it is the same cause which prevents men's receiving the revelation of the divine will, and which makes them occasionally mistake each other's meaning in natural things—namely, the indistinctness and obscurity of the directions. But the scriptures account for the world's not receiving the word, and being unable to *see* it, from a very different cause indeed.

As long as you maintain the principles which you avowed this evening, I release you, my dear child, from all further agitation of the subject. Should a change take place in your views, you will of course communicate it to me. But till then, I am obliged (though with a bleeding heart) solemnly to renounce all fellowship with you in your religion, and to view you—however amiable and dear to me in the flesh—as one rejecting the word of the Lord, and savouring not the things that be of God—but the things that be of men.

Your afflicted but affectionate Father,

XXII.

FROM THE CHURCH IN D—— TO —— M——.

3rd June, 1813.

Dear Sister M.—Though many circumstances might naturally seem to repress our hope of recovering you to the principles of Scripture from which you have turned aside, yet in that word of the Lord which *commands us* to attempt the restoration of those who are found in any transgression, previous to renouncing fellowship with them, we have enough both to direct our conduct in your instance, and to support our *hope* also, that it may please God to bless the means which he commands us to employ. And however your mind may have been made up upon the subject, or whatever reluctance you may feel to be recalled to views which at present you regard with aversion, we would beseech you—as one whom we still hope to have restored to us as a sister beloved—not to withhold your attention, nor to turn away from what we are about to offer.

All departure from the holy commandments delivered from the Apostles must originate in a declension from their testimony concerning Jesus Christ: we are persuaded, therefore, that it is not superfluous to remind you, that the revelation of the glory of the only true God in the gospel, is as much opposed to all that is reckoned good and excellent among men in religion, as it is unspeakably joyful to the most vile and ungodly who discern it. While kept in the discernment of it, we shall see but one thing that is glorious, and shall therefore be delivered from the sentiments of false admiration in which we naturally hold the *persons of men*—either our own or others. We shall be kept, also, in that holy reverence of the name of the Lord, which will regard the revelation He has made as stamped with universal sacredness and divine authority, and will fly from the appearance of profaning that sacredness, or trifling with that authority. The fundamental principles in your present course are opposite to these essential features of the gospel of God our Saviour. Instead of trying all persons and characters by the word of the Lord, you subject his words to the characters of men. You set it down as a fixed principle, that such and such individuals must be considered as accepted of God, and conclude that the Scriptures cannot call you to renounce fellowship with *them*: and, in all the natural pride of false humility, you make a virtue of your disobedience, as not setting yourself above those, who (you have found) are so much better disciples than yourself. In this estimation of their characters, the great criterion which Christ himself points out (of hearing *his* voice and keeping his commandments) you wholly set aside. We are aware that you speak of fair *fruits* in them, as evidencing their discipleship. But the basis of your present union with them is the ungodly maxim, *that ye may receive each other in the charity of the Gospel, though each live in open disobedience to what the other professes to acknowledge as a command of the Lord Jesus.* And thus there is not a command *peculiarly* HIS, the authority of which you do not deny. We say, peculiarly his,—for, when you profess not to hold in your fellowship drunkards, and thieves, and murderers, &c., we would remind you, that Heathens themselves acknowledge these evils to be inconsistent with excellence of moral character. And if you would indeed put away (as we doubt not) *such* wicked persons from among you, have we not reason to believe that it would be rather in the spirit of the religious world, and to keep your own characters fair in the sight of men, than in real obedience to the word of Christ? For if you acknowledge yourselves bound, in that instance, by the authority of his word, with what consistency can you consider the authority of the same word not equally binding in every other instance when it reveals his will? or, though you say that the *drunkard, &c. ought* to be put away from among disciples, would you hold yourself at liberty to continue in a connexion where such characters were retained? If you would, on what ground of consistency can you separate from the Establishment, or any of the most openly antichristian connexions upon earth? If you would not, and own that you could not, without being a partaker of their sin, you own that one part of the scriptural regulation of Christ's house is so binding, that united obedience to it is essential to Christian fellowship:—and then, with what consistency can you deny the same character to belong *to every other* part?

Thus, in conceiving that nothing affects the Christian character of professors but breaches of that moral law, the work of which is written in every man's conscience, you set aside all that peculiarly rests upon the authority of Christ:—and when you justify their disobedience to the revealed will of Christ, on the ground of their conscientious ignorance, you reject the mark which he assigns as distinguishing his sheep—that of *hearing his* voice *and following him:* and set up the varying rule of men's opinions in opposition to his immutable word. We are aware that you put forward the *doctrine* of Christ, in contradistinction to his *precepts*, as the one thing in which it is essential that the members of a Christian society should be agreed. How far some of those with whom you have joined yourself, even professionally, hold the unadulterated gospel, we shall not stop to inquire. But it is important to observe, that the distinction thus put forward is altogether unscriptural and ungodly.

The *doctrine*, or *teaching*, of the Apostles (in the scriptural import of the word) includes all that they declare, both of the work of the Lord Jesus and of his will. See Matt. xxviii. 20. and 1 Tim. vi. 3, 4. And part of what they teach is, that he who *even bids God speed* to the man that brings any other doctrine, or teaching, than theirs, is "a partaker of his evil deeds." 2 John i. 10, 11. The use you make of the Apostle's words, in Phil. iii. 15. is a melancholy evidence how deeply you are imbibing the spirit of the popular gospels; which have each their private revelations, distinct from the revealed mind of God. We earnestly call on you to consider, whether it be any thing short of profane to represent the Apostle as there telling the Philippian disciples—"If any of you be at present living in disobedience of the commands which I have given you in the name of the Lord, God will bring you to a perception of your sin (if it is to be called sin) before you die." Without entering at all upon the real meaning of the passage, which (though pretty evident) a Christian may have to own he does not see—we confidently say, that any one standing in the fear of the Lord must reject with abhorrence such an interpretation, as soon as his attention is called to its ungodliness. It is, however, well matched with the sentiment, that continued disobedience to all the precepts *peculiarly Christian*, is consistent with the continuance of Christian fellowship. We conclude this our admonition, commending it to the blessing of Him who alone can make it effectual for your recovery. We hope to be favoured with a communication from you without any unnecessary delay.

Signed in the name, and by desire of, the church in Dublin.

XXIII.

FROM THE CHURCH IN D——— TO THE SAME.

———1813.

We are sorry to observe that your speedy answer to our letter appears to have been written without the least consideration of what we offered, or any sober attention to the admonition we conveyed. We wish once more to observe the weakness of your arguments and the ungodly nature of your sentiments. You commence with stating most truly "that all believers should be united together outwardly." But when we agree with you in saying that they SHOULD, *we* mean that the word of God commands it, and that they who hold the expediency or lawfulness of their not being so, maintain a doctrine contrary to the apostolic rule, and are persons with whom we can have no fellowship without being partakers of their evil deeds: you professing in words the same principle, infer from it the lawfulness of leaguing yourself with those who deny and disobey it. Holding the principle with any scriptural consistency, you should reject as heretics (or sect-makers, causing divisions and offences) all who are not outwardly united with those whom you have joined, according to that passage in Rom. xvi. 17. to which you justly refer, as marking a character of men whom Christians are to put away from among them.—But, in fact, by the outward union of believers you seem to mean little more than all good people acknowledging each other in that character, by making light of their differences and occasionally worshipping together. The outward union of believers that we are taught from scripture to regard as of divine authority, the work of God, is their united profession of the one truth, and united subjection to the revealed authority of their one Lord. You, and those whom you have joined, are awfully united in representing all the peculiar precepts of Christ as what believers may continue to disobey, without any impeachment of their Christian profession; and where you vindicate this by the question "where is the person that sinneth not?" you really hold a language more like that of the professing world, than what might be expected from a disciple. We urged various scriptural arguments upon your attention, not one of which receives the least notice. But what do you put forward? why—an assurance that you have been solely influenced by the word of God—a testimony in favour of those with whom you are at present connected, as "having all heard the voice of Christ calling them," &c. as "seeking with a single eye to know his will," &c.—as "desiring to do all things to his glory"—and a declaration that, "after much earnest and humble searching of the scriptures, you find no warrant for rejecting those who profess the faith of Jesus, *though they may interpret some* passages of scripture in a different manner from what you do." Alas! what a paraphrase is this, for those who live in disobedience to the revealed will of Christ, and who refuse to hear his church admonishing and reproving them for their sin! In similar treachery of specious words you say of those from whom the word commands disciples to *withdraw* and *to have no fellowship* with them, 'that they are to be patiently forborne with, and to be discountenanced in their act of disobedience to the apostolic rule.'—When you talk of a *revelation of the divine will* as that which must be the *most joyful feeling a disciple can be sensible of,* you seem to have quite rejected our testimony against the meaning in which you use the word *revelation*. But we would again warn you that the revelation of the divine will is already made in the scriptures, and *he that hath an ear to hear, will hear what the Spirit saith unto the churches.* We pass by your intimation that we "profess to know ALL that we are commanded to do," as that which is contradicted by your consciousness of our professed sentiments, and which is too like the language of one sitting in the seat of the scorner. Looking for the mercy of the Lord to be displayed, in recalling you to the fear of his name, we beseech you again to consider your ways, and not to reject our repeated admonition. Signed, &c.

XXIV.

TO ———.

Dec. 11, 1813.

You probably know that, when I re-introduced this subject to the church, it was under the same impression of the immediate meaning of all the five passages—as desiring the conveyance of the *Apostle's salutation*; but convinced that—even upon that supposition—the inference was plain, and binding on Christians to the end of the world. For, if we find the Apostles adding to the salutations they desired, *an express injunction* that they should be conveyed *by a kiss*, and this, in writing to churches situated in the most various countries, and where this mode of salutation was not more general, *as a national custom,* than among us;—I did, and do, conceive that there would be in this a decisive indication, that the Spirit of truth meant to establish among Christians universally that most significant expression of brotherly affection: especially when it is considered, that it would be manifestly absurd for any one to desire his own correspondent to salute, in his name with a kiss, one whom that person was not in the habit of saluting with a kiss in his own name. And, if it were admitted, that the first Christians in *Rome* and *Greece*, &c., were accustomed to salute each other with a kiss, it must have been a custom peculiar to them *as Christians,*—(for in those countries it confessedly was not the national mode) and, therefore, must have been a custom derived to them from the same source of apostolic regulations, from which they derived all their other Christian practices.

But the clearer views, produced on the protracted discussion of the subject, have led me to quit the ground of this interpretation altogether, and, from the fullest conviction, to revert to the original view of the passages, which would strike any plain reader, as desiring the Christians—not to convey the apostolic salutations—but literally, as the words run, *to salute* EACH OTHER *with a kiss*. And here, before I state the arguments I employed last Sunday, let me call on you to consider whether the form of expression—*salute* EACH OTHER—can, by any fairness of interpretation, be construed into—"*present my salutations to all.*" I might desire—I have desired a person to salute another with a kiss in my name; and I, therefore, can conceive that I should desire him to salute twenty others with a kiss in my name. But can you conceive any one, in his senses, desiring the twenty persons to salute EACH OTHER with a kiss in his name? to salute *each other* with a kiss in testimony—not of their *mutual* affection, but of the affection of the writer to them all? The thing is so utterly unnatural, and the interpretation so forced, that it ought at once to be abandoned without further argument. Yet it has been so pertinaciously maintained, upon the ground of supposed *Jewish* custom, that I proceed to repeat what I urged last Sunday. First, then—however customary salutation with a kiss was among the Jews, what evidence is there that it was *customary* with them to salute with a kiss *by proxy?* We have fuller accounts from various sources of Jewish customs, than of the customs of any other nation. Yet of this there is not a vestige of tradition: while, according to the interpretation I contend against, it must have been so VERY COMMON, as to account for two Apostles—in five different letters—desiring this proxy-kiss, and not merely to this or that individual, but to the whole body of Christians.

But 2dly, supposing this to have been so common with them, how can it be accounted for, that the Apostles NEVER desire an *individual* to be thus saluted; though the instances of salutation sent to individuals be so extraordinarily numerous? Here, then, we have positive scriptural evidence against that commonness of the practice, which the interpretation would require.

And 3dly, we have various epistles *to individuals*, in which salutations are desired to single disciples, and to the whole body collectively: but in no one instance does the expression, "*with a kiss*," occur in this connexion.

Now, I say, that those, who still after all this maintain that interpretation of the texts, maintain it against a body of evidence, greater than we could expect to have accumulated upon such a point.

If that interpretation be given up, there only remains the other simple view of all the passages, that the Apostles do direct the Christians to express their mutual affection by salutation with a kiss. And while we walk in the fear of the Lord, and trembling at his word, I conceive that this must at once carry decisive authority to us,—so decisive as that we shall address ourselves to obey the direction without murmuring, and shall no longer urge *objections*, however we may propose inquiries.

What is, then, the fair inference from the *connexion* of all the passages, and from the *repetition* of it in 2 Cor? Simply this—that in none of these passages are the Apostles *establishing* a *new* practice in the churches, but referring to one of established existence among them. And, in this view, what is more natural than the connexion? How suitable, when the Apostles are conveying expressions of their love in salutations to various individuals, that they should incidentally remind them of the standing expression of their mutual love, by salutation with a kiss? And, as to the *repetition* of this, in different letters to the same church, is it more surprising than if they concluded twenty letters with—"my love to such and such. *Brethren, love one another.*" If they were establishing a new rite, or reproving the neglect of an instituted practice, we might certainly expect the direction to occur in another connexion:—but the present connexion, and the repetition, simply indicate the customary existence of the practice.

I confess, also, that I am more and more strongly inclined to think, that the reference in all the passages is to a *stated* practice in their meetings, on the first day of the week. For, as has been justly observed, it seems not likely that the church at Rome would have waited, perhaps for a year after the receipt of the Apostle's letter, before they obeyed the direction—waited for the occurrence of one of those rare occasions, of the return of a brother, after long absence, &c. We have decisive historical information, that the churches, about 60 years after the time of the Apostles, did observe such a practice in their meetings, and professedly in obedience to these apostolic directions. I am apt to think we have sufficient evidence from the Scripture that, in this instance, they understood the word aright.

And let me remark that, if such be the allusion, there would be no room for the objections you hint at borrowed from *propriety, &c.* If at the end of worship each brother saluted the brethren next him with a kiss, and each sister the sisters,—the world might scoff, but would have no just occasion to speak reproachfully. It would be, as directed, *universally* practised by all the brethren, while there would be in this no human *limitation* of the thing enjoined; for I am sure that no fair interpretation of the passage could conclude that any disciple was to salute with a kiss *all the rest.*

XXV.

TO M—— R——

—— 1814.

My dear R.—I have read your letter, as you may suppose, with much interest. I am grieved at the distressing account you give of your body; but if you be made acquainted with the joyful and faithful testimony of God concerning his son Jesus, all is well. Upon that question, it is not for me to judge, except so far as your professed sentiments accord with, or oppose, the revealed truth of God. The greater part of what you wrote on the 4th instant, particularly on that passage in Rom. x., would lead me to suppose that you had been mercifully led to see what God exhibits to us in his word; and all who see it live for ever. It is the distinguishing mark which he puts upon the vessels of mercy, which he has before ordained to glory; and the effect that you there describe, as following your view of the passage, is such as must follow from the belief of the gospel—peace and assured hope towards God. But then you afterwards sadly fly from this, when you come to your doubts and uncertainties whether you believe the gospel or not. God declares in his word that he sent his Son into the world to save sinners, to die for sin—the just for the unjust: he sets him forth to a guilty and ruined world as the propitiation or atonement for sin, which he himself provided when no other sacrifice could take it away, which he has accepted as completely magnifying his righteousness and truth, and which he has proved his acceptance of by raising him from the dead. Whosoever believeth this divine testimony (according to the same word) shall be saved: he is jutified from all things, and has that eternal life which is the gift of God in Christ Jesus. This glorious gospel, which thus reveals to us the character of the only living and true God—as just and the justifier of the ungodly—the just God and the Saviour, manifests at the same time the exceeding sinfulness of man; and this not only in the greatness of that atonement for sin which it exhibits, but also in the reception it meets with from man.—The carnal security and ungodly pride and earthly-mindedness of our hearts lead us all naturally to reject this divine testimony; and the rejection of it is manifested not more by careless indifference in many, than by the religious anxiety and religious exertions of others to make their peace with God—i. e. to do for themselves that which it has declared that Christ has done for sinners. Hence all the corrupted gospels that overspread the world, and the arguings and blasphemies of devout unbelievers, against the unadulterated gospel of God. So that, wherever any are brought to the knowledge of the truth, God is found of those who sought him not. But can they consistently doubt whether they believe the gospel or not? If a thing is declared to me, and I doubt whether I believe it, this is certainly the same as to doubt whether the thing declared be true or not. Yet I know there are many religious, who will gravely declare that so and so is the gospel of God, but that they fear they have not faith or do not believe it. This, in the plain and true meaning of the word faith or believing, is profound nonsense. Yours, &c.

XXVI.

TO J—— F—— G——, ESQ.

Jan. 25, 1815.

Dear Sir,—I am ashamed of having been so tardy in acknowledging your favour of last month. But my engagements are such, that I could not take up my pen till now to thank you for the kindness and candour which prompted your communications. I was not at all surprised by the terms in which I am marked in the printed leaf you enclosed; and I conceive Mr. K—— has more cause to complain of being undeservedly brought into such company. I have no right to complain. For opposed as I am to the religious world, I must expect that the religious world will be opposed to me. What they esteem best I think Antichristian, and what I hold as the precious faith once delivered to the saints, they brand with every opprobrious name of Antinomian, or empty speculations.

I do not well know how I should set about answering the writer of that paper: he observes that "*all the serious people* acquainted with the circumstances are now agreed that my leaving the establishment has been a curse instead of a blessing to Ireland." So far from denying that sentiment, I confess that I believe it is very true—taking "all the serious people" in the sense in which he uses the phrase, as comprising all those who seriously hold *any such gospel* as that, to the cause of which he says the Wesleyan Methodists are devoted, and to which that writer is evidently devoted with them. I doubt not but they would have been much better pleased with me had I remained in the most Antichristian connexion, violating the plainest principles of Christ's kingdom, and darkening that glorious gospel, which I even then at times inconsistently put forward; and I am well persuaded that any satisfaction some of these serious folks at first felt at my quitting the establishment, was only in the expectation of my falling in with some of those other ungodly sects, regulated, as much as the establishment, by the traditions of men. But while I am aware of all this, and cannot think of shrinking from the opprobrium which the writer marks as attached to me, I deny the competence of those most *serious* people to form any scriptural judgment about my conduct or my sentiments. Another matter, however, which the writer states, I can contradict,—namely, "that the grand object of my pursuit is to disunite the people of God, and to divide the churches of Christ." This is utterly false, though I can hardly conceive that the writer believes what he states. But the uniting of all the people of God, i. e. of all who believe the one and only gospel of his son Jesus, is an object that lies, and will lie, very near my heart, and never shall I think that the works of the man of sin are consumed, till *all that believe* in every place *are together*, as they were of old, walking by the same rule and speaking the same things. In the progress of that consumption, however, the peace of the Antichristian churches will be disturbed from time to time, and one and another poor sinner will be snatched by the mercy of God from their ungodly ways: and this will make the serious adherents of the man of sin mourn while believers will rejoice. This will make the word of Christ be considered as causing divisions and causing fire on earth, and those who profess it cannot scripturally expect any favour from men. I had some melancholy opportunities last summer of witnessing what the writer terms "the *flourishing* state of the Independent Churches in England," and avow, without any scruple, that I should rejoice to hear of their present peace being disturbed, and their present flourishing prosperity being marred by the introduction of scriptural principle among them. Thus you see, my dear sir, that I could not answer the writer's assertions but in a way which must aggravate the indignation of him and all like-minded with him. I am well aware that, essentially as I differ from such men in all my views of divine truth and precept, I might yet escape the bitterness of their animosity, if my views allowed me to regard or speak of them as good men; but viewing them as very ungodly and wicked men, on account of their opposition both to the priestly and kingly character of the Lord Jesus, I hope I shall never be allowed to court their friendship or to fear their enmity. Thanking you sincerely for your kindness, I remain, &c.

XXVII.

TO R. M'N——.

May —, 1815.

My dear M——,—It has grieved me much to have your letter of the 24th ult. so long unanswered. But it found me very ill; and I am still so much of an invalid, that I am little qualified for entering as largely into the subject as its importance demands. May the few observations I can offer be blessed to check what, I am persuaded, is a very serious error. Just at the time your letter came, we were engaged on the same subject with B—— B——. But, in some respects, his grounds are different to yours; for he insists that μηδὲ συνεσθιειν—*not even to eat with him*—means, not to eat the Lord's supper with him! Upon your interpretation of the passage, as if it forbid civil intercourse with the person *while under admonition*, I would remark, that while he is yet *under admonition*, he cannot be treated as one of the black characters enumerated in that passage. For instance—if a brother falls into an act of drunkenness, the church is not at once to consider and treat him as a drunkard. If so, they should put him away from them at once; for that is the line of conduct expressly enjoined toward such wicked persons. They are to proceed in the merciful labour of restoring their fallen brother; and if he hear the word of reproof and admonition, they are to rejoice over him and confirm their love towards him: but if he reject it, then he appears in the black character of the wicked whom they are to put away from among them. And do consider what is that interval during which you are to suppose the offender precluded from civil intercourse with his brethren. But a deep ground or error lies with you as well as with B—— B——, in the supposition, that when a person is put away from a church of Christ he is then to be viewed and treated completely as one who had never belonged to it. I would refer you to the Apostles' words about the incestuous person—"that the spirit may be saved in the day of the Lord Jesus,"—marking plainly, that the very same spirit of love and hope of mercy towards the offender which were to regulate all the former efforts to call him to repentance, were still to influence the church in the last act of discipline toward him. Accordingly, when this gracious design appeared to be accomplished in that wicked person, was he received back into the church as if he never belonged to it? No—for, if so, he would have been received on the ground of his professing the faith of Christ, without any inquiry into his repentance for any particular evil of his conduct. His verbal profession of the truth never appears to have been interrupted, and in his return to the church never to have been inquired into. He was received back as a recovered brother, just as he would have been retained if he had heard the reproof of his sin. And how suitable to that view of his recovery, under which they were called to put him away, was the merciful injunction that they should not even eat with him; that they should thus mark their abhorrence of his evil, and their affectionate concern for him. In that other view, which would cast him off (in one sense) from hope, and say, "I no longer look at a person who acts so wickedly with any idea that he can have known the truth"—there is, I am persuaded, awful pride of heart, and a sentiment very opposite to the influence of the truth in ourselves. As to the passage in Matthew, I have only time to say, that your argument would go as much against the prohibition of religious as of civil fellowship. For certainly Jesus would have as soon held the former with a publican as with a Pharisee. On the passage in Thessalonians, I can but formally avow my persuasion, that the view of it I have given in my "Apostolic Traditions" is the only scriptural one.

My love, &c.

XXVIII.

TO B—— B——.

—— 1815.

My dear B——,—It was with great concern I heard last Sunday that I—— B—— and his wife dined with you. In this I am persuaded you have been associating with those, with whom the divine word plainly calls us to keep no company: and I had hope after the long discussion which the subject received that we were all of one mind upon it. It is so uncertain when I may have an opportunity of talking it over with you, that I adopt this mode of suggesting some considerations, though probably none of them will be new to you. I believe we agreed that almost all the directions of the word are such as naturally arise out of the Gospel, and commend themselves to the new mind by their close connexion with the faith and hope of Christ,—such as we might be supposed to infer from the foundation of Christian fellowship, (if we were not so carnal) even though no precept had been given on the subject. Now, consider in this view our deportment towards those from whom we have solemnly withdrawn on account of their not hearing the word of Christ; how unsuitable is it that we should continue to indulge in social intercourse with them, and shew that we have pleasure in them, whether we consider the tendency of this in its effect on their minds, or the state of sentiment and feeling that it indicates in ourselves. Can we be taking that serious view of their evil, or be under that loving concern for their recovery, which becomes us, when we entertain this complacency in their society? and does not the manifestation of it directly tend to make them think light of what has separated them from our fellowship? Suppose, on the very day in which I have taken part with the brethren in putting away a wicked person from among us, I should bid that person to my table for the purpose of enjoying his company; could I be under scriptural views about his sin, and the solemn act in which I had professed to mark it? And if, instead of doing this on the same day, I do it after the lapse of months or years, does it not appear that I have lost sight of the principles on which I before acted towards him? Agreeably to these plain considerations I find the Scriptures speaking a uniform language about those put away from the Church of Christ. "Let him be unto thee as an heathen man and a publican." Matt. xviii. 17. "With such an one not to eat." 1 Cor. v. 11. "Have no company with him that he may be ashamed." 2 Thess. iii. 14. Not knowing by what misinterpretation you at present get over these passages, I shall not attempt to enlarge on them; I hope and pray it may not be necessary, but that you will be led to see the plain import of them, pointing to a deportment alike mercifully calculated to keep alive in our minds a serious sense of the evil which we are called to abhor, and to present it continually in the same serious light to the mind of the offender. My indisposition continues with so little, if any abatement, that I know not whether I shall be able to go to the meeting to-morrow. But, if not, I hope to send this by M——.

XXIX.

TO B—— M——.

March 21, 1815.

My dear M——,—A packet which P—— received last week from B——, has given us much trouble. It would seem that the church meeting in his house has been pursuing a course of discipline with you and Mrs. M——, which from the spirit in which it was conducted and met was likely to terminate in the most lamentable disunion. May the Lord in rich mercy prevent or heal the breach, and convince both sides of the evil, that, as we think, attaches respectively to each. P—— writes to B—— about the unscriptural ground which we think they have taken in their admonition—namely, the supposition that the word does not countenance the existence of two Churches so near each other as three miles and a half. Some other things in the spirit and manner of their admonition pain us much. But my object in writing to you is to present the subject to your consideration in the form in which, I think, there was much room for at least brotherly expostulation and remonstrance. I should suppose you would agree with me that all *needless* multiplication of churches is unscriptural and contrary to all that principle of Christian unity and brotherhood which should influence disciples, and inconsistent with that manifestation of their oneness in the Lord which is an important design of their meeting. Does not the question then come to this—is the present a case of such *needless* multiplication? Upon this, I beseech you, dear M——, and I beseech L——, to deal honestly with yourselves; and say are the petty hindrances to her meeting with the brethren at B——'s such as ought to prevent her? Are they such as would prevent her if your hearts were warm in the object? What difficulty can there be in having a common car for her conveyance such a trifling distance? You will not understand me as controverting the principle that, if two disciples be in a place where there is no Christian church accessible, they are called to observe together all the ordinances which they can observe. But I think it perfectly consistent with this admission to assert, that any such meeting falls very short in various respects of what a church of Christ is designed to be, either in the public exhibition of the truth, or in the means of mutual edification and profit: and I cannot but fear that your minds are little alive to the importance of the scriptural objects of a Christian Church, when you prefer such a meeting to what appears so easily attainable. Another weighty consideration I would suggest to you. However close your earthly connexion with L——, your Christian connexion with her is no closer than with any other disciple.—Ask yourself this, if it were not your wife, but some other disciple in your neighbourhood that was prevented from meeting with the Church at B——'s, would you act the same part? Supposing the hindrance of that other disciple real, (which I confess I do not think the present case) how far it would be within the limits of Christian lawfulness for you to act as you do, I am unwilling at present to decide; for I do not think the decision of that question necessary: yet it may be worth your while to consider, whether one of us, who meet in Stafford Street, would be warranted in absenting himself in order to meet with an individual who, from sickness or any other cause, could not attend. I should hope I have said enough, under the divine blessing, to convince you both of the evil you have walked in, and that we shall have the joy of hearing that it is corrected.

XXX.

TO G—— T——, ESQ.

Dec. 1815.

Dear Mr. T——,—The Christian like candour and sobriety with which you expressed yourself when I met you lately in the Bank, induces me to address to you the following brief observations on the pamphlet lately published by one of your society upon the subject of the Salutation.

If a thing were harmless in proportion as it is weak, there could be no occasion to say a word on the subject. But it is a melancholy truth, that what is very weak may be very mischievous; and it is therefore often a necessary, though always an irksome task, to expose disingenuous imbecility. The Remarker chooses to produce a number of Greek and Latin quotations, which he says he has been at much pains to collect; while the veriest smatterer in classical learning could have easily furnished him with dozens of passages as much to the purpose. Perhaps he will suppose that this declaration adds strength to his argument. Let us see. For what purpose does he adduce these passages? In the first place, in opposition to a supposed assertion which he *knows* we have never advanced, though he marks it with inverted commas as if a quotation of our words, namely, "that it was *no more customary* at Rome, for instance, to salute with a kiss, than it is now in this country." (p. 10.) Now, it is a serious charge to bring against the Remarker, that he *knows the falsehood* of what he states, in saying that this has been asserted by us. But you, my dear sir, are a witness to the truth of this charge. You must well recollect, that in the meeting at Cutlers' Hall we stated distinctly, that salutation with a kiss was no more the ordinary salutation in Greece or Rome than it is here; and that when Mr. B—— attempted to confound this statement with the essentially different one, that it was "*no more ordinary*," or "*no more frequent*," he was distinctly recalled to observe the broad difference between the two assertions; upon which occasion my brother P—— remarked, that the question was not at all whether they kissed each other *more frequently* at Rome than they do here. Accordingly, the Remarker betrays his consciousness of the dishonest weakness of the ground which he had occupied in that paragraph; and proceeds in the next to glance at the real statement which we had made. This he contents himself with attempting to invalidate, by asking us " to bring forward the *proofs* of the assertion;" and adds, " certain it is, kissing was an ordinary mode."

Whether the former challenge originated in real ignorance or in pretended, I will not venture to pronounce. (You will perceive I view the Remarker as one towards whom I am called to deal out reprehension in no measured language; and I shall submit to the charge of unwarrantable severity, if I do not in the course of this letter prove his character to be such.) If any other seriously asked the question, I would refer him to any writer upon Greek and Roman customs. But if he be not already acquainted with what every schoolboy knows, that the stated form of salutation was by expressions equivalent with our " Good morrow," as *χαιρε, ave, salve*, &c., and that when those were accompanied with any action it was commonly *by giving the hand:* if he be not acquainted with this, even from the stated use of the Greek word *δεξιοῦσθαι*, and the Latin *prensare*, the common expression for the salutation offered by candidates for magistracies to those whom they accosted, I would probably observe to him that the inquiry is one for which he is not qualified, and which he ought to leave to those who are competent to judge.

" But," says the Remarker, " certain it is that kissing was an *ordinary* mode." That confident assertion I meet with as confident a denial. It is certain that it was not an ordinary mode—in the sense in which alone that expression can be fairly understood; and to prove this, I shall not travel out of the Remarker's quotation. What do we call an *ordinary* mode of salutation in any country? A mode of salutation commonly practised on common occasions. Now what are the Remarker's three first quotations? Instances of a kiss given to intimate friends on the extraordinary occasion of their return from distant countries, and after long absence—(I make no remark on the ridiculous ignorance of calling Tiro Cicero's pupil, &c. ignorance which, if accompanied with modesty, ought to have restrained the Remarker from meddling in public with Greek and Latin classics.) Of a somewhat similar character are his quotations from Pliny and Suetonius. But upon these it is to be remarked, that besides their being instances of the kiss practised on occasions of going abroad to a distant place or returning from it, they are instances of the mode in which the Roman *emperors* took leave of or met the senate on such occasions. Now what should we think of a writer some centuries hence, who should adduce the many records of the king's giving his hand at levee to be kissed by his courtiers, as a grave evidence that *kissing the hand* was an ordinary mode of salutation in this country, and in these days? I think we should certainly pronounce him ludicrously deceived himself or an intentional deceiver of his readers. The same is to be said of the quotation from Dion Cassius, while the Remarker's dishonesty in misrepresenting the meaning of the word ορχηστας in that passage would deserve severe animadversion, were not this instance lost in others of much greater magnitude.

But what shall we say to his quotation from Justin? to his adducing, in proof of salutation with a kiss being an ordinary mode of salutation in Greece and Rome, the instance of Antiochus offering so to salute the Roman ambassadors on his arrival? Ignorant as the Remarker shews himself, he is certainly not so ignorant as not to know that Antiochus was neither a Greek or Roman, but a king of Syria—an Asiatic. Yet even this is put forward to the simple and unlettered, to bolster up his imposition. No doubt, it would really make nothing for his argument had Antiochus been a Roman, and had Justin's authority been of any historical weight. But I ask any candid and competent judge, what terms of rebuke are too severe for the man who could attempt to pass such a cheat upon the ignorant, in the case of a scriptural question? What he means to intimate by the true remark which he adds to this quotation—that Livy, relating the same narrative, says, he *offered him his hand*—I am at a loss to conjecture. But the obvious inference to any unprejudiced mind is plainly this, that Livy, a Latin writer of the Augustan age, relating the offered salutation, expressed that mode of salutation which was customary in his time and country; and the argument is strengthened by the supposition, that the mode of salutation actually offered was such as Justin relates. But we need no argument of that kind: and I hasten from such trifles, and pass his pretty quotation from Arrian, with the brief assertion that he either does not understand it or designedly misinterprets it; while I leave him the full benefit of the passage with his present interpretation of it. I have hitherto only shewn, that his quotations do not go one step towards proving that salutation with a kiss was an ordinary practice at Rome or in Greece. But I come now to the proof afforded by his quotations "that it was not." For this, I confidently refer to his quotations from Martial and many others which might be adduced of the same character, as well as to his second quotation from Suetonius. "What," you may say, "does not Martial there describe persons whom he calls *basiatores*—kissers—kissing every one they met in the street? and does not Tiberius prohibit daily kisses by an edict?" Yes, indeed; but it happens that Martial is a writer of epigrams; and that in these and similar passages he is satirizing and ridiculing those who attempted to introduce the practice. And I would be glad to know, what more decisive evidence can be afforded that this mode of salutation was not an *ordinary* mode, than that those who practised it were distinguished by the name of *kissers*, and ridiculed in epigrams, and at one time even put down by an imperial edict. If some of our travelled gentry (like those bucks at Rome) were on their return from the Continent to attempt introducing the frequency of continental embraces, there would probably be many an epigram made on them. But the man who would hereafter introduce these epigrams as a proof that saluting with an embrace was an ordinary custom of this country, and who would tell the simple that these epigrams "described the prevalence of kissing in Ireland," (p. 21.) that man must be either most weak or most unfair. I would pass by the ridiculous absurdity with a smile, were it not for the wicked purpose for which it is employed.

I now quit the disgusting task of sifting the Remarker's learning; and gladly leave unnoticed in it abundant matter for similar rebuke. While I have thought myself called on thus briefly and strongly to expose his dishonesty, I must add—what is more important—that if the fact were as he falsely states, it would not in the least affect the authority of the apostolic precept—a precept which stands independent of the varying manners of the various countries and ages—part of that word of God which "abides for ever." And to you, my dear sir, I would say, that it is an awful thing for a professor of the gospel rashly to set any learned statement of ancient customs in opposition to the plain meaning of a divine precept. The Remarker, I know, with that kind of special pleading which pervades his whole production, urges that there are precepts, the import of which may be illustrated from ancient customs, and which are not to be taken in the literal sense of the words; he instances the precepts, Mat. vi. 17. John xiii. 15. What he means by saying, that "it is agreed on all hands that these precepts *do not apply to us*," (p. 5.) is for you to consider. They do apply to Christians now as much as to those to whom they were at first delivered, and they apply to us in the very same sense in which they were then to be understood. Every one who is influenced by the scriptural fear of God will seek to know the *real* sense or meaning of the precept delivered and truths declared in his word. In these two instances, and many others which might be adduced, it is evident from the context that the *literal* meaning of the words is not their real meaning. Here, therefore, it is perfectly fair to adduce a temperate appeal to temporary or local customs, in order to account for the literal phraseology.

But how ungodly is it to infer from this, that every precept and (by analogy) every truth declared in Scripture may be invaded at pleasure by misapplied or pretended learning? Yet to this, the Remarker's argument evidently goes. "No principles," says he, "can be *more plain* than these;" yet, as he thinks, a bit of learning shews that they *do not apply to us*;—or, as I would say, the whole context shews, that the *literal* is not the real meaning—while a slight acquaintance with the customs of the country accounts for the mode of expression. *Therefore*, the Remarker infers that another precept equally plain, and without any thing in the context or nature of the thing to set aside the literal and obvious meaning, may with impunity be assailed by his learning; and so radically assailed, that he not only opposes the plain and obvious meaning, but gravely tells us, that it is no matter what the meaning is. (p. 9.) The man who fears God and trembles at his word, will abhor such sentiments. In the variety of fancied interpretations which the Remarker half puts forward, while he shrinks from asserting any of them, the same dishonesty appears as in the whole of his pamphlet. All he is zealous for is, that the precept may not be acknowledged or obeyed—but afterwards he is quite indifferent in what sense you understand it; while to his various readers he throws out the bait of various senses, which he does not himself believe to be true. "He is not prepared to say with certainty," (page 8.) that the Apostle's salutation is conveyed in the passages; but even that is to be thrown out to those who choose to swallow it, and is gravely argued for. It is true, we never heard of a man writing to a number of persons and bidding them *kiss each other* in token of his love to them; no more than we have heard of, or can conceive, a man in the same circumstances bidding those to whom he writes give his *love to each other*. Yet even this idea, contrary to all known custom, and intrinsically absurd, is to be covered by the sage observation—that we never knew a letter written by an Apostle except the apostolic letters which we have. (p. 8.)

But we have a concession also from this Remarker. "The passages do indeed shew, that kissing was in use at the time of the Apostles." (p. 8.) This concession is impudently profane, and such as we might rather expect from an open scoffer at revelation like Voltaire, than from a serious professor of evangelical truth. I would thank him to tell me when kissing *was not in use*. But let him go on, and observe upon the institution of the Supper, and on all the passages where the mention of it occurs, that they indeed do shew that *taking bread and wine was in use at the time*; but in use as a civil and not as a religious ordinance:—and in order to set aside the ordinance by his learning, let him remark, that the passages are not *more plain* than those, Mat. vi. and John xiii. But lest any of his readers should not be able to digest the interpretation, which represents the mutual kiss of the brethren as the Apostle's salutation, a couple of other equally reasonable interpretations are thrown before them, among which they may suit their several tastes and judgments. (p. 9.) The act may have been "enjoined only to be done on the receipt of the letters;" that is, a man might direct a number of persons to kiss each other *in token of having received a letter from him*. Or if that will not go down, it may have been "a general precept given with respect to the salutations of Christians." Now, for a moment supposing this—then they are commanded in their general salutations to salute each other *with a kiss of love*. Well; we might expect that the Remarker, if he thought this were the meaning, would address himself to obey it in his general salutations of his brethren. But, no: it is no matter "whether this be the meaning or not." Let the precept only be disregarded by Christians at this day, and the Remarker is content. However, with respect to this interpretation, which he intimates *may be* the true one, it is obviously contradicted by the whole nature of the apostolic mission; which was not designed to interfere with the *manners*, or merely civil customs of any men. It would be as reasonable to suppose they prescribed the kind of bow that Christians should make to each other, as that in their general salutation they should salute each other with a kiss. And as it is undeniable that they do *enjoin mutual salutation with a kiss*—(or as the Remarker chooses with his usual ingenuousness to express it, (p. 11,) that a "certain mode of salutation *was mentioned by the Apostles*,")—the conclusion remains plain to any disciple who will receive the instruction of the Word, that the mutual kiss enjoined was *not a civil but a religious ordinance*. The Remarker, according to his own expression, may "be prepared to say" (for indeed he seems prepared to say any thing) that the Lord's supper is *sufficient* for shewing the *unity* of Christ's people, (p. 15); and that a *periodical* kiss is utterly inconsistent with "*the spirit of salutation*." (p. 13.) But his sayings cannot prevent me from acknowledging the divine wisdom in instituting a stated expression indicative of brotherly *love*, which is suitable to that unity; nor prevent me from seeing what the essential spirit of salutation is, that it is an outward act indicative of either love or respect—with which the *periodical* kiss (as he is pleased to term it) is perfectly consistent—as consistent as the periodical return of the Supper is consistent with its spirit. The argument which he chooses to misrepresent so much, in order that he may combat it more successfully, (p. 6), is simply and briefly this; that the act enjoined is a mutual act, in which *all* the disciples are commanded to take a part; and, therefore, must point to the only time when they are all assembled. Indeed it might be added, that the precept *could not* otherwise be obeyed; since, except when they are assembled, they cannot *all* salute *one another* with a kiss. The argument is so plain that it may safely be left to its own force, by the side of his vain efforts to becloud it; while it would be easy to shew, that most of the precepts from which he argues as parallel instances are essentially dissimilar, as not enjoining all to take part in any mutual or social act. But the hardihood of his *assertions* is strikingly exemplified in that paragraph. He asserts, and marks the assertion with Italics to make it more emphatic, "that there is not in Scripture any mutual act enjoined on all disciples, which particularly points to the first day of the week." I leave it to him to maintain this assertion, either by denying that the participation of the Supper is an act in which disciples *mutually* join—or by denying that it is enjoined on *all* disciples—or by denying that it particularly points *to the first day of the week*.

While every page of the pamplet would afford matter for similar reprehension, I here dismiss the Remarker. In his present mind, I think it perfectly unimportant whether he oppose the principle or profess to obey it. Nor could I walk with him if he withdrew his opposition to-morrow, unless it were accompanied with a distinct profession of repentance for the complicated wickedness of his production. How awfully blinded his mind has become to the first principles of Christian fellowship, appears even from his idea of Christians separating "by mutual consent" upon a divine precept, and retaining their esteem and charity for each other unabated. About the contrary sentiment he may use bullying language, and say, "*let not any one dare* to attribute it to the word of God." But if ever he be brought to a scriptural discernment of the real nature of *Christian love*, instead of printing such language against disciples, he will contentedly be the object of it from the unbelieving world.

Amidst the plain severity of open rebuke, which I have thought myself bound to employ towards him, I desire to remember with thankfulness and abasement, that but for *mere mercy* I might now be acting his part, and employing the dishonest arts of sophistry and false learning in opposition to the precepts which I have been led to acknowledge and obey.

I have already written more than I designed when I took up my pen, and more than has been quite consistent with the nature of my other engagements. How shall I rejoice if what I have written should be blessed to extricate you or any disciple from the entanglement by which subtilty endeavours to perplex the word of God. I would thank you to communicate this letter to the Remarker, and to any others you may please.

I remain, dear Sir, &c.

P. S.—Some of my brethren to whom I have communicated this, have expressed a wish that I should enlarge it, and extend my animadversions to other passages in the Remarks, which I have left unnoticed, and which they see equally worthy of exposure. It would, in one sense, be an easy task; but, for the present, I decline prosecuting it. Besides the little time I have for writing on such subjects, and the length to which I should be led by a minute exposure of all that deserves exposure in the pamphlet, I confess to you that it is to me a disgusting task to rummage such materials as compose it, and that I feel disposed to wash my hands out of the dirty work as quickly as possible. But I will add, that I have not intentionally passed by any thing which I conceived might carry even apparent weight;—and that if you, or any of those connected with you (except the Remarker), should say, "We give up what you have noticed; but here is an argument unnoticed, upon which we rest as the ground of our opposition to the precept;" I will then, if life and strength be spared, meet that point; and I do not apprehend that I shall have any difficulty in proving it as weak as what I have distinctly refuted.

I have softened some of the expressions in my Letter (all that I honestly could) in compliance with the wish of one of my brethren. And here I would add, that while I have charged the Remarker not only with ludicrous absurdity but gross *dishonesty*, and have abundantly proved the charge, yet I gladly acquit him of that kind of dishonesty which is conscious to itself, at the time, of its departure from truth and candour; I can easily believe that, even in the grossest instances which I have marked, he wrote without thinking, and therefore did not discern the impositions which he attempted to pass upon his readers. But this is what I view as so awful in his character, while it is quite congenial to the character of *my flesh* as well as his; to treat a question of divine precept with *head-over-heels* opposition which musters every thing that can be said against it, and regards not or thinks not whether what is advanced be true or false, but only whether it carries a colour to the readers. This (however a lawyer may think it fair in defending the cause on which he is retained) is a most awful departure from Christian integrity.

XXXI.

TO J—— G—— S——.

Jan. 16, 1816.

My Dear Friend,—I really feel ashamed at being so tardy in acknowledging your two packets of Oct. 21, and Dec. 3. Need I say that both were very acceptable: and that, hitherto, I do not find (and, indeed, do not suspect) the least difference between us on the one grand point—" Grace reigning through righteousness unto eternal life by Christ Jesus." I have not yet had time to look at poor Mr. Chalmers's production; and, at any rate, would defer it till I have the whole. The very title sufficiently indicates how unscriptural his views are at present. Whether it be the obscurity of one beginning dimly to discern, or the darkness of a benighted adversary to the truth, time will discover: and if the Antichristian falsehood of his present views be scripturally exposed from the press, it will serve as a test of his character. When one considers the society by which he is surrounded, particularly his clerical brethren, and their seductive arts, the thought might damp all hope, did we not recollect to whom it belongs to teach sinners his way. But with that before our eyes, who can say but the Rev. Mr. C. may yet be a despised witness of Him, " who is despised and rejected by men—who has no form nor comeliness—no beauty, that we sinners should desire him," Is. liii.—though he came to save sinners, even the chief, and is the brightness of the father's glory. As to ——'s wish, that I should write a reply to Mr. C., my various necessary occupations will not allow me to attempt it at present. But, if I had time, I should have much inclination for such a work. I do not know any more profitable mode of bringing forward to the world the great controversy, than by setting the truth in contrast with the sentiments of the various popular theologians, whose works appear from time to time. And often have I planned for this purpose a kind of theological review. But, perhaps, the Lord sees in my wish to be so engaged plenty of vanity and self-seeking, which he mercifully counteracts, by keeping me to the oar of business. Often have I cause to think of that word—" He that seeketh his glory that sent him, the same is true, and no unrighteousness is in him, John vii. 18:" and ever must we own that the character is exemplified only in the one who spoke the word. Yet, according as He keeps us in the view of his own glory, and in the knowledge of the things that are freely given to us of God, we shall live not to ourselves, but unto Him who has loved us, and given himself for us; and shall rejoice to be nothing, that He may be all in all. In what an opposite way from the *divines*, do the Apostles exhort and animate to a conversation becoming the Gospel—setting the glory of that Gospel before them, reminding them of the high dignity and unspeakable blessedness which is put upon them—of its divine nature, its wonderful price, its glorious consummation.

"Ye are a chosen generation, a royal priesthood, an holy nation: that ye should"—what? endeavour to make out some title to this character, or evidences of its belonging to you, by a supposed work of faith? O, no—but "that ye should *shew forth the praises* of Him who *hath* called you out of darkness into his marvellous light." "Behold! what manner of love the Father hath bestowed upon us!" "Beloved, now are we the sons of God." "These things have I written unto you that believe on the name of the Son of God;" that ye may *know that ye have* eternal life, and that ye may believe on the name of the Son of God." Well may we say—this is not the manner of man.—I was here obliged to lay aside my pen, and can now only subscribe my name. Believe me ever truly yours.

XXXII.

TO J—— P——.

April, 26, 1816.

My Dear Sir,—I am sorry that so many months have elapsed before I could write to you. But I wished to write at some length: and being overloaded with business, I could not take up my pen till now. I have read your letter with attention; and with some satisfaction. It gives me pleasure to find any professor of the Gospel expressing himself heartily concerned, as you do, for the outward union of *all* the Lord's people. I can truly join with you, in saying that this is an object which lies near—very near—to my heart: and my anxiety for it is increased by a confident *expectation* of it,—from a persuasion that it is *promised* in the word of Him who cannot lie, and for whom nothing is too hard. As to the men, who can without scruple multiply divisions among those who verbally profess the truth, and lightly set up synagogue against synagogue; I see in them very little of the scriptural character of disciples, however highly they are esteemed by the religious world. Among such I reckon some, with whom (I believe) you are connected in this city, and who have been, for some time, zealously gathering disciples to them, on the principle of *forbearing with each other in matters of divine command*.—(You will excuse me for writing with much freedom and plainness.)—Proceeding on that principle, they had consistently no occasion to form a *new* society. They might have joined P—— S—— congregation, for instance, and would have only had to exercise *forbearance* with its present members in the few matters on which they differ. But, indeed, it would be found that no consistent reason could be assigned for their quitting the most grossly corrupt communion, in which they had been before: nor do they seem to have been directed in their conduct by anything but private fancy, and zeal against the only scriptural principles of Christian union. *That union* must always appear in a form the most contemptible and odious to men; contemptible as from other causes, so from the smallness of the numbers embraced by it; and odious, as standing in steadfast opposition to all the fairest forms of the religion of the world. None can have a relish for it, but those whose minds are subjected by divine mercy to the yoke of Him who *is despised and rejected by men*, who has *no form nor comeliness* to the natural eye, and who plainly tells us of the way that leadeth unto life—"*few* there be that find it." I quite agree with you that there is a *fault*, a very awful fault, on one side or the other: and I should always rejoice to meet the inquiry, where it lies. If those you speak of in K——— have been gathered together in the mind which you describe, I trust that they and I shall not be long asunder. But excuse me for saying that they *may* have left the Established church "from *conscientious* motives," and yet upon no solid scriptural principle. Conscience, and religious conscience—is a very deceitful monitor, unless where it is regulated by the word of God. The Established church no doubt presents a striking spectacle of the setting aside of the laws of the King of Zion, and the introduction of a code of human regulations in their place. Did you break off from that fellowship in submission to the binding authority of the divine word, or in the discretionary gratification of some kind of *religious taste*? If the former, how can you contend for maintaining fellowship with any, in whom the same evil appears of not obeying *any* precept of the word? Is it the *number* of precepts disobeyed in the other connexion, that made it obligatory on you to leave it? The man who holds that non-obedience to *any* divine command may be made a matter of mutual forbearance, ought to be prepared to say, before he quits the Establishment, how many instances of it may not be forborn with:—or he ought to state distinctly (as I have often urged such persons to do, but always in vain) what the precepts are, to which continued disobedience cannot be forborn with in a Christian church, and what those are in which it may. Indeed it is no wonder they do not like to be called on to explain themselves here: because, if they gave a plain answer to the question, the ungodliness of their system would be more strikingly manifest to any one who *fears the Lord, and trembles at his word*. It would more plainly appear that they invade the whole authority of the divine word, by marking any of its precepts as matters which the members of a Christian church may agree to set aside. Such a union is not a Christian union, but an Antichristian confederacy; which, however, I know may make a great shew of liberality and love, and will commend itself to the taste of the religious world, by the very characters which make it an object of abhorrence to disciples.

You seem to select the matters mentioned in Acts ii. 42, as including all things necessary to Christian union. And, understanding the passage aright, I would heartily agree with you. But, I dare say that you, like many others, confine the import of the Apostle's *doctrine*, or *teaching*, to the Gospel which they preached. Against that common perversion of the word, I might refer you to Matth. xxviii. 20. Rom. xvi. 17. 1 Cor. iv. 17. 2 Thess. ii. 15. iii. 6. But supposing for a moment that the doctrine of the Apostles implied only the things they taught *concerning the work of Christ*, and the way of a sinner's salvation,—allow me to ask how you would reply to a clergyman of the Establishment objecting to your secession from it as schism, and employing your own text against you. He might say—you own that I preach the Apostolic *doctrine* of Christ crucified, and on the first day of the week we continue in it, and in "*prayers*, and in the *fellowship* or contribution, and—(he might add if it be a Cathedral)—also in the *Lord's Supper*." You would probably be at no loss to vindicate your secession, by pointing out various objections to his religious connexion; and among them, perhaps, you would mention the setting aside of all the laws of *discipline*, which Christ has established in his house. But are *these* of indispensable obligation, though not mentioned in your text? Why should you not forbear with their non-observance, for the sake of peace and union? Do you exclaim at the idea of thus joining to cast contempt upon the divine authority of the King of Zion? 'Tis very good:—but with what consistency then can you object to us, who profess to regard *all* his laws alike as sacred; and who think it a *profanation* to talk of *forbearing* with continued disobedience to *any* of them?—Do you reply in that language, which I know is common in your connexion—"yes, they are all to be held sacred *as far as they are seen*: but all disciples do not see alike; and we cannot expect the maturity of knowledge in a weak babe. Shall I, then, break off from one, of whose *sincerity* I am *persuaded*, because he does not *see with me* in all things? Shall I withhold Christian fellowship here from one, with whom I hope to have everlasting fellowship above?"—Alas! the plausibility with which the father of lies dresses up his opposition to Christ and his kingdom! It would require more than the compass of a letter to shake out, and expose, all the ungodly lies that are contained in that language and argument. But the shortest way for detecting its fallacy with *you* may be to suggest, that the clergyman (whom I have just now supposed to argue against you as schismatic) might urge you with the self-same topics. "I do not *see*—I cannot *see*—the unlawfulness which you assert in the Establishment: and you own that many *sincere* disciples have lived and died in it. Why, then, should we not still walk together, though we cannot *see alike* in all things?" How *you* would answer him I do not know. I should be at no loss to tell him, that the authority of the divine precepts does not depend on our *seeing* them or not seeing them; though certainly they cannot really be obeyed without a discernment of them: and that, as to men's *sincerity* of opposition to them, it no more extenuates their disobedience, than their *sincere* rejection of the Gospel as a lie can vindicate their unbelief. I should be at no loss to tell him, when he put himself forward as one who must be acknowledged a genuine disciple, that whatever he might be in the sight of God, he could not scripturally be manifested as such to me, but by hearing the voice of God in his word: (John x. 27.) and that while the word assures me that believers themselves, through the wickedness of our common nature, might be found in courses the most evil,—yet the same word debars me from taking part with them in the evil, or *touching the unclean thing*, by holding fellowship with them till they repent. But while my reply to him would be to this effect, the grounds of it lead me necessarily to address the same language to every other professor, whatever be his religious connexion, who persists in walking contrary to any of the precepts of the Lord: and I am compelled to reject with abhorrence all proposals from them for an amicable compromise of our differences. The discussion of any particular precepts, on which you and I are at present disagreed, would be idle, and worse than idle, as long as the principles of unscriptural *forbearance*, adopted by your connexion, strike at the authority of all the precepts of God. And that connexion, formed in opposition against the few in this country who consistently assert their authority, I cannot view as a union of disciples:—though I freely admit there may be disciples in that Babylonish house, and it is my earnest prayer that such may come out of it. It will rejoice me to find you savouring the things that are of God, and not the things that are of men; and taking part with his despised and calumniated followers in the kingdom and patience of Jesus Christ.

I am, dear Sir, with best wishes,
Your willing Servant,

XXXIII.

TO J—— G—— S——.

May 23, 1816.

My Dear Friend,—Three or four days ago I received your packet, containing remarks on the 25th Psalm, &c. I have only had time to look at it here and there, but what I have read I like much. O! what a mine of joy to sinners is in that little verse, the 11th.—In our natural blindness, what a strange reason does it seem to urge for forgiveness of iniquity—"pardon mine iniquity—for *it is great*." And all our *natural* religion runs on the opposite idea, striving to reduce or conceal the quantity of our iniquity, that it may seem *small* enough to be pardoned. This is that *covering of sin*, of which it is written, that he who does it *shall not prosper;* he never shall succeed in the attempt. But when mercy opens our eyes to see Him who speaketh in the psalm,—Him, who was *made sin* for us, who took upon himself, as his own, the sins of many, and confessed them as his own before his Father whose name he came to glorify by fulfilling the work of putting them away by the sacrifice of himself, —when we hear the words as *his;*—"for thy name's sake"—for the glory of that name of thine, which I have come to manifest in a sinful ruined world—Jehovah the *Saviour*—just and the justifier of the *ungodly*—"pardon mine iniquity, for it is great"—great as all the exceeding sinfulness of the many brethren whom I have come to redeem; when we see the full cancelling of all that great iniquity certified in the acceptance of his sacrifice, and by his resurrection from the dead; then, and not till then, do we *confess our sins*, and see, that in the greatness of our iniquity, there is so far from any bar to the divine mercy, that it is only the more gloriously displayed in our forgiveness. But I must stop. I only took up my pen, to prevent you laying down yours, as you threatened. I fear poor —— will give but a very imperfect reply to Dr. Chalmers, though he may probably expose many errors. Unless he write with a single eye to the one thing needful, he might better spare his labour.

Believe me, dear friend,

Affectionately yours.

XXXIV.

TO ———.

April, 19, 1817.

Sir,—I should have replied to your letter immediately, had I not been more than ordinarily hurried with a press of business, as indeed I still am. Any freedom of expression you have used does not at all offend me. You will allow me to imitate you in this respect, which I may do with the less reserve as I address a mask: you must blame the disguise you have assumed, if I treat you with less ceremony than I might perhaps think needful if I knew to whom I write. But I have not the smallest wish to break through that disguise, and shall observe the secrecy you desire—only remarking, that we could go over more ground in two hours' conversation than in two days' writing. I would enter with you more cheerfully on the discussion you propose, if I were assured you possess as strong reasoning powers as you seem to attribute to yourself. But I have much doubt of that. In a little parenthesis, you express a very foolish dissatisfaction with my charging half-a-guinea for one lecture. If you thought the charge exorbitant, you ought to know that the evil would bring its own remedy; and you might as well blame a man for asking too high a price for his corn. But, in fact, while that mode of payment is more convenient to some students who have only a few lectures, it is less productive to me than if I charged twenty guineas for an examination—the terms of the private tutors who possess not my qualifications. If you apprehend that I am in danger of getting too rich, when I tell you that with very hard working I do not make quite 300*l*. per ann. you may be at ease on that score. Again—you say that the Christian religion "has only found its way with women or timid men, or rogues, or madmen." I think this also a very foolish observation. Newton, Locke, Bacon, Boyle, Sir Mat. Hale, &c. are names that, with every person of candour and information, must screen, at least from that imputation, any opinions they adopted after strict examination. I do not know which of your epithets you would mean to apply to them, unless perhaps "timid men;" and if all who are not rash be timid, they certainly were timid. But let me observe to you, that if a hardy contempt of danger constitutes courage, the blockhead that will leap for a shilling from the top of Patrick's steeple is the bravest man in the world. The man that thinks himself entitled to fling such epithets as you do against such men as I have mentioned, must consider himself possessed of extraordinary mental powers indeed. But that is a small instance of what you assume to yourself, in comparison of your imagining that you have proved too wise even for the Supreme Being. You more than intimate, that He intended we should *think* ourselves free or accountable agents; but you conceive that you have got behind the scene, and discovered the imposition. I think this, also, about as wise as it is modest. Thus, when I look at the reasoning in your letter, and the sketch you give of your system (if system it may be called), I own I see nothing that argues much depth of thought or acuteness of mind. Every dabbler in metaphysics will find puzzling difficulties floating on the very surface, which any one may pick up and no one can fully solve. But it is the mark of a very prejudiced mind to see the difficulties only on one side of a question, and the mark of a very shallow thinker to consider the certainty of any thing invaded by the difficulty or doubtfulness of some questions that may be asked about it. You say the Christian religion is "completely contrary to reason, experience, and observation." If you really have an understanding capable of meeting the rational discussion of it, I would undertake to demonstrate that it is the only system consistent to sound reason, while, among numberless evidences internal and external of its divine original, it contains one in proposing a system which (so far from being such as men were likely to forge) is such as no man of himself could possibly have thought of. I am not sure what you mean by saying it is contrary to *experience and observation*. But I am sure, that in addressing men as accountable beings, it speaks a language that is consistent, by your own confession, to the feelings they experience; and I think I may engage, that all your philosophy will not enable you to divest yourself of those feelings. You try to persuade yourself that you are a mere machine, composed of air, earth, and water: but you are *conscious* all the while that you are not a machine, but possess properties which neither water, earth, or air possess, nor can acquire by any composition of them: and this consciousness breaks out in the same sentence, when you express an expectation that *you* will be called into some other mundane system after your bodily particles have gone into their respective elements. Why should you call that new thing that may be made up of the same particles, "YOU," if you did not apprehend that you will retain your individuality after their dissolution? You express your doubt whether a savage is troubled with conscience; very little *troubled* with it, perhaps; but it no more follows that he is destitute of that internal sense, than it follows that you have no eyesight because you do not see in the dark. Yet, comparatively dormant as the faculty may lie in the savage, I believe you have never yet found an *authentic* account of savages destitute of all religion; and I know not how you will separate all exercise of conscience from that. Indeed, if you examine that self-praise and blame which you confess make part of our nature, you will find them little else than other names for this troublesome principle. I heartily wish you a better prop for your conscience than your system affords: else your conscience will sink when a dying hour brings the great and righteous Lawgiver more nearly to its view. The Christian religion, in addressing man as a creature not only endowed with conscience, but needing a better stay for his conscience than he could himself supply it with, coincides with multiplied experience and observation, and marks a knowledge of what is in man; while the kind of relief and support which it proposes, at once lays bare the root of his disease, and applies an effectual remedy. In maintaining that you are a voluntary, and *therefore* accountable agent, and that you are conscious of this, however you try to disguise it, I by no means intimate, what you vainly think must follow—that the Creator will suffer you to defeat any part of his great plan. No—you are under his effectual control; but you as vainly endeavour on that account to throw off blame from yourself, because He *suffers* you to do evil. That old book, that you think so foolish, has anticipated your reasoning in stating the objection—" Why doth he yet find fault, for who hath resisted his will?"

And now, sir, consider what kind of a god you acknowledge—one that not only has hitherto been doing nothing but amusing himself with the play of puppets, but is incapable of forming any creatures, the subjects of moral government;—for, according to your system, they cannot be the subjects of that, unless he give up all control of them, i. e. unless he ceases to be the supreme governor of his creatures:—unless he do this, whatever they do, they are but " obedient to the great system of fluctuating particles," and therefore not to be called to account; and this is the system which eleven years' leisure has produced. A creature forced by the works of creation to infer the existence of a being great, wise, and good, strives to throw off the yoke of divine authority from his mind by reasoning himself into a lump of earth, air, and water. You ask my free opinion on your principles. I freely say (however unphilosophical the declaration may appear to you) that I see in them an awful instance of the folly and wickedness which the Scriptures describe to be in man, and which I am conscious are in myself. But while your system leaves you groping in the dark, what I have learned from the Scriptures furnishes me with a solution of all that is passing in this world, and with a clear and joyful prospect into the next; at once discovers to me a God, whose glory is indeed strikingly contrasted with the vanity of your idol, and makes my conscience not afraid to discern his glory; preserves me undegraded from the rank of an intelligent and voluntary being, while it brings me into the posture proper to such—of acknowledged and willing dependence upon him, and subjection to him. I am, Sir, yours, &c.

XXXV.

TO J. R. K———, ESQ.

Nov. 20, 1817.

Dear Sir,—Your letter was delayed for some days, by being brought to College. The particular address which I prefix to my reply will prevent any mistake for the future, if you should favour me with any further communications; and to despatch such an unimportant subject, I would briefly observe, that I am not entitled to the distinction of "a minister of the Gospel"—except so far as every believer of that gospel may be called a happy servant of it. I have long since renounced all clerical character, and hold no official station in any church. Your letter has affected me with a good deal of surprise and with some pleasure:—my surprise is, that among all your religious friends you had none to warn you against communication with a man so long and generally obnoxious as myself. My pleasure is connected with the hope that you may prove indeed a partaker of that precious faith which is every where spoken against. It is a hope not forbidden by any thing in your letter; and I shall rejoice to find it confirmed by more explicit language hereafter. Formerly, I own, I should have been more sanguine in drawing immediately the most satisfactory conclusions about your views; but the experience of many years has taught me, what I ought to have earlier known from the scriptures, that *few* indeed are on the side of the truth of God; and that many are its keenest adversaries who held at first a very fair language, and are generally esteemed its most zealous friends. A little further exchange of sentiments (if you can bear with my plainness) will bring us better acquainted with each other.

Though I am mostly shut out from knowing what passes in the religious world, yet some indistinct echo of the noise made by your proceedings reached me, and excited a degree of interest to know more about you. That interest was damped by soon hearing of you and some others as clergymen and Baptists. But I am glad to find the latter part of the report unfounded with respect to yourself.

However, not to fill my paper with my hopes and fears, I would remark that it is in general contrary to my principles and practice to enter on the discussion of any Christian institution, except with those who profess agreement with me in the faith of Christ. I should think it calculated to mislead others, to becloud the grand essential difference between us, and dishonour the God whom I serve by confounding his holy name with the gods of the unbelieving world. You were rightly informed that my views differ from the general opinions of what are called the evangelical dissenters. But they differ upon much more essential points than water baptism. They differ upon the nature of a sinner's conversion, upon the faith of

Christ, the hope of the gospel, regeneration, sanctification, and in short the name and character of the only true and living God. The difference is most favourable to the evangelical dissenters, as far as every thing creditable and respectable in the eyes of man is concerned; for my sentiments must ever appear abominable and vile, except to the few who are likeminded with me, and find their life in what the world abhors. The scriptural account of conversion is very short and simple. Acts xiv. 1. Paul and Barnabas "went both together into the synagogue of the Jews, and so spake that a great multitude both of the Jews and also of the Greeks believed"—believed the things spoken by Paul and Barnabas concerning Jesus of Nazareth (see also Acts xxviii. 24.) This is all the plain account of the matter. Those men were at once Christians, converted to God, born of God, saints in Christ Jesus.

But the mere believing or crediting the things testified in Scripture concerning Jesus Christ, is made nothing of by the evangelical dissenters—it is the faith of devils—it and its few advocates have every opprobrious name heaped upon them; and any one who looks at their numerous accounts of so-called conversions and experiences, will find indeed a very different story. Great and glorious must have been the things believed by the first Christians, when the mere belief of them produced such great effects. But in the popular systems, all that greatness and glory are made but subsidiary to the series of religious exercises and feelings, which their disciples are brought through in their progressive efforts to attain to righteousness, till they are supposed at length to arrive at it by some private revelation of what is no where declared in the word of God.—An Apostle also tells in few words what that gospel was which he preached in every place, 1 Cor. xv. 3, 4. "That Christ died for our sins according to the scriptures; and that he was buried, and that he rose again the third day, according to the scriptures." Many an evangelical professor says in his heart about such a gospel when it is proposed—"and is this all?" Yet it is all, and it is enough. The sinner, whoever he be, that believes this knows *that* God whom to know is life eternal, has a good hope that maketh not ashamed; and boldness of access into the holiest. He sees that which a *sinner* wants—that propitiation for sin which God hath accepted, and which (as of his provision) is adequate for all the ends designed. He rests in what God is well pleased with, and discerning the glory of God in the face of Jesus is passed from darkness into light, from death to life, and from the bondage of sin into the glorious liberty of the sons of God. The same light that discovers to his view the glory of divine righteousness, discloses to him the bottomless abyss of human ungodliness and ruin. He rejoices in Christ Jesus, and has no confidence in the flesh; he is called to hold the *beginning* of his confidence and rejoicing of hope firm unto the end, to stand fast in the liberty wherewith Christ hath made him free, and to contend earnestly for the faith once delivered to the saints; his hope and joy indeed are suited to the publican and the harlot, and throw contempt upon all that is most highly esteemed amongst men as abomination in the sight of God. He can therefore expect no favour from the world—the religious or the irreligious world; and the former, as abounding most in those highly esteemed abominations, he may expect to find his most embittered foes; yet he has nothing to boast over them; he sees displayed in them only the enmity of his own heart against God, and he has cause to know more of its continued deceitfulness, ungodliness, and pride, than of theirs; he has a blessedness indeed which they yet know not of, but all centering in an object which they only need to see in order to be partakers of its blessedness with him:—with the little flock partakers of like precious faith he is prepared to walk in the fellowship of the gospel, in the enduring bond of christian unity, receiving as little children the gracious directions which their heavenly head affords them in his word, building up each other in their most holy faith, taught of God to love one another with a pure heart fervently, bearing each other's burdens and comforting each other's hearts with the prospect of the second appearance of the Lord without sin unto salvation, when the righteous shall shine forth in the kingdom of their father.

And is it so, dear sir, that you are subdued by the divine mercy to take part with this despised flock in their sorrows and their joys? Is it so that the propitiation which emboldened the prayer of the publican and the thief upon the cross is seen by you as the only spring of hope and relief to your conscience, and *sufficient* to fill with joy unspeakable, and full of glory, the very chief of sinners? Is it so, (as a sentence in your letter would seem to import) that you perceive the gods of the professing world around you to be *idols*, and their votaries to be wearying themselves in the greatness of their way, and rejoicing in the work of their own hands? Is it so, that you have come out from among them? that the snare is broken to you of all the deceivableness of unrighteousness in them? that the glitter and parade of their religion have lost their attractions to you, in the view of the one thing that is needful for a sinner, and divinely glorious? O, if it be so, with my whole heart I bid you God speed, and pray that he may fill you more and more with the knowledge of his glorious name, and with the knowledge of his gracious will, fulfilling in you all the good pleasure of his goodness, and the work of faith with power. If it be so, you will not be displeased or offended with my freedom, nor wonder that I have left so little room to answer what forms the main topic of your letter. I have published two pieces on the Baptist controversy, but they have been both for some time quite out of print: nor have I been yet able to find a single copy of either. But I shall make every inquiry, and expect very soon to transmit them to you. The first is very short, and I long wished to reprint it, with some observations on a review of it by Mr. Haldane; but circumstances have hitherto rendered this and other similar schemes impossible. The second piece is considerably longer, and was occasioned by the attack of one who had left our fellowship on the Baptist principles, but has been, for many years blessedly reunited to us as a brother beloved. The manner in which the Baptists have been generally opposed by Pædobaptists affords them great advantages; and certainly in their argument on the first view there appears a specious plausibility well calculated to ensnare disciples.

"The members of all the first Christian churches were dipped in water; and why should not all, who profess to be followers of those churches, imitate them in this rite?" It sounds fairly, and calls for fair consideration. But, looking beyond the surface of their argument, I find them introducing a rite, for which, I am bold to say, there is not a single precept nor a single *precedent* in the word of God—the baptism of persons who have never professed but to believe the apostolic testimony concerning Jesus of Nazareth. In this view their conduct is but a farcical child's-play in imitation of what the Apostles did. But in other views I find it vitally erroneous; I find it employed to mark, in a professing Christian, the epoch of a supposed transition from a spurious to a genuine profession, and this connected with the worst systems of popular conversion. I find it directly opposed to the important precept, which calls a believer "to bring up his children in the instruction and admonition of the Lord," Ephes. vi. 4; and in the contempt which it pours on the idea of the discipleship of such little children, I find all the high-mindedness of Antichristian profession which strikes at the very truth of Christ.

For my more enlarged views on these topics, I must refer you to the pieces, which I hope to send very soon. Let me just remark on the asserted difference you mention between Jewish baptism and that practised by the Apostles, that it goes to assert, that many of the Apostles (such as Peter and John) never had Christian baptism; "for Jesus himself baptized not:" and it is plain that these Apostles followed Jesus without any other water-baptism than they had received from John: and I would add, that the supposition of Christ's having commanded his Apostles to baptize with water, in the commission given to them, is directly inconsistent with Paul's language on the subject, 1 Cor. i. 14. The history of the disciples in Acts xix., contrasted with the account of Apollos in the preceding chapter, I think you will find fully accounted for in the second of my pamphlets. It is idle to represent the Lord's Supper as standing on the same footing, when we have a direct account of Christ's institution of that ordinance, and (besides recorded precedent) express information, that disciples are so to shew forth his death till he come. Hoping soon to be favoured with another and a longer letter from you, I gladly subscribe myself, with affectionate interest for the truth's sake, yours, ——

XXXVI.

TO THE SAME.

Dec. 21, 1817.

Very Dear Sir,—Your letter was most welcome and gratifying. Indeed it has afforded to me and others much matter of praise and thanksgiving to Him, whose "mercy endureth for ever," and has excited lively hopes that the Lord is visiting benighted England with the light of unadulterated truth. The epithet, by which I have been led to characterize your country, would surprize and offend the generality of your professors. But it is an awful character that forced itself on my mind in all my latter views of it. I have seen there the reign of the clergy of various denominations in great splendour and power, and multitudes blindly following their corrupt ways; but had to mourn that I could not even obtain a hearing, except in very few instances, for the despised gospel, while they have societies—for what (I believe) they call evangelizing Ireland. And let me not be mistaken, when I speak of hopes, that the Lord is mercifully visiting the country: I by no means think myself warranted to expect that the believers of the genuine gospel will there, or elsewhere, be any thing but a little flock, contemptible in the eyes of the world both religious and profane, and objects of its hatred, as disturbers of its peace, testifying against all that it reckons most respectable and good. It is not till the Lord Jesus shall appear in his glory, that his collected people will *appear* glorious in the comeliness that he has put upon them. Till then, they will present to the eye of man similar characters with their Head in the days of his flesh —"a root out of a dry ground," "having no form nor comeliness;" and all this only illustrates to them continually the essential opposition of fallen man, in all his ways and thoughts, to the ways and thoughts of God. That flourishing state of Christianity, which the popular religionists dream of, countenanced and supported by the great and respectable of the earth, is one of the idols they have formed to themselves and very consistent with the false gospels they embrace, but utterly inconsistent with the true. Yet how cheering is it when we see any new instances, in which the word of the Lord is made powerful to subdue the stout-hearted, to enlighten the blind, to turn into the way of peace, and righteousness, and life, those who were wandering in the shadow of death; where we unexpectedly find one and another new voices swelling the chorus of those, who in heaven and on earth celebrate the sole worthiness of the Lamb that was slain. I do indeed rejoice to think that we are agreed, nor do I see any thing in your letter to excite an apprehension of the contrary:—agreed in the one thing needful for a sinner, discerning that in Him, to whom all the testimony of God points, "behold my righteous servant—behold the Lamb of God, that taketh away the sin of the world—this is my beloved Son, in whom *I am well pleased.*" O blessed testimony—displaying the glory of the only true God, and that in such a way, that the chief of sinners instead of being terrified rejoices in the discovery and is at once ***blessed in Him.*** Who, indeed, teacheth like Him? I think now we could talk for ever upon the glorious theme, and that the sentiments of each would be reechoed by the new mind of faith in the other. How it would delight me, in a long conversation face to face, to compare notes with you upon various passages of Scripture, which the cunning craftiness of those who lie in wait to deceive has perverted. But I must recollect that I am confined at present to communicate with pen and ink, and that you desire my views "of the covenant and the Trinity." You will find me a very poor *divine* upon both. As to the covenant, all I know or desire to know is that blessed new covenant ordered in all things and sure, in which Jehovah has engaged,—"I will put my law in their inward parts, and write it in their hearts," (even the law which has gone forth out of Zion), "*I will* be their God, and they *shall* be my people: they shall all *know* ME; for I will forgive their iniquity, and I will remember their sin no more." Of this new and everlasting covenant Jesus (the true David or beloved) is the head—the mediator: with him it was made (speaking after the manner of men) in the eternal counsels of peace; "in him all its promises are yea and amen." "Once have I sworn in mine holiness that I will not lie unto David." His blood of atonement is the blood of this everlasting covenant, and those "sure mercies of David" are in Him sure to all the seed, the many sons and daughters who all are indeed one with him.

But besides this, what more, dear sir, do we want to know about the covenant? Professors of divinity may write learned volumes upon the covenants, and bewilder their hearers in a labyrinth of words. But what have we to do with their vain speculations? I own I was startled when you come to offer an explanation of (what is called) the Trinity, though soon relieved by finding so very little, if any thing, that could be objected to in what you said, and especially by the short concluding remark with which you check yourself—"perhaps, after all, we may be anxious to go beyond what is written." It is a check indeed suitable to the sobriety of mind which the truth imparts. How awful have been the presumptuous attempts of man to scan the infinity of God, while there is not a particle of matter surrounding us but presents mysteries inscrutable to human sagacity! The very name of Trinity I must discard as of human invention, with all the blasphemous farrago of scholastic philosophy which has been so rashly put forward to explain it. But to those who exclaim with Job, "O that I knew where I might find him!" is not the reply of the Lord Jesus to Philip in point, "have I been so long time with you, and yet hast thou not known me, Philip? he that hath seen me, hath seen the Father: and how sayest thou then, shew us the Father? no man hath seen God at any time: the only begotten son, which is in the bosom of the Father, he hath declared him." His name Jesus is identical with Jehovah the Saviour: He is Immanuel, God with us. In him dwelleth all the fulness of the Godhead bodily, and every one who is of the truth will with Thomas hail him—"my Lord and my God." But why should we vainly want to know more of God than is revealed in him? When I was last in Glasgow I had some long conversations at his desire with a young Scotch Minister; and he seemed puzzled to know what to make of me, finding that I protested against the Athanasian language. I was not a Sabellian, much less an Arian or Socinian; but simply adhering to the plain word of scripture, and pressing its truths upon his conscience. In short, I am afraid always of saying too much upon such a solemn subject. The presumptuous rashness of man, attempting to rush into that before which Angels veil their faces, is awful. But where the divine testimony concerning the work and office of Jesus is simply received, it at once decides the controversy about his character, informs the sinner of all that he needs to know, and checks the proud speculation that would inquire further.

And now, dear sir, that I have (however imperfectly) replied to your inquiry, suffer me to mention a topic about which I am very solicitous to obtain information from you.

I observe that you refer in both your letters to a number of persons with you, who seem to have received and to rejoice in the same truth. How do you and they walk together? Is it as the first churches of God which in Judea were in Christ Jesus, meeting together on the first day of the week to break bread and to edify one another, and joining together in all the institutions and ordinances of christian fellowship? do you attend to the appointed discipline by which evils that appear from time to time are met and purged away? It may be a subject to which your mind perhaps has hitherto been little directed: but it is so closely *connected* with the truth, and the scriptural principles of it are so simple and harmonizing with the pure gospel, that I trust they will quickly recommend themselves to your conscience. Indeed, until believers are gathered together to walk in one by the rule of the word, they neither have the proper edification designed for them, nor is the character of professors tried and manifested. I am glad to hear that you have never received any kind of ordination, for there is so much less of clerical prejudice to be overcome.

I shall not be surprized if, of those whom you think at present agreed with you in the truth, several be yet found to differ from you essentially. Of Mr. C——, whom you mention as my countryman, I do not recollect to have ever before heard; and the little that you now tell me affords me no satisfaction. I think he might just as well have stayed where he was. As he "intends to have a liturgy," no doubt he intends to be a clergyman still, and between a dissenting clergyman and a clergyman of the Establishment I know no difference worth contending about. To be the head of a religious congregation has certainly many allurements to the vanity and worldly-mindedness of man; but such ministers of religion have been and are the greatest agents of Antichrist.—It is time for me to have done. To the rich mercy and all-sufficiency of God our Saviour I heartily commend you; praying that we may prove to be perfectly joined together in one mind and one judgment on all his revealed will. I shall anxiously look for the favour of future communications from you. I am, dear sir, &c.

XXXVII.

TO G—— M——.

Jan. 2, 1818.

DEAR BROTHER M——,—I have communicated your letter to brother F——; and he agrees with me in opinion that, although it now unequivocally appears that you have renounced our fellowship, we are not yet at liberty to report to the church an ultimate failure of the commission we received from the body. If, therefore, you recollect the principles by which we are regulated, you will not be surprized that (as long as the merciful effort to restore you goes on) we still address you in the hope of the gospel as a brother beloved for the truth's sake. Your declining to address us jointly is perfectly consistent with the step you have taken of departing from our communion. But while I meet your wishes so far as to address you as an individual, I wish it to be distinctly understood, that I still act in execution of the commission received from the body, and in communication with the brother united with me in it. Indeed, should that commission at any time terminate unfavourably, I shall certainly feel no disposition to keep up an epistolary controversy with you upon baptism.

I regret (though I do not much wonder) that so small a part of your long reply bears any relation to the letter we addressed to you. By the topics to which we confined ourselves, you might have better judged on what " our views of the subject rest," than from any misrepresentations of your honest, intelligent, and anti-scriptural baptist author. I should certainly object to him as an interpreter of my language or sentiments on the subject.

At the outset, I cannot conceal from you my suspicion that you still remain *unbaptized*, though you have departed from the fellowship of your brethren on the ground of baptism. It is an inconsistency which I have known in other instances; and many particulars in your language lead me to think it is the case with you. *If it be so*, let me solemnly call your attention to the ungodliness of your conduct, and to the ungodly principles from which it must originate. *If it be so*, under the pretence of bearing testimony against those who (you say) " are united in making void a command of God," you remain yourself making void that command by not obeying it. Your sin in attempting to impose upon us what we are persuaded is no divine command, and have proved to be none, is combined with the hypocrisy of asserting the divine obligation of that which you continue not to obey. I forbear to enlarge on the awful consideration, from the degree of uncertainty which I feel whether or not I be mistaken as to the fact. If the supposition on which I have penned this paragraph be unfounded, I must only beg that you will consider it as cancelled.

You now professedly abandon the idea of employing baptism,

either to mark the transition from a spurious to a genuine profession of the Christian faith, or the era of our connexion with a particular scriptural church. You professedly abandon both of those positions as untenable, and yet to one or other of them you *immediately resort*, in saying, that "baptism is the scriptural commencement of a scriptural profession." This, which you now substitute for the former as your present opinion, carries with it no meaning (in your application of it) but what is coincident with one or other of the former. A scriptural profession (in the meaning of the words) imports a profession of believing that Jesus Christ died for our sins, and is risen again from the dead. It is evidently not in this sense that you use the words, as you admit that you always professed to believe this. And indeed of old, baptism was so far from being the commencement of this profession, that, *until this scriptural profession was made*, baptism was not administered (at least to adults), and did no doubt therefore *mark the commencement* of this profession, or the transition of the proselytes to it. But the words, in your use of them, must either import that transition from a spurious to a genuine profession of the Christian faith which we spoke of (and in reference to which we called you to speak plainly, and say *when* it took place in you)—or must import the commencement of a Christian profession in connexion with a particular scriptural church. This, indeed, appears to be the sense in which you employ them (as far as you have any determinate meaning), from the preceding part of the paragraph, where you talk of baptism *qualifying* the believer to join in worship with a scriptural church. But using them in this sense, what mean you by denying that you now consider baptism as marking the commencement of church connexion? and how could you wholly pass unnoticed the plain evidence we adduced, from the history of the believing eunuch, that baptism was not of old employed for this purpose? as well as our remark, that the notion is inconsistent with the *possibility* of the re-appearance of any scriptural church since the time of the Apostles? Perhaps, the latter remark (plain as it is) was put too briefly. Let me therefore confirm it by observing, that if baptism is to mark the commencement of connexion with a scriptural church, the church must exist to warrant the baptism; and, on the other hand, there must be baptized persons to form the church; so that, as soon as scriptural churches ceased to exist (as they did very soon after the age of the Apostles) they never could again exist according to this system. If there be any air of trifling in the argument, it is only occasioned by the absurdity of the hypothesis which it refutes. But let me seriously put it to you, dear M——, whether the repeated shifting of your ground and wavering of your mind about the just view of baptism, ought not to suggest to you the suspicion of an inherent weakness in the foundation of your system? And for what purpose is it, that all this shifting and wavering appears? To evade the plain and incontrovertible position which we put forward, that in every instance of Christian baptism recorded in the scriptures, the rite marked a transition to the profession of the Christian faith in a person who had not before professed it, or marked *the commencement of his*

Christian profession. But do we need the testimony of Jewish rabbins and German divines to authenticate the truth of that position? While you attempt to evade it, will you directly deny its truth or certainty? And why do you wish to evade it? Because the admission of it immediately puts down the baptism for which you contend (of those who have never professed any other than the Christian faith) as a human invention, without precept and without precedent in the word of God:—a religious farce, in which people amuse themselves by playing " Philip and the eunuch."—You may perceive therefore if you will, that the practice of Jewish proselyte baptism, which you are anxious to drag into the question, has nothing in the world to do with the ground of our argument. I incidentally mentioned it in my pamphlet (when I did not suppose that any were so absurd as to deny the fact—nor do I yet know that any *scholar not a baptist* has called it in question)—because it throws light upon the subject in the way of illustration. But with those who choose to dispute the fact, I have no occasion for the illustration, and will not be turned aside from the ground of scripture to argue about it:—though I know that persons would be less absurd in denying the most acknowledged customs among the ancient Greeks and Romans, than in denying the existence of that Jewish custom, for which more multiplied testimonies of Jewish writers are extant, than there are of Greek or Roman for any one custom among them. Indeed I might say, that if we had not a single testimony for its existence, any one who considers the various baptisms (or washings) notoriously practised by the Jews, could have no rational doubt that they would employ a washing on the reception of a Gentile convert to their community. And as to Dantz's *ideas*, which you say some man calls " contortissima et oppido ridicula," if you had either looked at my pamphlet or his collection of Jewish testimonies, you would see that *his ideas* have not the remotest leaning one way or the other upon the question. Indeed, what his ideas are I neither remember nor care. But I almost regret that I have stopped to say even so much upon the matter. You beat the air in trying to *prove*, either that *all* the first proselytes were baptized, or that many of them were not baptized *by the Apostles*. We never thought of calling in question either of these facts. But we did refer you to Paul's language in 1 Cor. i. 14. as an evidence that the right of baptism is no part (as you assume it to be) of the apostolic commission in Matt. xxviii. 19. And when you, with all other Baptists, evade the plain force of that evidence by urging that the Corinthians were baptized, though not by Paul, and that he thanks God only " that he had escaped an imputation by not baptizing them" himself;—you urge what has no manner of real force. For in any other thing *really* included in the apostolic commission (such as preaching the gospel to all nations, teaching the believers, &c.) can we suppose that Paul could without profaneness use similar language, and gravely thank God that he had escaped imputation indeed, by being so little exercised in doing what his Lord had commanded him to do? What you mean by saying, that the commission in Matt. xxviii. 19. was not *exclusively* apostolic, I am at a loss to conjecture;

but, important as it is in some views, I cannot stop to inquire;—no more than into what you mean when you talk of *pouring water upon the baptized*. You say you are not aware of any passages in which John's baptism with water is contrasted with Christ's. Look at Acts i. 5. xi. 16. Matt. iii. 2. Mark i. 8. John i. 26, &c. You talk of the case of a Socinian, &c. I can make no distinction between a Socinian brought to the knowledge of the truth, and a Moravian brought to it; save that in the antecedent profession of the latter there was a great deal more of the "deceivableness of unrighteousness." But you are quite mistaken in saying, that the Socinian "never professed to believe that Jesus is the Son of God." There is not a Socinian in the country that does not profess to believe it, while he nullifies indeed the declaration by the sense in which he understands it; just as the Moravian professes to believe the scriptural testimony of the atonement, while he undermines its truth by his sentiments about the way in which that atonement is applied to the conscience. I must pass over many other things in your letter, in order to make some remarks on the most important passage of all: and I have to regret that my remarks must necessarily be so brief. We referred you to the plain and most important precept in Eph. vi. 4. as that which is necessarily set aside by the Baptists: and in the little that you say on the subject, it too evidently appears that you are infected with the worst leaven of their principles. "On the *religious* education of children you have nothing to say." But *we have* to speak from the Scriptures of their Christian education. And though *you* have nothing to say on this, you have something to say on that about which the Scriptures are totally silent—the salvation of all who die in infancy. But then comes something also that you have to say *against* the scriptural precept referred to. "The *religious prattling* of your children is surely no evidence that they do really believe" that gospel, in the instruction and admonition of which they are brought up. Such is the contempt that you and all the Baptists pour upon the divine precept and divine truth. The children are to be brought up in the *instruction* and in the *admonition* of that simple and glorious truth; but though it is explained to them intelligibly, and they professedly acknowledge it, their acknowledgment of it is *religious prattling*, that affords *no evidence* of their *really believing it*. But not so the statement of gospel doctrine which *you* make in your letter. That, I suppose, I am to consider as evidence of your *soundness* in the faith. But I must tell you plainly, that the young child, towards whom its Christian parent faithfully observes the divine precept, affords me in that profession of the truth, which you so much despise as *religious prattling*, more evidence of its genuine discipleship than you do at present under such unscriptural sentiments. You may think your joke about the Swedish army a good one. But when you ask me to point out the scriptural ground for our idea of the discipleship of the children of believing parents, I confidently refer you to that precept on which you observe that you have nothing to say. Those who give that precept any interpretation, which is consistent with the parent's not regarding as a disciple the child whom he is *bringing up in the instruction and admonition of the Lord*, really set at nought the precept while they acknowledge its words. And when you call for the confirmation of the idea from *experience*, I cannot conjecture what the experience is which you conceive ought to have afforded the confirmation you demand. Is it that of the Moravian societies?

Should this letter also fail in convincing you in any degree of the evil of your sentiments and conduct, we would not trouble you to make any reply to it; as we have no wish to maintain a disputation. I shall not imitate your unbrotherly language, by expressing a hope that you will not repel that conviction as "derogatory to your dignity." I still look to Him who alone can bring us into and keep us in the simplicity of His truth, so to bless the admonition and reproof offered you, that I may be able always in confidence to subscribe myself,

Your affectionate brother.

XXXVIII.

TO R. L. C——, ESQ.

Jan. 14, 1818.

Dear Sir,—When I read the first words of your letter, telling me that you were "an inquirer after truth," a fear immediately struck me that you were a religious unbeliever; for I apprehended you meant by *truth* that great doctrine of God, which leaves no room for a sinner's inquiry after it; of which we are naturally not only ignorant but so opposed to it that none ever seek the knowledge of it; and which, when discovered to the conscience, supersedes all inquiry, "what is truth?" by the evidence it carries of its own divine certainty. But though the fear I have mentioned occurred to me at first, it was soon changed to very different feelings in the progress of your letter; and, unless I mistake the sentiments you seem to intimate, I think you will agree with me, that the man who is inquiring what *the* truth is must be considered as not only a stranger but an enemy to it. Your inquiries, however, into the scriptural directions for the regulation of a believer's walk are indeed very suitable to one who knows the truth of God. It is odd enough, that yours is the second letter I have very lately received from England on the subject. Mr. K——, of ——, wrote to me a few weeks ago expressing a wish to receive my tracts on Baptism, upon which subject he differs from many of his friends. He said so little in his first letter on the more fundamental subject, that I thought it needful in my answer to state my views of the gospel itself pretty fully, and this brought forth from him a reply, which has indeed afforded me considerable satisfaction; though (if he abide by the truth he has expressed) I believe he will soon find that some of his religious friends differ with him much more essentially than he is at present aware. I have since sent him various pieces that I have published at different times, and among them two or three on the Baptist question. But I am sorry to tell you, that those have been so long out of print that I had much difficulty in obtaining second-hand copies of them from a friend who possessed them. A single copy of them I had not myself, and know not at present whether I shall be able to procure them for you. I shall do what I can for the purpose; but if I fail, perhaps you could obtain from Mr. K. the use of the copies I sent to him.

It is a matter of much joy and thanksgiving to find one and another in England appearing to be delivered from the snare of the religious world. May "He, who stands and feeds in the majesty of the name of Jehovah," display his glory in keeping and guiding them continually! Since I have felt any interest about those, who have lately left the Establishment in England, (i. e. since my communications with Mr. K.) I have felt the same solicitude that you express, lest they should remain much astray on the principles of Christian fellowship; nor can I wonder if at present the minds even of believers among them be much beclouded on that subject. As I hope very soon to have the opportunity of sending you one or two pieces, in which my views of the matter are detailed, and am much limited at present in time, I shall here only say that our correspondence in Dublin and the few sister churches connected with us in the country is indeed most unpopular. It opposes all that passes current in the religious world as a charitable and forbearing spirit. While we find much exercise for real forbearance, we consider what goes generally under that name, as an ungodly conspiracy against the divine precepts. We are, in that respect, much like the Glasite or Sandemanian societies, though in other respects we materially differ from them. We conceive that they have retained much of the leaven of clerical domination under the name of Elders; and that, in making the presence of two Elders necessary for authorizing believers to act together as a church of Christ, they err radically in the constitution of a church and the nature of the Elder's office. We are indeed without Elders to the present day from the want of any brethren who meet the scriptural characters marked as necessary. But mentioning (as you have done) Glas and Sandeman, and fully agreeing with you that their works contain most important truths on the characters of the gospel and Christ's kingdom, I cannot omit that we differ essentially from some fundamental principles which S. (with whom I am best acquainted) puts forward. I allude to his sentiments upon the *assurance of hope*. Precious as his vindication of the truth appears against the corruptions and perversions of the popular divines, we conceive that he himself afterwards awfully perverts and corrupts it, in representing the gospel as calculated to afford a sinner joy at first on believing, only as satisfying him that he *may peradventure* be saved because *any* sinner may be saved, but leaving him doubtful whether he believes it or not, till after a course of painful exertion in the work of faith and labour of love he is led to discover in himself some good evidences of his faith, which afford him personal confidence towards God. The glorious truth, that S. elsewhere seems so blessedly to contend for, teaches us to say to any man advancing such a doctrine "get thee behind me, Satan." I must, in justice to the Glasites, add that I know an Elder in one of their societies, (at Liverpool) who seems uninfected with that Antichristian sentiment. But I do believe that in their body it has been a root of bitterness and leaven of ungodliness.

I received the other day a short tract written by Mr. Evans, (one of Mr. K.'s friends) which confirms your remark upon the style of high Calvinism, into which some of them have run. It is a style very different from the sobriety of scriptural language, and indeed very different from the language of Mr. K.'s last letter; but I mean to write to him at large on the subject.

I find I have almost filled my paper, without saying any thing upon Baptism; and I think it better to say nothing on the subject at present, than to treat it so very imperfectly as I should be obliged to do in this letter. I hope, however, along with the pamphlets which I mean to send you next week by a private conveyance, to send also the copy of a letter lately written in the name of the church here to one of its members in Edinburgh, who has adopted the Baptist sentiments. It comprises in a moderate compass our leading views on the topic; and affords matter for enlargement in our future correspondence, if any points in it should appear to you obscure or doubtful.

I am glad to find that you express yourself cautious at present about joining any society of religious professors; while I look forward with hope to our yet proving perfectly joined together in one mind and one judgment upon every thing relating to christian faith and practice. These two things are most closely connected together; and all the corruptions of each introduced by the man of sin would separate what God hath joined. That man of sin it is declared that the Lord will consume by the spirit of his mouth; and this declaration supports my confident hope against all discouragements, that the time shall return when all that believe in every place shall again be together in one, having given them one heart and one way by Him who alone maketh brethren to dwell together in unity. I am aware that they will even then be found a little and despised flock—a sect every where spoken against. But they will then be found maintaining the inviolable sanctity of all the divine precepts, while the ruling principle of their fellowship one with another will ever be that glorious MERCY of God through which they are made partakers of eternal life. I am reluctantly obliged to break off, but hope soon to resume my pen in your service; and shall be very glad to be favoured with renewed communications from you.

I remain, dear Sir, &c. &c.

XXXIX.

TO J. H——, ESQ.

——, ——.

My dear Sir,—Your letter of last July was forwarded to me when I was on a visit in Glasgow. Some friends there, and several here, have shared with me in the pleasure which it afforded. It is a great joy to any who are of the truth, to hear of others in a distant country taught to speak the same things. That I have been tardy in acknowledging your kind communication, has arisen from what I now believe was a mistake. Different persons in Scotland told me, that no vessel would sail for Halifax till spring: but I have lately heard that there is a general packet from some port of England. If so, I regret that I have suffered so much time to elapse; but I hope that will not discourage you from renewing the correspondence, which I shall be very glad to continue, as long as I find the same mind in you that as yet appears so pleasingly.

Your remarks on the inconsistency of my Address to the Methodists perfectly accords with the views of it I have been led to for some years past, and have since, as far as opportunity served, avowed. My sin (for there can be no sin greater than unfaithfulness to the truth of God) I cannot even palliate by the plea of mitigation you suggest—that I used the word *brethren* only as indicative of the common brotherhood subsisting between man and man. I fear I meant Christian brotherhood, and was led away by a vague hope, that there were a few in the society, who did not really hold the principles which as a society they all profess. But it was a false and wicked hope, partaking largely of that false charity of the world against which you so justly protest. While men profess sentiments contrary to the truth of the gospel, we have no right to suppose that they do not believe what they profess, or that they believe what they gainsay. Indeed, when I wrote that piece, and my Letters to Mr. Knox, the inconsistency of my language was even exceeded by the inconsistency of my practice. I held the awful character of a clergyman in the Establishment, even while I was latterly attempting with a few others to meet on the first day of the week in church fellowship. I may truly own with shame, that I have been a most slow and wayward scholar; while I may own with thankfulness the mercy and patience of the heavenly teacher. It was still many years before the production you first met, that the account of E. C. was published: and I can readily conceive (though I have forgotten the particulars, and have not a copy of the piece,) that you must have perceived in that even a greater ambiguity of language. Yet I believe my leading object was to set forth sovereign mercy. There were some other things formerly published which I would wish burned. I mention this only that you may not judge of my present sentiments from my earlier productions, if others of them should come in your way. A friend in Glasgow has promised to send you, by a vessel which is shortly to sail from that port, a parcel of my later pamphlets; and I confess I shall wait with some solicitude to hear from you after you have received them, that I may know more fully how far we are of one mind. The more flattering present appearances are, the more anxiously must I hope (if it be consistent with the Divine will) that nothing may ultimately occur to prevent our scriptural union. The account you have given me of the churches in America is very interesting. I had been led to suppose, that Mr. Sandeman's visit to America had been without fruit. With his writings I became acquainted during the course of my Letters to Mr. Knox; and his memory has ever since been dear to me. Yet, I confess, your disconnection from the Glasite churches in Great Britain appears in my view to have been mercifully ordered. I trust it has been, and will be, the occasion of leading you to prove all things by the Word, more fully than the members of their societies seem to be allowed. I have had some intercourse with them, and I own they seem to me sadly in trammels to a system laid down for them by a man. At all events, you had the scriptures most plainly with you in the immediate ground of your separation. Whenever we cease to love mercy, or act contrary to it, however we may mask our sin, there is an awful departure from the fundamental principles of the Word. Besides your just observations on the sentences you quote from their pamphlet, relative to that rule of discipline, suffer me to remark on the expression—" which has in fact been proved to be *hypocritical*"—that even in the melancholy case of a brother relapsing into an evil, for which he had before professed repentance, we cannot scripturally say that his former profession of repentance has been proved hypocritical. He that will presume to say this, must suppose himself exempt from the possibility of falling again into any evil, for which he has been given repentance; and ill, indeed, does such a notion become us. The account which you gave me of the practices observed by the churches in your connexion is in general pleasing; and there appears, in most respects, a great similarity between us. But this leads me to notice some things in which, at present, we differ. The churches in this country are still without elders; but we do not on that account forbear acting in every respect—partaking of the supper on the first day of the week, and observing the institutions of discipline—different brethren in rotation presiding at our meeting. A contempt of the ordinance of elders is imputed to us,—but I trust falsely. It is humbling to say, that we have not as yet found any man among us whom we could scripturally call to the service, as manifesting in some degree all the characters pointed out in the letters to Timothy and Titus. In this matter we are yet lacking; and it is indeed a serious want. It may probably be very contrary to your present views, that Christians in such circumstances should observe the Supper: but, from the general spirit of your letter, I trust you will give the subject a candid consideration. To us it appears very plain from scripture, that it is not for administering the Supper elders are designed; that the idea of an administrator, as it were, representing the divine Institutor, is nothing short of profane; that churches must exist in general before they receive elders; and that the notion of churches existing, but not meeting on the first day of the week to break bread, has no warrant from the Word. The feasts of charity we do not consider a divine institution; though we did, as long as we could, practise something of the kind for promoting mutual acquaintance and brotherly love. That the Corinthian church had a meal in some way connected with the Lord's Supper, appears pretty evident. But does it not appear from 1 Cor. xi. 34, that the Apostle does not treat that as an ordinance of God, but as that which circumstances might render it more expedient to omit. The subject of salutation was under our consideration for several weeks on my return from Scotland, and we were on the point of adopting it as an ordinance, when a view presented of all the passages by one brother checked and obliged us to suspend. Of the justice of this view I confess myself at present satisfied; though it had never struck me before. It is this—that the Apostles in these passages send their *own* salutation to all the brethren, and desire it to be presented by each to the other with a kiss. Consider the import of Phil. iv. 21; and then consider whether 1 Thess. v. 26. is not justly to be interpreted in precisely the same sense.

I am obliged to be brief on these subjects; but whatever you may have to offer on your side, I trust you will find us ready to weigh with serious consideration. I do not at present see any thing else in which I have reason to suppose we differ. On whichever side any error remains, may the Lord mercifully remove it! It is equally important not to receive any human fancy as a divine ordinance, and not to overlook or reject any of the ordinances really delivered by the Apostles of Jesus Christ. Our profession has hitherto been attended with much reproach and much trial; nor do we expect that either will cease till the second coming of the Lord. The reproach of narrow bigotry and uncharitableness is necessarily connected with the doctrine we avow, and with our total separation from all other religious connexions. Yet our numbers have multiplied to a degree that fills us with grateful surprise, and may perhaps startle you. In Dublin we somewhat exceed one hundred; and there are six or seven little churches in the country parts, amounting to about one hundred more. Among us are, I suppose, a dozen who were formerly clergymen, and above twenty who were formerly Baptists.

XL.

TO R. L. C———, ESQ.

Feb. 23, 1818.

My Dear Sir,—Your letter of 28th ult. did not reach me till last Wednesday. I am very glad to have received the communications it contains, as they may give an important direction to my future correspondence with Mr. K., if it should be continued: but he has been for some time a letter in my debt. Your letter was also very acceptable to me, as seeming to confirm the opinion I had formed about your views of the great truth; particularly the few words you add, by way of postscr'pt, *upon the true grace of God*. This is the grand subject for our communications, as it will be the grand theme of all the redeemed above through eternity. "Looking for the mercy of the Lord Jesus unto eternal life," is the common character of that new mind, which is given them in the knowledge of the truth. They shall not be ashamed of their hope: for the only living and true God is the God of this hope, its author and its object. They shall find "mercy of the Lord in that day." To becloud this hope, to turn aside the minds of men to some other, no matter what or how dressed up, is the great object of the father of lies: to keep the minds of the elect in the discernment of it, of its sole sufficiency, and of its glorious fulness, is the great work of the Spirit of truth. I am glad to observe the cheerfulness with which you accede to the idea of our continued correspondence, discovering it as additional evidence of the agreement of our views; and if there be that fundamental agreement which, I hope, you will not be displeased at my writing with the utmost plainness, and exploring every corner in which any latent disagreement might lurk. To the same plainness of dealing I heartily invite you. Now, though there is nothing in your letter, but what may be understood in a meaning most true and important; yet there are one or two expressions about which I wish to inquire. You speak of the "imaginary union with Christ before all worlds." You do not, I trust, mean to controvert the divine purpose of mercy to the redeemed *from everlasting to everlasting*, or their being given to Christ in the eternal counsels, to be effectually brought to glory by him. If any one mean no more than this, by the term "eternal justification," far be it from me not to assert the *thing* with him; while the phrase I object to as unscriptural. My objection to Mr. Evans's tract on the "Lamb of God," lay not so much in its containing any thing that I could say was false, as in its putting certain truths of scripture altogether out of their place, and not putting forward at all the simple gospel, as a divine proclamation of glad tidings to any sinner whatsoever. His gospel in that tract seemed to be, "*if you be an elect sinner*, I have good news for you: Christ has died for *you*, and you shall be saved." I have long known the zealous advocates of such a gospel among the most bitter opposers of those glad tidings, which were sent to all nations and sinners of every description, for the obedience of faith. But I must add, that I read his short tract, which you kindly sent me, with much more satisfaction; and saw in it nothing to bar the hope that he might mean right. No doubt I read it very cursorily; and having lent it to a brother, who called on me, I have it not now at hand. But if you perceive any thing objectionable in it (besides the general indistinctness of statement,) I should thank you to point it out. I tell you candidly I ask this, rather to know *your* sentiments, than from feeling much interest about Mr. Evans; for while he continues a clergyman, and the head of a religious congregation, I cannot view him with any satisfaction. To Mr. K., if I should have encouragement to write again, I mean to write largely on the system, which some of those whom he regards as brethren have adopted. I was *startled* (as I have told him in my last) by a short passage in his second letter, which he commences with observing, "how to explain the Trinity is a subject of much difficulty;" but closes with a better remark, "perhaps, after all, we may be anxious to go beyond what is written." In my reply, I enforced the suitableness and importance of that sobriety of mind, which seemed to dictate the latter check to his speculations. In the same letter he speaks of the doctrine of *union*, as seeming to be the "key of the house of David;" but what he proceeds to state upon the union of God and man in one Christ, and the union of Christ and his church, appears to me very excellent. I would transcribe it, but that I am afraid of exceeding the limits of my paper. I called his attention, in my last, to the principles of Christian fellowship, and the simple way in which disciples should walk together, as they did of old. I only regret that I then addressed him with too sanguine confidence of his agreeing with me about the faith of Christ. However, if he be walking in the same high mind with the generality of religious leaders, (and from which nothing can keep us at any time but the abasing view of the mercy revealed in the gospel to the chief of sinners) my letter contained some things, which have probably rubbed the skin off him.

For you, dear sir, I am chiefly anxious, lest, discovering dangerous in those you were lately connected with, you should fly into some errors errors in the opposite extreme. To this we are always prone, from the radical opposition of our own hearts to the unadulterated gospel of the glory of God. I observe in both of Mr. Evans's tracts, a principle intimated, which, in its right connexion, is most important, —the necessity of the peace of God reigning in the conscience, to any truly Christian walking. Those who mistake, for that peace, the personal confidence, built on the assumption that they are elect sinners united to Christ, eternally justified, &c., have fallen indeed into a radical mistake. But they mistake as radically, who think that peace is to be attained or kept by any strivings or workings of the sinner: the revealed testimony of the name of the Lord is sufficient, at all times, to afford it; and "the joy of the Lord is truly his people's strength." May you grow in the discernment of the glory continually presented to our view in the divine testimony concerning the friend and saviour of sinners! May you be filled with all joy and peace in believing it! When I can get a copy of it, I mean to send you a letter on the subject, written some time ago, to a person in Lancashire.—I thank you heartily for your kind invitation of me to your house in London, and shall rejoice, if circumstances should enable me to accept it. I shall cherish the hope, though I forsee a difficulty from some printing business, which is likely to call me to Edinburgh. But perhaps I may be able to accomplish both. I have had thoughts, if I live to take another summer's tour, of bringing my daughter with me, as I did in my last visit to Scotland. May I ask whether you are so circumstanced, that this would be consistent with my accepting your invitation—in short, whether you are a married man? Do not attribute my freedom to Irish impudence, but rather to the openness with which a Chistian deals with one that he hopes is a fellow Christian.—I hope you will not be frightened by the length of my letters. If you knew how little time I have for writing, you would see in it an evidence of the interest I feel in your correspondence. I have said nothing on the important subject of church-fellowship, waiting for your promised inquiries: you are also in possession of my leading views on that in print; and I conceive, that where there is real agreement on the foundation, there will seldom be ultimate difference on the way in which Christians should walk together; supposing that either party discerns the scriptural course, that they continue to communicate on the subject with patience, and in the fear of God.

XLI.

TO THE SAME.

March 5, 1818.

My Dear Sir,—Your letter was most welcome to me, and rendered more so, perhaps, by the little delay of its arrival; for which, however, I am ashamed that you should think it necessary to account. But I am somewhat aware of the many engagements one in your circumstances must have, and shall not entertain any unpleasant thoughts at an occasionally lengthened silence. Need I say also, that I hope you will use the utmost freedom of remark, or (when you see necessary) of opposition, upon any sentiment in my letters, or in my publications, which you think controvertible. I ought to admit that, as it is a liberty which on those subjects I always assume. Indeed the sacredness of them requires it from Christian fidelity.

Since my last, I have seen some publications of Mr. Evans, on which I have been anxious to offer some remarks to your attention;—the more so, because you have intimated a unity of view on doctrinal matters with him. You will not, I hope, think my observations prompted by hypercriticism. Every believer of the unadulterated truth must be jealous to maintain it uncorrupted. The first of Mr. Evans's pieces to which I allude is "on the Lamb of God," designed for general circulation, and professedly exhibiting the gospel. Now I candidly own, that I do not think the gospel put forward in that tract is that which the Apostles preached, and still preach, to all nations. I have it not now at hand; but I distinctly recollect that the leading tenor of it is this—"Reader, you may perhaps be an elect sinner, and if so, I have good news for you; Christ has died *for you*," &c. It never was thus the Apostles addressed their fellow sinners. They delivered their testimony concerning Jesus as glad tidings—*to sinners* (from heaven) proclaiming peace made by him—without any doubtful *if* or *perhaps*, to make the minds of their hearers question whether it was of joyful import to *them*. When I say that Mr. Evans appears, what is called, a high Calvinist, do not suppose that I am an advocate for that insidious and absurd attempt to hold the doctrines of election, predestination to eternal life, &c., in a modified or qualified manner. Every believer of the gospel must be decided in his mind on those doctrines in the most unqualified sense. They are interwoven in the very tissue of that gospel of salvation which he believes. But indeed a man may be a high Calvinist, and yet unacquainted with the genuine gospel, and the hope which it imparts. The kind of gospel that seems put forward in that pamphlet, would be very apt to lead a man, who received it, to say —"I am an elect sinner, and therefore Christ died for me, and has taken away my sins, and I shall assuredly be saved eternally;" and while he would say in this what is true of every believer, and while he might, according to his views, be most fond of his doctrine of atonement and salvation by grace alone, he would avow a confidence resting on a foundation quite aside from the revealed testimony of God,—that contains no declaration about his being an elect sinner, no declaration about him individually, distinct from every other sinner in the world. Many, I am persuaded, have been quite sure of their being elect sinners, who were not, and who manifested that they were not, by stumbling at the simple gospel. That gospel is the decided and immutable truth of God, whether men believe it or not, and the hope of the gospel rests upon its naked truth, and therefore on a foundation which cannot be moved. It exhibits from heaven to the sinner, *as such*, all that the chief of sinners needs, for emboldening him to draw nigh to the holiest, crying Abba Father—the perfect work of righteousness, which God has accepted for the justification of the ungodly—the propitiation for sin, which has taken it away, and made peace for the rebellious. Never, I hope, shall I be afraid of commending the all-sufficiency of that propitiation to a fellow sinner, through my doubtfulness whether he is among the number of the elect. I have no doubt that it is sufficient for him, and for any sinner upon earth—sufficient to fill him with all hope and joy in believing the divine declaration concerning it, and sufficient to support that hope which it inspires;—while I am very sure that none will believe that declaration but those who have been ordained to eternal life. Those who see not enough in that divine declaration to warrant their hope towards God, are anxious to find something in their hearers to complete its joyfulness, by enabling them to testify that they are among the number for whom Christ died; and perverting the scriptural language of a ransom and price paid for the redemption of the elect, they strain it to a representation, as if Christ must have suffered more, had one more sinner been given to him—as if the atonement he has made, though sufficient indeed for what he undertook to effect by it, were insufficient to afford hope to any others than a certain number of sinners. But the sinner who disbelieves the gospel, rejects the counsel of God against himself, and perishes in his sin, not for any insufficiency in the propitiation which God has exhibited in his word. The faith of many an high Calvinist is nothing but a hardy confidence that he is among the elect for whom Christ died; but the faith of the gospel is the belief of that which is revealed from heaven in the word of God.

In the other piece of Mr. Evans's, ("the old man and his grand-daughter") he has a note in p. 16, to explain what believing on Christ is; and instead of simply saying that it is believing the testimony which God has given of his son, 1 John v. 1, 9, 10; after quoting various scriptural figures, in which the exercise of that faith is described, he seems to think that he has a better account to offer, by a figure different from what the Scriptures any where supply—"all which may be reduced to *venturing upon Christ for salvation*." When a man sets about an explanation of the meaning of faith, and employs ANY *figures* in explanation, I think the odds are that he has yet to learn the simplicity of its scriptural import. But really Mr. Evans's figure seems to me most objectionable. I should feel myself more warranted by the word of God, to speak of the venturesomeness of disbelieving, than the venturesomeness of believing. What are we to think of the idea of a sinner's *venturing* not to make God a liar? *venturing* to believe that what God has said in his word is true? But no—this was not Mr. Evans's idea—but some *act* or *exercise* in the sinner's mind, connected (I fear) with an indeed venturesome assumption, that he has been given to Christ to be saved eternally. O! what a mass of Antichristian ungodliness is contained in this idea of faith! and what a copious field for all the wicked arts of pretended ambassadors of Christ, working up their hearers to that state in which it is supposed they may safely believe in this sense, and thus encouraging and directing them to put forth this venturesome act of faith. I know nothing of Mr. Evans except from his writings, and they contain less *open* falsehood than most religious compositions: but to the dearest brother I have, holding such language as he holds, I would say, 'Get thee behind me, Satan'—while I would cherish the hope, as long as facts allowed it, that he might be found yielding to the reproof and correction of the word.

I have enlarged so much upon that fundamental subject, that I have little time or space to enter upon others. I read your remark upon the popular idea of the now certain and progressive sanctification with much pleasure. Those who think of a work of grace that makes them better, or less wholly evil, than they were by nature, know little of the true grace of God.

On the important subject of church-fellowship, I should be far from wishing to precipitate you, and I approve much, in general, of the caution you express. But while I say this, I must own that I do not like the idea of your delaying to act according to any scriptural principle that you do see. On your monthly communion, you say, "Every week would I now think be scriptural, and therefore right and profitable." If you annex just ideas to the word *scriptural*, we may substitute for the terms "right and profitable"—'binding on the authority of the great Head of the church.' But dismissing that and other particulars, I should wish you to consider, in general, what you mean by examining in what way Christians ought to walk together in fellowship. If you mean the exercise of your judgment and discretion in devising some rules for the purpose, I shall think you very unprofitably and wickedly occupied in the speculation. But if you mean by it, examining what the word of God directs on the subject, under a conviction that it is directed, and that its authority is sole and paramount, then I would look for prompt obedience from a disciple, to any part of the divine rule that he discerns: and if he defer this till he shall discover a perfect system or rules, or if he evade it, through fear of abridging his usefulness, he ceases to act like a disciple. I am persuaded that very little examination of the subject would be sufficient to convince you, that the meeting of a church of Christ, on the first day of the week of old, was a very different scene from what is exhibited in your meeting. How you will act under that conviction, I shall wait with some solicitude to observe; but would not hurry you, if I could. As to what is commonly called *forming a church*, it is the work of man; and, like all his works, abominable. A church of Christ is of his formation, and all its rules are already made and delivered by him. I shall not, by any apologies, increase this enormous letter. Commending you to the riches of that mercy which reigns through righteousness unto eternal life, by Christ Jesus, I remain faithfully and affectionately yours.

P.S. I have some hopes of visiting England this summer, if life be spared.

XLII.

TO M. B———, ESQ.

March 25*th*, 1818.

My Dear M——,—I have been so occupied since I got your letter, that I could not sooner sit down to answer it. My mind is not changed at all upon the *general inexpediency* and unsuitableness of a believer's marrying one not of the household of faith. But the scriptural ground on which we thought ourselves called to deal with the person who did so, as acting against an express rule of the word,

I no longer discern in the same view as heretofore, and therefore could no longer take part in an act, which, without the divine authority to support it, is an awful mockery. We were accustomed to rest our conduct on the expression, 1 Cor. vii. 39, " only in the Lord," conceiving that the words meant *only a believer*. Now, *that* I am persuaded is not their meaning. The expression occurs in many other places, but it will be sufficient to refer to a very few in order to determine its import. In Eph. vi. 1. children are enjoined to obey their parents *in the Lord*: that is, not their parents *who are* in Christ, or believers, but to obey their parents with an eye to the Lord's will and glory—as becometh those who are in the Lord. In Rom. xvi. 2. the church is directed to receive Phœbe *in the Lord*; and the phrase is immediately interpreted by the following words— " as becometh saints." So when the Apostle declares the liberty of the widow to marry *whom she will*, he adds " only in the Lord"— as a Christian woman, who is called to do this, as every thing, in the name of the Lord Jesus. In Col. iii. 17, 18. the truth and justice of the interpretation, which I have offered as presenting the real meaning of the passage, has been generally admitted even by those who continued for a time to contend most strongly for the intrinsic unlawfulness of a Christian's, in any case, marrying an unbeliever. But indeed those who took that side have not been able to adduce any scriptural ground for their assertion. I have been charged with inconsistency in admitting and asserting the *general* inexpediency of the thing, and consequently its general evil, while I deny our warrant for applying the discipline of the Lord's house—even where there is most reason to fear that it springs from the fleshly mind. But this is in many views fallacious. What is in general inexpedient, and cannot be done without *evil* by the Christian *when it is inexpedient*, may in some circumstances be *right*, and that which the Christian walking in the fear of the Lord can do as unto Him. A Christian may be in circumstances—(although this also has been strangely contested)—in which it is his Christian *duty* to marry, 1 Cor. vii. 2—9, and yet certainly may be unable to obtain any Christian partner—much less one in any respect suitable. But besides such a case of obvious and direct necessity, if I expostulated (for instance) with a sister on such an occasion, and she replied that really she wished to marry, and not finding any brother for a length of time propose for her, nor any likely to propose, she had taken a man, not of the body, with whom she thought she could be happy,—I confess my mouth would now be stopped; I dare not impose on her a burden which I do not find the Lord has imposed. I might have been better pleased, and thought she acted more expediently, if she could have been content to remain single; but I cannot find what precept of the word she has transgressed. I look back with shame and compunction at the instances in which we have proceeded to the removal of brethren in such cases: but I trust I should sooner be removed myself from the body, than again concur in such an act;— unless some scriptural warrant for it should appear which has not yet been produced. However, I was glad to observe last Sunday more pleasing appearances of approaching agreement. On the subject of oaths I have not yet brought forward any thing: nor is my own mind sufficiently settled to speak with full decision. I can only say that, if I were summoned to-morrow to give my evidence on oath, I should decline being sworn till I had explained the only sense in which I could take the oath—namely, as a solemn appeal to God for the truth of my testimony. But if there must be understood by the words—"so help me God"—any thing of an *imprecation* of the divine vengeance to visit falsification, I should decline the oath, and am persuaded it is unlawful. I was long willing to understand the words as a prayer for the divine help, though I knew many things against the interpretation. Still I find so many others adopt the same conception of their meaning, that I should be willing to propose it. But I suspect that no judge would admit the interpretation. Look at the beginning of the article "*Oaths*" in the Encyclopædia. That the system of swearing in these countries is a most awfully wicked one is indubitable. If we should ultimately have to bear a testimony against it, it will be at much worldly loss; but I trust the Lord will not allow us to shrink from the trial.

Your truly affectionate,

XLIII.

TO R. L. C———, ESQ.

March 31, 1818.

My Dear Sir,—I received your letter of the 28th ult. but a few days ago, and take advantage of the return of the same gentleman who brought it, to enclose a few lines for you to my son.

Your letter was quite satisfactory on the points about which I inquired your sentiments; and accounts sufficiently for the language you held about the Seceders. But I confess I have been made sick at heart by hearing of the blasphemous extravagances of expression and sentiment into which they have run. Wherever I find professors using such language as you describe, I should turn away from them as heady and high-minded speculators: nor dare I allow my mind to be disturbed from the simplicity of the great truth, by plunging into the discussion of the particular sentiments, even for the purpose of exposing their falsehood. I hope you will not be dragged into such discussions: they might make you a disputatious theologian, but would be little calculated to build you up in the faith and hope of the gospel. I hope you will be on your guard against theological writings. Your views of scriptural doctrine are such as would of course lead you to reject the *gross* trash that is published under the name of evangelical: but there is at present plenty of a more insidious kind, with a sprinkling of important truth occasionally intimated, but that truth only profaned by the trash with which it is mixed. Shall I own to you that I reckon such publications as Mr. Jones's of the number? The very community of interest which pervades it, with all the varieties of evangelical professors, stamps it with the character of the "deceivableness of unrighteousness." Nor can it well be otherwise, where a professor, of something like the gospel, undertakes to cater monthly for the appetites of the *religious world*. Christians, while walking in the spirit of the holy truth, will leave such work to others whom it befits. But no doubt any monthly magazine, conducted according to the principles of the gospel, would be a very losing speculation to its printer.

Out of the variety of questions you propose to me, I must for the present fasten on that which is the most vitally important—the assurance of hope. Yet to the Christian little need be said upon it. The hope of the gospel enjoyed in the mind must keep pace at all times with the belief of the gospel, from which alone it springs. Those who speak of one existing without the other, speak a language inconsistent with the true nature of both. The man who talks of being fully persuaded of the truth of the gospel, but at the same time is a stranger to the hope full of immortality, and not possessed of peace and joy in believing, is certainly deceiving himself or others; probably, under correct language, attaching some false meaning to the expressions of the gospel, or mistaking the ability to discourse about it correctly for the inward persuasion of the truth: and if under that profession he is diligently exercised in the *endeavour* to bring forth Christian fruit, that he may have some good evidence about himself to encourage his confidence, he is engaged in a course of strenuous exertion against the truth and glory of God. Yon seem to speak with a timidity that I do not like about obedience to the divine precepts: decidedly, that also will keep pace with the faith of the gospel. It is that glorious gospel which bringeth forth fruit, Col. i. 6.—all the genuine fruit of the spirit,—and just in proportion as any man is kept in the discernment of its glory, and persuasion of its divine certainty, he will be kept walking with God in full subjection to his authority, and as a little child receiving at his mouth, from the scriptures, every intimation of his gracious will: while much of the influence of that gospel on his spirit and his conduct will appear in forms, which the religious world, so far from acknowledging as good, will reckon to proceed from the influence of sin. But its friendship is enmity with God. As to the observation, which some suppose the believer thus walking takes of his own fruits, and the increased boldness in the sight of God, which they conceive he derives from observing them, it is an idea that supposes him not to hold fast "the beginning of his confidence and rejoicing of hope." It is an exercise indeed very congenial to the pride and self-righteousness of our deceitful hearts: but any believer, who looks at himself at any time in the light of the gospel of the glory of God, will only have such an abasing view of his vileness as would leave him without hope, were it not for the sufficiency of that grace which is revealed to sinners. It is remarkable that, in the Lord's description of the transactions in the great day, his sheep are described as unconscious of that evidence, by which they are marked as his indeed; while those on the left hand are described as contending that they are not destitute of it. Who indeed can see the glory of the divine truth, and not feel that his faith and all its fruits are less than a grain of mustard-seed? and not see the suitableness to him of the publican's prayer, "God be merciful to me a sinner?" I am, and have been for some time, so extraordinarily hurried with business, that I am obliged to refer other matters in your letter to a future opportunity. It would take many long letters indeed to answer it all fully. I thank you very heartily for your kindness in permitting me to bring my daughter with me, if I should be able to visit London this summer. But some of the circumstances on which that depends are so uncertain, that I must request you will not allow the prospect of my visit to interfere with any engagement, which you might otherwise be disposed to form, and which perhaps would lead you from London at the time. Yet I feel more and more how much preferable one or two days' conversation would be to the longest epistolary communication.

XLIV.

TO THE SAME.

April 23, 1818.

My dear Sir,—Though unable to write at any length, I hasten to send you a few lines, lest you should delay the publication of the tracts you mention. I only regret that you thought it necessary to consult me upon the subject. It will be perfectly agreeable to my wishes to have them republished in London, in whatever form you think best. They were originally printed separately here, and I have regretted that I combined them in the last edition. The paragraph to which you allude, I think, may be wholly omitted. I have sometimes wished to reprint the discourse prefixed to the "Remarks on certain Questions," &c. in the form of a tract, No. 3. You will consider yourself at equal liberty there. All I object to in the republication of those pieces is the introduction of such alterations and additions as a tract society in Glasgow adopted when they professed to print the tract, No. 1. It gives me pleasure to hear that any thing is likely to occasion your visiting Dublin; and though the accommodations I can offer are very humble, yet if you can content yourself with them, I shall be very happy to have you under my roof during your stay. In Scotland you will be in the very land of theology. I hope you may get out of it without loss. I hear with regret (though not much surprise) the determination of your mind on the Baptist question. As to myself, I should doubt the grounds on which I have formed my judgment, if I ever closed my mind against the reconsideration of the argument. But indeed some points in it only appear the more decisive the more I consider them; while on others, subordinate questions may be started, on which I have always avowed my inability to speak with decision, and am therefore desirous of waiting for more light. You think that the simple reader of scripture would come to the conclusion that all the disciples were to be dipped in water, as a confession of the faith of the gospel. Now let me beg of you, dear sir, to consider seriously from the scriptures alone, whether we have any reason to suppose that the children of the first disciples, born to them after their conversion to the faith of Christ, ever were baptized. If you have read with any real profit what I have offered upon that subject, you will be certain that they were considered and brought up as disciples, of whom they must have formed a very numerous class. But what scriptural ground we have for supposing that they were baptized, I know not. For such a baptism is there any scriptural precept or precedent? But I must abstain from enlarging. Let me only add that I am mistaken by those who think I have raised *any argument* from the practice of Jewish proselyte baptism. I but mentioned it as an illustration; and I am sure the illustration is not really liable to the objection which you suppose. I do not recollect that I have read what Glas or Sandeman say upon the subject; I always thought them so unwarrantable in contending for sprinkling as baptism. Hoping soon to enjoy a personal interview with you, I remain, &c.

XLV.

TO THE SAME.

June 13, 1818.

My dear Sir,—Forgive me for saying, that no one of your letters has afforded me so little satisfaction as the last. It too much indicates a mind filled indeed with theological questions and strifes of words, but little occupied with the glory of the gospel and kingdom of God. Tract and Bible societies, the religious diet of unbelieving men—endless diversities of scriptural churches—Christian fellowship confined within one limit to-day, and extended far beyond that limit to-morrow, &c.—these are poor topics for me to take up in reply; and so far as I do so at all, it will be only with the view of recalling you to that one great object from which our wicked hearts are continually prone to start aside. As to tract societies, I should think that those, who are scripturally united and walking together in the truth of the gospel, will find no occasion to travel out of the fellowship for printing any short statement of the gospel for general circulation. But this is an age of religious associations. They afford a natural channel for the false charity and zeal of the religious world to follow in; they supply a pleasing religious bustle, and come in as a pleasant succedaneum in place of the scriptural union of disciples. They have a shew and a respectability, which never can attach to a company of believers, earnestly contending for the faith, and holding fast the traditions of the word of God as their only rule. Far be it from me to dissuade you or any from contributing to the most extended circulation of those scriptures, which are able to make a sinner wise unto salvation. But I frankly avow that I could not attend any meeting of the numerous Bible societies, without raising my voice in the most explicit testimony against the blasphemies that are commonly uttered there. Suppose I had been present a few months ago at the meeting of the society in London for supplying the army and navy with Bibles, where a Royal Duke presided, and bishops and archbishops made their motions and speeches; could I have heard the utility of the object enforced from its tendency to make soldiers and sailors brave warriors, and illustrated by the success with which Mahometans employ religion to animate the courage of their troops—could I have heard this and been silent? or could I have restrained my reprobation of the sentiments, from observing that they were uttered by Mr. Wilberforce? It is, no doubt, only a newspaper report that I have; but I know that language equally profane is employed at every meeting of the society in this country, by our most evangelical divines. Or could I, as a Christian, join with the society in trumpeting forth our good works—in bedaubing with thanks and praises every member more elevated in rank than the rest—and in exulting at the growing liberality which merges all sects and parties in zeal for the extension of *our common religion?* You will say my language is cutting. I cannot help it: divine truth is very cutting to its adversaries. While in my right mind, I shall never wish to give offence, or to cut for the sake of cutting; but neither shall I shrink from appearing, for the truth's sake, the keenest and narrowest bigot upon earth, an object of annoyance and contempt to all parties, but above all to half-hearted professors of a half gospel. May you, dear sir, be guarded against their cunning craftiness and lying in wait to deceive! May you be valiant for the truth of God, and disregard the traditions of men! It becomes a sinner, who has his life in the divine truth, to contend *earnestly* for its sanctity and glory *as for his life.*

I have looked at the passage which you quoted from my Essay on the Apostolic traditions, and attentively read it in its connexion. When I read only the insulated sentence quoted in your letter, I thought I should have occasion to bid you expunge the passage, as seeming to make the binding authority and obligation of the divine law depend on the moral capacity of the creature to fulfil it—a sentiment, however, which I am conscious of having abhorred no less when I wrote that piece than I do now. But after attentively reading the whole passage, I see no sentiment which, fairly interpreted, I could retract: while I regret the ambiguity and metaphysical subtleties unavoidably connected with the scholastic phraseology which I oppose. The thing which I oppose is distinctly stated in—[see vol. i. p. 252. med. "Now, I say," &c.] The sentiment opposed to it, for which I contend, is as distinctly stated in—[ib. fin. "The revelation," &c.] If any man chooses to express the unchangeable purity and authority of that divine law, of which all sin is the transgression, by saying with you, that *it is the duty of fallen men and fallen angels to be perfect*, I have no objection to the sentiment; while I am sure the strange phraseology has not been derived from the scripture. Nor, in a similar sense, have I any quarrel with those who choose to say that it is the *duty* of all sinners, to whom the gospel is sent, to repent and believe the gospel; while I prefer to say that their impenitence and rejection of its testimony is the crowning manifestation of the wickedness of their hearts. But when men, who neither keep the law nor believe the gospel, inquire further about their other duties (and it is plainly of those supposed other duties I am speaking in the passage you quote), I have nothing further to tell them on the subject, but that they are deceiving themselves with the proud and ungodly notion of having a capacity to do something well pleasing to God. That this capacity is more or less implied in the talk of their particular duties, appears even from Mr. Fuller's statement, that it is not the *immediate* duty of unconverted professors to partake of the Lord's Supper. They are not in a capacity for doing it, but it is their sin that they are not; and in any sense in which they can maintain, that prayer is their immediate duty, I will maintain, that partaking of the Supper is their immediate duty. But whether you admit or not that, in your talking of the duties of unbelieving men, *you* connect with the language any idea of their capacity more or less to discharge them—(though in the instance of promoting the circulation of the scriptures you seem very plainly to do so)—can it be doubted that such language must and does convey the idea to every unbeliever to whom it is addressed? If I urge upon a man, who has been just before gainsaying the glorious gospel, the *duty* which lies upon him to circulate the scriptures, to pray, &c. &c. do I not speak (to say the least) an insidious language, which he indeed would be glad to hear, which in its obvious meaning falls in with all his ungodly principles—and which, while it excites him perhaps to address himself to the performance of those *his duties*, strengthens him in his wickedness and unbelief? Ah! dear sir, I have followed you too long into the entanglements of scholastic phrases. It only needs to have the eye opened to the distinctive glory of the gospel of God, in order to be extricated from the labyrinth, and to turn with abhorrence from the treachery of that disguised opposition to the truth which would involve us in its mazes. I am sure my brother B—— never intended to intimate that sinners, who have never heard the gospel, shall not be righteously condemned for their sin. But if he marked the unbelief of others as the one awful ground of their condemnation, I fully concur with him, and what is more important, I am sure the scriptures in various passages speak the same language. (John iii. 18. 19. 2 Thess. i. 8, &c. &c.) How just is the language, and how consistent with the certain truth, that unbelief alone binds every other sin upon the guilty soul—in what blessed harmony with the word which proclaims to a sinful world, "WHOSOEVER *believeth* shall be saved." It would require the metaphysics of Mr. Fuller (or his humble imitator Mr. Jones) to trace any resemblance between this principle and the Quaker system.

Should you settle in any such system of doctrine as admits the mind to be occupied with those subtleties, (among which I reckon your distinction of positive and moral duties) I should think it very unimportant what principles of church order or fellowship you may adopt. But I would just remark that you are not mistaken in supposing that our practice of not joining in social worship with any, but those in full communion with us, is connected with the sentiment that we are the only scriptural church in Dublin. What churches there may be, unknown to us in other parts of the world, agreed with us in faith and practice, I cannot say. But all who walk by any other rule than we have received from the word of God we must judge unscriptural; and we find ourselves debarred by that word from having any fellowship with them, till they repent of their present opposition to it, and in fact become one with us. In avowing this I am well aware of the disgust and indignation which the avowal is calculated to excite in the religious world. But it moves me not; and I distinctly add that any church, however specious, which shrinks from avowing itself the only scriptural church in the place, does in that very circumstance in my view avow itself an unscriptural and antichristian society. If instead of five you could enumerate fifty churches that each claimed the character, it would matter nothing. The claim of each must be tried by the word of God: but any who do not claim the character certainly do not possess it. I believe however all those you mention, except the Sandemanians and ourselves, have too much humble modesty and liberality to advance the claim. However we may add the Church of Rome, the great mother of harlots—whose master knows more of the characters of Christ's house which he imitates, than many of its children. Much as I have written I am obliged to leave much of your letter unnoticed. I am very sensible how severe and cutting my letter must appear, if it be not made profitable to you: but I am conscious that I only discharge the office of true charity. Whenever my freedom becomes disagreeable, the slightest hint will check my pen. About my visit to London I am still uncertain. If I were to say nothing on your admonition about baptism, you might perhaps think me moved by it. I just say therefore that I am persuaded, in calling me to be baptized, you call me and the baptizer to a childish imitation of what was done in the apostolic days, to play Philip and the Eunuch without any real sameness in the thing. You have not told me whether you conceive the children born to the first proselytes after their conversion—that numerous class of early disciples—ever were baptized—or if they were, when they were baptized.

Believe me, dear sir, with the best wishes for your best interests, faithfully yours,

XLVI.

TO THE SAME.

Aug. 29, 1818.

And so I have been more than a week at home, and have not yet written to my very dear and kind Mr. C——; yet I can truly say, no day has elapsed since we parted that I have not thought of you and yours with the most lively interest: and where our fellowship is with the Father and with his Son Jesus Christ, you know how that interest is expressed. But I have had such a noise in my head since my return as almost unfitted me for writing, and I knew that my daughter had despatched a letter to dear Mrs. C——.

I dare say that letter contained a full account of our voyage, &c. &c., upon which therefore I shall say nothing, but that all the circumstances of them were as mercifully and tenderly ordered as we could wish. On the Sunday morning after we arrived in Glasgow I went to the meeting of the Scotch Baptists, of which Dr. Wall is an elder, partly to meet a person in that connexion, who had bid us to his house, and partly in the hope of being offered the use of their place for speaking. In the latter I was disappointed. But I heard two sermons, under the name of exhortations, from members of the body, which sufficiently shewed the lamentable state in which they are. One took his text from Ephes. vi. 5, 6; and after a philosophical disquisition on the division of labour, argued largely, on natural principles, against the evils of idleness, stealing, &c.; but as to the grace that makes sinners the servants of Christ, and capacitates them for doing the will of God from the heart, was silent. The whole of his discourse, which I suppose occupied half an hour, was evidently a written essay which he had committed to memory. When the second took his text from Ps. xxxiii. 18. 'Well,' thought I, 'surely we shall hear something of the gospel now, something of that mercy in which sinners have hope, something of the nature of the scriptural fear of the Lord.' But indeed I was mistaken. The "hope in His mercy" the speaker never even mentioned after having repeated his text. He was wholly occupied in a vague declamation on the blessedness of *God's people*, as having his eyes always on them, and the awful state of those who are not his people. I was glad to find that a few had lately separated from the body on the subject of evidences assuring the hope of the believer. It is indeed an important subject; and I am more and more satisfied that wherever the leaven of the Glasite doctrine upon it (which I conceive not essentially distinct from Maclean's) has been fully received by any individual or body, it must necessarily turn away their view from the glory of the unadulterated truth. Is it not plain indeed that if a religious professor be walking in apprehensiveness that he is not at peace with God, he must (if sincerely religious) be seeking satisfaction on that most important point, or in other words must be seeking to get peace with God, i. e. must be going about to establish a righteousness of his own, though under the most evangelical phraseology and modest profession, that it is only MERE *evidence of his interest in Christ* he seeks. But in all his religious diligence and strictness, the only genuine spring is wanting: it is all employed that he may have some ground of hope and confidence which he sees not at present. I do believe indeed that with the greatest number of even evangelical professors, who have imbibed the doctrine, there is no great seriousness of Christian thought about the matter. They go through life without the answer of a good conscience toward God, and yet without much uneasiness of conscience. They are connected perhaps with what is considered a scriptural church (shall I say—perhaps with the Scotch Baptists); and it is a received principle in their connexion that believers commonly have not that peace and confidence towards God, of which this member is conscious that he is destitute. But he quiets his conscience with this very principle, and with the other pleasures which his church connexion affords him; is anxious on that account to maintain that connexion; and goes on to the end in a lifeless round of attendance on ordinances, a sober, decent worldling. No wonder if such a man feels the contention for the truth (when it comes across him) an attack upon himself. You see I am still led, in my communications with you, to dwell upon the foundation—not, I may say, because I think you do not know the truth, but because I trust you know it, and that no lie is of the truth. 1 John ii. 21. Since my return, I have been reading for the first time John Barclay on the assurance of faith—an expression which he seems to substitute for the assurance of hope. It contains many excellent things: yet some of his language seems to me incautious, and some of his sentiments doubtful. He expresses himself, at times, as if it were the consideration of his own faith that gave him boldness toward God; and if that were his mind, there is a common ground of error between him and those whom he opposes; while I am sure that the enjoyment of scriptural confidence toward God is inconsistent with the conscious uncertainty whether we believe the truth or not; for that is at bottom an uncertainty about the revealed truth itself. But our vain hearts would rather walk in a kind of confidence derived from the fixed principle that we are believers, than be continually emboldened altogether by that divine testimony, which supersedes all consideration about ourselves but as sinners, and by its all-sufficient fulness of glorious hope, warrants at all times the fullest confidence of the chief of sinners. That Barclay himself walked in much of the enjoyment of this hope I have little doubt; but I have reason to fear that many of his followers have swallowed rather what is doubtful or inaccurate in his language. The more I look at you as of one mind with us in Ireland upon the great truth, the more I lament the things that still keep us asunder, and I believe that when I write next I must devote my letter to the painful subject of our differences. Yet, who knows but the necessity of it may be spared? I shall earnestly look for your promised visit to Dublin. Did I not understand that you had some leisure about Christmas? Though we parted so lately, I already feel the want of some hours talk with you.

XLVII.

TO THE SAME.

Sept. 1818.

My very dear Friend,—Your letter led me before the Lord in wonder and praise. When I see any thing in man accordant with the truth of the gospel, I see the finger of God; and have cause to admire his work. Whatever I see contrary to that truth in myself or others, I see the working of a principle as ungodly as the devil, and may well abhor it. From all the communications we had in London upon that grand topic, I did expect that you would soon find yourself out of your place in your connexion with Red Cross Street. But that it should be so soon—and followed by such prompt decision of conduct! I can only say, Blessed be God! I was observing yesterday to some of my brethren, among other remarks on the subject—how despicable to the fleshly eye, but how wonderful in ours, is the fact of two disciples having then (for the first time I believe in that monstrous city) met together in the simplicity of scriptural principle. I trust—indeed I doubt not—it will prove that then the standard of the glorious truth of God was erected, and that there will be a gathering to it—however small—of those who are indeed on the Lord's side. In all the weighty solemnity of the season which you justly feel, the whole analogy of faith speaks the same cheering language to the weakest disciple which the angel spake to Daniel of old—"Fear not, O man greatly beloved—be strong—yea, be strong!" All indeed that you have known hitherto of the opposition of the world is far short of what you may now expect. But while our eyes are kept open to the glory of Emmanuel's name, we shall see that "they that be with us are more than they that be with them." 2 Kings vi. 16. It is noted as the sin of the Israelites (in all whose rebellions we have but a picture of our own unbelieving hearts) that "they tempted the Lord, saying, Is the Lord among us or not?" Exod. xvii. 7. Numb. xi. 20. Let us not so tempt Christ, but be strong in faith giving glory to God. But I must restrain myself—for I am very limited in time, and have many things to notice.

You ask me whether I am still of my former mind as to the admission of persons, &c. I suppose your question refers to a very bad sentence at the end of my letter to Philo. (See vol. 1, p. 307.) Almost as soon as it was printed I saw its evil, and commonly erased the passage in any copy I gave away. We never acted upon the sentiment, nor indeed had I the formed sentiment when I wrote the words which seem to convey it. How could a man maintaining baptism walk with us, without making a supposed precept of Christ a matter of forbearance? But truly I do expect your speedy abandonment of the matter, now that you are unshackled by your late connexion. Think only, my friend, was your baptism like any thing you read of in Scripture except in name and form? or *could* it have been so at any period of your course? If Timothy was born after his mother Eunice's conversion to the faith of Christ, think have you any ground in Scripture to suppose that he ever was baptized? The practice is quite suitable to those who want to mark some stage in their Christian profession, to which their minds may revert with complacence: but indeed it is out of place with those who have ever professed to believe that apostolic gospel, which is all that they now have to assign as a reason for their hope. I have often wished to incorporate and abridge the two pieces on baptism; but I know not how I can set about it. If you publish the shorter, use your discretion in annexing to it extracts from the longer.

You ask about our order of worship. It is, a hymn—prayer—reading the Scriptures—a hymn—the Supper, preceded by a very short prayer and giving of thanks before taking the bread and the wine—a hymn—mutual exhortation—the contribution—prayer—the salutation with a kiss—a hymn. Do we differ now on the subject of promiscuous worship? I should hope not. For instance—if you had an unbelieving servant or one not in fellowship, would you call him in to what is termed family worship? The Lord our God is holy. Would this be sanctifying his name? or is it reconcileable with the principles in Rom. x. 14. 2 Thess. iii. 6, &c.

If I should not find an earlier opportunity of sending them, a dear brother (Doctor M——, a young physician,) will be going to London in less than three weeks, and I shall rejoice in the occasion of making him known to you. Your intelligence about Mr. S—— rejoices me. There is an end of his chapel and popularity as a preacher, and, I trust, the commencement of a scriptural course. Surely the Lord is visiting England in mercy. Could I see my way, I should be ready enough to run off to you: and indeed my flesh would be too ready to conceive of it as of some consequence that I—(ah! that big vile I)—should be busy at present in England. But the Lord does not need me for his work; and the new mind leads me only to leave myself in his blessed hands, that he may make any thing or nothing of me, as he thinks best. For all the abundant kindness and substantial affection in your letter, how shall I thank you? I thank Him who teaches us to love one another with such a love as nothing but his truth produces. *At present*, my place is here; and it is enough for us to know our *present* place. The departure of a very few pupils, without others coming to supply their room, may perhaps very soon mark my path in another direction. If the Lord send me to you, it will be well—if not, it will be well—he is himself the all-sufficient God. You will find me, when you come, ready to meet your kind invitation of opening my mind to you freely on every thing. But it is a subject that may be postponed till we meet. Remember, I shall expect you to take up your abode with me, humbly as I can accommodate you.

There are some exceptions to Mr. G——'s rule about want of righteousness or want of money. I can hardly say that the latter occasioned any part of my depression when with you, for I scarcely thought of it. But my son was much in my thoughts—and my dear daughter too, not in fellowship with me, though I think she ought. I have some hopes that her mind is rather engaged about the point on which we differ. You do not know how trying it is to be an alien to those of your own house.

XLVIII.

TO THE SAME.

Sept. 17. 1818.

My Brother, my beloved Brother,—My heart rejoices to exchange the endearing appellation. I have received your letter about an hour ago, and it has left me scarcely fit for writing, yet I cannot but write. Blessed for ever be our redeeming God—the God of all grace—the God who doth wondrous things! How did my heart often sigh when you went down after breakfast, when I heard your voice in the front parlour and could not outwardly join one who I thought ought to walk with me. But now we should pour out our souls together before the throne of grace. O blessed privilege for creatures altogether sinful to enjoy! O blessed union which the truth of God produces! in which his name is sanctified, and none of its glory profaned by being yielded with ungodly forbearance to the evil of men. It is because I see our unity of sentiment the fruit of his blessed truth, and therefore of God, that I have joyful confidence of its lasting: for otherwise what hope would there be of that, considering what we both are as sinners? But his mercy endureth for ever—it is from everlasting to everlasting. He will perfect that which concerneth us, and not forsake the work of his own hands. And what should our song be while on our way to the heavenly Zion, but the same which it shall be for ever when we arrive there; the song of praise and thanksgiving to Him who has loved us and washed us from our sins in his own blood? O! what an essential difference there is between full attention to all the gracious revelation of his will from this principle of glorifying him, and the vain strictness of exertion to glorify ourselves by obtaining something in our hearts or lives to prop up our hope towards God? "Ye *are* a chosen generation, a royal priesthood, an holy nation, a peculiar people; *that ye should* shew forth the praises of him who hath called you out of darkness into his marvellous light." Our foolish minds are continually inverting this order, and would be doing something *that we may be something*. Before this reaches you I hope you will have received a little parcel which I sent you by a person who sailed last Monday night, with a few hasty lines in reply to your former letter. That letter is not immediately in my possession, which I regret, as there remain in it some things unanswered. I recollect your inquiring about a Mr. W—— of K—— L——. We have formerly exchanged several letters, the particulars of which I forget; but the general impression left on my mind was pleasing; and I have often wished and designed to visit the place. I am disappointed to find that your coming to Dublin is postponed till November—and I half envy my brother M—— that he will enjoy a meeting with you before myself:—I shall gladly give him your kind message, and I doubt not he will gladly do what you desire, unless it be prevented by his having a companion, a young man about sixteen, with whom he travels.

I see you are hot upon removing me to London; and you may well suppose that our complete union disposes me to some such change even more than before. But I candidly own that all my mind revolts from the idea of being burdensome to you. I have been thinking of a trial for a year without removing my family immediately. I know not what encouragement there might be with you for some kind of day school on liberal terms, or for private pupils in the mathematical sciences and classics. Were I independent of labouring for my bread, or had to labour only for my own support, I think I should be apt not to reside permanently in any one place, but after a residence for a year or two, according as there appeared work in the Lord's vineyard, should move my quarters. But here am I involved in talking of my foolish schemes. I have committed and do commit my way in this matter to the Lord, and I desire to rest it with him, daily praying that he may not leave me to my own will or wisdom. Your zeal in the circulation of tracts I hope will provoke us to jealousy here. We greatly need to be stirred up to more exertion for spreading the truth. For the last three or four weeks we have been engaged in a renewed attempt on Sunday evenings to call the attention of the world to the Gospel. Very few attend; but still sufficient to warrant the continuance of the effort I am a little jealous of your seeming inference from the immense multitude of inhabitants in London, that there must be very many who have an ear for the word. Of all that multitude, how few are there who are not at present lending a willing ear to the grossest doctrines of Antichrist; and of the rest who make a more refined profession, how few perhaps would be found, when the unadulterated truth is laid before them, to close with it cordially, without wishing for some change in its statement or for some addition to it. No doubt they have scarcely yet been tried in this way; and how many people the Lord may have in that great city it is not for us to speculate on. But his ways are so sovereign that it might be, that more would be found in some country village than in all London; and to that revealed principle of his kingdom it is always wholesome for us to attend: "Few there be that find it." It is well calculated to beat down that carnal vanity which would always lead us to seek something that would make a figure in the eyes of men: and equally calculated to support our spirits in patience and hope, while we find so few to join us; and to keep us rejoicing in the prospect of that coming day, when the Lord shall appear to be glorified in his saints. I do not carry these ideas so far as I believe the Glasites do; for I fancy if they saw a few hundred disciples gathered together in London, they would be ready to conclude that it must be on Antichristian principles. Yet what a little flock would that be!

XLIX.

TO ———.

——— 1818.

Sir,—The letter you favoured me with, did not reach me till my return to Dublin, and it is but lately that I heard through Mr. K. how I should address an answer to it. Suffer me now to offer a few plain observations to your attention. Two things struck me with some surprise in your letter; the manifest inconsistency between the first paragraph, and almost all that follows;—the other—your taking offence at expressions used by me, which I am confident I never employed in my discourses, because they are a style of language that I have long thought unscriptural. The Scriptures are explicit in assigning the salvation of the righteous to the Lord, tracing it from the purpose of his grace, of which they were the objects in Christ Jesus before the world began, to the effectual working of his power, bringing them by the word of truth to the knowledge of him, in whom they are made partakers of righteousness, and the adoption of children, guiding them by the spirit of truth, and keeping them through faith unto that glory of which they are heirs. The scriptures, I say, explicitly reveal this great salvation as his work, who has power over all flesh, that he should give eternal life to as many as the Father hath given him. But they no where speak of the perdition of the ungodly as the effect of a divine decree that they should not believe and be saved: for this indeed would imply what is directly contrary to the truth,—namely, that they are all so well disposed, that if they were let they would gladly come to Christ that they might have life: whereas the carnal mind is so opposed to the true God, that it is impossible a single individual should ever come to Christ, unless drawn by the Father. It can hardly therefore require the exertion of his power to keep any back. Plainly as these things are revealed, I know they are opposed and blasphemed by the whole world, by religious and profane, have ever been so, and ever must; the world, thoroughly unintentionally, confirming that word that they reject: and no objection against it is more constantly bandied in various forms than that, "Why doth he yet find fault? Who hath resisted his will?" 'If the work of a sinner's salvation from first to last be God's work, those whom he does not save, may equitably arraign him as the author of their ruin.' And truly I know not any specimen of human wickedness in this world coming nearer to what we may conceive exhibited in the regions of outer darkness, than this objection.—While those who hardily make it, are wilfully rejecting that salvation which is revealed, and clothing their blasphemous sentiments in devout hymns and sermons. But what surprises me, sir, in you is that you appear, in the first sentence of your letter, unequivocally to assert that doctrine, against which this objection is brought. But I own to you that I fear there must be some latent fallacy in your mind, and that you have not weighed the import of the words that you employ in that passage, or I think you could never have written as you do in the remainder. Think with yourself again, are you indeed persuaded that any sinner *whatsoever*, who believes the divine testimony concerning Jesus of Nazareth, is justified in him, and shall be eternally saved by him—that their faith, or knowledge of that testimony, is the gift and work of God—that they can do nothing, either to promote their acceptance in his sight at first, or (as you express it) to assist in their final salvation—and that none, who persist in disbelieving that testimony, shall escape final condemnation. Why, sir, if you are persuaded of these things, we are agreed; and what is it you are objecting to? You know that, in this case, your creed differs from that of all the surrounding world—that they are indeed a *little* flock, who have received repentance to the acknowledging of this truth;—and may you not then answer your own objections, and the difficulties you start against the divine mercy from the number of those who perish. But consider again, I beseech you, what all these objections amount to. Is it to this? If God save not the majority of mankind, his character appears to have more cruelty than goodness? and will you really maintain this language? then, of course, if he save not *all*, he is but imperfectly good. Indeed, I would have supposed, from the tenor of your argument, that you held that fashionable lie of the final salvation of all men and devils, were it not that the first sentence of your letter appears to disavow it. But I cannot but fear that your notions of the divine mercy are altogether unscriptural; and that, like many others, you mean by the term something, the non-extension of which to sinners, would derogate from the divine equity and goodness; i. e. something that is not *mercy*, but which sinners may claim as a right, while they think it safer to pass the compliment of *calling* it mercy. If ever the word of truth, that declares the true grace or mercy of God in Christ Jesus, gain admission into your mind, I doubt not but it will bring down the high thoughts that are now exalting themselves against the knowledge of God; and while it discovers to you the distinctive glory of Him who is the only true God and eternal life, just and the justifier of the ungodly, will satisfy you of the importance of testifying against all that is called God, and that is worshipped by those who believe not the testimony of his name. You will see that your argument, about worshipping the *true* God *falsely*, is but a play on words. I have the decided authority of the Scriptures for asserting that none but those, who believe the revelation he has made of his name, do or can call upon the true God; and that whosoever calls upon him, shall be saved. Your argument, that Christ cannot be said to have destroyed the works of the devil if only a few of mankind be saved, has been already sufficiently answered. As to the number of the saved, I know nothing but what the Scriptures inform me. I know that when all are brought together they will form a multitude that no man can number; but I know also, from the same authority, that their number on earth, at any particular period, has hitherto been small indeed, in comparison of those who tread the broad way. Indeed, all who believe the gospel, will find how few they are that think with them. What, therefore, do you mean by wishing me to represent the majority of men around me as in the way of salvation, when I see them despising and hating the testimony of the Saviour? This does not look as if you were persuaded that none but those who believe the truth will be saved. Excuse the plain fidelity with which I have written, and which, however it may displease you, has been dictated by the truest concern for your welfare. I am, &c.

L.

TO ———.

——1818.

Sir,—On my return from the country, I have received your letter of the 26th ult., which you tell me is the fourth you have written without receiving any answer. I beg you will forgive me this appearance of neglect. I think some of your former letters must have miscarried; for I do not recollect receiving any other from you except one last year from Mr. D——, of Glasgow, accompanied with a pamphlet, "The ancient doctrine of the Seceders," &c. My silence upon that, partly arose from the nature and multiplicity of my engagements, (which forbid my attempting to hold epistolary correspondence with all who might desire it) but chiefly from your pamphlet leading me to apprehend that you are betrayed into a rashness of speculation in which I dare not follow you. Yet I confess that I then entertained more hope than I do now, that there was something of an unity of mind between us, upon the great truth of the Gospel. Your last letter, in which you explain your sentiments on the doctrine of a sinner's justification before God, leaves me only to wonder how you could so much mistake my mind, as to wish for communication with me. I am not altogether a stranger to the comforts that are connected with fellowship of brethren united in the gospel. But to that comfort unity of view, with respect to the doctrine of the gospel, is essentially requisite; and there, it appears from your letter, that we essentially differ. You would agree with me in *saying* that the Gospel is a revelation of righteousness to the guilty and ungodly; but we do not mean the same thing by the words. You mean that it communicates to them a mind and nature agreeable to the righteous and holy will of God; by participating in which, you conceive that men are justified in the sight of God. I mean that it reveals that perfect righteousness fulfilled by another, which God declares he has accepted for the justification of the evil and wicked before him. The hope of your Gospel must be a hope derived from the supposed perception of the new nature in you: the hope of the Apostolic gospel is derived solely from the perception of the work of righteousness, finished by the Lord Jesus. The perception of this, (or the belief of the divine word that reports it) will indeed produce a new mind; but this mind, and all its correspondent fruits, are the "*fruits of righteousness*," not the righteousness, nor the cause of the righteousness of those who are saved. Of course, as you deny Christ made righteousness to his people by imputation, I suppose you deny their sins made *his* by imputation; and I confess, sir, that judging of your sentiments from your own statement of them, I am obliged to consider you as a stranger to the true grace of God. At the same time I thank you for your expressions of kindness and good will towards me, and will be happy to render you any service in my power. I am, &c.

LI.

TO J. B———.

—— 1818.

I HAVE read your letter twice, with as much attention as you could desire: for (while in my right mind) I can never be averse to examine the scriptural grounds of my conduct and principles, from whatever quarter the call to that examination may come. I received none of the *shock* from your sentiments which you seemed to apprehend, for the avowal of them did not surprise me. I had long conjectured that you were of the mind which you now express; partly collecting it from your former communications, but still more from knowing how closely connected is opposition to any of the divine precepts with the abandonment of the *sanctity* of them all. As I am also aware how closely connected this is with a departure from the truth of the unadulterated gospel, I seriously think that I can make you no kinder return for the trouble you have taken in trying to convert me to your ungodly system, than by sending you the enclosed tract, which I entreat you to read with close attention. I am persuaded that, if ever you be effectually arrested in that downward course which you are pursuing with such accelerated velocity, it must be by the sanctity of that truth (in which the only true God makes himself known to us) being brought more clearly to your view and more powerfully to your conscience.

I am at a loss to conceive why you thought the scriptural union, which the great mercy of God has lately produced in my family, was likely to dispose me to the unscriptural union which you so zealously contend for. But I hope it *has* led me to look with more confidence of expectation to Him, with whom nothing is impossible, to display the same mercy and power in other instances, according to his sovereign will. It is only in the hope of that divine blessing, that I proceed to make a few brief and detached remarks on your letters; but without any design of entering into a detailed reply. Your criticism on the singular form of the word *tradition* in 2 Thess. iii. is like many of the other criticisms of which you ought to be ashamed. I would just refer you to Matthew xv. 2, 3, 6. Mark vii. 3, 5, 8, 9, 13. Col. ii. 8.—in every one of which passages the word is singular, and evidently equivalent with a *system of doctrine*, or code of precepts delivered. It might be well for you also to consider what the Thessalonian church *must* have understood, when they read the sixth verse of that chapter, and before they proceeded to read the subsequent passage, in which the apostle applies that general direction to a particular instance of disobedience to apostolic tradition. It would be as easy to expose your mistranslation of the word σημειοῦσθε, in which you confound two verbs essentially distinct, σημειόω and σημαίνω. It is observable indeed that in the Syriac version (one of the most ancient that we have)—so full was the translator's mind of the general direction in the passage, that he renders the words "note that man" by "let him be separated from you."

But I pass these topics, on which really the question does not turn with you. The fundamental question,—however you conceal it by vague declamation and specious words, is whether there be a King in Zion who has delivered to his subjects a *sufficient* and *authoritative* revelation of his will in the scriptures: or whether his subjects be left to walk after their several fancies and to do each what is right in his own eyes. There is fully implied a denial of the former in your palliative paraphrases for continued disobedience to the plainest precepts of his word, after full and patient admonition for the sin—as "a *difference* with regard to particular practices or the *meaning* of particular precepts." It is at once charging the sin upon a supposed *obscurity* or uncertainty in the word of God; and involves the common ungodly sentiment that ignorance, or non-perception of a divine command, neutralizes the disobedience into an innocent infirmity. I would recommend to your serious attention the passage in Levit. v. 17—19. and I would observe that there is a very short step to be taken, in order to extend this ungodly forbearance to the very truth of the gospel. A Socinian urges just the same *principle*, that even if he be wrong it is but a difference of opinion about the meaning of words—a harmless *mistake*. It is truly curious to observe some of those precepts which you talk of as so *obscure* and *doubtful* in their meaning. The word of God commands the churches of the saints—"salute one another—all the brethren—with an holy kiss—a kiss of love." It again solemnly charges his children—"swear not at all—by any oath." (I am by no means restrained from bringing forward this instance by the shortness of the time since I was myself, in the ungodliness of my flesh, rejecting this divine command.) Now, I say that these precepts are as plain as words can make them,—as intelligible to a child as to a philosopher. "No"—say you—"I cannot for the life of me *understand* them. I do not see their *meaning*. And will you withdraw from me for a mere *mistake* and a little *ignorance*?"

But I must add, that you are only playing the deceiver in urging this,—the deceiver of yourself probably, as well as of others. For it is manifest from your interpretation of that passage in Thessalonians, that you do not consider the most *wilful* and avowed rejection of *known* apostolic precepts—persisted in after repeated admonition—inconsistent with the offender's being kept in the fellowship of the church. Any man there, who persisted in his idleness certainly could not plead that he did not *understand* the apostolic injunction; and yet you assert that this idler was to be kept in the fellowship—in the closest and most endeared fellowship of the kingdom of heaven:—only the disciples were not to be *intimate* with him!

You gravely tell me indeed what cases of disobedience you would *forbear* with, and what you *would not*. Of the latter you give but one instance, namely, worshipping with persons who remain in the establishment: as if there were any more wickedness in this than in all other breaches of scriptural rule. If ignorance of the sin may be pleaded in other cases, I should be glad to know why the plea should not be admitted in this. But the whole shews that you take no other rule, but your own fancy and religious taste.

Even in the cases of open and acknowledged immorality, to which you professedly apply the prescribed discipline of the house of God, I apprehend that the real grounds on which we would remove the offender are essentially different. It is his *refusal to hear the correction of the word of the Lord* that scripturally stamps him with any of the characters enumerated in 1 Cor. v. 11. and the same rejection of that word is found in the characters whom you would retain in the body. With respect to the offender himself also, the last solemn act of discipline scripturally proceeds, not at all on the pharisaic notion on which you rest it, that the person guilty of such wickedness *plainly manifests that he* IS NOT *of the truth*—that he IS NOT *of the kingdom of heaven*; but in the hope that he is, and with the merciful view, "that the spirit may be saved in the day of the Lord Jesus." With respect to the body indeed, it is (as you truly intimate) that the old leaven may be purged out—that leaven which would be likely to leaven the whole lump. But pray is there no similar danger to be apprehended from leaving in the body the standard of rebellion erected against the authority of any of the laws of Christ?

You rightly conceive that I would confidently refer to that passage in 2 Thess. iii. as expressly prescribing a course opposite to the laxity for which you contend. But I as confidently say, that the person who thinks the divine obligation of that course rests upon the interpretation of this particular passage, does not yet discern the scriptural grounds of it. It rests on the whole nature of an apostolic church, and the divine authority of the apostolic precepts. The former your principles would transform from a body joined together in the maintenance of the word of Christ, into a confederacy against every part of it: for the same systematic rejection of one precept which you would tolerate in any one member *must* extend in principle to every precept and every member alike. And I tell you candidly, that if I were to adduce any *particular* passage of the word in support of my withholding fellowship from you, it would not be that passage in Thessalonians, but much rather such a passage as that in

1 Tim. vi. 3. Your sin in disobeying particular precepts has long merged in the additional iniquity of becoming a ringleader in teaching contrary to "wholesome words—the words of the Lord Jesus Christ, and the doctrine which is according to godliness." I know that you, with multitudes of others, are accustomed to apply that word *doctrine* (or teaching) exclusively to what the scriptures declare of divine *truth* for the obedience of faith. But the very passage to which I refer, as well as many more, ought to correct the misapplication.

I shall take no notice of the imputations which you so liberally throw out against us—of *strife, and enmity, and pride, and high-mindedness, and hypocrisy:* nor of your very false insinuation, that we LIGHTLY AND HASTILY *sever* the bond which unites disciples with us, if they do not IMMEDIATELY SUBMIT *to our authority.* Most of those with you have abundant cause to know the falsehood of such a charge. As to the other *melancholy* effects which you so often refer to, of what you call the present system, I really know none of them. I think it a great mercy that in your present mind you are not with us. And if (as you intimate, and I know is the case,) there are other bodies in town like-minded with you, from whom you yet walk apart; this only shews your common inconsistency. You all talk speciously about unity, and yet go on without scruple to multiply your synagogues without any reason but your several fancies.

Yous attempt to confound the systematic *rejection* of a divine precept with the *short-comings* which every believer will acknowledge, of conformity to them all, is a sophism so gross that it deserves no answer.

When you apply the apostolic exhortations to follow the things that make for *peace,*—to keep the unity of the spirit in the bond of *peace*—to avoid *questions which engender strife*—when you apply these to the union which you plead for with those who persist in disobedience to the precepts of God, there is abundance of sophistry in this also; but indeed there is much worse. I must plainly say there is awful *profaneness.* And is it so, that the apostle who solemnly delivered the ordinances of the kingdom of Heaven in the name of its King, at the same time instructed his subjects to avoid the introduction of these matters, *as questions that engender strife?* In holding this language about them, I am aware that you mean to assume, that the matters which we hold as preceptive are not really so: and this is a palpable *begging of the question.* But at the same time, the whole of your argument goes to prove the duty of your forbearance about them, *even on the supposition of their being what we hold them,* and therefore justifies me in conceiving that you extend the same language to them, even in that view. *If* you really do not mean this, will you admit that the precepts—"Swear not at all"—"Salute one another with the kiss of love," &c. are parts of the *doctrine according to godliness*—the wholesome words, the words of the Lord Jesus Christ, to which those who consent not are to be removed from the fellowship? No: unless the Lord give you another mind, you will not admit this; for then there would be no difference between us on the nature of Christian forbearance. We are as forward as you can be to assert the wickedness of putting forward as divine precepts what are not truly so.

But then comes your distinction between the present time and the time of the apostles:—" they *could not* have given us directions referring to the present cases, because there was no room for *uncertainty* about the *meaning* of their precepts then." This is indeed a sweeping principle of ungodliness, that would persuade us we are without rule in the scriptures—rule either of *faith or practice:* for an *insufficient and uncertain* rule is equivalent to none. The apostles were indeed better taught, than to give any direction *involving the supposition* that their precepts to the churches were of that uncertain and doubtful character which you attribute to them. But while in all that part of your argument, you rest on our present *ignorance and liability to mistake* the meaning of their precepts, you prove (as I have before noticed) by your interpretation of the passage in Thessalonians that this is *not your real ground:* and that you would extend the same forbearance to the disobedience (to use your own language) " which arises from want of submission to what is *known* to be the will of God."

I have witten much more than I intended, though in a very random and hurried way. I am sure that what I have written will afford you abundant matter—(if you be not brought to repentance)—for renewing your imputations of pride, and high-mindedness, and strife, and uncharitable severity. You seem to have quite lost sight of the real nature of the charity, and lowliness, and peace of the gospel. If what I have written be blessed to you (and it is only in that *hope* and *prayer* that I have written so much), you will form a very different estimate of evil and of good; and will see that it is not with the fire of the sanctuary your *lights have been burning*.

I am, dear John, with affectionate concern,

Your real well-wisher,

May I beg that you will shew this letter to any to whom you have shewn yours? Should you through rich mercy be convinced of the ungodliness of the principles contained in your letter, I shall be glad to see you or to hear from you again. Should you not, I do not see any end to be answered by continuing a *private controversy*.

LII.

TO THE SAME.

———, 1818.

Dear John,—Your last communication would not require any further notice from me, but for one passage in which you refer to a wicked sentiment in my piece on baptism. I am a good deal surprised to hear from you that you are not sure I have ever fully renounced that sentiment. Let me now assure you that my attention was no sooner called to it—(I believe not a month after the publication of the pamphlet)—than I fully renounced it with abhorrence, and have ever since taken every opportunity to protest against it, commonly expunging the passage from any copies of the work I circulated, regretting that no opportunity has yet offered of *publicly* renouncing it.

I might very suitably close our correspondence here; but as I have been obliged to take up my pen again, I shall add one or two brief remarks. You talk of one *having a scruple* about the salutation with the kiss of charity; evidently meaning one who *doubts* at once the *lawfulness* of omitting the practice, and the *obligation* of observing it. Such a man certainly cannot obey the precept, however he may profess to do so in the outward act: and as certainly such a man would be most hypocritically wicked in pretending to press upon his brethren a matter which he does not himself see to be of divine authority, or in pretending not to forbear with their disobedience to it. But you really much mistake, if you think we have adopted the practice (or any other in which we require unity of mind in those with whom we walk) as a matter of doubtful opinion. With your system, it is very suitable to talk of all the peculiar precepts of Christianity in that light, and to substitute the term "*ignorant* disciple" for one who rejects the plainest instruction of the Word, after it has been patiently and solemnly laid before him.

That *instruction* is the dealing called for with any disciple *ignorant* of any part of the divine will, there is no question between us. There is as little question that all the precepts of the gospel are stamped with the character of *mercy:* and if ever you be brought to see the true nature of that mercy, you will see it as much in the last act of discipline as in any of the preceding. Your misinterpretation of 1 Cor. v. 5. is sufficiently refuted by 2 Cor. ii. 7. Certainly, if the church removed that offender as one who had plainly manifested that he was not of the kingdom of heaven, they removed him under a mistake. But probably you have an interpretation for doing away the plain meaning of the latter passage also.

You refer me to your Paisley Letters for your reasons for not uniting with those who worship privately and occasionally with persons in the Establishment. I wanted no additional reasons to prove *their sin:* and I have found no grounds on which you can reconcile your conduct towards them—supposing them (to use your own language) *ignorant* of their sin—with your conduct towards those who persist in disobedience to any other part of the divine rule. I suppose that, for any thing for which you *refuse admission* into your synagogue, you would also *remove* from your synagogue; though indeed you are in such a labyrinth of-wicked inconsistency, that I do not know whether I ought to suppose it.

One thing, however, in your letter marks it quite superfluous to attempt the exposure of any of your inconsistencies. You hold your interpretation of 2 Thess. iii. and at the same time deny that you consider wilful and avowed rejection of *known* apostolic precept consistent with the continuance of Christian fellowship. Now the only way in which these two things can possibly be reconciled, is by your maintaining that the idler remained *ignorant* of the apostle's *meaning* in testifying against the evil of his idleness, and enjoining the opposite course. I do not conceive that any continuance of *argument*, with the man who will assert this, is at all likely to be productive of any advantage.

I am sorry to add, that I consider your confession of faith to Mr. M—— much more like that of a *theologian* than that of a simple Christian; and one turning point of it at least very ambiguous. But that you may not again charge me with passing over any matters, I must expressly tell you that I neither have now, nor had when I last wrote, any intention of answering you at large. I neither have time for the attempt, nor if I had would I think it useful. It will rejoice me at any time to find your zeal receiving a direction *for* the word of God instead of *against* it.

I am, &c.

LIII.

TO THE SAME.

Dec. 12, 1813.

Dear John,—You will perhaps be surprised at hearing from me again; but no matter: let it at least mark the concern I feel at the course you are pursuing. I have just returned from C——, where, at your mother's desire, I communicated to her your letters and my replies. In reading the latter, I perceived a passage which I felt very obscure from the brevity which I used; and as I had to explain my meaning in C——, I think I may as well explain it to you also. It is in the passage where I observe, "that I suppose that, for any thing for which you refuse admission, &c. you would also remove," &c. My meaning is this: you refuse to take into fellowship the people in Stephen-street, on account of an evil in their course, on which they are deaf to admonition, and avow that they cannot see the evil: it is not yet *revealed* to them that it is evil by that private spirit, which so many set above the Scriptures. Well; if one of those, with whom you are at present walking, should fall into the same evil course of occasional and private worship with persons in the Establishment, and if he should prove deaf to your admonition upon it, is it not to be supposed in common consistency that you would remove him from your fellowship? You would not make this evil a matter of forbearance, though he should plead that you were removing an *ignorant disciple*, instead of instructing him. That is, you would in this one instance professedly pursue the same course with us, but certainly not on the same grounds; it would be at your own fancy and religious taste. If it were in maintenance of the word of the Lord, you would have done with your forbearance in other matters, where the authority of that word is invaded. In removing him also, or in not receiving the Stephen-street people, according to your avowed principles in your first letter, you conclude that they are all manifested as not of the kingdom of heaven. I know you do not mean this; though I do not well know what you do mean: yet I suspect that I know it as well as you do yourself. But it is more important to remark, that I have lately found to a certainty, what I had long suspected, that the Stephen-street people forbear upon the truth of the Gospel itself; that many of them avowedly maintain, and erroneously contend for, that deadly part of the Sandemanian doctrine, that a believer walks in doubt whether he is a child of God or a child of the devil, till he observes evidences in himself, that satisfy him he is a genuine believer. From your repeated attempts to obtain a junction with them, I am apprehensive that you are of one mind with them in this; or think this also a matter of forbearance. If so, all communication with you about the walk of disciples is very much misplaced. I shall only briefly add, (lest my silence upon it should be misconstrued) that I have very long questioned the correctness of the interpretation, which I offered in my Apostolic Traditions, on 2 Thess. iii. 15; and that, for some time, I have been convinced of its incorrectness. The Apostle must be understood as there guarding the church against a precipitate withdrawing from the offender, without a previous effort of love to bring him to a sense of his evil by admonition. But all admonition from the church, collectively, must cease after his removal, though individuals may occasionally renew it as opportunity offers, while his verbal acknowledgment of the truth continues. I think I have now said all that I feel needful: may the Lord (if it be his sovereign will) bring you back to the reverence of his holy name and word. Your sincere well-wisher,

LIV.

TO J. A———. AND T. D———.

Dec. 1818.

We are directed, beloved brethren, by the church in Dublin, to communicate to you some of the sentiments which have been suggested to our minds by our hearing of the trying division that now keeps asunder those who have walked together in C——. By a letter received from our brother C——, we understand that he, as well as our sister W——, is now through divine mercy of one mind with us and you on the subject of oaths. But his objection to some of the sentiments and practices contended for by those with whom you have lately formed a junction, keeps him asunder from you. In this it appears to us that he is right, and that you were precipitate in forming a union with persons not agreed with us on the divine rule by which we are called to walk. If they, when they offered themselves to your fellowship, were conscious of the existence of any such disagreement, and still more if you were conscious of it, we think there was a very evil departure from the essential principles of Christian union in your forming the junction, and that a step which ought never to have been taken cannot be too soon rectified. We should deeply regret an additional evil, if it appears that your minds are infected by the vain extravagancies which, we learn with pain, your new associates have run into. We allude not merely to the affectation of particular modes of diction opposed to the ordinary language of common life, but also to the misinterpretation of the words of Christ in Matt. xxiii. 8. 10. and John xiii. 14. In the former, the word rendered "master" is literally a guide or leader; and what our Lord forbids to his disciples in the passage is evidently—not the addressing of men in civil society according to any of those distinctions of rank and circumstance with which his kingdom was never designed to interfere, but the assumption of any titles or character of religious superiority above their brethren. In the latter passage our Lord, teaching by expressive acts as well as by words, as on other occasions—(see for instance Mark ix. 36.)—conveys to us a blessed lesson of readiness at all times to the lowest service of love to our brethren; a lesson which is altogether perverted by those who consider it as the institution of a ceremonial act which we are to make opportunities for observing. But it is not our object to enter into a detailed exposure of any of these errors. We think it much more important, dear brethren, solemnly to call your attention to the bitter root from which such idle questions and vain janglings originate. It is when our minds get from under the sobering but blessed influence of the glorious truth, that they are ready to run after every novel shadow, and to feed the vanity of the flesh with the admired inventions of our own fancies. Even if those who have adopted these vain conceits were now professedly to abandon them, we should not view the change with any satisfaction, unless they discerned that most evil root of their error which we have marked: and if you, brethren, discern it and are aware that these differences of sentiment were known to either side or both, when your junction was formed, we are persuaded that you are called immediately to dissolve that union which ought not to have taken place. We commend you, dear brethren, to God and the word of his grace, praying that you may be mercifully disentangled from every snare of the adversary, and kept abiding to the end in the simplicity that is in Christ Jesus.

LV.

TO J. L———.

Dec. 28*th*, 1818.

My Dear Sir,—Nay, I must say—brother—till I find you (which I hope and believe I never shall) turning away from that glorious truth which appears to dwell in you. Your letter has refreshed me and all the other brethren here to whom I have communicated it; and I dare say several pray for you. It is refreshing to see the work and teaching of *God* in any of our fellow sinners. May the mercy and power of the Lord be more and more displayed in you and all his people for the glory of his own name, uniting our hearts to fear and love and rejoice in his holy name alone, and keeping us from all the deceivableness of unrighteousness which surrounds us, and which is always so congenial to our religious flesh! Do I not know you a little personally? Are you not the man whom I once heard exhort in the Leith Tabernacle, and who accosted me very affectionately in the gallery? This is only a question of curiosity, and very unimportant: for I think I know your mind—the mind of the spirit of truth in you—from your letter. What a hubbub that truth makes, when it gets among a number of decent orthodox professors, who doubt not but they *believe* enough and are occupied with going on *to do!* who are ready perhaps to say of the clearest statement of the gospel that "*it is all very true; but*"—aye; but they see not in its truth all their life and all their glory. Very truly you observe, that but for God's own work the knowledge of his name would long since be extinct upon earth:—would indeed at any hour be extinct. Every thing in man—in us and others—is essentially opposed to it. And what a view does this give us of our own continued ungodliness! a view that puts down for ever all the common notions of some progressive betterness in believers than in others, or than in their former selves: that he who glorieth may glory in the Lord. And seeing the revelation He has made of his great name, do we not see enough to glory in, and *enough* to cheer our hearts amidst all the reproaches we may be called to meet with for his name's sake? The world that knows Him not cannot know us,—cannot understand our meaning: and they naturally view us as disturbers of their peace, and opposed to all that they think most excellent. Can we boast over them? No, in no wise. While we are in nothing moved by the adversaries, but set our faces as a flint contending earnestly for the faith of God against all the lies of man, let it be "with meekness and fear:" not that ungodly fear in which they walk, reasonably afraid of the *insecurity of their ground* after all their doings; but in that godly fear which will abound so much more in the glorified spirits of the redeemed before the throne, than it ever does in them here.

Your account of Mr. H—— does not surprise me, coinciding only with what I had myself observed in him, and lately heard of his course when in London. There were at one time pleasing appearances in him; and I set it down that either they would become more decisively pleasing, or that he would go *back*. For many years he has seemed to me to retrograde. I fear he has never seen the glorious sufficiency in the revealed character and work of God our Saviour to give the fulness of peace and joy and *assured hope* to an ungodly sinner, and its exclusive sufficiency to afford us any good hope at any time, and to work *effectually* in all them that believe the report of it. Where this is not discerned,—where this is not enjoyed, —we are at most but endeavouring to imitate the features of a living Christian: and the imitations at this day are, indeed, many of them admirably executed. The imitators naturally take fire, when any poor sinner (snatched as a brand from the burning by divine mercy, and glorying in that holy name which is his all) attempts to examine their image, and questions whether there be in it the breath of life, and exposes some of its corruptible materials. And, indeed, the jealousy and alarm they feel at any impeachment or doubt of their own profession is one of the decisive evidences of its hollowness. What is it to me if all the world questioned my christianity? And if I were supposed to speak any thing contrary to the truth, or of dubious import in our meeting, I know not why I should be hurt at any brother's noticing it? If I know the certainty and glory of the things which I believe, I must be glad of the opportunity of asserting them, and well pleased at my brother's jealousy about them. There is a sentence near the beginning of Mr. H——'s review of my piece on baptism, in his magazine, that would long since—if his church were standing in the truth—have led them to call on him for a public recantation of it. He told me no doubt in a conversation, when you saw me last in Edinburgh, that he did not mean what he has said: but if words have any meaning, he broadly asserts in the passage that sinners are justified *for their believing:* and he might just as well assert that they are justified for their works. But I confess that the liberality of his *forbearance* about the precepts of God I have commonly seen connected with a correspondent liberality about the gospel itself. It must spring from not discerning the *sanctity* of the word of the Lord. And no doubt if men will be ambitious of a large and respectable party in the religious world, they must adopt that liberal and forbearing course. But I trust the scattered sheep of Christ shall be given progressively to hear his voice in his word, and shall flow together to that *goodness* of the Lord, (Jer. xxxi. 12.) which is the rallying point for them all. Let all who love the true peace of Zion call upon him, to whom alone the work belongs, to glorify his name by consuming the man of sin with the spirit of his mouth, by gathering his sheep that have been scattered in the cloudy and dark day, "eating that which their shepherds have trodden under their feet, and drinking that which they have *fouled* with their feet." (Ezek. xxxiv.) "Give ear, O shepherd of Israel—shine forth—stir up thy strength—turn us again and cause thy face to shine! Let *thy work* appear unto thy servants and thy glory unto their children! And let the beauty of the Lord our God be upon us!" This is our suitable prayer. But that I may not quite fill this paper without a brief allusion to the present bar between our fellowship as brethren,—what think you now of your *baptism?* if, indeed, you have nothing now to profess but that blessed report in the Word, which you have professed to acknowledge from your infancy. But if it be a *profession about your profession*, perhaps you should be baptised again. Have you any precedent in scripture for such a baptism as your's? And what think you about the young child brought up in the instruction and admonition of the Lord, and professedly believing that Jesus Christ *died* for our sins and has *risen* from the dead? Do you look with scorn now upon the profession, or do you not acknowledge it the same as your own? But I abstain from enlarging; satisfied that the truth about which you appear to write so pleasingly is that which alone can set you to rights on this and every thing. If ever you go to Glasgow, try and make out Mr. J. G. S——, one of the few in Scotland that I have confidence in as a disciple. Most of your professors are to a sad degree *theologians*. I feel much interest about you, and hope soon to hear more of your course. Have you a family? In what business are you? The good Lord bless and increase you more and more!

LVI.

TO THE PEOPLE CALLED BEREANS, WHO ADDRESSED A LETTER TO THE CHURCH OF CHRIST ASSEMBLING IN STAFFORD STREET, DUBLIN.

March, 1819.

Dear Friends,—Your letter was put into my hands by A. C——, and read to the church last Sunday, after the usual exercises for which we meet. It was heard with pleasure; and I have been directed to communicate with you in reply.—If I do not address you immediately by the title of *Brethren*, it is because we consider the Christian use of that term confined to those, who have

received each other in the Lord, and walk together in one way according to his revealed will. I do cherish the hope, both from your letter, and from what I have otherwise known of your professed principles, that there are among you those who are partakers of like precious faith with us: and wherever I conceive the children of God to be scattered abroad, I *look* for their being gathered together in outward unity again, as they were of old. Their scattering from each other has been the work of the adversary, acting upon the common ungodliness of our flesh, and turning them aside from the good old paths appointed by their Lord, and marked in his word. Their gathering again must be, like every thing *good*, the work of the Lord—of his mercy and his power. But I see it *promised*, in the denounced *consumption by Him of the man of sin*. The instrument, also, which he employs for effecting this,—and indeed every thing else of "the good pleasure of his goodness" that he works in his people, is marked—*the spirit of his mouth*,—that word which is quick and powerful, *the sword of the spirit*. And, therefore, any opportunity of communicating with our fellow-sinners on the principles of Scripture, we are accustomed to embrace with joy, in the name of the Lord.—Writing, however, on his truths, and as before Him, I must use great plainness of speech. And, in order to bring what I have to say within the compass of a sheet, I must study brevity. But this may perhaps be but the *commencement* of further communications on scriptural subjects.

I have already intimated our general satisfaction with the language of your letter, and with your professed agreement with us on the glorious Gospel, which we endeavour to put forward to attention by the circulation of tracts. But when you use the expression—"unto all that believe the record that he hath given of his son, *through the holy spirit manifesting the same in their hearts*,"—do you mean to intimate that any sinner can, *at any time*, believe that record without the holy spirit, &c.? We are certain that none *can* at any moment: though men may profess it with their lips, may talk about it, and even talk quite correctly, while they are still under the power of darkness. We hope you have no false meaning attached to the words you used; though I have thought it safer to inquire.

You express a wish that, in future publications, we should "direct our attention, more particularly, to the nature of the faith which is the operation of God." Perhaps we may. But our views of the Gospel, and of the nature of faith, lead us in general to say very little on the mere question—*what is faith?* Every one knows what it is to believe a thing that is told him: and we think it highly important to mark that we use the term *faith*, or *believing*, as applied to the Gospel, in no other but that common English sense of the word, which all can understand in a moment. But the matter on which we are led to enlarge is—the truth declared from heaven to all in the Scriptures for the obedience of faith. In that truth "the only true God" reveals his glory: and they who believe that truth know his name, and *have eternal life* as his "gift in Christ Jesus." And we are sure that, according as that truth dwells in them—they will bring forth "fruit unto God." We have no *apprehension* or *jealousy*

mercy and divine power could keep me, at any moment, from turning this short corner upon the truth. But I have met with two men, who called themselves Bereans, in Glasgow, who were manifestly to me infected with this leaven. I know, my friends, the opposition which you make, and rightly make, to the *doubting system* of some, who use fair words at times about the Gospel, but really blaspheme the truth in denying its sufficiency to afford an ungodly sinner the fulness of *assured joy and peace*—till he finds this and that about him—(if ever he does) to warrant his concluding that he has the faith of God's elect. Far be it kept from me to countenance such blasphemy! But it is our constant common character—in running from one deadly error, to run right ahead upon another. And errors, apparently the most opposite, will commonly, when traced, be found to have a common principle, as they always indeed spring from a common source. I could point out the common principle of the two deadly errors, which I have here noticed, if space allowed. Let not those of you, who are mercifully kept from the error, which I suspect to work among you, conclude that the caution is not needful in the body. With the same plainness with which I have written throughout, I would observe that I recollect, in my first visit to Scotland, two or three interviews with one of your preachers Mr. D——; that for a length of time all his conversation delighted me; but that I ultimately parted with him, apprehensive that he was not walking in the truth. With him the immediate ground of this apprehension was my finding that he not only *had been* a busy meddler in political agitations against the government of the country, but that he was then altogether deaf to the reproof of the word upon the subject. Such a man we would not keep in our fellowship. I tell you plainly, (though it must spoil my political character with *him*) that the only principles here, which I can acknowledge as consistent with *Christian duty*, are those stigmatized by the phrase—*passive obedience, and non-resistance*. Mistake me not, my friends, as if I drew an unfavourable conclusion against you all, from any thing unpleasant I may have met with in some. I have long cherished the hope that there are many *disciples indeed* among you: and with such I look forward to that *full union*, in which such ought to be outwardly connected. I have my fears that you are at present very lax, and much astray, as to the principles of church-fellowship: but this is a subject on which I would not wish to enter, till other more fundamental matters have been fully treated. I would add, that when I was in Glasgow, in the summer of 1815, I met a dear old Berean, a shoemaker from the neighbourhood of Stirling I think of the name of M'Bean, with whom, as far as I understood him, I think I had perfect unity of mind on the faith and hope of the Gospel. I have lost his address, or mislaid it, among the multiplicity of my papers. But if you should know of such a person, and have any opportunity of communicating with him, it would gratify me that you should send him a copy of this letter, with my love. If you wish for further communication, I hope you will write with all the freedom and openness of which I have set you an example. Peace be with all those of you who love the Lord Jesus Christ in incorruption! Let them say continually, "Let the Lord be magnified!" Amen.

LVII.

TO J. L——.

March 27, 1818.

What must you have thought, my dear friend, of my leaving both your letters so long unanswered? They were forwarded to me from London; for I have been from various circumstances unexpectedly detained here, and am still uncertain how much longer I may be detained, though *I think* (if I live) I shall now very soon leave Dublin. But for the last two months or more, I have been so busy preparing for the press "Seven Letters on Primitive Christianity," that I have got into sad arrear with all my correspondents. I have also, indeed, been very ill (often what is called *dangerously*) with unsettled gout. I have just sent off the "Letters" to London to be printed; and you are now the second person to whom I have since taken up my pen. I let a party of *Bereans* in Edinburgh, from whom we received a letter, take precedence of you. By the bye, if you know D—— K——, or whether you know him or not—if you introduce yourself to him as a correspondent of mine, he would probably shew you my letter; and I should be well pleased that you got at their sentiments as much as you could upon its contents. If you see the letter, you will see what I hope and what I fear about the people. Any thing you can communicate to me from your own observation or knowledge I should be glad of. Mere hearsay about them I don't mind. I confess I have long had an eye upon them, and am well pleased at an apparent opening for epistolary intercourse. You will find them holding a most opposite language to that of the *Glasites*; and yet I fear the mass of both parties are infected with a *common* error,—namely, deriving their hope from *looking at their faith*; the one, very confident about their faith, and *therefore* having a very confident but false hope; the other very doubtful about their faith, and therefore similarly wavering in their hope, but both alike aside from the truth, and from the fulness of divine hope to an altogether sinful creature in believing that truth. However, I look for disciples appearing yet more manifested both from the Bereans and Glasites, though I am sure that any disciples at present among the latter must be very stunted in their growth; and fear that among the former, they must need a great deal of pruning. I know intimately a dear old man in Liverpool, a Glasite elder, whom I have always heard with delight, and always on one theme. But what a contrast between him and his fellow-elder! They are generally all under sad *trammels*, and as afraid to submit their system to examination as the Papists. Yet one would think that it might strike them as a strange and ugly symptom, that ever since their commencement in the days of Glas and Sandeman, they have not learned an iota more of scripture principle, or found out that their system had been wrong in any one particular. I am very glad to hear that you have got into conversation with any individual among them. It is not easy to get it with them upon Christian topics; and I beg you will not indulge your disposition to silence and loneliness; but while he is willing to speak upon his views of the faith and hope of the gospel, be as communicative of yours: and who knows what simple word the Lord may bless for breaking to pieces all the ungodly shackles of his system? We have been extraordinarily busy here for some time past in personal communication with various professors, who used to keep us at arm's length: and we have the joy of finding one and another added to our body; among them one of the parish clergymen of Dublin, and several who were till very lately keen Baptists, but now look with abhorrence at their Baptist principles—as I rather hope you will by and by. When I say *several*, do not mistake me: all our additions, in the extraordinary stir and ferment there has been within the last few months, are I suppose within fifteen. (But that is a wonderful number with such a contemptible set as we are.) I do not mean to enter on the subject at present. Indeed I have neither time nor room: and you will shortly (I hope) see our leading views in this and other matters in the piece I have sent to press. But meanwhile I would suggest to your consideration the following simple questions:—1. Whether you have not ever *professed* from your infancy to believe the apostolic testimony concerning Jesus of Nazareth? 2. Whether it was not upon taking that profession on them for the first time that men were baptised of old? in short, whether it did not in every recorded instance mark the commencement of the Christian *profession* of the person baptised? 3. Whether you have a single precedent, or a single precept in scripture, for the baptism of any whose Christian profession has been hereditary, like yours and mine, and Timothy's, and multitudes of others in the apostolic days, even all that were born to the first proselytes after their own conversion? 4. Whether any child can be *brought up* in the instruction and admonition of the Lord (Ephes. vi. 4,) without being considered by its believing parent, during all that course, as a disciple of the Lord? If your faith be as simple as in general I hope it is, I should recommend these questions to your serious reflection. If it be not, I should wish to confine our communications to other topics. If you answer the first question in the negative, I should desire to learn what you mean by your *present* Christian profession. If you answer the fourth in the affirmative, I should wish to know what you think of the religious *training* of an adult who is not considered a believer of the gospel. The whole matter, indeed, is so plain, when viewed in the light of the simple truth, that I should not wonder if your next letter announced that you were no longer a Baptist—without our having any argument upon the subject. And, indeed, this would give me great joy; for I must always view the profession of a thorough Baptist with great suspicion—without knowing any thing more of him than that he is a thorough Baptist. At the same time, I own that I have often wondered that all the conscientious and thinking professors who do not know the one truth are not Baptists.

Yet why should I wonder how they get over it, when the Glasites, with all their professed regard to scripture, are content with their infant sprinkling as baptism? Your interpretation of Acts xix. 5, I think very wild and forced—that kind of jumping through scripture, to which I should always prefer acknowledging that I did not understand the passage. To give you my views of that passage would occupy too much space. They are stated in the larger of my pieces on Baptism, some copies of which I am pretty sure lie at Mr. D——'s, in Glasgow. But I have not one of them myself.

I am curious to ask you, whether your business in the Excise connects you with the administration or the taking of *oaths?* Much as I am pleased with all your letters in general, there is one bitter bad sentence in your second; and so inconsistent with the rest of your views, that I stared with surprise when I met it. I just quote it, and leave it to the observation of your better mind. "Can we glory over them? No, in no wise." (So far good.) "Can a sentiment or feeling at variance with that answer exist in the mind of a Christian?" I imagine that I see you, at this moment, staring at the wickedness of your own question. But, after all, if you deliberately repeat it, or do not abhor it,—I can only say with a sigh, that we have quite mistaken one another's meaning; and would let you into a secret, that there is no sentiment or feeling so diabolically ungodly as not to exist in my mind—that my own heart in all its movements *is* as proud as Lucifer's, and substantially denies *that God is;* and that I never expect or *desire* any other sentiment or feeling from it till I die: and yet that the consciousness of all this does not disturb my peace and confidence towards God a tittle. Blessed be His glorious name for ever! But indeed, my dear friend, I do not suspect you at present of meaning any thing else than I mean, in spite of that wicked question. Yet I repeat it, that I am sure we mean quite different things, unless you now see its wickedness. The feeling from which that question came was one of those fleshly feelings, all of which (in the believer and unbeliever alike) are proud in their most humble form, and Atheistic in their most devout.

There are only about seven walking together as yet in London—hardly enough to walk together in all Christian ordinances, according to the Glasite plan. The letters that are coming out will make me still viler than I am in their eyes: yet I hope some of them will give them a reading. I must have done. The more I look at your letters, the more I think I do know you, and the more I love you for the truth's sake. The good Lord ever keep you liable to the reproach you mention, of looking only at the *one* thing—*the sinner's hope!*

LVIII.

TO THE SAME.

June 11*th*, 1819.

My Dear Friend,—How glorious that gospel that warrants a creature, altogether sinful, to commit all his ways for life and death to the gracious ordering of the living God! My time has been and is much occupied; and before the arrival of your letter to Mr. C——, I had postponed writing to you till Mr. D——'s return to Glasgow, but that letter shews me that I must not longer delay. You are impatient for my letters on primitive Christianity. It has been strangely delayed by the printer, but will be out the beginning of next week. I shall be anxious, indeed, to hear your sentiments after you have read it. I have forborn to enter on the question of baptism with you, in the prospect of your seeing what I have to offer on the subject in that publication. My vain flesh would suggest that with your professed views of the truth you could not resist what I say. But I know that you will, *if you are let*. There is one who can thrash the mountains with a straw. *His* will be the work and the glory if the little piece be made profitable to any of his people: though in spite of the conviction of that truth, *my own heart* would fain rob him of the glory and lift up itself against him. You are doubtful whether D—— and you understood each other. I am sure *he* did not understand *you*. Any man who thinks *himself* improved in his own character, and no longer altogether wicked and ungodly, must be aside from the truth. I quite agree with you as to the general suitableness of confirming such statements from the word of God. But I wrote to the Bereans, not so much to prove to them what is truth, as to ascertain by a brief declaration of sentiment, whether we were of a mind or not. The apostle uses the expression "his *flesh*," as synonymous with *himself*, (Rom. vii. 18.) and gives such an account of it as does not look like any improvement: and in Gal. v. 17. he plainly describes it as wicked as the devil, for worse cannot be said of the mind of Satan, than that it is contrary to the spirit of God: and all expectation of any change in it he puts down in Rom. viii. 7. Compare 1 Cor. xv. 10. (not i) and Gal. ii. 20. All the texts that Mr. K. thinks inconsistent with the idea, really establish it when rightly understood, i. e. when seen in the light of the glorious Gospel. I am sure there is no unity of meaning between him and me: nor should I ever think of talking to him (while he is of his present mind) about the principles of Christian fellowship in the churches of the saints. Yet I can easily conceive that there may be disciples entangled in that connexion, and I am glad to hear that my letter has been answered, as that will tend to counteract Mr. D.'s effort to smother it. But how disingenuous of them, after writing to us in Dublin, and receiving our reply, not to communicate to us any thing they have to say against our sentiments.—I know that, on the point alluded to, the Glasites seem much more scriptural in their view: and they commonly speak a blessed language about the Gospel, as suited to the relief of creatures so totally and desperately wicked in themselves. But then comes the leaven in their system, corrupting and dishonouring the glorious Gospel, under the idea of *guarding it*, as if *it alone* could afford a sinner nothing but a precarious and uncertain hope, without being sufficient to give him assured confidence, and filial boldness, before God. This system, wherever it is indeed received, must as effectually turn aside the person from the hope of the Gospel, as the *Berean confidence about their character as believers*. Indeed the language I have heard from some Glasites in prayer, makes me uncertain how far they do not, in their system, approve of the *desire*, and *wish* for some improvement in their own hearts. Yet I must maintain that any such *desire* can spring only from the flesh: while I own that my flesh is continually prompting it. I must hasten to a close. You alluded to some circumstances of trial in your family. Do they continue? Was it sickness? or what was it? What blessed pregnancy of meaning is there in the words—"how much rather shall we be IN SUBJECTION to the Father of spirits and live?" And what madness of wicked rebellion does it mark in our own hearts, that would ever be ready to take our concerns out of his own blessed hands! And what but the unchangeable display of his mercy, reigning through righteousness towards creatures so unchangeably stubborn and rebellious in themselves, ever produces the new mind which says, "Thy will be done?" The one mind in fact is altogether good, and nothing evil comes from it, for it is not ours, but the mind of the spirit of God—the spirit of the Truth, and the life in Christ Jesus: the other mind is altogether evil, and nothing but evil proceeds from it; for it is our own. "Let Israel rejoice *in Him* that made him, let the children of Zion be joyful in their King."—If I live a little longer, it is not unlikely that I shall see you. My heart embraces you for the truth's sake: and I am not discouraged by your present firmness in your baptism, from looking to the Lord for full union with you. I see, from the short observation you made, where your error lies. After you have read what I offer in my pamphlet, proceed vigorously and plainly to oppose me, wherever you think me wrong. But do not defer writing till you get the work. You may communicate any part of this to Mr. K.

LIX.

TO THE SAME.

June 21, 1819.

My very dear Friend,—On receiving your note, (for I shall not count it a *letter*) I was quite vexed with myself for having said a word on the subject of my ailments. I have been considerably better since, and quite agree with you, that it *may* be the Lord's design to leave me here longer than I generally contemplate. We may well leave all that with him, and rest in the *certainty* that his cause on earth shall suffer no loss by my death, whenever it takes place. He will raise up and qualify instruments for all the work in which he sees fit to employ them in his church: and further than he sees fit to work by us, we can do nothing. What blessed weight in the words, "Thine is the kingdom, and the power, and the glory!" And in the view of this truth, how suitable to his people, at all times, the admonition given to Ahaz—"Take heed, and be *quiet; fear not*, neither be *faint-hearted*." If we had faith as a grain of mustard-seed!

I am glad to hear that you are likely soon to meet Mr. S——. I think you and he will understand each other on the great Truth: but I would apprize you that, in an attempt which he lately made to walk with a few in Glasgow, I think he has taken it up on false principles —more in the way of gratification to his taste, than under the authority of the divine word, and in the view of every thing in the fellowship of a Christian church being divinely ordered, so that there is no room for continued diversity of mind or practice. He, at present, differs with me upon some ordinances, but would fain compromise the difference. Yet this is so inconsistent with his other professed sentiments, that I am looking for the appearance of better things in him. From his disappointment among the Glasites, he seems at present to abandon the idea of a *full* return of disciples to Apostolic rule. Yet, where that idea is abandoned, their fellowship cannot be maintained upon scriptural principles. Indeed, the idea at once impeaches the divine sufficiency, or unchangeable authority of the Scriptures. You may be curious to know something more about us here. We are a most contemptible set to profess to be *the* church of Christ in London;—only seven compose the body, but they seem united in the glorious truth. Yesterday we had to put away a woman, who plainly understood not the profession of faith on which she had been received. You will at present be sorry to hear that my hosts, and another member, are apostates from the Red Cross-street body. Yet, whatever you may think of their abandonment of baptism, you will be pleased to hear that it was their perception of the falsehood of the faith, held in the R. C. street body, that first decided them against it. The adversary is awfully working in this country, in spreading lofty

voice in his word, and shall flow together to that *goodness* of the LORD, (Jer. xxxi. 12.) which is the rallying point for them all. Let all who love the true peace of Zion call upon him, to whom alone the work belongs, to glorify his name by consuming the man of sin with the spirit of his mouth, by gathering his sheep that have been scattered in the cloudy and dark day, "eating that which their shepherds have trodden under their feet, and drinking that which they have *fouled* with their feet." (Ezek. xxxiv.) "Give ear, O shepherd of Israel—shine forth—stir up thy strength—turn us again and cause thy face to shine! Let *thy work* appear unto thy servants and thy glory unto their children! And let the beauty of the LORD our God be upon us!" This is our suitable prayer. But that I may not quite fill this paper without a brief allusion to the present bar between our fellowship as brethren,—what think you now of your *baptism?* if, indeed, you have nothing now to profess but that blessed report in the Word, which you have professed to acknowledge from your infancy. But if it be a *profession about your profession,* perhaps you should be baptised again. Have you any precedent in scripture for such a baptism as your's? And what think you about the young child brought up in the instruction and admonition of the Lord, and professedly believing that Jesus Christ *died* for our sins and has *risen* from the dead? Do you look with scorn now upon the profession, or do you not acknowledge it the same as your own? But I abstain from enlarging; satisfied that the truth about which you appear to write so pleasingly is that which alone can set you to rights on this and every thing. If ever you go to Glasgow, try and make out Mr. J. G. S——, one of the few in Scotland that I have confidence in as a disciple. Most of your professors are to a sad degree *theologians.* I feel much interest about you, and hope soon to hear more of your course. Have you a family? In what business are you? The good Lord bless and increase you more and more!

LVI.

TO THE PEOPLE CALLED BEREANS, WHO ADDRESSED A LETTER TO THE CHURCH OF CHRIST ASSEMBLING IN STAFFORD STREET, DUBLIN.

March, 1819.

DEAR FRIENDS,—Your letter was put into my hands by A. C——, and read to the church last Sunday, after the usual exercises for which we meet. It was heard with pleasure; and I have been directed to communicate with you in reply.—If I do not address you immediately by the title of *Brethren,* it is because we consider the Christian use of that term confined to those, who have received each other in the Lord, and walk together in one way according to his revealed will. I do cherish the hope, both from your letter, and from what I have otherwise known of your professed principles, that there are among you those who are partakers of like precious faith with us: and wherever I conceive the children of God to be scattered abroad, I *look* for their being gathered together in outward unity again, as they were of old. Their scattering from each other has been the work of the adversary, acting upon the common ungodliness of our flesh, and turning them aside from the good old paths appointed by their Lord, and marked in his word. Their gathering again must be, like every thing *good*, the work of the Lord—of his mercy and his power. But I see it *promised*, in the denounced *consumption by Him of the man of sin*. The instrument, also, which he employs for effecting this,—and indeed every thing else of "the good pleasure of his goodness" that he works in his people, is marked—*the spirit of his mouth*,—that word which is quick and powerful, *the sword of the spirit*. And, therefore, any opportunity of communicating with our fellow-sinners on the principles of Scripture, we are accustomed to embrace with joy, in the name of the Lord.—Writing, however, on his truths, and as before Him, I must use grêat plainness of speech. And, in order to bring what I have to say within the compass of a sheet, I must study brevity. But this may perhaps be but the *commencement* of further communications on scriptural subjects.

I have already intimated our general satisfaction with the language of your letter, and with your professed agreement with us on the glorious Gospel, which we endeavour to put forward to attention by the circulation of tracts. But when you use the expression—"unto all that believe the record that he hath given of his son, *through the holy spirit manifesting the same in their hearts*,"—do you mean to intimate that any sinner can, *at any time*, believe that record without the holy spirit, &c.? We are certain that none *can* at any moment: though men may profess it with their lips, may talk about it, and even talk quite correctly, while they are still under the power of darkness. We hope you have no false meaning attached to the words you used; though I have thought it safer to inquire.

You express a wish that, in future publications, we should "direct our attention, more particularly, to the nature of the faith which is the operation of God." Perhaps we may. But our views of the Gospel, and of the nature of faith, lead us in general to say very little on the mere question—*what is faith?* Every one knows what it is to believe a thing that is told him: and we think it highly important to mark that we use the term *faith*, or *believing*, as applied to the Gospel, in no other but that common English sense of the word, which all can understand in a moment. But the matter on which we are led to enlarge is—the truth declared from heaven to all in the Scriptures for the obedience of faith. In that truth "the only true God" reveals his glory: and they who believe that truth know his name, and *have eternal life* as his "gift in Christ Jesus." And we are sure that, according as that truth dwells in them—they will bring forth "fruit unto God." We have no *apprehension* or *jealousy*

voice in his word, and shall flow together to that *goodness* of the LORD, (Jer. xxxi. 12.) which is the rallying point for them all. Let all who love the true peace of Zion call upon him, to whom alone the work belongs, to glorify his name by consuming the man of sin with the spirit of his mouth, by gathering his sheep that have been scattered in the cloudy and dark day, "eating that which their shepherds have trodden under their feet, and drinking that which they have *fouled* with their feet." (Ezek. xxxiv.) "Give ear, O shepherd of Israel—shine forth—stir up thy strength—turn us again and cause thy face to shine! Let *thy work* appear unto thy servants and thy glory unto their children! And let the beauty of the LORD our God be upon us!" This is our suitable prayer. But that I may not quite fill this paper without a brief allusion to the present bar between our fellowship as brethren,—what think you now of your *baptism?* if, indeed, you have nothing now to profess but that blessed report in the Word, which you have professed to acknowledge from your infancy. But if it be a *profession about your profession,* perhaps you should be baptised again. Have you any precedent in scripture for such a baptism as your's? And what think you about the young child brought up in the instruction and admonition of the Lord, and professedly believing that Jesus Christ *died* for our sins and has *risen* from the dead? Do you look with scorn now upon the profession, or do you not acknowledge it the same as your own? But I abstain from enlarging; satisfied that the truth about which you appear to write so pleasingly is that which alone can set you to rights on this and every thing. If ever you go to Glasgow, try and make out Mr. J. G. S——, one of the few in Scotland that I have confidence in as a disciple. Most of your professors are to a sad degree *theologians.* I feel much interest about you, and hope soon to hear more of your course. Have you a family? In what business are you? The good Lord bless and increase you more and more!

LVI.

TO THE PEOPLE CALLED BEREANS, WHO ADDRESSED A LETTER TO THE CHURCH OF CHRIST ASSEMBLING IN STAFFORD STREET, DUBLIN.

March, 1819.

DEAR FRIENDS,—Your letter was put into my hands by A. C——, and read to the church last Sunday, after the usual exercises for which we meet. It was heard with pleasure; and I have been directed to communicate with you in reply.—If I do not address you immediately by the title of *Brethren,* it is because we consider the Christian use of that term confined to those, who have

received each other in the Lord, and walk together in one way according to his revealed will. I do cherish the hope, both from your letter, and from what I have otherwise known of your professed principles, that there are among you those who are partakers of like precious faith with us: and wherever I conceive the children of God to be scattered abroad, I *look* for their being gathered together in outward unity again, as they were of old. Their scattering from each other has been the work of the adversary, acting upon the common ungodliness of our flesh, and turning them aside from the good old paths appointed by their Lord, and marked in his word. Their gathering again must be, like every thing *good*, the work of the LORD—of his mercy and his power. But I see it *promised*, in the denounced *consumption by Him of the man of sin*. The instrument, also, which he employs for effecting this,—and indeed every thing else of "the good pleasure of his goodness" that he works in his people, is marked—*the spirit of his mouth*,—that word which is quick and powerful, *the sword of the spirit*. And, therefore, any opportunity of communicating with our fellow-sinners on the principles of Scripture, we are accustomed to embrace with joy, in the name of the Lord.—Writing, however, on his truths, and as before Him, I must use great plainness of speech. And, in order to bring what I have to say within the compass of a sheet, I must study brevity. But this may perhaps be but the *commencement* of further communications on scriptural subjects.

I have already intimated our general satisfaction with the language of your letter, and with your professed agreement with us on the glorious Gospel, which we endeavour to put forward to attention by the circulation of tracts. But when you use the expression—"unto all that believe the record that he hath given of his son, *through the holy spirit manifesting the same in their hearts*,"—do you mean to intimate that any sinner can, *at any time*, believe that record without the holy spirit, &c.? We are certain that none *can* at any moment: though men may profess it with their lips, may talk about it, and even talk quite correctly, while they are still under the power of darkness. We hope you have no false meaning attached to the words you used; though I have thought it safer to inquire.

You express a wish that, in future publications, we should "direct our attention, more particularly, to the nature of the faith which is the operation of God." Perhaps we may. But our views of the Gospel, and of the nature of faith, lead us in general to say very little on the mere question—*what is faith?* Every one knows what it is to believe a thing that is told him: and we think it highly important to mark that we use the term *faith*, or *believing*, as applied to the Gospel, in no other but that common English sense of the word, which all can understand in a moment. But the matter on which we are led to enlarge is—the truth declared from heaven to all in the Scriptures for the obedience of faith. In that truth "the only true God" reveals his glory: and they who believe that truth know his name, and *have eternal life* as his "gift in Christ Jesus." And we are sure that, according as that truth dwells in them—they will bring forth "fruit unto God." We have no *apprehension* or *jealousy*

voice in his word, and shall flow together to that *goodness* of the Lord, (Jer. xxxi. 12.) which is the rallying point for them all. Let all who love the true peace of Zion call upon him, to whom alone the work belongs, to glorify his name by consuming the man of sin with the spirit of his mouth, by gathering his sheep that have been scattered in the cloudy and dark day, "eating that which their shepherds have trodden under their feet, and drinking that which they have *fouled* with their feet." (Ezek. xxxiv.) "Give ear, O shepherd of Israel—shine forth—stir up thy strength—turn us again and cause thy face to shine! Let *thy work* appear unto thy servants and thy glory unto their children! And let the beauty of the Lord our God be upon us!" This is our suitable prayer. But that I may not quite fill this paper without a brief allusion to the present bar between our fellowship as brethren,—what think you now of your *baptism?* if, indeed, you have nothing now to profess but that blessed report in the Word, which you have professed to acknowledge from your infancy. But if it be a *profession about your profession*, perhaps you should be baptised again. Have you any precedent in scripture for such a baptism as your's? And what think you about the young child brought up in the instruction and admonition of the Lord, and professedly believing that Jesus Christ *died* for our sins and has *risen* from the dead? Do you look with scorn now upon the profession, or do you not acknowledge it the same as your own? But I abstain from enlarging; satisfied that the truth about which you appear to write so pleasingly is that which alone can set you to rights on this and every thing. If ever you go to Glasgow, try and make out Mr. J. G. S——, one of the few in Scotland that I have confidence in as a disciple. Most of your professors are to a sad degree *theologians*. I feel much interest about you, and hope soon to hear more of your course. Have you a family? In what business are you? The good Lord bless and increase you more and more!

LVI.

TO THE PEOPLE CALLED BEREANS, WHO ADDRESSED A LETTER TO THE CHURCH OF CHRIST ASSEMBLING IN STAFFORD STREET, DUBLIN.

March, 1819.

Dear Friends,—Your letter was put into my hands by A. C——, and read to the church last Sunday, after the usual exercises for which we meet. It was heard with pleasure; and I have been directed to communicate with you in reply.—If I do not address you immediately by the title of *Brethren*, it is because we consider the Christian use of that term confined to those, who have

received each other in the Lord, and walk together in one way according to his revealed will. I do cherish the hope, both from your letter, and from what I have otherwise known of your professed principles, that there are among you those who are partakers of like precious faith with us: and wherever I conceive the children of God to be scattered abroad, I *look* for their being gathered together in outward unity again, as they were of old. Their scattering from each other has been the work of the adversary, acting upon the common ungodliness of our flesh, and turning them aside from the good old paths appointed by their Lord, and marked in his word. Their gathering again must be, like every thing *good*, the work of the Lord—of his mercy and his power. But I see it *promised*, in the denounced *consumption by Him of the man of sin*. The instrument, also, which he employs for effecting this,—and indeed every thing else of "the good pleasure of his goodness" that he works in his people, is marked—*the spirit of his mouth*,—that word which is quick and powerful, *the sword of the spirit*. And, therefore, any opportunity of communicating with our fellow-sinners on the principles of Scripture, we are accustomed to embrace with joy, in the name of the Lord.—Writing, however, on his truths, and as before Him, I must use great plainness of speech. And, in order to bring what I have to say within the compass of a sheet, I must study brevity. But this may perhaps be but the *commencement* of further communications on scriptural subjects.

I have already intimated our general satisfaction with the language of your letter, and with your professed agreement with us on the glorious Gospel, which we endeavour to put forward to attention by the circulation of tracts. But when you use the expression—"unto all that believe the record that he hath given of his son, *through the holy spirit manifesting the same in their hearts*,"—do you mean to intimate that any sinner can, *at any time*, believe that record without the holy spirit, &c.? We are certain that none *can* at any moment: though men may profess it with their lips, may talk about it, and even talk quite correctly, while they are still under the power of darkness. We hope you have no false meaning attached to the words you used; though I have thought it safer to inquire.

You express a wish that, in future publications, we should "direct our attention, more particularly, to the nature of the faith which is the operation of God." Perhaps we may. But our views of the Gospel, and of the nature of faith, lead us in general to say very little on the mere question—*what is faith?* Every one knows what it is to believe a thing that is told him: and we think it highly important to mark that we use the term *faith*, or *believing*, as applied to the Gospel, in no other but that common English sense of the word, which all can understand in a moment. But the matter on which we are led to enlarge is—the truth declared from heaven to all in the Scriptures for the obedience of faith. In that truth "the only true God" reveals his glory: and they who believe that truth know his name, and *have eternal life* as his "gift in Christ Jesus." And we are sure that, according as that truth dwells in them—they will bring forth "fruit unto God." We have no *apprehension* or *jealousy*

stances, of a marriage being so conducted by a clergyman, as that submission to it should not be considered as absolutely at variance with Christian duty.

Brethren, we feel ourselves called upon to rejoice; and we trust that you are prepared to partake in our feelings, that the necessity of discussing such a question—a question of remotely possible lawfulness—is thus superseded. And we exhort you, henceforward, to take, with us, the plain and unambiguous course, which a knowledge of the above fact opens to us in all such cases.

LXIV.

TO J. L———.

Jan. 9, 1820.

MY VERY DEAR FRIEND,—Your letter was, as usual, very acceptable and refreshing to me. It is refreshing to hear from any one a decisive language, accordant with the great truth. It does not appear to me at all *extraordinary* that you should feel little desire for a more extended fellowship. My flesh would be very glad to pick out about a dozen pets of fellow disciples, and shut myself up with them in a snug corner. But when the new mind remembers Him who pleased not himself, we shall rejoice in every new display of his victorious mercy in our fellow sinners, though, as our connexions with them multiply, assuredly our trials will multiply likewise. But the period of our trials is very short, and passing fast. Those who have in prospect to be FOR EVER with the LORD, may well endure hardship for a few days. One of the greatest trials I have had in my course, has been connected with the calling of my brethren's attention to that precept on which you and I yet differ. To give up swearing myself, at whatever loss, would have been nothing in comparison of being instrumental in leading others most dear to me to incur the loss of all their livelihood. With you, at present, I do not desire to say much on the subject. I do not think you have looked it in the face: for if you had, how could you talk of its merely prohibiting profane swearing in common conversation? "Neither shalt thou swear by thine head, *for* thou canst not make one hair white or black." I suppose this is true only when we swear lightly, and irreverently, by our head. J. H—— (though he talks plenty of wicked nonsense upon the subject) is perfectly right in referring to Numb. xxx. 2. for the illustration of it. The Jews were there taught, that when a man swore an oath *to bind his soul with a bond*, he was not to break his word. The Lord Jesus teaches his disciples, that they are not to bind their soul with a bond at all, by swearing any oath. What that awful bond is, under the forfeiture of which men are now understood to bind their souls in swearing, may be collected, (if we choose to look at it) even from the published speech of the Attorney General, at the opening of Carlile's trial; where, referring to the oaths of the Jury he speaks of their having "*pledged their hope of eternal life*, arising from Christianity, for the truth of their verdict." Let me only add, that if any choose to call it an oath, if I answer under an adjuration by the living God, I shall not fight about words. I am as certain as Mr. H., that this is not the thing forbidden in the text; and have not the least scruple about its lawfulness. Enough of this subject, to which I do not think I shall return till you invite me. What ailed you, when you penned that sentence, in which you talk of Satan's empire promising "to be completely and universally established?" Were you forgetting on whose shoulder the government is: Satan, and all that is in the world, and all that is in the flesh of disciples themselves, have formed in all ages one league against the truth of God. But the kingdom is the LORD's, and his arrows are sharp in the hearts of his enemies; and his word shall stand good, which declares that one generation *shall* declare his works to another; which says to the church—"instead of thy fathers shall be thy children;" "shall I cause to bring forth, and shut the womb, &c.?" There never would have been a seed to serve him in this world of sinners, but that he can raise up children unto Abraham from the very stones: and when the last of his elect are gathered in, the stage of this world shall be taken down. I have given Mr. H.'s Strictures one hasty reading since I received your letter, and found, as you suspected, much need to look up. My proud flesh was continually prompting the thought—"I will give this man a good trimming." Surely he cannot, in one sense, say worse of my spirit than it deserves. There was one, and but one, who could say of himself, "I seek not mine own glory." "He that speaketh from himself, seeketh his own glory: but He that seeketh his glory that sent him, the same is true, and no unrighteousness is in Him." The mind of faith in his people, is the mind of Christ; and truly in this and every thing, it is opposite to their own. I think I shall shortly reply to Mr. H. on the subject of the truth. I do think his pamphlet very weak and very wicked, but a masterly production for the purpose for which it is designed, of raising a clamour against the truth and making his peace with the religious world. Surely Mr. H. must sorely repent having published my letters to Knox: for in them many of the principles, which he now holds up to the execration of his readers, are explicitly asserted. I think he has quite receded from the profession he made when I first knew him. What does he mean by the *marked separation* with which he charges us? If I mistake not, there is more *marked* separation in his Tabernacle, than in S—— s——. His dexterity I admire, in raising a dust about other questions, and escaping from them under cover of it. However, he will assuredly have the best of all the argument in the eyes of those for whom he writes. I am quite like you, in being better pleased to receive ten letters, than to write one. So that, from my punctuality in replying, you may judge that I wish to hear from you. That I may make this letter worth the postage, let me just add—compare Levit.

xvi. 16, 19. with Haggai ii. 10—14. and Hebr. x. What a view does it present of our own uncleanness, of the holiness of the Lord, and of the greatness of that atonement by which we have access unto God. The Lord increase in us the good hope, which this revelation of his name affords to the *chief of sinners!* If you take these for the texts of your next letter, you will be at no loss for a subject.

LXV.

TO THE SAME.

March 1, 1820.

My very dear Friend,—I see a month has elapsed since I received your last welcome letter, and that is too long an interval. I have just finished a long letter to D—— K——, and four of his associates, who sent me, some time ago, a strange kind of epistle in reply to my former. Theirs is rather abusive, and filled with the most ridiculous cavils, but betraying a mind and sentiments much aside from the truth. I shall be glad of your calling on him shortly, to ascertain whether he has received it, and how he meets it. Unless it please the Lord to bless it to them, I dare say it will increase the irritation they manifest, at my moving any question about the soundness of their profession. But till they shut the door to further communication, I am unwilling to drop them altogether, they verbally acknowledge so much important truth. Well does it become such as us to be "*patient towards all men.*" See if they will communicate to you both the letters, theirs and mine. They make, or pretend to make, the strangest mistakes about my meaning. Explain it patiently, as long as they will let you. As to my intended reply to Mr. Haldane, I have not yet commenced it, and it is uncertain when I may. It is, indeed, a nice and solemn thing to publish any thing on the subject. So you have been preaching; and you are half sorry for it, and doubting whether you should have done so. It reminds me of a question, which you put to me in one of your first letters, which, I believe, in the press of more important matter, I never answered. I can enter fully into all your feelings on this matter. A disciple, sickened by the religious world, seeing the mass of iniquity that goes on under their so-called preachings, and that is mainly promoted by them, is very apt to turn with disgust from every thing that passes under the same name. But we are always ready, in running from one evil, to bolt right ahead upon another. Now let us consider—(putting out of our thoughts the sentiments, both of the Glasites, and of the popular religionists)—on what scriptural ground a Christian could be warranted in declining to tell his fellow-sinners, when they are willing to hear him—either in public or in private, according to his abilities and opportunities—what he has learned from the word of God. Shall he decline it because they have Moses, and the prophets, and the Apostles, authoritatively declaring to them, at all times, the things of God in the words of God; and because we, so far as we speak aright, can never speak but the same things which they testify? Specious as this may appear to some, yet, legitimately followed up, it would bind disciples in never opening their mouths on the truth, either among themselves or others, but in the very words of Scripture. And I have heard of a little party in your country (I know not whether now existing) who did go this length, and confined themselves in their own meetings to the reading of the Bible. But, in fact, there is absolute scepticism as to what is truth at the bottom of this, under the show of exclusive reverence for the words of the most High. If I see and am convinced of the divine truth, in any of the numberless passages of Scripture which have been awfully perverted by the cunning craftiness of men, (for instance in Hebr. xi. 6.) shall I be afraid, either by writing or speaking, of protesting against their ungodly perversions, and asserting its true import in any words the most intelligible, and best calculated to convey my meaning? Is it in the mere articulate sounds of the words of Scripture—as *words*—that any charm or importance lies? and not rather in the glorious things meant and intended by those words? I am aware of what some may say—"O! then the vain man thinks his own words better than those of the Holy Ghost." Let that be followed up; and it is in *Greek* and *Hebrew* the Scriptures must alone be read to men. But, as I said, the objection, under a show of reverence for the *words*, despises and questions the things of God. But, perhaps, your doubts and difficulties on the subject have arisen rather from your consciousness of the workings of your own vain and deceitful flesh in preaching. Shall I, then, decline speaking to my fellow-sinners on the great salvation, because my own heart would, at any time, make an ostentatious display of my zeal or eloquence, or my knowledge, and sacrifice to its own drag, at the very time that it pretended to be setting forth the glory of the Lord? If this were a good reason, I might well never open my lips: and I confess, that long as I have been what is called preaching—(I hate the name if I could obtain another)—I have uniformly found it, on this account, the most trying engagement that I can attempt, and have peculiar cause to say, before engaging in it, and during and after the engagement—*God be merciful to me a sinner*;—while I scruple not also to avow (what would stamp my character with a Glasite) that many is the watering I get in watering others. But to drop myself—a *bad* subject every way—are you at any loss to see the rankness of pride and unbelief concealed under that *humble* objection to a disciple's speaking to his fellow-sinners upon the one thing needful? Of course, I suppose, in any other matters in which he does venture to engage, either alone or with others, he is *free from dangers from his own heart*. Away with the thought! Shall I then lastly decline it, because some persons conclude, when they hear of my preaching, that I am led to it by the religious flesh, and am saying—"come see my zeal for the Lord." I am sure they cannot suspect too ill of *me*:

but what hypocrisy and seeking to please men would there be, in my accommodating my conduct to their views? I consider my preaching but as talking to a greater number at once. Many are offended at my being engaged in it so little, and others at my being engaged in it at all. What have I to do with the opinion of either party? I confess I hold the preaching opportunities very cheap in comparison of *conversation;* and I have often endeavoured to combine the two; as I find a quarter of an hour's conversation generally conveys my *meaning* more than twenty sermons. But many will hear me preach, who will *not* converse. When I say many, observe that my audience at 3 o'clock on Sundays when I speak, seldom exceeds a score, and is often smaller. You treated me better in Scotland, but I fancy it was because you did not understand me. I am half vexed at having filled my sheet with this subject: yet having entered on it at all, I was anxious to guard you against what I think a snare in the Glasite views. There may be a great deal of hypocrisy in our trying to avoid the appearance of hypocrisy. I shall be glad to hear of your being much engaged in talking to your neighbours, as long as you tell them the truth: while I am sure that you will talk to them in the mind of the truth, only so far as the mercy and power of God keeps you in the perception of its glory. When we lose sight of that, it is little matter whether we talk or be silent. Be strong, dear friend, in the Lord; and care not whether others think you carnally strong;—"Remember that Jesus Christ has been raised from the dead:" what more do we want, at any time, to bring us into the presence of the living God, crying Abba! Father! It will be a fight to the last, especially against our wicked hearts, bent to depart from Him, in departing from this truth. But the time is short: Salvation belongeth unto Him: and He increaseth strength to those who have *no might.* We talk of our *weakness,* as if we had some little—though *too little* strength.—But remember our character—NO might. Remember His—the *mighty God* —the God of Jacob. Write often. I like to hear from you.

LXVI.

TO THE SAME.

May 1, 1820.

MY VERY DEAR FRIEND,—I am ashamed of having so long delayed answering your last; and that which I now write must be rather a note than a letter. I am about leaving town to-morrow morning for Dublin, and shall probably be absent for nearly six months. The uncertainty of my plans till within these few days partly caused my silence; but along with that, the circumstance of my being deeply engaged and fully occupied with a reply to Mr. Haldane. I have now nearly finished the rough draft, but in transcribing shall have carefully to prune away every thing that might irritate him *needlessly*—such as a remark that he has much more *marked* separation in his tabernacle than we have in any of our churches—the evidence that he has formerly *seemed* to countenance, by republishing my letters to Knox, many of the principles which he now most keenly opposes, &c. Yet my reply will abundantly confirm his abhorrence of my spirit and my sentiments, unless the God of all mercy open his eyes. The chief point I enlarge upon is the sameness of character in the hearts of believers and unbelievers—of *man* in all circumstances. And I find increased reason for thankfulness, for having had the occasion to take up my pen again; though I am sure that the more clearly my meaning is developed, the more it will excite a general feeling in all religious parties—"away with such fellows from the earth."

Dr. M—— set off for Ireland last Saturday. He was disappointed with you on one point; and though I say little on it, I am much pained. I do not wonder at your discerning the indisposition in your own heart to look the subject in the face. If you gave a different account of *yourself*, I should not believe you. But when I see a professed disciple of the Lord walking after his own heart, in shrinking from the close consideration of a divine precept to which his attention has been called, I sigh and wonder just in proportion to the apparent clearness of his professed views of the truth. I do not at all wish you to lose sight of the wickedness of our interpretation of the precept, if it be wrong, nor of the carnal bias which you justly observe might prompt to it, even if it be right. But, my friend, if you see the glory of the only true God, and have life in His name, take that part of his divine word and consider *what it means*. It has some one definite import; look steadily what it is; and do not longer turn away your eye from it, contented to vibrate between various fancied interpretations, in no one of which you settle. If you once settle in an interpretation of it different from ours, in the love and fear of the Lord set about reproving and correcting us. If you should be convinced with us that the thing allowed under the law of Moses, but forbidden under the gospel, is—*the swearing of any oath to bind our soul with a bond*, with respect to what we shall say or do; but remain of opinion that the oaths administered in your country are not of such a nature, avow this: and then we shall know the ground of disagreement between us, and it will be narrowed for subsequent examination. At present, I do not know where to meet you; and I do not think I shall mention the subject again till you say in what sense you understand those words of the Lord—"Swear not at all." I have written more than I thought I should have been able.

Farewell, dear Friend.

LXVII.

TO MESSRS. D. K——, &c.

March 1, 1820.

DEAR SIRS,—I have had some doubt whether I ought to make any reply to your letter, from some of the characters which it bears. But I have had so much satisfaction lately in reading some pieces of Mr. Barclay which I had not before seen, and such increased confidence that he contended earnestly for the truth, and was a happy partaker of its blessedness, that I am unwilling hastily to drop the correspondence of those who *profess* agreement with him in sentiment. However, while I continue to write I must continue to write with plainness. That there may be no needless misapprehension of meaning between us, let me distinctly mark, that the man who prays, "God be propitiated to me, a sinner"—in the sense which you choose to affix to the words—conceiving that God is *yet to be* propitiated through the sinner's "pitiful approaches"—or through any thing else, is decidedly an unbeliever. But I must say, that this sense is so plainly opposed throughout the tract on which you endeavour to animadvert, that your opposition to it might seem to indicate more disposition to cavil than jealousy for the truth. However, to avoid as much as possible all ambiguity of language in any future edition of the tract, I shall expressly protest against your construction of the words, and substitute such a paraphrase as this—be propitious to, or deal mercifully with me, a sinner—i. e. according to that mercy which thou hast revealed as belonging to thee, flowing to the chief of sinners through that propitiation for sin which thou hast provided and hast accepted. (See vol. 1, 543.) Such was the publican's prayer, and such will be the prayer of every believer to the end of the world. You think that he is described as an unbeliever, offering therefore the sacrifice of a fool; and yet in a more hopeful state, "more accessible to the words of truth than the proud pharisee." Here is, indeed, a fundamental difference of sentiment manifested between us. I shall come by and by to the perverted scripture by which you support your sentiment. But at present let the contrasted opinions be brought distinctly under view. You plainly intimate either that a profligate unbeliever, or that one who has very lately been a profligate unbeliever, but is now becoming piously, but unbelievingly, exercised and solicitous about obtaining what he calls mercy, is more accessible to the words of truth, is in a more hopeful way—and, as you say, more to be justified—than the man who has long been a strict religious unbeliever. I say they are both alike dead in sin, without God in the world; and that none but he who quickeneth the dead, and calleth things that are not as though they were, and to whom nothing is hard, can give his truth entrance into the minds of either. But you refer to the Lord's words in Mat. xxi. 31, as containing your sentiment, very much as Mr. Haldane understands the publicans to have been a much better disposed kind of sinners than the Pharisees. In these words, the Lord states *a fact* illustrating the divine sovereignty, and the character of his kingdom; and well calculated to beat down the pretensions of those whom he addressed—the fact, that He who hath mercy on whom he will have mercy, and hardeneth whom he will, called into his kingdom many of those who were thought the most worthless, while he left to their hardness and impenitent heart those who thought themselves most worthy. But does this warrant the inference that the former were "*more accessible* to the words of truth" than the latter? I should be glad to find you manifesting something of the character of the ingenuous *believing* Berean, in abandoning the sentiment unequivocally.

After endeavouring to fasten on me the charge of *viewing God as yet unpropitiated*, and *putting some work for the purpose into the sinner's hand*, you go on to charge me with having used the word *offer* in p. 16. of the letters, "instead of *declare*, as it ought to be." (See vol. 1. 363.) When I first read this, I wondered, if I could inadvertently have employed any language which could, by any ingenuity of misinterpretation, be conceived to countenance the popular idea of the gospel as an *offer* of mercy, &c., an idea against which I have long publicly and privately protested as inconsistent with the truth; and indeed I was somewhat amused as well as surprised on reverting to the passage of my letters to which you refer as involving that sentiment. Why, sirs, any person acquainted with plain English may see, (if they will) that the passage has no more to do with that sentiment than any other line of the work you could have quoted at random. When I there speak of persons yielding a verbal assent to "*what I offer*," the expression is plainly equivalent with the words, "what I lay before them;" as we talk of *offering* remarks—*offering* observations, &c. And this is so obvious, that I really should be ashamed to vindicate myself against your criticism, or to notice it all, but that it plainly stands connected with another error in your minds. You conceive of me, or of some men now on earth, as *officially declaring* the gospel: and accordingly you conclude with a hope of my being "made more abundantly an able *minister* of the new covenant." I own not any man in that office but the apostles of the Lord Jesus Christ. THEY *declare* to us and to all the world his gospel officially, as commissioned by him for the purpose. I am glad of any opportunity of telling my fellow sinners, either in private or public, either orally or by writing, what I have learned from the apostolic word; and calling their attention to the divine truth declared by the Apostles. But indeed I am as far from assuming to myself, or from admitting in others, any *office* of *declaring* what the gospel is,—almost as far as from making what divines have called a *gospel offer*, in their presumptuous claims to the rank of negotiators between God and man. From a short passage in one of Mr. Barclay's pieces which I lately read, I think he would have joined me in protesting against that clerical leaven, with the influence of which I fear you are infected.

In what follows of your letter there is a great deal so *like* railing, that I should decline replying to it, even if I had room and time. I shall therefore confine myself in the remainder of this letter to some general remarks, which I shall be glad to find you receive with more patience and candour than you have my former. In my last I really meant not to bring any accusation against you. I know but little of you, and I aimed at coming to a fuller knowledge of your mind. I made inquiries and offered remarks. I candidly expressed the hopes and the fears which I felt about your profession. I now acknowledge that your reply makes me stand much more in doubt of you, and for this among various other reasons: you evidently seem piqued and hurt at my having made any question about your soundness in the faith; really, I look upon this as a very black mark. The man who comes to me avowing his doubts whether I believe the truth, says nothing at all calculated to disturb or offend me while I am in my right mind: he gives me an opportunity, always pleasing, of putting forward that truth which I believe, and which I am sure he can never shake or overturn. If he attacks it, is it *me* he attacks? If he sift my meaning at all points, and be not satisfied with the soundness of my profession, without proposing ever so many forms of falsehood to see whether I reject them, is that offensive to me? No, verily. And if he add ever so many cautions against the deceivableness of unrighteousness, and the deceitfulness of my own heart, he speaks the language rather of a friend than of an enemy, in reminding me of dangers of which I would never (in one sense) lose the fear, while in the revealed *salvation of God* I see a sufficient shelter from them all. But I have long found that professors who have fallen into that snare, my mention of which you think so strange, of substituting a confident persuasion about their having faith, or their being among the number of the elect, for the gospel, are offended and irritated when any disciple calls this *their* gospel in question; and I do not wonder at it. It is a thing no where testified in the word of God. The ground is hollow on which they build, and they are up in arms lest the building should tumble about their ears. The confidence of such a professor has for its basis the principle, "I am a believer, and therefore there is no fear of me." The confidence of the believer rests on that immoveable truth, *God is*, that God which the word from heaven reveals him to be. I put to you a question, the very proposal of which seems to have displeased you much; and I cannot but observe that, while you multiply words about it as if to shew that it was unnecessary, you have not throughout your letter answered it. It was whether you conceived that any man can believe the *written* testimony of God concerning his son Jesus *at any time* without the Holy Ghost. Mark, I say *written* testimony—which does not contain one word about Duncan King or John Walker specially. Instead of answering this distinctly and cheerfully, you tell me what every Calvinist (of the most corrupt form of popular profession) would tell me, that it is God alone who *calls, enlightens, manifests*, or *begets again*, &c. O, very true!—though we may be quite disagreed as to the inquiry who are the called, enlightened, begotten, &c. But besides your appearing thus to shy a very plain and simple question, I observe afterwards a language which increases the necessity for pushing it—"Were they sanctified through the truth, *manifesting their sins forgiven*, as Mary was who believed in him who was the propitiation for the sins of many?" This language at least looks very like that popular doctrine of appropriation which Sandeman well exposes, while he afterwards sadly and awfully beclouds the subject by representing the gospel itself insufficient to afford the chief of sinners the fullest personal confidence towards God. The appropriators and he agree in that; as the most apparently opposed errors often meet. The scheme of which Sandeman talks at times, would supply the supposed insufficiency of the revealed testimony of God, by sending the sinner to pore over himself for some good evidences to buttress up his hope—and the appropriators would supply it by sending him to look for some supplementary revelation of a thing, not contained in the divine testimony—that Christ had died *for* HIM—his confident persuasion about which they call justifying faith.—You talk of the truth which Mary believed as *manifesting her sins forgiven*. Sirs, that truth manifests the Saviour of sinners: and they who know his name will put their trust in him. He and He alone, in that revealed work and character in which the word testifies of Him, is that fulness of Jehovah's house with which his people shall be satisfied, and in which He calls the sinful and the evil, the wicked and unrighteous, to delight their souls continually. Isa. lv. Ps. xxxvi. Our hearts are continually like a deceitful bow, bent to backsliding from him, and to go a whoring after our own inventions. But He will keep the feet of his saints abiding in the way of peace, will keep them holding fast that hope, which the publican and the harlot and the pharisee need only to see, in order to be happy partakers of it. This is that work of faith which He fulfils: while indeed the heart of man, left to its workings at any time, is abundantly competent to keep a sinner feeding on ashes, in a high evangelical profession, at the bottom of which is a confident persuasion "that he has been ordained to eternal life."—Such professors will be very apt to object to me as some do—"*you are always afraid of yourself*," and will think themselves very strong in *faith* because they are not afraid of themselves; and will be unable to see the consistency of a perpetual fear of myself with perpetual peace. But in truth there is a fear which is very different from being fearful, as there is a confidence very different from the assurance of faith.

Another ungodly symptom that I am sorry to observe in you, is your inability to discriminate between things the most essentially distinct, your confounding some of the plainest truths of scripture with the grossest falsehoods. For instance, you think that my assertion of the continued ungodliness of the flesh (or of his own heart) in the believer, is equivalent with an assertion that the believer is carnally minded; and your views on this important topic appear to be just the same with Mr. Haldane's and those of all the religious world. My assertion that unbelieving men cannot suitably be addressed with any of the precepts or exhortations directed to disciples (or as you choose to express it, "are unprepared for them") you confound with the systems which hold a progressive preparation in the sinner for the gospel, and a preparation which is to be forwarded by human exertion. But I must add on this head, that if I could detect no error in your professed sentiments, I should view as a black mark on your profession, the contempt with which you treat the revealed will of the Lord concerning the walk of his people. Attention to that revelation, you set aside, as "*breaking our teeth upon shells*," while you set in opposition to it your fancied persuasion of the truth, as "*enjoying the kernel*." Any supposed enjoyment of the truth that is set in such opposition, I must consider but a fancied enjoyment: and I suspect that, if you spoke out, you could point to passages in the tract No. iii. which you dislike as much as any thing else in my writings.

You say that "I do not see eye to eye with you on that subject." There is much truth in the old vulgar saying, that none are so blind as those who do not choose to see. I suspect you are forced to see more than you choose, on the discrepancy between the course of your sects, and the divinely ordered course of the first (disciples)—the first christian churches. That discrepancy happens to be too clearly marked in my letters: (see Vol. 1. 370.) and I dare say your *minister* has a decided objection to its removal. Choose then what you will hear.—But till you manifest an ear for the word of the Lord, notwithstanding all the high ground you take, your professed knowledge of Christ and rejoicing in him, I must suspect that a deceived heart has turned you aside, and that there is a lie in your right hand. But believe me it will give me great joy to have my suspicions scripturally removed. Remaining, dear sirs, your real well wisher,

---

LXVIII.

TO MRS. L. S. G——.

April 18, 1820.

Dear Madam,—I am not quite sure that I may not presume too much in addressing a written communication to you: but I am quite sure that, even if I do, your kindness will forgive me, from a consideration of the motive; and that your professed views of scriptural truth will plead for my writing with all plainness, when I write at all. I have not seen any of my brother C——'s communications to you, but I have seen with much pain yours to him: your short note of yesterday looks too much like a *finale*, occasioned by the tenor of his last to you. Perhaps from his natural quickness he may have employed a language somewhat too summary; though, from our perfect unity of mind, I cannot suppose that he has expressed any sentiment in which I do not fully concur. The truth of the gospel of the glory of God, as the divine testimony concerning the Lord Jesus Christ, his person, work, and office, is a sacred and inviolable truth, not admitting any change or alteration. It is one, woven from the top throughout without seam; and any attempt to rend it, any avowed rejection of any part of the testimony, whether in the form of taking from it or adding to it, must be regarded with abhorrence by the believer standing in the truth, as a profanation of the holiness of the Lord. Even the profession of subjection to it *for ourselves* (as some speak) in its uncorrupted integrity, but accompanied with the false charity *for others*, which would admit them to be right enough, though they hold some other doctrine under the name of gospel than that which we profess, is utterly inconsistent with the real discernment of the truth. How far your notions of the gospel come at present under either of those cases, I really pretend not to pronounce; but I must unequivocally pronounce, that the sentiment you have adopted concerning the laws of Christ's house, (that subject on which I perceive my brother has forborn to enter) is altogether irreconcileable with the real nature of his kingdom. It is very little I am about to say upon the subject: you seem to require some text of Scripture expressly informing us, that the precepts issued from the King of Zion through his apostles to his disciples, and recorded in the scriptures of the New Testament, are of binding authority on his disciples at this day: and you will perhaps be confirmed in the sentiment which rejects them, when I tell you at once that I can refer to no such express declaration as you require. But may I not more suitably require from you the divine revelation which has repealed them? Is not the ungodliness of your sentiment sufficiently marked to a believer by all the scriptures, which do expressly describe the Messiah's kingdom as one "which cannot be moved;" of which "not one of the stakes shall *ever* be removed, neither shall any of the cords thereof be broken." Is. xxxiii. 20. Heb. xii. 28. And observe, dear madam, as in the last quoted passage, that this is one of the characters by which it is expressly *contrasted* with the Mosaic dispensation which was to be removed, and which has passed away. (It is remarkable, indeed, that it is in that very epistle to the believing Hebrews, which announced to them the termination of the earthly kingdom, that the express warning occurs, not to forsake the assembling of ourselves together.) Accordingly, with those apostles whom He commissioned to teach his disciples in his name to observe all things, whatsoever he commanded them—with these apostles He declares that he will be—binding what they bind, and loosing what they loose, even unto the end of the world: that stability is sufficiently ascertained to us, in opposition to all the corrupt glosses that would confound it with the end of the Jewish dispensation, by the permanent nature of that kingdom that was to remain after the other vanished away, as well as it is distinctly marked in 1 Cor. xv. 23, 26. But, in short, your sentiment immediately strikes at the throne of Him who is seated as a king upon the holy hill of Zion; and if it nominally leave him a lawgiver and king, (Isa. xxxiii. 22.) exhibits him as a lawgiver without laws, and a king who allows his subjects to do whatsoever is right in their own eyes. And here, dear madam, I must briefly mark an inconsistency—(one of those inconsistencies with which error is prolific)—which appeared in your language as we walked together, and which is repeated in one of your letters to my brother C——. You profess to see much sin in the course in which you lately walked, in a kind of fellowship with other professors. But according to the sentiment which you maintain, (and which on the day I saw you, I hoped was but the perplexity of an agitated mind), what sin after all was there in it? or what sin would there be in your returning to the Establishment—if you like it? If indeed it be so, that the rule which was formerly binding on disciples in the apostolic word has ceased to be binding now, I cannot understand what sin there is in walking contrary to that rule; and I am sure no other revelation from heaven has been given since, which they can transgress. You continued in that kind of fellowship while you liked it: you gave it up when you ceased to like it; and you may resume it, or any thing in its place, when you like. Where is the harm in any part of this course? where lies the sin that you mean to acknowledge and take shame for? But I do not wonder that many who were engaged in such an attempt should find it much more comfortable, and (as they will say) more profitable, to abandon it. You did seem in some points pleasingly distinguished from them: but, indeed, you now seem just of their mind.

Praying the God of all mercy and power, that if you be one of his, you may receive the reproof of his Word,

I remain, dear madam, yours faithfully.

LXIX.

TO THE CHURCH IN C——.

July, 1820.

Beloved Brethren,—We write to you at the desire of the church in Dublin, about a matter in which we have all to acknowledge much unfaithfulness heretofore. Our attention was called above a year ago by the church in C—— to the intrinsic unlawfulness of our *employing a clergyman to solemnize our marriages*, in any circumstance, or under any supposable modification of their religious rite. At that time, most of us conceived that we had sufficiently come to a scriptural settlement of mind upon the subject, because we were professedly agreed upon the utter inadmissibility of the thing, *in the circumstances in which we are placed*; having an opportunity of obtaining an equally legal validity to the marriage contract without having recourse to any antichristian priest for the purpose. And satisfied with that kind of *hollow* unanimity of sentiment, which we flattered ourselves would produce a unanimous abandonment of our former wicked practice, we most unwarrantably (with the exception of a few brethren) deprecated the agitation of the question—whether circumstances might not be at least *imagined*, in which, *if* we had no other way of having our marriages legalized, we might have it effected even by the intervention of a clergyman;—*provided* that he either forebore the usual *religious* exercises on the occasion, or received our explicit declaration that we did not mean to join with him in them.

A marriage that has recently taken place in the church at L—— has again forced our attention to the subject: and we would lay before you the plain considerations which now make us avow the full conviction—(with shame for our past slowness to admit it)—that the thing is *in itself absolutely inconsistent with our allegiance to Christ.* We beseech you then to consider, brethren, that—although marriage is in its nature essentially a *civil* contract—yet the *solemnization of marriage by a clergyman* is essentially and avowedly a *religious* rite; in which the clergyman acts *officially* as such, and in his capacity of *a priest of his religion*: that when, therefore, we apply to him under any circumstances *to solemnize our marriage*, we necessarily call upon him to act for us *in that capacity*, to exercise his *clerical function* for us; and that no explanation we could offer, nor any indulgence he could afford, can possibly make us throw off the *fellowship*, which we do thus hold with his antichristian system. This position we shall confirm by taking a case the most apparently favourable to the opposite view which can possibly be imagined.

We shall suppose that a good-natured clergyman, in order to meet our scruples, not only consents to lay aside *all* religious exercises or expressions upon the occasion, but even dispenses with our appearance in what is called his *church*; that he merely pronounces the parties man and wife, on their declaring that they receive each other in that relation, and upon this gives them the usual certificate that he *has solemnized their marriage*: now, would not the parties, in submitting even to this, have employed that clergyman to perform for them, *in his clerical function*, that which none but a person sustaining this function is considered capable of doing? Would they not have had their marriage PROFESSEDLY *solemnized according to the rites of his religion?* And would they not vainly put a cheat on their own consciences by pleading that these rites indeed have not been really observed? Allow us to illustrate this (if it need illustration) by putting another perfectly parallel case. The law of the country requires men to qualify for various offices by receiving what is called their *sacrament*. We should all look with horror at the idea of this conformity, whatever might be the worldly temptation. It is well. But let us suppose that the same good-natured clergyman agrees to lay aside every tittle of *religious* ceremony on this occasion also,—merely to give us some bread and wine, which (he says) we may innocently receive from any man,—and upon this to furnish us with a certificate of having *qualified*,—a certificate of our having committed the most awful abomination. Could we seek it? Could we receive it? Could we, without the most hypocritical treachery against the King of Zion, concur at all in the wicked imposture? Yet, to mark the case as perfectly parallel with the former, it is only needful to add, that—according to the principles of that religion of which that clergyman is a priest—the *administration of their sacrament* is not more essentially a *religious rite* than *their solemnization of marriage*.

We are persuaded, that nothing more needs to be said on the subject for deciding the minds of all who are kept standing fast in the truth, and therefore "sanctifying the Lord God in their hearts." We only beg it may be distinctly observed, that we should not conceive the decision rested on scriptural grounds in the mind, if the circumstance of our being able to have our marriages legally ratified otherwise, were allowed to enter at all into the considerations which produce it; if we stood not prepared in the strength of the Lord to encounter every loss that could possibly be incurred by our adherence in this matter to the principles of the divine Word. We have to confess in this (as in every thing) our own awful unfaithfulness; and to praise him for that mercy which endureth for ever. We pray that you may all be "kept in the love of God, looking for the mercy of our Lord Jesus Christ unto eternal life:" and hoping soon to hear from you in reply, we remain, &c.

[A brief remark or two on the answer of one of the members is added.]

His decision seems to consist of two parts:—1. That it is intrinsically unlawful to employ a clergyman to solemnize our marriages. 2. That in a certain supposed case it would be better to commit this sin than a greater. In the first point, the matter on which we wrote would seem given up. But is it given up *honestly*? with a manly—a Christian acknowledgment of antecedent error, in opposing our admonition as *altogether unscriptural in its tenor*? Alas! what poor work we make when we want to preserve *our consistency*! But on the second point, I must say, that a most unscriptural principle is put forward. According to the whole nature of the revelation from the living God, I am not at liberty to suppose that it ever leaves me to *a choice of evils*—to choose which part of his revealed will I shall violate.

I believe I was sufficiently distinct in marking, that our assertion of the wickedness of employing a clergyman to solemnize our marriage, never was to interfere with our *marrying*, where the Word points it out that we ought to marry. And when any one says against this—'What, if I can *get no woman* to live with me as my wife unless I will join in a sacrifice to Jupiter to *solemnize* the marriage?'—he says what is *absurd* in the supposition, and what is *profane* in the application: profane in implying that our heavenly Father, who has given us the two precepts in the Word—"FLEE *fornication*," and "FLEE *from idolatry*"—will yet place some of his children in circumstances in which they *cannot* obey both—but *ought* to balance in their judgments the *comparative importance* of the precepts, in order to decide which of them they will violate *in the name of God*. No other answer ought to be given to the argument.

LXX.

TO MR. J. HALDANE.

Jan. 1821.

MY DEAR SIR,—Having at length decided on replying to your strictures publicly, I have just finished the rough draft of an introductory letter to you. But I find that in it I have been obliged on one point to employ terms of reprehension, which I think it safer to communicate to you in the first instance in private. No doubt the blessed rule of dealing among fellow disciples, given in Matt. xviii. 15, is not in some views applicable to us, as we have never walked together as brethren; yet the spirit of it, as well as other principles which I need not enter into, lead me to think this the more expedient course: I shall therefore proceed without further preface or apology to extract the passage to which I allude.—" As to your grossly calumnious," &c. and down to " sacrificing his truth to gain your approbation." (Vol. 1. 434.) Such, my dear sir, are some of the observations which I find it necessary to make in my introductory letter. Greatly should I rejoice if they were made the occasion of leading you to consider your ways in the light of the revealed will of God. Any other consideration of them is a vainer thing than you suppose. Very different indeed is the course you and I are pursuing, (so different that one or other of them must be very evil) as well as the views and spirit with which we write. By and by we shall both stand before the judgment seat of Christ; and there the opinion that men have formed of us, will be a matter lighter than vanity. In your jealousy for the characters of " excellent men"—in your so rapidly retracing the steps, by which you formerly seemed to approximate towards the assertion of most important scriptural principles—in your joining and now heading the popular outcry against them,—in all this I am sure you think yourself engaged in a course of christian *usefulness*; and I suspect the unscriptural ambition of that, has long been your great snare. But I *know* that the spirit which prompts it, is a very evil one; for it is our own, though in a very fine dress. You think you are promoting God's service, in cultivating a friendship which is enmity against him, and the wickedness is covered from your view, under the specious motive of winning the religious world to some shreds, which you retain of professed principles like scriptural truth. Yet with all the increasing respectability of your character, and increasing obloquy attached to mine, I am happy, and I do not think you can be so. I doubt whether the popular teachers do not still look at you with something of a jealous eye, on account of your former approaches to that same Sandemanianism; and whether you must not recede still farther and more openly from the profession you once made, before you can fully satisfy them that you also are not, or were not, one of that sect everywhere spoken against.

You have gone far indeed towards clearing yourself from the imputation: but can you be quite at ease between the conflicting considerations, that still more is needful to wipe it off thoroughly, and that any more explicit recantation may hazard the loss of those "excellent men," whom you have hitherto attached to you? Ah, dear sir, if ever you be brought to the mind of seeing nothing glorious but the name of the Lord, the object of your contention will be changed; you will have all the world against you; but you will find in the light of His countenance what will outweigh all worlds. But let me not increase the enormous length of this letter by further remark. Only let me suggest to you that it is an awful state which is described in Hos. vii. 9; and that all that kind of self examination, which I dare say you diligently employ, or at least earnestly enforce, never can prevent or detect it. Yours, &c.

LXXI.

TO J. L———.

Jan. 1821.

My very dear Friend,—You must indeed have greatly mistaken any expression of mine, from which you inferred that I wished to terminate our correspondence. Your intelligence of having now a few connected with you, is very interesting to me; and I think the better of *their* profession, from their being desirous to canvass with us the only point of difference. That is but consistent with their conceiving us to be of one mind with them on the faith and hope of the Gospel. The existence of any difference is very—very painful. But let us make it a matter of joint petition, that it may be *scripturally* removed, and not fear but that the prayer shall be answered. Coming with any legitimate request to Him to whom sinners have access, what but our hardness of heart and unbelief ever makes us doubt of being heard? Matth. vii. 7—11. Mark xi. 24. John. xiv. 12—14. xvi. 23, 24. 1 John v. 14, 15. These are great words: but not too great for the warrant of a *sinner's* drawing nigh *to God*.

There are just two points to be considered in the question—(I do not mean to argue either of them now.) 1st. Whether the thing forbidden us in the word be not a *pledging* ourselves before the Lord, that we will act so or so, under any *forfeiture*, however small.—2dly. Whether all oaths in this country, and indeed in every country, be not such a pledge; and whether this be not the essential difference between an oath and a simple affirmation, however solemn. Now, dear friend, resume your pen to me; and tell me all particulars about your course, and those with you. I expect, ere long, to address you, as brethren beloved, in the full fellowship of the Gospel. But for the present, if you do not choose to say anything about our difference, be silent on it, and write only about the grand point of agreement. With the most affectionate interest, yours,

---

LXXII.

TO THE SAME.

April, 1821.

My very dear Friend,—Believe me, I never had an idea of putting out of view the question so painfully at issue between us, though I wished to hear of your course, even though you should, for a time, say nothing upon it. Your letter of Feb. 8th, though *professedly* giving a view of the meaning you attach to the precept in Matt. v., really left me quite at a loss to know what you mean. I have sufficiently marked that I understand it to be a prohibition against *binding* ourselves, as to our future conduct, under the imprecation of any forfeiture, however small, or by any *pledge* that we stake for our acting as we engage to do. At times you would seem to intimate that all such binding of our souls by a bond, is inconsistent with Christian principles. Yet, at other times, you seem to have a different idea. What do you mean by quoting the Apostle's language—"I call God to [record] witness *upon my soul?* Do you think, with many, that Paul intended to imprecate the divine vengeance on his soul, in case he spoke falsely—in short, to say *may God damn me* if it be not so and so? The plainness of the dress in which I put the sentiment does not at all increase its profaneness. Do you ask how *I* interpret the passage? As usual I say, in the first place, I am *sure* he had *no such* meaning as this. In the next place I say, that I *think* he uses the word soul here as equivalent with the *inward man*. What he was assuring the Corinthians of, was not any thing cognizable by man—any thing of *outward* conduct—but the *inward* motives which influenced his conduct; and he suitably appeals to God as the *witness* of *them*. I smile, and I sigh, at the fight you make about the import of the *promissory oaths* in this country. And let it be observed, that *every* oath administered in this country is essentially a promissory oath, as much as the oath of allegiance. But do you deny that the oath administered in England and Ireland to all nations, except those of the Scotch Kirk, is *expressly imprecatory* in the words, "So help me God!" or, as it ran originally, "So help me God at the judgment day?" The special clause in an Act of Parliament which provides for swearing those of the Scotch Kirk here, according to the Scotch form, proceeds not upon any difference in the import of the two forms, but upon their scruples to *kiss the book*, &c. And truly, any one who chooses to see, may easily see precisely the same import in the phrase, "*As I shall answer* before God at the great day of judgment." You quote various persons, lawyers and others, who loosely speak of an oath, as the *most solemn* of all appeals to God, or modes of affirmation; without their marking in what its *peculiar* solemnity consists. Does that go one tittle against the uncontradicted interpretation of those who do precisely mark what the others admit? And are they *divines* merely? Was it as a divine that Archdeacon Paley wrote? No: it was as a *civilian*. Were the compilers of the article *Oath*, in the Encyclopædia Brittanica, and Rees's Encyclopædia, divines? One of the Barons of the Exchequer in Ireland, distinctly admitted to me last summer the *imprecatory* nature of every oath; and confirmed it, by mentioning the form in which (I think) a Japanese was lately sworn in our courts, by holding up a china dish, and dashing it against the ground: just as Livy, detailing the form of *Oath* by which the Romans ratified their treaties, describes the priest knocking out the brains of a ram, with an imprecation that Jupiter might so destroy the party who should violate the terms of the league;—and agreeably to old *Varro's* express declaration, that *every oath terminates in an imprecation*. Yet, I would observe to you, that I am by no means sure that all the things called oaths, under the old Testament, were of this nature; or were, some of them, any thing more than such a simple appeal to God as the witness, as any Christian may employ. I was pained, my friend, by an appearance in your last to me, as if you were disposed to *cut this subject short*. If you write again, keep in view the distinctness of the two questions,—1. What the thing prohibited in Matt. v. is.—2? Whether the oaths of this country be a thing of that nature? Still affectionately yours, for the truth's sake,

---

LXXIII.

TO THE SAME.

June 11, 1821.

I bear you on my heart before Him that heareth prayer, in whose gracious presence we sinners are set by the revelation he has made of his glorious name. I cannot but say, that I think your flesh has been struggling against plain scriptural principle. You now *doubt* the lawfulness of what men call you to. Under even that *doubt*, I trust you will see your course plainly marked, not to do the thing. How can my friend express himself so undecidedly upon the clause, "So help me God!" "It is an *ill* phrase—but is a person necessarily obliged to subjoin what is not expressed—*but not otherwise*?" And does that need to be *expressed*, my friend, in order to expose the wickedness of our saying—"So may God help me, as I shall bear true allegiance to," &c. If that be not binding ourselves, under a curse that we *shall* act so and so, I know not what is: and you have professed to abhor the thought of this. That this is the design and intention of every oath administered in this country, I think has been fully established, whatever be its form: but when the form is as above, I know not how it can be disputed. And is there any instance of such an oath being enjoined, even under the law of Moses? Or is this, by any subtility, to be confounded with a solemn declaration of an antecedent fact, as in the presence of Him who searcheth the hearts? But if you bring the *oath of cursing*, enjoined in Numb. v. 21—22, as parallel, I must say you might as well bring the meditated slaying of Isaac by Abraham, or the extirpation of the Canaanites by the Jews, as justificatory of similar acts now. The *divine* COMMAND rendered that right which, without it, must have come from the evil one. I have already marked the passage of the law, to which the Lord's prohibition decisively refers: and the binding of the soul there was *voluntary*; and I hesitate not to say even then came from evil—from the hardness of their hearts—on account of which it was permitted, just as the putting away a disagreeable wife was permitted. But I have done. I have been corresponding with one A. M'——, a baker in Cupar Fife, and, from his last, I hope the Lord has opened his eyes. To the riches of his abounding mercy I commend you and yours.

LXXIV.

TO THE SAME.

July, 1821.

"How good and how pleasant it is for brethren to dwell together in unity!" This also is the LORD's doing, and it is marvellous in our eyes, like all his works. Our hearts embrace you all—yourself and your wife—brother F—— and his—with unreserved affection, as beloved in the Lord, fellow-heirs of that glory which is about to be revealed, and fellow pilgrims in a world in which we are warned that we shall have tribulation. Tell me what may be the value of your present employment. We need not trouble ourselves with calculating the probabilities of your being allowed to retain it. The LORD knows and has determined how that shall be. He knows, also, what you have need of for food and raiment: and shall he withhold that from those, to whom he has given eternal life and the adoption of children? I shall now be *weary* to see you all; and if it please God to continue the amendment which appears in my health, I think it likely that I shall strain a point to get to Leith before the end of the summer. One of my proposed objects in giving up my establishment at Dublin was, to be more at liberty to go about. Perhaps there was much of the working of fleshly vanity and pride in the wish. "He knows the things that come into our mind, every one of them;" (Ezek. xi. 5.) and knows that every one of them is evil—every imagination of the thought of our hearts: and it is on such a black ground he displays the glory of his rich grace and great salvation. You mentioned brother F——'s family as with you. Tell me the particulars of his family—of what it consists. Be not cast down at any prospect of the spoiling of your goods. Take it joyfully, remembering Him who is "GOD with us," and who has said, "I will never fail you nor forsake you." To his rich mercy and mighty keeping I commend you all.

LXXV.

TO THE SAME.

Sept. 18, 1821.

MY VERY DEAR L——,—It affords us matter of thanksgiving to find that you were kept so still and unanxious in your trying circumstances. O yes—*kept:* and it is an easy thing to the Lord to keep us so in circumstances the most trying. What a little glimpse of his glorious name is sufficient to effect it! Well may he say to us—"If ye had *faith* as a *grain of mustard seed.*" I was thinking lately of what a West-India planter once told me, of the comfort of the *slaves*, in having no care about providing for themselves or their families in sickness or in health, knowing that all this will be done by the master *whose they are.* "Ye are not *your own;* for ye are bought with a price." How wonderfully is our full blessedness and security interwoven and incorporated with the most constraining motive to glorify God with our bodies and our spirits, which are God's. "Be still; and know that I am God." Yes; every thing opposite to that stillness is the working of those atheistic hearts of ours, which deny that God is. The Lord be with you all, and keep you glorying in his holy name.

LXXVI.

TO THE SAME.

Oct. ——, 1821.

Your last letter, my very dear L——, afforded us much matter of praise and thanksgiving to Him "who alone doeth great wonders." For surely it was He that gave you favour in the eyes of Mr. ——, He that turneth the hearts of men whithersoever he will. After such a deliverance, we are often ready to say, in the elation of our minds, that we shall never distrust the Lord again. But that word describes us to the end—"Then believed they his words: they sang his praise. They soon forgot his works: they waited not for his counsel." (Ps. cvi.) Well; that other word describes *Him*—"But He being full of compassion forgave their iniquity, and destroyed them not." (Ps. lxxviii.)

I conceive the fortnight spent at C—— has been of service to me. While there, I had much fighting with a set of professors—(——— at their head)—in whom the deceivableness of unrighteousness assumes the novel form, of combining Arian or Socinian views of the person of Christ, with a very plausible language about his work, and such an outward accommodation to some scriptural principles, that Mr. —— has for some time preached without the usual accompaniments of singing and prayer. He is a very amiable and interesting man; but holds every thing with such laxity, that not only J. Haldane's profession, but John Wesley's, appears very good in his eyes. We found one or two of his people apparently very differently minded: and perhaps it may please God to make the coal of fire thrown in among them burn. Mr. —— candidly avowed a state of mind which I believe is very common, though generally concealed. He sees two sets of scriptural passages, which he thinks speak an opposite language. He balances one against the other; and according as either scale at different times preponderates in his view, he is strongly *inclined* to adopt one or the other set of sentiments. Such a state of mind is almost unavoidable in a serious inquirer, not persuaded by divine power what is truth: while the man must frequently study to conceal his scepticism from himself as well as others. Such are the men who have two strings to their bow. The Lord himself keep us all holding *fast* the faith!

I hope you have not been over hasty in calling —— —— to fellowship in all the ordinances. I am sure that no precise limit of age can be marked for this. It must vary according to different circumstances and characters. But there are two opposite errors (as in most cases) which we should equally guard against—a premature reception of them into church membership—(I use the phrase for brevity—not that I like it, but you know my meaning—) and such an unwarrantable delay of calling them to it, as would leave them to grow to men and women in a neutral kind of character. In one of the Irish churches, a short time ago, they fell into the former mistake; and were for calling children of five or six years old to join in partaking of the Supper. But it has been eventually blessed for bringing the minds of all there to a more scriptural settlement on the subject. Not to insist at present on the principle that the Supper is exclusively a *church* ordinance, not to be separated from the other acts and exercises of the collective body, when they come together on the first day of the week; nor to insist on the plain fact, that mere young children cannot really take any part in all those acts and exercises; and that it is only making them young hypocrites if we lead them to pretend to do so; does it not evidently accord with all the principles of divine wisdom in the Word, that during the period of early childhood, the child should be under the exclusive and absolute control and management of its parents? When it joins the full fellowship of the church, that species of absolute control, which it has been so important previously to maintain, ceases. And though there is a parental authority and filial subjection which continue, yet it is obvious that the exercise of the former becomes very different from what it was before. The young disciple must now be supposed to think, and act, and judge for himself in the concerns of the kingdom of God, and must be treated accordingly. It might be very important (for instance) to whip a young child soundly for naughty conduct or temper; and any thing which would exclude that kind of treatment during the proper period, would be utterly inconsistent with all the principles of due parental discipline. But I certainly think any such mode of discipline is excluded as soon as the child passes into church-membership. If any thing improper be observed by others in the child previously, it is the parent and not the child that is to be dealt with on the subject. The evil of the opposite error, I need not enlarge on. On the whole, if we are kept adhering to the general principles of the Word, I think we shall be at no great loss about the proper period: and I should scarcely expect it to appear much below the age of twelve or fourteen years: and certainly I should not expect it to be much after the latter age, if the child has indeed been brought up in the instruction and admonition of the Lord. I believe I should have scarcely entered on the subject, if I thought it would have occupied so much of my paper.

The account you have given of the two actually added to you, and the three likely to be so, is most interesting, and makes me impatient to hear from you soon again. And so a Presbyterian elder seemed likely to become a fool for Christ's sake? O, how glorious does he appear reigning in the midst of his enemies, and making his arrows sharp in their hearts! We have very little increase as yet here; and are, indeed, a most sorry set to put ourselves forward as *the* church of Christ in this grand city. But one and another now and then, from the lowest classes, are brought in; and some a little more respectable are *unsettled* from their former profession, but not yet settled in the true. They are *considering:* and when it comes to a sinner's considering whether he shall believe and obey the word of the Lord, though divines think him in a very hopeful way, and he thinks himself engaged in a very good process, we know that it is only divine mercy and power that can turn the scale to the truth. I have been asked before by some very specious professors in Ireland, *how* they should proceed to get at a scriptural decision on this and that point: and they have stared at me when I have told them that I knew of no rule for the purpose. I have been for the last two months engaged in an afternoon preaching (so called), chiefly on the Psalms. And surely John Barclay has been honoured to do good service there. From a dozen to a score of outliers attend, but few of the same persons twice.

I have often thought that, if I had means, I should like to publish a revised edition of all the scriptural pieces I wish to survive me, in order to put down some of the earlier productions of my pen. As to the Address to the Methodists of Ireland, I have mentioned in my Reply to Mr. Haldane that I am willing that any one should reprint that and the Letters to Mr. Knox, (they must go together) provided he print along with them castigatory notes, which I shall be ready to furnish. With these, I should be glad of the republication; for there is much important matter, particularly in the Letters to Mr. Knox: but without the antidote of the notes, I protest against the reprint. Could I, for instance, now countenance the pages of wicked nonsense in which I expostulate with the Wesleyan Methodists for their *bigotry* in not co-operating with the Calvinistic Evangelicals in spreading the gospel? There are strange inconsistencies in that piece, a conflict between light and darkness: I get clearer towards the close of the controversy with Mr. Knox; but I could not agree to the separation of the address from the Letters. Next comes the Address to Believers, &c. to which I must for the present demur; at least to its republication without the Appendix, or without the addition of two or three pages which I think much wanted in that piece. It says too little distinctly about the gospel of Christ; and on the conversation becoming the gospel there is a serious omission, on the topic of *obedience to the peculiar commands of the King of Zion.* These omissions at present commend it to many who would dislike it if they were supplied.

The bookseller, who you say is apprehensive of injuring the circulation of this piece by attaching to it a name in such bad odour with the religious world as mine, is at liberty to substitute for it, "An Apostate from the Church of Antichrist."

What will Mr. Haldane say to Mr. O——'s circulating the wicked doctrine, in the Address to the Methodists, of the total and invariable corruption of the human heart?

Tell me how you have got on at Cupar. My prayers are offered up for you all, that the Lord may fulfil all the good pleasure of his goodness in you and the work of faith with power. Let us be remembered by you in the same way.

LXXVII.

TO THE CHURCH IN LONDON.

March 17, 1821.

Being doubtful whether I shall be able to meet with the brethren next Sunday, I am led to put on paper the substance of what I wish to offer on the subject which has been introduced, and which some appear disposed to press, or push forward, to a precipitate decision. In the first place, let it be well observed, that the relation subsisting between man and wife, is in itself altogether of a *civil, temporal*, and earthly nature; and not at all intrinsically a religious connexion. The opposite view has obtained great currency from priestcraft, and from the religious rites which are generally made to accompany the solemnization of marriage. And I readily admit the marriage connexion is the most lasting and closest of all earthly connexions. But I repeat it, that it is essentially as much of a purely civil and earthly character, as the connexion subsisting between a master and his apprentice, or between two partners in trade.

And the truth of this statement is put beyond all contradiction, by the Scriptures of the New Testament. For they expressly acknowledge the marriage relation as subsisting in full force and permanent obligation between a believer and an unbeliever. (See 1 Cor. viii. 1 Pet. iii. 1.) Now, between such parties, there could subsist no *religious* connexion or *religious* fellowship. And it is quite idle to urge against this, that such were instances of marriage formed *before either of the parties was a Christian*. Be it so. Yet it is indisputable, that when one of them became a Christian—if the marriage connexion be to a Christian of a religious nature—the marriage relation must have been immediately dissolved between them. But we know, on divine authority, that it was not; and the inference from this is incontrovertible. I push this very plain point so much, because I am sure, when it is duly considered in the light of the word, it goes very far indeed towards a determination of the question now agitated. At least I am warranted to say, that, after this principle has been once established, when we recollect that the Christian dispensation leaves us at liberty to form and maintain all other civil connexions with those who believe not, we ought to require the most decisive scripture authority, before we admit the idea of an absolute law, prohibiting a Christian from forming the merely civil connexion of marriage with any, except one united with him in the faith. And here, in the second place, let me notice the vanity of all those references to the Old Testament Scriptures, and the law given to the Jews, with which divines abound on the subject, but which ought not to be heard from any of us. Have we yet to learn that essential difference (among others) between the law given by Moses, and the Christian dispensation,—namely, that the former was for a people *outwardly* separated, by temporal enactments, from the rest of the world, and restricted from intercourse with others, even in the things of *this life*. But that this external and civil separation of them, as a nation, from the other nations of the earth, was but an *earthly* shadow of the higher separation unto God, of those who belong to that kingdom of heaven, introduced by the Gospel. It was in perfect consistency with this, that the Jews were commanded even to put away unbelieving wives whom they had taken, but that to the Christian such a step is prohibited. But, in the third place, (in order to prevent, as much as possible, all mistake of my meaning) I would remark, that what I spoke just now, of our being left at liberty by the Gospel to form and maintain connexion with the children of the world *in things relating to this life*, I spoke of "a liberty which we have in Christ Jesus;"—a Christian liberty, which leaves us not without law to Christ in these very matters; and the exercise of which is to be regulated by all those general principles of the word, which call us, whether we eat or drink, or whatever we do, "to do all in His name, and to His glory." And, I would add, that while all our engagements, connexions, and intercourse with the world will be restricted and regulated by those principles, just according to the indwelling of the glorious truth in our minds; so it is peculiarly important that we should be thus regulated in forming the closest and most permanent of all earthly connexions. Else, we shall be found "abusing our liberty for an occasion to the flesh." (Gal. v. 13.) This is a sore evil, which the Lord will visit with correction in his children, and which often proves the occasion of manifesting evils deeper and more radical. But I see an equally awful evil, manifested by those who would vainly attempt to guard against this abuse of Christian liberty, by making (as it were) a complete code of laws square at all points, and (as they think) providing for all cases. All such attempts to enforce the particulars of Christian conduct, which nothing but the influence of the blessed Gospel can produce, originate in the presumption and ungodliness of our flesh. Now, the considerations are obvious to the mind of faith, which mark the general high expediency and desirableness of a Christian's forming the marriage connexion only with one like-minded with him in the things of the kingdom of God; the desirableness of having in his partner through life a comfort, and an help in matters of the highest concernment, instead of a discomfort and an hindrance, and especially the importance of having one who, instead of counteracting his paternal labour in bringing up his children in the instruction and admonition of the Lord, will aid and co-operate with him in the work. I think it more consistent with sobriety of mind to express myself thus, than rashly to say, what I have heard some advance, that a Christian who marries an unbeliever, incapacitates himself for the discharge of that solemn parental duty. This would be in effect to say that the Apostles gave a general command to Christian parents, which some of them, at that day, were incapable of observing. These considerations I would urge upon the attention of any believer thinking of marriage. If he be thinking of it in the mind of Christ, and from the influence of scriptural principles, I am sure he will not be insensible to their weight: but I am not equally sure that he yet may not eventually marry one that is an unbeliever; for I am not sure that he will *be able* to obtain any sister in Christ; much less am I sure that he will be able to obtain any sister at all *suited* to him in age, education, &c.; circumstances which it is idle to say, are indifferent and unconnected with the comfort of the marriage state. And, truly, those who would make an absolute law that he *shall* marry a believer, if he marry at all, may find it needful to have another law, making it compulsory on the sister whom he asks, to accept him. But if they say, (as I have heard some say)—*let him remain unmarried,* if there be either no unmarried female in Christian fellowship with him, or no one who will marry him, they greatly err in this, and manifest their forgetfulness of the plainest sayings of the word of God. For that it is not good to marry, is a saying which all cannot receive, save they to whom it is given; (Matth. xix. 11.) and again, "to avoid fornication, let every man have his own wife, and let every woman have her own husband." (1 Cor. vii. 2.) Mark well the 7th, 9th, and 37th verses. But this, indeed, is not the only instance in which the wickedness of setting up laws of human tradition goes hand in hand with setting aside the laws of God.

In the fourth and last place I would say a few words (for many are not needed) on the passage in 1 Cor. vii. 39, which is adduced as an express prohibition against a Christian's marrying any but a Christian. And here I confess, that if the Apostle give such a prohibition to a Christian widow, it does appear to me that, by all fairness of inference, it must be considered as extending to every disciple. But those who apply the passage in this way, are obliged to insert words that are not either in the original or the translation. Fastening upon the phrase, of "being in Christ Jesus," (which frequently occurs, and confessedly imports *being a Christian*) they would read the latter part of the verse, as if it ran—"she is at liberty to be married to whom she will, *if* only *he be* in the Lord. Now, I forbear every observation upon the original, which indeed is literally rendered in our version. But it is undeniable that the words, which they would supply*—'*if he be*'—are an arbitrary insertion of their own; unwarrantable, if the passage admit an easy interpretation without them; and utterly to be rejected, if the introduction of them affix a meaning to the passage, which contradicts any of the rest of Scripture, as I have shown this interpretation does.

To illustrate this—let us suppose that any one should take it into

* J. M'C——, on hearing this read, observed that he did not consider there is any ellipsis, but that the phrase of *marrying in the Lord,* must mean, according to the analogy of Scripture language, *marrying a Christian,* and proceeded, as usual, to refer to the phrases of receiving and saluting such and such persons *in the Lord.* It was replied, that while the persons described to be thus saluted or received, were confessedly Christians, yet it is certain, that saluting or receiving in the Lord, cannot mean in itself, saluting or receiving a Christian; for that, if so, an infidel saluting or receiving *me,* might be said to salute or receive me in the Lord; which he himself admitted could not be said—and that, besides, even a Christian might salute or receive a fellow Christian, and yet not do it in the Lord, but on principles of natural civility, earthly attachment, or self-interest. So that it is plain the words, *in the Lord,* in these phrases, (just as much as in Eph. vi. 1.) really import the Christian mind, principles, and grounds, on which the disciples were commanded to salute or receive their brethren. But to this obvious and indubitable remark, he was as deaf as to every other.

his head, that believing children are bound only to obey *believing* parents, he might—with equal justice—adduce, in support of his opinion, the Apostolic words in Eph. vi. 1.—"Children, obey your parents in the Lord:" and might turn them, by a similar insertion, into—obey your parents, *if they be* in the Lord. We should be at no loss to reject his corruption of the passage, to deny his right of adding arbitrarily to the text, and to mark the obvious sense in which Christians are spoken of as *acting* so or so in the Lord,—namely, in a Christian way—from Christian principles, and as becomes disciples of the Lord. What has now been said, at once suggests the real meaning of the Apostle's language relative to widows: but it may be set in a still clearer light, by bringing the latter part of the verse into immediate connexion with the previous expression, to which I am persuaded they refer—"*She is at liberty—only in the Lord*—to be married to whom she will." Let us compare with this the expression in Gal. ii. 4—"who came in privily to spy out our liberty, which we have in Christ Jesus." And that in Gal. v. 13—"ye have been called unto liberty, only use not your liberty for an occasion to the flesh." And now, how plain and how suitable is that restrictive guard which the Apostle throws in upon the consideration of the Christian widow! He asserts, indeed, her *liberty* to be married to whom she will; but immediately suggests to her attention, that the liberty which he speaks of, is a liberty which she has in Christ Jesus—a Christian liberty, and therefore not to be used for an occasion to the flesh, but exercised, or abstained from, under the regulation of Christian principles, and with a view to the will and glory of the Lord.

Fully persuaded that the views, I have put forward in this paper, are accordant with the Scriptures of truth, I have every confidence in the Lord that they will commend themselves to the new mind of all my dear brethren; and that through the abundant mercy of our God, we shall be all found of one mind upon this, as upon other scriptural subjects.

LXXVIII.

TO J. G. S——.

April 4th, 1821.

There was one who could say—"I am a *stranger* upon *earth*." All that surrounded *him* in this sinful world presented no attractions to him. We are of the earth, earthly; but this is the victory that overcometh the world, even our faith, turning worldly-minded sinners into strangers and pilgrims upon earth, according to the mind of Christ. Well for us that the word of Jehovah has gone out, not to be recalled—"rule thou in the midst of thine enemies." Ps. cx.

2. His power seems blessedly manifested here (though in a way the most quiet and contemptible to man), giving his word entrance into the heart of one and another sinner—almost all in the lowest ranks of life: and hitherto I have the joy of seeing that the little body gathered in this great city, rest and rejoice simply in the one work of redeeming mercy finished on the cross, as all their glorying before God, and a sufficient ground of glorying for the chief of sinners. They are not such theologians as your Scotch folk. It is well ordered for the pride of my heart that I have little or nothing to do, even instrumentally, in the work that is going on. Those who have received the word tell their friends and acquaintances of the great thing it reports, and the Lord opens the heart of others at once to see and rejoice in the glory of it. When I write thus, you are to understand that the number gathered does not exceed thirty. Most of them (and the most satisfactory of them) are persons who never had made before even what is called an *evangelical* profession. The only one of the body who plagues us occasionally, talking of *duties*, is an old Scotch professor.

Now that I have told you all about our course here, I shall expect you will communicate freely to me all about yours, and those that you know I would wish to hear of. Are you still for making the Lord's ordinances matters of mutual forbearance? Oh! my friend, that may carry a fair show to the flesh; but it cannot consist with real obedience to the word of the Lord. Is it in obedience to that, you take up the attempt of walking in fellowship with any? or is it in the indulgence of a kind of private taste or fancy? But I have done. Very truly yours,

---

LXXIX.

TO THE SAME.

June 12, 1821.

My dear Friend,—As I have to dispatch a packet to Mr. D—— to-morrow, I now sit down to give all the answer I can to Mr. ——'s inquiries about Messrs. —— ——, &c. The only one of them, of whom I have had any personal knowledge, is Mr. E——, a pleasing intelligent gentleman, but quite the clergyman still. I have not kept up any acquaintance with him since his last publication. Mr. K—— at one time opened a correspondence with me on the subject of baptism; which I of course turned to the grand fundamental topic. On this he wrote once or twice very pleasingly; but very soon got tired. He never replied to a letter in which I marked the error of the *high Calvinists*, who mistake for faith a strong persuasion that they are among the elect of God. Some observations that I offered upon that, seemed evidently to touch him on a sore point. And I have otherwise reason to apprehend that the error I noticed widely pervades their connexion, though some of them have got to speak a correct language about the meaning of *faith*. But as far as I have had opportunity of observing, they generally seem more occupied with the talk and consideration of the love of God to *them* individually, than with the glorious mercy revealed and testified in the word. And indeed it is amazing what a plausible language the deceivableness of unrighteousness sometimes assumes in such professors, and what zeal for doctrines that sound most like the truth. There are many subordinate differences of sentiment and practice among them; but none (as far as I have heard) that have at all disturbed their amiable brotherhood; for on all the principles of christian fellowship, they are as lax and tolerant as Mr. —— or any such could wish. They all however agree in direct and open opposition to the truth, in the person of the Lord Jesus. Mr. E—— and Mr. B—— have published books upon the subject; but I confess I have not read a page of either of their productions, for I abhor the proud speculations in which they fearlessly indulge, and which are too congenial to my own ungodly heart. They seem very vain of their system, as if it were a *new* discovery that reconciled all difficulties; though I believe it to be abundantly old. As far as I can understand, it is a kind of compound of Sabellianism and Socinianism. They allow to Him who was made flesh, a kind of angelic human nature created before any thing else; and apply to him the epithets and character of God, from the most High *dwelling in him* as his temple. One of them (a disciple of Mr. E——) attended one of our meetings, and getting into conversation with some of us afterwards, expressed (as they usually do) the greatest satisfaction with all that she had heard—excepting (she added) one little expression. This on inquiry proved to be some expression, in which a brother had intimated the proper Godhead of Him who came into the world to save sinners. I proceeded to expostulate with her, and asserting that He who was made flesh was indeed God over all, she keenly interrupted me with—"No—he who was made flesh was not God." Here I thought she had involved herself in such a direct contradiction of the express testimony of the word, that she might at any rate be made *ashamed*. I therefore calmly referred her to the declaration that *the word was* God—*and the word was made flesh:* but I soon found that she paid no more regard to that declaration, than if it were quoted from the Koran. Mr. S—— of C—— is the one among them all who presents the most pleasing appearances: but even he is carried away with their philosophy and vain deceit on this point. He visited Dublin some time ago, and after attending a meeting of the church in Stafford-street, got into close and long conversation with some of my brethren, in which he expressed the greatest delight with what he had heard and witnessed, and afforded them equal delight by the apparent clearness and simplicity with which he confessed the truth; till one of them, who had heard of these speculations, introduced that subject and inquired his views. He was very unwilling to bring them forward, for he seemed quite anxious to present himself as fully of one mind with us: but when pressed, he avowed himself quite of a mind with Messrs. E—— and B——; and went into a long disquisition in defence of their sentiments. I have heard also from a sister who heard him at C———, that though he had often spoken agreeably to the truth, he on one occasion expressed principles in direct opposition to it. Some of them have discovered that the ordinance of the supper and all other things delivered to the churches formerly, have no decisive authority now;—that christians now are under a *higher* dispensation than was in the apostolic age; that this was the dispensation of the *Son*, but that now is the dispensation of the *Spirit*, &c. But enough. What I have said is sufficient to intimate to —— in what light *I* view them all. He probably will think it very happy that they are not bigots in matters of church fellowship.

On the morning after I wrote to you in reply to your letter of the 6th, I was seized with a slight paralytic affection, which among various other symptoms promises the religious world a speedy release from one of its plagues. But He, before whom the walls of his Zion are *continually*, will accomplish all his own work, and be at no loss for instruments—will make his arrows still sharp in the hearts of his enemies, so that one generation shall declare his name to another, till the great controversy is finally decided by his coming in his glory. Even so, Lord Jesus, come quickly!

Affectionately yours,

LXXX.

TO THE CHURCH IN DUBLIN.

May 27th, 1821.

Beloved Brethren,—We have received the letter which you commissioned two of your members to send us, and have read it with that attention which the importance of the subject demands. We receive it as an expression of your godly jealousy for the truth, and of your love to us and to the brother with whom you call us to deal, and for whose "unscriptural language" and "avowed error" on the subject of repentance you say we are *accountable*. Accurate expression of our meaning upon every scriptural subject, we acknowledge to be very important; and still more important the accurate interpretation of scriptural language. It must be held so by all who truly fear the Lord and tremble at his word. But we have to acknowledge also how short we all come in this; and how prone we are either to mistake the meaning of the divine word, or to express our sense of it incorrectly. To be watchful over and helpful to each other here, is indeed one of the most important exercises of brotherly love. We acknowledge also that every church of Christ is so far *accountable* for any manifested departure from the purity of the faith in any of their body, that if they suffer that "root of bitterness" to remain among them, they are partakers with the offender in his sin, and betray their own allegiance to the truth. But we confess, brethren, that even supposing our brother's interpretation of repentance to be erroneous—(and if it be, we must observe that it has been avowed in much earlier publications from him, than the one you refer to—see, for instance—) (Note I. Vol. i, 554)—we do not view his error as inconsistent with the faith and hope of the gospel, though its correction cannot be unimportant: and we do not therefore see it an occasion for that dealing with him from the collective body, which we conceive ought not to be taken up unless where it ought to be pursued, if necessary, to the last stage of discipline. We would not be understood as by any means declining the serious consideration of the subject presented to us in your letter: but we hope that, on the grounds which we have stated, you will allow us to refer the immediate discussion of the question to a communication between the brother whose sentiment you reprehend, and some individuals of your body.

We are the more led to this course, because we are almost all of us very young in scriptural knowledge, and incompetent to nice verbal disquisition; and because we have to acknowledge that there are parts of your letter which we do not understand. We would rather for the present set it down to this cause, that some passages of it strike us as very objectionable, than suppose that it arises from unscriptural sentiments in those, of whom we have every confidence that they are of one mind with us on the things of our common salvation. We do not, for instance, understand what you mean by pronouncing, that "*there is a sense* in which repentance may be scripturally said to *precede* faith, but *no sense* in which faith can truly be said to go before repentance." The only sense in which we can understand that repentance may be said to precede faith is this—that till a sinner's mind is changed he believes not the gospel: and in this sense we conceive it may be as truly said that faith precedes repentance, inasmuch as there is no true repentance till a sinner believes. But we confess that all such questions—as whether faith precedes repentance or repentance precedes faith, we consider among the foolish and unlearned questions which we are called to avoid; because we cannot acknowledge any period when a sinner has repentance without having faith, or has faith without having repentance.

Whether, in the scriptural application of the term repentance, the change of mind to which Jesus Christ came to call sinners, and is exalted to bestow upon his people, refers exclusively to the change in their judgment, understanding, and discernment, in opposition to our natural ignorance of God,—or whether it refers generally to that new mind of the spirit, which in all its characters is opposed to the mind of the flesh,—is a question on which we would forbear pronouncing a decisive judgment, till we understand better what you mean to urge against the latter sentiment.

We all, however, desire firmly to maintain, that it is in believing the unadulterated truth of the gospel, and according to the discernment of its glory, that all the characters of that mind, in which we are called to walk towards God and towards men, are produced and are maintained;—not by our willing or striving—but by God working in us both to will and to do;—and this in the same way from the beginning to the end;—at first giving the word of his grace entrance into the mind, and throughout the believer's course keeping the same word abiding in him.

We pray that He may bless all our communications to our mutual edification and to the glory of his name:—that He may at once keep us all vigilant and jealous for the purity of his truth, and at the same time keep us from departing from scriptural simplicity in the pursuit of unscriptural refinement:—that we may be all found speaking the same things, and with one heart and one mouth glorifying God for that mercy, which reigns through righteousness by Jesus Christ.

Signed in the name of the Church assembled in
Portsmouth-street, London.

LXXXI.

TO T. M———. AND T. P———.

May 26, 1821.

Very dear Brethren,—Were it not for the consideration that every circumstance is wisely and graciously ordered or controlled by Him who numbers the very hairs of our head, I should greatly regret that I was not present at the dealing you had, some time ago, with brother H———; as it might have enabled me better to understand your meaning. But except a very general account of that occasion, and the quotation of some expressions of his, which obviously appeared to carry an unscriptural sense, I heard little or nothing of what passed. And yet I recollect that some of the few things I did hear, struck me once with a passing apprehension that there might have been on the other side something of an unscriptural refinement embodied with a just opposition to his language. Probably, I ought not then to have let this apprehension give way to that general confidence, which I am accustomed to repose in your scriptural judgment. And believe me that, on the present occasion, I have found myself in more danger of yielding an unwarrantable deference to that, than of lightly resisting you. I do not mean to say that I have not had to guard jealously against the latter also. After the closest examination of your letter, it is with great pain I say, that there seems to me something more of difference between us, than mere difference of expression. And, in order that we may get to the bottom of it, I must write with great plainness, and at some length. If I write on one point a little more metaphysically than there ought to be occasion for, you must attribute it to your own launching into such considerations as that—*with what mind* we believe the Gospel. Ah! dear brethren, is such a vain and subtle question fit to be thrown before a church of young disciples? Your letter was read to them at our last meeting, and such an answer offered them, as I mentioned my intention of proposing. But it was justly observed that, before they agreed to send it, they ought to have an opportunity of more closely considering your letter, each for himself. That has been afforded them by the multiplication of copies passed from one to another during the week; and what the result may be at our next meeting, I know not yet. But, while I could not consistently deny the justice of affording them all that opportunity which one called for, I tell you candidly, that I think they have been very unprofitably and very dangerously employed. And, from the language which I *hear* that one of them has used of apparent acquiescence with you, in opposition to the sentence, commencing with—"Every thing called repentance, but antecedent," &c. (See "A brief Account of the Separatists," &c. Vol. i. p. 558.) I am not without fears that he has been stumbled—probably mistaking you as well as the Scriptures. However, I look to Him who can turn into a blessing things apparently the most adverse.

But to the point. And I must commence with some remarks on the meaning of the expressions—the *mind*—and *change* of mind; because I think undigested views on that subject lie at the bottom of our difference. By the *mind*, I can understand nothing but the *inward* man in opposition to the *outward:* and by the inward man, I mean simply all that passes within us, comprising not only our *thoughts* and judgments, but our *desires, affections, intentions, &c.* And I mean this, in contradistinction to all idea of the *substance* of the mind, of which, I repeat it, that I know absolutely nothing—have no more notion of it, beyond these *mental characters*, than an infant. Accordingly, when a man is said to *change his mind*, it will import as various changes as the things in the inward man, to which a a reference is at different times made; but without ever importing any further *change* than—a judgment, intention, desire, &c., *different* from what he had, before his mind was changed. For instance, suppose a man says—"I thought very ill of you once, but I have changed my mind:"—or—"I intended to ride to-day, but I have changed my mind:"—or again—"I was desirous to marry her, but I have changed my mind:"—we have here three distinct references, according to which the phrase, *change of mind*, will convey a change either of *opinion*, or *intention*, or of *wish* and inclination. And does it, even in common language, convey any thing more? What would you say, for instance, to my proposing the question—"and *with what mind* is it, that you now think well of me?" &c. It is not, dear brethren, either for cavilling, or for parrying your censure of *my* language, (to which I shall come by and by)—that I wish to direct your attention most closely to that passage of your letter, where, in order to prove a change of mind (in one sense) *antecedent* to faith, you say "that it is not *with our own minds* we believe," &c. It is because that here, if any where, I think the real difference between us must lie. And I confess, that were I not so well acquainted with your sentiments on the truth, I should, from that sentence, and the sentence beginning with—"We have no hesitation in saying, &c."—apprehend the existence of a most serious difference indeed. I should apprehend that the writers so conceive of the order of God in a sinner's conversion, as if there is first given him a certain *spiritual mind*—in opposition to the fleshly,—*with which* (when the sinner has it) he then believes, to the saving of his soul. And in this, I should see exactly the system of Fuller, and almost all the mass of evangelical professors. I have indeed no apprehension, but that you will reject with abhorrence all such ideas. Yet—as we are continually prone to receive, both in our language and our thoughts, a tincture of every ungodly leaven—I would beseech you seriously to consider, whether there were not at bottom, in the language you have employed, some floating half-formed notions bordering on this.

The *belief* of any thing, brethren, is seated in the *mind*, or is one of the characters of the *inward* man: and in this sense alone I can understand the phrases—believing *with the mind*—or *with the heart*, in opposition to the mere outward profession of believing. Now, as we are all naturally ignorant of God, and at any moment, left to ourselves, would become blind to his glory, there must indeed be a *change* of mind, or a *new* mind, where any sinner believes that Gospel which reveals his name. There is a *new* character in the inward man—in his *judgment, understanding, discernment*. And greatly indeed do you mistake me, if you suppose that I consider not *that change*—without reference to any other—repentance unto life:—so that, wherever that is, the sinner is alive unto God, and where that is not, the sinner is still dead in sins. The assertion of this is indeed embodied in our maintenance of the essential truth—that whosoever *believeth* shall be saved. And it is truly most important, that we should maintain the simplicity of the meaning of the word BELIEVING, without involving in it any reference to the *fruits* of faith. But passing this for the present—you will observe the *only* sense in which I can admit that any *change of mind goes before faith*,—(while even in this sense the proposition is so dangerously ambiguous, that I should never think of so expressing myself)—namely—that as we are all naturally ignorant of God, there must be a great *change* in our minds before we believe that God is. It would certainly be much more accurate, and less ambiguous, to say—that there must be a great *change* in the sinner's mind *when* he believes: and this I now mean, not in any reference to the *influence* which the knowledge of the truth has—not in reference to any *other*, though concomitant change in his mind,—but to the mere circumstance of his believing that which he before disbelieved;—in reference to his antecedent ignorance of God. And here, dear brethren, I do think that I express myself more correctly than you, when you write thus:—"to say that repentance *precedes* faith, only implies that, when God opens the eyes, we see his glory," &c. It does not (I conceive) immediately and truly imply any thing about the *author* of repentance—about its being a *divine* gift and work. But that passage in your letter might be so easily understood, as equivalent with what I say myself, that I should not think of noticing any inaccuracy in it, but for its *connexion* with other passages. And that makes me fear, you might have had some floating notion of a divine work *first* opening the sinner's eyes—giving him a kind of new spiritual faculty,—and then giving him *with the eye-sight he has got*, to discern the truth. Yet I trust that, on reconsideration, you will acknowledge with me, that the only true and intelligible sense of your proposition—that repentance (or a *change* of mind) precedes faith—is in reference to the antecedent unbelief of the sinner who now believes. I hope, also, that you will see with me the great and serious danger of expressing even that meaning in any such language. But will you still maintain that "there is *no sense* in which faith can truly be said to go before repentance?" Is it not true that a sinner must believe the Gospel before he has any such change of mind as repentance unto life imports?—true in this sense —that till he believes the Gospel he has no such change of mind? I honestly declare that I think it essential to maintain this: nor do I doubt that you really maintain it along with me,—though I am wholly unable to interpret your language in consistency with this. But the longer I live, the more I see of the ambiguity of words, and of the mischief which it produces.

I pass now to what you conceive an error in my language about repentance. You think that the import of the word refers exclusively to the change in our *judgment, understanding, discernment*, when we are brought to the knowledge of God. I have long been accustomed to speak and write of it in a more comprehensive sense, as referring not only primarily to this fundamental character of the *new* inward man, but to all the other features of the new mind—the mind of the Spirit—consequent on faith: while I have long also been anxious to maintain (as well as I could) their inseparable connexion with faith—so as that it is not only *in believing* the truth they are first produced, but *in* continuing in the faith, as we first believed, that they are all maintained, and *in* our growth in the faith that they all grow. Now I confess that, after the closest review and consideration of my sentiments and language upon the subject, I see no reason from the scriptures to alter either,—bating that imperfectness with which I may have expressed my meaning, either in the passage on which you animadvert, or in various others which you might as well have selected. I have already noticed the *comprehensive reference* in which, in common language, we speak of *changing our mind*. And surely you will not deny, that the word rendered *repentance* has in its proper meaning a reference as comprehensive. You will not say that the proper meaning of the Greek word μετανοια refers exclusively or particularly to the *judgment, understanding, discernment*. This would be contradicted plainly by its use even in the New Testament scriptures. It would be sufficient to adduce against it Luke xvii. 3, 4. When the brother who has trespassed against you is described as turning again, saying, "*I repent*," it is evidently an avowal of a change—not merely of *judgment* and *understanding*, but of *disposition* towards you—a mind towards you opposite to that from which the wrong originated. But then you conceive that whenever *repentance towards God* is spoken of in connexion with *faith toward our Lord Jesus Christ*, it is to be understood in that *exclusive* reference. And why, dear brethren, should you think it important or right to narrow the general import of the word here? The self-same ministry of the gospel which the apostle expresses, as a testifying of "repentance towards God, and faith towards our Lord Jesus Christ," he elsewhere expresses as a beseeching of sinners to be "*reconciled* unto God." Writing to *you*, I am not solicitous to vindicate myself from the false ideas attached to the latter phrase by unbelieving religionists. But I must say, that it seems to me plainly to refer to men as of a mind—not merely without the *knowledge* of God, but ill-affected towards him, full of *hatred* of his name, as well as *ignorance* of it. Need I say, that among all the black features of our natural mind—the mind of the flesh—I admit, and I assert, that ignorance of God—or the *power of darkness* under which we lie—may well be (as it often is in scripture) pre-eminently and emphatically marked? because, from the nature of the gospel, when *that* is removed—when the *knowledge* of God is communicated—there is a new creation; "all things *are become* new;" there is a mind opposite in all its features to the mind of the flesh. So that, without at all confounding *faith* with love, joy, &c. or involving in the import of faith the idea of any of its fruits,—I think it perfectly warrantable to speak of the *mind of faith*, as being the new mind of the spirit in *all its characters* of absolute dependence upon God, reverential rejoicing in him, and unreserved subjection to him: because every one of these *new* mental characters is so inseparably connected with the belief of the truth, that every thing contrary to *them* springs from the mind of the flesh, or the mind of *unbelief*: much as we would say that the *avaricious mind* is a mind of *selfishness*, of *hard-heartedness*, &c. without at all involving any of these characters in the meaning of the word *avarice*. But I have somewhat digressed.

It is indeed very important, brethren, to express ourselves correctly, and (as far as we can) unambiguously, upon divine truth. But it would be a vain idea to expect, that by any precautions here, we can prevent the inconsistencies of misinterpretation which unbelieving men will fall into. And it would be a sore evil if, in pursuing our precautions, we kept back or concealed any parts of that truth, which is in itself one uniform and consistent whole. Now I do think that you are in some danger of falling into this evil, when you would insist on interpreting such passages as these—"I have come to call *sinners to repentance*"—"exalted a Prince and a Saviour to *give repentance*," &c.—as *exclusively* referring to a change in the sinner's *judgment, understanding, discernment*. *If*, indeed, this be the correct scriptural import of the word in such passages, no doubt you are quite right to insist upon it. But if it were, might we not rather have expected, in the former of the passages quoted, that the characters contrasted with the *sinners*, whom Jesus came to call to *repentance*, would have been designated, not as the *righteous*, but as the *wise* or the *understanding*? But I would rather say to you, *think*—(divesting yourselves, not so much in one sense of *system*, as of our little human solicitude to preserve consistency of system)—think candidly and seriously what was conveyed and intended to be conveyed to the hearers or readers by the word *repentance*, or change of mind, in these passages:—think whether the word did not simply refer to the *general ungodliness* of mind in those whom He came to call to a new mind, and on whom He bestows it:—think whether we be not in these expressions called to see Jesus as the minister of that new covenant, of which the promise, as revealed by one of the prophets, ran—"A *new heart* also will I give you, and a *new spirit* will I put within you," &c. And however important it is to maintain that this *is done* wherever the gospel is *believed*, and nothing of it done where that gospel is disbelieved,—think whether there would not be more of theological hypercriticism than of scriptural accuracy, in denying that the reference in that promised *change of mind* is as comprehensive and general as the characters of ungodliness in our own minds. Just as I conceive the same thing expressed by the apostle, when he declares Jesus as sent to bless his people "in turning every one of them from their iniquities:"—or just as another apostle opposes that "*renewing* in the spirit of our minds," which we are taught, to the "old man which is *corrupt* according to the deceitful lusts." Eph. iv. 22.

And here, I confess, I am a little jealous of your sentiments:—not at all (you will readily believe) as the evangelical world would be jealous of some *Antinomian* aspect in them; but on another point. Perhaps my meaning will be at once conveyed, and (I should hope) commended to your better judgment, by the following brief suggestion:—If I see myself called at this day to a continual *renewal in the spirit of my mind*, but in declaring the gospel to the greatest infidel, I thought it inconsistent to call *him* to the same *newness of mind*, in the same comprehensive sense, would there not be reason to suspect that I had one gospel for him and another for myself? or that *I* was pursuing some newness of mind different from that to which he would be brought, in merely believing the gospel? or that I was pursuing it in some other way than in holding fast that gospel which I call him to *believe?* Certainly my meaning is quite misunderstood by those who conceive that—in speaking of the new mind as *consequent on* faith, and yet not in the sense of *subsequent* to faith—I intend something following faith at a *very short interval*. The apostles, in preaching the gospel, call on their hearers to repent and "be *converted*," or *turned* to the Lord: and believers are exhorted, that with purpose of heart they should *cleave unto the Lord*. Now, if we be walking in Christ Jesus AS *we have received him*, surely we shall see that either call is obeyed in *believing* the Word, which reveals the name of the Lord: that "a right spirit"—right towards God according to all the characters of the mind of Christ, can be "renewed within" us continually only in the same way in which it is first given to the man who never before believed the truth:—that *we* can *cleave* unto the Lord only in the same way in which a sinner can first *turn* to him. Yet, shall we say, that *conversion* or *turning* to the Lord refers exclusively to the *judgment, understanding, discernment?* Indeed I must say, that it refers to our natural character, as not only *ignorant* of God, but estranged from him, and indisposed to him in the whole inclination and posture (so to speak) of our minds, just as much as the call in Is. lv. 6, 7. Nor am I afraid of having my *orthodoxy* questioned by you for saying this, unless there be some more real difference between us than I at present suspect.

But perhaps you say—' Are there, then, *no* passages of scripture in which repentance is to be interpreted as referring exclusively to the change in the sinner's *judgment, understanding, discernment*, when he believes the truth?' O yes, decisively there are: and among them I reckon that passage—" if God peradventure will give them *repentance to the acknowledging of the truth*;"—which you hesitated about adducing, for some reason that I cannot for the life of me comprehend. And I should be disposed to mark Acts xvii. 30. as another instance of that exclusive reference, on account of the immediate connexion in which the word there stands with—" the times of this ignorance," &c. And in several other passages, from a similar connexion either nearer or more remote, I should think it very *fair* to understand it in that exclusive reference for which you contend; while I own that in several even of these passages, I should have no quarrel with a brother merely for his interpreting the change of mind as referring more comprehensively to the general antecedent ungodliness of mind described in them. But I have, indeed, sadly failed of conveying my meaning, if you think that, in admitting *ever so many* passages, in which the word refers exclusively to the change in the sinner's judgment and understanding, I have admitted any thing inconsistent with what I have before urged; or inconsistent with the avowal that I do *not* think it was intended in the same exclusive reference in that summary of Christ's preaching—" *repent* and believe the gospel"—or in his words—" except ye *repent*, ye shall all likewise perish"—or—" one sinner that repenteth," &c. &c. In these and other passages, I do conceive that the *change of mind* spoken of refers to *all* the ungodly characters of the mind of fallen man, as not only *ignorant* of God, but proudly rebellious against him and turned from him. At the same time, this is a point which I would not *fight* with you; being quite sure that any whose *judgments* or *understandings* were changed, or who *believed* the gospel, had all the repentance to which they were called. But I cannot see it equally unimportant to contend against your apparent idea of a new *mind* first given to a sinner, *with which* he then believes; and against your supposed *priority* of repentance to faith: for which I consider the mere order of the words in that passage—" repent and believe the gospel"—a very weak argument. When two phrases were employed, it was necessary that one should be expressed before the other: and I should see strong objection to saying—*believe* the gospel *and repent*. It would be at best pleonastic, and would too much seem to intimate that some other change of mind was intended, than the belief of the gospel brings with it:—while the other order, I think, suitably intimates the present ungodly character of those to whom the call is addressed, and the joyful testimony of God sent to them as such, and calling them to turn to Him and live. As to what you say about " confounding the *manifestations* of the new mind with that *mind itself,*" you will be at no loss to answer it yourselves, if I have succeeded in conveying to you what I offered in the early part of this letter, on the meaning of the term *mind.* Of the MIND ITSELF, either old or new, we know literally nothing but its *characters;* and among the characters of the new mind certainly are those mentioned in the obnoxious parenthesis. I call them also *characters,* rather than (with you) *manifestations.* The new *mind,* or characters of the *inward* man, are *manifested* in the conduct of the *outward* man. Do you mean, by calling these mental characters *manifestations* of the new mind, that they manifest a believer's faith to *himself?* I should hope you would reject *that* meaning of the expression, and really I know not any other.

I think I have said as much on the general subject of your letter as ought to be needed. But let me add a few words on the particular passage in the "Brief Account" which you censure. I see nothing in the whole which, fairly interpreted, is open to just objection. But when I define repentance to be "the new mind which the belief of the gospel produces," if any one should conceive that I mean either to exclude the belief of the gospel from its distinguishing features, or not to mark that as its leading feature, he would certainly much mistake my meaning. And I readily admit this mistake might be somewhat guarded against by substituting the words—"the change of mind which takes place in a sinner's believing the gospel." I do not, then, know any thing which I should wish to alter in the following paragraph, which seems to have most displeased you; unless that I would (if publishing it again) substitute *subjection* for *devotedness;* and instead of "the sole work of God," say—what I meant—"the work solely of God"—or something to that effect. If you read that paragraph with a view to the general scope of it, you will see that, after having stated in the former paragraph the scriptural sense of faith and repentance, considered in themselves and independently of their divine Author, I then proceed to state that God is the sole giver and maintainer of them, and that his revealed word is the instrument by which he works them. There is nothing in the sentiment that I could honestly alter or retract. But now I say ultimately, if what I have offered fail of reconciling you to the little pamphlet, let it be *called in.* The copies in Dublin can easily be so, as they were sent over by brother C——, and I shall buy up the copies in London from the bookseller whose property they are. Were it not that the pamphlet professes to be a statement of our sentiments as a body, I should not think myself warranted to call it in, on any objections that have been yet stated. My engaging in it did not originate in my own thought or wish. Indeed I was for some time very averse to it; and after I undertook it, I should have been right glad to have had an opportunity of submitting it to some of you previous to publication. Still I think it usefully calculated to suggest important points of scriptural truth to scattered disciples. But if we be not agreed in the sentiments which it contains,—(claiming only for the expression of them that candour of interpretation which every human composition needs)—it certainly ought not to remain before the public. I shall only add, that I pray God to make you quick to discern, and able clearly to expose any thing which I may have said contrary to the purity of scriptural truth.

Yours, very dear Brethren,

Most affectionately for that truth's sake,

P.S. (May 27th.)—Well—I have just returned from our meeting: and right glad should I be, brethren, that without any interference on your side you could have heard what passed on the subject of your letter. I think you would have been ear witnesses of its most injurious tendency. I should particularly like you to have heard an old shrewd Scotsman—(who was the individual that last Sunday desired a week's delay, that the brethren might consider and *try* to understand your letter)—that you could have heard him to-day avowing that he understood your meaning very well, and proceeding to explain it. I did not wonder at all when he explained it in the broadest way, as a *new mind first given by the Spirit*, and then the sinner believing *with this new mind*. I could only assure him, from all my long and intimate knowledge of your sentiments, that *this* was not, could not be your real meaning: that I am persuaded you would be among the foremost to reject that sentiment with abhorrence. I should be glad to have seen in *him* more prompt and marked abhorrence of it. But I am sorry to say, that under this conception of your meaning, he had in the course of the week spoken of the difference between us as only *verbal:* I should consider it as going to the very root of the gospel. But though utterly unable otherwise to interpret that extraordinary paragraph, in which you speak of our not believing *with our own minds*, but *with* or *according to* a new mind,—I shall not yet admit the fear but that you will explicitly disclaim all such notions. Dear brethren, might you not as well say that *a believer does not himself believe*, as that he does not believe with his own mind? Indeed, the former is the only intelligible sense of the latter; and that sense strikes me as very like nonsense. But let me not add to the length of this letter. The Church ultimately concurred unanimously in sending the reply which goes in their name. May it appear that they indeed hold fast the principles expressed in it! I have not yet read to them this private letter of my own. But I shall think it needful to do so: though, alas! it unavoidably involves them in considerations with which they ought to have nothing to do.

I need scarcely say, that I cannot be quite easy till I hear from you. May your next afford more satisfaction than your last! If you perceive the dangerous tendency which I have marked in your language, you will of course calculate some of your future communications—not merely for satisfying *me*—but for confirming the minds of young and weak disciples *against* the errors which you have *seemed* to countenance. And for a particular reason, I wish you to say very distinctly whether you concur or not with what is expressed in the sentence of the pamphlet, beginning, "Every thing called repentance," &c.

LXXXII.

TO A. M'I———.

June 12, 1821.

DEAR SIR,—I should not have been so slow in replying to your letter of the 8th ult., but that I have been ill and much hurried in settling my family in a house which I have lately taken in London. At the same time, now that I take up my pen, I feel at a considerable loss how to address you. I find you have been reading different publications of mine; and the general approbation which you intimate of the sentiments they contain, is in some degree pleasing; but it is very indistinct. On the subject of church fellowship at least, you must greatly mistake my views, or you would not have thought it necessary to propose the question, whether I think you *ought to join* the Baptists in your place. You speak of having some time ago separated yourself from one of their societies; but you do not mention on what grounds you took that step.

If you take up and lay aside Christian fellowship as a matter of taste and individual fancy, it is of little consequence whom you join. I am rather surprised at your intimation that the Berean Baptists with you, agree with the doctrinal sentiments put forward in my late publications: for I have had a good deal of communication by letter with several individuals of that connexion in Edinburgh, who decidedly differ from me as to the fundamental truth. The idea that a man's own heart is as wholly evil, after his believing the gospel as before, they avow to be unintelligible to them: and they deride all attempt to distinguish between the good hope towards God, brought to a sinner directly by the testimony of his name in the gospel, and that confidence in which he builds himself up by the consideration that he is a believer. I have, therefore, every reason to fear that their boasted confidence rests on the latter sandy foundation. With respect to church order also, in which you say there is no difference between me and the two meetings in Cupar, there is such a great difference between me and the Berean Baptists of Edinburgh, that they do not come together on the first day of the week to break bread. But, indeed, they seem not to consider *divine authority* in the matter at all: and this may probably account for a considerable difference of practice in their different societies, without any interruption of the connexion which, I suppose, subsists between them all. If so, however, I think no better of the Bereans of Cupar than of the Bereans of Edinburgh. Your objection to them, "that they make Baptism the door of their church, because," &c. I think a weak objection. If their Baptism rested on scriptural grounds, they would do very right in not receiving a person who refused to be baptized. Do you think that a person, however professing to believe the Apostolic word, and desiring to be received into one of the first Apostolic churches, would not have been rejected, if he, at the same time, declared that he must be excused from observing the Lord's Supper weekly? Or, do you think that the weekly observance of the Supper could therefore be fairly said to be the door of admission into the church? No—there is an ungodly inconsistency in the idea of any man's wishing to walk in fellowship with a christian church, but not to walk in the same way, or by the same rule, with them. The man who desires it, and the churches that yield it, are alike proceeding on antichristian principles. You speak of some Glasites meeting in your place. I should like to know what you think of them and of their doctrine, and why you do not seem to entertain the idea of joining that body. On the general principles of church fellowship they certainly have more scriptural notions than most others, and also, as far as I know, speak more clearly on the grand subject of grace reigning through righteousness by Jesus Christ, till they come to separate the assurance of faith from the assurance of hope, and so bewilder themselves with another hope, than that which the gospel brings to the guilty. How stands it with yourself here? Do you see in the revealed testimony concerning the work finished by Jesus Christ enough to satisfy your conscience; — enough to give peace and confidence of approach into the holiest to any other sinner who believes the report of it, as declared to all alike in the scriptures? Some talk very fairly about the work finished by the Lord Jesus; but after all it appears that they do not see enough in it to satisfy their consciences and give them peace with God: and they go on to get this secret something, as yet unpossessed, by trying to walk so as to find out in themselves evidences of genuine faith. Others appearing for a time fairly to oppose that error, go on to substitute for the faith of the gospel a confidence that they are believers. The faint hopes of the former that their faith may perhaps be genuine, and the full persuasion of the latter that their faith is genuine, are much more nearly akin than the two parties imagine. But they are alike remote from the soul-satisfying peace, which the grand thing revealed in the gospel, affords to the sinner who discerns it. Blessed are their eyes that see this; that see the real character of the mercy, which the gospel reveals as belonging to the only true God, in something of the glory of its fulness, freedom, and sovereignty, and in its awful holiness, brought in and brought to light through the wonderful propitiation for sin, which has taken it away. They, indeed, see the heavens *opened*, and the angels of God ascending and descending upon the Son of man: they see that fulfilled which was set forth of old in vision to Jacob; and in the discovery of it have their feet set in the way of peace, and in the gracious presence of the living God. If any two or three sinners in Cupar be brought by divine power to this view, they are called to walk together and build up each other in this most holy faith, just as if there were two or three hundred of them. You call on me for my foundation from scripture, for saying that two or three disciples may be a church of Christ. I might more justly call on you to produce any scriptural warrant for the idea, that the obligation of disciples to obey the rule of the word, depends upon their numbers. The rule is abundantly plain, that disciples of Christ are to come together on the first day of the week, to shew forth the Lord's death in the breaking of bread, and to observe the other ordinances as delivered by the apostles. Put the question, whether two or three disciples can be a *church* into plain English, by asking whether two or three disciples can assemble themselves, or come together thus into one place; and perhaps the magic and mystery enveloping that ecclesiastical term *church* may be dissolved. I forget now what is the smallest number which the Glasites and others say can constitute a church—suppose seven. Well, let there be seven disciples in any place joining in church fellowship. Are they bound by *divine authority* to come together and observe the ordinances as the first churches of the saints did? Are all of them alike so bound? Well—one of them dies in the course of the week. Can the divine rule be now abrogated to the other six? As to those who talk of one or more *elders* being necessary to dispense the ordinance of the Supper, they are but bringing in priests and priestcraft under another name. But you object (with many others) that two or three cannot form a church, because they cannot attend to the discipline as delivered in the scriptures. And shall the possible occurrence of circumstances, in which they must cease to walk together as a church, prevent their so walking together till such circumstances occur? Why—the same objection would equally prove that the seven disciples, or any other number which can be assigned, cannot constitute a church. For an evil either in sentiment or practice may appear among them, in which every individual but one may take a part and be involved; and after the reproof and admonition of that one has been rejected, the ordinary and stated course of Christian discipline for purging out the evil cannot proceed: but all which the one who stands for the Lord can further do, is to leave the body—just as if there were but two disciples, and one of them failed of restoring his fallen brother by admonition, he could then only turn away from him. You ask me about the time when we observe the Supper. It is sufficient to reply, that we know of no meeting of a christian church on the first day of the week but one, when we observe all the ordinances.

The multiplication of religious meetings is altogether borrowed from the religious world, and makes a fair shew of edification by observances not divinely appointed, but resting on human tradition.—That is always accompanied by a rejection of the appointments of God. I shall rejoice if any thing I have written be serviceable to you, and am, dear sir, yours faithfully,

LXXXIII.

TO THE SAME.

June 30, 1821.

Dear Sir,—I have received your letter of the 12th inst. with much pleasure: the reasons you assign for not thinking of joining the Glasites are abundantly conclusive, and the view you take of that people seems quite to coincide with my own; yet I cannot but hope at times that there will be found, both among them and the Bereans, scattered disciples, who cannot however be manifested as such on earth, till they come out from their present connexion. When I speak of the Glasites as having juster views than most others, of the principles of church fellowship, I refer particularly to their *profession* of holding sacred all the institutions delivered to the first churches, in opposition to the ungodly liberality which, in most other societies, tolerates disobedience to them. In this Glas and Sandeman had quite the advantage of John Barclay. The latter (as far as I know, or can judge from his followers that I have known) appeared not to trouble his head about the divinely appointed order in the churches of the saints: probably under the idea of confining the direction of his zeal to the maintenance of the uncorrupted gospel. This certainly is the only topic on which I should ever wish to insist against those who deny it: but in walking with those who confess it with me, if we thought it released us from solemn attention to all the revealed will of our heavenly Father, as delivered to his children in the apostolic writings, we should certainly be setting the revelation of the Lord's glorious name in opposition to the reverence and godly fear which it commands from all who know it: and those who do so, however clearly they may talk of the truth, are not walking in it. Those who confess Christ before men, must confess him with reverential subjection as the king of Zion, as well as with godliness of heart, as the great high priest who has taken away sin by the one offering of himself in the place of the ungodly. I fancy that John Barclay would have been quite willing to remain in connexion with the Kirk of Scotland to his dying day, if he had been allowed: probably his flesh caught at the corruption of *doctrine* in the Glasite societies, as a pretext for turning away his ear from their testimony for other points of the divine word; and probably the Glasites were hardened in their rejection of his testimony against their corruption of doctrine, by observing his open disregard for divine institutions. I have formerly read what John Barclay wrote on the assurance of faith, and in general with much pleasure; though I recollect thinking one or two passages ambiguously expressed, and suspecting that the Bereans have taken them in a sense different from what I believe the author intended. But I am much better acquainted with his work on the Psalms, and esteem it highly. As to the expression in the Glasites' prayer which you mention, and on which you desire my opinion, I have no hesitation in saying that I think it very bad, and indicative of a mind quite aside from the truth, under a fair shew of lowliness; but it corresponds with what I have often noticed in their prayers; that they seem to study to pray, *as if they did not think themselves believers;* as if they did not think themselves at present children, and possessed of eternal life in Christ Jesus; but hoping some time or other to become so. This is altogether opposite to the prayer of faith; opposite to the mind in which Christ taught his disciples to pray, saying, "our Father;" opposite to the persuasion that God is what his word declares him to be; for he that professedly calls upon God, and is at the same time *doubting* and questioning whether he is heard, and comes with acceptance before him, must at bottom be questioning whether the god, upon whom he calls, be the only living and true God, who has revealed himself as the justifier of the *ungodly*, through the redemption that is in Christ Jesus—the Saviour of *all* that call upon him. Those who use the phrase you mention, "if thou wilt thou canst make me clean," appear wholly to forget the declaration of our Lord Jesus to his disciples, "Now ye *are* clean through the word which I have spoken to you;" appear to avow their doubt whether his blood *has* taken away sin, whether it be true that he saves to the uttermost *all* who come to God by him. I think it very likely that many of them have no distinct idea annexed to the words which they use; but employ them as an unmeaning cant which they have been taught to think very modest and humble; but it is too probable that others, by the *cleansing* after which they groan, mean some change for the *better in their own* hearts, of which I am bold to say that the man who asks it, gravely asks God to falsify his word. The full Glasite system upon the assurance of hope, where it is fully imbibed, I consider utt r y inconsistent with all prayer, as well as with all *praise;* that blessed exercise to which the Gospel calls continually all those who are brought nigh to God by the blood of the covenant, and for which the man, who was to the last moment a blaspheming infidel, but is this moment convinced of the great things of God reported in his word, has all the same ground and warrant with an apostle I have met with one Glasite, a dear old man now dead, an Elder of the body in Liverpool, who, in prayer and conversation, seemed to have that peace of God in his conscience which the Gospel gives; yet he was evidently restrained by the trammels of the system, so as to be half afraid of speaking as if he had it: he used to admit me also to a freedom of conversation with him, which is very unusual in their connexion. I confess that I often *regret the repulsive stand-off* manner by which they commonly shut the door against free and patient discussion.

And now, my friend, opposite as the Berean confidence appears to be to the doubting system of the Glasite, I apprehend that the same principle is at bottom of both; while the evil is much more refinedly disguised in the former. The thorough Glasite prays doubtingly, because he is doubtful whether *he has faith.* The thorough Berean prays confidently, because he is confident *he has faith:* in each case is *not our faith* considered the warrant of our confidence? The Gospel calls the evil and the lost to draw nigh with boldness to the throne of grace, *because* the grand things which it reports from heaven are assuredly true; because Christ has once suffered for sin, the just for the unjust,—and has risen again from the dead—because God is such a God as he has revealed himself to be. The divine certainty of these things warrants the fullest confidence towards God in any sinner on earth: but I have to acknowledge my own evil heart continually working in opposition to the divine glory of God; and have nothing fine to say like the Bereans, about the high degree of believing confidence in which I actually walk: when it is strongest it is less than a grain of mustard-seed, in comparison of the *greatness* of the things of God which excite it; while I bless him that his real glory and truth so much over-pass the narrow limits of my faith.

You tell me that the Bereans with you object to the expression of my reply, "while kept standing in the truth, I can never," &c. (Vol i. p. 456.) I need no more information about them to mark to me their mind, high and lifted up with a presumptuous self-confidence altogether different from the hope of the Gospel. So then they would have me say absolutely, 'I never can have any difficulty in avowing that I believe, and that believing I have eternal life:' the professor, who would deliberately say so, I would consider as advancing a boast as vain as Peter before he fell: there is no depth of unbelief into which *I could* not, or should not plunge, if but left to my own heart. Yet this consideration cannot in the least disturb my rejoicing in the hope of the glory of God, while kept in memory (you see I again use that offensive *while*) of that salvation which belongeth to the Lord. I would observe to you that I have no wish for the concealment of any thing I write upon Scripture subjects, or indeed any thing I think, so far as I have formed a judgment upon them. I should be very glad that both the Bereans and the Glasites with you would give a patient reading to what I have written; you are surrounded by a great variety of professors; and your country is the most theological country I ever knew. Guard against your mind being occupied, and your attention being distracted from the simplicity of the word, by the various systems of men. Human theology, in its most shining form, is a thing essentially different from the light and understanding, which the entrance of the divine word giveth to the foolish, and such are we continually.

P.S. Some expressions in pages 24 and 25 of J. Barclay's Assurance of faith, I think very bad.

LXXXIV.

TO T. A——, ESQ.

Oct. 24, 1821.

My dear T——,—I dare say you will be surprised at getting a letter from me, but let me hope that you will not be displeased, even when you find it a letter of serious admonition and reproof. To the language of faithful reproof, we are all naturally averse. The pride of our vain and wicked heart rises up against it: and while we are striving to cover our evil ways, even from our own view, we regard any attempt of any other to expose the evil to us, as intrusive and offensive, though it is really the most important expression of true affection. There is solemn weight in that divine declaration, "the ear that heareth the reproof of life abideth among the wise;" but "he that refuseth instruction sinneth against his own soul." Prov. xv. 31, 32. But let me come at once to the immediate occasion of my writing.

You have, I dare say, heard of the rich mercy that appears to have been extended to ———. I say appears—because God alone knows whether that word of eternal life which he now confesses, does indeed dwell in him. Every appearance at present is most gratifying, and I trust will be progressively confirmed by the practical fruits in his conduct; though he must probably, throughout his life, smart under the temporal effects of his former wickedness. That is a small thing, if his spirit be saved in the day of the Lord Jesus. He mentioned to me, some days ago, his having met you several times before he left Dublin, in one of those gambling houses which he frequented—not (he admits) either playing yourself or betting. Being then in that mind which rejoices in iniquity, he states that he rejoiced to see you there—rejoiced in the idea of your having thrown off the trammels of the Christian profession; and it was with considerable surprise that he learned here, that you are still in outward fellowship with us. He observes truly, that though you did not at the time engage in the gambling which you witnessed, yet the almost inevitable consequence of your frequenting such scenes must be, that you will be drawn in to take an active part in them: and the temporal ruin of this I need not enlarge on. Indeed, it is far the least important part of the subject.

But, my dear T——, supposing you were never to be led on to that further step, is a notorious gambling house a suitable scene for a disciple of the Lord to frequent? As children of the light and of the day, we are called to "have no fellowship with the unfruitful works of darkness, but rather to reprove them." (Ephes. v. 11.) We are called "to let our light shine before men" to the glory of our heavenly Father (Mat. v. 16. 1 Pet. ii. 9.); and if we attempt to reconcile with this, our seeking amusement in the haunts of the grossest wickedness, avowedly appropriated to the prosecution of the works of darkness—and to reconcile the two under any pretence of exercising our Christian *liberty*, we are plainly turning the grace of

God into lasciviousness, and might, with equal plausibility, vindicate our seeking amusement in a brothel. But even the persuading you to abandon all such practices would fall quite short of my real aim in writing. That is, to direct your attention to the root of the evil—to the character of the unbelieving fleshly mind, after which we must be walking, when we walk in such a course. We must then have lost sight of the great things of God testified in the word from heaven. We must have fallen into a lifeless formal profession of the faith, in which we cease to be persuaded of the divine realities of the kingdom of heaven, though a remaining suspicion that they may turn out true, perhaps prevents our expressly renouncing the faith. But are we not then living to ourselves, and not unto Him whose we profess to be? Are we not then really walking after the flesh, after the imaginations of our own evil hearts, and not in the truth? Are we not deceiving ourselves with a name that we live, while we are dead? "For if we say that we have fellowship with the Father and with his Son Jesus Christ, while we walk in darkness, we lie and do not the truth." 1 John i. 6. Is it not a fact, T——, that your intimate associates and pretended friends are young men of notorious profligacy of manners? And how can we fairly account for your complacency in them and their complacency in you? If, in your intercourse with them, you were acting and speaking as a disciple and witness of the Lord, they would soon be sick of your society. But is it not the fact, that in the idle vanity of imitating their licentious dissipation, you would be ashamed boldly to confess the Lord Jesus before them? And it is a solemn word which he has pronounced against those who are ashamed to confess his name before men. Well—I do not conceal from you that I think your state is a very awful one,—marked with the characters of an evil heart of *unbelief* in departing from the living God. Yet I view it with a hope derived from the nature of his glorious gospel, that he will open your ear to the reproof of his word—to the instruction of that divine wisdom, of which it is pronounced, "happy is the man that findeth her." Prov. iii. 13. O that you may hear "the voice *behind* you"—the voice of Him on whom you have turned your back—wooing you, in the accents of sovereign mercy, to turn to Him and live. His presence surrounds you while you read these lines. His faithful word testifies the rich mercy that is with him, the great salvation that belongeth to him—"Incline your ear and come unto Him; hear and your soul shall live." Is. lv. 3. Read the whole of that chapter, and read it as the voice of Him that speaketh from heaven, in connexion with the apostolic testimony of him "whom man despiseth," but who is set for the salvation of God unto the ends of the earth;—once made a curse in the place of transgressors, that sinners, even the chief, may be blessed in Him and brought to eternal glory by Him. Brought back to the remembrance of His glorious truth, you will feel the force of that language—"Ye are not your own, for ye are bought with a price: therefore glorify God in your body and in your spirit, which are God's." I shall wait in anxious expectation of hearing from you, and in the hope that your reply will afford me joy and not grief.

LXXXV.

TO MRS. M———.

——— 1821.

Dear Mrs. M.—I feel myself, on various accounts, at a loss in attempting to reply to your inquiry. You know that I do not think you, in your present mind, competent to judge upon that subject; and how far any of the parties are, about whom you are interested on the occasion, I am ignorant. However, I can have no objection to express my own views on the general question: and if any one should desire further communication with me in explanation of them, I believe you know that I am easily accessible.

Persuaded as I am that the Scriptures afford a rule sufficiently directive and divinely authoritative for the regulation of Christ's disciples, both in their individual and collective capacity—a rule which never has been annulled, and never can to the end of the world; I consider the precept in 1 Cor. v. 11. as binding on me now, as it was on the Corinthian believers when Paul sent them his letter. But this view binds me to consider the real meaning of the apostolic direction from the context, and from the whole analogy of Scripture; and thus I am led to view the precept as restricting the civil intercourse of disciples—not with those of the world, who have never walked with them in the fellowship of a Christian church—in which alone disciples can walk together scripturally—but with those who have appeared of that household of faith, but have been removed from it, according to the scriptural discipline by which its purity is to be maintained; and I consider the civil intercourse with such, which is prohibited, as that, which indicating complacency in them, would convey—on the side of the disciples who should indulge in it—that their minds had ceased to be impressed with an awful sense of the evil, which had occasioned the separation of the offending brother from their fellowship, and would thus be injuriously calculated to weaken the solemn testimony of the body against it in his view. With respect to the Antichristian world around me, with whom I have never walked in the scriptural fellowship of the gospel, I do not think that this Apostolic precept bears at all on my social intercourse with them. But even in the case where it does apply, and where I and my brethren aim at observing it, I have another remark to make. From the whole analogy of Scripture I am sure that neither it, nor any precept rightly understood, will be found to trench upon any of those duties, which are connected with the various relations of life. I am, therefore, persuaded that the precept would be misunderstood, if a disciple took it in all cases *literally*. A husband and wife—a parent and child—a master and his apprentice, may be so circumstanced, that the wife, the child, or the apprentice, shall be called to be regulated by that precept, in their deportment towards the husband, the father, or the master.

Now, I conceive they would greatly mistake, if they thought themselves actually forbid to sit at the same table and eat with those, towards whom they stand in such an intimate relation, the duties of which may require that they should do so. And, although those who wish to set aside all the peculiar precepts of the divine word, may think that, in saying this, I concede a case in which one of them cannot be obeyed, it is really no such thing. Such a case is as supposable when the apostle wrote, as at this day; and only proves that the thing really forbidden, is that *voluntary needless* intercourse which is sought for the purpose of *mutual satisfaction*, and indicative of mutual complacency. I should not, therefore, consider myself debarred at all by the precept, from remaining at the table of one of the world who had bid me to a feast, though I found seated at it a person who had been removed from the fellowship of the church, and whom I, therefore, could not ask as a guest to my own; and though I should literally eat with him in such a case, yet, if I bear in mind the divine direction in its real import, it will importantly regulate my deportment and demeanour towards him, though certainly not so as to produce moroseness or incivility. He knows that I have not sought his society, and nothing in my manner should lead him to think that I *enjoy* it. When I have marked voluntary *needless* intercourse even in civil life, as the thing forbidden in that passage, I mean to include all that intercourse which does not arise from, and is not connected with, the duties of the various relations in which the providence of God places disciples; and among these duties there is, I think, a degree of kind correspondence and occasional intercourse with those, with whom I stand in other very close fleshly relations besides the few I have mentioned. I have two sisters, for instance, who once stood in Christian fellowship with me, but have long ceased to do so, from their turning aside to the religions of the world. Our intercourse is in consequence very little, very *dry*, and unsatisfactory: yet I occasionally write to them; and were I in their neighbourhood, would think myself called to see them; or if they came to London I should have them, if they needed the accomodation, at my house: and yet I might all the time be regulated by that divine precept, which I am sure was not designed to interfere with the natural kindness due to such near relations according to the flesh. As to the precept in 2 John 10, I think it simply forbids disciples to extend that *hospitality* to *teachers* of another doctrine, which would indicate a desire to forward the objects they have in view. Disciples were called to be helpful to those who were indeed engaged in the ministration of the word of Christ; and, as in other ways, so in receiving them into their houses, and affording them such accommodations of lodging and of food as they might need. But this help they are forbidden to afford to any one who taught differently from the apostles, lest they should even appear to countenance "his evil deeds." I conceive that I might occasionally have at my table, in the way of courteous neighbourly intercourse, one of the clergy or preachers of the religious world, who are teaching (I am sure) in direct opposition to the word of the apostles, and yet without at all violating that precept in John: because it would not even appear to be done for abetting his evil deeds. Yet I own that in proportion as I observe any of them calculated to deceive, by an approximation of language and profession to the truth, I am disposed, and feel myself called in general, to avoid them.

LXXXVI.

TO ———.

———, 1821.

You ask my opinion on the letter which you gave me to read, and the character of the writer. The general complexion of the letter is indeed bitter bad, for it seems to be an attempt to encourage some one, who spoke the language of unbelief, to entertain some favourable opinion about his state and character. Any attempt so to encourage any one (believer or unbeliever) is contrary to the truth—as much so as the state of mind that needs such ungodly encouragement, that wants to see something favourable about them, in order to come to God with confidence. It is true, that the encouragement afforded in many passages of the letter, would appear to be derived from the consideration of the revealed truth of God—the mercy that is with him. But how inconsistent with that is the idea of *encouraging* a fellow sinner, to whom the divine testimony is sent, to believe what God reveals. The apostles, in setting forth Jesus Christ as the propitiation, warned men indeed of the awful consequences of disbelieving the record which God hath given of his Son; but when did they set about *encouraging*, and coaxing, and entreating, and charging them "to receive into their hearts the joyful tidings" —or, in plain language, to believe it? The idea is more suitable to those who mean, by believing, some venturesome act (as they call it) of the mind: which is nothing more or less than a presumptuous venture to believe that they are believers. Its inconsistency with the scriptural simple meaning of faith will be manifest, if we apply it to a human testimony, from the reception of which the apostle illustrates the reception of the divine. 1 John v. 9. "Ah! do believe what I have told you." What nonsense in the affairs of men! What wicked nonsense when applied to the things of God! But one encouragement plainly suggested in the letter, is plainly contrary to the truth—'Has he not given you to *wish* to be delivered from it?' That is thorough language of the insidious teachers of a gospel that is not the gospel of Christ—daubing the wall with untempered mortar. Whether the person addressed was encouraged by the supposed discovery of that *wish* in his heart, or continued mourning at not being able to find it, the person addressed was alike in either case astray from the hope of the gospel, and the encouragement which it affords and conveys to any ungodly sinner who believes it. The writer of the letter would seem then to have no gospel, no glad tidings, nothing joyfully encouraging to lay before a man absolutely so wicked, as to have no wish that is not opposed to the truth of God. Yet to such the apostles published their gospel, and all, that believed what they told, rejoiced. Their gospel to be sure is only fit for such. When I am asked my opinion of the state or character of the writer of the letter, I suppose I am asked whether I think him a believer or not. Reading some parts alone (such as the parenthesis in the second page) I should hope that he may: reading others alone I should conclude that he is not. And reading the whole, I can only say, that if he does not receive the reproof of the Word, when the wickedness of the general tenor of the letter is pointed out to him, and reject with abhorrence the sentiments in it that oppose the truth, I must conclude him a stranger to the faith and hope of the gospel. But I must add, that this part of the question proposed to me, seems to originate from a mind that looks more at the characters and reputation of men to determine what is truth, than at the word of God. With persons of this mind, corrupting the word of God is a venial error, but invading the character of a man is an unpardonable sin.

LXXXVII.

TO MR. J. C. G——.

Oct. 14, 1821.

Sir,—You were not mistaken in supposing that I would receive with readiness any such communication as you have favoured me with. Few things would gratify me more than that those who differ from me at present most widely, should yet afford an opportunity of amicably discussing our differences; and I often regret that this is so generally denied me. But before I reply to the immediate subject of your letter, allow me to observe upon it in general, that although I hold the question of oaths to be one of very great importance to disciples, (as I consider every thing relative to the revealed will of their God and Saviour) yet I by no means consider it of *primary* importance. In that rank I hold but one thing —the faith and hope of the gospel: and till there appears agreement in that, I have no desire to labour for agreement on any points relative to the conduct of disciples.

I am not sure that I quite understand what you mean to put forward against my views of the unlawfulness of all oaths to a Christian; and certainly I do not understand at all the sense you affix to the precept "Swear not at all." You say that I hold my own views "*in opposition to all explanation.*" Now I confess that I have never found proposed any explanation of the passage, opposite to its obvious meaning, which would stand a moment's critical or rational examination. You ask me, "is not such a most solemn affirmation as I admit to be lawful, something more than the *literal* yea, or the *literal* nay prescribed by our Lord as the limits of our communications?" Now I never intended to convey that the Lord confined his disciples to any particular form of words in expressing their affirmation: but I conceive that he confines them to affirmation, and that the simplicity of mere affirmation is not at all affected by its solemnity. The *simplicity* of mere affirmation I consider as standing opposed to the pledging of ourselves, under any forfeiture, to the truth of what we declare, or to the certainty of what we promise. It is the latter, indeed, against which the Lord's prohibition is immediately pointed. I by no means say that the precept points particularly to *judicial* oaths; but I say that it points to oaths in general—oaths properly so called—in which men "bind their souls with a bond" that they will do so or so; (see No. xxx.) and I say that every oath administered in this country, even to the swearing of a common affidavit, is such: and I candidly own to you that this —while it seems to me clearly the very thing against which the Lord's precept is pointed, is a thing so inconsistent with all the principles of revealed truth, that I now dare not do it, if there were no such express prohibition of it as I see. When you speak of the *literal* precept as violated by a *judicial* affirmation, as much as by a *judicial oath*, I suppose you must refer to the *solemnity* of the affirmation. But if you refer to this as constituting a violation of the precept, it is plain that the *judicial* occasion of it has nothing to do with your position; and how you then *reconcile* the solemnity of some of Paul's affirmations with the precepts of his Lord, I am quite at a loss to conjecture. But it is very possible that, from a misconception of your meaning, I may be fighting in the dark; and I am persuaded that an hour's conversation would go farther towards producing a mutual understanding, on this and other points, than ten hour's writing. Have you any objection to afford me such an opportunity? * * * * * *

LXXXVIII.

TO THE SAME.

Nov. 6, 1821.

Dear Sir,—My answer to your last has been delayed longer than I could wish, by bad health and much occupation with business. Let me indulge the hope, as long as nothing appears to forbid it, that you are not mistaken in supposing we are essentially agreed on the faith and hope of the gospel. On that I would only say at present, that there *can* be *no* disagreement there, that is not an *essential* disagreement. But on the immediate subject of our correspondence, we certainly do not as yet understand each other. In such cases I commonly find it advantageous to mark distinctly *how far I agree* with the person, with whom I am engaged in discussion, that it may appear more distinctly where our disagreement lies. I therefore say, that I quite agree with you, that it is to the *real meaning* of the passage we are to attend, and not to the mere sound of the *words;* and that, in considering the real meaning of this passage, we must fairly take into account both the *preamble*, by which the prohibition is introduced, and the *reasons* by which it is enforced.

Again, I quite agree with you that the preamble refers to Num. xxx. 2. and gives us not *partially*—but *wholly*—the subject matter on which the Lord intended to comment.

Again, I quite agree with you, both that it may proceed from *evil* if we employ any peculiar *solemnity* of affirmation on an unsuitable occasion, and that it may in other instances not proceed at all from evil, to make the *most solemn appeal to the Searcher of hearts for the truth of what we say:* and I would add, that I hold this to be so, not merely in a case of *life* or *property*, nor merely when we are *judicially* or *publicly* called on to do so—(the cases to which you seem to confine the lawfulness of the thing)—but in other cases also; such, for instance, as those in which we find an apostle thus solemnly confirming the truth of what he declares.

And, lastly, I quite agree with you, that no abuse by others of a thing intrinsically lawful can impeach the legitimate use of it by us.

But now I could wish that you had not broken off so abruptly towards the close of your letter, when you say that the Lord's "own *reasoning* comes decisively to our aid in judging of his intentions, and clearly leads to the real object of his animadversions and legislation." I could wish that you had proceeded to mark distinctly what that *real* object in your view is, so as to distinguish between it and all that is now strictly and properly called an *oath*. As well as I can collect your meaning, however, it is this—that the Lord forbids to his disciples all VOLUNTARY *solemnity* of confirmation when they declare any thing as true, beyond a simple assertion that the thing is or is not so or so: and I think you use the word VOLUNTARY here, in opposition to those occasions on which a magistrate or judge requires such solemnity of confirmation at our hands. Now if I be right in my conjecture that this is your meaning, I can confidently undertake to prove that you are mistaken. In the first place, let me remark, that in an important sense—no act of mine is the less *voluntary* for being done at the requisition of a magistrate. Suppose Nero commanded me on pain of death to go and burn incense on the altar of Jupiter. If I do so, I do it *voluntarily*. I have the alternative—the choice proposed to me—to do so or to suffer death; and I chuse the former. If I be dragged indeed by force to the altar, my being there is no act of mine, and nothing voluntary. But even then, if I take the incense in my hand and put it on the fire, this is my *voluntary* act. However, if you chuse to use the word *voluntary* merely as opposed to what is done at the command of a magistrate, I shall not contest your right to do so, though I think it a misapplication of the term. But then I know not how you can reconcile with your interpretation, the solemnity of Paul's declaration, made neither *publicly* nor at the requisition of any magistrate.

But in the next place I would observe, that your interpretation is utterly at variance with that *preamble*, which you justly refer to as marking the general theme of the Lord's discourse. From that we find indisputably it relates, not to any solemnity of *declaration* of what is *true*—not to any asseveration of a *fact* that *has* taken place, —but to *engagements* under which men bind themselves with respect to their *future* conduct. This, I think, cannot be controverted, whether we look merely at the Lord's words in the 33d verse, or at Numb. xxx. to which his words plainly refer. I would observe, also, that I think you mistaken as to what you call the Lord's *reasoning* in the passage. He has condescended to enforce his precept by assigning *reasons*; but those reasons do not lie in the words to which you refer. (v. 37.) These words are but an authoritative declaration of the evil from which every departure from his precept originates. The *reasons* are given in the three preceding verses—namely, that none of the things are our *own*, under the forfeiture of which we would pledge ourselves to act so or so, and that over the *least* of them we have no power. Now, my dear sir, if this reasoning be admitted to have any force, it applies as forcibly to such an engagement made at the requisition of a *magistrate* as to one made ever so *voluntarily*: it concludes the intrinsic unlawfulness of *all* such engagements, by which we would *bind our souls* with respect to our future conduct: and no earthly magistrate can convert into lawful what is *intrinsically unlawful*. I have been assured by one who long served in high rank in the East Indies, that it to this day is no uncommon mode of judicial swearing among the natives there, to swear by the head of a near relation, a wife or child, (the juror placing his hand upon the head of the person) and that the meaning is well understood to be the staking of the life of that person, as devoted to fall a victim to the anger of the gods in case the juror fail of what he engages. Well, *suppose a magistrate* called on me to pledge in this way, swearing *by my own head*. Would the reason which the Lord assigns against the thing cease to apply, because a magistrate commanded it?

The only remaining question to a disciple *ought* to be—Are the oaths taken in this country engagements of such a nature as the thing prohibited? (For I readily allow that the mere *name* of *oath* should not decide the matter.) I say—yes—every one of them. Every one of them is an *engagement* binding the juror's soul as to his future conduct under the most *awful of all pledges*, over which he has no power; while he presumes to stake it, and expresses his desire to *forfeit* if he fail of fulfilling what he engages to do. I will do so and so; and may God *so* help me as I shall fulfil my engagement. As a Christian, I acknowledge the Christian duty which I always owed to the king and the constituted authorities of the state. But could I, as a Christian, pledge myself under the forfeiture of the divine favour, that I *will* discharge that duty the next hour? or that I *will not* commit murder to-morrow? I believe I need not trouble myself to prove to you, that the oath of *testimony* in those countries, and even the swearing of an affidavit is as much a *promissory* oath as the oath of allegiance; and you are well aware what is the course of examination of a child, to ascertain whether it understands the nature of an oath—and what is the only reply that is looked for to the question—'And what do you think will be the consequence if you should not tell the truth after swearing to tell it?' 'I shall go to hell.' Yes—the poor Japanese, when he dashes the china plate to the ground in his form of swearing, probably contemplates only a similar destruction to his body, which he prays to light on him if he should swear falsely. The so-called Christians have just learned from the scriptures to sport with a more tremendous stake. But the disciple of Christ, who remembers that "a man's goings are not from himself," will shrink from pledging himself absolutely as to any thing in his future conduct: much less will he desire that the salvation of his soul may be taken off from that ground on which the scriptures rest it—("not of him that willeth or of him that runneth, but of God that sheweth mercy")—and made to rest on his own adherence to the engagements which he forms.

Let me add a brief word on the two passages to which you refer—Exod. xxii. 11. Numb. v. 19, 22. They are dissimilar from each other, but both alike essentially different from all engagements with respect to future conduct. In the former, there is mentioned "an oath of the Lord that *he had not* put his hand unto his neighbour's goods;" and here I have no reason to think that any thing more is intended *than a solemn appeal to the* Lord—or declaration of the fact as before the Lord—to which on a suitable occasion I make no objection. In the latter passage, decisively "an oath of cursing" was enjoined in the case. But let it be remembered, that it was enjoined by *divine* authority, and connected with the *miraculous* effect assigned to the bitter water of jealousy, and that it also related to an antecedent fact, the truth of which the God of Israel saw fit to decide by his own interposition. Now had it pleased the Lord to command his disciples, under the new dispensation, to appeal to him in any similar way to decide a controverted fact, I say that in such an appointment there would not have been a tittle of inconsistency with the prohibition in Mat. v. 34, which we are discussing: yet I acknowledge that, without such a divine appointment, it would be most evil and presumptuous to appeal to him for any such miraculous interference. I remain, sir, with best wishes,

Yours faithfully,

LXXXIX.

TO HIS BROTHER, JAMES WALKER.

—— 1821.

My dear James, * * * * * *—You say that *if* my ideas of religion lead me to believe that primitive Christianity may be again revived, yours is the very country (Tennessee, U. S.) where I may be useful. Yes, my dear James, I believe, and am sure, that primitive Christianity shall be again revived; nay, I witness its revival, though in a very small and despised way. The ground on which I express myself with so much confidence, is that word of the Lord "which abideth for ever." He has said that he will consume the man of sin with the spirit of his mouth, 2 Thess. ii. 8; and "is any thing too hard for me, saith the Lord?" Every departure from primitive Christianity, either in doctrine or in practice, is the work of the man of sin—the effect of human ungodliness corrupting and setting aside the word of God; and by that word, as "the sword of his spirit"—"the sword which proceedeth out of his mouth," he is bringing back the flock of his pasture to the good old paths from which they have been turned. It is one of the signs of the times, an indication of the approaching appearance of the Lord from heaven. There are many adversaries: but he laugheth them to scorn, and his is the kingdom, the power, and the glory. All of *man's* that has been displayed on earth since the entrance of sin into the world, has been one exhibition of ungodliness, and of besotted blindness—of rebellion, stubbornness, and ingratitude: but on that dark ground the mercy and the power of God are exhibited, accomplishing that work of saving whom he will, which is his own exclusively, and in which he displays all his glory. I should be very glad to send you some of my publications on the subject, and I hope yet to find an opportunity of doing so. I think I will enclose in this letter a smaller tract—very short—but simply putting forward that fundamental divine truth, of which it is declared, "whosoever believeth shall be saved." All return to primitive Christianity must commence there. As long as men disbelieve the truth of God, and are left to strong delusions that they should believe any of the lies which pass under the name of Gospel, but are not the Gospel—all their religion is vain, and all their very sacrifices abomination to the Lord. And such *false religion* is one of the main instruments in the hands of the man of sin for leading his captives to destruction. In the revealed truth of God there is one thing alone excellent and glorious discovered, the glory of the Lord—as just, and yet the justifier of the ungodly—the just God, and yet the Saviour of sinners, even the chief, through the redemption that is in Christ Jesus. He appeared once in the end, or last age of the world, to put away sin by the sacrifice of himself, Heb. ix. 26. He has *finished* that work; it is done; and the divine acceptance of that, his one offering for sin, has been proved by his resurrection from the dead. The Gospel is sent preaching or proclaiming to the rebellious peace by Jesus Christ—peace made by the blood of his cross, who bore the sins of many, and was made a curse for them, that men might be blessed in him. The same divine word brings nigh this righteousness and salvation of God, to every one *alike* to whom it comes in the declaration, not that whoso doeth this or getteth that to forward himself to it—but that whoso believeth the testimony of God shall be saved—not put into a salvable state (as many profanely talk) in which he may save himself *if* he bestir himself sufficiently in the work—but *shall be saved* unto the uttermost by him, who is the captain of salvation appointed to bring many sons unto glory. The belief of this of old gladdened the heart, enlightened the eyes, and made wise unto salvation even the betrayers and murderers of the Lord of glory. They were then taught by the apostles how they ought to walk and to please God, as children of the light and of the day, as heirs of the kingdom. And those apostolic instructions are still given in the New Testament Scriptures, and in the record of the way in which the first churches walked in the fellowship of the Gospel. "He that hath ears to hear, let him hear." * * * * It is now many years since I have renounced with abhorrence the title of *Reverend*, and the whole of the clerical character connected with it. That character, under whatever name or modification, is one of the ungodly fictions of the man of sin, and one of the main pillars of Antichrist's kingdom.

XC.

TO DR. F.

Dec. 8*th*, 1821.

MY VERY DEAR DR.——.—Though I should in general be glad to take up my pen to you at any time, yet I own that on the present occasion there are considerations which would make me very averse to it, if I dare yield to them. But as I see that I ought to encounter the task, let me set about it cheerfully; in the hope that it will end in the profitable correction of error, on which ever side that error exists at present. Poor B—— has naturally and necessarily transmitted to our brother C—— your two letters, with a copy of his reply to your first. You will, in the first instance, be confirmed in your apprehension that our minds "need some regulation on the subject," and that we "have still to learn what the scriptures teach about church-bounty," when I tell you honestly that I dislike your letters very much; that I think they are very like giving a brother a stone when he asks for bread; and seem to me to assert principles with great confidence as scriptural, which—from their plain opposition to the spirit of brotherly kindness—I am persuaded the Word does not sanction. Observe, that however I may have occasion to advert to B——'s case for the purpose of illustration, I write not to press that case upon your attention, but to sift the general principles of the Word. You say that his case "is not such as *can scripturally* be met with the bounty of the church:"—that "the objects of church-bounty are such as may be said to be *past labour* and desolate;"—referring for the proof of this to 1 Tim. v. 4, 5, 9, 16. Now, if this language (in the connexion in which it stands) have any meaning, it must mean that this passage marks the *limit*, beyond which church-bounty *cannot scripturally* extend. And I conceive that you might as reasonably adduce the same scripture to prove, that no poor saints but *widows* are to have their necessities supplied by the church, and no widows but those who are at least sixty years old. As to the 9th verse, if you can point out to me its precise meaning, I shall be glad; for I confess myself doubtful about it: but I am quite *sure* that it does *not* mean what you seem to adduce it to prove. As to the 4th and 16th verses, if you can shew that B—— has any near relatives, who are able to relieve his wants and are believers, *their* attention ought to be directed to the plain instruction there given. There remains only the 5th verse, which I believe you will scarcely say has any thing to do with the question: and I am utterly at a loss to conjecture what part of the entire passage you mean to say proves that B——'s case "*cannot scripturally* be met with the bounty of the church." As to *desolate*, if you had taken any trouble to inquire, you would have found that he has long been so desolate, that but for the bounty of an individual brother he might have *starved* in a gaol. And it does seem to me extraordinary to assert, that what any *individual may* scripturally do in such a case, a number of the brethren, or the whole body, *cannot scripturally* assist in doing. What mystic charm is this you have discovered in the word church? Besides that passage in Timothy, you refer in proof of your assertion to Rom. xii. 13. Now, in the whole of the latter passage, from the 9th verse, it does appear to me that the apostle treats of the conduct and tempers of *individual* believers one towards another, rather than of any thing to which he calls the church in its *collective* capacity as a body. And if I judge rightly in that, and you judge rightly in thinking that the 13th verse amounts to a *prohibition*, on those addressed in it, to supply B——'s wants, it must exclude him from the bounty of any *individual* brother, at least as much as from *church-bounty*. I confess I think you had not any right to rebuke poor B—— so sharply for not yielding to the *force* of what you put forward as scripture principles. But I am sure you had every right to rebuke him sharply for his worse than foolish language about brother C—— and myself; and also to expose the unsuitableness of his applying to any church for a *loan*. But observe, my dear F——, (I think it not unimportant to note it, in order to call your attention to the kind of mind in which you wrote)—observe that you quoted Rom. xii. 13. as excluding his case from the bounty of the church, *before* you had got any of that proof against him, which you *think* his reply affords, that it was not for *necessities* he sought relief, but that it was in "a worldly speculation" he desired the church to aid him. You *think* his reply affords you proof of this; but it is because you misunderstand it: and your mistake might easily have been prevented or rectified by a communication with P——. For bread to eat and raiment to put on (which I think are *necessaries*) he *must* have continued dependent on the bounty of his brethren. I am ashamed of the special-pleading question which you put—"are your *pupils* saints?"—as if he thought of *their* being supported by the bounty of the church. He does undoubtedly "hope to make gain of them;"—if that be sufficient to put down his object as a "worldly speculation." And so would a shoe-maker hope to *make gain* of the leather which he bought. And therefore, I suppose, a christian of that trade, but so poor that he could not buy leather, could not *scripturally* apply to the church to aid him in the purchase; nor *could* his case scripturally be met with the church-bounty. If he did apply, it would certainly be very fair and right for the deacons to exercise a sound discretion in judging, whether it would not be better for him to seek journey-work: but I can easily conceive the circumstances to be such, that he *could not* get any journey-work, from not having served a regular apprenticeship, or various other causes: and to say that it would then be unscriptural to apply to his brethren, either individually or collectively, to enable him to get the materials by which he has a prospect of earning his own bread;—to say that the scriptures "*prescribe limits* of church-bounty," out of which he lies, because he is not *past his labour*, or because he aims at *making a gain* of the materials, &c., does appear to me, I confess, a gross abuse and perversion of scripture. When I read in scripture of a christian church, that none among them *lacked*;—when I hear an apostle saying, "bear ye one another's burdens and so fulfill the law of Christ;"—and presenting to the attention of disciples on the subject, that principle of the word—"he that gathered much had nothing over, and he that gathered little had no lack;"—I ought to be very jealous of your language, as indeed a *worldly speculation*, when you talk about the *limits* of church-bounty *prescribed* by scripture. I know no limits, but the ability and willingness of the church on the one hand, and the real good of the brother to be aided on the other. 'But if the church were to aid B—— in carrying into effect his worldly speculation—for earning his bread,—they would be employed in raising bounty, to put one member much above most of the others.' Well;. I shall allow some force to that argument when you shew, either that B—— is aspiring to any situation above that "wherein he was called;"—or that he *can* earn his bread in *any other* situation. I am intimately acquainted with him and with his affairs; and I confess I know not any way in which he could set about earning his bread different from the present,—or on a more moderate scale,—or with any thing like so fair a prospect of successful exertion. I am sure you could not expect a man near seventy years old, who has never worked as a day-labourer, to earn his bread by digging. And yet he might be immediately connected with a church, in which every other member was a day-labourer. If *they* affected to become farmers and to live in slated houses, it might immediately appear that they were forgetting that truly important word, which calls us "not to mind high things but *conform* to low:" while *he* might be perfectly warranted by scripture in seeking means for doing so, as the only way in which he could make the legitimate effort to *eat his own bread*. But why is he—not only to be refused the aid he sought, but made an *offender* for seeking it? If he meant by *calling on* the church in Dublin, or by having a *claim* on them, any such claim as it was *compulsory* on them to answer,—(but I am sure he did not)—he meant very wrong indeed. Christian bounty, I conceive, is in *all* cases a matter of bounty and not of *necessity*. The only compulsion in it is the constraining influence of the love of

Christ; the only necessity, that which the law of love binds upon the conscience. And here also I believe we differ. You seem to conceive that a church, however abounding in means, is not to be applied to for the relief of necessitous brethren, unless in some extreme cases which you contemplate, and in which you think the applicant is warranted to say in effect "you *must* supply me, or I will bring you under discipline." Every part of the idea I protest against, as contrary to the real scriptural nature of christian bounty. If a man in any case be warranted so to apply to me, he would apply to me not for *bounty*, but for his due *right*. I believe that you have lately had one error on the subject corrected in your mind: but think well, my dear F——, whether you have not been running right a-head into another. That is the way of us all. It is very strong language you use, that the nature of B——'s application "would only need to be known" by the church in Dublin "to be *resisted*, if *the scriptures were attended* to." And has it really come to that with the church in Dublin? I can only say, that—if it be so—however proud they may be of some supposed *knowledge* of scripture principles,—I fear it is a knowledge which puffeth up, and not the love which edifieth. Now, do not suppose that I have any quarrel with you for declining to lay B——'s application before the church; or with the Dublin brethren for declining to take any share in the burden of relieving him, with the individual on whom it has lain so long. No: I dare not call you or them to account for the free exercise of your judgment in the matter. But to say in effect, that attention to the scriptures must *bind* the Dublin brethren to *resist* the application, does indeed appear to me awful. Certainly the new scheme that you have discovered, seems well calculated for saving the pockets (and hardening the hearts) of the Irish brethren; as well as for draining the pocket of the only one here, who can exercise christian bountifulness.

Though my letter is enormously long, I have much that I could wish to add on the subject. But if the Lord bless what I have written, it will prove sufficient for bringing us to one mind on *principles*; and believe me always, in the love of the truth,

Your attached brother,

XCI.

TO J. L———.

—— 1822.

The opposite objections to your doctrine from the Baptists and Bereans, are—just as it should be. That there is some lie (though hard to be detected) in the Gospel of the latter, I have no doubt;

if it were only from their general indifference about the laws of the heavenly kingdom: and I fancy that it is, with many of them, nothing but the old appropriating system of a private revelation, &c. dressed up in a more specious garb. But I can easily suppose that there are disciples among them: and in that, and other views, I am very glad to learn that you are likely to have more communication with them. While any are willing to communicate with us patiently, we ought to be forward to meet them. I need scarcely say, that there is a mode of using the word IF—in our professing the hope of the Gospel, which believers of the truth might well object to. The sinner, standing in the faith and hope of the Gospel, has the hope of *eternal life*, without any IF: but that hope is derived from the character, which he knows belongs to the only true God, not from the reflex consideration that he has this knowledge or discernment. In the fondness of the Bereans of speaking about their own hope without an IF, I consider them as speaking very confidently—not about the revealed truth of God—but about their being believers of it: and the more boastfully they speak upon that subject, the more I am disposed to question their pretensions.

We meet but the once, like you. It is plainly the only meeting of divine authority; and to multiply religious meetings, while it makes a fair shew in the flesh, would be very like impeaching the wisdom of the divine appointment.

In your letter of Dec. 14th, you mention a woman who had drawn back after fair appearances. It is less marvellous when any draw back, than when any come forward, and hold on cleaving to Him who is despised and rejected by men. The latter is the wonderful work of God. The former is but the natural developement of what is in man. Who would not wonder more at seeing a piece of iron rise from the bottom of the water and swim, than at seeing it remain at the bottom or sink?

It will be matter of great joy if Mr. ———'s partner in life be subdued by the truth: and I do not wonder at all at her brother's indignation being excited by any appearances tending that way. The religion of Jesus is a very sorry thing for a *lady* or *gentleman* to be brought down to. But what a change they must think (if they thought at all) has taken place in the world since the days, when Christ spoke of people being *ashamed* to confess him before men, &c. The thing put forward on all sides as Christianity now, is a thing which even the Deists are generally ashamed of not confessing. And, indeed, as it turns in its most refined forms, upon that which is most highly esteemed among men—human goodness attained to in a supernatural way—it would be surprising if the world were not rather proud of professing it. But the friend of publicans and sinners—the Saviour of the lost—God just and justifying the ungodly—is, and must be, a stone of stumbling and rock of offence to the end of the world, unto all but those of the king's enemies, in whose hearts he makes his arrows sharp to subdue them to his word—and this because he hath mercy upon whom he will have mercy. I was very glad to get even the names of our dear brethren with you. I trust our sister T—— will be brought *well* through the trial of her faith which you speak of. It is a *little trial*: but the least would be sufficient for our flesh to stumble at. If she be kept mindful of the *ground* on which she and our brother come together on the first day of the week—mindful of the great things of God which they shew forth in it—the death and rising again of the Lord Jesus;—she will think little of the contempt of the world for their meeting. Our flesh turns into a snare the observers of our assembly, whenever our thoughts are occupied about them. May you all be kept with that as the motto of your union—*Thy God thy glory!* He ALL our glory! He our sufficient glory in the deepest circumstances of trial and abasement. What garbage are our vain hearts ready at all times to feed upon. Handful as we are, we would be for glorying in our numbers or our greatness. And so some of you have got it in your heads that I am a *great man*—you ought not to have told me so; for I should be ready enough to believe that there must be *some* ground for the imagination. But this I can tell you, that I know an effectual recipe for making a little and contemptible man even of the greatest: and any among you, that have had any respectability in the world to lose, are in the high road to get rid of it.

What blessed *levelling* that is which James speaks of, i. 9, 10: and what he applies immediately to the rich and the poor, is equally applicable to the learned and unlearned, the wise and the foolish.

XCII.

TO J. H——, ESQ.

March, 1822.

VERY DEAR SIR,—I again find myself a shameful defaulter in my correspondence with you, and have need of all your kind indulgence to forgive me: I received in due course your favour of May 20th, 1820, a short note from yourself, but inclosing copies of three long letters, two of them apparently addressed to you, and one to Mr. I. M——. In your note you tell me that you were then copying a letter which I should receive very soon; but no communication from you has reached me since: I heartily hope your letter has not miscarried: the expectation of its arrival prevented me from taking up my pen immediately. I was also, for the latter six months of 1820, very much unsettled, by going over to Ireland, with my family on a visit; and since my return here I was attacked early last spring with an illness, which almost incapacitated me for all business; and for some time appeared likely to terminate my earthly course: for the last four or five months it has pleased God to restore my health to a wonderful degree, but I have been so busily employed in preparing a classical work, which I have now sent to press, that I got into arrear with all my correspondents, and you are one of the first of them I now sit down to address.

The kind patience and labour which you and your friends bestow on me, call for my hearty acknowledgments; and I can truly say, that I feel an affectionate interest in you all, though mixed with much pain that there should remain any difference between us, to prevent our full union in the fellowship of the gospel; but is any thing too hard for me, saith the Lord? He is the God that doeth wonders, and it is his work to make brethren dwell together in unity.

The oftener I read over Mr. C——'s letter to you of Sept. 27th, 1819, the more of almost unmixed satisfaction does it convey to me; and that satisfaction is heightened by the postscript, in which he says that all his brethren at Preston professed entire agreement with the sentiments expressed in it. From that letter alone I should have no doubt that the writer agreed with me substantially, in all that I am contending for, on the assured hope toward God, which the gospel is calculated to convey—alike to any sinner whatsoever believing its report—according to his faith; and the writer was then eighty-four years of age. Probably he has before this changed faith for sight: if not, may the Lord fulfill in him all the good pleasure of His goodness, and the work of faith with power.

But why did I say that my satisfaction from that letter was *almost* unmixed? I will tell you, in order that nothing may be left unnoticed on this fundamental topic: I think some of the expressions even in that letter too weak; for instance, "and in holding the beginning of his confidence fast unto the end, *he is safer* than in labouring for a source of greater consolation in any thing he conceives of in himself." Are there *two* safe ways here, of which we can say that one is safer than the other? I do not suspect the writer meant this; but the expression is dangerous: and perhaps the tenderness of the language originated in the thought of some highly esteemed individuals, who had sought, or put others upon seeking that supposed higher consolation in the unsafe way: but let God be true and every man a liar. Again, quoting a passage from one of my writings, he says, "it is, if I understand him, designed against those self-righteous doubts and fears, that proceed, as such fears *often* do, from not having in view the truth we profess to believe:" when I look at the sentence immediately following this, I cannot doubt but the writer would agree to change *often* for *always*.

Again, "as to what is said of an assurance of hope, proceeding from a consciousness of loving from the heart, it appears to me not only not *worth contending* for, but to appearance implying a trust in one's own heart;" is not this also too weak? It does appear to me worth contending against to the last extremity; and when the writer, in a former part of his letter, says, "no one, I suppose, will presume to say that the perfection of his faith consisted in a consciousness that he was obeying God in what he did, or that his joy arose from such a consciousness;" could he be ignorant that Palemon, in the sixth of his letters to Mr. Harvey, has repeatedly held such language? as when he says, "if our hearts condemn us not as destitute of love to that truth which the world hates, then have we confidence towards God; *even as much confidence as the testimony of our own conscience can give us:"* * * * * "such a testimony of one's own conscience must give no small confidence; yet this is but one witness and needs to be supported," &c. He then goes on, misinterpreting, I am persuaded, the text Rom. viii. 16, to describe an *additional* testimony of the spirit of God, supporting this testimony of our conscience; and adds, "thus that love to the truth, which formerly wrought in the way of painful desire, attended by many fears, is perfected by being crowned with the highest enjoyment it is capable of in this mortal state;" * * * * "the assurance of faith, then, arises from the evidence carried in the divine testimony to the conscience of the ungodly; the assurance of hope arises from experience in the hearts of them that love God and keep his commandments:" and his meaning here manifestly is, arises from their consciousness of loving God and keeping his commandments, corroborated by a supposed testimony of the Holy Spirit, to the same fact.

Again, "to have the Holy Spirit as the Comforter and Earnest of the heavenly inheritance, is an attainment far beyond the regenerating work of the Spirit, by which men are at first brought to the knowledge of the truth, and taught to love it:" * * * * "it presupposes the work and labour of love, and the testimony of our conscience, that love is the spring of our work and labour." * * * * "By this proof men come to know that the joy they had on their first believing, was not the joy of the hypocrite;" * * * * "and thus they receive an additional knowledge and certainty about the truth, in the way of experience, by perceiving that it works effectually in them, producing its genuine effects."

Indeed, my dear sir, it is not from any desire of picking holes in Mr. Sandeman's writings, that I quote these passages, but I do think that they contain rank poison, which I fear has altogether corrupted the truth in the minds of many who profess to be his admirers. I do think that they describe the advanced believer as rejoicing in a hope altogether different from the hope of the gospel, and as having done with the ladder by which he had painfully ascended to it: and shall I screen such passages from exposure, or regard them with less decisive abhorrence, because they have been penned by a man whose memory is otherwise endeared to all the lovers of the apostolic gospel, by the clear statements and bold assertions of it which he elsewhere makes? No: I should detest such sentiments as much, and be even more forward in exposing their wickedness, if I had penned those passages myself.

Wherever the principle is maintained, that the assurance of faith, or assured faith, must not always be accompanied with correspondently assured hope and confidence towards God, the mind must be looking for a hope and confidence derived from something else than the revealed truth of God. So far as the conscience at any time is not relieved from *the fear that hath torment*, by the glad tidings testified in the scriptures, it will, and must be looking for relief to some other quarter. Mr. Sandeman employs in support of the doctrine which I oppose, the words of the apostle John:—"If our heart condemn us not, then have we confidence towards God," and considers this as applying, not to the believer who is but now called to the knowledge of the truth, but to those who have passed through the long course of painful desire attended with many fears, in the supposed self-denied obedience and labour of love, and have now obtained that highest enjoyment, the testimony of their own conscience and of the Spirit of God, that their love is genuine. Now it might be well to observe the preceding words of the apostle; "If our heart condemn us, God is greater than our heart, and knoweth all things:" he seems here to treat with very little ceremony those who have not that confidence toward God; he seems to consider them as not standing in the truth, though according to Palemon's application of the following verse, every believer must long be in that state, in which his heart condemns him. And when the apostle says afterwards, "these things have I written unto *you that believe* on the name of the Son of God, *that ye may know that ye have eternal life*, and that ye may believe on the name of the Son of God," he does not seem to consider that, which he so strongly calls the *knowledge* that we have eternal life, as the peculiar attainment of a few believers, but rather as the common blessedness to which the gospel calls all who believe it. As to the believer's hope and confidence being perfected and assured by his becoming satisfied, that the joy he had upon his first believing was not the joy of the hypocrite, I must say that this is a hope and confidence quite aside from the hope of the gospel, and resting as much as any of the false hopes of the appropriators, upon something nowhere revealed in the scriptures; and indeed it is a sandy foundation. If I were to look at any time to the joy which I have from believing the truth, in order to assure my present confidence toward God, and if my conscience were at the same time made honest, I could find nothing but what is calculated to plunge me into the most painful doubt, and even in absolute despair: there is such a deceitfulness of the flesh mixing itself with all *my* joy, *my* faith, *my* hope, and transforming itself into a very angel of light, that I can only say in that view, "God be merciful to me a sinner." But, blessed be his name, the hope which the gospel reveals and brings to me, is each moment a hope wholly independent of and unconnected with the question, whether I ever before believed it. It is a hope resting on a foundation, about which there is no uncertainty; which is at all times equally and unchangeably sure, even the truth that God is; and while the Word that reveals his distinguishing character and glory, as the just God and the justifier of the ungodly, with whom there is forgiveness, yea plenteous forgiveness, and to whom salvation belongeth; unto whom no sinner can come, upon whom no sinner can call, without being accepted of Him and saved by him; while that word stands true to my conscience, I care not whether I ever believed it before; I want nothing more to assure my heart before him, and to bring me to his mercy seat, with the boldness of a child, and with the sacrifices of praise for his unspeakable gift.

Observe, my dear sir, that it is not about that confidence and joy, which I actually derive at any time from the revelation of God, that I speak great things; far, very far from it: in the clearest perception of the glory of God, in the face of that Son of Man whom he has made strong for himself, the greatness of the things of God only shows me the littleness of my faith, as indeed less than a grain of mustard seed; but I am not afraid to speak great things of the fulness of hope and confidence towards God, which the gospel warrants to any sinner alike; and which the gospel, the great instrument of the Holy Ghost the Comforter, is adapted and sufficient to afford; and I therefore know not any exercise of that office of the Holy Ghost, as the Comforter, distinct from his fulfilling the work of faith with power in God's people. Mr. Sandeman speaks of a joy which a sinner has on his first believing the truth, and which he long after discovers was not the joy of the hypocrite: well, I should think then that it must have been the joy of the Holy Ghost; but no, to have the Holy Ghost as the comforter is (according to him) an attainment beyond the work of the Spirit, by which men are at first brought to the knowledge of the truth; and certainly the kind of comfort which he afterwards attributes to the Holy Ghost, is quite a different thing from all peace and joy in believing: yes, it is in believing in Christ the disciples are declared to rejoice with joy unspeakable and full of glory.

It gives me great pleasure to find Mr. C. in different passages, appears to disavow all idea of the comfort of the Holy Ghost, distinct from his taking of the things that are Christ's, and showing them unto his people; distinct, in short, from the work of faith; but I must candidly own, that there are other parts of his letter to Mr. M———, which I dislike much, but in which the inconsistency with the good parts appear to me so glaring, that I trust the truth which he generally professes, will burn up the chaff which is mixed up with it. A passage at the close of that letter involves so much of the matter in debate, that I shall at once quote it, and proceed to offer my remarks upon it with that plain freedom which the nature of the subject demands:—"Nor can I see but the supposition that the belief of the gospel is always connected with an assurance of one's own salvation, is in effect the same as supposing faith to consist in such an assurance; they do either of them debar all the comfort of hope from the man who entertains fears for himself, lest he should in time of temptation fall away; and such fears the scripture itself appears to me calculated to excite." Yes, indeed, and blessed is the man that feareth always; but Mr. C. expresses himself at times as if such warnings in scripture, as "be not high-minded but fear," "let us therefore fear lest a promise being left," &c., were only addressed to those who apprehend, or ought to apprehend, that they have not the faith of God's elect, but not to all believers at all times; especially not to those who (he says) have attained that greatest perfection which a sinful man can attain to in this life, to be made sure of the favour of God. Thus, for instance, he speaks in another passage, "I can hardly think he (Mr. Walker) is contending for a doctrine, that were it scriptural, would render all warning useless as to believers: for, were *all such sure* that they should never fall, there would be no propriety in warning them of any danger they were in of the contrary." Do not these words more than imply, that there are *some* believers so sure, that they shall never fall, that to them the scriptural warnings of the contrary danger cannot with propriety be considered as addressed?—Now this sentiment I utterly protest against, and abhor; be the man who is supposed to have got above these warnings, an apostle just finishing his course, or any other man: and I do hope that you and Mr. C. will renounce it also. Can the most advanced believer for instance consider himself as not included in the import of that warning, "Let him that thinketh he standeth, take heed lest he fall?" assuredly any man who conceives that such warnings cannot with propriety be addressed to himself, is filled with that pride that goeth before destruction. If so, and if it still be admitted that there are (or ever have been) some believers, professing personal filial confidence toward God, and assured hope of eternal glory, does it not inevitably follow that all such warnings, and the Godly fear which they are calculated at all times to excite, are perfectly consistent with the fullest assurance of hope? Indeed in the whole of that cleaving to the Lord with purpose of heart, holding fast the truth, and flying for refuge to lay hold on the hope set before us in the gospel, there is intimately included a perception of perpetual danger, to which we are exposed; from the *tormenting* fear of which, the gospel is at all times calculated to relieve the mind of a sinner; but from the godly awful apprehensions of which, it never was designed to release the most advanced believer: on the contrary, it impresses and enforces this fear, and is the grand instrument by which the Lord fulfills that promise of his mercy to the heirs of salvation: "I will put my fear in their hearts, that they shall not depart from me." And here, that I may not be misunderstood, let me remark that I consider any boasted assurance of a man's own salvation, as nothing but presumption and ungodly confidence, if it disjoin in his mind the idea of departing from the Lord and destruction. Well, now what view do the scriptures present to every believer, whether the weakest and youngest, or the strongest and most mature? what view of *himself?* what but that of a sinner in whom, that is in his flesh, dwelleth no good thing—but a body of death, every tendency of which at all times is contrary to the Lord, and to the truth which reveals the glory of the Lord. This I trust you will agree with me is the only view which the scriptures warrant any man to take of himself; the unaltered and unalterable character of every sinful man: but to such radically ungodly creatures the glad tidings are sent from heaven, revealing the righteous and holy God as the Saviour of such, and bringing nigh that salvation of God to all alike in the divine testimony, that *whosoever* believeth its divine report is a partaker of that salvation; a salvation absolute and perfect like all the works of God; one complete whole from the first justification of a sinner in His sight to the crown of righteousness in heaven. Now if there be but one gospel declaring the same divine testimony to all alike, and revealing the only ground of hope to any sinner; those who have the most assured hope and joy must derive it from that gospel, and not from the consciousness of any circumstance of difference between them and any of their fellow sinners; which they could not thus derive, if the gospel were not in itself at all times calculated to communicate the fulness of hope and joy to every sinner alike who believes it. Accordingly when the apostle prays that the God of hope would fill the disciples with ALL joy and peace, he marks that it is *in believing* they must thus be filled. In short, if the gospel of the glory of Christ he not adapted and sufficient to give the most assured hope toward God to every sinner alike, those who have the most assured hope must derive it from something else than the gospel. Can it be necessary for me to add, that I by no means assert that all who believe the gospel have the same degree of assured hope from it? or the same believer has at all times? This would be to assert, that all who believe are equally strong in faith, equally clear in their understanding of the truth, and firm in the persuasion of it. But I speak of the proper effect of the gospel where it is believed, and according to the measure of faith: every thing contrary to which proper effect I must trace to one evil root—*unbelief*: and this without at all "supposing faith to consist in the assurance of our own salvation." Every thing like that sentiment I renounce and abhor, and have no doubt that many have perished in their sins, filled with an assurance of their own salvation. Mr. C. and Palemon himself admit that some believers have, what the latter calls the assurance of hope; though I trust he was never allowed to get what he describes under that name. Now if this assurance of hope be had by them *in believing the gospel*, as I am glad to find Mr. C. at all times asserting, why should he apprehend, that the assertion of the perfect adaptation of the gospel to convey it tends to confound the faith of the gospel with the possession of that assured hope? but why also should he say that my assertion "debars all the comfort of hope from the man who entertains fears for himself, lest," &c.? Ah! if I could convey to you all my views of the deep poison that I think is in that sentence of his letter! What is that comfort of hope which he is afraid of men's being robbed of? is it not the hope, that although they have not the answer of a good conscience towards God, they yet may be believers, and therefore accepted of him? But is that the comfort or hope of the gospel? No, positively; no, it is that deceitful looking for comfort and hope to their own faith, which is perfectly consistent with the most abasing complaints of unbelief. Suppose that any of these fearing professors—(I have before explained the sense in which I admit and assert that every believer is called upon to fear, yea to fear lest in time of temptation he should fall away; and I am sure that any man that does not, cannot really join in the prayer, "lead us not into temptation;" but I am now speaking of the fear that hath torment;) suppose, I say, that any of these fearing professors came to be assured, that to the last minute *he had not believed the truth*, does this overturn his comfort of hope at this minute? If so, I must say that it had better be overturned in time, for it is built upon the sand. But does this debar him from the comfort and hope of the gospel? Not a whit; on the contrary, it is Palemon's doctrine in the assurance of hope which indeed debars from it; which shuts up (as far as man can) the abundant fountain of everlasting consolation and good hope from the poor ungodly sinner: and instead of allowing him to hear the voice from the mercy-seat, which calls such "to drink, yea to drink abundantly," teaches him, that the spring indeed is there, but that to get at its rich supplies he must go through a course of painful desire, till he arrives at "a consciousness of loving God, and keeping his commandments." O yes; it is this that keeps him under Egyptian bondage, and sends him to make bricks without straw. That hope is worse than faint,—it is of a spurious kind—which can be damped or extinguished by the plainest assertion of the fulness of hope, which the gospel ought to inspire. I am not afraid that this, scripturally maintained, will discourage the weakest believer; it has quite the contrary tendency, even when it most exposes to him the unbelief of his own heart. I remember a period of my course, even after I spoke freely and clearly on the way of a sinner's justification before God, when I used to attempt to comfort and strengthen two persons in whom I was much interested, and who professed agreement with me in sentiment, but were often in perplexity and doubting *their own interest*, from the apprehension that they had not the faith of God's elect; when I used to attempt to comfort and strengthen them by insisting on the evidence which then satisfied me that they did believe the truth. You will probably agree with me that in this I pursued a very unwarrantable course; yet if any believers are to have their hope assured by observing such evidences in themselves, I really do not know why another, conceiving that he observes them, should not point to that spring of consolation and encouragement. But, blessed be God! those two persons were not suffered to take that deceitful comfort; and I was soon cured of administering it, from being brought to more scriptural views myself. I was led to deal with them just as if they had never believed the gospel; to put the question of their faith wholly out of consideration, and to direct their attention to the glorious sufficiency of the thing revealed for all the wants of the chief of sinners. Almost as soon as I did so, the comfort of stable hope flowed in upon them: and I have every reason to believe that they were kept rejoicing in it to the end of their course. Mr. C. no doubt, in different passages of his letter expresses himself so, that according to the most obvious meaning of his words, there ought to be no controversy between us on the subject; and indeed I have a lively hope that there will not ultimately be any. But even in those most excellent passages, comparing them with others, I am led to apprehend some ambiguity of meaning. He says, "He that says he has found enough in the gospel to set his mind at rest as to the way of peace with God, but is still saying with the many, "who will shew us any good?" or with the young man, "what lack I yet?" is ignorant both of himself and the extent of the grace and mercy of God:" and again, "they whose minds are not relieved from every anxious inquiry after conversion, faith, or whatever they term it, whereby they think to be saved, it is certainly folly for them to pretend to believe the Gospel;" from such passages I should conclude that we were quite agreed; but how can I reconcile them with Mr. C.'s contending elsewhere, that a believer of the gospel, by which I mean not one who has formerly believed the truth, but one who is now standing in it, may yet be apprehensive that he has not the faith of God's elect? So far as he apprehends this, can his mind be really relieved from every anxious inquiry after conversion, faith, &c.? can it be set at rest as to the way of peace with God? must it not be still secretly saying "what lack I yet?" If there be any ambiguity in the good language I have quoted from this letter, I think it must be in the words "set at rest as to the way of peace with God;" at least I know some who would assent to the statement, but mean by it only this, that every one, in believing the gospel, must be satisfied that there is no other way of peace with God, but that which the gospel reveals, and that this is a sure way of peace to those who know it, and are in it; while yet they conceive, that the believer may be ever so apprehensive, that he does not know it, or is not in it. Now really if this were the case, the gospel would be little calculated to set the mind of any sinner at rest; it would only tantalize him with the view of a thing very blessed perhaps to others, but without bringing any of that blessedness to him. And here I am obliged to revert to that passage in my letters on Primitive Christianity which Mr. C. has quoted with disapprobation; "the man who with his mouth confesses the gospel to be true, yet avows his apprehension that he has not faith, talks but wicked nonsense." I should not have expected opposition to this from the man who said in his shorter letter to you, "when the gospel commends itself to one's conscience in the sight of God, it can leave one in no doubt whether what he has in view be really the truth of God or not." Would that his letter to you on this subject had been subsequent to his letter to Mr. Mansfield: but that offensive assertion I can neither retract nor qualify; I penned it deliberately; and deliberately do I say, I hope to be kept maintaining it till I die. That such a man talks nonsense, I have somewhere in my writings sufficiently proved; and what on every other subject all men would perceive to be nonsense. Is it not nonsense to say, I am sure such and such a thing *is true*, but I apprehend that *I do not believe it*? that is, I am sure it is true, but I fear I am not sure it is true. Yet this is what the man says, who professes that he is persuaded that so and so is the gospel of God, and at the same time declares his apprehension that he has not faith. We know that many so called evangelical professors would vindicate themselves indeed from the charge of talking nonsense in this, by shewing that they use the word faith in a meaning subversive of the truth of the gospel. But if another, who adheres to the scriptural meaning of the word faith, attempts to vindicate himself from the charge by explaining, that he is not sure what is the true gospel of God, but is only disposed to suspect that it is such a testimony as I say it is; then I can no longer consider him as confessing with his mouth that the gospel is true: at the most he only confesses that it is probable; and in fact makes that avowal of his unbelief, which it would ill become me to contradict. All I can do with such a professor, is to lay before him again the scriptural evidence of the gospel, connected with the divine declaration, that whosoever believeth it not, shall be condemned.

But I have called the language which I describe not only nonsense, but wicked nonsense; because it plainly speaks of faith as something distinct from the belief of the gospel. And let us not, my dear sir, be surprised at detecting wicked nonsense sometimes in the language of disciples themselves: what else do we speak, whenever we speak according to the imaginations of our own hearts? Mr. C.'s argument against my position I have already noticed. In fact, if it disproved what I have advanced, it would equally prove that no believer would be justified in conceiving that he had faith; there being no believer who is not addressed in such language as this, "be not high-minded but fear." I can honestly assure you that I abhor the thought of anything that would undermine the force of such at any time, as much as I abhor the thought of saying any thing derogatory to the glorious joyfulness of the gospel. I would never be so anxious to shew the consistency of different parts of scriptural truth, as to maintain them all in their true meaning and legitimate extent. I am sure they shall be all found consistent, and in perfect harmony with each other. I think I see these two points which I must say Mr. C.'s argument would set at variance, are thus consistent: I think I find them so in my own daily walk. Whatever degree of joy in the Lord and of godly fear I am led in, they always keep pace with each other, rise or sink together. But I must distinguish between the godly fear, to which every principle of the word calls every believer at all times, and the fear that hath torment. Those who are not walking in the former, I am sure are not walking in the comfort of the Holy Ghost, whatever may be their boast or their actual presumptuous confidence; and those who are walking in the comfort of the Holy Ghost, I am sure are not walking in the latter, that is, in the fear that hath torment. And let me assure you (I say it in order to remove, if it may be, groundless suspicion of my meaning) I find myself as much involved in controversy with the people called Bereans, and against their confidence, as ever I have been with the people called Glasites, and against their doubting system. As to the former indeed, (not to speak now of the gross appropriation among the high Calvinists of this country, who mean by faith a confident persuasion of their own election;) even before I understood things as well as I think I do now, I suspected something unsound in their professions, not only from their general diregard of the peculiar precepts of the word, but also from their being led to speak so continually about the strength of their own confidence; an effect which I never find produced by the views I contend for. In short the Berean gospel seems to be; 'I am sure I am a believer, therefore I am safe.' They professed for a time to like much what I said; but for some time past they have discovered that there is a grand difference between us; and while they object to an IF which they find in my writings, suffer me candidly to say, that I do not like Mr. C.'s language in the passage where he says,—"the certainty of each one's salvation is evidently suspended upon the event of his keeping the commandments of Christ." In the connexion in which this stands, I can well conceive he means nothing wrong; and there is so much of important truth to be contended for, that I would earnestly avoid all mere verbal controversy: yet the expression strikes me as so ambiguous, and so calculated to convey ideas always congenial to our foolish hearts in their religious mood that I should hope Mr. C. will not insist upon it. Part of that salvation wherewith the remnant according to the election of grace are saved by the Lord, and in the Lord, is their keeping the commandments of Christ, and walking in his good ways, hearkening to the voice of their shepherd in the word, and following him. In the chain of their salvation we may well distinguish various links; but they are all links of one chain, which cannot be broken, and which is suspended wholly from the mercy-seat of God. Accordingly, while Christ says to his disciples, "*If* ye keep my commandments ye shall abide in my love," all the inference which our vain hearts would be ready enough to draw from the words, (as if our abiding in his love were suspended upon our keeping his commandments, and so turning the very law of faith into a law of works) is elsewhere set aside expressly by the plain language of the new covenant; as when the LORD, who calls the things that are not, as though they were, declares it to be the unchangeable counsel of his mercy towards his true Israel, "they *shall* also walk in my judgments, and observe my statutes, and do them." Ez. xxxvii. 24. It is because the whole of their salvation is the exclusive work of Jehovah, not suspended on any conditions to be fulfilled by sinful man, that we may be certain that wheresoever there is any one link of the chain, there will be found the whole: in which sense it is, that I understand such language as "*If* we believe," "*If* we call on the name of the Lord," "*If* we love him," *If* we keep his commandments," "*If* we endure unto the end we shall be saved," &c. I do not suspect, however, that we really differ here, unless perhaps Mr. C. intended by the expression I have noticed, that the certainty of a believer, that he shall abide in the love of Christ, depends on, and is derived from, his finding that he has kept, or does keep, the commandments of Christ: and in this view I do think that the sentiment would be very objectionable, and too well calculated to remove a man from the one and only sure ground of confidence and assured hope, and to build him on the sandy foundation of what he has observed, or thinks he observes, in or about himself. But it is time for me to draw to a close this important subject, after I have made one more attempt to communicate my meaning.

Among the many things which please me much in Mr. C.'s writing, one is, that his mind appears exercised with some of the great words of the Lord, encouraging his disciples to confidence in prayer; such as that, "if ye abide in me, and my words abide in you, ye shall ask what ye will, and it shall be done unto you." Oh! it is for our profit to hearken diligently to such words; while they are well calculated to rebuke us for our hardness of heart and unbelief: it is when we have most of the confidence which such wonderful divine sayings ought to inspire, that we are most constrained to ask only according to the revealed will of our heavenly Father; and most restrained from asking according to the will and desires of our fleshly minds. See also John xiv. 12—14. xv. 16. Mark xi. 24. 1 John v. 14, 15. 'Aye'—says the flesh—'but all these words are addressed to *disciples*; and if I could but be assured that I am a disciple, a partaker of the faith of God's elect, then I should be encouraged by such words.' No; the man who is so encouraged to come with boldness, is not really encouraged to come to the throne of grace by the view of the great High Priest over the house of God, whose blood has opened a new and living way into the holiest for sinners; but is encouraged by the self-complacent view of certain characters, which he thinks distinguish him from his fellow-sinners.

And now, dear sir, let us direct our attention to another word of the Lord, Matthew vii. 8, 11, "every one that asketh receiveth; if ye then being evil know how to give good gifts unto your children, how much more shall your Father, who is in heaven, give good things to them that ask him." Taking these words in their connection with that revealed propitiation for sin, through which God is thus kind to the unthankful and the evil, just and the justifier of the ungodly, I say that they afford a sufficient ground of hope at all times for emboldening the chief of sinners to come unto God, nothing doubting, for all the good things of his salvation; and this with the most assured confidence of receiving all that, for which he calls on the name of the Lord; a confidence resting wholly upon the revelation which he has made of his name. Dear sir, do they not afford such a ground? and what but unbelief can make any one look for any more or any other encouragement? In the light of the glorious security and fulness of the divine warrant, and foundation for filial confidence in drawing nigh unto God, let the whole controversy about the assurance of hope be viewed, and is it not decided? I remember, many years ago, before I had read a line of Mr. Sandeman's writings, a conversation I had with one who was familiar with them, and had imbibed all Mr. S.'s sentiments, at least all the bad part of them. The question was stated by him, 'who are warranted by the word to put their trust in God?' I maintained, to his great surprise, *every soul of man alike to whom the word is sent;* and I maintain it still; while assuredly none, but those who believe the report of the word, will see that blessed warrant which it affords, or enjoy that everlasting consolation and good hope which it is abundantly sufficient and adapted to convey.

Since I have been engaged in writing this letter, I have received one from a brother in Dublin, Mr. T. M——, now an elder of the church there, which among other articles of intelligence, contains one communication so connected with the topic I have attempted to treat, and illustrative of it, that I think I may as well transcribe the passage; though you would mistake me much, if you suppose that I rest my views of the subject on any human anecdote. My correspondent writes thus:—"How little we know who the Lord's people are, or where they may appear; but surely when they do, we are called to glorify him for his mercy; and you will join with me, I am sure, in this exercise, when you hear of the striking display of that mercy in the case of one of our boarders, a Miss G——, who died the beginning of last month." (Mrs. M—— keeps a boarding-school.) "She had been brought up in the church of England religion, or rather no religion at all; for she knew nothing of the modes or terms of it. She had been pretty healthy during the time she was with us, nearly a year and a half, till within a few weeks of her death, when she looked delicate; but was not much more than a week seriously ill, in which time the real nature of her disease appeared. It was pulmonary, and made rapid work indeed. She died on a Saturday; the Sunday evening previous to which my wife intimated to her the probability of her not recovering. She shewed the natural workings of the natural mind; said, if she was but prepared, wanted to have prayers said, &c. Mrs. M—— spoke to her of the gospel; she was anxious to hear, and during the night made many inquiries, but still appeared not like one receiving the truth. In the morning, however, particularly after directing her attention to some portions of the word, and speaking a while on it, she saw the great salvation, and all its blessed effects appeared; her countenance, her language, almost every thing she did, expressed the happy change; and from that period, till her death, all was most delightful: she seemed like one that had found a pearl of great price, the very hope that she wanted, simple, satisfying, and divinely given: her triumph over death was complete, and her only anxiety for herself was to be gone. She wished to see her sisters, and her aunt, Mrs. F——: they came accordingly, and she at once stated her object to be, to tell them of what gave her such joy and cómfort. It was quite affecting to hear her, a creature who, but a few hours before, was uttering words of ignorance and despair, now testifying of the one sacrifice for sin, and shewing its efficacy to give peace to a dying sinner. You would have been delighted to hear the many things she said, which I could not attempt writing, and to observe the increase of light in her mind during the short period she remained; for, to use her own expression, she had been rejoicing in the gospel but one day and one night. It was, indeed the Lord's doing; and thus he seeks out and saves his lost sheep; and whether called at the eleventh hour, or to bear the burden and heat of the day, is a matter of no consideration. The mercy in which an apostle rejoices after fighting the good fight, and finishing his course, and ready to depart, brings equal blessedness to the sinner, who, but the hour before he expires, is visited with the light of its glory."

Well, my dear sir, that young creature seems to have found no deficiency in the gospel itself, for supplying a sinner with the most assured hope towards God: she certainly had no opportunity of getting it in the way Palemon describes. Some, I am aware, would evade the force of such an instance, by saying, that the Lord departed in it from his ordinary way of proceeding; but I trust you will agree with me, that there is nothing to be seen in it, but the genuine and proper effects of the revealed truth believed. In the hope that full unity of mind will appear between us on this fundamental subject, I now dismiss it, and must hasten to bring this long letter to a close. I must, therefore, in a great measure, postpone the two other topics which Mr. C. treats on, to perhaps another opportunity; only making a few remarks for clearing the way to them.

On the subject of oaths, I quite agree with Mr. C. that if

they be not forbidden by the Lord, my misinterpretation of Matt. v. 34, involves along with many other evils, that of disobedience to magistrates; and that disciples need to look well to it, before they refuse obedience to earthly rulers in any particular; and to be well assured that the case is one in which they cannot obey them, without disobeying their heavenly king. But, indeed, independently of this, the attempt to add to his laws, by binding what his word does not enjoin, is quite on a par with the attempt to take from his laws, by loosing what his word does enjoin: either is an awful display of human wickedness and presumption; and I have to plead guilty of both. Mr. C. thinks that the passage forbids the use of oaths *in the church*. But whatever the thing forbidden be, is it not manifest that it is absolutely forbidden; and that grounds are assigned for the prohibition, which remain invariably the same, whatever be the occasion or circumstances of the oath? (it is a point of distinct inquiry what we are to understand by the oath or swearing, which is thus absolutely prohibited.) For instance, when the Lord says, "neither shalt thou swear by thy head, because thou canst not make one hair white or black;" without now at all inquiring into the precise import and connexion of those words, (though I do not think them obscure) must we not own that this reason stands as good against swearing by our head, out of the church as in the church, at the requisition of a magistrate, as without such requisition? and this simple remark, I do conceive, is quite sufficient to set aside Mr. C.'s interpretation of the passage, as well as many other interpretations which I have heard, whatever may be said afterwards upon its real meaning.

I do not understand the grounds on which he has previously said, "that, unless when required by civil rulers, there can arise *no doubt* of its *unlawfulness* upon *all occasions*." Supposing (but not admitting) that the divine prohibition regarded only oaths between disciples in the church, there might easily be conceived occasions for a disciple's confirming by oath his engagement to those that are without, where yet human laws did not command him to do so; and if the thing be not forbidden in the word, or be not a thing intrinsically opposite to the principles of the word, why should a disciple scruple to do so? and if it be forbidden in the word, or be a thing opposite to its principles, can the command of civil rulers legitimate it? I might add, that nine-tenths of the cases, in which oaths are taken without scruple, and in which, I believe, Mr. C. as yet thinks they may be taken by disciples, are cases in which civil rulers do not require them: for instance, if I should take an oath for recovering a debt or getting a draw back from the custom-house, can I reasonably or truly vindicate my conduct, by pleading that I do it at the requisition of the magistrate, or in obedience to the laws of the land? certainly not; I do it to get my money, which I am justly entitled to; but the law does not command me to prosecute my right; it only says, if I will do so, I must swear: but it will not, in such instances, even impute to me the civil criminality of disobedience, though I should abstain from the swearing, and forfeit my rightful property. Ah! it is hard to argue in a bad cause. I rather suspect Mr. C. has not yet caught the precise view of the passage which I mean to put forward. I conceive that the thing absolutely forbidden, is the vowing that we will do so or so under some pledge or forfeiture, which we stake to confirm our engagement—which is called, in Numb. xxx. *the binding our souls with a bond*, for the performance of what we undertake. That such is the intention of every oath administered in this country, even the oath of testimony, I think, is indisputable; though I long wilfully shut my eyes against it, not so much for sparing myself, as for sparing others; and I am persuaded that the more the thing is examined by disciples in the light of the truth, the more will it be found revolting, not only against the passages of scripture, in which it is expressly forbidden, but against all the principles of the gospel. Though such an oath was not expressly forbidden under the law of Moses, yet I do not at present recollect any instance in which it was commanded. The thing most like it, perhaps, was the oath of cursing, which attended the administration of the waters of jealousy; but that was a divinely instituted appeal to the God of Israel, for his miraculous interference to authenticate the truth of an antecedent fact. As to its being necessary to the nations of the world, that men should bind themselves under a great curse with respect to their future conduct, I am aware that political writers are apt to speak of such oaths as the grand bond of society; but I consider it as one of those principles which pass current in the world without examination, though utterly without foundation in truth. Do you really think that any man was ever restrained from acts of treason, by the consideration of his having taken the oath of allegiance, and in that had imprecated against himself the forfeiture of the divine aid, in case he should fail of keeping it? But I have been betrayed into more argument on this subject than I designed.

I pass on to a few remarks on the question of Baptism. I could wish that Mr. C. had only seen, or only attended to what I have offered on that point in the seventh of my Letters on Primitive Christianity. I there aimed at divesting the subject of every thing which I conceive can be at all fairly questioned; of every thing on which my own mind is not quite decided: for I have no hesitation in confessing, that I profess not equal decision of judgment on some questions, which may be raised about the subject, in some of its bearings. I have written chiefly against the baptism of the so-called Baptists in these countries; and I am fully persuaded, that it has no warrant or precedent in the word; that it is a mere human figment, and very wicked in the principles connected with it. I am sure, also, that although I was sprinkled by a clergyman in my infancy, it would be vain to think of instancing that rite as any thing like what I read of, as practised in the apostle's days. I am sure, therefore, that I have never been baptized with water, as the first christians generally were; and I find myself wholly unable to see from the scriptures, how I could either now, or at any period of my life, conform to the rite, which confessedly was then practised, except in some farcical imitation of it.

Mr. C. says, " one convinced that he ought at some time to have been baptized would, without trying to determine exactly when that time was, desire, without further delay, to have it now done;" and I have often heard a similar remark, but I confess it appears to me to have more of plausibility than force. I cannot be convinced that I ought at any time to have been baptized, without knowing in general who ought to be baptized, and on what occasion; for surely it might be shown, even from the acknowledged ordinance of the supper, that a disciple may live and die in circumstances, in which he cannot and ought not to practice it. The same divine authority which marks the ordinance, marking also the occasion on which it is to be observed. But here, in order that I may not waste arguments in the dark, I should like to know what your practice is: some of Mr. C.'s language would lead me to suppose, that, when you receive additions to your churches from the antichristian world, you call them to be baptized with water: I speak not now of the children born to you subsequent to your own church membership. But I should conceive that you do not acknowledge, as christian baptism, any rite under the name, which had been practised towards your members previous to their connexion with you: for Mr. C. says, "as to those who never professed that faith, (and he has sufficiently marked that he means by profession here, that profession in which there appears nothing that nullifies it) nor were baptized at the request of parties who did profess it, I cannot think they were ever entitled to baptism, or that any thing they received under the name, ought to be considered as such." I am not disposed at all to controvert this; but as it seems to me to point to a practice, quite different from what I understand to be the practice of the Glasites in these countries, I wish to ascertain whether I mistake the writer's meaning or not. I never conceived that Mr. Glas or Mr. Sandeman had any other baptism with water, than what they had received under the name, in the church of Scotland. You will not suppose that in making this remark, I mean to insinuate that you are disciples of men. I rejoice to think that you have manifested a very different mind. We certainly appear to differ greatly in our application of the phrase *professors of Christianity;* and I think the scriptures will bear me out in speaking of the *profession* of the christian faith, in connexion with real opposition to it, as constituting that which is properly antichristian. I do, therefore, consider the whole antichristian world as *professors* of christianity: does not Paul take the same view of them in 1 Tim. iv. 1—3. and in 2 Tim. iii. 1—5.? are we, in such passages, to understand him as describing the blindness and ungodliness of men, not even professing the christian faith?

I confess that I feel a weakness of judgment and indecision of mind, whenever I am pressed with the question, "What would you do if you were among heathens, and any of them received the truth? would you call on them to be baptised with water? I have no legitimate motive for concealing that indecision, and the remaining ignorance of scriptural rule connected with it: yet I see no reason for retracting in the least my position, that in the commission given to the apostles in Matt. xxviii. 19, the Lord did not command them to baptise with water; and bear with me when I say that I do not see any force in Mr. C.'s argument for establishing the contrary. I by no means wish to suppress the reason, which Paul assigns for his having baptized so very few, " lest any should say I baptized in my own name"—but I do not see how that, or any similar consideration of expediency, could account for his thankfulness to God, that he had so seldom done what the apostles are supposed to have been commanded to do. Apply such a reason to the preaching of the gospel, and what would you think of it? and as to the supposition of any thing distinct in Paul's commission from the rest of the apostles, Mr. C. justly admits, that we have more recorded instances of persons baptized by Paul, than by all the rest of the apostles. Now I allow that the administration of baptism was no more exclusively confined to the apostles in the primitive practice, than the preaching of the gospel; but if they were charged in their commission alike with both, I cannot understand how an apostle should thank God that he had been so little engaged in one.

As to Mr. C.'s objection, that my view of the commission would produce an unmeaning tautology, it might be so if we were to stop as he does at the word baptizing them; but I think not at all, when we connect these words with the following. Suppose it had run thus, " go ye therefore and disciple, not men of the Jewish nation only, but men of all nations, baptizing them, not unto Moses, but unto the doctrine of the Father, and of the Son, and of the Holy Spirit;" would there be any unmeaning tautology, although we took the word baptizing in the same sense which it obviously bears in 1 Cor. x. 1, 2? I think not; and I think the passage last referred to, would be sufficient to authenticate the sense in which the word baptism, or baptizing, was to be understood. The expression in Heb. x. 22, which Mr. C. adduces as indisputably importing baptism with water, I really do not think refers to any such thing; except so far as there is an allusion certainly to the Jewish washings, the substance of which shadows, believers are declared to have; and I would beg of you to consider in connexion with that the passage in Eph. v. 26, and the words of Christ in John xv. 3: in all these passages I think our attention is directed to that, which all the Jewish washings or baptisms typified. But I feel rather uncomfortable at taking up the subject in such a hurried way at the close of my letter. By the length at which I have written, you will judge that I feel no small interest in your correspondence. May it issue, to the glory of the Lord, in the correction on each side of whatever is contrary to His revealed truth and will.

Believe me, dear sir, &c.

XCIII.

TO MR. B———.

Dec. 2, 1822.

My dear Sir,—* * * * Much of your language is pleasing. It appears pleasing that you profess approbation of such plain and offensive truth as you have met in my reply to Mr. Haldane. But excuse me for saying honestly, that in the greater part of your letter, you seem to be less occupied with the greatness and glory of the unadulterated truth of the gospel, than with the display of some supposed discoveries, which you think you have made in the interpretation of the Old Testament scriptures. I mean to return to that subject before I conclude; but, at present, let me observe that we are all vain creatures naturally, seeking our own glory and trying to set off ourselves in all that we do and say; nor do I know any class in which this vanity is more strikingly predominant, than in religious professors of long standing. I do not mean by any remarks of this kind, to disavow the hope that you may prove to be a disciple of the Lord. I would cherish that hope as far and as long as the Word of God warrants. But, according to that rule, I cannot return the language of brotherly confidence with which you address me, till your profession is authenticated by something more than words. If you had all knowledge, so that you could understand all mysteries, and interpret the most difficult passages in the law of Moses and the prophets with critical exactness, it is yet possible that you might not have love, by which faith works, and which can be manifested only in keeping the commandments of the Lord. You say you have been a *professor* of the name of Jesus for near forty years. Probably you have been long a *professor* of that name; but I dare say you mean by professing it—a profession of the uncorrupted gospel: perhaps you mean that you have been so long a partaker of the precious faith of God's elect. I should like to know how that has been manifested, what are the fruits that have evidenced it. Probably the fact is, that you have been so long a very serious professor of what is called *evangelical* religion. Well: this country abounds with such; and so far as I weigh most of them in the balance of the sanctuary—(false weights and a deceitful balance are an abomination to the Lord)—I know not any greater enemies of the cross of Christ. In general, the doctrine they profess and teach, when their meaning is stripped of the spurious disguises which conceal it, proves to be another gospel than that which the apostles preach; and, accordingly, when the latter is brought forward plainly against their corruptions, I know not any who avow more unequivocal hatred of the truth. From such a disciple I cannot look for any of the genuine fruits of faith. But there are some others, and their number is at this day increasing, who appear to confess with their mouth the same unadulterated gospel, which whosoever believes shall be saved. Yet their profession is nullified in my view, because it appears to be only talk, and they prove themselves, by their works, destitute of the fear and of the love of the Lord. Themselves and their admirers would think this a very extraordinary charge for any one to bring against them, because they are often eminent for what is called piety and strictness in their religious life—hold fast the traditions of their elders, what is called *family* duty, and the observance of the Christian *sabbath*, and the hearing or preaching of plenty of sermons, &c. &c. But talk to those men of the special commandments of the Lord—of the way in which the apostles teach disciples to walk together in the closeness of Christian fellowship—and of the divine institutions by which that fellowship is to be regulated; and they are found utterly deaf to the reproof and instruction of the Word, and as zealously making it void by their traditions, as the Scribes and Pharisees of old. That such professors have not the love of God in them, and that the fear of God is not before their eyes, the scriptures bind me to conclude; just as much as if I saw them living in drunkenness and adultery. When I therefore find a man, who tells me that he has professed the truth as it is in Jesus for forty years, supposing him to be really a man of truth, I should rather expect to find this statement accompanied with an avowal of shame and godly sorrow, for having long taken part with the antichristian abominations of the religious world: I should expect this, because I know how widely these have overspread the country, and how even disciples have been infected by the deceivableness of their unrighteousness. But passing this—my first inquiry from that professor would be—what he has been professing as the truth? and here my great object must be to get out of words and phrases, at the real meaning which he attaches to them. If he stands that test (and very few do), my next inquiry must be—have you been, or are you, holding fast the tradition of the apostles (2 Thes. ii. 15), or the precepts delivered by them to the churches of the saints? are you walking with the disciples by that rule; or, if you can find none to walk with you by it, are you standing alone, in absolute separation from any religious fellowship with all others? You have said so little distinctly in your letter about the truth which you profess (though what you have said is pleasing), that I am disposed to ask your meaning in that expression, —" None ever received him yet unto salvation but *sinners*." I ask it, because I well know the meaning of the words, as employed by the evangelical world, and they mean a lie. By sinners they understand what they often term *sensible sinners*—sinners who have been previously brought to acknowledge their need of such a Saviour as the gospel reveals; and this they mean to mark as, what they call, the first work of the Spirit of God, which they say is in a man prior to his believing the gospel. The same professors commonly mean by *receiving* the Lord Jesus Christ, something else than receiving the testimony of God in the scriptures concerning him, or, in short, believing that testimony; and the mere belief of that they reckon a thing of very subordinate importance. Now if any thing like this be your meaning, you certainly do not yet profess the truth of the gospel, any further than almost all the inhabitants of Great Britain profess it. But if you only mean that all men are sinners, and that none but *sinful men* receive the Lord Jesus, it is decidedly true: for unto none others is he sent. It is equally true, if you mean that the belief of the truth, as it is in Jesus, always includes or brings with it a discovery of the real nature of sin, and our own character as sinners.

Let me add a few words upon the two texts, about the interpretation of which you say you differ from me. You judge quite right in supposing that I have no pretensions to infallibility in the interpretation of particular passages of scripture. In fact, there are many on which I can honestly say nothing, but that I do not understand them; and others, of which, though I may conjecture their meaning, I am quite doubtful, and would much rather learn than teach. But I own that I see nothing in what you have offered on Numb. xxx. to make me change the language I have held on that passage. Whatever may be said of your view of the *typical* meaning of the regulations given to the Jewish people in that chapter, it would be quite wild to deny that it literally contained directions about what vows were to be considered binding, and what were not. To take another instance, we know, from infallible authority, that the passover was a striking type of Christ; yet would you deny that the Mosaic directions about the observance of the passover were to be literally attended to by the Jews, while the Levitical law continued? Now, on that chapter in Numb. I believe I have simply remarked, that there is an obvious allusion to the 2nd verse, in the introduction of Christ's prohibition against swearing; and have introduced the passage as illustrative of the nature of the oaths prohibited. But perhaps you would like so to spiritualise the Lord's prohibition, as to leave yourself at liberty to take as many oaths as your worldly interest called for. As to Phill. ii. 13, I do not recollect that I have said a word upon that verse, though I know I have at some length asserted the real meaning of the preceding verse, against the divines and our translators. Upon your interpretation of the 13th verse I do not think it worth while to raise an argument. It is very certain that the Lord's people are made a *willing* people in the day of his power.

I am glad to learn the general view you take of the book of Psalms. David was a prophet, and spake not of himself, but as the spirit of Christ that was in him did signify, of the sufferings of Christ and his following glory. There is no part of scripture more devoutly wrested to their own destruction, by ungodly religionists, than that book; and none more glorious, when it is seen in the light of that interpretation which the Spirit of Truth gives in the New Testament scriptures. But you are quite mistaken, when you suppose that others have not maintained, and publicly maintained, the same view. If ever you meet with honest John Barclay's work on the Psalms, you will find it blessedly asserted. To be sure he was reckoned mad in his day, as those who are made wise to salvation may expect to be reckoned; the servant is not above his master. However, I fancy I should never be able to keep pace with you in your interpretations of the book of Job, &c. I see strong, and at present insuperable, objections to view Job as either identified with, or typical of, the man Christ Jesus. If you marked him, as to be seen in Elihu, perhaps you would speak much more correctly. But really such critical disquisitions on difficult scriptures I should decline, even if we had a personal interview. I am mostly occupied by what is plain in the word, as plain to any old woman as to myself: and I do not find that real scriptural knowledge is promoted, by exercising our vain fancies in squeezing some evangelical interpretation out of every part of scripture. At the same time, I know that the testimony of Jesus is the spirit of prophecy; and am therefore sure, that if I had more of the spirit of wisdom and revelation, I should see Him in many a passage where I do not now. But why should I pretend to be wiser than I am? * * * *

Yours, &c. &c.

XCIV.

TO S. W——.

Jan. 6, 1823.

Dear Brother,—We have been commissioned by the church to convey to you their solemn and affectionate admonition on the evil of your conduct; and we adopt this method of doing so, from the apprehension, that we should at present find insuperable difficulties in the attempt to obtain a personal interview. For a long time now, those who have observed you most closely, have mourned over the many symptoms of your declension from the faith; but the immediate evil which was laid before the body at its last meeting, is your having determinately refused to afford to some of the brethren any opportunity of inquiring into a *report*, which we had heard, of your being lately married, and in circumstances which necessarily excited the apprehension, that you have had your marriage solemnized (as they call it) in the common way, by the intervention of a clergyman; as well as probably preceded by the *affidavits*, which the law in such cases requires. The object, however, of our present dealing with you, is not at all to inquire whether that report and those apprehensions be or be not well founded. It is to call your attention, in the name of the Lord, to the undeniable evil of which you have been guilty, to your violation of every principle of brotherly love, in obstinately refusing to afford your brethren an opportunity of obtaining satisfaction from you, by either sparing a few minutes when we last saw you, or by appointing any time (as you were intreated to do) when we might meet you on the subject. You must have become, indeed, awfully blinded to the principles of our Christian fellowship, if you think for a moment that such conduct is consistent with them. It is conduct which can spring from nothing but pride of heart, indifference to your brethren, or desire to cover your sin. Deceive not yourself, brother, by *saying* that you have faith, and *talking* about the glorious gospel, when you manifest that you have not that *love* which is one of the first works of faith. But, blessed be God, that gospel which you too plainly are letting slip, still abideth the same and unchangeably true; still proclaiming to you from heaven peace by Jesus Christ, who has died for our sins and risen again according to the scriptures. Whatever be the depth of varied iniquity in which you may be found, this is still suited to restore your soul, to heal your backslidings, and to lead you in the paths of righteousness and peace. Remember from whence you are fallen, and repent: "for it is a fearful thing to fall into the hands of the living God;" and He has said, "If any man draw back, my soul shall have no pleasure in him." We commend this our admonition to the blessing of Him, who alone can make it effectual for your recovery; and still cherish the hope that you will be restored to our confidence.

XCV.

TO THE SAME.

Jan. 13, 1823.

We *once* more address you, dear brother. We address you as a poor sick brother, at the point of death. We address you with the words of eternal life. It is a faithful saying—"He that hateth reproof shall die:"—"He that despiseth instruction despiseth his own life:"—"He that being often reproved, hardeneth his neck, shall suddenly be destroyed, and that without pity." Prov. xv. 10. 32. xxix. 1. If, indeed, you have ever tasted that the Lord is gracious, if you have ever had your fellowship with the Father and with his Son Jesus Christ, may we not appeal to your own conscience, that it is even now an evil thing, and a bitter, to depart from the living God. For where is now the blessedness you have enjoyed, your peace and joy in believing, your glorying in the holy name of the Lord, your standing in the light and liberty of his glorious gospel? In place of those things, is there not darkness, and the shadow of death, and vexation of spirit, irritation and pride of heart, while the recollection of the divine truths which you have acknowledged, only haunts your conscience, and produces a kind of anticipation of that worm which dieth not? But is there no balm in Gilead? Is there no physician there? Does not Wisdom still cry aloud to the most foolish and the most rebellious, "Turn you at my reproof;"—"Return unto the Lord, for thou hast fallen by thine iniquity;"—"Take with you words and turn to the LORD; say unto him, Take away all iniquity and receive us graciously; so will we render the fruit of our lips." He that indites such words to backsliding sinners, will assuredly *in no wise* cast out *any* that come unto him. But beware lest that come upon you that is written—"Because I called and ye refused," &c.—"Our God is a consuming fire." If we should not hear from you before the next meeting of the church, or if we see you not before its termination, we must infer that you still reject the admonition offered to you in the name of the Lord: and you will sooner or later know that it is an awful thing—(however impatient for it you may be in your present mind)—to be cut off in his name from the fellowship of a church acting under the authority of his word.

XCVI.

TO MR. P. C——.

March 21, 1823.

MY DEAR SIR,—I regret that I have been so tardy in replying to your letter of the 28th ult. from bad health and much business, and the necessity I feel of replying at considerable length; as you may perceive from the enormous sheet of paper I have taken. I read your letter with considerable satisfaction, a satisfaction connected (as you may suppose) with the appearance which I see, of your discerning the great truth as it is in Jesus, in contradistinction to the various counterfeits which pass under its name. I have long been convinced that a great majority of those who profess to like many parts of my writings, and to agree with me *in general* on the way of a sinner's acceptance in the sight of God, really mistake my meaning; and themselves mean quite a different thing from that which I desire to put forward. I cannot, therefore, but be pleased when any thing I say proves the occasion of manifesting that difference, which I am sure exists, and which they are dishonestly anxious to cover. This has been the case with those parts of my Reply to Mr. Haldane, which assert the unchanged and unchangeable character of *ourselves*. Many of the evangelical world are willing to admit in words the totality of human corruption in a sinner, on his first hearing and believing the truth of the gospel, and deriving from it relief to his conscience, and hope towards God. But when they are told that this is the only good hope which a man can *ever* have, and that the gospel speaks no comfort to the oldest believer, but that which it speaks equally to the publican and harlot; they immediately shew their animosity to the truth, and view it with just the same aversion and disgust as it excited in the Scribes and Pharisees of old. They conceive they stand upon a much higher ground and firmer foundation than is laid for *absolute sinners*; and wonder how any, whose words they were before disposed to admire, can assert a doctrine, which seems to them to subvert the very basis of morality and good works, especially that good work which they mean by *sanctification*. Their views of what they call sanctification in themselves I have been accustomed to illustrate, from supposing that the mass of *iron*, which the prophet caused to swim, was endued with consciousness, and occupied with admiration of its having lost the properties of iron, and become *cork*. However, we know that it was *iron* still when at the surface of the water, just as much as when at the bottom: and nothing but the same divine power, which raised it from the bottom at first, kept it afloat afterwards—kept it from its own continual tendency to sink. I confess I should need no more to convince me, that any man's hope was the hope of the hypocrite, (however plausibly and clearly he might appear to speak about the truth), than his telling me that his nature was less corrupt and ungodly than it had been. At the same time I am sure that, while I assert these sentiments, I must be regarded by the most refined professors with a jealous eye, as indisposed to the *interests of holiness*. They do not know what the "*holiness of the truth*" is: and they conceive that a believer's flesh—or his proper *self*—can be no further evil, than as he is *left to walk after* its lusts. Its lusting also against the Spirit they recognize only in those overt acts of wickedness, which all the world agree in reprobating: but it is not till the mind is subdued by that great truth which reveals THE GLORY OF GOD, that we discover the evidence of our own ungodliness, in the continued opposition of our minds to that divine truth, and in our continual propensity to let slip the things which we have learned. As to your *brother's* boasted evidence of his nature being sanctified, it ought reasonably to check his confidence to consider, that Socrates, and many another heathen, might have given the same account of himself with equal truth. But to tell the truth, I should not be at all surprised if the man who made the boast—(supposing that he ever had a taste for the *mountain dew*)—went to bed that night as drunk as Bacchus; and if he be a vessel of mercy whom God has ordained to glory, I can readily conceive such a thing to be mercifully permitted, in order to plunge his fancied holiness in the mire. But unless I pull in the reins, I shall fill my sheet, without entering on any of the topics of inquiry which you propose.

The unsettlement of your Baptist principles I hear of with satisfaction, only as they appear to be shaken by the breaking in of the great truth upon your mind. I would not give a bawbee to convert all the Baptists in the world from their baptism, if they did not give it up by being converted from their false gospels. As to the passages of scripture which still stick with you, little needs to be said. You say that you have "no difficulty in getting over the other passages in the Acts of the Apostles," &c. Now probably you *mean* very right: but let us be much upon our guard against attempting to *get over* any passage of scripture. I would always desire to give the fullest and freest scope to every thing contained in the Word; certain that to attempt maintaining any thing in opposition to what is there declared, is an attempt as vain as it is wicked. And if any passage of scripture comes and knocks to atoms any system that *I* have maintained,—I would only say, Blessed be God! and blessed be the power of his Word. That the modern Baptism—(I must call it so)—is utterly without scriptural foundation, I am sure. But there are various questions that may be proposed on the subject of primitive Baptism, on which I would much rather learn than pretend to teach. And I would desire to have my mind kept open to all further instruction from scripture on the subject; without the slightest apprehension that any new scriptural information will shake the principle upon which I am decided. You say that you are still at a loss how to understand the passages which you quote, "as applying to any professor in our day." *In one respect* they are not all applicable to professors in our day,—so far as some of them intimate that the persons addressed had been dipped in water, when they first professed the gospel; and the professors in our day had not been so:—few comparatively have been so dipped at any period of their Christian profession. Now many a Baptist would think that in saying this I concede a great deal to the Baptists. I care not about that: I say so far *truth*; and I am not afraid of any just inference from it. But what can they fairly infer from my concession? Is it, that in order to *make these passages applicable*, they are to practise a baptism—in such circumstances—and for such purposes—as the Scripture nowhere commands or relates it to be practised? That assuredly would be a strange inference. But are these the only parts of the apostolic addresses to their converts, which are not applicable (in some respects) to the professors—or to the real disciples—of this day? I am sure they are not: and I am as sure that the assertion—seen in its real import and bearing—does not at all impeach the unchangeableness of that word of the Lord, which endureth for ever. What think you of the latter words in Eph. i. 13? I am aware of the popular interpretation, which applies that *sealing with the holy spirit of promise*—subsequent to the belief of the gospel—to some fancied private revelation to the believer, of a thing nowhere declared in the word—his own personal acceptance. Every one standing in the truth will reject that interpretation: and it seems to me, that no one acquainted with the apostolic language can have any just room to doubt, that the *sealing with the promised holy spirit* there mentioned, refers to the miraculous gifts of the spirit communicated by the laying on of the apostle's hands. And what would you think of professors now pretending to those miraculous gifts, in order to *make* that passage *applicable* to them? I might adduce various other passages, in which the apostles address the first disciples in a language *not applicable* to professors at this day, even while the truth inculcated in their addresses continues applicable to the end of the world: as when they refer to their Jewish converts as having been literally circumcised, and to their Gentile converts as having been literally worshippers of dumb idols. And does this take off from the real force of such passages to me and to you? Not the least. If, for instance, the Thessalonian disciples were "turned to God *from idols*"

(1 Thess. i. 9.), it was in believing that apostolic gospel which reveals "the living and true God;" and I am taught that I can no further serve HIM, than as I am kept abiding in the same apostolic word; and that every thing called god, and worshipped by those who are not of the truth, is no better than an idol:—while it would be nonsense to say, that you or I—even when most ignorant of the truth—have ever been worshippers of the image of Jupiter or Diana. A grave Baptist elder once remonstrated with me very seriously for saying, that I considered their baptism—in one view—as *futile* a thing as the sport of children, agreeing to *play Philip and the eunuch.* But really I can say nothing *better* of any thing done for the purpose of making passages of scripture applicable to us, that are really inapplicable. I would now say a little more upon the particular texts you refer to. One of them—1 Pet. iii. 21, tells me expressly, that the washing with water is NOT the baptism intended in the passage. "The antitype-baptism to which doth also now save us, by the resurrection of Jesus Christ." And lest we should dream of water-baptism as the thing alluded to, the apostle throws in this guard—"*not* the putting away of the filth of the flesh, but the answer of a good conscience towards God." Whatever is to be said of the rest of the passage, this cautionary explanation satisfies me that we are not to think of the washing with water as at all comprehended in it. It *seems* to me that the passage is to be illustrated from Matth. xx. 22. The apostle has noticed Noah and his family as saved by that very water which executed the vengeance of God upon an ungodly world. And even so, elect sinners now are saved from condemnation, and have the answer of a good conscience toward God, by that very *condemnation of sin in the flesh,* which was fulfilled in the baptism of suffering unto death, wherewith Christ was baptized. But whatever may be said for or against this illustration, I must believe the apostle that the passage has nothing to do with washing with water. As to Rom. vi. 3—5. and Col. ii. 12. I am aware that all commentators give into the notion, that the apostle intimates some typical similarity between the *immersion* in water and Christ's death, and the *emersion* from the water and Christ's resurrection. But I confess that the idea seems to me most puerile and fanciful, without the least support from the passages fairly interpreted. In both the apostle reminds disciples of the import of their Christian profession,—that they professed to be dead with Christ to sin, and risen with him to newness of life. And in this respect they are applicable to disciples—yea, to all professors of Christianity—to the end of the world: however little the great mass of professors are aware of the real import of their profession. The apostle indeed marks the Christian profession of those whom he addressed, by the phrase of being *baptized into Christ:* in which I acknowledge an allusion to that rite of washing with water, by which they had taken on them the profession of Christ's disciples. But the only *typical* significancy in that rite which I can acknowledge, is its *cleansing* import. "Now ye are clean through the word which I have spoken unto you." Those who, for the first time, professed to believe that word, professed to have passed from their former state of uncleanness

in unbelief, to the state in which they were cleansed from all sin by his blood: and in their washing with water, I can see nothing else typified. In the passage of Colossians I think there is a mistranslation, which has contributed to countenance the fanciful interpretation that I reject. The 11th verse begins—" in whom"—i. e. in Christ —" ye are circumcised," &c. Now, the expression in the 12th verse, rendered " *wherein*," and applied to baptism, is precisely the same with that before rendered " *in whom* ;" and ought. I am persuaded, to be so rendered there. But if I even could believe that there was an allusion to a distinct typical significancy in the *immersion* and the *emersion*, I must be certain that the apostle alludes to the rite of baptism, only as indicative of the import of their Christian profession, and not in reference to any virtue in the rite itself. Therefore, all the lesson that he really teaches in the passages, I see *applicable* to you and to me at this day; while I must think that we should be worse than idly employed in practising some imitation of the rite, in order to bring ourselves into circumstances more exactly parallel with those of the first converts. On the remaining passage, 1 Cor. xv. 29. I have only to say that *I do not understand it at all*; —(do you?)—and that I have never met an interpretation of the phrase—" *baptized for the dead*"—in which I could satisfactorily acquiesce.

I must despatch very briefly the two remaining topics which you propose. You ask me whether I am " decidedly against a disciple's bearing arms in every case." If I mistake not, I wrote my mind upon that subject lately to my brother, J. L———, whom, I hope, you will soon know, if you do not already. The substance of what I can reply to the question, is this. I cannot conceive a disciple walking in the truth, and *taking upon him* the profession of arms. Indeed, in this country, that is put blessedly beyond controversy, as no man can become a soldier without being *attested*, or sworn before a magistrate, i. e. without directly violating the express command of Christ. But a man who *is in the army*—(or who is a public hangman)—may be called to the knowledge of the truth: and in that case I find myself without warrant in the word for dealing with him as an offender against the law of Christ, even though he continue in the profession of arms;—while I should, without hesitation, urge him, on the grounds of Christian expediency, to quit it *if he can*. I find a military officer at Cæsarea received as a disciple by an apostle, and no intimation given of any injunction to him to lay aside the use of arms. As to the abstract question, whether I would, in any case, think myself justified in resorting to the private use of arms—(even so far as the taking away of life)—in self-defence,—I am not fond of debating it. I think disciples may peacefully look to their heavenly Father, never to place them in any such circumstances as alone could justify it. But if pressed for an opinion on the abstract question, I must frankly say that I can *contemplate* cases in which I think that I would, without any scruple, shoot a ruffian, and consider myself in doing so, only as the executioner of the laws: just on the same ground as—if I were in the office of Sheriff—I might be legally bound to hang a criminal with my own hands. But really I should rather decline arguing the point, if any thought differently from me: and I do not conceive that a difference of theory on such a question could bar our Christian fellowship for a moment, till it came into practice.

The question about the marriage of believers with unbelievers, is one that must more necessarily come into practical operation: and if the little that I have room to say upon it here should not satisfy you, I can send you at another time a copy of a longer paper on the subject. All our churches were once of the same mind about it that you incline to: and whenever such a case occurred among us, we took it up in the way of discipline, as any other case of violating a divine precept. The scriptural ground upon which we rested was 1 Cor. vii. 39.—assuming that the expression, "*only in* the Lord," meant—*provided he be a disciple;* and fairly inferring that there could not be one rule for Christian *widows* in the matter, and a different rule for other Christians. In one instance we removed from our fellowship a dear sister, who would not profess repentance for the thing; and she died, not in outward connexion with us, but I believe in the Lord. I say it to our shame. But I well remember that the other cases, in which the discipline terminated in a profession of repentance from the party, used always to leave my mind more painfully dissatisfied: because I could not honestly believe that they would not do the same thing again (if it were yet to be done), or that they really regretted having done it: and because the latter is a state of mind which I could not *wish* to produce in a married person. However, I shut my eyes against all such difficulties; thinking that we were following the plain authority of the word. But it is now some years since we have been convinced, that we misinterpreted that passage in 1 Cor. vii. on which we had grounded our practice. The expression is not—"she is at liberty to be married to whom she will, only *to one who is* in the Lord;" but—"she is at liberty—only in the Lord." And I would connect the latter words with—"*at liberty:*" as if he said—'she has the *liberty* —only let her remember that I speak of the liberty which she *has in Christ Jesus*, as a disciple of his, and which she is therefore called to use to his glory, and not to the mere indulgence of the flesh.' Compare Gal. ii. 4. and v. 13. Others connect the words "only in the Lord," with the expression—to "marry whom she will;" and fairly illustrate the expression of "*marrying in the Lord,*" by such language as that in Eph. vi. 1, where believing children are called to "obey their parents *in the Lord,*" i. e. from Christian principle, with a regard to the will and glory of the Lord;—certainly not meaning that they are to obey their parents, only if their parents be disciples. Taken in either way, the import of the passage is much the same: and while it admonishes disciples not to lose sight of their Christian character and rule in forming that most important connexion of marriage, it certainly lays down no general law against their taking an *unbelieving* partner. This having been the only portion of the New Testament Scriptures on which we rested our former practice, our practice of course changed with the changed view of its meaning. It would be a profane mockery of Christian discipline, to apply any thing under the name, for binding that which the word of the kingdom hath left loose. And now that my judgment is released from the shackles which our former misinterpretation of the passage imposed on it, I cannot but admire the divine wisdom in *not* having laid down such a law as we had imagined. How inconsistent would it be with some other parts of Scripture! Nothing is more clear in the word than that there are circumstances in which a Christian man will find himself absolutely *bound* to marry, as the appointed preventive against fornication and other acts of uncleanness, which are opposed to the possession of our vessels in sanctification and honour. But who can say that he will always and everywhere be able to find any woman with whom he can have religious fellowship? or any who can be prevailed on to receive him as a husband? And let it be well noted that the marriage connexion, though the most intimate and lasting of all human connexions, is yet decisively one not of a religious but of a civil nature: else the relation of husband and wife could not subsist—(as we know from the word that it may)—between a Christian and an heathen. But after saying so much in vindication of our opinion, that there is no absolute law on the subject to Christians, let me add that I am persuaded, if a Christian use his liberty in this matter as a Christian,—if he proceed on Christian principles in choosing a wife,—he will generally, *if possible*, seek a believing partner. The considerations that enforce the general *expediency* of this are obvious, if we reflect either on his comfort or his profit, or especially on the scriptural care and treatment of their future offspring. But there are various things in which we may most suitably urge on a brother considerations of Christian expediency; and yet we should act most sinfully if we attempted to bring him in as an offender, even though he may act differently from what we think expedient.

If you be not frightened at the length of this, I shall be glad to hear from you again. Its length may shew you how much I am your friend and willing servant for the truth's sake.

XCVII.

TO THE SAME.

June 10, 1823.

Dear Brother,—Your letter of the 11th ult. was very welcome. It found me very ill, as I have been indeed most of the spring; I am now better: but very busy. Most of the leisure time I used to have, is now occupied with writing for a review, and must stand as my excuse for being such a bad correspondent; but as I expect an opportunity to-morrow of sending you a few lines free of postage, I must no longer delay writing, however briefly. I rejoiced (but was not surprised) to hear of your junction with the brethren at Leith. May we grow up together in the knowledge and love of God, content to have *Him* alone for our glory and defence. The contemptible appearance in the world, which a Christian church must make, is one of the trials at which our carnal hearts would always be ready to stumble. We might be willing enough to submit to it for a time, in expectation of some respectability being hereafter attached to us, from increasing numbers, &c.; but to be to the end of our course a poor, little, despised, and hated sect, the objects of indignation and contempt to all the finest and most esteemed people around us, this is very hard to the flesh. One thing, however, makes it and every other trial easy, when our eyes are kept open to the Glory of the Lord—when our ears are kept open to that voice which speaketh from heaven in the word, "Behold me, behold me!" (Isa. lxv. 1.) I have had for some time Mr. Sang's pamphlet, but really I have not yet read it. I looked at one page, in which I found misrepresentations of my sentiments so gross, as to be scarcely worth exposing. Whether I shall ever notice the piece I cannot yet say. I have spoken to my brother C—— to send the tracts which you desire, and should hope you will soon receive them. I quite agree with you that what I said about a christian in the office of sheriff was perhaps very untenable, but we need not trouble ourselves with such supposed cases.

You speak of the disappointment of the brethren in Leith at my not visiting them last year. My desire to do so is (I think) fully as strong as theirs can be; and I may now say that I indulge the hope of seeing you and them in the course of next month, or beginning of August. Let us remember that there is but one who can make our meeting a mutual blessing, and that needeth not any of us as instruments of blessing to the rest. The prospect of conversing with you so soon, face to face, reconciles me the more to the necessity I find of concluding this letter abruptly.

My hearty love to J. L—— and the other brethren at Leith, when you see them. The Lord Jesus be with your spirit.

XCVIII.

TO ——.

Aug. 22, 1823.

My dear Friend,—Agreeable to your desire I sit down to give you some account of myself, and of my interview with ——.

The Monday after my arrival I sent a note to ——, and he very kindly called the next day. We sat together in close and unreserved communication for nearly three hours. I found in him no *Glasite* backwardness to converse freely on scriptural topics: and we came at once to the grand point of Sandeman's doctrine on the assurance of *hope*. You will be surprised to hear that he unequivocally renounced it, and avowed a full unity of mind with me on the subject, expressing himself as abhorring the idea of a sinner's deriving any hope towards God, at any period of his course, from the contemplation of any good evidences about him, or from any thing but that one glorious truth which speaks peace, and gives hope to the most guilty and ungodly of the sons of men. He also as unequivocally spoke of that truth as sufficient to afford the most assured hope at any time to a sinner, and of all attempts to separate the assurance of *faith* from the assurance of *hope*, as striking at the very root of the gospel. This was very pleasing: but what surprised me more, and in some views damped my satisfaction, was that he spoke of this as *now* the common mind of the Glasite societies. He seemed scarcely aware that the opposite doctrine had been put forward in Sandeman's writings; talked of having seen it with much pain in some letters of a Mr. ——, who was engaged in the *Perth* controversy: and of his son having been lately brought under discipline in the church in ———, for reviving the sentiment in some of his exhortations. He described this as terminating in his professed repentance. —— seems a very intelligent as well as candid man: so that I cannot doubt but that a stand has been made against the deadly error in ———. But in a subsequent conversation nearly as long as the first, I pressed on his attention the evidences, that the false doctrine on the subject has been to a *very late period* publicly asserted by Glasite writers, and that the world had every reason to consider it as generally held by their body. He admitted that he may perhaps have too much taken the contrary for granted, but repelled all that I offered on the obligation of their making their repentance and disavowal of the doctrine as public as their sin, on the ground that *all* human publications on scriptural subjects are to be deprecated: I am satisfied that there is something bad at the bottom of that. Since these two long conferences, he dined here; when our conversation was more general, but still mostly on scriptural subjects. On various other points he is not a thorough Glasite: and I find that they are covering up differences in their society, which will, however, I trust, break out. He was, till a few weeks ago, an elder, but displaced on his marrying a second time. He then told his fellow-elders plainly that he is not at all satisfied on the truth of their interpretation of the passage—"the husband of one wife." He also gives up that cursed part of their discipline of not receiving any profession of repentance, from one who has been twice put away. And he admits that their interpretation of the "two or three," as meaning the two or three *elders*, is untenable. *You* will not think the worse of him for all the *forbearance* that he must be exercising for peace-sake among the Glasites: but indeed *I* do. I am glad to have been able to write some intelligence, which I think will prove interesting to you. It interests me very much.

Believe me always very affectionately yours.

XCIX.

TO ———.

Aug. 25, 1823.

My dear Sir,—Any hopes I had entertained of being able to call on you before my departure are at an end. I have been advancing pretty steadily towards convalescence since I had the pleasure of seeing you, but so very slowly that I cannot yet manage a walk of more than half a mile. I am to sleep on board the steam packet to-morrow night, and in bidding you most heartily farewell, I scarcely know how to thank you for your kindness, for the quantity of your time you have indulged me with, and for the satisfaction you have afforded me in so much free and unreserved conversation. Very, very gratifying to me has been most of that conversation. I cannot perceive a shadow of difference between us as to our professed faith and hope towards God; though I do seriously apprehend that you too much take it for granted, that the rest, who are in fellowship with you, have got freed from the leaven of that sentiment, which would ground *assured* hope towards God on something else than the bare revelation of his glorious name—a sentiment which would lead us to end in the flesh after beginning in the spirit. Passing this, suffer me to say (with the same openness with which all our communications have proceeded), that reflecting on what you have said on other topics, I do fear that you are pursuing a false *peace* in your societies. There are three points on which you do not seem agreed (at least fully agreed), with what is considered the Glasite system (I use the phrase only for brevity). The interpretation of "the husband of one wife"—the *unmerciful* rule of withholding readmission from a person twice excluded—and the interpretation of Matt. xviii. 19, 20. The latter bears closely on the question on which we are at present divided—whether the administration of ordinances comes within, or belongs exclusively to the office of elders; (that idea which seems to me plainly a remnant of *clerical* leaven;) or whether disciples gathered together to the name of the Lord, are not warranted and bound to observe *all* his appointed ordinances, even before they receive the gift of elders. Dear sir, be not afraid to look the question in the face, and consider whether even, according to your present views, you be not adopting an unscriptural *forbearance* in not calling your brethren to consider their ways on these subjects. As the coming of the Lord draweth nigh, the call to his disciples becomes louder, to remove the stumbling-blocks out of the way, which prevent the full manifestation of that unity of mind and way for which he prayed. The fear of *appearing vain* in my imaginations (and I cannot appear more vain to any than all the imaginations of my own heart are), must not restrain me from avowing the expectation, that disciples are to be gathered more closely and brought more generally into the old paths than they have been yet: and it would be most unsuitable for you or me to prefer the interests (as it were) of the several societies with which we are connected, to the divine prosperity of that Zion, which her children are called to love, and to mourn for, and rejoice with. It becomes us rather to pray that, if there be any false sentiment or way retained among us, on either side, upon which our respective societies will not bear the reproof and instruction of the word, that word of the Lord may break them to pieces. You will forgive me, I know you will, for all the freedom which I use. Knowing how your time is occupied, I do not think of taxing you with any reply to this, though I shall always be most happy to hear from you on any occasion. I was interrupted yesterday in writing this, and conclude it under the painful feelings of temporary separation from those who are greatly endeared to me. Farewell, dear sir, and believe me always with lively and affectionate interest,

---

C.

TO R. L. C——, ESQ.

Sept. 18, 1823.

Dear Brother,—* * * * I found our brethren here in general as well as usual, and retaining an affectionate remembrance of you. You know they have been engaged in a trying discussion with the church at C——; and it still hangs as a dark cloud, which none can disperse but He, with whom all things are possible; and who has formerly scattered many another cloud, which seemed big with mischief. I am necessarily a good deal occupied in my thoughts with the subject, and am therefore disposed to give them to you on paper.

The principle, that it is unlawful for Christians to employ a person of the world, or allow him to be employed in any service for them, in executing which he will have occasion to take an oath, seems to be now avowed with so much positiveness, and propagated with so much zeal by some, that it obviously threatens a speedy breach among the churches. If those who scruple the thing were contented to abstain from it themselves, without imposing on their brethren a law which is destitute of all scriptural authority, in that case others would be called not to interfere with their weak consciences. But this not being the case, it becomes necessary that all, even those whose conduct in life is least affected by the question, should have their judgment formed on the subject. Perhaps it may please God to bless the following observations for producing or confirming a scriptural decision on it.

If I know that an unbelieving man is about the commission of murder, or robbery, or any act by which injury would be done to others or to himself, and if I have any means of dissuading or preventing him, it would obviously be my duty to endeavour to dissuade or prevent him. "That love which worketh no ill to his neighbour," and which is therefore "the fulfilling of the law," must prompt us to prevent harm to our neighbours, if we can, as well as not to do it. Yet, even in such a case, if I were to set about dissuading the unbeliever from the meditated act, on the ground of its sinfulness, and as if to prevent his violating a divine command, I should act most inconsistently with Christian principles, and in a way calculated to build up that unbeliever in some of his most deadly delusions.

Accordingly, heretofore we have been all accustomed to acknowledge, that it would be most unsuitable for us to present any of the divine precepts to the attention of the world for observance, and peculiarly so, to call them to observe any of those precepts, which are exclusively addressed to disciples of the Lord for the regulation of their conduct. Such is certainly our Lord's prohibition of all oaths to his disciples: and while *they* are debarred from the thing forbidden by the divine authority of the word, and may no doubt observe the inconsistency of the thing with the principles of that gospel which they believe, on what ground could they endeavour or *wish* to prevent unbelieving men from taking an oath every day—from pledging themselves to any conduct under the forfeiture of the favour of their gods, whether called by the name of Jupiter or any other name? It would be impossible to mark any harm done by their swearing, to themselves or any others: and greatly must we have lost sight of the word, if we should attempt to deal with them on the ground of the command given to disciples: of obedience to that command they are at present incapable; and denying its authority, it signifies nothing whether they never swear or swear every hour.

Now, if these things be admitted, they immediately expose one of the grossest fallacies of the main argument put forward in the communications from the brethren at C——. They speak of the two things as parallel—the employing of a worldly man to murder or rob for us, and the employing of him (as they say) to swear for us. Supposing for a moment that the latter part of the representation were a fair one, it appears that the two things are not at all parallel; since the one is an act of his which we should be bound to prevent, if we could, while it would be inconsistent with our Christian principles to try to prevent the other. The whole argument, therefore, which they raise upon that assumption, falls to the ground.

But there is an additional and very gross fallacy in their language—of employing another *to swear for us*—or, as some of them have expressed it, *our swearing by proxy*. Assuredly, the man who swears, swears for himself, to confirm his own testimony or declaration; and neither swears, nor is considered to swear, as the proxy of any other. And if they abandon that absurd language of our swearing by proxy, and explain the expression, swearing *for us*, as importing only *for our benefit*, so that we expect some advantage (pecuniary or personal) from his swearing, they introduce a circumstance into the question which really cannot affect it at all; or alter the nature of the thing. If I might lawfully call on a worldly man to bear evidence, for the purpose of proving the innocence of a third person falsely accused of murder, and this in a case where I have no personal interest in the matter, then assuredly I may as lawfully call on him to bear evidence for the purpose of establishing my right to a thousand a year; and it is nothing but palpable sophistry to perplex and throw a false gloss upon the subject, by involving the general question in the consideration of his swearing *for us*.

But in the next place it is utterly unfair to represent us as employing or compelling any man *to swear*. This will perhaps appear more clearly by attending to some other cases to which the sweeping principle asserted by the Church at C—— applies. Let us take one, to which they have themselves adverted. Suppose a Christian man possessed of an estate, for the management of which he appoints a man of the world as his agent. A law is now set up, that he shall not appoint that agent but in a *qualified* way; i. e. no doubt, under the restrictions that the agent shall not distrain or eject a tenant, or take any step in which his swearing would be necessary; otherwise the Christian is represented as employing the agent *to swear for him*. Now (not to repeat what has been already said on the evil of that solicitude manifestly to prevent, as it were, unbelievers *from committing sin*), can it be said with any fairness that the Christian employs his agent to swear? No, indeed: he employs him to manage his estate, to collect his rents, &c.; while, perhaps, he is aware, that in effecting those purposes for which alone he is employed, he certainly will swear. In like manner, when I ask a worldly friend to let me name him as an executor to my will, is it fair to say that I ask him to swear for me? I do not. I ask him to administer to my effects; aware that he cannot do this without swearing. Or if, being drawn for the militia, I procure a substitute, this is really providing him, not to be attested for me, but to serve in the militia; which he cannot do indeed without being attested: and even so, if I apply to a man of the world, or even summon him to prove a fact, or send a clerk to the Custom House to effect the clearance of a ship, the thing which I aim at having done, and which I call those persons to do, is perfectly innocent, though the way in which they must do it, is one which *I* could not adopt, but one which the witness or the clerk is perfectly consistent in adopting. Do any ask, but am I justifiable in employing another to do a service for me, which I know he will do in an unchristian way? Really, those who will answer this in the negative, cannot consistently employ an unbelieving labourer to plough his field.

When Paul was brought to Rome, in consequence of his appeal to Cæsar's judgment-seat, let us suppose that he was called with his accusers to plead his cause before one of the heathen tribunals, and that in the course of his defence he saw a heathen soldier in the court, who could disprove some fact that was falsely laid to his charge: might not Paul, consistently with every principle of the heavenly kingdom to which he belonged, refer to that soldier's testimony, and call on the court to examine him upon the fact? And this, even though he should know that the man, if he were examined, would lay his hand on the altar of Jupiter, and confirm his evidence in the way customary with heathens? Was the man any more an idolater if he did this, than if he did it not? Could Paul fairly be said to call him to that act of idol worship? and how unsuitably would Paul have acted if he interfered to stop the witness from giving that confirmation of his evidence by exclaiming—"Pray do not swear by Jupiter, for in doing so you will commit a great sin." It was a very different thing when he and Barnabas resisted the people of Lystra from offering sacrifices to them; for this was connected with a testimony against the general principles of their idolatry, and with a setting forth of the only true God. Let us imagine that we live in a heathen country, where none were allowed to travel a particular road without making an obeisance to an idol-image by the way side. A Christian would find himself debarred from going along that road. But if he had a message to be delivered, or business to be transacted on it, who will say that he might not lawfully send one of the heathens on his message or business? And could it justly be said that he sent that heathen to make obeisance to the idol.

Nothing seems to mark more clearly the falsehood and the danger of the principle taken up by the brethren of C——, than this consideration, that none who adopt it can consistently stop short of endeavouring to restrain unbelieving men from swearing, or to make them, as it were, observe a precept given exclusively to disciples of the Lord. For example, a few days ago I had occasion to call on my attorney, for the purpose of signing a pair of leases, the deed of surrender of another lease, and the memorial of one of them for the purpose of being registered. The attorney rung the bell, and desired one of his clerks to come in, that he might witness the signature. This certainly was with the view of his making the necessary affidavit to get the memorial immediately registered, and of his being competent to prove the execution of the other papers legally. Now, if I had declined to *allow* him to be present for this purpose; (and one of the C—— brethren expressly says—"If I either ALLOWED or engaged a man to swear for me, it would be virtually the same thing as if I did it myself;) if I had said that I would not allow him to witness my signature, lest in proving it he should commit the sin of swearing, would not this have been directly interfering to prevent that man's swearing? an interference, which any who are standing fast in the truth, must see to be altogether unsuitable to it. But if, on the other hand, I was fully justifiable in *allowing* him to be called in by my attorney for the purpose of witnessing my signature, must I not have been equally justifiable if I had called him in myself, or brought him with me, for the same purpose? What essential difference there is between the two things it would be very hard to point out.

On the whole, the C—— sentiment strikes me as having nothing to countenance it, but the unfair and sophistical form in which it is put forward, and as involving a mass of the most dangerous errors—such as the idea that unbelieving men are more or less evil according to the number of their evil *acts*; and that Christians are called either to prevent their transgression of divine precepts, or to engage their observance of them while they still remain in unbelief. That scruples on the question should be excited in the minds of some disciples by the fallacious forms of proposing it, is not surprising; but that they should continue after that fallacy has been exposed, will be surprising and very lamentable.

In coming to the consideration of such questions, we need to remember that it is not merely against the *worldly* bias of our fleshly minds we have to be guarded; that there may be a morbid apprehensiveness of this; and that the vanity of the flesh may equally operate in leading us to encounter worldly trials to which we are not called.

I confess I feel a great deal of satisfaction in having been led to a full settlement of judgment on this subject.

If you see any weak point in what I have suggested, you will of course not spare it.

Yours affectionately,

CI.

TO THE SAME.

Nov. 23, 1833.

Dear Brother,—I will aim at simplifying the question, of the lawfulness or unlawfulness of playing at games of chance, by presenting to your consideration a particular case. Suppose you and I should amuse ourselves by throwing dice, and decide by the highest throw which shall pay the other a penny. I say this is essentially resorting to the lot to determine the matter: and I have little doubt you will be at once sensible of this, if the thing to be determined were of higher importance. If, for instance, a tyrant decreed that one of us should die, and left us to decide which should be the sufferer: in case we could not otherwise agree on the point, we might decide by lot; and if we did, we ought to feel that we were leaving the decision to the Lord, in the persuasion that "the whole disposal thereof is of Him:" and might we not as freely employ the dice for the purpose as any other form of lot? We know not exactly the form of lot by which the apostles chose between Joseph and Matthias; but whatever was its form, could it be essentially different from the highest throw on a pair of dice? Now, if so, have we any right to employ the same lot in the way of amusement for deciding a matter so trivial as a penny? That those who do the latter intend not any appeal to the Lord I allow, and that they may not be at all serious on the occasion, but merely diverting themselves. But the question is, whether such diversion be suitable to Christians who remember what is said of the lot. Those who do it appeal to *something* for the decision of the matter—to something wholly beyond their own control, and the result of which no human judgment has any means for conjecturing or regulating. This something they are accustomed to call *chance*. What is that? You will observe that, to simplify the question at present, I suppose the two persons who are proceeding to throw the dice, do not continue any such amusement through a number of throws, but that each throws but once, and that but one penny is to be decided at the time. Before either A. or B. has thrown, there is no more reason to conjecture that either will be the winner than the other. Perhaps A. throws sixes, he has then certainly calculated the chances (as it is called) against B. It is 35 to 1 that he will not win; 35 to 2 that he will lose; however, the matter is still uncertain. He has a *chance* of winning, to which he appeals; and contrary to all our calculations of probability he throws sixes. If we were seriously employing the lot, on an occasion that warranted our appeal to the Lord for his decision, even after the one had thrown sixes, it would not become us to calculate any probabilities about the ultimate result; but when we amuse ourselves with the lot, we put out of consideration Him with whom the whole disposal of it is declared to be, and employ rational calculations of probability, while we are forced to own that in any one instance chance or luck may run counter to them all. Is not this same chance or luck one of the idols of the world? You attempt to distinguish between the lot in scripture and throwing the dice, &c. for amusement. "The lot," you say, "is merely a renunciation of our own judgment in the act we are performing." Consider whether, in this respect, it does not exactly coincide with the scriptural nature of the lot. It would certainly be unsuitable to employ the lot in any case, where we have rational or scriptural rule for the regulation of our judgment. That the lot *ought* to be a most serious appeal to God, and *ought to be* connected with the persuasion that we are acting in conformity with His will in the appeal, is certain. But this cannot be admitted as constituting any essential difference between the lot and throwing the dice for a penny, without assuming what is the question, that we may lawfully amuse ourselves with the most light employment of that, which (when we employ it at all) ought to be employed most seriously. In weighing what I have offered, put out of the consideration altogether whether many, or few, or any, agree with me on the subject. If you think there is an essential difference between a game at cards or backgammon, and the case I have proposed of deciding by the highest throw on the dice who shall pay a penny, state it as strongly as you can. I cannot at present see any. "The lot," you say, "is not forbidden, and we may look for the divine blessing, while amusing ourselves with the lot, as much as in any other act which is neither forbidden nor enjoined." You perceive that, in stating this argument, I substitute for your words—"whilst playing a game at cards or backgammon"—a plainer phrase, which, according to your present concession, is equivalent. And now I readily admit, that in any *intrinsically lawful* amusement or relaxation, a Christian may well use it as to the Lord with thankfulness to him and looking for his blessing. I am sure also that the lot is not forbidden: but is not its nature sufficiently intimated, and the occasions on which it is to be employed sufficiently marked in scripture; to debar us from making it a matter of amusement? Honestly speaking, should we amuse ourselves with it, while we really recollect and believe what is said of it in the Word of God? I should wonder much if any Christian would throw the dice for amusement under that recollection, and conscious that he was then taking the lot. I rather think the matter might be left to you there, and that further argument is but calculated to entangle the subject. However, you go on to remark, and most justly, that the disposing of *every* event is as much of the Lord as the lot, even where our own judgment is exercised ever so properly and prudently. It is a blessed truth, the remembrance of which is calculated to make us "in all our ways acknowledge Him." Yet in ordinary cases this is not only consistent with the prudential exercise and use of appointed means for arriving at the end proposed, but the right view of the one binds and encourages us to the employment of the other. I conceive that the inference which you meant to be drawn from the remark is this, that there is no such particular solemnity in the use of the lot as I conceive. But I think its proper solemnity remains unshaken, when we consider that it immediately involves that "renunciation of our own judgment" which you have marked, and in this virtually includes the looking for a determination to some other and higher direction.

CII.

TO MR. Y——.

Dec. 10, 1823.

Dear Mr. Y——,—You had no cause to apprehend that I should consider you as taking any *liberty* with me in writing. I thank you for your letter, in which, I doubt not, you designed my profit; and if I do not go to the same length in reply, it is only because I think I have exhausted all I have to say upon the subject.

Though you speak of having read what I have offered on it in print, you seem not to understand my meaning yet, or you would not speak of me as representing a law of Christ's kingdom to have become obsolete by the lapse of years. The thing that you contend for and practise under the *name* of baptism, I positively deny to have been at any time a law of his kingdom, or practised at all in the apostolic days: I mean the baptism of a person who has *never but* professed to believe that Jesus of Nazareth is the Messiah. Whether that baptism of *proselytes* to the Christian faith, which confessedly was practised in the apostolic days, was observed as a Jewish washing, or as an institution of the Lord Jesus in the Kingdom of

Heaven, is a question which it really is not necessary for me to go into at all, *as immediately affecting my own practice*; any baptism that I could observe being essentially distinct from that of the apostolic days; and indeed involving in it a lie—that I had not before *professed* to believe in Jesus of Nazareth. At the same time—on that question—I must utterly deny all force in the remark by which you and so many others attempt to get over my argument from 1 Cor. i. 14. The administration of baptism, you say—and very truly—was not *peculiarly apostolic*. But no more was the preaching of the gospel. But who could admit the idea of Paul's thanking God (on any account) that he had preached the gospel to very few of the Corinthians? You equally mistake my meaning, in seeming to think it necessary to maintain, *as against me*, that all the proselytes to the Christian faith in the days of the apostles were baptised, or washed with water, on their conversion. I really never thought of denying it. I wonder much at your selection of the two passages, 1 Cor. xv. 29. and 1 Pet. iii. 21. as supporting your views. As to the former, I have to confess that I do not understand at all what *baptism for the dead* means. Do you? As to the latter passage, it contains a very explicit declaration that the apostle is not speaking of baptism with water at all. Notwithstanding the apparent approximation of our views on the subject of children, I suspect there is some essential difference still latent. For though you now talk of acknowledging your young children as disciples from their first instruction in the truth, and only making baptism with water a part of that instruction and admonition, in which you would bring them up, I fancy you would have your young child to collect, as well as it was able, from your *statement*, that it ought to ask for baptism, instead of plainly calling and exhorting it to the rite. If you do the latter in plain English, I am sure your children would readily receive the washing; and then all I could say against your practice would be, that we have no intimation in the New Testament Scriptures of any such baptism being commanded or practised, though it is certain that there was in the apostolic age a most numerous class of such young disciples. And in all this, I think I make a most *direct appeal to the Word*. But you seem to forget that, when I am engaged in proving that a doctrine is NOT in the scriptures, which some falsely derive from it, (as, for instance, the popish doctrine of purgatory,) I am unavoidably involved in a line of argument somewhat different from that, by which I prove that a doctrine *is* in the scripture. If I were a Baptist, I should certainly quote a much greater number of texts in supporting the error, than I now do in opposing it: but you are quite mistaken when you infer that I should therefore make a more direct appeal to scripture.

Looking to Him who alone can *well* bring us to one mind on this and every other part of his truth, I remain,

Yours, with sincere interest,

CIII.

TO F. C——, ESQ.

Feb. 24, 1824.

My dear Friend,—In one of your letters you expressed a wish to know wherein our fundamental difference consists.

Perhaps some of the little pieces which I sent you may have already answered that inquiry. Do you not perceive that we do not believe the same gospel? that while we both bear the Christian *name*, we do not mean the same thing at all by Christianity? Our difference of sentiments and opinion upon this subject, is in your view of no essential importance; nor, in fact, is what you call Christianity, if you were to look honestly at the state of your mind. In my view, any difference of opinion on this subject is fundamental indeed. If we believe not the same gospel, we do not worship or serve the same God. You say it has always appeared to you "that the Christian road to salvation was *a broad* one, designed to embrace all descriptions of believers." Now, if you were to ask yourself seriously—what you mean by *salvation;* and what you mean by the *Christian road* to it; perhaps you would find that you had never attached any distinct ideas to the phrases. But, on the opinion you express about the broadness of that road, ought it not to strike you that you avow your disbelief of the plain declaration of Christ, Mat. vii. 13, 14:—"Enter ye in at the strait gate; for wide is the gate, and broad is the way, that leadeth to destruction, and many there be which go in thereat: because strait is the gate, and narrow is the way, which leadeth unto life, and few there be that find it." When such a passage is quoted, folks commonly run to a commentator (if they have one) to see what he says upon it. Why so? Is it because there is any obscurity or doubtfulness in the import of the words? No: there cannot be any language more plain and unequivocal in its meaning. But they do not like the meaning; and at the same time they do not like to avow their rejection of the scriptures. They want help to get over the meaning, and they therefore apply to the commentator for assistance to affix some other meaning to the words of scripture, to twist them into a sense opposed to their real import; and they commonly succeed in finding what they look for—some support and authority for the lie they love. This has been the grand business of the *commentators* for ages. When you add that the Christian road to salvation was destined to embrace "all descriptions of believers," there is a sense which your words might be supposed to have, in which I should cordially concur with you. All, of whatever description—who *believe* the divine testimony in the Scriptures, have everlasting life, and shall be saved eternally. But nothing of that kind was your meaning. You mean that persons who believe every variety of doctrine under the name of Christian, shall alike participate in what you call salvation, provided they possess those characters of personal goodness which you think the essential point, and which at bottom you conceive will equally lead to salvation the infidel as well as the Christian. Indeed, if *varieties* of faith, under the common *name* and *profession* of Christianity, be alike consistent with salvation, it is idle to talk of the Christian faith being essential to it. The Christian is one, and invariable; (and here, in order to shut out, if possible, a class of questions and speculations not immediately affecting ourselves, I would remark that I, throughout, wish to be understood as speaking of the case of those alone to whom the word of God is sent, and who, therefore, either believe or disbelieve the testimony which it declares.) But the fact is, that the great mass of professors in these countries have no persuasion of the divine certainty of that revelation which they say they believe. They have found the profession of it general around them, and creditable—provided it be not a serious and scriptural profession. They have been brought up themselves under the Christian name, and certain religious forms that they call Christian. They are, perhaps, also aware that the evidences of the divine origin and authority of Christianity are such as no infidel has been able successfully to assail, and such as have extorted the acknowledgment of the most able men who have examined the subject most closely. They find also, that—as might be expected in a real revelation from heaven,—the belief of it is declared to be of vital importance: that the words run—"he that believeth shall be saved," and "he that believeth not shall be condemned." On all these accounts they have a suspicion at times that it may be true, and are partly ashamed, and partly afraid, to own the lurking suspicion that it is false—to own it even to themselves. Yet so far as they examine the Scriptures at all, they find things in every page, at which their incredulity stumbles, declarations which they accordingly disbelieve. They find, however, other passages, which they think—(because they misunderstand them)—consistent with the principles which they have adopted as indubitable and good. Of such passages, therefore, they are often forward to express great admiration, while anxious to turn away from the former as dangerous and false. Their occasional language about them as unintelligibly obscure, is only a more civil method of saying that they think them false. Their minds having never been subdued to the authority of the divine word, they derive not their sentiments from it, but will make it bend to their sentiments, or reject it when they cannot. Thus they commonly contrive to keep the whole subject at a convenient distance from their minds. Their serious attention is engrossed by the various objects of the present life, which have in their view a certainty and reality which the others have not: while the latent suspicion that, after they have done with the present life, they may perhaps find substantial realities in another, leads them to maintain what they consider a decent and prudent regard to what they call religion. Do not, however, suppose from this language that I should think any better of their course, if (as sometimes is the case), they were ever so intensely and exclusively occupied with what they call religion. So long as the only true God is unknown and denied, man's religion (be it much or little, cold or fervent), is idolatrous and vain. The only true God has discovered his character and glory in the testimony He has sent from heaven concerning his son: and it is life eternal to know him, or to believe that testimony. John xvii. 3. He conveys this knowledge to whom He will, even to all whom He has before chosen out of the world and ordained to eternal life. Compare Matt. xi. 25, 27. John vi. 37, 44, 45. x. 26—28. Acts xiii. 48. Those are the sheep for whom Christ has laid down his own life—stooped to be made a curse for them, that they might be blessed in him. The gospel is a testimony of the glory of God in their salvation—in that salvation which is absolutely and exclusively his work. In the divine truth, of which they are convinced by divine report, they are brought to the knowledge of that living God, whom they had before disowned and denied, and from the life of whom they had been alienated; and while this discovery shows them the utter evil of all that they thought best in themselves, —the idolatrous character of all their former religion—while it abases them in their own sight, it also exalts them and gives them "everlasting consolation and good hope," 2 Thess ii. 16, from the character in which God is discovered, as the justifier and saviour of the ungodly;—from that propitiation for sin which he sets forth in the one offering of his own Son bearing the sins of many;—from the evidence which his resurrection from the dead affords that he has finished that work, which he willingly humbled himself to undertake, and that God is well pleased for his righteousness sake; and from the divine assurance, which brings this righteousness and peace nigh unto those who are farthest from righteousness,—that those who believe—not those who *do* this or that to attain unto righteousness—but those who believe the word that testifies the righteousness of God, are accepted in the beloved, are justified from all things, and *have* everlasting life. I forbear enlarging on this topic, because my views of it are detailed in several of the little pieces that I sent you. If there be any point on which you desire further information about my sentiments, use all freedom in calling on me to afford it.

CIV.

TO J. F——.

Feb. 9, 1824.

My very dear Brother,—Though I am ill able to write, yet a letter I have just received from H. F—— marks the necessity of my communicating with some of the church at L—— on his case; and on some accounts I think it better to write to you than to L——. I had heard with much grief of the contest and disturbance of mind which he had produced among you: but when he informed me by letter that he had *left your fellowship!* on account of your singing the Psalms, I immediately wrote to him, not to argue the question about the comparative expediency of singing the Psalms or Hymns, but to call his attention to his wicked trifling with the ordinances of God, in making a difference of judgment on any such question the ground of his forsaking the fellowship of the body. By his answer I find he makes quite light of the reproof, and continues utterly insensible to his sin. I had expressed my hope that the church at L—— would pursue the scriptural course for calling him to repentance: but some of his language in his last leads me to apprehend that nothing has been done in that way. When any one quits our fellowship, is not the church whose assembly he forsakes called immediately to pursue the same course of admonition and effort to restore the offender, as in any other case of manifested evil? And observe well, that in dealing with H. F—— on his sin, ye are called to decline all discussion with him of the question, whether it would be better to sing the Psalms or Hymns. His sin consists in making agreement on either side of that, or any such question, one of his terms of communion. And really, when the fellowship of the saints is so trifled with as to be made to turn upon such points, there is an awful indication that the person does not see its really divine ground and limits. You will perceive, that according to the views which I offer, the church is not at all disqualified for acting together in applying the discipline of Christ's house to H. F——, from the circumstance that you and others have been brought over to think *with him* on the question between psalms and hymns. Though you might prefer hymns—(and, indeed, I understood that you were waiting with some degree of impatience for the Dublin hymn-books)—yet I trust you abhor the idea of saying, "I will not walk in Christian fellowship with any *who will sing the Psalms of David.*" I regret and wonder that such arguments as H. F—— puts forward should carry any weight to your mind. But all that is a very subordinate matter; the weakness of his argument is lost in the wickedness of his conduct. Yet is it not disgusting to read this as one of his weightiest arguments in his last? "We cannot use language *as our own*, which the Lord by his prophet speaks of himself." And which of the brethren did he find doing so? *There*, indeed, he would have found an error worth contending against. In his former letter he urged the question, how could we sing, "Lo, I come to do thy will," &c. taking for granted that in singing such words we must *personate* the Messiah. He might as well say, that when you and S—— were singing "Scots wha hae wi' Wallace bled," you were both intending to personate Bruce. But all this discussion should be for the present put wholly out of sight. H. F—— says, in his last, "All the church, I believe, with two exceptions, are of the same opinion now. *We* are to have a meeting on Sunday, and I hope all will be *brought to one mind.*" Whether ye all concur or not in preferring hymns to the Psalms, or the Psalms to hymns, I comparatively care not a rush; and it is awful to find him persisting to talk of such agreement as the unity of mind to which the Lord brings his people by the influence of the truth; but I should be sorry indeed to find, that you had received him back in any *such way* as he intimates in that sentence. It would be covering his sin and countenancing it. You are all agreed that you may use some of the psalms. You are all agreed that you may use some hymns. There is no fair room, therefore, for any dissension here. But I trust you will be all agreed in marking your abhorrence of the conduct of him who would rend the body of Christ on such a question; and that, unless he be brought to repentance for his wickedness, you will agree in that language which I, from the heart, pronounce—though he thinks that none but an apostle ought—"Let him be accursed." I have been very ill for several weeks; and can only add, that I shall anxiously wait to hear of a *scriptural* termination to this business. The good Lord bless and keep you all in the simplicity of faith and love.

Your affectionate brother,

CV.

TO THE SAME.

March 3, 1824.

It is with grief of heart, my brother, I find, by a letter received this day from our dear L——, that H. F—— has neither been brought to repentance for his iniquity, nor been put away from among you. In the former, I see the continuance of his sin; in the latter, I see the rest of you acting the most cruel part towards him, and the most unfaithful towards the Lord, in taking part with his sin, or suffering it upon him. I am sorry that I happen not to have your letter at hand, but I remember the substance and general tenor of it; and I observed them with great pain. For though you professed to agree with me that H. F—— had acted in some degree wrong, in quitting the fellowship of the body because you sing the inspired songs of David, you yet evidently sought to extenuate his evil by sharing the blame (as it were) between him and another who has opposed him; and were only anxious for a kind of deceitful *settlement of the difference between them*. My brother, whereinsoever you think J. L—— has sinned in the business, reprove him, marking his sin distinctly. I know not yet wherein you think it consists. But is any evil in him (supposing ever so much can be established) to be used as a set-off against the gross, obvious, and continued wickedness of the other? (I wish H. F—— to see all that I write.) Ever since he came among you, instead of seeking his edification and yours in the common faith, he has appeared to amuse himself with distracting and subverting your minds. He at length abandons your fellowship *because you sing Psalms!* and sufficiently marks his object in this step, as expecting to be a ringleader of schism, by coolly observing to me, that indeed you and others of one mind with him *had not yet left the body*, but that he expected you soon would. Though you appear to have been sadly infected with this leaven, I trust you will be found *not* of one mind with him. But, indeed, I am jealous over you with a godly jealousy. You seem to think J. L—— unwarrantably severe in expressing doubts of H. F——'s standing in the truth. This is one of the bad symptoms of false charity in yourself. But I wish you distinctly to understand that I fully coincide with J. L—— there. When I see a man—no matter if he were my own son or brother after the flesh—making such a profane plaything of his connexion with a Christian church, and rejecting and making a mock of all reproof offered to him,—when I see him for months exerting himself in the service of the devil,—labouring to divide and rend asunder the body of Christ, can I have confidence in such a man as a brother? can I take the talk of his lips about the truth in opposition to his conduct? No. From the bottom of my heart I say—would that he were cut off who troubleth you! And I see in that course, as much the course of mercy to him—if he be a vessel of mercy—as of profit to the body and faithfulness to the Lord. And what mean you, dear F——, by allowing him or any one this week to abandon your fellowship, and the next week to rejoin it, without even any profession of repentance? Think you that, in any case, this can scripturally go on in a Christian church? His present conduct is much of a piece with (but worse than) a former instance, in which he left the church in London, because we would stand up (instead of keeping our seats) while blessing and giving thanks before taking the bread and wine! That was bad enough; but, indeed, there is something more profane in the present case. The songs which were given by inspiration of God to the sweet Psalmist of Israel, and all, from the first to the last, celebrating—not David—but his Lord,—put by the royal prophet into the hands of Ethan, Asaph, Jeduthun, &c. to record, and to thank, and praise the Lord God of Israel, (see 1 Chron. xvi.)—he gravely tells us, are unfit for the purpose to believers! Surely, then, he must suppose that David, and the singers he appointed, must have sung them in unbelief. And if any of the singers then had his mind enlightened to see the import of the lxxxixth Psalm, for instance, as David's mind certainly was, (Acts ii. 30, 31.) he would, I suppose, take his hat and walk out when Ethan raised that Psalm in the sanctuary. I write in great haste and in much bitterness of spirit, seeing that the unavoidable and speedy consequence of your not purging out the evil from among you, must be that any one who sees and abhors it must leave your fellowship. My love to J. L——, and tell him that I must remain in his debt a little longer; as I am but slowly recovering, and have a press of business on me at present.

Ever, with true affection, yours,

CVI.

TO THE SAME.

March 7, 1824.

Alas! my dear John, the melancholy intelligence which your letter brought me yesterday is only what I expected to hear. Indeed, I know not what else J. L—— could have done. All his efforts had proved vain to engage the body in a dealing of scriptural discipline with H. F——. Ye took part, and still take part, with his ungodliness. In such a case, any disciple who sees and abhors the evil, has no part left but to turn away from the body who will not purge it out from among them. Some may say that J. L—— should have waited a week or two longer. I really cannot pronounce on this: but it seems to me, from the whole course of the business, that it would have been but another week or two of vain jangling, and that he has been very far from precipitate. What you say of the kind of *acknowledgment* which you were unanimous in receiving from H. F—— only proves, how deeply and universally you are infected with the leaven of his sin. He would not, forsooth, have left the fellowship, if he had been satisfied that the *objectionable Psalms* would be discontinued! Words cannot more plainly avow his impenitence. What is it but to declare that he still sets it up as a term of communion, that those with whom he will condescend to walk shall not sing (for instance) the lxxxixth Psalm? And this is received by you all as a profession of repentance! I am sure, I wonder not that my brother L—— suspects he has erred, in trying to select the Psalms that ye would not *object* to. I am sorry to remark that you, dear John, seem infected not only with H. F——'s immediate principles, but with the radical principle of the popular forbearance. You seem in one of your letters plainly to intimate, that he was justified in leaving the body because he could not *conscientiously*, in his present views, sing the lxxxixth Psalm. This is just setting up the worldly notion of men's *consciences* being the standard of right and wrong. However, he has now succeeded in effecting the schism which he seems to have worked hard for from the beginning: and all who know the circumstances must take one side or the other. *I wish it to be distinctly understood that I stand with J. L——.* I cease not, however, to pray for you and H. F——, that ye may be led to see and to abhor your iniquity; and particularly that you, dear John, may be given to see the evil of that false *good-nature* which has proved such a snare to you in this business.

CVII.

TO THE SAME.

April 9, 1824.

My very dear F.—The letter which I received from you on the 20th ult. afforded me great joy. It found me very busy; and I have since been postponing my reply in the daily expectation of hearing from J—— L——. How comes it that he does not write? Besides my solicitude to hear how the Excise business has terminated, he must surely be aware, (if he thinks) that I *need* some communication from him about the state in which you are as to Christian fellowship. I trust that, before this, you and he are again walking together; that the breach between you, which Satan was allowed to make, is fully repaired; and that I am therefore no longer to have the most painful feeling, that, in maintaining my Christian union with one of you, it is interrupted with the other. The sacredness and closeness of that union is seen only in the light of that divine truth which produces and cements it. While kept in the discernment of this, we shall see and abhor two apparently opposite evils, but equally profane, and springing from the same root of bitterness. The one, and perhaps the more common, is that of sacrificing divine truth, or divine command, in order to maintain something under the name of church connexion. Such union is the unity of confederates against the glory of the Lord. The other evil—(less common, because it can be developed fully only in those who stand, or have stood, in outward connexion with a scriptural church)—is that of lightly rending the visible body of Christ, and sacrificing Christian union and fellowship to the maintenance of our own whims and fancies. Both evils must alike originate in a mind blind to the divine nature and sacredness of the unity of brethren in the faith; must originate, in short, in that common spring of all evil—unbelief,—that insensibility to the one revealed glory, which leaves a man under the power of his fleshly mind to follow his idols, and the vain imaginations of his own heart. It will rejoice me to hear that your dealing with poor H. F. has been blessed for calling him to repentance;—to find that his sickness is not unto death. If his eyes be indeed opened to see his sin, he will no longer be found justifying himself by attacking others. In his last letter to me—chiefly filled with railing invectives against dear L——,—he reprehends me sharply for reviving the recollection of his former evil, and mentioning to you his having abandoned the fellowship of the brethren here for a similar vagary. Circumstanced as we are, I cannot acknowledge that I did any thing wrong in mentioning it. If one, who has been called a brother, turns away repeatedly, again entangled in the same evil for which he has before professed repentance, it is idle to say that the recurrence of his sin must not revive the recollection of the former instance of it, until scriptural repentance appears anew. Whenever this appears, it would be indeed very unwarrantable to remember or rake up against him any thing that has passed. Though I have written so far, I am not decided whether I will despatch this letter to-day; I feel it so unsatisfactory to write, without knowing what has taken place since your last.

Monday (12th.) Still no letter: but, perhaps, this day's post may bring one. At any rate I cannot longer delay sending this, as I fear you must think my silence strange. There have been a few lines on business from H. F. to Mr. C——; and from the style of his address, and his total silence on the subject of his conduct, it is plain that he had not then repented of his evil deeds. I have little doubt that he looks for support from some in D——; and that, in his present mind, he will aim at spreading the schism wider, which he succeeded in producing among you. It is an awful spectacle. If all those, who have walked together at L——, be really brought to the mind which you express in your letter, I doubt not that the breach has been repaired before this. But I apprehend there may have been some difficulties to J. L——'s re-uniting himself to the *collective body*. Certainly I conceive that each of you, when led to see your sin, was called to *seek re-union with him*; and not to wait till he could seek it with the body. It is not from any idle punctilio that I mark this. But, as I consider that he was divinely bound to act as he did in leaving you, I must consider that the standard of scriptural truth moved with him, and ceased to be with the rest of you. Round that standard any who were afterwards brought to repentance, should immediately rally. Among all the profitable lessons of instruction and reproof which this melancholy business is calculated to impress on disciples, that is one—the importance that each—male and female—from the oldest to the youngest, should have their judgments formed for themselves from the Scriptures, so as to adhere to that rule, *at all cost*, in the fear of the Lord, unswayed by personal influence and regards. I expect this will go to you under Mr. D——'s cover; and you and L—— may avail yourselves of the same for some time in writing to me. Write without delay, and tell J—— to do so likewise, whether his Excise business be decided or not. My love to your dear partner, and the children. Grace be with you all!

Very affectionately yours, for the truth's sake,

CVIII.

TO J. L——.

Jan. 9, 1824.

My very dear L——,—So it seems that, at the very time I thought your trials about oaths at an end, they have begun again, and with a more formidable aspect. It is well, my brother:—all right; for it is the Lord's doing. Has he not told us that the hairs of our head are all numbered? Does he not say—"It is *I*; be not afraid?" Does he not mercifully rebuke our unbelief in such language—"Do ye not remember? Are ye yet without understanding? O ye of little faith!" You say you feel yourself "less able to refight this battle than when it first began." No matter: it is not your's. Remember that word—"When I am weak, then am I strong." But you are really weary of such a contention, and ashamed of it, as it is deemed to spring from enthusiasm or imbecility, &c. It is a sad affair, to be sure, when such *clever* fellows as J. L—— or John Walker are laughed at as *fools* for Christ's sake: and there is but one effectual remedy for that pride which kicks at it, and would make us faint under it—to *consider* HIM who endured to be called mad, and to be the song of the drunkard.

March —, 1824. * * * * Have you ever read, dear J——, of certain women which ministered to him of their substance? To whom? do you know? 'Aye, aye; it is written, Luke viii. 2, 3. I know that passage very well.' Say, my brother, do we not forget the *thing*, however we may recollect the *words*, when we kick so proudly, as you seem to do, against the idea of our possibly becoming dependent on our fellow sinners. That the flesh will kick at it, I know: I am well acquainted with the feeling: but let us not be imposed on by it, as if it were a good and proper feeling.

There is a spirit of independence which the Word enjoins, of eating our own bread, &c. But if He, whose we are, be pleased to say—"I see it best that you should be unable to earn your own bread, for I see the pride and naughtiness of heart which lurks under your independent spirit. Go—I have commanded the ravens—or a widow-woman—or such and such brethren, to sustain you"—would it not become us to say—"Good is the will of the Lord?" But all this while you are fretting and fuming under an imaginary trial in possible prospect. You have discovered it to be false, I suppose, that "sufficient unto the day is the evil thereof." O, J——! let us rather be *in subjection* to the Father of Spirits, that we may live. "Be still: and know that HE is GOD."

It grieves me much to hear that F—— is disturbing you with questions that minister strife rather than godly edifying. I well recollect how much comfort and food I had singing the Scotch version of the Psalms of David with you. I believe I checked your impatience for the new hymn-books, thinking that you are better off as you are. But really I should think myself ill employed fighting with any brethren, *which* should be used. While the Psalms are used, in the mind in which they were indited, they are a feast of marrow and fatness above all hymns that ever were composed by man. I smile at his objection to the version on the ground of *taste*. I should decisively object to the more poetical English version, or to Dr. Watts's. I do view with pain and surprise our brother's objection to the language in Gal. i. 7, 8, as if unfit for any believer except an *inspired* apostle. May it be the language of our whole heart and soul unto the end! But as used by the apostle or by us, I really have never conceived the words, "Let him be accursed," as denoting a prayer that the curse of God should ultimately fall upon him (though we must be sure that it shall, if he be not given repentance to the acknowledgment of the truth), but as a direction that he should be regarded by us as an accursed thing, as one (however specious and highly esteemed) upon whom the wrath of God lies. He that will not heartily join with the apostle in the solemn words, must be animated by some spirit very different from that of the truth. May you all follow the things that make for peace, and the things whereby ye may edify one another.

April —, 1824. * * * * Thanks for your interesting letter of the 14th. It relieved and rejoiced me in many views. How tenderly does our Heavenly Father deal in allowing you to retain your situation in the Excise! It is what I expected: but to find my expectations realized, is delightful and calls for praise. So also does the termination of H. F——'s business. It had a very threatening aspect for some time; but I trust will be turned into a blessing. Dear J.'s last letter prepared me to expect a happy result, though I scarcely flattered myself that you would be so soon re-united to so many. I trust that mutual confidence and love will be more than ever strengthened and abound among you.

July —, 1824. * * * * It rejoices me to hear that you are all going on in the peace and comfort of the gospel. O! it is indeed a good and a pleasant thing for brethren to dwell together in unity. And the restoration of that blessing must be considerably endeared by its late interruption. Your account of our sister ——'s health, and the pecuniary prospects of the family, ought to excite our sympathy and prayers. May they acknowledge the rod, and Him who hath appointed it, and be profitably exercised under his correcting hand! How cheering are the assurances that whom the Lord loveth he chasteneth; "that when we are chastened of the Lord, it is that we may not be condemned with the world." I believe many of the pecuniary trials of Christians originate in their not attending to the plain rule given them—"Mind not high things, but conform to low." Rom. xii. 16.

I am at present threatened with an attack of gout. But I have had a longer interval of freedom from it than I have been accustomed to for some years. I labour also under a new disease, which I thought would have subjected me to a painful surgical operation. I felt very cowardly at the prospect, but I found great comfort from the consideration of that word—"We are members of his body, of his flesh, and of his bones," Eph. v. 30. (It is *out of* his flesh;

taken out of it as Eve from Adam's). No man ever yet hated his own flesh, but nourisheth and cherisheth it, *even as the Lord the church*. Surely, if we had faith as a grain of mustard seed, the closeness of this union which subsists between the members and their Head, is sufficient to make us yield ourselves to him and his gracious dealings at all times and in all circumstances, in implicit reliance on his tenderness, and care, and wisdom. He does not willingly afflict or grieve us; but he loves us too well to leave us without chastisement; and has too high aims for us, to let us take up our rest here. "Blessed be the Lord God of Israel from everlasting to everlasting; and let the people say, Amen."

CIX.

TO MRS. C———.

May —, 1825.

* * * *—. And now I must dismiss my nonsense for the present. He was indeed a wise man that said—"Even in laughter the heart is sad," Prov. xiv. 13; and, perhaps, even in nonsense the heart may be sober; driven to the nonsense from not knowing how to bring forward the sober verities that press upon it. But there are circumstances which will force them out head foremost. You are going to spend (I think) three years at P——; and I am sure I do not think my life worth three years' purchase. You may, on your return, find me vegetating where I am; but I think it more likely that I shall by that time have done with this life, and have got behind the scenes. You think that I shall be in a state of insensibility, or, in fact, of temporary non-entity. I am sure I shall not! for I am sure the scriptures plainly oppose the notion, and I know nothing at all about the matter but what the scriptures testify. They have spoiled me as a philosopher, and they have spoiled me as a man of prudence and respectability in the world. In short, they have made (what the world thinks) a fool of me. Yet, if I had to begin life anew, and were allowed one wish, it should be to be "yet more vile," 2 Sam. vi. 21, 22, in the same way. What folly would it be to make any of the objects of this life the matter of any one wish; for which of them is it that is not like a passing dream? But, my friend, you would mistake me much if you should think that I aimed at exciting in you or myself such a moralizing fit as has led many, under a general conviction of the emptiness of every object in this world, to devote their main solicitude to the supposed concerns of another world. One may be so exercised to any degree of earnestness, and yet be occupied with a more unreal shadow than the irreligious sensualist. If the irreligious world are walking in a vain shadow, the religious are walking in the *shadow of*

a shade. The Christian alone is a child of the light and of the day: "he alone is *awake*, and knows whither he is going." And when I speak of the Christian, I mean that man or woman who believes the truth declared from heaven in the gospel of God the Saviour. That revelation discovers the character and glory of the *only true* and only living God. It is the light of life; and as every Israelite who saw the brazen serpent lifted up by Moses in the wilderness was healed (Numb xxi. 8, 9. John iii. 14, 15), so every man that sees the truth revealed from heaven in the gospel, is restored to eternal life. Probably, my friend, you would wish me to throw in some qualification to this assertion, to modify it in some way, to insert some proviso or condition. If so, it is because you do not believe the statement, and hold some doctrine which represents the attainment of eternal life as hanging upon something which the sinner has to do for the purpose. And this is the universal thought of man's heart, so far as man thinks at all upon the subject. "What shall I do that I may inherit eternal life?" is the question which man's excited conscience suggests: yet he does not like the only answer which is in point to the inquiry—"If thou wilt enter into life, [thus] keep the commandments of that righteous holy law, which enjoins perfect love to God and to man, under the penalty of death." He has a secret misgiving that he is a sinner against that law, and will be so to the end. Hence it happens, that in the part of the world called Christendom, a private gospel has been introduced, which represents an imaginary Christ, whose office it is in some way to make up for the deficiencies of good and well-disposed sinners, and to reveal a spurious mercy in their false god, which consists in indulgence to sins so small as theirs. So far as they can contrive to twist the scriptures into a coincidence with this deism (and here they have all the tribe of commentators and divines to help them), they are ready to admit the Bible to be a very good book, though they conceive that they could do very well without it, and that many do. Many think it an unsafe thing to call in question its divine origin, and therefore take pains to conceal, even from themselves, their scepticism on the subject. But when they meet plain passages of scripture, in point blank opposition to their fundamental principles, they do not hesitate to blaspheme the doctrine of scripture as very wicked doctrine, and the God whom it reveals as unreasonable and unjust. The parts of scripture which they like (for instance, the Sermon on the Mount), they like because they misunderstand them. Other parts they cannot for the life of them misunderstand, even with all the aid of their commentators: and those, therefore, they pronounce bad and dangerous. Indeed, when I consider the essential opposition of the human mind and all its principles to the revelation of God made in the scriptures, my wonder is not, that so few believe the report, but that any do believe it, and in this I see not any betterness of disposition in those who believe, but the power of God, whose word shall not return to him void, but shall accomplish all that for which he sends it. (Isa. lv. 11.) It has pleased God, by the foolishness of preaching [of the apostles' preaching], to save those that believe. (1 Cor. i. 21. Acts xiii. 48.) "It is not of him that willeth, or of him that runneth, but of God that showeth mercy;" (Rom. ix. 16), and the mercy that he showeth is indeed mercy "higher than the heavens," such as a creature altogether evil needs: while the perfection of this mercy is revealed in full harmony with the perfection of righteousness, and holiness, and truth, through that propitiation for sin which is set forth, as provided by God and accepted of Him, in the one offering of his Son dying the just for the unjust, and stooping to be made a curse in the place of sinners, that sinners (consistently with the divine glory) might be blessed in him. Here the revelation of God shows to man what is indeed good—that with which God *is* well pleased; and thus the gospel testifies the righteousness of God—that work of righteousness accomplished, on account of which God is just while he justifies the ungodly. The good hope which this gospel affords, it brings as near to the murderer on the gallows as to me or to you. He that believeth the report shall be saved, whoever he be; and he that disbelieves it, whoever he be, shall be condemned. And as to the grave apprehension, that such a doctrine will encourage men to commit murder, &c., it only shows that the person committing them, rejects the counsel of God against his own soul, and is of just the same mind with those who reproached Christ in the days of his flesh with being a friend of publicans and sinners. It is quite time to release you. I could mention circumstances which have led me, particularly at this time, to give you one plain testimony against that "philosophy and vain deceit" which corrupts the gospel of Christ. However, it at least is designed in true kindness; and if we should not meet again in the flesh, consider these as the last words of your faithful, though unphilosophic friend,

P.S. Why should I leave the ends blank, when I shall perhaps never communicate with you again upon the subject? You are a rational philosopher, and you think me irrational, because I disregard all the supposed discoveries of human reason about God and the ways of God, and consider the revelation made in his word as the one and only decisive oracle of divine truth. But let me not be misunderstood here. Far be it from me to undervalue right reason: but I am sure there is no right reason in these matters, till reason is *rectified*, by the mind being subdued to the acknowledgment of the truth and enlightened by its precepts. (How forcibly does the apostle *reason* against the reasoners on that subject in 1 Cor. ii. 11.) I know and am sure that *my* reason, or the intellectual faculty as exercised by myself, did lead me, and would have led me (if I had been left to its guidance), for ever to reject all the essential principles of divine truth, and to build one and another religious system of vanity and lies: in supporting which I might have gone through this world with great eclat and prosperity, but would have lived and died without God and without hope; i.e. without the only true God and without the only good hope. But I am equally sure that my views were then as irrational as they were unscriptural. And now that I see and am convinced of what is declared in the Word of God, I do see that this is the only thing consistent with *right* reason;

and that every system opposing it, *is* not only ungodly but irrational. I admit that difficult questions may be pressed on various points, which I cannot answer but with an honest avowal of my ignorance, because the scriptures do not inform me on the subject. But I say that the philosophers are unreasonable and unfair in urging these difficulties against the truths of scripture: for it would be easy to show that whatever system they embrace, is pressed with equal difficulties. The objections, for instance, which most derive from questions about the origin of evil, about the consistency of the creature's responsibility with the divine foreknowledge, &c.—these objections, legitimately followed up, would lead the objectors into downright Atheism; and I am sure that with that they would find themselves embarrassed with as many difficulties as they have attempted to escape. Instructed in all that I need to know, as a sinful creature, for my guidance and support, I am content to be ignorant about a great many matters of curious inquiry, and acknowledge the divine wisdom, as well in the limits of revealed discovery, as in its extent.

CX.

TO MRS. T———.

Aug. 6, 1825.

Though scriptural principle will not allow me at present to address you as a sister in Christ, yet I am ready to reply to your letter of the 25th ult., and to acknowledge that I am pleased with the general sobriety of mind which it manifests. I had heard of the distractions at C——; and am quite uncertain whether, if I were there to-morrow, I could unite with any of the little parties that remain. The breaking up of the church there I did not wonder at, as I know the state in which it had been for some time. When once a church is turned into a debating society for the agitation of curious questions, under the pretence of seeking increased knowledge in the good ways of the Lord, the sooner it is broken up the better. The adversary (often in the form of an angel of light) has succeeded in turning away their ear from the truth. They have become tired of the heavenly manna. To have "nothing at all besides that manna before their eyes," (Num. xi. 6.) seems to them a poor thing; and, therefore, they seek out many inventions! This is the continual propensity of all our hearts. But when an individual or society is left to that mind, they are as much walking after the flesh, while engaged (as they think) in prosecuting scriptural *inquiries*, as if they were walking in drunkenness and adultery. I have never thought of C—— for some years without a sigh: but "the Lord knoweth them that are his;" and will in his own time make them manifest.

Your carnal policy in maintaining religious fellowship with your husband, while he denied a divine command which you acknowledged, —in short, in loving him more than Christ,—has been rebuked. You seem to see that it has; and therefore I pass to the other subjects to which you call me. As to a believer's marrying an unbeliever, I do think that there is no rule in the New Testament against it; and I abhor the sin, of which I was guilty with others, of making a law which Christ has not made. And yet I am sure that the principles of Scripture mark the *general inexpediency* of such a connexion, if *it can be avoided*. That the marriage connexion is a *civil* or *earthly* connexion, and not a religious,—(though it is the most lasting and intimate of all mere earthly connexions)—is certain from this;—that the connexion continues in unabated obligation between those who can have *no religious fellowship*. The unbelieving husband is declared to be sanctified by the wife, and the unbelieving wife by the husband: that is, the marriage connexion with the unbelieving party is lawful to the believing. (1 Cor. vii. 14. see also 1 Pet. iii. 1.) And herein appears as plainly the difference of the law under the Gospel of Christ and under Moses. The Jew was bound even to *put away* a heathen wife with whom he had cohabited. But can we wonder at this, when we know that the Jews were debarred by their law from *civil* intercourse, from eating and drinking, with the unbelieving world. And those false teachers, who would refer us to the Jewish law in this and other matters, ought consistently to call a Christian husband to *put away* an unbelieving wife. The only passage of the New Testament Scriptures—(and to them alone Christians are to look for their rule)—which I formerly thought warranted the opposite inference, is that in 1 Cor. vii. 39. —" she is at liberty to marry whom she will, *only in the Lord.*" As if this meant—provided it be *to one who is in the Lord*, that is, to a fellow-disciple. But this in fact was inserting in the text what it does not contain. And the expression *in the Lord*, or the liberty which we have in *the Lord*,—is sufficiently illustrated by a reference to Eph. vi. i. and Gal. ii. 4. v. 13. At the same time I wish to say distinctly, that if a disciple act in this matter, of choosing a partner for life, *in the Lord*, (that is, as a disciple of the Lord, with an eye to his will and his glory)—I am sure he will choose a believing partner, *if* he can obtain any such at all suitable: and this, from the considerations which you justly suggest, especially those connected with the bringing up of the children. But I am obliged to put in the "*if*"—that I have inserted. For I must say that a Christian man may be so circumstanced, that he would *be bound* by the authority of the Lord to marry an heathen woman. He might be in a heathen country, where he had not one fellow-disciple; or, if he was in a church of fellow-disciples, none of the females might be unmarried;—or none of the unmarried females might be willing to take him for a husband; or none of them might be such as would make a wife at all suitable for him. And as to those who would say —' let the Christian man in those circumstances remain unmarried;' —they are only acting consistently in setting aside a divine law, in order to establish their own tradition. The Christian man, so circumstanced, may be *bound* by the divine law *to marry*. (1 Cor. vii. 9. Heb. xiii. 4.) But this divine law worldly religionists think of less authority than a law of worldly *prudence*, and of *pretended* superior *purity*, which they substitute. I pass to the other subject to which you call. On this general question about the distinction of *the law* into moral and ceremonial, which *the divines* run upon, I would briefly remark that, as they apply it—I think it only calculated to darken counsel by words without knowledge. In the ordinary scriptural use of the phrase—"the law"—we are plainly to understand that law which "was given by Moses"—*generally*—without any such distinction as they would introduce: though it is certain that, in the law given by Moses, there is included that law called moral, the work of which is written in the hearts and consciences of all men, charging them with guilt for doing evil. But, to come to the point for which you seem to introduce the other question, I acknowledge not any religious observance of the first day of the week obligatory on Christians, but that of coming together on that day, as the first disciples did, to shew forth the Lord's death in the Supper, and to observe the other ordinances of Christian fellowship. I was too long deterred from speaking a plain language on the subject, partly from being myself infected with the popular doctrine on it,—(though I could never rightly make out the scriptural authority for a *Christian Sabbath day)* and partly from worldly policy, unwilling to shock the prejudices of the world. But I must now say that the idea of a Christian sabbath-day, succeeding the Jewish sabbath, and to be observed by cessation from the ordinary business of life, is one which is utterly destitute of scriptural authority, and which the man of sin has introduced. Here also full well do the corrupt professors of this day, like the scribes and pharisees of old, set aside the commands of God, that they may keep their own traditions. Look at one of them, on the first day of the week, running to this or that religious meeting, to hear this and that preacher, or perhaps himself to preach; but altogether deaf to the instruction and reproof of the word as to the real observance of the day. The hypocrite challenges you for letting your children *play* on that day. (I do not know that even a Jewish child was restrained from that on the Jewish sabbath.) But I suppose he would be still more shocked if he saw you darning your husband's stockings on Sunday. And what has he to offer in support of this? Nothing, but a human tradition! 'Under the Christian dispensation there is a *change* of the sabbath from the last day of the week, which was appointed to the Jews, to the first day of the week; and now the first day is to be observed by Christians as the last day was by the Jews, and they must do no manner of work on that day;—not even (as the tip-top professors say) so much as to shave themselves.' Well: if a poor disciple of Christ may ask the question, I would beg to learn from these good gentlemen what ground they have for asserting this *change* of a sabbath day, and the continued obligation of *any Sabbatical* observance to Christians? 'O! as to the change, all the divines are agreed—Dr. Doddridge, and Dr. Watts, and (I suppose) Mr. Kelly, and all the *good* people, that the change *must* have been made by divine appointment: and though the New Testament Scriptures are *silent* upon the subject, yet it was probably made between the resurrection and ascension of the Lord. And as to the observance of a Christian *Sabbath* none but enemies to all religion and godliness can disregard it.' Thank ye, gentlemen; my blessed master was ranked in that class before me. A Christian standing in the light of the truth and adhering to the word of the Lord, can need nothing more to embolden his rejection of the current tradition on this subject, than to find that it has no foundation in the Scriptures of the New Testament, and that they plainly declare the cessation of all Jewish observances, on account of the *accomplishment* of that good thing, which these shadows typified—the Redeemer's entering into his rest on the completion of his work. Those who believe the testimony of that, have a *Sabbath* indeed; but not on any one day of the week more than another. Though I do not think any further remark on the subject necessary, yet I would briefly add that, according to the popular system, we must suppose that *two different* sabbath days were observed in the first Christian churches: nothing is more certain than that the Hebrew Christians continued to observe the law of Moses, and assuredly this special precept of it. *They* kept the sabbath, of course, on the only day on which it could be kept—the *last* day of the week. But the Anti-christian *divines* would persuade us that the Gentile Christians had *another* sabbath, which they kept, and were bound to keep the *first* day of the week. So that, in fact, the Jewish disciples were weekly breaking the *Christian sabbath*, and the Gentile disciples *the Jewish sabbath*. This absurdity may be swallowed by the besotted followers of the man of sin: but Christians are called to maintain the one observance of the first day of the week, which was delivered both to Jewish and Gentile converts—the coming together on that day into one place to eat the Lord's Supper. This, and all the Christian fellowship connected with it, appears a contemptible thing in the eyes of worldly professors. But they really despise Him whom God hath crowned with glory and honour. You see I have readily set about replying to your inquiries. I have done so, because you seem to make them with a view to scriptural re-union with the disciples of the Lord. The last pieces I have published, are "Seven Letters on Primitive Christianity;" and "A Sufficient Reply to Mr. J. Haldane's Strictures" on that work. If you have not seen them, I believe they may be had at Tims's, 85, Grafton Street, Dublin. If not, I would endeavour to forward you copies.

I remain yours in the hope of the Gospel,

P.S. I received a long time ago a letter from J. D——, to which I did not reply, because I could not without making myself a party in a division, upon which I had heard only one side. It seems a very dubious ground for any man's departing from a Christian church, that they do not manifest enough of love. He seems pretty plainly to say—"I manifest enough of love."—That "*great* I" is a great devil.

CXI.

TO THE SAME.

Dec. 20, 1825.

Dear Mrs. T——,—A few days ago I received your note of the 9th instant, and now send you two copies of the Letters on Primitive Christianity, the Reply to Haldane, Thoughts on Religious Establishments, and each of the seven tracts. Accept them as an expression of warm affectionate interest. I have an indistinct recollection of Kelly's pamphlet that you allude to; but I never answered it. I was quite satisfied with the evidence which it afforded that we differ on the fundamental truth; and was willing that professors should be left to manifest themselves by taking such side on the question as they thought right. It would be easy to expose the sentiments which Mr. K. advocates, so that probably himself, and certainly others, would have been led to *modify their language* on the subject. But this I do not think desirable. The greater part of the most *specious* religious profession in Ireland, has been occasioned by the *exposure* of antichristian doctrine, obliging its adherents to paint their mask more nicely. I am glad to hear that the mask is (to disciples) taken off from some of the professors in C——, by thus openly advocating the popular notion of sanctification as an improvement in *ourselves*. Concerning some of them who can speak the most plausible language, I have long been quite sure that they are of Antichrist, from their persisting, after many reproofs, in distracting the Church of God by turning it into a debating society. But the sentiment which some of them now avow, leaves no room for any believer of the truth to doubt their character. Whenever a talker about the gospel tells me that he thinks *himself* a better kind of body than he was before his supposed conversion, or that he hopes to become so, I can be at no loss to conclude that he needs yet to be converted to the truth, and is at present ignorant of it. He is looking with secret complacency at a thing that is all unclean, and is blind to the one object in which the fulness of the divine good pleasure centres. I have sometimes illustrated the subject (I know not whether in any of my publications) by the narrative in 2 Kings vi. 6. When the iron was made to swim and floated on the surface, it was still as much *iron* as when it had lain at the bottom of the water: and this would have been manifested by its sinking at any moment to the bottom, if the miraculous power that raised it had ceased at any moment to keep it afloat. If we suppose the *iron* indued with consciousness, and imagining (in the contemplation of its swimming) that it was turned into *cork*, we should have a little image of the delusion of those professors, who have imbibed the popular doctrine of sanctification. I wish you had mentioned the names of some of those in C—— with whom you are united. Is

J—— D—— among them? The smallness of your number need not dishearten you, if (as I would hope) ye have the truth with you. "He that is coming will come and will not tarry;" and at that day "the rebuke of his people will he take away from the face of the earth."

Affectionately yours, dear Mrs. T——,
For the truth's sake,

CXII.

TO THE SAME.

May 6, 1826.

My dear Sister T——,—I think I need no longer hesitate about addressing you as one standing in that endeared relation. My hesitation before arose chiefly from my apprehension that you were in fellowship with T—— G——, with whom I could not walk till he is brought to repentance for a long course of wickedness, which he has imposed on himself and others as very good. I scarcely know any wickedness more awful, than that of stumbling and distracting disciples by the agitation of questions ministering strife, the discussion of which he has seemed to think the grand business of a Christian church. I consider his character the more dangerous, from his ability to express himself most plausibly as to the great truth, both in speaking and writing. But enough of this. Your letter found me confined by a fit of gout, partly to my room and partly to my bed. It has left me still very weak upon my limbs: but I must no longer delay to make you some reply, though a very imperfect one.

I am pleased to find that you perceive Sandeman's error, on what he terms the assurance of *hope* as distinguished from the assurance of *faith*. The attempt to distinguish them, as if the one could subsist without the other, is an ungodly attempt,—goes to the subversion of the fundamental truth for which he in general contends so clearly and ably. The uncommon excellence of most of his writings renders this leaven in him the more dangerous, and I am sure that it has wrought all kinds of evil in the churches with which he and Glas were connected. While they speak clearly and blessedly about the gospel as affording hope to the chief of sinners, they seem each to look for something further to warrant him in entertaining this hope, and to fear that it is presumptuous to entertain it confidently. And indeed it would be presumptuous, if the confidence of hope were to be derived by discovering good evidences of our faith. You call on me to give you my thoughts on *evidences*, &c. But I am scarcely aware of any thing that I would add to what I have written on that subject. Besides the passage that you refer to in my "Sufficient

Reply," I would direct your attention to the tract No. 3, on "The Scriptural Fear of the Lord," particularly the *three paragraphs preceding the two last*. At any moment that the great truth revealed from heaven *evidences itself* to my conscience, the peace, and hope, and joy, which it affords, stand perfectly distinct in their foundation from all evidences either of my faith or of my unbelief the moment before! and those are corrupters of the truth who would set in opposition to this such texts as 1 John ii. 3. This is that "*beginning* of confidence and rejoicing of hope," which we are called to *hold fast to the end*; and therefore all talk of *additional consolation*, of a confidence derived from another source, is to be rejected with a "*get thee behind me, Satan*." But while evidences of my faith stand quite aside from the foundation and spring of my confidence towards God, I think it important to mention, that the only conclusive *evidence of faith* which can be adduced—evidence of abiding at any time in the truth—is the fruits of faith, that fruit of the spirit which is "love, joy, peace, long-suffering," &c. While I assert this, and plainly add that I have much more *evidence* to adduce of my "hardness of heart and unbelief," it does not shake my confidence or disturb my hope at all. You quote the language of the apostle in Rom. viii. 16. and naturally quote it according to the current English version—"beareth witness *with* our spirit." But I think it not unimportant to remark, that the passage ought to be rendered—"the Spirit itself beareth witness *to* our spirit that we are the children of God." According to the present version, and the manner in which it is handled by the popular divines, it is often supposed that there are two distinct witnesses described as assuring Christians that they are the children of God: on the one hand, their own spirit conscious of certain good evidences of sonship about themselves; and, on the other hand, the Spirit of God helping out that consciousness, and making a kind of private revelation to them, that they have a clear title to heaven. And in this way the words of the Apostle have been commonly employed to subvert the apostolic gospel, and to introduce altogether another hope and comfort than "the *comfort of the scriptures*." (Rom. xv. 4.) But, in fact, the apostle is speaking of the effect and influence of the *Gospel of Christ*, as contrasted with the law of Moses, in completely *relieving the consciences* of those who believe it, and giving them *filial confidence* towards God; which filial confidence (or spirit of adoption) is produced, not by any private revelation to them of something no where written in the scriptures of truth, but by the power of God bearing testimony to the *word of his own grace*, or opening their eyes to see the glory of that High Priest of our profession, in *whom* we have *boldness* to draw near into the holiest. (Heb. x. 19—22. iv. 16.)

CXIII.

TO THE SAME.

June 27, 1826.

Dear Mrs. T——,—I feel your letter of the 18th inst. a kind of reproach to me for my silence. But the inclosed unfinished letter will show you that I *began* to reply to yours of the 9th April. And why did I not finish and despatch it? I will tell you candidly. I heard from pretty good authority, that a sister from the church in Dublin had been some time ago at C——, and met on the first day of the week with some there who were considered in fellowship with us; but that she found them so trifling with the ordinances of the Lord, that some of them observed the ***salutation with an holy kiss,*** as of divine appointment, and others declined it. This information discouraged me, and I threw aside my letter unfinished. In fact, I was long uncertain whether there were any in C—— with whom I could scripturally consider myself in Christian fellowship; and the intelligence I have alluded to checked the rising hope that I might so consider you and those connected with you. Perhaps, however, you were not of the party with whom the Dublin sister met, or perhaps your principles and practice have since been changed. As to those who tolerate rebellion against the laws of Christ's house, under the name of Christian *forbearance,* I make nothing of their profession, however fairly they may talk about the hope of the gospel. The holiness of the name of the Lord—the infinite distinction between the character of the *only true* God, as revealed in his word from heaven, and all that is called God and worshipped by the world—this is the ground and spring of the holiness of his people, who are *separated* unto him by the truth made known to them; and while they are kept sanctifying Him in their hearts—hallowing his name—they will hold fast the traditions delivered to them in his name by the apostles of Christ, and will abhor the thought of considering any of them as matters about which they may agree to differ. Many things in the former of your letters I must for the present leave unanswered, being much straitened in time, and afraid that Mr. Y—— might leave town if I were to delay sending this. I am sorry to say that I have not a copy, and know not where I could procure a copy, of one of the pieces you mention. Even the seven tracts are out of print, except the third and seventh. Of these I shall take an opportunity of sending you some copies. But the weather is so very hot at present that I really cannot walk so far as Fleet Street; and the parcel would be too large for the twopenny post.

Excuse haste; and believe me, with affectionate interest,

Yours, &c.

CXIV.

TO MRS. B——.

Jan. 10, 1826.

VERY DEAR MRS. B——,—I do indeed heartily thank you for both your most kind and welcome letters—that of July 4th and Dec. 9th. The particularity of information they afforded me was the more gratifying, because I have been so long unaccustomed to it. You may suppose how little intelligence I receive about Irish friends, when I tell you that I never heard of your illness two years ago till your letter informed me of it. So we are both likely to go off the stage in a somewhat similar way. I have often looked at it as a pleasant and tender mode of removal to a Christian; since it saves all the trouble of the *process of dying*. But in whatever form he may arrive, Death is included in the inventory of our inheritance —among the all things that belong to us in Him who is head over all things to his church. Your account of young M—— and C—— (there is the fruit of calling a son by the father's name, the father becomes inevitably *old* on the entrance of the boy into the world,) gives me great pleasure; particularly the intelligence that they are walking in the truth. Give them my love; and tell them that very soon (if they live long enough) they will be as old as I am. To such little creatures as we are, and earnestly occupied by such little things, the interval appears very long in prospect; but looking back, it seems to me but as last year that I was a lad in college like them. The world is passing away—generation after generation; but "the word of our God abideth for ever." *There* is a substantial and blessed reality. Every thing that occupies men, aside from *this*, is but the agitation of a dream. But those who are awake to the great things of God declared in the Word, are awake indeed; and all that engages them is to be consecrated to Him whose they are, and to be pursued in the prospect of that glory which is about to be revealed at his second coming. His mercy and power alone can keep us in that mind; and his truth, which testifies the salvation that belongeth to Him, is the great instrument by which he keeps the heirs of his salvation awake and walking in the light. Let us give *diligent heed* to the things that we have learned, lest by any means we let them slip. "When the Son of Man cometh, shall he find faith on the earth?" His coming is very near, and blessed are the few whom he shall find watching. It gave me joy to hear of L——'s addition to you. What greater joy is there as yet, than in witnessing such instances of the LORD's power reigning in the midst of his enemies? I well remember the fairness of L——'s verbal profession; but I am more and more convinced, that wherever there are a few gathered together to the name of the LORD, the verbal profession of those who hold aloof from their fellowship is to be utterly disregarded; fully as much so, as if we knew them to be walking in a course of the grossest immorality. I have said that I recollect L——. My memory is quite failing for the passing occurrences of the week. I forget one day what I said or did the day before. But old circumstances remain as fresh in my memory as ever, and, I think I may say, *old friends*. Dear ——— and ———! I remember you well. I remember the wintry drive with M——. I remember the blazing fire and the kind countenances that received me at the end of it. I remember—every thing.

CXV.

TO J. L———.

Feb. 12, 1826.

So you are released from the Excise, and are in business for yourself. Well: I trust you will be enabled to make both ends meet. How cheering and quieting the assurance that our heavenly Father "knoweth that we have need of these things," Mat. vi. 32.—of food and raiment. His are the cattle upon a thousand hills, Ps. l. 10.: and all things are ours, 1 Cor. iii. 22., in Him who has redeemed us sinners unto God by his blood. But he loves his children too well to let them have their inheritance here in their own management. "Whom he loveth he chasteneth, Heb. xii. 6.; and surely that word ought to make us endure chastening submissively and cheerfully. A beggar full of sores expiring at a rich man's door amidst surrounding dogs, seems to the fleshly eye a melancholy spectacle, and scarcely to be reconciled with the idea of his possessing all things. But what a wonderful revolution is there when he is carried by the angels into Abraham's bosom.

I have been thinking a good deal lately of that word in Joel ii. 26—"Ye shall eat *in plenty*, and be *satisfied*, and *praise* the name of the Lord your God, that hath dealt *wondrously* with you." Such words will certainly have their fullest accomplishment when we shall have entered into the heavenly rest. But it is indeed only our hardness of heart and unbelief that at any time prevents us from finding them blessedly accomplished at present; so abundant is the fatness of his house into which we are brought; so plenteous its provision for all that an utterly sinful creature needs; while the voice of the king himself, presiding at the feast, announces "all things ready," and speaks continually—"Eat, O friends: drink, yea, drink abundantly, O beloved," Song v. 1. "What would ye that I should do for you?" Mat. xx. 32. When he asked his disciples of old—"what was it that ye disputed among yourselves by the way?" we are told that they "*held their peace:* for by the way they had disputed among themselves who should be the greatest." (Mark ix. 33, 34.) They were ashamed to tell their master what their consciences told them was so contrary to his mind and spirit. It is so with us, whenever we are harbouring desires that we cannot bring to Him. The flesh would conceal its lustings from Him, and obtain their gratification without Him. But He knows all its workings, as he knew the dispute of his disciples; and graciously reproves and corrects our folly. Whatever desire we can bring to Him, as according with his will, we may bring to Him with the fullest confidence of receiving what we ask; and this surely ought to *satisfy* us—unless we would have something *contrary* to his will. O! if we had faith but as a grain of mustard-seed, how should we praise him continually who hath dealt wondrously with us indeed, in spreading such a feast for the poor and vile, in bringing the ungodly near to the living God. Our eyes are holden (till he opens them), so that we do not see the well of living waters that is beside us. And the moment after we have seen and drank from it, we would forget that it is there, if we were let. To "know the things that are freely given us of God," 1 Cor. ii. 12. is the work of his spirit: and his word is the sword of that spirit; the word which reminds us continually of the blessedness which we are called to inherit in Him who became a curse for us. "They which believe ARE *blessed* with believing Abraham." "Ye ARE *blessed* of the Lord which made heaven and earth." "*Praise ye* the name of the Lord."

March, 1826. * * * While you are exchanging the psalms for hymn-books, I should rejoice if we could get rid of all our hymns for the psalms. —— feels with me strongly on the subject: I have not talked about it to others. How miserably meagre are all the compositions of men in comparison of the divine word! Have you ever seen the version of the psalms without *rhyme* which the Glasites use? I do hope that something of the kind will yet be introduced in our churches; though I shall probably not see it.

June, 1826. * * * * The church here goes on much the same way,—too contemptible in point of numbers, and every thing else, to excite attention. Yet, occasionally, one or another individual is unexpectedly called, so as to supply the place of others who fall away: and though the instances are very rare, yet they sometimes strikingly exemplify the power of Him who "reigns in the midst of his enemies," so as to cheer us, and remind us "what work he did in the days of our fathers, in the times of old." Ps. xliv. 1. "Awake, why sleepest thou, O Lord? Arise for our help"—Ps. xliv. 23.—is a suitable prayer for his church; though it will not be fully answered till He come in His glory. Yet, previous to that day, I do look for a greater gathering of his redeemed out of Antichristian Babylon, and a more signal consumption of the man of sin.

CXVI.

TO MR. J. H———.

Sept. 8, 1826.

Dear John H———,—I do not wonder that you should be surprised at not having heard from me sooner since I left B———. On my return to town I proceeded to join my wife and daughter at Ramsgate; and both then and since we have again settled in our own home, I have scarcely had a week's freedom from gouty attacks; and even when most free from them, I continue so infirm on my limbs, that I could not possibly walk to the coach office with the parcel for you: that office is above three miles from my house; and I now hire a messenger to leave the parcel there, as I know not when I may be equal to the walk myself, if ever I should again. I am sorry to say that all our stock of tracts is exhausted, except Nos. iii. and vii., some of which I send you along with the Letters on P. C. and Sufficient Reply.

But though I have been long prevented from executing your commission, be assured I have not been unmindful of you. Indeed, it is, and has been, one of my daily petitions to the throne of grace, that ye may be approved to be the Lord's husbandry, a plant of his own planting, by his watering you with that river which makes glad the city of God, the blessed streams of his heavenly truth; and by his causing you, under its blessed influence, to increase in fruit to his glory—not in such spurious fruit as those by which the religious of the world display their zeal and piety—but in the fruits of righteousness, of which the world cannot take cognizance—peace and joy in believing the divine report—steadfastness of adherence to it, as to that which is our life, and abhorrence of all that *deceivableness of unrighteousness* which is opposed to the sanctity of the divine word.

You know, my dear John, that I aim at not passing by unnoticed any *ambiguous* language that falls from you. It is one of the most important exercises of brotherly love to watch over each other with that godly jealousy, which takes alarm at any thing that appears opposed to the truth of God.

At the close of your letter, you speak of not forgetting to pray that, "the important truths contained in the word may become the power of God to the salvation of our souls, and the souls of our fellow-sinners." Now, whatever meaning there may perhaps be, in which the prayer described in these words might be scriptural, their most obvious meaning seems to me to describe a prayer very unscriptural;—the prayer of one who professes to believe the divine truth testified in the word, but is looking for something further to make it *become* the power of God to his salvation. The Gospel of Christ is the power of God unto those that *are* saved, even to those who are called to the belief of it, 1 Cor. i. 18. 21. 24. God HATH saved the believer, and called him with an holy calling, 2 Tim. i. 9.; and how can such an one consistently pray that the Gospel may *become* to him what it *is?* This is very consistent with the popular systems, according to which a man may be ever so far from salvation, though believing the divine report: but it becomes not those who are brought out of darkness and death into light and life by the belief of the truth. As to the prayer, that the word may be made the power of God to the salvation "of the souls of our *fellow-sinners,*" I would remark briefly that we there also need to be kept in remembrance of the revealed will of God, that we may pray according to that will. We shall then not ask for any universal or general conversion of our fellow-sinners; for this would be asking God to act contrary to his revealed counsel—in fact, asking him to falsify his word—it is a remnant that shall be saved—few that are chosen.

But certainly it is most suitable for the believer to pray, that the word of our God may be glorified in being made to work powerfully in those that have believed through grace, and in being made effectual to the calling of those whom he has ordained to eternal life. All this, indeed, is included in the import of that petition which his children are taught, "Hallowed be thy name."

You know, my dear John, that in writing to you as I do, it is not under the supposition of your being any otherwise minded than according to the truth (See 1 John ii. 21.): but no admonition to hold fast the faith in its purity, can ever be unsuitable to those whose own hearts and thoughts are ever and altogether opposed to it. I inclose a few lines to our dear Peter H. My love be with you all.

CXVII.

TO P. H———.

Sep. 9, 1826.

As I dare say our brother H——— will communicate to you my letter to him, I shall not repeat here the account of my long silence. I beg you will never talk or think, as if you used unwarrantable freedom in writing to me. I should not have thought it any freedom, even before we were united in Christian fellowship;—but now recollect that we are brethren—one in Christ Jesus; our communications with each other cannot be too free. John has given me an intimation of one of the objections which you find brought against us by the religious world—namely, that we do not exert ourselves more to publish our principles, and win converts to them: and this objection is strangely brought against us by men who have heard all that we have to offer, and still remain unconvinced and disobedient to the word. It does indeed become us to be always ready to give an answer to every one, that asketh us a reason of the hope that is in us; —to contend earnestly for the faith, and against every antichristian corruption of it. But the followers of him, who "did not cry nor lift up, nor cause his voice to be heard in the street," cannot suitably employ the noisy and ostentatious zeal which the world admires. We have but one simple, though grand topic, to which we can consistently direct the attention of our fellow-sinners; and are precluded by the truth from all that effort of preachers to work upon the passions of their hearers, and to get them into a course of religious training. We have also to remember that those, to whom we speak at any time, have Moses and the Prophets, Christ and the apostles, preaching to them in the scriptures, and that we can but plainly point out what they say, and testify against the false interpretations that are current of their words: nor shall we think this simple reference to the scripture testimony insufficient, while we recollect that God honours his own word, knows who are his, even while they know him not, and will assuredly call every one of them in his own time to the belief of the truth. While I make these remarks, I should be very far from intimating that we have not to take shame for much remissness and indifference to the object of holding forth the Gospel; but I am sure, that when we are most engaged in it scripturally, the religious world will think us quite deficient in zeal and exertion. But in truth we are not to trouble ourselves about their objections and fault-finding. They manifest their blindness and antipathy to the word of God, by urging any circumstances (whether truly or falsely) in the conduct of those, who assert its truths and precepts, in vindication of their own unbelief and disobedience.

CXVIII.

TO MR. J. H——.

Nov. 9, 1826.

Dear Brother H——,—I have too long delayed replying to your letter received by Mrs. B——, along with P—— S——'s book and letter to S——. I have read them both, and to those who are of the truth, his character and spirit are sufficiently manifested in them. The poor man seems quite beside himself with religious vanity. "God has revealed many things to me which come to pass according to my predictions"—"my predictions are sure to come to pass"—"the rising generation will see my predictions fulfilled in the family of ——," &c.; and then the low scurrility of personal abuse in which he vents his spleen against individuals, and the glee with which he contemplates their final condemnation! All this, indeed, is small in comparison of his blasphemies against the faith of the gospel—"a moonshine faith"—"a mental way," &c. While he thus rails at the belief of what God has declared in his Word, he no where (as far as I see) distinctly states what he means by *faith*; and, in general, professors of his class are studious to keep a veil of mystery about that. Yet it is sufficiently evident that here, also, the grand thing in his mind is *self*. "The blessed Spirit revealed the Redeemer's sufferings for *my* sins." "*God revealed his everlasting love to my soul*," and that he had "*loved* ME from everlasting." The Lord shewed me that he had *loved* ME, and chosen me in Christ before the foundation of the world."

Thus, it is plain that his faith is a confident persuasion that he is one of the elect, and that to produce that persuasion in his mind is what he means by the work of the spirit, or, in other words, to reveal to him a matter about himself which is no where declared in the scriptures. He decries the belief of what is declared from Heaven in the Word, as a "moonshine faith, with which a man may go to hell like Judas;" and he cries up the belief of what may, indeed, be a "mental whim;" what is not to be found in the word of God, and what may be nothing but a suggestion of the father of lies. It is no wonder that such a man as this P—— S—— should make so light of the scriptures in his letter to S———;—"As to differing from the scriptures, *it is according to man's opinions. Some take the scriptures one way and some another*." And no wonder he is so indignant at those who oppose his spirit as delusive and his faith as baseless: he is, in short, a genuine specimen of the so-called high Calvinists of this country. But I am very far from thinking it expedient to meet this pretended prophet (who has such private revelations about himself and others) in the way of public controversy. I think it would be quite unsuitable for our brother S——— to pretend to put himself forward in print. It was very well that he should oppose S——'s errors in the way of private communication either by letter or word of mouth. But when the other so arrogantly spurns that kind attempt, and challenges to a public controversy, I should be disposed to say, "Let him alone." As to myself, *I* have often thought of writing a tract against that class of professors: and perhaps I may yet put it in execution. But I should not think of selecting that man for my antagonist. Doctor Hawker would be a more decent opponent; and though he is one of the reverend gentry, I am sure he has not so much of the high clerical airs and arrogance, as the illiterate P—— S——. There is but one thing I should wish to have an opportunity of marking to that gentleman: that by the simple belief of the written word against which he rails, we are very far from meaning the mere acknowledgment or belief that the scriptures contain a divine revelation. Of this many are strongly persuaded who yet disbelieve the most important truths declared from heaven in that sacred volume, just as the carnal Jews, &c. But while I should like to mark this distinction to him, I dare say there is no occasion: he probably is well aware that we do not consider the mass of those, who acknowledge the Bible, as partakers of the salvation testified of in the word;

though he chuses so to misrepresent our mind: and while he talks of almost all the people in this country as having the faith for which we contend, it is very clear that he has it not himself. For it is an essential part of the divine testimony, that "whosoever believeth that Jesus is the Christ, is born of God." But this declaration he evidently doubts and scorns. What a revolution the entrance of the truth into his mind would produce in him! How much would he abhor what he now admires, and admire what he now abhors! Well, when we consider the essential contrariety of the heart of man to the truth of God, we may indeed admire his mighty working in keeping that truth from becoming extinct in the world; and may rejoice in that faithful promise made unto him, in whom all the promises are yea and amen,—"My spirit that *is upon thee*, and my words which I have put into thy mouth, SHALL NOT depart out of thy mouth, nor out of the mouth of thy *seed*, nor out of the mouth of thy seed's seed, saith the Lord, from henceforth and for ever." Is. lix. 21. The Lord be with your spirit! My hearty love to our dear brethren P—— H—— and S—— B——.

Yours, with true affection, &c.

CXIX.

TO MR. J. S——.

January, 1827.

MY DEAR S——,—I have been for some time much grieved at hearing of the state of affairs between you and the church at E——; and though I continue much a stranger to the *particulars* of what has passed, I yet am led to write freely to you my view of the *general* subject. If I do not mistake, your brother D—— refused to practise the enjoined salutation with a kiss of charity, on occasions when he was the only *brother* in the meeting, declaring that he would not then observe it unless it were *always* interchanged between the different sexes in our meetings. Now, if I be right in forming this general conception of the origin of the strife, I cannot hesitate to say that his conduct and his language were most ungodly, as resting his conformity to a divine command on the conduct of others. He would obey the precept at one time, *if* others would practise the thing enjoined in a certain way at other times! Is not such a sentiment utterly opposed to the fear of the Lord, and to all real obedience to any part of his revealed will? If he thought the churches falling short of conformity to the word in this matter, he ought to have called their attention to it in faithfulness and love, by the admonition of that word which is profitable for correction and reproof and instruction in righteousness: but instead of this—to say substantially—" I will not obey the word, unless ye obey it in the way that strikes me as right"—is this like a disciple? Is it not a plain expression of that fleshly mind, which is indeed *our own*, and ever in direct contrariety to the mind of the spirit? Now, what the intermediate steps were, which the brethren at E—— took with D——, I am quite ignorant: I therefore cannot take upon me to pronounce that they proceeded scripturally and are free from blame in the matter. But this I say, if his conduct and sentiments were such as I have been led to conceive, and if they proceeded scripturally to admonish him on the ungodliness of his sentiments and conduct, but failed of bringing him to repentance, they were perfectly justified in putting him away from among them as a wicked person. In their dealing with him, I conceive that the brethren at E—— ought to have determinately refused the admission of any idle controversy about the order of sitting in our assemblies, as a circumstance which none can pretend is decided by scriptural rule, and which therefore none can propose as a matter of divine obligation to others. But if any one would make that circumstance a subject of vain jangling, and persist in doing so after admonition and reproof, I should view him as manifesting in this a mind opposed to the truth: but how much more if he professed to make his own obedience to a divine command hinge upon his brethren's accommodating their practice to his fancy in a thing indifferent. Now, if the general view which I take of D——'s sin be correct, it is indeed a very awful matter that you and the L—— brethren should make yourselves partakers of his sin, and produce a schism in the body of Christ, by continuing to hold him in your fellowship. This is as inconsistent with true love to him as with love to your brethren, and fidelity to the word of the Lord. But let me own to you candidly, that there are various expressions and sentiments in your last letter to Mr. B—— which make me fear for you, dear S——, that you are sadly turned aside from the principles of the word to the latitudinarian forbearance of worldly religions. I have not that letter before me, but I am clear in my recollection of the general purport of what I allude to. You say that no one should be put away from our fellowship, but for the breach of a command as explicit and express as—" thou shalt do no murder." Now the fact is, that we shall look in vain for *any* code of positive christian ordinances drawn up with that legal precision. Take the very first and fundamental ordinance of christian fellowship—our coming together into one place on the first day of the week to *shew forth the Lord's death in the supper*. You professedly observe this: but what do you mean by observing it? If you mean only to do a thing that *you* think right or pleasant or expedient, but that you conceive others who think differently from you may innocently let alone, I would at once say that you might just as well let it alone yourself, and that there is no real obedience to the word of the Lord in your present practice. But if you mean to avow that you act in obedience to the divine authority of that word in what you do, it is so far well: but let me ask you in what part of the word do you find it written, " thou shalt observe the Lord's supper on the first day of every week?" But while it would be vain to look for any such passage, disciples need be at no loss to produce as sufficient scriptural grounds for their practice, in the recorded practice of the first churches regulated by the apostles of Christ. Acts xx. 7. 1 Cor. xi. 20. To those who fear the Lord and tremble at his word, there is sufficient intimation of his will, and it never was designed to extort the reluctant conformity of others by legislative enactments. There are indeed some who object to any such *inferential* use of the scriptures; but they are inconsistent only in professing to make any use of them at all. You say that none ought to be put away from among us, but those whom we put away as wicked persons; and indeed there I agree with you. But in the conclusion which you evidently mean to draw from this principle, you seem to forget, that wickedness is the natural character of us all—our own proper character at all times, and that there is no greater manifestation of human wickedness, than the obstinate refusal to hear the admonition and reproof of the word of God. To take up in the way of discipline any thing which is not opposed to that word, would be utterly unwarrantable; and it would be as unwarrantable not to employ the patient labour of love, in applying the admonition of that word to the correction of the evil which is opposed to it. But when this ultimately fails, however trivial many may conceive the evil on which the dealing of discipline originated, its particular circumstances are all merged in the one general evil of non-subjection to the authority of the divine word, which proves the person to be walking after the imagination of his own wicked heart; and whenever we look at this as a small matter, while we regard as a more decisive evidence of wickedness, his walking in what all the world agrees to be evil—drunkenness, adultery, &c., it only proves that in our minds we are savouring not the things that be of God, but the things that be of men. I have said nothing of the spirit of vain contentiousness manifested in the business; and upon that shall only now say that a disciple, walking in the peace and lowliness, and love of the truth, could never think of agitating the church by a strife about the order of sitting in their assembly.

CXX.

TO MRS T———.

July 18, 1827.

My dear Sister,—I am glad of an opportunity of telling you that all matters of uneasiness about you, which I expressed in my last letter, have been long since removed: and I trust that our gracious Lord will keep us all in such simple subjection to his divine word, that nothing shall be allowed to disturb our unity.

I think there is something of fleshly wisdom in the difficulties which are perplexing you. I have just looked over my former letter, and I confess I see not any thing in it which I would wish to alter. You observe that it seems to "sanction different modes of observing the salutation as allowable." Now, the thing in which no difference is allowable, is that which is enjoined by the word of the Lord—namely, that all the brethren should salute one another with an holy kiss: in order to which, it is obvious that this salutation must be interchanged when all the brethren are assembled,—that is, in the meeting of the church. But if agreed in this, why should we attempt to lay down any law regulating other circumstances not determined by the word? as, the particular time of meeting when this ordinance is to be observed—the arrangement of the seats, which will in some degree regulate the individual persons between whom the salutation actually takes place, &c. &c. Why should not each church exercise its right of judging on such points? That there is *in general* an *expediency* in an order of sitting which separates the sexes, has seemed to me very obvious. Yet if another church thought that this savoured more of worldly policy than of Christian simplicity, I know not what right we should have to lord it over them in the matter. But this I would say decisively, that any arrangement of seats is unlawful, which would prevent *any* member of the church (whether male or female) from observing this ordinance. The general principles of Christian prudence and discretion can never sanction the breach of a positive command. In the case which you describe at C——, there seems to me no real difficulty; and it is foolish to perplex ourselves with the difficulties of imaginary or supposable cases. (We may say, sufficient to their time is the difficulty of such.) The brother who is sometimes the only male in your assembly, is, I understand, married, and his wife a sister. Why should not the sittings be so arranged, that she should take her place next him? If the unbelieving husband of another married sister were likely to feel dissatisfaction if *she* sat next a brother in the assembly, I should recommend that his most unreasonable niceties should be humoured, while they can be so without involving disobedience to the word. But you doubt whether one brother and any number of sisters can constitute a *church*, because they cannot proceed to matters of discipline, females not being able to give their testimony, as not being allowed to speak in the church. Now, supposing the one brother not to be the subject of the discipline, there is no difficulty in the case. For after *he* has laid the matter before the body and borne his testimony, he may call on any sister who is acquainted with it to confirm his testimony by standing up, without opening her mouth: though I confess that I should not think her saying distinctly—"I confirm our brother's testimony"—would be any departure from the real meaning of the scriptural rule, as there would be no *teaching* or *usurping of authority* in this. But what is to be done if the brother be the object of the discipline? Why, plainly this: after the failure of all private admonition and efforts to call him to repentance, the sisters must withdraw from fellowship with him, and cease to meet as a church. But why should the possibility of this prevent their meeting with him as a church before such a case arises, which may never occur? If it should, it would follow, by the same argument, that any number of sisters, with *two* or *three brethren* (or ever so many), cannot constitute a Christian church: for it might possibly happen, that all the three brethren should be partners in a common transgression (one of these perhaps directly, and the others indirectly by countenancing him in his sin); and in this case, as well as in that which you have stated, if private means failed, the sisters must withdraw, and the church would be dissolved.

As to my health, it is better than it was last autumn, though I sensibly feel the advances of old age, and my eyes begin to fail much. Our earthly tabernacles must be dissolved, as the leprous house: but, blessed be God, our spiritual bodies shall be fashioned like unto the glorified body of our exalted Head.

Mercy and peace and joy be multiplied to you all.

Your affectionate brother,

CXXI.

TO THE SAME.

Aug. 20, 1827.

DEAR Mrs. T——,—Your letter of the 13th has grieved me much, and the sentiments avowed and contended for in it, are such as manifest (the natural mind of us all) a mind quite opposed to the fear of the Lord and the trembling at his word, and therefore such as must completely nullify in my view your profession of the truth; though you say that you think we *could not refuse fellowship with you* if you were in London. But how striking is "the *deceivableness* of unrighteousness" in you, when you talk of *fully concurring in what the spirit saith to the churches* on this subject, and of *allowing the divine obligation to salute one another with a holy kiss* when we are all assembled. The whole of your extraordinary argument upon the supposed indecency of the observance in certain circumstances, proves that you do not allow that divine obligation; and though I dare say you have imposed upon yourself so as to think that you do, yet you have sufficient acuteness of intelligence to be undeceived on this point—after one or two remarks—unless you wink hard indeed to avoid conviction. Suppose the one brother who attends your assembly had not a wife who is also in connexion, and with whom certainly he might exchange the salutation (not as with a wife, but as with a sister), what, in that case, is to become of his observance of the ordinance, according to the wise argument you raise? If he then obey the precept at all, he must exchange the salutation with a female not his wife, and this you have discovered to be contrary to decorum, shamefacedness, chastity, and I know not what—though passing in a solemn public meeting, in avowed obedience to divine command, and in professed indication of Christian brotherhood. I do not mean at all to degrade the divine authority and wisdom of the institution, by entering into any refutation of the futility of your objections. I would only remark, that your objections go absolutely against the divine obligation of the institution, and not merely against any particular circumstances of observing it. One other observation I would briefly make, in confirmation of this. You have discovered it to be indecent that the different sexes should exchange the salutation with a kiss in the Christian assembly. I have known others who, with at least as much plausibility, have insisted on the indecency of *men kissing one another*. You and they may settle that question together, if the God of all mercy bring you not to another mind. But those who are so wise as to argue against the wisdom of God, shall be taken in their own craftiness.

Your language, in some parts of your letter, would seem to indicate, that you had been led to see the sin of having allowed your brother to continue so long in disobedience to the command, and that you were proceeding to correct the evil. But it is quite manifest, from the tenor of all the rest of your letter, that though you would have only cunningly covered your sin by an alteration of your practice, it would not have been in any real repentance for it, in any real subjection to the word, or humiliation for your disobedience of it, but because you thought a way was pointed out, in which it might *seem* to be obeyed *decently*.

And now, perhaps, you may be ready to ask why I have still addressed you in this letter as a sister, though in the language of plain rebuke. I will tell you. Your letter leaves me in some uncertainty whether brother A———, and those with him, have proceeded altogether scripturally in their separation. I fear they may have been somewhat over hasty, and not sufficiently patient and yielding, in pursuit of the things that make for peace. Peace certainly cannot be truly pursued by yielding any atom of divine truth or precept. But if the breach could have been prevented, by yielding, even to the weakness and unreasonableness of any, a mere arrangement of the seats, while the divine command should be observed by all, and its binding authority acknowledged by all, I think any such concession ought to have been made. Mark—I say IF this could have been; and I must add that, according to the sentiments avowed in your letter, I could not now cover up the difference with you by yielding any such arrangement, without an explicit profession of repentance on your side, which should mark that you considered that arrangement, not as essential to the observance of the institution, but merely as what you thought more expedient or satisfactory to your feelings. If I came to one of the sister churches, where the sexes sit promiscuously, I should violate the word, if I made this a matter of contention with them; and still more awfully, if I broke off from their Christian fellowship on account of it. But, on the other hand, if one of them came to us, I should think him as unwarrantable if he insisted upon our sitting promiscuously, and we should take him into discipline, if he made that a matter of strife, but still more if he made it an occasion of breaking the unity. I should thank you to shew this letter, or at least the latter part of it, to A———. I commit it to the blessing of Him who alone can make it effectual for good. If there shall be no change of mind in you, there will be no occasion for you to write again. But rather let me hope that I shall hear from you with joy, and so be able still to subscribe myself affectionately yours, and for the truth's sake,

---

CXXII.

TO MR. J. G. S———.

Nov. 8, 1827.

* * * * While in Dublin, I saw a private letter from Mr. T—— of L——— (whose pamphlet you shewed me), which in my view quite decides his character as a teacher of lies. He states the sense in which he understands the expression of Christ's having *redeemed* his people, and explains it as including only this—that he has delivered the Jews from the yoke of the Mosaic law, and the Gentiles from *natural death*. But the blessedness of the *forgiveness of sin* to his people, by his being made sin for them, suffering in their place, does not seem at all to enter into his contemplation. His letter also confirms what I had heard before, that he carried off his congregation with him from the Presbyterian Kirk, and is getting a new meeting-house built by them at considerable expense. Indeed, his pamphlet seems to me marked with those characters of acute subtlety and hardy self-confidence, which fit him well for a ringleader of any new-fangled heresy. Well is it for sinners that there is one, who will not suffer his own elect to be deceived by the false Christs and false prophets: and when it is considered how congenial to our own hearts is every thing contrary to the truth, it may well seem more marvellous, that any are brought into and kept in the narrow path, than that they are so few. In you, my friend, it always appears to me a great inconsistency, that while you maintain the sacredness of the heavenly doctrine, which reveals "grace reigning through righteousness by Jesus Christ unto eternal life," you yet object to those who maintain the corresponding sacredness of all the precepts and institutions delivered from heaven to the children of the kingdom. I see not how there can be more forbearance, or tolerance of diversity of mind, in the one than the other, without alike invalidating the authority of that divine word on which all alike rest. I understand that you would not retain in your fellowship any one who does not acknowledge the divine obligation on disciples, of coming together on the first day of the week to shew forth the Lord's death. It would be well to examine the ground on which you would

act in that case; and to consider whether it be not an equally stable ground for similar rigidness in the case of every other real precept and institution of the kingdom of heaven. If you profess to admit this general principle, but object to me as holding things which are not *really* preceptive, this would alter the question at issue between us, and would call us to consider seriously, in each instance, which of us is adding to or taking from the word. The believer must tremble at the thought of any such interference with the laws of the King of Zion. These few hints you will receive as a token of affectionate interest from your sincere friend.

CXXIII.

TO A—— C——.

Nov. 15, 1827.

Dear A——,—It was with much pleasure I received your letter of the 8th inst. and I very gladly comply with your wish that I should write to you. I heard of your having been in town, and witnessing one of the meetings of the church in Portsmouth-street. I apprehend that, in the conversation which you had with some of the members, there was a mutual misunderstanding of each other's meaning. But that will easily be removed on a future occasion by a little patient explanation, if (as I hope) we be indeed of one mind on the great truth. That being the one great bond of our union, we of course think it needful to ascertain (as far as we can) that there is unity of sentiment with us upon it, in those whom we receive into our fellowship. We have but one inquiry to make,—namely, whether they believe the testimony sent from heaven in the scriptures concerning Jesus of Nazareth. But all the terms, in which that testimony is conveyed, have been so long and so awfully perverted from their real import, that some sifting of the meaning attached to the words is found needful, and especially in the case of those, who have been much engaged with the religious world. This was not so in the apostolic age; but all who professed to *believe that Jesus was the Christ* were at once received on that confession into the Christian body; because no diversity of meanings had yet been attached to the words, or had obtained currency among those who bore the Christian name.

I am very glad to understand that you have given up the idea of quitting your present situation. It was part of the apostolic advice to Christians "that every man should abide in the same calling wherein he was called." 1 Cor. vii. 20. It would be vain for a Christian to expect, by any change of situation, to escape the reproach of Christ; and we are taught rather to rejoice if we be counted worthy to suffer shame for his sake, and are called by patient continuance in well-doing to glorify Him before those, who falsely accuse our good conversation in Christ. Indeed, when we are told that "they did *spit in his face*," that they said he "*had a devil and was mad*," that "he was a *gluttonous man and a wine-bibber*," &c. a Christian may well loath himself for the pride and naughtiness of his heart, in thinking much of any scorn or hard speeches to which he may be exposed on account of his Christian profession. You seem to begin to find what a different thing is that charity (or *love* of the truth) by which faith works, from the thing called charity in the religious world, and which proceeds upon a kind of agreement to hold the persons of men in admiration. Christ was reckoned very uncharitable by those who remarked,—"in so saying thou reproachest us also." But if he had shewn himself a respecter of the persons of men, he would have been as much a favourite with the scribes and Pharisees, as he was the object of their aversion and contempt. And just so at this day: the Christ who speaks the good and comfortable words of mercy and eternal life to sinners—to those who have before God no character but that of evil and ungodly rebels—that Christ is despised and rejected by the religious and devout of the world; while they are zealously attached to the various false Christs put forward by the false teachers, who make their livelihood by corrupting the gospel. One has well illustrated the nature of the thing called *salvation* in the popular doctrine, by comparing it to a ladder let down *within a short distance* of a person at the bottom of a deep pit, by catching at which he has a chance of being extricated. The *exertion* necessary to avail himself of the means of relief thus offered, some preachers represent as very great, and others as very small. But there is an exertion necessary to be made, and their doctrine is designed to rouse one class of hearers to set about it, to encourage others in making it, and to comfort and animate some, with the consideration that they have made it successfully, and are either clear out of the pit or in a fair way of being so very shortly. And such is the miserable hope and consolation to which the popular preachers lead their deceived hearers, and in which they build them up, while they dress out their several systems in the phrases of scripture, and often speak in high terms of a Christ and his atonement, &c.; but still as subsidiary to that mental exertion of the sinner which they describe as the *act of faith*, and by which he must avail himself of the means of relief *offered* to him in their gospel. Wonderful indeed is the revolution which takes place when a sinner, who has been vainly wearying himself in this unrighteous labour, or as vainly comforting himself with his supposed success in it, is arrested by the mercy and power of God, and given to see HIS *salvation* as proclaimed from heaven in the Word—that salvation wherewith HE saves his people unto the uttermost; to see that peace which *is* made for the rebellious—that sacrifice which *has* taken away sin—that righteousness which is "not of him that willeth or of him that striveth," but is "unto and upon all them that believe" the divine report of it: so that the sinner believing that report finds himself—not put upon any effort to get peace with God, and righteousness, and eternal life, but at peace, invested with perfect righteousness and possessed of eternal life. "Blessed is the people that know the joyful sound: they shall walk, O Lord, in the light of thy countenance." Ps. lxxxix. 15. When you say in your letter, "I do trust that God has in mercy given me to see the truth as it really is"—I am led to ask, whether you mean to intimate any degree of uncertainty upon that subject, any dubiousness of what is really *the truth* in Christ Jesus? Farewell, dear A——, &c. &c.

CXXIV.

TO W. C—— AND J. M'G——.

Jan. 19, 1828.

Dear Sirs,—Your letter of the 18th ult. arrived when I was labouring under an attack of gout: and since that attack has gone off, I have been more than ordinarily busy. Let this stand as an apology for my not replying to you sooner. But now that I have taken up my pen for the purpose, I apprehend that my reply will but very imperfectly satisfy the expectations you have formed. You desire a full and scriptural answer to three theological questions which you propose; and I am not at all in the habit of discussing theological questions, nor disposed to discuss them even with those with whom I am in religious fellowship. The objects of a Christian church and of a divinity club are utterly different. In the latter, the Word of God may be employed as an exercise of intellectual subtilty, and (pardon me for saying it) I think Scotland peculiarly abounds with that profanation. But to disciples of Christ that Word is the power of God to lead them walking in the way of peace and righteousness, as the blessed subjects of the kingdom of heaven. While I write this, I fear that my expressions (if sifted) may appear to you very incorrect or ambiguous.

I really can hardly believe you serious in asking me, "Whether Christ's coming into the world was to procure the love of God, or was the effect of that love? I fancy you are well aware that I ever consider and speak of Christ, as the "*unspeakable gift of God*," while it is only as viewed in him, and redeemed unto God by his blood from *deserved wrath*, (the sentence of which was irrevocable) that his church is or could be the object of the love and complacency of a holy and righteous God. But really I must check myself from enlarging at present on a topic, on which you are fully aware of my sentiments.

If you believe the plain testimony of scripture, that the people of Christ are saved from wrath through him, (1 Thess. i. 10.) from that wrath which awaits the enemies of God, you can be at no loss for the import of the term reconciliation in such passages as Rom. v. 9, 10, without my laying down any formal definition of it. But perhaps you are of a mind with those, who confine the meaning of the word reconciliation to the removal of the enmity of the sinner's mind to God. *If so,* I assure you that you are substantially rejecting Him, who is set forth from heaven as "a *propitiation* through faith in his blood," as having put away sin by the sacrifice of himself. But if indeed you know him who speaks throughout the book of Psalms, "*Mine* iniquities are more than the hairs of my head:" Him who indeed was without sin of his own, but stooped to be *made* sin, to have the sins of all that were given him out of the world, made to meet on him; who undertook to answer for them as his own, and to be smitten by Jehovah in the place of his sheep; if indeed you unequivocally allow these principles, how comes it that you would make my brother L—— an offender, (for I know that it is to him you allude) because, as you tell me, he maintained in conversation with you, that "Christ has taken the sins of his people upon him, made them his own, and *in this sense* was chargeable with sins, and received the divine forgiveness?" Really, it is in the justification, release, or acquittal of their surety from sin, that the justification of all his seed is assured from heaven. But why do I talk of this to men, who seem plainly to deny that Christ became "in any sense chargeable with sin," and therefore deny the imputation to him of his people's sins? For I think that to impute and to charge to one's account is one and the same thing. It is expressly declared, that God *imputed not* their trespasses to his people, 2 Cor. v. 19. Those, therefore, that deny that their trespasses *were imputed* to Him who was made sin for them, must attribute to the Most High a connivance at sin, and a receding from the word that revealed the sentence of wrath and condemnation against it. Such men may talk highly and speciously of the divine compassion and mercy, &c.; but I am bold to say that they lie under a deadly mistake as to the nature of the forgiveness which there is with God. As to the expressions which you object to, of Jehovah's being *pacified*—his *wrath* removed or turned away, it is enough to say that they are scriptural expressions, while the believer knows, that all the language which attributes change of mind or human passions to Jehovah, is to be understood as spoken after the manner of men. There is one expression that you attribute to my brother L.,—namely, Christ came into the world *to procure the love* of God to man, that I would be far from vindicating, as it would be too likely to convey ideas contrary to what is declared in John iv. 9, 10, and throughout the scriptures: though I can conceive the language might be employed in a sense indubitably true—namely, that without the work of Christ no sinner could have been the object of the love of God. But let me add, that the particular expression is so unlike any thing I have ever heard from J—— L——, that I must suspect you to be under some mistake in the matter, till the statement is confirmed by himself. I readily admit, however, that I have known divines to talk much about Christ's *appeasing his Father's wrath*, &c., in a way which I consider very objectionable. But I have far exceeded the length of communication which I had proposed; and shall only add frankly, that while you are of the mind, which your letter *seems* to me to indicate, I think your outward union with the church at L—— very undesirable. I remain, with best wishes, your's faithfully,

CXXV.

TO J. H——

March 11, 1828.

My dear brother H——,—You should have heard from me sooner, but that it has pleased God to visit me with long-continued illness. For the last ten weeks I have had a succession of gouty attacks, the last very severe, which have so enfeebled me, that I can scarcely creep along the room with the support of two sticks. Blessed be the God of all mercy that we sinners can view the loosening of the earthly tabernacle, as but the approaching answer to that prayer of the redeemer—"Father, I will that they also, whom thou hast given me, be with me where I am." When he was *parted from* his disciples, and *carried up into heaven*, (Luke xxiv. 51.) they had a striking evidence indeed that his *kingdom is not of this world*, and that it was not the prosperity and glory of *this world* they had to look for, but blessedness with him in heaven. Yet we read in the same passage, that "they returned to Jerusalem *with great joy*." Now the spring of their joy was—not any thing they saw in or about themselves, distinguishing them from other men—but the *fact* of which they just had decisive evidence, that the *Lord was risen indeed*, and that thus there was a divine proof and attestation that He was indeed the Messiah, of whom all the prophets had spoken, to whom all the sacrifices under the law pointed, and in whom they all received their full accomplishment. Having offered himself through the eternal spirit unto God, it was now proved that this his sacrifice for sin was accepted, that there remaineth no more sacrifice for sin, and that there needs no more; that the work of putting it away is finished, and everlasting righteousness brought in for the justification of the ungodly. The view of this great redemption might well send the disciples back to Jerusalem with *great joy*; and was well adapted, and sufficient, to impart the same joy at all times to us Gentile sinners. The risen and ascended king of Israel has "received the heathen for his inheritance," and is set for the salvation of God *unto the ends of the earth*. His kingly glory, in which *all things are put under his feet*, assures the security of all that concerns his redeemed ones. While He is head *over all things* to his church, *all things* must work together for their good. Things present and things to come, life and death—all are theirs. Whether I shall be allowed to see you again in the flesh, appears very uncertain. My last attack seemed to have gone off so well, that I was able to meet with the brethren last Sunday: but I have since had a degree of relapse. I trust to hear from you shortly, that you and our dear brethren at C—— are well, and kept walking in the truth, in nothing discouraged by the smallness of your numbers, or the multitude of your adversaries. We have had a very pleasing addition to our body lately, in a woman of the name of A. C——, whom I met in the walks at B—— in the year 1826. I think I mentioned to you at the time that I had got into conversation with her, and given her some of the tracts, &c. It appears that she was then half distracted with the jugglery of the popular gospel. But their snare is broken, and she is blessedly delivered.

My hearty love to our dear brethren. Mercy and peace be multiplied richly to you all!

CXXVI.

TO R. L. C———.

June, 1823.

In the following few remarks which I am about to offer on P——'s letter, I wish to be understood as referring exclusively to the general law he promulgates: "that it is unlawful to read the scriptures to or with those who do not appear to believe them." With the particular circumstances under which any individuals may have practised the thing, or may still practise it, with the expediency or inexpediency of the practice under such circumstances, I do not at present directly meddle; and let me premise that Miss G—— in her letter did state the general principle most fairly. Her words are, "they say it is unlawful to read the scriptures to or with unbelievers." The rest of her letter treats of the particular circumstances under which she reads them in her school. It was upon the general principle that I briefly remarked in reply, that the position seemed so monstrous, that I conceived she must have mistaken their meaning. I am grieved to find she did not mistake it, and that P—— declares himself and those with him *prepared to maintain* that general position, in the unlimited extent in which he distinctly lays it down. I have purposely refrained for some days from putting pen to paper on the subject; but after the most serious consideration of it, I must now declare myself prepared to resist the imposition of this law to the uttermost, as manifestly opposed to some of the most indubitable principles of the Word.

In thus declaring myself, it is with my eyes open to the melancholy consequences which must ensue, and speedily, if the diversity of mind remains unremoved.

In the last chapter of the Acts, we read that Paul, addressing an assembly of his countrymen, expounded to them and testified the kingdom of God, persuading them concerning Jesus, both out of the law of Moses and out of the prophets, *from morning till evening:* and some believed the things which were spoken, and some believed not:

and when they agreed not among themselves, they departed, after that Paul had spoken one word—"Well spake the Holy Ghost by Esaias the prophet unto our fathers, saying, Go unto this people," &c. "Be it known therefore unto you, that the salvation of God is sent unto the Gentiles, and that they will hear it." Now, if Paul, instead of quoting from memory (as he probably did) those verses from the sixth of Isaiah, had opened the book (as our Lord did in the synagogue at Nazareth), and had read the same passage to those unbelieving hearers, whom he evidently addresses in that part of his discourse, would Paul have done that which was unlawful? But during the whole of the preceding discussion, which was continued from morning till evening, and in which he expounded the things of Christ out of the law of Moses and out of the prophets, may we not be certain that he had the book before him, and read the scriptures to and with his audience, though many of them manifested their rejection of what he offered, by contradicting and opposing him, and in this manifested that they really believed not that Moses in whom they trusted, John v. 45—47. We find Paul in like manner disputing daily in the school of one Tyrannus both with Jews and Greeks;—"and this continued by the space of two years." Now, some at least of the Jews with whom he thus disputed were the unbelieving Jews, from whom he had separated the disciples when he quitted the synagogue; and never do we find him contending for the truth of Christ against his unbelieving countrymen, without appealing to those scriptures which they professedly acknowledged in the controversy. Whether that appeal was made by quotations repeated *memoriater*, or read to them from the book, certainly made no difference; and I am aware that those, with whom I am contending now, have too much acuteness to maintain that it could make any difference either then or now. This, however, leads me to remark incidentally, that it is plain we have not yet all the law which they mean to impose on us. We are forbidden at present to *read* the scriptures to any but apparent believers of them; but they must certainly intend to forbid likewise all *quotation* of them or reference to them, in conversation with one ignorant of the truth; and it is scarcely necessary to add that this involves a prohibition of all communication, oral or written—private or public—on any scriptural subject, in vindication of the truth or in exposure of error, with any of our unbelieving fellow sinners in these countries. How far the spirit that would dictate such a law participates of the mind of him, who has compassion on the ignorant and on them that are out of the way, let them who are spiritual judge. I am aware that P. (in the last paragraph but one of his 4th page) appears to make a reservation in favour of "*the way of oral utterance.*" But I must candidly say, that I do not think he intended in that passage to concede any thing contrary to the broad principle which I shew to be involved in his law. He is much too shrewd to advance a distinction between the oral utterance by reading, and oral utterance by repeating from memory. If then he would really allow me to speak with an Arminian professor, for instance, in defence of the truth, he must mean to debar me from all reference to the scriptures with one who upholds his ungodly sentiments by scripture misinterpreted. The Arminian would quote Heb. ii. 9. to prove that Christ died for those who perish in their sins. And I may indeed, by "oral utterance," assert the contrary, but I am prohibited from opening the Bible and referring to the perverted passage in its context, and proving from that very passage that Christ brings unto glory all for whom he tasted death. I am prohibited from this, for "it is unlawful to read the scriptures to or with those who do not appear to believe them." I reject the ungodly law with indignation.

When P—— quotes 2 Tim. iii. 16., and in his usual manner asks,—*Would it be monstrous* if a disciple looked upon this passage as including *every lawful purpose* to which the scriptures can be applied? I reply, that I am as ready to admit as he can be to assert, that we may well consider the ends for which the apostle there declares the scriptures to be profitable, as a complete enumeration of the purposes for which they were designed, or to which they can be lawfully applied. But before he infers by implication, that it is therefore unlawful to read the scriptures to those who are at present ignorant of their true import, he ought to shew that such unbelieving professors do not need *reproof, correction, instruction in righteousness.* Paul certainly thought so, when he employed those very scriptures as he did, in contending with his countrymen for the faith of Christ. But Paul declares the ability of those scriptures to *make a man wise unto salvation:* whereas it seems, according to the principles now sought to be established, that a man must be first made wise to salvation, before the scriptures can be lawfully laid before him. What the *means* are by which P. himself would profess that he was made acquainted with the way of salvation, I know not. But if he would assign the scriptures as the instrument which God had made effectual for the purpose in his own instance, I know not how he can assert the unlawfulness of an attempt to apply them to a similar purpose in other instances. No doubt, the ultimate design of God in giving the scriptures is "that the *man of God* may be perfect." They are given, like all other things, *for the elects' sake.* But it would be as reasonable to accuse the Apostles of acting in unlawful inconsistency with this truth, because they preached the word of salvation indiscriminately to all, as it is to charge me with acting unlawfully in reading the scriptures (and expounding them also) to an assembly the most mixed.

But P. intimates that this is to represent the scriptures as "*designed for unbelievers.*" There is manifold and mischievous ambiguity in that language. I have already marked, that in the highest view they are designed for the benefit of God's elect alone. It is also certain, in another view, that none but those who *professedly believe* the scriptures, or acknowledge them as a divine revelation, can consistently be addressed and reasoned with in the way of appealing to the scriptures. But it is fully within the design of the scriptures, that they should be so employed in opposing the errors of such, and laying before them instruction in righteousness. Nor is there a passage, however directly preceptive to disciples alone, that may not be employed for the purpose of reproof and correction, to those who are at present manifestly not disciples. I have written as much as my strength will admit, and as much as ought to be necessary.

CXXVII.

TO MR. J. H———.

Sept. 26, 1828.

Dear Sir,—I thank you for your letter, and for the plain avowal which it contains of your sentiments. As to your frequenting the synagogues of the Establishment, I assure you I have no worse opinion of them than of the mass of the dissenting meetings. Indeed, when you yourself compare them to the house of the idol Rimmon, you say as bad of them as I have ever said. You mention various matters, in some of which you think that you agree with me, while in others you declare that you differ. The fact is that we differ essentially and radically, even when we most seem to agree. Your letter manifests that your religion is taught by the precept of men, and regulated by your own fancy, not by the word of the Lord. You *think* that you are likely to get more benefit by attending antichristian synagogues than by staying at home. You *think* that our meeting but once on the first day of the week to break bread, looks "as if we were afraid of *serving God* too much." You *think* that "one-seventh portion of our time is not too much to devote," &c. You forget to add, that you think the scriptures of the New Testament a very defective rule for Christians. The only argument that you attempt to offer from scripture for the continued observance of a seventh-day rest from the business of life – and that in direct opposition to the plain decision of the apostle, Col. ii. 16, 17—would equally prove that Christians should continue to offer *sacrifices of slain beasts*; for certainly the divine appointment of such sacrifices was long antecedent to the Mosaic law. But those who are of God will hear the apostles of Christ: and those who hear *them* well know that all such observances were *shadows of the good things* which were then to *come*; and that now to continue adherence to those shadows would be virtually to deny that the substance *has come*. Nor will they find it necessary to refer to *Ignatius*, for proof that there is an observance of the first day of the week which disciples were and are taught by the apostles, nor for instruction how they should observe it.

Pardon me for saying that my abhorrence of such religion as yours, is not at all lessened by the fondness you express for a great deal of *religious* talk, by your dislike of conversing about bullocks, &c. &c. There are many blaspheming Wesleyan Methodists—nay, many Turkish Dervises—who would beat you all to nothing in the appearance of *such* sanctity.

I perceive, by a copy of your verses, that the variety of sects and parties in the religious world distracts you, and leaves you utterly at a loss to guess what is truth. It is quite natural that they should produce such an effect, wherever the mind is not brought under subjection to the divine Word; and this is the work of Him alone who makes " his arrows sharp in the hearts of his enemies." When the disciple is established in the doctrine of the *grace* of God, this gives him a settlement of mind, and unravels for him all the perplexities of the religious world. What a revolution would it produce in you, if the God of mercy and of power ever give his word entrance into your mind.

I am, dear Sir,
Your sincere well-wisher,

CXXVIII.

TO J. L——.

Dec. 12, 1827.

THANKS, my very dear J——, for your comfortably long letter. In the account of your fleshly vanity in those engagements, (where its workings are most vile) I only find, what the scriptures always teach us, that your heart is a counterpart of mine: there is no greater plague to a disciple. Yet it is needful that its appearance should not make us fume and fret, at finding ourselves so vile: for that is only another form of fleshly vanity: but just on the moment send us to our strong-hold—to the mercy-seat—loathing ourselves in our own sight. It is indeed pleasant work speaking for the Lord to ever so many of our fellow-sinners, where he is pleased to keep down our own hearts, by the overbearing power of his own glory: there it may be truly said that it is not we that speak, but the spirit of our Father. As to not seeing fruit from our preaching, mind not that: the word of the Lord shall not return to Him void: and it may be, after *many* days, that this bread, cast upon the waters, shall be found again. We have an encouraging instance at present in A. C——, whom I met at B—— nearly two years ago: she was then sick in soul and body; had suffered (it seems) many things of many spiritual physicians, and grew worse and worse. I said a little to her, and gave her some tracts. We have had two most pleasing letters from her lately, by which she appears a happy partaker of the hope that maketh not ashamed.

Do you know that I was pleased, and somewhat relieved, to hear that you had not parted with poor ———. A fear had sometimes occurred to me that I was too harsh with him; and that, instead of merely stigmatizing his language as the language of ignorance, I ought to have laboured patiently to point out to him with all plainness, how it went to the subversion of the truth. His language certainly, if it came from one offering himself to our fellowship, would in my mind warrant us to decline receiving him. But when a person has been received among us, he seems to possess an additional claim on us for all patience of instruction; and it is hard to mark the degree of mere ignorance manifesting itself, which would authorize us to remove him, *so long* as he professedly yields to the instruction of the word. On the whole, I am very glad indeed that you at length found so much glimmering of the truth in him, as enables you to keep him: who shall despise the faintest glimmering of that? it is the light of life, and will issue in eternal glory. Give him my love, and say that I desire he will forgive me, if I treated him too harshly.

As to the two theologians who have been making advances to us, I am thankful to God, that ye have hitherto escaped union with them, for from the short account you give me of their language, I am satisfied that they belong to a class of professors whom we are specially called to avoid. Nothing is more abominable than the turning of the Gospel of the grace of God into a subject of theological disquisition and metaphysical jangling. In this such men disport themselves without fear, and their word indeed eats as a canker. We really do not need those philosophers to inform us, that the church of Christ has been the object of the Father's *everlasting* love, that his mercy is *from* everlasting *to* everlasting upon them that fear him; nor to teach us what the word of the Lord pronounces with so much majesty—"if thou sinnest, what doest thou against Him? or if thy transgressions be multiplied, what doest thou unto Him? If thou be righteous, what givest thou Him? or what receiveth He of thine hand?" (Job xxxv. 6—8. xxii. 2, 3.) But when they come insidiously to set these undisputed principles in opposition (directly or indirectly) to the word, which declares the wrath of God revealed from heaven against all unrighteousness and ungodliness of men," and his people *saved from wrath* by Him who suffered it in all its terrors in their place, dying the just for the unjust,—the one beloved *in whom* they *are made accepted*, and in whom alone they could at any time be viewed with acceptance by a holy God;—then these disputers are unmasked, and their best words and fairest speeches are proved to be but the cover of rebellion against the most High. My love to all the brethren. . Peace be with you all!

CXXIX.

TO THE SAME.

May 12, 1828.

Blessed be God for that hope which death cannot shake! for that eternal life that he hath given us in Him who was dead, but is alive again and liveth for evermore. What riches of grace and glory given to the evil—to those who have no other character of their own but evil! Accordingly, it is worthy of notice, that in the language of Scripture, what is *our own* is put as of the same import with what is evil and contrary to God. "They ceased not from THEIR OWN doings, nor from their stubborn way." Judg. ii. 19. "A rebellious people, which walketh in a way not good, after *their own thoughts*." Is. lxv. 2. Ezek. xxxvi. 17, &c. All the natural religion, which is agreeable to man, proceeds on an effort to disguise this our own character, or to shake it off, by arriving at some betterness in ourselves, so that our own doings, thoughts, and ways, shall cease to be so utterly and exclusively evil. Such an effort after goodness must be highly esteemed by men; and it must be highly offensive to them to be told, that it is all an unrighteous labour and vain, and that it matters nothing whether they be much or little occupied in it, whether they be comforting themselves with the idea of success in their object, or weighed down with sorrow at the thought of their failure in it. Nothing indeed but the rod of his strength, who rules in the midst of his enemies, can reconcile us, and keep us reconciled, to the revealed character of God as *kind to the evil—justifying the ungodly—saving sinners*. And then how blessed is it to come before the throne of grace confessing our sin, but to come for the good things that he giveth liberally to the sinful; and to remember, that we may confidently plead—"*he* is worthy for whom thou shouldst do this,"—while we see in ourselves no worthiness, but to be left to perish in our own ways. But the religious world cannot see, how the unvaried continuance of our own unabated evil character is consistent with our being kept and delivered from the evil, and led in the ways of righteousness and peace. I heard with interest of our sister B——'s blessed departure. When I saw her, it seemed little likely that she should be called away before me. I rejoice to hear that your little body are kept walking together in the unity of the spirit. My Christian love to all the brethren.

CXXX.

TO THE SAME.

Dec. 18, 1828.

A few days after I despatched my last letter to you, I received a large packet from ——, containing copies of his letters to you, (except the last) and of your letters to him, with a note intimating that I must take part with him, unless I had turned aside from the faith. I see no cause to doubt that the right course has been pursued with C——, and the course best adapted to recall him to a sober mind, *if* he be of the truth. His letters are full of railing, and all the manifestations of theological high-mindedness. I thought it not suitable to make him any reply; so that of course I am set down in his books as a Pharisee. As the best way of filling my paper, I proceed to express some of the thoughts suggested to me on the occasion.

People may learn theologically a sound language about many *parts* of divine truth, and yet never know the truth. And their ignorance will manifest itself in their conception, that the *parts* of divine truth, for which they seemingly contend, are at variance with others to which they are disaffected, and which they wish to suppress. And thus from the different parts which men professedly patronize, and the other parts which they manifestly oppose, there is a great variety of forms of false profession—Calvinistic, Arminian, &c. in all their shades and modifications. But it is very remarkable, that erroneous sentiments, apparently the most opposite, will be found to spring from one and the same mistake,—not merely from the one principle of ungodliness in our hearts, but from one principle of falsehood in doctrine. Thus J. C—— thinks himself in his theology much opposed to J. H——; and yet (speaking of the former's sentiments as they *appear* in his writing) they evidently to me set out from one common lie: namely, the supposition, that if the hearts of disciples be as utterly wicked as those of any other sinners, this must imply that disciples walk after the same mind as unbelievers. J. H——, *seemingly* having his eye to all the Scriptures that declare the contrary of the latter, regards those who assert the former (the unchangeable ungodliness of the heart of man) as enemies to what he calls holiness and practical good works. And J. C——, *seemingly* having his eye to the scriptural testimony of the utter and invariable evil of the heart of man, regards those who assert such Scriptures as Rom. viii. 5—14. as Pharisees. But thus it is plain, that C—— and H—— agree in one common principle of error; and each, by setting one half of Scripture against the other half, shows that he does not understand even that half for which he seems to be zealous. Each thinks, that if a Christian be the temple of the Holy Spirit which is in him, if the word of Christ dwell in him, &c., his heart cannot be quite as bad as it was in the days of his unbelief.

C—— has learned to talk of the latter, and thence denies the former; H—— to talk of the former, and thence denies the latter.

There is something very bad working in Ireland in the way of questioning our *authority* to put forward the Gospel to the world. It has been opposed determinately, and by those who abhor, as much as the patrons of the sentiment, all usurpation of *peculiar* authority here, such as belonged to the Apostles. But no man, who is fully persuaded of the *truth* of the Gospel, will be at a loss for the *authority* for asserting and maintaining it in public and in private. The divine authority of the Word is his authority for this. I consider the opposite idea as connected with absolute scepticism as to all divine truth.

CXXXI.

TO THE SAME.

March 17, 1829.

The faith which stands not in the wisdom of man, but in the power of God, is single-eyed. It is not distracted with the various inquiries—what will this or that man do or say? who will concur with me? what will be the consequences? "Thus saith the Lord," decides every thing; and shuts out all consideration about other persons, and all calculation of consequences. "Where the word of the king is, there is power," Ec.viii. 4.:" and it is indeed in the midst of his *enemies* that he reigns. It is with his rod—the sceptre of his power—that he feeds his people. (Mic. vii. 14. Ps. cx. 2.) The word, rendered *feed*, includes the reclaiming them from their wanderings, and every other exercise of the *pastoral office*. And he is indeed glorious, "standing there and feeding in the majesty of the name of Jehovah." (v. 4.) I heard it remarked lately, that when we read in the Old Testament of the wonderful interferences and glorious displays of Jehovah in his dealings with his people Israel, of the pillar of a cloud by day, and the flaming fire by night, &c. &c., our foolish hearts are secretly disposed to look back at these, as more glorious than any thing we know of now. But we may consider the thought rebuked by that word of the Lord—"Except ye see signs and wonders, ye will not believe." John iv. 48. We are expressly taught that the greatest glory of the law of Moses was as nothing in comparison of the things now revealed to us, but revealed (not as the former glories) to the senses, but to faith—that faith which is the conviction of things not seen. The former kingdom is called *carnal* and *earthly*, in comparison of that *heavenly* kingdom into which we have been brought. And the superior excellence of the glory of this, consists in the superior clearness with which the same God of Israel has revealed, and does continually reveal to us the same name, or character which He proclaimed, when his servant Moses entreated to be shown his glory—" Merciful and gracious, forgiving iniquity, transgression, and sin, and that will not make a full end;" (for so the words ought to be rendered) but will leave *a remnant*, in whom, as the vessels of mercy before ordained unto glory, He will "make known the riches of his glory," as the just God and the Saviour. The clear discovery of the way in which His mercy reigns through righteousness unto eternal life, through the redemption that is in Christ Jesus; this is all the glory of that house which is his own, Heb. iii. 6.; and blessed are they that dwell in it, Ps. lxxxiv. 4. Well may they be still praising Him, and saying—" Blessed be His glorious name for ever; and let the whole earth be filled with His glory, Ps. lxxii. 19.

CXXXII.

TO MISS F———.

April 24, 1829.

Dear Miss F.—I had written the additional remarks, which I send you, before the receipt of your letter this morning. I am not a little surprised at your thinking any knowledge of the Greek original necessary to ascertain the correctness of what I offered, when you surely must be aware that the English phrase, which our translators have employed, "*no not* to eat," is of precisely the same import as "not *even* to eat." I am equally surprised and pained at your saying, that if it mean "not even to eat"—you are "quite incapable of understanding the meaning of the chapter:" for, surely, whether you admit the meaning asserted or not, you cannot deny that it is perfectly *intelligible*; as intelligible as the direction of another Apostle, that I should not "*receive into my house*" (2 John 10.) a person whom he describes, nor bid him God speed. We may contend against the reasonableness of such precepts; we may reject the meaning assigned, as not the real meaning: but to talk of being incapable of understanding it, is indeed very unreasonable.

You quite mistake one of my remarks, when you suppose that I intended to impute to you any want of activity in circulating the view you have adopted. But indeed, now it appears that you were never of one mind with us on this divine command. You may perceive by M——'s letter that I am in communication with the Dublin church on the subject. But I have no idea that the case of scriptural discipline in the church here (however similar) should be stopped, till the brethren in Dublin come to some decision of a controversy, which they have allowed to be raised among them. If they will not concur with us in maintaining the precept, of course our connexion with them also will cease. The prospect is very melancholy, but not so melancholy as it would be, that some outward connexion should be kept up by our compromising the laws of the kingdom of heaven. However, He, to whom nothing is impossible, can yet dispel the black cloud that impends.

REMARKS ON 1 COR. V. 11. REFERRED TO IN THE PRECEDING LETTER.

HERETOFORE I had supposed that we were all of one mind upon the apostolic precept given in 1 Cor. v. 11. and there are few (if any) of the divine precepts on which there appears less room for any difference of judgment among disciples. But I am sorry to find that there has been privately adopted a misinterpretation of the passage, which amounts to an absolute rejection of it: and this is circulating privately, and spreading like leaven. It would be more suitable to the principles of Christian fellowship, that when any individual in the connexion adopts a view of any part of the divine rule, different from that in which the body are *professedly* united, this diversity should be openly avowed to the brethren. The opposite course is more suitable to those religious sects, who agree to differ amicably upon the divine commands. But waving this for the present, I would proceed to expose briefly the falsehood of the interpretation assigned by ———, and in which ——— appeared to concur. They interpret the expression "with such an one *no not to eat*," as referring to *the eating of the Lord's supper* with such a character. Now, in the first place, there cannot be found throughout the New Testament any instance in which the simple expression of *eating with* a person, is used for *eating the Lord's supper with him*; while there are several instances of the same word being employed in its obvious signification of *joining with persons in civil intercourse*, as when the disciples and their Master are reproached *for eating with* publicans and sinners. But, secondly, the plain force of the expression "NO NOT to eat," or as it would literally be rendered, "not EVEN to eat with such a person," is utterly inconsistent with the notion that the *eating* intended is the eating *the Lord's supper*. Would it not be really profane to represent as a small and ordinary thing, that most solemn act of Christian fellowship, in which disciples join together in showing forth the Lord's death, and exhibit their heavenly union in him with one another? Yet such decisively would be the profane import of the language as so misinterpreted. "I enjoin you not to associate with those called brethren, but fornicators, &c. &c.—with such an one not EVEN to eat the Lord's supper." But, thirdly, the misinterpretation is still more abundantly refuted by the connexion of the 11th verse with the 10th. There we find the apostle expressly allowing to Christians that companionship with such characters of the world—and marking the impossibility of our avoiding it without going out of the world—that companionship which he forbids us to maintain with the same characters when appearing in the Christian. But did he mean to allow them to hold fellowship in the ordinance of the supper with fornicators of the world?

The three verses (9. 10. and 11.) are most closely connected, and plainly amount to this: 'I enjoin you not to associate with fornicators, &c. not even in convivial intercourse: but when I say this, I intend such characters only, when they have appeared in your Christian body, and not fornicators of the world. For how could you avoid their society, unless ye were altogether to go out of the world? Nay, if any of the infidel world bid you to a feast, and ye be disposed to go, use your liberty. But not so if any one called a brother, &c.' Now, taking the 11th verse in this connexion, from which it cannot be disjoined, how can any one say that the eating which is *allowed* to Christians *with a fornicator*, &c. of the world, *but forbidden* with a *fornicator called a brother*, is the eating of the Lord's supper?

I hear so many extraordinary things, that I should not be much surprised if I heard some such objection as this, against the view which I have contended for—'And is it only in civil companionship that we are forbidden to associate with fornicators, &c. appearing in the church, and are we allowed to keep them in the Christian fellowship?' Any one starting such an objection must willingly overlook what has gone before and what follows. In the 4th and and 5th verses, the apostle has expressly commanded the Corinthian church to put away such a character from their Christian fellowship; and he briefly recalls their attention to that command at the close of the chapter: distinct from this, though closely connected with it, is the direction which he gives in the 11th to regulate their deportment towards such an one, *even* in the civil intercourse of this life.

The wisdom of the latter direction is disputed. ——— urged against it—" What additional punishment is there in not having him at our table, after we have removed him from our Christian fellowship?" It is a very awful thing to set up our wisdom against the wisdom of God; and when we attempt it, it is no wonder that our wisdom should be found folly, as it obviously is in the present case. What can be more suitable, what more adapted to keep alive on our minds a due sense of the awfulness of the case of one, who has rebelled against the divine word—as well as consistently to present to him our solemn testimony against his rebellion—than that we should be enjoined to abstain from all that intercourse and companionship with him, even in the things of this life, which would import complacency in him and satisfaction in his society? And this at once exposes the futility of an objection which some have started, as if the precept were impracticable, as inconsistent in many cases with the duties which are imposed on him by the various relations of life? 'Should a husband refuse to eat his meals with his wife, or a wife with her husband, a parent with a child, or a child with his parent, if one of the parties be a disciple, and the other has been put away from the church?'—Is there, in such a case, any of that convivial intercourse which the apostle really forbids, and which is sought from mutual complacency in each other? I would freely say, in reply to such cavils, that while I contend for the apostolic precept in its real and obvious import, I should not think that I violated the precept at all, by actually partaking of a meal (in many cases) at the same table with one of the characters described. I dare not, for instance, either ask him to an entertainment that I made, or accept of his invitation; in doing so I should break a plain command. But if I were invited to dine by one of the world, and found at his table one who had once been in Christian fellowship with me, but was put away, should I therefore leave the table? I have known some that would, and I respect their adherence even to the letter of the Word, though I think it not enjoined by the spirit of it. Have I sought his society? In my remaining at the table, is there any thing indicative of my complacency in him? or is there any thing that contaminates me, any more than in dining in the same house with him, or in the same city? No—I should remain at the table without scruple, while guarding my deportment against even the appearance of familiarity with him, or of pleasure in his society.

CXXXIII.

TO THE SAME.

April 25, 1829.

In addition to the paper of remarks which I sent you yesterday, on 1 Cor. v. 11, allow me now to request your attention to the following, suggested by ———'s letter to you. Her communication makes me more acquainted than I was before with the extraordinary ground taken by her and others, for their rejection of the apostolic command. But before I notice that, let me remark how awful it is that she has not condescended to take the slightest notice of the Apostle's words, " not even to eat with such an one"—or to give the least intimation what she conceives to be their meaning, but absolutely passes them over, as if they were unworthy of consideration. " *Whatever the dealing was there ordered*, it could only be so long as the offender was called a brother, which he certainly is no longer after he is put out of the body. Paul says, What have I to do to judge them that are without," &c.

The Apostle had commanded the Corinthians to have no fellowship with fornicators; and he now remarks, that this prohibition related not to fornicators of the world, but to the case of such a character appearing within the Christian body—such as had now occurred in the incestuous person; proving thus, from the remark, that he had nothing to do to judge them that were without, and that the Corinthians must needs go out of the world if they were not to associate with *its* fornicators. With respect to such a character appearing within the church, and therefore *at that time* called, or bearing the name of a brother, and therefore a proper object of the apostolic judgment, he repeats and enforces his command, that they should put him out of their body, and abstain from all companionship with him, even in the convivial intercourse which they were allowed to hold with heathens. O yes, says Miss H——'s argument in effect—obeying one part of your injunction in removing him from our *Christian fellowship*, we may, in opposition to the other part, hold as much good fellowship with him as we please, in the social intercourse of this life; for he is *then without*, and you say that you have nothing to do with judging those that are without. Really, such pitiful special pleading would be ludicrous in common matters; but, on a scriptural subject, it is very profane. Admitting that the Apostle had nothing to do to judge them that were without, yet Miss H—— might allow it to be within the apostolic province to instruct and command those that were within; and what she calls the *dealing* ordered with the fornicator, Cor. v. 11, is simply a prohibition to the disciples against eating with him. A little more modesty might have made her pause before she virtually denied his authority for this.

If Miss H——, by the words "not even to eat with such an one," understands eating the Lord's supper with him, combining this with her assertion, that the "dealing ordered" could only have been so long as he was within, she must imagine that there was some such practice then, as what has since been called *suspending a person from the communion*. If she mean that while he was still within the body, and therefore joining the body on the first day of the week in all Christian ordinances, the church were yet forbidden to eat an ordinary meal with him, I would ask Miss H——, *how long* she conceives a fornicator is to be *retained* in the church? I would tell her that he is to be put out forthwith, as soon as his wicked character has appeared.

CXXXIV.

TO THE SAME.

April —, 1829.

Believe me, dear Miss F., it went to my heart last Sunday to be obliged to call you to such a trying interview in the present weakly state of your health. I fear the very sight of my handwriting must now be painful to you. But can you wonder that I am unwilling to omit any effort for averting the sad result which seems so fast approaching? Allow me, therefore, to return to one point, which is capable of being put so as must command your assent, unless the

Lord has said—"Let her eyes be holden;" or (what I consider perfectly equivalent with this) unless you are left to shut your eyes wilfully against the clearest light. The point I mean, is this—that the English phrase *no not*, is exactly of the same import with *not even*, and therefore that it does not require, as you intimate, any knowledge of the Greek, to be satisfied that the *eating*, mentioned in the 11th verse, is not the eating of the Lord's supper. I have sometimes attempted to illustrate the force of "*no not*," by supposing that I told you of a person from whom I had expected a legacy, that he *left me nothing*, NO NOT *sixpence*. I have appealed to you, whether you, and every one acquainted with English, would not understand by that expression—not *even* so *small* a sum as sixpence. It is discouraging enough that this appeal has not carried conviction with it. But perhaps, if I pursue the illustration in a somewhat different form, it may strike you more. Suppose you asked me how much has he left you? and I replied—"nothing—no, not *two thousand a-year*." I now call on you to think whether you would not be disposed to say, why that is strange language; as if 2,000 a-year would have been a small legacy;—whether you would not at once feel that the phrase "*no not*"—in connexion with the mention of a legacy so great—was improper and absurd.

There are one or two other remarks which I would offer; but yet, if you still conceive that the words in the 11th verse "*no, not to eat with such an one*," refer to the highest act of Christian fellowship, there is obviously no use in saying anything more.

CXXXV.

TO MR. W. C——.

May 7, 1829.

DEAR BROTHER,—I need scarcely say that your letter afforded me joy, and matter of thanksgiving to Him, who maketh men to be of one mind in an house—in that house which is indeed his building. I should make very little of the intelligence that the W—— brethren had ceased to be baptized, had it not appeared that this change is connected with one much deeper,—with a clearer perception of that glory of the Lord, which confounds and lays low all the fancied glory of man *at his best estate*, Ps. xxxix; (Mark the emphasis of the Psalmist's language in the passage referred to; *Every*—not some, or many, or most men—but *every man*;—not in some circumstances and unfavourable conditions, but—*at his best estate*;—not—is beset with much vanity—but *is altogether vanity*.) which at once furnishes us with an infinitude of substantial glorying in His redeeming mercy, and faithfulness, and power, and at the same time discovers to us our own utter vileness at all times, the utter contrariety to God of all our own thoughts and ways, and willings and workings. The salvation, wherewith he saves us from *ourselves*, is great and wonderful indeed. "*Bent to backsliding from me,*" is the character which he gives of his people; not the character (as so many think) which *was* theirs, but which *is* theirs unvariedly to the end. Yet in such rebels he accomplishes that word of his promise—"I will not turn away from them to do them good; and I will put my fear in their hearts, that they shall not depart from me." The various and gross corruptions of the revealed truth of God throughout Christianity, in those days of the Gentiles, present an awful display of human wickedness, as just similar to that of the Jewish people. But there is a still blacker display of it, and of crowning malignity. It is this. Let us only be left to ourselves to make our own use of the gospel of the grace of God, in the purest form in which words can convey it, and there is no one of us that would not abuse and pervert that glorious gospel, into an occasion to the flesh in any of its most loathsome forms; talking perhaps most excellently about the truth of God, and at the same time walking after our own lusts, led blindfolded by the father of lies with a lie in our right hand. Well, how blessed is that hope, which, even this view of the malignity of our own hearts, does not shake or in the least affect. Any hope is false, that would be shaken by the conviction that we are fully capable, even of the wickedness last described; not only capable of it, but that it is one of the forms of ungodliness, to which our own hearts continually tend: the hope, which such a conviction would shake, must be a hope that we are not quite so bad. But blessed be God, the way into the holiest is so made manifest for such sinners, that we can at all times come boldly unto God, with full boldness, confessing our sin, without any attempt or wish to cover it; loathing ourselves, but giving thanks to his holy name, and glorying in it; satisfied with his goodness, and looking to him confidently to fulfil in us all his good pleasure, even to the end. But I must check myself, in order to add one or two remarks. You introduce the phrase, "workers together with God," which is borrowed from our translation of 1 Cor. iii. 9. In the original, it is not—"labourers together with"—but fellow-labourers, and not "with God"—but "of God"—in the employ of God; and happily a little attention to the context will be sufficient to satisfy any disciple of this, though wholly ignorant of Greek.

The apostle had sharply reproved the Corinthians for the schisms and parties that were among them. They classed themselves under different leaders, according to the different instruments through whom they had been called to the belief of the Gospel, as Paul, Peter, Apollos, &c., and some, no doubt, thought they stood on much higher ground, as having been called under the personal ministry of Christ himself. The Apostle strikes at the root of this carnal glorying. "Who is Paul, and who is Apollos," but mere instruments in the work which is exclusively God's, and in which the instrument employed is *nothing*, but that God, who works by any he pleases, is all; and how unreasonable to make any difference between Paul and Apollos, &c. the occasion of divisions among you, when we all possess one common character, are all FELLOW-*servants* of the same Lord. I believe I need not say more to satisfy you that the idea in the passage, is—not "workers together with God"—as if God and the Apostles were fellow-workers, but fellow-labourers one with another, employed by the same God in the same work. It is the more needful, however, to insist on this correction of our translation, as we know what a handle the Wesleyan Methodists and others make of the text, for giving a countenance to their profane atheistic idea of a sinner's *co-operating* with God in the work of his salvation; and indeed it is an idea which is at the bottom, not only of the Arminian blasphemy, but of most of the Calvinistic orthodoxy—in short, of the creed of all who would reject the sentiment, that every work and thought of the mind, and motion of the will, that springs from the believer's own heart, is from first to last *opposed* to the only true God—so far from being in any *co-operation* with him. Blessed be God! in such HE worketh both to will and to do, and his mercy *reigns* victorious unto eternal life. To his faithful care and keeping I commit you, and all the dear brethren at W——, to whom, though unknown in the flesh, I desire my affectionate salutation.

CXXXVI.

TO R. L. C——.

June 8, 1829.

P—— need not endeavour to enlist *feelings* on his side. It is unnecessary, and the attempt is unscriptural. He really writes like one utterly ignorant of the nature of Christian admonition and scriptural reproof. He talks of them throughout as an exercise of *jurisdiction* on the side of those who offer them, over those to whom they are offered. He takes for granted that a *Christian Church* has the right of *exercising jurisdiction* over its own members, and that we attempted to exercise it over the body in Dublin. The whole of this idea is monstrous. The only jurisdiction over Christians, either collectively or individually, in matters relating to the kingdom of God, belongs to the king of Zion; and the moment any *church*, or any member of a church, thinks of exercising *jurisdiction* in the affairs of His kingdom, there is indeed an usurpation of Christ's authority.

Take the last act of discipline in a church,—the removal from among them of an unreclaimed offender. It is an act which their *king commands*, and in taking which they but *obey* his authority, but exercise not the slightest authority themselves. In obedience to his commands, they cease to walk with that wicked person;—they cease to hold him in their fellowship. But let us look a little closer at the nature of Christian admonition and reproof. To *admonish* a person is to *put him in mind* of something: and this implies that the person has before known, or professedly known, that of which we put him in mind. In doing this, do we exercise any jurisdiction over him? For *Christian* admonition there is *always* room from a church or an individual disciple towards *any* other disciple or church: there is *always room and ground* for it, on account of the *continual tendency* of our hearts to let slip the things which we have been taught; and therefore the apostles speak of it as an exercise of brotherly love, in which it is well that disciples should *always* be engaged. Col. iii. 16. Rom. xv. 14. And when they are thus blessedly engaged in *admonishing one another*, are they *exercising jurisdiction* over each other? But when any one, with whom we are in Christian connexion, appears to *have let slip*, or to *be letting slip*, any of the Christian principles he has professed, then there is a more special call on those who observe this, to *admonish* him, to *put him in mind* of what he is forgetting; but not a whit more exercise of jurisdiction or authority over him. Now, suppose that I send a *letter* of Christian admonition to a brother in those circumstances, with whom I have not an opportunity of a personal interview, what should we think of him, if, instead of meeting my brotherly labour of love in a similar mind, he were to throw my letter unread into the fire, and manifest that he was affronted and irritated at my *officious interference?* What should we think of this, if he even tried to vindicate it, by saying that, indeed, before the arrival of my letter he was beginning to recollect the principles, to which I aimed at recalling him? Nay, I will give P—— more advantage. I shall suppose that I wrote my admonitory letter under misinformation or mistake; and that my brother was really at the time kept in full remembrance of the principles, of which I put him in mind;—if it were really so, would he be more likely to burn my letter, or to be affronted at the receipt of it? Indeed, he would not.—And what I have to say of one individual Christian writing to one, I say of twenty associated, writing a common letter to twenty others associated; whatever mystic meaning P—— may annex to the term *church*. But of this more hereafter. But is not the exercise of *jurisdiction* implied in any attempt to *reprove?* Not at all necessarily, according to the scriptural import of the word, any more than in the attempt to admonish. The Greek word, commonly translated to *reprove*, is the same which in Matth. xviii. 15. is translated "*tell him his fault;*" in which passage all idea of the exercise of *jurisdiction* or *authority* is excluded by the whole spirit, in which the disciple endeavours to gain the brother who has trespassed against him. The strict and literal meaning of the term is—to *prove the character* of a thing—(generally its evil character)—by *bringing it to the test* by which it should be tried. In scriptural reproof, that test, by which we show the evil that we reprove, is the divine word. *We* exercise no jurisdiction or authority by referring to that tribunal, to which all the authoritative decision belongs. But where the reproof is scriptural, it constitutes one of the highest exercises of brotherly love, in that family where "all are brethren" on one common level: and truly there is reason to apprehend some great mistake in the mind of those, who repel that exercise of love as the attack of an enemy. P—— seems to admit that we have scriptural authority for the idea of sister churches—*i.e.* churches so acknowledging each other as holding the same faith and walking by the same rule, that a member of one visiting the other, joins its fellowship of course, on being recognised as a member of the former. In fact, it is evident that the apostolic churches were generally thus connected: and the connexion naturally (I may say) arises from the nature and ground of Christian connexion. But according to the nature and ground of that communion, how can this connexion be scripturally maintained, without allowing the freest communication between them, on all things concerning the kingdom of God,—without the most open door to the interchange of Christian admonition and reproof: no more than the Christian fellowship of two individuals in the same church can be maintained, if either close the door against the other. It would be but the *name* of brotherhood that would then continue; and disconnected from all the grounds that are essential to its real existence. Is this less true of two collective bodies of Christians, than of two individuals? Is not mutual confidence as to the unity of their faith and way, essential to their acknowledged connexion? And does it consist with the maintenance of this confidence, that one of them should reject a Christian communication by letter from the other, and repel it indignantly as "*a wanton creating of a cause of probable disunion?*" Really, such conduct and such language invade every principle of Christian fellowship; and only prove that it was high time for us to adopt the course which we have taken.

But what reason had we to think it *probable*, that a disunion would be occasioned by our sending that letter of brotherly admonition to a body, with whom we professedly stood in Christian connexion? could we have calculated on such an unbrotherly rejection of it by all of them? I certainly should not have been surprised if the same party, who openly opposed the divine command, should also oppose the reception of our letter exposing their sin, and the sin of the adverse party, who had tolerated their rebellion for so many months; nor should I have been surprised if this had accelerated a separation, which ought to have taken place so long before. But that the nominal asserters of the command should also concur in rejecting our admonition, is what assuredly we could not have anticipated. And now who have made that letter the *occasion* of our disunion? We or they?

But how unfair and unfounded is P——'s representation, that we have cut them off *for not reading that letter in the church assembled!* He seems to have penned that representation for the sake of the *point*, that "we admonished them for one offence, and cut them off for another." From my letter to M—— informing him of our procedure, P——, if he looked at it (but perhaps his indignation would not allow even this), must know that the ground of our procedure was, their non-repentance of the evils on which we admonished them. —(as far as M——'s reply conveyed any information of their mind; combined certainly with their closing the door against communication with them as a sister church.) But if the language of M——'s reply had afforded any scriptural ground for hoping that they really saw the wickedness of the course in which they had been so long walking—instead of affording evidence to the contrary, would their mere refusal to receive our letter have led us, who reported the result to the church, to mark the course which we did, as that which alone remained, or have led the church to adopt it? You, my brother, know and can testify the contrary. Yet undoubtedly, even then, the rejection of our letter would have formed a subject of the most serious remonstrance and expostulation; nor could I think of continuing in connexion with any church, that would *continue* to adopt and vindicate such unbrotherly conduct. But certainly every communication which we have as yet received, affords accumulated proof that they remain utterly insensible to the radical evils on which we admonished them.

But what right have we "*to proceed to an act of discipline to a distant church?*" An act of discipline! Shame that P—— should employ the phrase in the way of mystery or charm, for beclouding a most simple subject. If we are warranted by the word to acknowledge a distant body of disciples as a sister church, must we not of necessity be warranted in declaring that connexion dissolved, when the grounds of it and of the brotherly confidence essential to it are removed? Or, having once acknowledged that connexion, must it continue *of course* for ever? No, P—— himself says "that he would not absolutely charge us with evil, had we thought fit to withdraw from them three months ago."—(Why he fixes upon that period I know not, it being now more than five months ago since H. made his speech disowning the precept, and was tolerated in it.)—So, had we dissolved the connexion so long ago, without previously making any effort to recall them from their evil ways, all would have been well, in P——'s view. Not so in mine. I should never have consented to break off a connexion so close and of such long standing, without an attempt at reclaiming them by scriptural admonition. And what does P—— mean by saying—"Do not think I dispute your right to take every means in your power to convey instruction to other churches, or to *point out evils in which ye may find them walking.*" What more did we do in that admonitory letter, and from which he has chosen to be affronted, and which it is plain was rejected by the body through *his* influence and misleading? And now he raises an outcry against *us* for a rupture, of which he has been himself the author; which he appears so anxious to perpetuate, that he is about retiring from the Stafford Street body, because (it seems) they are about employing some means for healing the breach which he has occasioned! But really the more I examine the whole of that passage in his letter, the more inexplicable it appears,—or rather, the more irreconcileable with any true principles of Christian union. He goes on to say, "Had you sent us, instead of your *admonition, information* that you could not continue to countenance our course by walking with us,—you would have very speedily heard that we had put an end to this course, *attended with probably as ample a confession of evil on our parts* as you would have desired." Really! But now (this is the necessary supplement intended) ye shall have no confession of evil from us, but we shall stand on our defence and on a vindication of our evils, because ye presumed to offer us brotherly admonition upon them! And this man talks of the evil of making Christian fellowship turn upon straws! Had we merely given them the *information* that we could not continue the connexion, without endeavouring to point out the evils to their attention, P—— might have had some pretext for charging us with employing a *threat*, as he does now for accompanying our admonition upon them with a remark, that their continuance would be inconsistent with continuance of our connexion as sister churches. As to his accusing us of *knowing*, when we sent the admonition, that "the distracting matter was just arriving at its close," I must tell him that we knew it not, either when the admonitory letter was ordered by the church, or when it was dispatched by us. But I must tell him further, that we know it has not arrived at a *scriptural close* to this day,—unless some *great change* has taken place since the writing of his letter, of which we have had no telegraphic account. The really *distracting matter* has been their profanation of the divine commands, by tolerating for more than five months the open disavowal of subjection to one of them in an individual member, and the progressive spreading of that rebellion through a majority of their body, as well as the turning of the Church of God into a *school of disputation*. For these evils we neither knew of any symptom of repentance, when we admonished them on the subject, nor do we know of any now, but have lamentable evidence of the contrary in P——'s letter. In the last of these evils, indeed, P—— seems to glory; when he boasts that himself and A. B. "all along stood unflinching in the *fore-front of the hot battle*;" and declares that "it ought to sink deep in our consciences," that such fine combatants should now (through their own pertinacity in evil) be likely to be separated from the Stafford Street body. I am sick of his letter, and drop it with one more remark. I have held P—— very, very dear, for the truth's sake: and it will relieve my heart from a load of pain, if he ever be restored to the same place in my brotherly affection or confidence which he has formerly possessed. But reflecting on the course, in which he has been, and is still engaged, I cannot at present regard him with any complacency.

CXXXVII.

TO THE CHURCH IN DUBLIN.

June 8, 1829.

Very dear Brethren,—Much endeared to us by the manifestation of the mind of Christ in your letter of the 3rd instant. That letter was marked with such Christian honesty and explicitness of candid acknowledgment, that we could not hesitate to lay it before the church, which we did on yesterday; and the church with as little hesitation joyfully declared the connexion restored between them and your body as sister churches, and gave us the pleasing commission to inform you of this with their most Christian salutations. Blessed be the good shepherd who is faithful to that promise—"*I* will seek that which was lost, and bring again that which was driven away, and will bind up that which was broken and will strengthen that which was sick." Ezek. xxxiv. 16. We doubt not but, through his powerful blessing, what has passed (though for the time not joyous but grievous indeed) will prove abundantly useful for knitting us together more closely, and leading us to watch over each other in love more faithfully. Excuse us for writing so short a letter at present. We are much occupied, and unwilling to delay sending this. Poor P—— will shortly receive a paper of remarks on a most painful letter lately received from him. That paper we wish you to see after he has done with it. And now, dear brethren, grace be with you, and keep us all walking in that heavenly wisdom "all whose paths are peace."

P. S.—Unity of mind is so essential to real Christian union, and any concealed difference of mind, covered up by a laxity of principle, is so surely productive in the end of every evil, that we think it at least safe (though perhaps not necessary) to state to you distinctly, that *we hold it lawful for a Christian to employ any means that come within the compass of his ability and opportunity, for exposing and refuting antichristian lies, by putting forward scriptural truth in opposition to them, either privately or publicly, either by speech or by writing.* If you note the terms we use, you will see them adapted to mark the legitimate use of scripture towards them that are without, in contradistinction to that which is illegitimate and evil. We should wish the church in Stafford Street to be clearly acquainted with our mind on this subject. If any hold that to be actually unlawful, the lawfulness of which we assert—(while we do not urge upon any, exertions which may seem to them inexpedient)—such persons certainly could not honestly walk with us. They would be tolerating in us what they think evil. If, as we trust, there is no such discordance of mind between us here, you will probably see it needful to use caution, in the reception into your body of others whom you may suspect to differ from us on this subject. You know the lengths to which some in Ireland have lately gone upon it.

CXXXVIII.

TO MRS. B———.

June —, 1829.

THANKS to my dear Mrs. B—— for so promptly sending me so satisfactory a letter—satisfactory, as giving me the information I desired, and, as part of that information, the restoration of the D—— to your fellowship, and the greenness of Mrs. N——'s old age. My heart's love to her. I should be ungrateful if I were not ready, as far as I can, to communicate my sentiments on any subject upon which you and M—— desired to know them; but I believe I need not say that I fully concur with you in holding it unlawful for us to read the scriptures to or with unbelievers, in any way that implies or involves religious intercommunity with them. But I confess I wonder that this has been agitated so exclusively as to reading the scriptures, there being so many other ways in which we may fall (and are in fully as much danger of falling) into the same evil;—for instance, joining them in that kind of vague religious talk and observation, which they are forward to introduce as good and spiritual. I wonder also that, if nothing more was originally meant than is now stated to have been intended, the church in Dublin should have been kept in hot water for so many months, by the discussion of a principle which at once commends itself to the conscience of every one, who knows and hallows the name of the Lord. I wonder also that the subject has been dropped in Dublin, without some more marking of the way in which, and the purpose for which, we may *lawfully* read the scriptures to unbelievers every day in the year—namely, for the express purpose of proving their *disbelief* of those scriptures which they profess to own as the oracles of God—exposing and refuting from the scriptures their ungodly misinterpretations of it. Does this involve or imply any religious intercommunity with them? Nay, the very reverse. The more we are faithfully engaged in such an use of the scriptures, the more shall we be considered "men of strife and contention," opposed to all the world in our religion. I do wonder, also, at many things, which I really cannot reconcile with the principles of common sense or common honesty, in those whom I have most highly esteemed. For instance, I wonder that P—— should now say he never thought of laying down a law for us, when he opened the subject in his first letter to Mr. C——, in these words:—"It is unlawful for a Christian to read the scriptures to or with unbelievers; this we are prepared to maintain:" and when, in his last letter to Mr. C——, he declares that the terms which he there employed had been stated and canvassed "in various private assemblages," before they were brought forward; and emphatically protests against the supposition that he does not still adhere to them to the very letter. I do wonder that P——, whose acuteness of intellect and studied accuracy of language we all know, should talk, as if the terms which he employed admitted any diversity of meaning, or as if they do not expressly lay down a law for Christians, which we should receive as a law of Christ, if it be sanctioned by the word, but if not, should reject as a human interposition. I do wonder that, after so long asserting the *general unlawfulness* of reading the scriptures to an unbelieving professor of them, and indeed without admitting any alteration to this day in the terms of that assertion, he should yet talk now of leaving the matter to each disciple's discretion; and I confess that, while these strange inconsistencies are persisted in, I must apprehend that the peace which has been patched up is hollow, and that much evil is covered up under it.

The unbelief of the professing world is (I may say) bottomed on scripture misinterpreted, and employed to support the lies which the world loves. Our controversy, therefore, against those lies cannot consistently be maintained, without a continual reference to those scriptures, the sacredness of which consists in the sacredness of that truth which they declare, and for which we are called "earnestly to contend;" and the sacredness of that truth is consistent with the most indiscriminate promulgation of it. It is utter nonsense to distinguish, in making that reference, between quoting these scriptures from memory and reading them from the book, or between reading a single verse and an entire chapter—to admit the one as lawful and condemn the other as unlawful. But, indeed, I apprehend that there are among us some, who secretly disapprove of all contention for the truth against the errors of the antichristian world around us, though they would allow us to communicate in a whisper on the subject, with such as should take the pains to cross-examine us. But let any Christian read such a passage as that in Acts xi. 19—21, and then say whether the first disciples made such a piece of free masonry of their faith—whether they did not rather act on the principle, "what ye hear in the ear, that publish ye upon the housetops." Matt. x. 27. Any principle opposed to this, I avow that I abhor. There is one more remark I would add.

I think there is much and mischievous *ambiguity* in the position that "the scriptures are *given* only to the church of God." The scriptures are, in a most important sense, given to all alike to whom, in the providence of God, they come; and I wish P—— would distinctly state what he means by saying, that they are given more specially to the Christian church in Stafford Street, than to the antichristian synagogues of Plunket Street or Eustace Street. It is, indeed, most true that the scriptures cannot *profit* where they are not mixed with faith; and that as all things are for the elect's sake, so in the divine counsels the scriptures are not designed to make any others wise unto salvation.

But those who would infer from this that the scriptures are not adapted to make wise unto salvation any, but those who already have received that wisdom without the scriptures, or any but those who are already *ostensibly* among the elect of God, draw an inference against which I protest as pregnant with the most ungodly enthusiasm. How did P—— and F—— and G——, &c. come to the knowledge of the truth? I read that faith cometh by hearing—or by having the truth set before the mind for the obedience of faith? Now, the scriptures (it seems) have not been designed and are not to be used for the purpose. Well, was it by what they heard from those in antichristian societies? (There were no others in Ireland.) They will scarcely say this. Or was it by what they read in such writings as Sandeman's? Why, the very same persons set their faces against all publications upon scriptural subjects, however scriptural. Or was an angel from heaven sent to tell them the gospel? Or were they brought to the belief of it without hearing it at all? If they mean that *they* are in the same circumstances with those to whom the writings of the New Testament were addressed, it is partly not true. They are not evangelists, like Timothy and Titus; nor masters of Onesimus, like Philemon, &c. 'But they are in connexion with ostensible believers, walking together by apostolic rule, like the churches of the saints, to whom many of the epistles were addressed.' This is very well, so far as it is true. But I hope it has been by the scriptures that their former antichristian disobedience to apostolic command has been corrected; and yet they tell me that the scriptures were not then *given* to *them*, nor designed for their correction! Indeed they were, just as really as they are *given* to them now.

REMARKS ON ACTS xi. 19—21. REFERRED TO IN THE PRECEDING LETTER.

In my correspondence with different persons here and in Ireland, I referred to Acts xi. 19—21. and especially to v. 20. as containing a divine instance of the gospel being preached by Christians bearing no apostolic character or mission, and preached not only to Jews but to Gentiles, while their warrant and ours for thus declaring the word of life indiscriminately, is established by the declaration—" that the hand of the Lord was with them." I have complained also to more than one, that as far as I could understand, P—— and his associates, in opposing this scriptural course, had never condescended to make the least reply to this reference, or to take the least notice of it. But I now find that P—— conceives he has succeeded in evading its force, by discovering that the *Grecians* spoken of in v. 20. were not Gentile Greeks, but *Hellenists*, or Jews,* living among the Gentiles, and using the Greek version of the Old Testament scriptures in their synagogues.

This assertion, it seems, he has put forward triumphantly to persons unable to examine whether it is true or false: and I dare say he *thinks* himself borne out in it, by finding in his Greek testament, that the word rendered Grecians is (Ελληνιστας) as in Acts vi. 1.—not (Ελληνας). But I must now tell him, that every one who has the least pretensions to biblical scholarship knows that the true reading is Ελληνας, and not (as in the vulgar text) Ελληνιστας.

* Such certainly were the mass of Jews born and resident in Antioch.

For this, he may find quoted by Wetstein, (in his folio edition) a host of MSS., ancient versions, &c., and among the MSS. two of the *most ancient and valuable* in existence—the *Alexandrine and Beza's*. Some of them also he may see adduced by Griesbach, who has even introduced (Ελληνας) into the text; what he never does except when he considers the vulgar reading unquestionably corrupt.

That it is so in this instance, the whole passage affords the most decisive internal evidence; and it is happily of such a nature that it can be laid before the mere English reader. In short, to admit the reading (Ελληνιστας) would make *nonsense* of the passage.

That the Hellenists, or Grecians, mentioned in Acts vi. 1. were not Gentiles, but *Jews*, is certain from the consideration, that at that period the gospel had not been sent to the Gentiles. But that the Grecians mentioned in Acts xi. 20. were *not Jews*, but Gentiles, is as certain from the connexion of the 20th with the 19th verse. "Those then who were scattered, upon the persecution that arose about Stephen, travelled as far as Phenice, &c. preaching the word to *none but unto the Jews only*. But some of them were men of Cyprus and Cyrene, who, when they were come to Antioch, *spake unto the Grecians*, preaching the Lord Jesus." Now, let any reader of common sense say, whether the *Grecians*, mentioned in the 20th verse, are not here plainly *contradistinguished from Jews;* and if they were not Jews, must they not have been *Gentiles?* Accordingly, Rosenmüller, in his commentary on the passage, justly remarks that "if these Cyprian and Cyrenæan Christians had taught the *Hellenists*, they would have done nothing else than what the others had done, of whom we read in the 19th verse, "the Hellenists also being *Jews*."

Though I have said so much in exposure of P——'s attempt to corrupt and pervert this passage, and though I should be pleased to find him *honestly* acknowledging the error, in so far as it might afford room to hope that there was some humbling of his mind; yet I avow that—if it were merely on the ground of this text, that he even gave up his opposition to the declaration of the Word of Life to those that are without, I should think very little of it. In all opposition to the freest exertions—either private or public—either by speaking or by writing—for circulating scriptural truth and exposing antichristian lies, there is embodied a mass of high-minded and false views of the gospel, and of the nature of the christian profession, and of the times of the Gentiles: and while those false views continue, it matters little how a man may interpret a particular text, or whether he opposes such exertions or not.

CXXXIX.

TO J. L——.

June 13, 1829.

At length, my very dear L——, I take up my pen to you, but I regret that it is upon a *debateable* question, instead of those blessed certainties which admit no debate between us, and which generally form the topic of our letters. I have reconsidered the case of Christian insolvents very seriously; and *that* you will understand as including a looking to the Father of lights and of mercies to be kept from the evil workings of my own will and wisdom. The result is a confirmation of my mind on the side on which I last wrote, and a comfortable expectation that you also will be led to the same.

When I wrote first on the question, I believe I allowed a kind of *feeling*, or *moral taste*, to run away with my judgment. I met the question too confident in the truth of *its* suggestions, and with too little jealousy of the *white* devil in my heart. This disposed me to bind on my brethren heavy burdens, which I now believe neither the Word of God nor right reason would sustain me in imposing. But before I proceed to meet the argument in your letter of June 1st, let it be well observed, that the only point at issue between us is, "whether there be *any* cases in which a Christian who has been insolvent can consider himself *conscientiously* released from his debts without having paid them in full?" If it can be shewn that there are or may be such cases, this must restrain us from laying down any universal rule on the contrary side, how many cases soever there may be, in which the debtor *ought* to feel that the obligation on his conscience continues; as I believe he ought, in nine cases out of ten of the bankruptcies that occur, and perhaps in every one of the four cases you have been dealing with. But having premised so much, let me now put the case of a man who has carried on business for years fairly, diligently, and successfully, but at length becomes insolvent through a casualty, or series of casualties, over which he has no control: for instance, through the unexpected breaking of banks, and several of his own debtors connected with those banks. He lays his affairs before his creditors, and every thing in them is found on examination straight and honourable. He gives them up all his remaining property, which affords a composition of 10*s*. in the pound, which they readily concur in accepting, and give him a legal discharge, leaving not the slightest stain upon his reputation. Now, I say that he has no longer any cause conscientiously to feel himself *in debt;* and therefore lies under no conscientious obligation to pay his former creditors the other 10*s*., even if in the course of his future life he should become able. Mark, I do not question the high *generosity* of such a step; but it is by that name I would now designate it, and not (as I did at first) by the name of true *honesty*. And is there not one consideration which at once renders the justice of this view probable?

Men's moral feelings are commonly quite alive to the conduct of *others* when *their own* interest is affected by it. But is there one of those former creditors who continues to look upon him as *still in their debt?* or who regards him as less an honest and an honourable man for resuming business for *himself*, and not as their agent or servant? or who wonders and complains, when he thrives in business, that he does not set about paying the other 10*s*.? No: however high in respectability his character stands, they will rather *wonder* if he does; and they will not term it an act of *honesty*, but an act of generosity.

Now does not this shew, that in the fairest mercantile transactions, there is always a *conventional understanding* between the parties, according to which A., giving credit to B., expects indeed that B. will pay him *in full*, if no unforeseen contingency disable him, but does not expect payment *in full*, if he should fairly become insolvent? This understanding is mutual between the parties. Each gives credit to others, and obtains credit himself, according to this tacit convention: and perhaps trade could not be carried on upon any other principle. (But however that be, it is in their *understood meaning* that all contracts are morally binding, and in no other.) And is it not a fair and equitable principle—as fair and equitable as that upon which the business of insurance proceeds? In each, it leaves men to regulate their charges according to the *risk* which they conceive they run. In each it subjects them to an *occasional* heavy loss, but more than compensates them by an accumulation of small but regular gains. Is it not fair and equitable in another view? I will suppose A. and B. *both* Christians. B. fails from such casualties as I have described above; compounds with, and is released by, his creditors; but the next day, in conversation with A., talks as conceiving himself still in A.'s *debt*, and bound to pay him the other 10*s*. when he can. Now, what ought to be A.'s reply? I think this: "No, my brother, your failure arose from a visitation of Providence, to which we are all subject, and which ought to be considered a visitation on your creditors as well as on yourself. It is not fit, therefore, that you should be the only sufferer from it. We all know well, that *if* your bankers and so many of your debtors should fail, you also must fail, and we as well as you must suffer. Yet, notwithstanding this *known risk*, we thought—and hitherto found—it our interest to maintain mercantile dealings with you. Events which we neither of us expected, but both knew to be *possible*, have occasioned that failure, and each is called to bear submissively the loss that falls to his share. But I cannot think of throwing my proper share of it upon you; nor *ought* you to consider the whole as belonging to you." Ought not A.'s language to be something of this kind?

Now, if I have succeeded in conveying my meaning upon that understood, though tacit *convention*, on which all trade *is*, and *must*, and *ought*, to be carried on, I think you will be at no loss to answer your own argument. "There is a difference, &c. The underwriter agrees to make up the loss that may be sustained, and fulfils his engagement: but the debtor *violates* his engagement—he gets 100*l.* worth of goods, and returns his creditor perhaps only the fourth part of the stipulated sum." This is really the fallacious argument called a *petitio principii*, or *begging the question*. You assume that he has engaged to pay the whole 100*l.* in case of insolvency, which I say he has not engaged to do. To save repetition, I suppose your debtor such a *fair* insolvent as I have described, and designated by B., and let A. be the merchant from whom he has got 100*l.* worth of tobacco at twelve months' credit, six months before his unexpected insolvency. Let his composition with his creditors be only 5*s.* in the pound. And now I say he *violates no engagement* in paying A. only 25*l.* instead of the full stipulated amount 100*l.*; and if so, the whole of your argument falls to the ground. Probably you will admit at once that he cannot be said to *violate any engagement* merely in not doing what, from unforeseen casualties, he cannot do,—not making a larger composition with his creditors. But, several years afterwards, becoming able to pay them the other 15*s.* with interest, perhaps you think that he then violates a *conscientious engagement*, if he does not do so. But neither can this be, unless there has been *an engagement to do so, either expressed or* MUTUALLY UNDERSTOOD.

May I not now appeal to you that there *has been no such thing*: and that the conception of any such engagement, is utterly contrary to the well-known principles on which all trade is carried on. But to put this, if possible, in a still clearer light: let us go back to the commencement of B.'s transaction with A.; and I shall suppose A. to be so cautious and so whimsical, that he will have various conditions *expressed* in their agreement which are generally *understood*, and tries to introduce others that are never either expressed or understood. B., knowing his oddity, humours him as far as he can, and the following dialogue takes place between them:—

A. "Well, friend B., you shall have the 100*l.* worth of tobacco on the usual credit that I give, twelve months. Do you *engage* to pay the 100*l.* punctually at the end of twelve months from the day of delivery?"

B. "Of course, or you may now draw on me at twelve months for the amount, and I will accept your bill, or I will give you cash now if you allow me 5*l.* for prompt payment. But I believe it is well known that I fulfil all my pecuniary engagements punctually?"

A. "I know it; and I have no immediate occasion for the money. But am I to understand that you engage *positively*, and without any mental reservation, to fulfil this contract—happen what will?"

B. "Really, you must excuse me. To make any such presumptuous engagement would be utterly inconsistent with my views of the uncertainty of life, and of every thing in life. I might die, and responsibility would be transferred to others. I might become insolvent, and——"

A. "Oh! you are afraid of that. Your affairs, I suppose, are in a ticklish state?"

B. "No. sir, my affairs are not in a ticklish state; nor have I any reason to fear that I shall become insolvent. And here I should take my leave, but that, knowing your oddity, I bear with you. You may, therefore, look at my books; and you will see, that when I balanced them a month ago, my credits exceeded my debts by many thousands."

A. "Sir, I meant no offence, and believe your word without looking at your books. I perceive that it would be unreasonable to ask you to engage *absolutely* to do, what you might *possibly* become unable to do, though it is highly improbable. But allow me to ask, will you *engage*, that in case of your becoming insolvent before paying me for the tobacco, and in case of your ever becoming wealthy after the settlement of your affairs, you will *then* pay me in full?"

B. "I will make no such engagement. I know not any reason for binding myself to that with you, which should not equally lead me to make the same engagement to all from whom I get goods. It would amount to an engagement, that in case of insolvency, from circumstances the most unavoidable and unforeseen, and after a settlement with my creditors and discharge from them, I should then *make myself over to them*, as their slave, for the remainder of my life, to labour for their benefit and not for my own. I should really decline trade altogether, if it were to be carried on upon such a principle. Let me ask, do you look for any such engagement from others with whom you deal? or do you *understand* them as *implicitly* making it, when they obtain credit from you? or do you consider yourself as making it when you obtain credit from them?"

A. "No, indeed, I cannot say I do."

B. "But *you favour me specially*. Good morning."

A. "Nay, stop, friend B., you shall have the tobacco without any such unreasonable pledge. It is but fair that I should be subject to lose by unavoidable contingencies, as well as you."

Now, I have made Mr. A. say things very absurd. But why are they absurd, except because they outrage the stated and well-understood principles of all mercantile transactions. Nor do I really see what can be fairly urged for holding such an insolvent as B. (after the settlement of his affairs) still conscientiously bound* to pay his former creditors in full. There is a *painful feeling*, indeed, which may very strongly prompt him to it. "I have been the occasion, though the innocent occasion, of loss to them." And it is an honourable feeling; yet even *it* may need to be *regulated* by the judgment. There might be just the same feeling in the case of loss sustained by the underwriters on a policy of insurance; yet should I not be rather quixotic, if this led me to reimburse them, at least if they were better able to sustain the loss than I. But I repeat it, that for one case of insolvency, such as I supposed B.'s, I am persuaded there are nine of quite a different character; in which the insolvent is not the *innocent occasion*, but the *culpable author* of loss to his creditors; and in which, therefore, conscience

* I think it may be shewn, that it would go to bar the *rightful* claims of his *future* creditors, by giving the former what is called (I believe) a *lien* on every thing he might acquire through life, as not his *own property* but theirs, till they were paid in full. But enough has been already said for exposing the principle.

ought to suggest to him that he is *bound* to repair the *injury* as far as he can. In general, I should think—(but must speak very hesitatingly on a subject with which I am so unacquainted) that the insolvent, to have his *conscience* justly released, must be able to shew, that in the fair prosecution of his business he has sustained unavoidable *losses* sufficient to account for his failure; and that, if this cannot be shewn, there is at least a strong presumption that he has failed from mismanagement, neglect, extravagance, or something worse. Can B——, for instance, assign the bankruptcy of any of his debtors to account for his? And if not, how can he account for his *insolvency*, when he now carries on the same trade of shoemaking —on reduced means—so effectively, as not only to support his family, but to lay by money?

I quite agree with you, that the fear of *encroaching on the property of others* is a most salutary one, which can scarcely be too much encouraged: and when a man, like you, trades upon borrowed capital, it cannot be doubted that *it is* the property of others he is managing. But, indeed, I could not wish you to be more impressed with this, than I have every reason to believe you are. As to C———, the gross falsehood and hypocrisy of his assertions are obvious, and of course cannot be passed over.

CXL.

TO THE SAME.

My very dear Brother,—Before I proceed to reply to any of your questions, I must notice what I think more important—a passage in your letter to B. C., which makes me think ye have acted wrong. B—— has been able to collect about 15*l.* of debts due to him, and has applied the money to his own use. Now, I wish you all to think—did that money belong to him of right, or to his creditors? Surely, to the latter: and what right had he to employ a shilling of it for his own occasions? he used it for buying leather, that he might earn more money. Very well—if his creditors agree, all of them, that he should do so: but without this, I conceive he could not justly keep a penny of it, any more than if it were money of another's, passing through his hands *in transitu*. And did not the body with you wink at this departure from moral integrity, (I must call it so, according to my present views, however common it be) in order to save their own pockets? It does appear to me that it is incumbent on the church to advance cheerfully, from time to time, whatever is necessary for enabling him to get materials for his trade, while he goes on diligently and economically.

And have you not here a definite object for your contribution, according to your several abilities? You see this leads me to one of your knotty questions. I have no idea of a pecuniary weekly contribution, either for the sake of form, or to make a fund against future casualties. But if there were in any part of Scotland a church, consisting of ever so few individuals, all of them in easy circumstances, I do not see why they should not still *remember the poor*, Gal. ii. 10. "The poor always ye have with you"—if not of the household of faith, yet of this world. But as long as our brother B., for instance, remains unable to render justice to his creditors, I should not think that any of the churches wanted an immediate definite object for their contribution—their weekly contribution. What—you will say perhaps—should we contribute to his creditors, many of whom may be richer than ourselves? No—I say it would be a contribution to him for his food and clothing, which he provides now by money that is not really his own, though the indulgence of his creditors may allow him to make this use of his earnings. If ye were able actually to support that man and his family, so that every penny that he expended, should come from the liberality of the churches, and every penny that he earned should be transferred to his creditors, I should think there was in this a definite object for your stated bounty importantly connected with the glory of God, and the profit of your body—more so, than if an individual were at one payment to clear off all his debts: because the other mode of extricating him would have a greater tendency to keep alive on his mind the true principle, that while he owes more than he can pay, he has no property of his own. Let me put it in this way—do you think that we could be justified in leaving our poor to be supported by the bounty of the world, so far as we had means for doing it? I dare say you all answer that with a decisive negative. Well—is not our brother B. supported at present by the bounty of his creditors? But supposing him completely extricated and independent, do you think there are not in the other churches several individuals, to whose necessities it would be most desirable to contribute? And if—what we have no reason to suppose—but if there were not—how many are there of the world, sick and in prison, to whom we should minister, as imitators of Him, who causeth the rain to descend on the just, and on the unjust? Talk no more of the want of *definite object* of contribution at any time. But should it be a stated weekly matter? You admit that it would be easier for most to contribute 20s. in forty or fifty payments, than all at once; and I think the evident truth of this may lead us to discern the wisdom of God in that direction to the churches, 1 Cor. xvi. 2. Is it not remarkable that the *first day* of the week is specified in that direction? But there, it may be said, the brethren are desired each to lay *by him* in store. Well, I should not strongly contest the matter, if that course were followed by any church, instead of each putting his contribution into the deacon's hands. Yet I think the apostolic direction in the passage would have been really observed, if the Corinthian brethren lodged their contributions with the deacons of the church, for the specific object which Paul called them to contribute to; while that object having been the supply of the poor saints at Jerusalem, through his ministration, I can easily understand why he distinguishes this collection from the ordinary and stated one, which I do think went on among the churches. Certainly, that passage which is rendered, "they continued steadfastly in the apostle's doctrine and fellowship"—should run—"in the apostle's doctrine, and in the *communication* or *contribution*:" (It is an adjective formed from the same word, which is rendered "ready to *contribute*.") and if I might hazard a conjecture—though as but a conjecture—I suspect, that what Paul learned from the Apostles at Jerusalem about the *remembrance of the poor*—was that stated weekly practice. It certainly was not the lesson of general bountifulness. But, as I said, if the members of any church preferred each to make himself his own store-keeper, I should not strongly contend against it; though I should wonder if they contended for this mode of depositing their weekly contribution, in case they saw that continual need which there is for the stated remembrance of the poor; and *there* is the point for which I am disposed to contend. I would deprecate contests about the particular mode and form of the thing. I would only recommend the simplest mode, and that least calculated to feed the hypocrisy and vanity of our hearts. I think such is that which we commonly practise, and at least suggested by the specific mention of the first day of the week in 1 Cor. xvi. 2. and by the mention of the *contribution* in connection with other stated observances of the church, one of which belongs exclusively to the assembly on the first day of the week. I trust we shall have no ultimate difference on the subject.

As to the other hard question in your last, it is very little indeed that I can say upon it. I have been myself often pressed with the same inquiry—and have only replied, that if ever I be placed in such circumstances, I trust I shall be enabled to see my way more clearly than I do at present; and I am sure it is important that brother C——, and all of us, should be ready to acknowledge our ignorance and inability to solve all difficult cases of casuistry which may be presented to us. If any man, professing the Christian faith, now baptize a Gentoo or Mahometan on his professing it, (I readily allow) he does a thing just like what was done of old in the days of the apostles—and a thing to which my arguments against the practice of the baptists, as employed in these countries, do not apply. This acknowledgment does not make me at all less undecided on the unscriptural nature of the practice, against which I have argued. I am quite certain that this has not either precept or precedent of the Scripture to support it. If I be further questioned why I do not express myself with equal decision, either for or against the other, I can only reply—because I have not the same clearness and decision of judgment, and do not like to speak much about the question, lest I should speak foolishly. I should therefore rather learn than teach; and I readily admit that this indecision of my mind betrays an ignorance, which needs to be removed and corrected; but which I do not think is to be removed by my allowing myself to be involved in a discussion on a case which, with me, is altogether hypothetical, and likely to remain so. You perceive that

any one who applies to me as an *oracle*, will find himself greatly mistaken. There remains yet another question in your letter of April 26, and I declare I am uncertain whether I have replied to it or not. But I believe not. You raise the question about the lawfulness of bearing arms for the defence of the country. I fancy we may save ourselves the trouble of canvassing that, for I believe no one would be allowed to bear arms for the purpose, without being attested or sworn before a magistrate. But here also there is a certain point to which we may go clearly; and if we be satisfied to stop there, we shall escape questions that are rather curious and puzzling than important.

CXLI.

TO THE SAME.

June 26, 1829.

My very dear James,—Mr. C. being called by business into Yorkshire, has commissioned me to pen some remarks on your letter of the 15th instant, addressed to the church here, and to assign our reasons for at *once* determining not to lay it before the body. In the first place, it was written under the supposition, that circumstances continued as described in our printed statement, whereas they have happily changed. You of course have heard before this, that we have been able to renew our connexion with the church in S——— Street, on the most satisfactory evidence of their repentance. (Observe, M——, and those with him, assemble in our old place of meeting in S——— Street.) Mr. C., calculating dates, thinks you must have had that information, when you took the step of separating from them. But I am persuaded there must be some mistake in this. You surely would not have taken the step under that knowledge. Their letter, of which a copy has been sent you, arrived the very day that our statement was printed off, so that on the following day we were able to acknowledge them again as a sister church; and though our separation from them was of such very short duration, yet I see the merciful hand of the Lord in allowing it to take place: and I doubt not he will make it productive of much good.

But now I will say that we had other cogent reasons for not laying your letter before the church. Any written communication from one church to another, ought not to contain debateable matter, and yours contained much, about the correctness of which I doubt. In the first place, you seem to make yourself a kind of party with Dr. Hamilton, and that without having heard both sides. (By the bye, of Dr. H. and his excommunication, a majority of the brethren

object having been the supply of the poor saints at Jerusalem, through his ministration, I can easily understand why he distinguishes this collection from the ordinary and stated one, which I do think went on among the churches. Certainly, that passage which is rendered, "they continued steadfastly in the apostle's doctrine and fellowship"—should run—"in the apostle's doctrine, and in the *communication* or *contribution*:" (It is an adjective formed from the same word, which is rendered "ready to *contribute*.") and if I might hazard a conjecture—though as but a conjecture—I suspect, that what Paul learned from the Apostles at Jerusalem about the *remembrance of the poor*—was that stated weekly practice. It certainly was not the lesson of general bountifulness. But, as I said, if the members of any church preferred each to make himself his own store-keeper, I should not strongly contend against it; though I should wonder if they contended for this mode of depositing their weekly contribution, in case they saw that continual need which there is for the stated remembrance of the poor; and *there* is the point for which I am disposed to contend. I would deprecate contests about the particular mode and form of the thing. I would only recommend the simplest mode, and that least calculated to feed the hypocrisy and vanity of our hearts. I think such is that which we commonly practise, and at least suggested by the specific mention of the first day of the week in 1 Cor. xvi. 2. and by the mention of the *contribution* in connection with other stated observances of the church, one of which belongs exclusively to the assembly on the first day of the week. I trust we shall have no ultimate difference on the subject.

As to the other hard question in your last, it is very little indeed that I can say upon it. I have been myself often pressed with the same inquiry—and have only replied, that if ever I be placed in such circumstances, I trust I shall be enabled to see my way more clearly than I do at present; and I am sure it is important that brother C——, and all of us, should be ready to acknowledge our ignorance and inability to solve all difficult cases of casuistry which may be presented to us. If any man, professing the Christian faith, now baptize a Gentoo or Mahometan on his professing it, (I readily allow) he does a thing just like what was done of old in the days of the apostles—and a thing to which my arguments against the practice of the baptists, as employed in these countries, do not apply. This acknowledgment does not make me at all less undecided on the unscriptural nature of the practice, against which I have argued. I am quite certain that this has not either precept or precedent of the Scripture to support it. If I be further questioned why I do not express myself with equal decision, either for or against the other, I can only reply—because I have not the same clearness and decision of judgment, and do not like to speak much about the question, lest I should speak foolishly. I should therefore rather learn than teach; and I readily admit that this indecision of my mind betrays an ignorance, which needs to be removed and corrected; but which I do not think is to be removed by my allowing myself to be involved in a discussion on a case which, with me, is altogether hypothetical, and likely to remain so. You perceive that

individual act, and of maintaining him in his seat among them! Is it not monstrous? I would not enlarge so much on this subject, but that I think it highly important that the false views should be corrected which Dr. H. evidently adopted, and which I think you have partly yielded to. I must add that I have never been acquainted with Dr. H., and that there are several passages in his narrative which I am wholly unable to understand. Do I say, that if he came to London, and desired to join us, he would not be received? I do not say so; but certainly not as a matter of course and of right, nor till he unequivocally professed repentance for his conduct in Dublin, gave up his disputing in the church, and also gave up the attempt of teaching things of which he knows so little as the millennium, as the locality of the new heaven and the new earth, where the glorified saints shall be for ever with the Lord. So full is he of curious inquiries into that and other subjects, that he plainly considers his views upon them as *terms* of Christian communion, (see his second paragraph); and I suppose his interpretation of the number of the beast, (whatever it may be) and of every thing else in the book of revelations, he would think himself equally entitled to make a subject of teaching in the church, and to force upon his brethren. O! what delightful discussions we should have then in every meeting. Of his sobriety of judgment in interpreting the scriptures, we have a very curious specimen, in his application of 1 John ii. 19., in p. 6.—Really, one might almost suspect he was making game.

You seem, in one passage, to return to an idea which you formerly threw out, "that *every thing* coming before a Christian church must be treated as a *matter of fact*, and be introduced at the mouth of two or three witnesses, for the information, and solemn and silent consideration and decision, of the body."

I rather suspect that you have in view the account given in Acts xv., and particularly the 12th verse; and it is indeed importantly instructive. But consider, dear J——, that, in this case, the *Apostles* and Elders were the persons consulted on the question, and who came to consider and decree, though the multitude of brethren were present. These, of course, kept silence, awaiting the decision of those, whose decision was to be binding on them. But when that decision was pronounced, was it delivered at all, as the two or three witnesses in Mat. xviii. testify the fact, "this man has trespassed against his brother so and so; we have laboured to call him to a sense of his sin, but he will not hear us?" Surely, no. The Apostles and elders declared what seemed good to the Holy Spirit, and to them: to them who had *authority* to declare the will of the king of Zion to his people, and whom his people are bound to hear with *implicit* subjection. But I trust we shall reject with abhorrence the attempt of any man or men to arrogate to themselves such authority now. Every matter of fact, indeed, cognizable by men, and involved in a case of discipline coming before a Christian church, must be brought before them, established at the mouth of two or three witnesses, and so established, that no question is to be admitted, whether the facts be or be not. But that is a very different thing from the authoritative decision by a few, of the question, what the revealed will of the Lord is, and that decision to be submitted to in silence by all the rest. If we were all fully informed on that which is so fully revealed, and if all our minds were in due subjection to it, undoubtedly questions about it would not arise. But it is not so: and though any such question arising certainly indicates the existence of an evil, we must yet beware of preventing its appearance by any usurpation on our part.

My meaning, perhaps, will be put more clearly by considering the case when all the churches in Ireland were deaf to the divine prohibition against oaths, till one, brought to repentance, called the rest of the brethren in Dublin to repentance on the subject. He certainly ought not, and I think did not, introduce the question, as what you call "a matter of free debate." He laid the subject before them as a matter decreed by the word of the Lord, and in the clear view that those who receive that decision could not continue to walk with those who should continue disobedient. But would it not have been most unsuitable if he, and the few who first concurred with him, had proceeded in the way of testimony as to a matter of fact, and claimed their testimony to be received by the rest in silent acquiescence? As we had been ourselves very slow to learn, and fruitful in inventing all fallacious arguments to set aside the divine command, I think we were bound to hear patiently, and answer distinctly, what others offered against it. But after its plain meaning had been sufficiently established, and the various attempts to evade it exposed, for which a very few conferences on the subject might have been sufficient, I am sure that any further protraction of the controversy was evil, and I am convinced that I allowed it to be protracted too long. I think it likely that I ought to have separated from the opposers in three weeks after the introduction of the subject.

In the next paragraph of your letter, you mention *artificial* speeches made "under the name of short and simple addresses." I am not sure to what you allude; nor do I think we have any such thing among us. But though nothing is more abominable than *artificial* speeches in the church, I should be afraid of saying any thing that could lead the brethren to refrain from the simplest address, however short. I think there are some among us of very weak utterance, who, if they would be content to speak a few words simply, might speak to the edification of the body. The simplicity that I mean is opposed to every thing artificial. I have in view some of our brethren, whose own souls are, I believe, exercised and fed and comforted with opening views of this or that passage of scripture during our meetings: and if such would then (*speaking because they believe*) just direct the attention of the body to the passage that is made food and life to themselves, without attempting to enlarge beyond the few words that they can utter without confusion, I then think it would be very desirable; and it is what I have often urged upon them. Indeed, I often hate myself for the multitude of words that I use. But do you know, my brother, that I have been somewhat startled by your quoting such a passage as Mat. x. 20. as "*fully applicable*" to any of us who now speak on the things of God. There seems to me in that some want of sobriety of language, and *perhaps* of sobriety of mind. Yet I find it hard to express my objection, without seeming to disclaim that gracious influence and aid of the spirit of truth in speaking, without which I would earnestly desire to be restrained from speaking at all. But in scripture, does not the phrase of "the spirit speaking in or by a man" generally, if not always, import one of those *extraordinary or miraculous gifts*, which we have no reason to think were continued after the apostolic age? And, observe, it was to the *twelve apostles*, when first sent out, that the words which you quote were addressed. So the Holy Spirit is said to have spoken by the prophets of old, by Balaam, by Caiaphas; and when the Holy Spirit fell on the assembled disciples, they spake with other tongues, as the Spirit gave them utterance. Probably, I need not add a word more, in order to suggest the need of some caution in applying the same phraseology to any speaker at this day. But it may be more profitable to remark, that I would infinitely rather speak of the things of God, under that divine influence of the spirit of truth which continues, and shall continue, with disciples to the end, than under that extraordinary or miraculous impulse which has ceased. "No man *can call Jesus Lord but by the Holy Spirit*." To speak under that work of the spirit, opening to the mind the glory of the truth contained in the confession that *Jesus is the Lord*, and turning the eye from every thing that the flesh would glory in,—that is more blessed speaking, than to speak with the tongues of men and of angels. We may *covet earnestly* that gift: and be sure that, when we have spoken most under that blessed influence, we have experienced little of it in comparison of what the glory of the truth and the power of the spirit of truth may afford; as well as that, so far as we have in any degree spoken so at all, we have spoken *not from* OURSELVES.

I must only add, in one word—that the question about elders never was raised in the church in Dublin. The report arose from one or two having intimated a *doubt* on the subject in private conversation. I believe those who talked as if a man must not eat with his wife, &c., were the opposers of the precept, who urged this as a consequence which they supposed must follow from it. On the subject of our warrant to put forward the truth in any way in opposition to the lies of Antichrist, we are (blessed be God!) of one mind here: and I have no reason to think that they are not so in S—— Street. But we have directed their attention to it. I know you will forgive any freedom of animadversion I have employed on your letter.

CXLII.

TO THE SAME.

Oct. 26, 1829.

A Mr. ——, a quondam clergyman, who, I hear, made a very fair profession, turned *Deist* while I was in Dublin; and so has, I under-

object having been the supply of the poor saints at Jerusalem, through his ministration, I can easily understand why he distinguishes this collection from the ordinary and stated one, which I do think went on among the churches. Certainly, that passage which is rendered, "they continued steadfastly in the apostle's doctrine and fellowship"—should run—"in the apostle's doctrine, and in the *communication* or *contribution*:" (It is an adjective formed from the same word, which is rendered "ready to *contribute*.") and if I might hazard a conjecture—though as but a conjecture--I suspect, that what Paul learned from the Apostles at Jerusalem about the *remembrance of the poor*—was that stated weekly practice. It certainly was not the lesson of general bountifulness. But, as I said, if the members of any church preferred each to make himself his own store-keeper, I should not strongly contend against it; though I should wonder if they contended for this mode of depositing their weekly contribution, in case they saw that continual need which there is for the stated remembrance of the poor; and *there* is the point for which I am disposed to contend. I would deprecate contests about the particular mode and form of the thing. I would only recommend the simplest mode, and that least calculated to feed the hypocrisy and vanity of our hearts. I think such is that which we commonly practise, and at least suggested by the specific mention of the first day of the week in 1 Cor. xvi. 2. and by the mention of the *contribution* in connection with other stated observances of the church, one of which belongs exclusively to the assembly on the first day of the week. I trust we shall have no ultimate difference on the subject.

As to the other hard question in your last, it is very little indeed that I can say upon it. I have been myself often pressed with the same inquiry—and have only replied, that if ever I be placed in such circumstances, I trust I shall be enabled to see my way more clearly than I do at present; and I am sure it is important that brother C——, and all of us, should be ready to acknowledge our ignorance and inability to solve all difficult cases of casuistry which may be presented to us. If any man, professing the Christian faith, now baptize a Gentoo or Mahometan on his professing it, (I readily allow) he does a thing just like what was done of old in the days of the apostles—and a thing to which my arguments against the practice of the baptists, as employed in these countries, do not apply. This acknowledgment does not make me at all less undecided on the unscriptural nature of the practice, against which I have argued. I am quite certain that this has not either precept or precedent of the Scripture to support it. If I be further questioned why I do not express myself with equal decision, either for or against the other, I can only reply—because I have not the same clearness and decision of judgment, and do not like to speak much about the question, lest I should speak foolishly. I should therefore rather learn than teach; and I readily admit that this indecision of my mind betrays an ignorance, which needs to be removed and corrected; but which I do not think is to be removed by my allowing myself to be involved in a discussion on a case which, with me, is altogether hypothetical, and likely to remain so. You perceive that

that God has sent such a child into the world (dying in its infancy) only "to receive that which *should make it meet for the inheritance of the saints!*" and who urges the necessity of its baptism, lest it should "*go out of this world without any visible way of blessing from God*"—is manifestly ignorant of the first principles of the kingdom of God. He has (as I observe well expressed in the preceding page) *set up his calf and dances about it.* I almost blame myself for having written a line to you upon this subject, when I see another of such prominent importance calling my attention. In sending us Mr. B——'s epistle to you, it is very plain you sent it as something you considered very good and Christian-like, as the production of a man who, as you express it, "possesses much clearer views of eternal realities" than others. Now, I request you will for the present lay down this sheet till you open his letter, and again attentively read the passage in the first page of it which I have marked in the margin. He continues the subject in the same style through the next page: but what occurs in the first page is sufficient—read it, I say, again attentively, before you return to my letter. Now, I beseech you to answer me candidly, and as before the searcher of hearts, what you think of that passage? What you think of the state and character of the man whose sentiments it expresses, and this, whichever be the case, whether he be rejoicing in that kind of assurance of hope which he describes, or mourning for the want and seeking to attain it? If his sentiments on the subject accord with your present views, I request a candid answer to one other question—were those, or anything like them, your sentiments when you joined our fellowship? If so, I must avow that we mistook your meaning, and that you have quite mistaken ours. Such a mutual mistake very frequently happens, but whenever it is discovered, the sooner the outward connexion which was formed upon it is dissolved, the better. Perhaps you may see the point of my inquiry more clearly when I propose it in this form:—Do you conceive that a man can be sound in the faith of Christ, who is seeking to obtain hope towards God in any way, or to have his hope confirmed by being assured that he produces the genuine fruits of faith? and do you think it any part of the work of the Spirit to testify to a man's mind that he does produce them? Do not be restrained by any disinclination to change your religious connexion, from answering these questions explicitly and honestly. If you, indeed, think with Mr. B——, you will be at no loss to find a religious connexion, not only more suitable, but more pleasant to you; and no doubt he will help you in it. If I could, I would have proposed these inquiries to you, without any intimation of my own sentiments, but it was impossible. If you reject his sentiments, and reject them with *abhorrence*, as all (I will not say disciples, but all) *agreeing with me in opinion* must reject them, there may then be room for my entering a little more on the subject. But, indeed, I think I have done so in some part of my Sufficient Reply, a copy of which I send you, lest you should not have one. But if you have, I shall thank you to bring mine with you when you come to town, as I doubt whether I possess another. I need scarcely assure you, dear Miss J——, that I shall rejoice to be always able to subscribe myself,

Your affectionate brother,

CXLIV.

TO THE SAME.

Oct. 31, 1829.

My very dear Sister,—My daughter and I returned about a week ago from an excursion of nearly seven weeks to Dublin and to Buxton. It was not till our return that I received your letter of last August; and I can't tell you with what joy I read it, and the more lively joy, because the first word which caught my eye, "*Sir,*" excited in me fear that all was wrong. But when I found you so decisively rejecting the poison in Mr. B——'s letter, "abhorring that which is evil, and cleaving to that which is good," it did indeed excite in me thankfulness and praise to the God of all grace, "who keepeth the feet of his saints and delivereth them from the snare of the fowler." It has endeared you to me more than ever as a sister and beloved for the truth's sake. Your blessed escape from the snare that was so insidiously laid for you, is (you see) not the fruit of our own wisdom or watchfulness, for you were ready to fall into it; but I trust it will prove the occasion of making you more jealous of that which the scriptures so emphatically and justly term "the deceivableness of unrighteousness:" never is that deceivableness greater and more dangerous than when it appears in a doctrine often approaching most nearly to the truth, but involved with sentiments utterly subversive of it. Such, assuredly, is Mr. B——'s notion, that it is the office of the Spirit of God to witness to his conscience that his works are the genuine fruits of faith, and so to give him assured hope and confidence towards God: nor can I conceive a more awful instance of human vanity and satanic delusion, than is exhibited in a man coming to the comfortable conclusion that he is a genuine believer, and shall be assuredly saved, from observing (as he imagines by the aid of the Spirit of God) the abundance and genuineness of the fruits which he produces. The Lord taketh pleasure in those that *hope* in *his mercy*, Ps. cxlvii. 11.—in that mercy which is revealed from heaven in the gospel, as reigning through righteousness by Jesus Christ unto eternal life. How different is such a hope from Mr. B——'s! The thief expiring upon the cross (according to Mr. B——) must either have died without any assured hope towards God, or must have got some hope by reflecting on the fruits of his faith! And yet Mr. B—— will talk grandly and speciously of the joyfulness of the gospel to a sinner, whom it finds ungodly and without strength; but it is only talk: for while he maintains that the assurance of faith is separable from the assurance of hope—(and truly he has a goodly company to keep him in countenance in this)—or in other words, that an ungodly sinner may be assuredly persuaded of the truth of the gospel report, and yet be destitute of any assured hope towards God, the hope that he proposes

any one who applies to me as an *oracle*, will find himself greatly mistaken. There remains yet another question in your letter of April 26, and I declare I am uncertain whether I have replied to it or not. But I believe not. You raise the question about the lawfulness of bearing arms for the defence of the country. I fancy we may save ourselves the trouble of canvassing that, for I believe no one would be allowed to bear arms for the purpose, without being attested or sworn before a magistrate. But here also there is a certain point to which we may go clearly; and if we be satisfied to stop there, we shall escape questions that are rather curious and puzzling than important.

CXLI.

TO THE SAME.

June 26, 1829.

My very dear James,—Mr. C. being called by business into Yorkshire, has commissioned me to pen some remarks on your letter of the 15th instant, addressed to the church here, and to assign our reasons for at *once* determining not to lay it before the body. In the first place, it was written under the supposition, that circumstances continued as described in our printed statement, whereas they have happily changed. You of course have heard before this, that we have been able to renew our connexion with the church in S——— Street, on the most satisfactory evidence of their repentance. (Observe, M——, and those with him, assemble in our old place of meeting in S——— Street.) Mr. C., calculating dates, thinks you must have had that information, when you took the step of separating from them. But I am persuaded there must be some mistake in this. You surely would not have taken the step under that knowledge. Their letter, of which a copy has been sent you, arrived the very day that our statement was printed off, so that on the following day we were able to acknowledge them again as a sister church; and though our separation from them was of such very short duration, yet I see the merciful hand of the Lord in allowing it to take place: and I doubt not he will make it productive of much good.

But now I will say that we had other cogent reasons for not laying your letter before the church. Any written communication from one church to another, ought not to contain debateable matter, and yours contained much, about the correctness of which I doubt. In the first place, you seem to make yourself a kind of party with Dr. Hamilton, and that without having heard both sides. (By the bye, of Dr. H. and his excommunication, a majority of the brethren

16—20. and you may see that they describe the appearance of the Messiah in these circumstances of lowliness and weakness—(" a worm, and no man")—which were opposed to all the grandeur and noise of earthly kings, as if he were unequal to effect even the smallest object, as the *breaking of a reed already bruised, or the quenching of smoking wick*—(so should the word be rendered). Compare Ps. xxxviii. 13, 14. with Is. xlii. 19, 20. That He, so poor, so weak, so despised, without form or comeliness, was set forth by Jehovah as the mighty Saviour, his anointed servant ordained to bring forth judgment to the Gentiles. From an examination of the context, and the Evangelist's application of the passage, I am satisfied that such is the real meaning of the words " a bruised reed," &c. But one of the many evidences that the teachers of the religious world have not the fear of God is, their utter want of reverence for his Word. What the real meaning of any text is, *i. e.* what is the meaning of the Spirit there, they commonly care not a rush, so they can but ingeniously find out a sense in which it may be applied or accommodated in what they call a spiritual and savoury way to some insidious doctrine. Dear H. G——, whose case I related in Vol. i. 473, of the Sufficient Reply, did not find that there was any harshness or cruelty in addressing her as an unbeliever, when she came to me lamenting that she was so. But then I had to lay before her that which is adapted and sufficient to convey at once the fulness of joy, and peace, and hope, to one that it finds in the depth of infidelity and darkness: while Mr. B—— knows not any gospel of that character, however speciously he may at times talk of its joyfulness. " It is presumption," says he, " and not the assurance of hope, if the believer's certainty of his own safety *arises from any other source* than the witnessing of the Holy Ghost to his spirit by the unerring rule of the Word, *that his fruits or works are the fruits of faith.*" Now, observe the cruelty as well as wickedness of this doctrine. It would go to shut out the believer from ever having the assured hope towards God, or rejoicing in God, and to incapacitate him from bearing any of the fruits of righteousness. " The joy of the Lord is the strength of his people ;" the hope of salvation is the helmet with which the youngest soldier of the cross goes out to fight the good fight of faith. 1 Thess. v. 8. All—including him who but the last moment passed from death unto life, believing the record of God concerning his Son—all are saints of God, and, because they are so, have the spirit of adoption that cries Abba, Father—the spirit by which they know the things that are freely given to them of God. Gal. iv. 6. 1 Cor. ii. 12. So is it according to the apostolic gospel, and effectually does that gospel work in all them that believe it. But not so is it according to Mr. B——'s gospel : his believer, however assured in faith, must not think of rejoicing in God as his God and Father, and rejoicing in the hope of glory, till, in a course of obedience and fruitfulness, he has got a supposed revelation made to him that he may now venture to conclude that his faith is genuine, and that he may therefore, without *presumption*, conclude that he is a child of God, and stands fair for heaven. Cruel doctrine, indeed! that sends his disciples indeed to make bricks without straw, to walk as children of the light of the day, as children of God, under the uncertainty whether they are not children of darkness and of the devil. "They may weary themselves in the greatness of their way" in the effort, and they may at length be encouraged, under Mr. B——'s wicked consolation, to think that they have succeeded, that their evidences for heaven are clear enough. But vain is the attempt to produce grapes of thorns, or figs from thistles. It is hard to know where to stop on such a subject. I must therefore stop abruptly.

My wife and daughter join in hearty Christian salutation to you, with, &c.

CXLV.

TO MISS T——.

Nov. 25, 1829.

Among the other characters of the God of Israel—the only true God—which are celebrated in the cxxxvi. Psalm, and which his people are called to recollect with thanksgiving and praise, I am forced to think of that mentioned in the 4th verse. "To Him who alone doeth GREAT WONDERS." And is it not indeed *wonderful*, that you and I should be brought into Christian correspondence on our mutual faith and hope, and into that intimate and endearing connexion which unity in these produces? Yes, we may well confess—"this hath God wrought;" and may well join in the corresponding language at the close of the lxxii. Ps. 18, 19. While every instance of the Lord's reigning in the midst of his enemies, and subduing them to him by the sword of his Spirit, affords matter of unspeakable joy, I confess, my dear Miss T——, that in your case my joy is greatly heightened from the consideration of *our* dear, dear sister L—— and of her joy. She will easily believe that my wife and daughter share in it largely, as I doubt not the whole church will, when they are put in possession of the intelligence. But when I mention the whole church, and think of the materials of which for the most part it is composed, and think of a *high-minded* young lady like you being made desirous to take part with such a despised set in the fellowship of the despised gospel, I am reminded of old Lear's remark (is it not King Lear's?) "that misery makes us acquainted with strange bedfellows." So, indeed, we may say, that the overbearing power of divine truth in the stoutest heart, brings us into strange company. Yet let us ever recollect, that there is only One of whom it can be said—in the most important sense—that he "*humbled* himself;" Him who, though the Lord of all, took upon him the form of a servant, and *descended* indeed that he might exalt the lowest. When we, through the knowledge of

Him, are most "clothed with humility," it is not that we descend from any rank of dignity which really belonged to us—(for all have sinned, and in that have become miserable, and poor, and blind, and naked)—but that we are *brought to our senses* out of the delirium of blind ungodliness and self-righteousness in which we had imagined ourselves very fine creatures. A patient in Bedlam who had conceived himself an emperor, if cured under the physician's care, would not descend from any *real* dignity, but only discover his proper character; and if he were then disposed to glory on this account over his companions that remained insane, might it not well rebuke the folly of such glorying to find, that, if he passed for a moment from under the physician's care, he was ready to relapse into his old dreams of imperatorial dignity. So is it with us. Let us but be left any hour to ourselves—to our own hearts—and we are ready to be as proud as Lucifer—proud of our fancied humility! So here am I prating to you on paper just as if we were old acquaintances. But while I have room left, I wish to offer you a few remarks suggested by some expressions in your letter. When you say, that through His righteousness we *shall* be justified, I doubt not that you will joyfully agree with me in desiring to alter the language to the *present* tense—" we *are* justified." I do not suspect you of having *meant* any thing else; indeed, other passages prove that you did not; but it is delightful and profitable to contemplate the language of the Holy Spirit concerning the *present* blessedness of all them that believe the testimony of God concerning his Son. "We *have* peace with God"—" we *have* redemption through his blood, even the forgiveness of sins"—" He *hath* made us accepted in the Beloved"—" He *is* made unto us of God, wisdom and righteousness"—"He *hath saved* us, and called us with an holy calling." So that the believer possesses all that righteousness and salvation which the votaries of Antichrist are seeking after and trying to get. Those are labouring to become what they are not as yet—righteous and holy, &c. We are called to walk as what we are—children of God, and "as children heirs—*heirs of God*, and joint heirs with Christ." We have received not the spirit of the world, but the Spirit which is of God, that we might know the things that are freely given to us of God—1 Cor. ii. 12; and corresponding with this is the language of the Apostle John—" these things have I written unto you, that believe on the name of the Son of God, that ye may know that ye HAVE *eternal life*." 1 John v. 13. Surely it is with reason that we are called to "offer the sacrifices of *praise* continually"—" to rejoice in the Lord always."

You say—" I am aware that constant watchfulness must *be exercised by me*, and probably to my last hour." I am sure you do not mean by this any kind of *condition that we have to fulfil*; and I dare say, intended no more than is contained in the Apostle's expression of giving earnest heed to the things which we have heard, lest at any time we should let them slip. Heb. ii. 1. That is blessed watchfulness indeed—being kept *awake* to the *glorious gospel*. In none can this watchfulness be found, but in the children of the light and of the day. Observe the striking language of the Apostle in

1 Thes. v. 4, 5, 6.;—" Ye are not in darkness. Ye are all the children of light and of the day. *Therefore*, let us not sleep as do others, but let us watch."

If a man lighted a thousand candles at midnight, it would still be night to him: nothing but the appearance of the *sun* can produce day; and so nothing but the shining of the light of the knowledge of the glory of God in the person of his Anointed, can make any sinner cease to be " of the night," and make him capable of watchfulness to that only true light. And it is thus that the Lord keepeth the feet of his saints, and holdeth their souls in that life which he has given them, even by keeping them awake to that glorious truth which they have believed—keeping them to the end by his own power through faith, so that he will not suffer them to depart from Him, as is the perpetual tendency of their own hearts. It is on this character of ourselves as a people, " bent to backsliding" from Him who has made us his people —Hos xi. 7.—ever prone to relapse into sleep by forgetting that truth in which the glory of the Lord is revealed; it is on this, our unchangeable character, that the repeated calls to watchfulness proceed: and we may bless the Captain of our salvation for sending us such animating and awakening calls as that, 1 Cor. xxi. 13, " Watch ye, stand fast in the faith, quit you like men, be strong"—" strong in the grace that is in Christ Jesus."

I must hasten to a close. It grieves me to hear that your health is not as we could wish; but I trust that even it will be benefited by the blessed repose of mind which the decision of your late inward struggle tends to produce. Mrs. W—— and M—— join me in kindest salutations to you and to our dear L———. Mercy and peace be multiplied to you both. Yours, dear Miss T——, with true attachment, and in (I doubt not) everlasting bonds.

CLXVI.

TO R. L. C———, ESQ.

Jan. 1, 1830.

The following are the leading considerations I would suggest on the subject of your note. The account we read of the first disciples at Jerusalem, that all who believed were together, seems naturally to have arisen from their intimate unity of faith, and from the brotherly love " wherewith they were taught of God to love one another." Those who are thus united in one mind and one heart (I may say) will naturally aim at being as much together as the circumstances of our present state will admit; and may look forward gladly to that future state of being, when the circumstances that now prevent their being all outwardly together shall end; when, being ever with the Lord, we shall be ever with each other. But that they cannot be so at present is obvious; however, it would seem that the same principles will lead them to be as much so *as they can;* and therefore that any light and needless multiplication of churches, and consequent outward separation of disciples, must originate in evil. This further appears, when we consider what the scriptures teach us of the Lord's wise and gracious designs in congregating his disciples into assemblies, consisting of many individuals of various characters and gifts, "differing according to the grace that is given them," but all needful to the well-being of the body, and designed for mutual service and edification. The illustration given from the variety of members in the one natural body is very striking, (Rom. xii. 4, 5, &c. 1 Cor. xii. 4, to end) and marks, I think, that the needless splitting of a church into distinct meetings would be to overlook or undervalue the revealed designs and appointment of the Lord. In that day of the Lord's power, when the Apostles penned their instructions to the churches, their language on this subject (as well as on others) was adapted to the state and circumstances in which they considered the churches as originally existing, without descending to the minute consideration of possible and occasional exceptions from those ordinary circumstances. It is adapted to the case of several disciples, male and female, associated and coming together into one place, rather than to the case of one brother meeting with one or two sisters. In these days, we have to mourn indeed over the comparative hiding of that divine power, which of old gathered and established the assemblies of the saints, but we have also to look for its renewed display in the progressive consumption of the man of sin, and have to avoid every thing that would be adverse to it. However, we must admit and maintain that, even in the Apostolic days, there existed *distinct churches* very near to each other, Cenchrœa, for instance, being much nearer to Corinth than —— to ——, and that some of them were comparatively very small, being spoken of as a church in the house of an individual. How small some of them might have been, even to the coming together of two or three disciples on the first day of the week, it does not become us to pronounce. But however short the distance was between two Christian meetings, or however small the number in any of them, we are not to admit any thing in such facts inconsistent with the principles before adverted to: we may be sure there was a need and just occasion for their meeting in distinct assemblies. All the remaining inquiry, therefore, resolves itself into the question, what constitutes such a need and just occasion for forming a distinct church? and indeed it is one of those questions which from their nature admit not such a precise answer as our vain wisdom might require; but, after a suggestion of the general principles bearing on the point, the matter must often ultimately be committed to the judgment and discretion of the disciple, while there are extreme cases in which the determination is plainly either favourable or unfavourable to the thing. I can easily conceive that the number of disciples at —— *unable* to meet in ——, might be so increased, as to mark the formation of a distinct church there as desirable; while I cannot pretend to define exactly the minimum of that increased number which would evidently justify it. On the other hand, you seemed to feel, when speaking together, that ——'s permanent inability to attend in —— would not justify me in withdrawing from that meeting, when I can attend it, to form a church in my own house, or in engaging others, who can and do attend in ——, to join me in such a plan. I doubt much whether this would be marked with any real difference in my instance, and in yours. In fact, I believe, that what recommended it at first to you was the consideration of your children, and your just attachment to Mrs C.; for if she and the children had been out of the question, you surely would not have thought of forming a church in your house, in order to afford —— the comfort of it on the first day of the week. Yet, in matters relating to the kingdom of God, I conceive that she and Mrs C. must be considered as standing on one level; and as to your children, the only one of them that has been joined in church fellowship does, and still may, meet with us in —— ; the rest have been but witnesses of our assembly, and would as yet be no more in your house. Now, however desirable it may be, that after a certain age they should have an opportunity of observing the meeting and practices of an assembled church, yet this is a very subordinate and comparatively unimportant part of the parental duty towards them; indeed, it can scarcely be considered as necessarily included in that "*instruction* and *admonition* of the Lord," in which they are to be *brought* up; and much less can it be considered as a legitimate substitute for the latter. Certainly, they are two distinct things, not to be confounded one with the other.

CXLVII.

TO D. L——, ESQ.

Jan. 23, 1830.

My dear L——,—You perceive that I see none of the inconsistency which you think attaches to such a style of address from me to you. It only expresses the affectionate interest which I really feel for you. I thank you for sending me Dr. Hoskins's pamphlet. I have read it with all the attention such a production required. I expected to find it weak and wordy, and from my knowledge of the side he has taken upon the subject, I knew I should find it wicked: but sorry indeed am I to find that he has gone so awfully far in emancipating himself (p. 9) from what he thinks weak scruples, but from what is the fear of God and reverence of his word,—that he occupies so boldly the seat of the scornful.

I observe but one sentence in his pamphlet that has any real bearing on the question at issue. I refer to that near the close of his paraphrase, on the chapter, p. 12.—"You shall not admit him *even* to that table, admission whereto is the *simple* recognition of profession, discipleship, fraternity, and fellowship." Such is Dr. H——'s interpretation of that part of the apostolic command—"with such an one no not to eat." Now, I must say plainly, that this is one of the most impudent forgeries on scripture that I have ever heard of, and as absurd as it is grossly impudent. Can he adduce any instance from scripture, or from any interpreter of scripture, either in Greek or in English, or in any other language, in which the simple expression of *eating with* a person is employed to denote *eating the Lord's Supper with him*? No; but he does not *scruple* to coin the meaning for his occasion; and this, though it goes to turn the apostle's language into profane nonsense. With such a man have no Christian fellowship, *not even* in the *highest and most solemn* ordinance of Christian fellowship, the supper of the Lord? Yes, Dr. H——, the highest and most solemn, though so *simple*. And all this profane nonsense and corruption of the word is maintained in despite of the context both preceding and following the command. For let Dr. H—— labour ever so hard to conceal it in a heap of words, the connexion of the 10th verse (marked by the word "for") is evidently this: I say, with *such* a person not even to eat, *for* as to fornicators, &c., of the world, I did not think of prohibiting your eating with *them*. Does not this put it beyond doubt (if there could otherwise have been any reasonable cause for doubt) what the eating is he intends to prohibit. In the 9th verse he permits that eating with the fornicator of the world, which he prohibits them maintaining with the same character found within the church. Did he permit them to eat the *Lord's Supper* with heathens? or did the Corinthian disciples ever fall into the mistake of supposing that he thought it necessary to prohibit this?

It is not to Dr. H. that I would suggest any such considerations. It is not argument, but the fear of God, that he wants: and all his scoffs and buffoonery of disputation (p. 19, 20, 30, &c.), I would meet simply with "the Lord rebuke him." More than enough has been said and written for others on so plain a matter. And what is the amount of all that ye urge against the divine command? Why, that there may be cases in which the literal act of eating in company with one removed from the body is unavoidable, from the relationships of life and the duties arising from them. A more sober inference from this would be, that the apostle did not contemplate such particular cases in the passage, nor think it needful to discuss them;—that such unavoidable companionship in eating is not the convivial intercourse which he intended to prohibit, but that which is needlessly sought for enjoyment in the person's society. In truth, the majesty of the divine word, in giving its precepts, does not descend to meet or provide against the cavils and objections of men, who oppose it.

Suffer me to put it to your conscience, whether you would think it consistent with the precepts in Rom. xvi. 17. to cultivate needless intimacy, even in social life, with the character there described?

Yet it might just as reasonably be objected, that a Christian wife cannot *avoid* her husband, nor a Christian child its parent, though of such a character.

But I have done. I do not cease to pray that He who alone can repair the breaches of Zion will make bare his arm for effecting that work in Ireland, by calling out his own children from the tents of ungodly men. Yet, in saying this, I must add an avowal that I consider it an eminent mercy to his church that he has caused the removal of some such persons as Dr. H.

CXLVIII.

TO MRS. B——.

July 26, 1830.

MY VERY DEAR MRS. B——,—The Lord's mercy has indeed been very great in restoring to us dear M—— B——, and a few others. Never, I think, has it been more strikingly exemplified how our eyes are holden and our hearts hardened against the *plainest* principles of the Word of God, than in the course of that rebellion in the Exchange; and as clearly is it manifest, that such a *ringleader* in the rebellion as our dear M—— could not be brought back by any thing but divine mercy and power. I long held him very dear; but he is indeed dearer than ever. And I trust the same mercy and power will yet be displayed in Mrs. M——. I have no doubt that she has *never yet read the passage* with that sobriety of serious attention, and that subjection to divine authority, which the word claims from every one that fears the Lord. And what work we do make, when, instead of hearkening to what the Lord saith, we give ear to the suggestions of our own wisdom, dictating what it is fit that he should say! With what *loathing* of themselves will any of them return, who are indeed brought to a right mind!

I saw your ———, in some respect, with great pain at the prospect of the trial that I think awaits you, though tempered by the blessed confidence that it will be all wisely and graciously ordered. I may be over-apprehensive: and assuredly the Lord who wounds can heal what appears the most deadly wound, and can avert the trial that appears most inevitable. But be prepared, my sister for giving him up. It will be comparatively easy, when you recollect that he appears to have been marked as one of Christ's sheep, and consider out of what a world he is to be taken. I dare say, many would blame me for thus frightening you by such plain talk; but we shall not be *frightened*, if our ear be but kept open to the voice that speaketh from the mercy seat, "Fear not!"

The vagaries you mention of the Hamiltonians and Burghites are, indeed, awful instances of the delusive power of Satan. I do not understand their notions any better than yourself: but I have seen and heard enough of them to make me sure that they are turned aside from the truth to fables. In several instances, they directly contradict the apostolic word: but in other points of a more doubtful character, connected with prophecies yet to be fulfilled, and specially connected with those in reserve for the Jewish people, I consider that they as decisively evidence the character of ungodly men, by their hardihood in making points of *doctrine*, matter of TEACHING, things of which they know so little—of which it is declared that so little is or can be known. "We know not yet what we shall be." And with all their rash and heady speculations, what do they know (more than you or I) about that *new earth* which shall succeed the present after it has been *burnt up?* or of the state of being when we shall be like the angels of God, without *marrying* or *giving in marriage?* Mr. Irving, indeed, one of the teachers of falsehood here, regardless of that PLAIN word (as they all appear to be) has published to the world, that his imagination riots in the thought of the intercourse of the sexes that shall take place in the new earth, and he has found many a silly woman laden with lusts to listen to his dreams. But the whole occupation of mind with these hidden matters, which those like H—— and B—— manifest, proves at once to the spiritually minded that they are not occupied with the glorious things that *are* revealed. Those who HAVE COME "to *Mount Zion*, to the city of the living God, the *heavenly Jerusalem*," &c. will not trouble themselves much with doubtful speculations concerning the earthly Canaan. But we may expect that evil men and seducers will wax worse and worse as the day of the Lord approaches; and their deceitful ways have such attractions for our flesh, that if the Lord himself did not keep them, his very elect would be deceived.

My love to all with you.

CXLIX.

TO MISS WALKER.

——, 1830.

You wish me, my dear child, to put on paper some of the remarks I offered upon your friend's letter. When you first showed it to me, I expressed myself little pleased with it; and now, upon a second and more attentive reading, I dislike it still more. I see nothing in the letter, or in the spirit which it manifests, that distinguishes the writer from the mass of pious and strict evangelical professors; very careful and troubled about many things, and in that very circumstance manifesting the want of perception of the glory of the one thing needful. Out of the abundance of the heart the mouth speaketh and the pen writeth. Is there a syllable in her letter, from beginning to end, upon the one glorious theme of heaven, and the only theme worthy to occupy the redeemed on earth? Perhaps, according to her views, that is a subject which may be laid aside where there is professed agreement on it. Yet professed agreement to the plainest statement of the truth is now carried so far by many, that the hollowness of their profession is chiefly discoverable from the circumstance, that their minds and their tongues are occupied about every thing else of a religious kind, rather than it. Her ready reception of every imputation against the disciples—down to that old reproach of sinning that grace may abound—is another very ungodly symptom. Her indiscriminate language about *the pleasures of the world* is most like the religion of the world—one of the highest pleasures of many. I suppose she is too "spiritually minded" (according to her views of spirituality) to take any pleasure in any of the same objects with the world. Probably she will call that a sneer at one adorning the doctrine of, &c. &c. I cannot help it: some of the imputations she retails against us are bad enough; but indeed I hope we shall be better employed than in defending *ourselves* against them. Her question about B—— is a very black one. Of course, before she would join the apostolic church at Corinth, she would have taken care to ascertain that the man who had been guilty of incest was not with them; indeed, she seems quite too good for a church of Christ. She hopes for a *pleasing account* of us, and our great improvement, from you: and what is the pleasing account she looks for? Not that we are standing fast in the faith, and in the liberty wherewith Christ has made us free, rejoicing in hope of God, and in nothing terrified by our adversaries, &c. but that we are not frequenters of balls and plays, and do not hold the possibility of being spiritually-minded in a ball-room. Of course, if Mr. V—— chose to give a ball in his house, and to require her attendance, she would lose all her spirituality and become carnally minded; or, more probably, she would be labouring to maintain some devout and religious frame of mind while the fiddles were playing; and little aware that in that very pious effort (on which her peace of conscience would hinge) she was really under the influence of that carnal mind, which (in its most religious form as well as most irreligious) is enmity to the only true God. I hope you will not gratify her with the account she looks for; for I fear it would be but gratifying her religious flesh. She gravely observes, that she could not join any church holding such principles as she imputes to us. I wish her distinctly to know, that we could not receive any professor of the mind of which she appears from her letter to be. I shall rejoice to find that she turns out such as you think her: whenever she does, I am sure that she will see I have not written too severely.

CL.

TO J. L———.

Oct. 1830.

* * * * STRIFE is placed in such a connexion in Galatians v. and elsewhere, that I conceive those who will persist in striving about words to no profit, and agitating questions that are not for godly edifying, should be put away from our fellowship, and avoided just as much as those who walk in any other of the acknowledged lusts of the flesh.

How rapidly, my brother, are the wheels of Providence revolving! "Behold, he cometh with clouds!" and we may almost hear the distant sound of his chariot-wheels. Is there not "upon the earth distress of nations with perplexity, men's hearts failing them for fear, and for looking for those things which are coming on the earth." How blessed that we are called at such a time to look up and lift up our heads, for our redemption draweth nigh. How blessed to hear the first-born among many brethren addressing the great congregation that he has received, in such language as that (Ps. lxii. 8.) "Trust in Him at *all* times: ye people, pour out your hearts before him: God is a *refuge* for us." Wonderful: a *refuge* for *sinners*, whose guilty consciences naturally would lead them to try and fly *from* him, but are now led to fly *to* him, and trust in him, and call upon him as their Father and their God! And all this blessedness brought to us "through the redemption that is in Christ Jesus"—who humbled himself and took upon him the form of a servant, and amidst all the sorrows of death that compassed him held fast his confidence in Jehovah, *trusted* in Him, and was delivered: and gives the privilege of being the sons of God to all that believe in his name: and "if children"—or rather—*since* children—" then heirs: *heirs of God*, and *joint heirs with Christ*." How briefly do those few words sum up the wonderful blessedness we are called to, and the wonderful way in which sinners are called to it! "Heirs of *God!*"—what an infinite inheritance! But how can a sinful creature have such a portion?—*joint heirs with Christ!* How slow of heart we are to know the things that are freely given to us of God. What a boundless field of discovery is there under the teaching of that Spirit, who alone searcheth all things—yea, the deep things of God! May you and I, and all his children, be led into it more and more!

CLI.

TO R. L. C———, ESQ.

After disposing of such cases, there are in others general principles which it is most important for a Christian to attend to. Whatever be the form in which he may have this world's goods laid by, he cannot be too suspicious of the workings of his own covetous heart: and if—for the purpose of either *keeping* or *adding to* his store—he shut up his bowels of compassion against the real wants of a necessitous brother, he is then absolutely in the snare of that covetousness which is idolatry. And this evil—though generally perhaps *secret*—may become so manifested by overt acts, as to call for the discipline of the house of God to purge it out.

But if I were to go beyond such general principles,—the application of which can be effectually produced in the disciple's mind only by the influence of the truth,—if I were to attempt (for instance) to lay down and enforce a law against a Christian's going into a *benefit society:* I should fear that I was presuming to be wiser than Christ, and to add to the laws of his kingdom. The following considerations, I think, justify me in saying so.

A man may have money *laid by* in various forms. It may be in Bank; it may be in Government debentures; it may be in the funds of a benefit society; it may be in the rent of a house; it may be in land. For let it be observed, that if I have inherited landed property of 1000*l*. per annum rental, all the value of that, which is beyond my wants for the present year, may be considered as so much stock in Bank, the interest of which is calculated to meet the wants of future years.

Dare any lay down a law, that a Christian must not *have* a landed estate? I think we should be opposed in the attempt by the explicit testimony of scripture. From the Scriptures of the New Testament we not only know that there were *rich* as well as poor in the Apostolic churches,—(the former of whom were exhorted indeed not to "*trust in uncertain riches*, but in the living God,—that they be rich in good works," &c. but no intimation given to them that they could not lawfully *be* rich)—but we know that in the first church at Jerusalem there were persons possessed of *lands and property*, the whole of which they might have kept without any censure from the Apostles (Acts v. 4.) The exercise of active love among them is indeed on record for our imitation, in those who sold this or that piece of ground or house, which they could spare, to supply the wants of their poor brethren: for this is what the original really imports, and not that each land-owner sold all his land, &c.

Well: if there was nothing necessarily inconsistent with Christian principle in their *having* lands, and *continuing* to have them, so as to be distinguished as rich brethren; neither could there be any *intrinsic* contrariety to Christian principle in their *obtaining* lands by purchase, &c.; still supposing that they did not, in order to effect such purpose, "withhold good from those to whom it is due."

Well: is not what I have said on landed property immediately applicable to money in the funds, or laid out in any way that we think prudent? The evil is not in having it, or in laying it out so as that we continue to possess a pecuniary interest in it. But it consists in regarding any such stock, as a *store not to be broken in upon*, even when the present real wants of a brother require it.

It seems to me that this view by no means trenches on the force of divine injunction in Mat. vi. 19—21, and that the apparently stricter interpretation which some have put forward—(as if it were forbidden to have any stock of worldly goods sufficient to meet future occasions, as well as present wants)—is untenable, contradicted by other parts of Scripture, and calculated to land in *hypocrisy* and various other evils.

You will see from what I have written, that—however needful Christian caution and jealousy of ourselves be in the matter—I think we have no business to attempt laying down a law, that a Christian must not put money (if he can lawfully spare it) into a benefit society. I was for some time afraid to express myself so decisively upon the subject: for though not engaged, nor likely to be engaged, in any thing of the kind myself, I felt what a snare the consideration of others might be; as well as how awful it would be for me to be a stumbling-block to them, by corrupting the rule of the word. But under the restriction and control of the general Christian principles, which the power of the truth only can enforce on the conscience, I now feel myself quite at liberty to say, that the thing cannot be pronounced unlawful in the abstract.

CLII.

TO ———

———, 1830.

You tell me that for some time past you have been very discontented and unhappy. That is a state into which, from our unbelief and hardness of heart, we are always prone to lapse under the various trials of our course; and it is always an alarming state, as indicating a dimness of eye to the one satisfying good thing shewn us from heaven, and is connected with a readiness to become "weary and faint in our minds," and it is only the strong power and care of the good shepherd that keeps us at such times from falling and turning aside with them who draw back into perdition, and He keeps us from this by recalling our minds to the good words and comfortable which He speaks to us from the mercy-seat. Is not this one of them? (Ps. lxii. 8.) "Trust in the Lord *at all times*; ye people, *pour out your heart before him*; God is a refuge for us." What a poor thing it would be to take these words merely as the language of the literal David, a sinner like ourselves. Do we not know the voice of the friend of sinners, declaring the name of Jehovah to his brethren in the midst of the congregation that he has received as his inheritance—setting forth before them the deep tribulation through which he passed in the days of his flesh, and the unshaken confidence that he maintained in God throughout all, and calling us to be followers of him in this, as joint heirs with him, heirs of God and all the blessedness that belongs to his children. "I ascend unto my father and your father, unto my God and your God." Trust in him at all times—" in the times of the thickest darkness, of the bitterest sorrow"—when your spirit is overwhelmed within you. (see Ps. lxi.) " Pour out your hearts before him," as the children given unto me, and whom I, presenting them before him, am not ashamed to call my brethren. " God is a refuge for us," a secure shelter and hiding-place from every evil, from every storm, from every enemy. Shelter yourselves in Him and fear not. Heaviness may endure for the night, but remember the glorious morning in which your expected joy shall come. In such language does he continually speak to us. And is there not enough in all this to banish discontent and unhappiness? Our consciences, testifying all the vileness and ungodly workings of our hearts, might well suggest objections against the idea of such blessings being ours, did we not see how it comes to us, that it is the glory wherewith He is crowned who is *worthy*. "*Heirs of God*." What an inheritance! but how can it be the portion of a sinful creature?—"*joint heirs with Christ*." " The glory which thou hast given me I have given them." Shall we not exclaim, these are the sure mercies of David. Blessed be the Lord God, the God of Israel, who only doeth wondrous things, and blessed be his glorious name for ever! And shall not that name be hallowed by those who know it? Shall they confound it with the various gods of the world that are but idols? May it be as ointment poured forth with mighty efficacy and refreshing fragrance to you.

CLIII.

TO THE SAME.

——, 1830.

I HAVE read your letter with some pain; and am startled, I confess, at what seems to me a kind of morbid tenderness or soreness of conscience, and at an apparent shaking of your mind upon scriptural principles, because you think they are not sufficiently exhibited among those you walk with.

" One of my strongholds is, that the spirit of truth produced unity in the believers of the apostolic gospel. If I see not this unity, *what is the inference?*" That is, indeed, ugly language; and before I advert to the two points in which you think you see in us something ontrary to the unity which the spirit of truth produces in believers,

I return your own question upon you—"What is the inference?" the inference which you mean to draw—supposing that this unity is not to be seen in us. Are you to infer that any scriptural principle you have scripturally held is to be relinquished? Or that any principle you have held strongly is not founded in scripture? It is by an appeal to scripture that it it is to be decided, and not by a reference to the practice or sentiments of any men, or to what is observable in any men. "Let God be true, though every man a liar"—is the language that expresses the mind of the Spirit. What then, I repeat it, is the inference you mean to draw? The only inference would be, that you can no longer *acknowledge as believers* those with whom you have been connected: and, indeed, it behoves us to be kept in a mind of readiness to forsake and hate *all* men—in that respect—for Christ's sake. Yet, ask yourself, was that the inference you secretly designed? – or rather, another, which you probably half covered from your own conscience? I freely say, that I think you in much greater danger from the amiable and respectable religious professors around you, than from those in whom you think you see those inconsistencies: and I do fear that your mind has been weakened and entangled, by lending your ear to the objections which they speciously raise against us as not acting *consistently* with our *own professed principles*. I would not descend to discuss that question with them. It would be a question about *ourselves*, and not about divine truth; and even about our professed *principles* of Christian fellowship we cannot consistently argue with any, but those who confess with their mouth the one everlasting gospel. We should generally find it our wisdom with false professors to "let them alone."

And now, a few words on your two points, lotteries—or games of chance—and defrauding the revenue. I wish to mark distinctly that I think there is an essential distinction between them. I think the former highly *inexpedient* and unsuitable for disciples: the latter, I am sure, is utterly *unlawful*. I cannot but admire the female sophistry in your desiring me to state the grounds for *non-observance of the precept*—render unto Cæsar, &c.; in which language you assume that either I do not acknowledge, or do not obey the precept, or that I walk with some who disown or disobey it. I confidently reply, that neither is the fact. I would as soon steal your purse as knowingly defraud the revenue, and would as soon walk in religious fellowship with a thief, as with one who practised the latter; and I can tell you, that I know not one who holds the precept more sacred—who obeys it at more sacrifice of worldly gain—than ——. But you *think* that he and I would have disobeyed it, if I had made him the bearer of a note to you when he lately went to Paris—a note which I should not think of sending you by post, perhaps from a feeling that it would not be worth a sous, and, in my sending which by him, the French post-office would not lose a sous. And yet, with what is indeed strange inconsistency, you admitted in our last conversation that we could not be said to violate the precept in bringing even to Paris an open letter of introduction, which it might be important we should personally present. If the French law be really designed to visit with punishment such an occasional departure from its letter, I am sure it must be for the purpose of espionage, and not of revenue; and I can conceive many occasions that would justify me in my conscience from risking the threatened penalty, in order to avoid that espionage. If your conscience had not the same freedom, you should abstain: but should you, therefore, set up your judgment as the standard to which others must bend? When I was removing from Dublin to London, I got over my books duty free, though certainly the *letter* of the act subjected them to duty. How did I effect it? I made interest with the Secretary of the Admiralty, whom I had known in college—he made interest with the heads of the Custom-house, and they took my affirmation that I was bringing over my library for my own private use, and not for *the purpose of sale*. Well, in that way I got them over without risk and without duty; because the commissioners were influenced to regard the spirit of the law, rather than the letter: but there was no provision for such a case in the act, nor any act granting them the power of remitting the duty. And would you think yourself at liberty to call them over the coals for this, as not obeying the precept of rendering to Cæsar, &c. It would require very little argument to prove, that you might as reasonably be charged with violating it when you got over a few letters and a couple of songs through the French ambassador. But, indeed, I am sick of pursuing a subject, on which there is all the substantial agreement between us that you ought to look for. Nor ought you to wonder that I shew no great respect to your over scrupulousness, when you recollect that the state of conscience that strains at a gnat, is generally the same that leads to the swallowing of a camel. You may perceive that I write under the influence of that jealousy which burns as "a vehement flame:" but that is necessarily connected with the love that I bear you. (Cant. viii. 6.)

On the subject of games of *chance*, &c., I am glad that you see, with me, that a Christian ought not to meddle with them: but I am sorry that you should think of imposing your view as a law upon your brethren who do not see it. Are you ready to exclaim at this language, as countenancing the ungodly *agreement to differ* of the religious world? It does no such thing. The ungodliness of their union consists in agreeing to differ about the revealed truth or precepts of the Lord. But can we say that there is any precept against spinning a tetotum—for determining some circumstances in, perhaps, a geographical game, or letting our children amuse themselves so? I would not do it—I dare not,—and I laboured long with ——— to convey to him my view of the unsuitableness and inexpediency of every thing of the kind. It grieved me to the heart that I failed, but I am sure that I should sin grievously if I attempted to *make a law* upon the subject. Perhaps another case will explain my meaning to you more distinctly. One, formerly connected with us in Dublin, got a silver ticket for the theatre, and frequented it more than weekly. What sober-minded Christian could hesitate about the inexpediency and unsuitableness of this? Yet, all remonstrances failed of convincing him of it: and could we pursue it further as a case of discipline? I think not, unless we are prepared to make a law with the religious world, or could lay down (what would be more difficult) how often a man may go to the theatre without doing what is sinful.

CLIV.

TO MRS B——.

Aug. 7, 1831.

CERTAINLY, dear Madam, you did not misunderstand me, when you conceived that I court inquiry into my Christian principles and practices; though not so as to continue any controversial discussion about them beyond certain narrow limits,—to which, however, you and I have not yet approached. The little that passed between us last Sunday se'nnight, was under circumstances very unfavourable. I would now, in the first place, notice the inquiry which you propose towards the conclusion of your letter of the 30th ult. viz.:—the nature of our *church-government*.

The *only* church government which we acknowledge is CHRIST'S. We have no other governor. Individually and collectively, we recognize no *authority* over us as Christians, but HIS: and it is in the word of his Apostles that we have his will authoritatively made known to us. The attempt of any man, under whatever name, to exercise any authority over us as Christians, we should repel, as a rebellious usurpation of Christ's prerogative. It is manifest, indeed, that if the laws of his kingdom—*all* its laws—are already made and promulgated in his word, there is no *room* for the exercise of any human authority in the things of that kingdom;—OBEDIENCE must be the only thing that remains alike for all its subjects. This applies just as strongly to the office-bearers in a Christian church, the Elders and Deacons,—as to any others.

I am aware, that most who designate these men as *officers* mean to convey, that they are invested with some *command* over the rest as privates—or laity. But real Elders and Deacons are *servants* in the employment of the body under the great head. Of these most of our churches have Deacons, very few of them as yet have Elders. Such servants to the church are *Christ's gifts*. He, according to his will, raises up one or another of his brethren, in whom all the qualifications are found, so minutely marked as requisite. We count it a great mercy whenever we are thus supplied; and feel it an humbling want, while we remain without these his gifts. But we dare not on that account draw a profane cover over the want, by investing with the *name* of Elders any who possess not, in some degree, all the prescribed characters.

As to your other inquiry, which you join with that relating to our *church government*, whether we have any other practices as a church, besides those with which you have been made acquainted, I can truly say that I do not know of any. *All* our acts as a church are open to the public eye. You have witnessed the *ordinary* and *stated* practices, in which we join on the first day of the week: and we have but the one meeting of the church. In it takes place, as *occasion* requires, the reception or exclusion of members. But I am led, by one expression in your letter, "the *sabbath*"—to apprize you of what, I believe, I have not been led to mention in any of my publications, that we regard not the first day of the week as a *sabbath*,—or (as divines call it) the *Christian sabbath*, which they pretend has succeeded to and taken place of the Jewish. Undeniably the Jewish sabbath was the *last* day of the week: and we are informed on good authority, that it, and all such Jewish institutions, were but *shadows* of good things then to come,—shadows that have *passed away* since the coming of the heavenly kingdom. As to the theological fiction, which divines so unblushingly put forward—that *the day was changed* to the *first* day of the week on the resurrection, and that Christ *undoubtedly* before his ascension instructed his Apostles about this change of the *sabbath*,—we reject it with abomination as a mere human tradition, destitute of even the shadow of foundation in the Apostolic word. In writing to *you*, I need scarcely add that there *is* an observance of the first day of the week, that we hold divinely obligatory upon all disciples. On it,—in memorial of that resurrection, by which they are begotten again "unto a lively hope," 1 Pet. i. 3.—the Christians of any neighbourhood are bound to come together into one place, to join together in eating the Lord's supper, and in the other appointed acts of Christian fellowship. I thought well to put you in early possession of our sentiments on this subject, as they greatly increase the bad odour in which we lie with the devout and honourable. But it is time for me to pass to some other topics on which you treat.

I intimated that I thought you quite afloat as to the divine authority of all the peculiarly Apostolic precepts. (I use the expression "*peculiarly* apostolic," to distinguish them from those *moral* exhortations, which many infidels will acknowledge to be very good and obligatory.) And I confess that nothing in your last changes my opinion. You do indeed quote my words with professed approbation—that "the word of the Lord is the only authoritative and only lawful rule of Christian conduct." But you evidently conceive that a person may very *innocently* walk contrary to this word in one or another instance, even after his attention has been called to it;—*innocently*, if he only THINK himself right. And you seem to conceive that I must admit this, because in my own church we did not formerly submit to some of the practices which we now hold sacred. And was the *evil of our disobedience* any the less, because it existed in my *own church*? When I was myself a clergyman of the establishment, and thus connected with all its antichristian abominations, I really *thought* that I did very right in remaining in such a connexion. Did this make it right? Does not any such notion immediately substitute each individual's mind and judgment, as the rule of Christian conduct, in place of the word of Christ? In fact, you might as reasonably say that Saul's persecution of the church was very innocent, because he then "verily *thought* that he *ought* to do many things against the name of Jesus of Nazareth," Acts xxvi. 9.

In your former letter you expressed yourself dissatisfied with my saying that the churches, with which I stand in connexion, include all whom I can *acknowledge* as disciples: and it is a declaration that must shock the charming liberality of the religious world. But your dissatisfaction resolves itself, in fact, into this: "Why should you not acknowledge *me* as a fellow-disciple, though I walk not with you or in connexion with your churches, because I *cannot* see some of the precepts which you hold as sacred?" My reply to any such inquiry must be—*just because we hold as sacred the rule by which we walk.* Any attempt to throw the blame of disobedience to it upon an imputed *obscurity* in the rule, we think to be substantially a denial of its authority. But indeed, dear Madam, when you are confident of your sincerity and innocence in substituting, for instance, a holy and loving curtsy for the enjoined salutation with the holy kiss of charity, you seem little acquainted with the self-deceiving power of the human heart, and of the degree to which our *will* naturally influences our judgment. I confess to you freely that there is no one of the observances, in which we join on the first day of the week, that my flesh would so gladly get rid of, as that of salutation—it exposes us so much to the derision of scoffers. And that this aversion to the thing was at the bottom of my supposed *inability to see* the precept so long, I have no doubt. That your judgment also in the matter is warped by your will, you afford decisive evidence in the circumstance, that your judgment is not the least shaken by the removal of the ground on which it *had professedly* rested.

"A kiss," you had said, "was at that period, *as is well known*, a common mode of salutation," &c. And thence you inferred, that the mode of salutation *common* at this period and in this country, might be substituted in the Christian observance of the apostolic precept. I had been well acquainted with the argument, and with the decisive refutation of it. This, however, you quote so inaccurately that I must repeat it. I was not so foolish as to assert, that the Romans were not in the habit of using the kiss as A mode of salutation. On the contrary, I expressly marked to you that I admitted there was no age or country, in which salutation with a kiss was not practised between close and endeared connexions. But I did say, that a kiss was *not the ordinary* or *general* mode of salutation among the old Romans, any more than it is among us at this day: and that the precept of saluting one another with an holy *kiss*, occurring notwithstanding in the letter to the church at *Rome*, your argument against the literal practice must fall to the ground. (I might have extended my remark to the Greeks as well as to the Romans.) But though the ground on which your judgment had professedly rested was thus removed, your judgment was not the least shaken in consequence; and you have now shifted your ground to the *pedilavium*. Upon that I shall not now say a word, in addition to what I have already offered in print; except that, if you really think—after reading my published Remarks—that the *literal* meaning of the apostolic precept concerning the salutation, can be shewn not to be its *real* meaning, in the same way as I have shewn the *literal pedilavium* not to be the thing *really* intended in John xiii.—if you really think this, I am sure it would be quite idle for me to say a word to change your opinion. But here I must remark, that from your language in your last letter, I am not sure that you have really given up the idea of the kiss having been the ordinary mode of salutation in ancient Rome; though you shrink, through a kind of politeness, from maintaining it in opposition to my positive denial of the fact. Now, madam, there is no doubt that real *courtesy* is not only consistent with Christianity, but is enjoined by it. But, really, Christianity quite spoils the kind of politeness that proceeds on deception, or that is inconsistent with the most steadfast assertion of every thing that involves scriptural truth. And be assured that your plainest avowal that you think me misinformed on that point of Roman manners, though it might make me smile, would not hurt me in the least. It is a point on which it requires very little scholarship to be rightly informed. If you can consult any one capable of examining a few passages that I should refer to in the Latin classics, I think I could satisfy yourself. Perhaps, I may even at present satisfy you, by telling you an amusing little anecdote. One of the *Scipios* (I think) was a candidate for an office at Rome; and canvassing the citizen electors, in *shaking hands* with one of them, he was annoyed by the *hardness* of his gripe. "My good friend," said he, "may I ask, do you walk on *all-fours*, that your hand is so hard?" It was an unfortunate joke, for it lost him his election. The candidate, during his canvass, was accompanied by a kind of agent called a *nomenclator*, who whispered in the ear of his employer the names and circumstances of the citizens; and it is in perfect correspondence with the above story, that a poet of the Augustan age describes one of these agents as whispering to the candidate—"that man has great influence in the parish;—*shake hands with him*." Now, I would put it to your own consideration, if salutation with a *kiss* were the ordinary or general mode of salutation now in England—whether a candidate for Westminster would not employ it with a voter whom he wished to gain—whether he would employ any less warm mode of salutation on such an occasion? Indeed, even grasping the hand was a more warm salutation than the *most ordinary* mode employed by the old Romans; among whom, as well as among the Greeks, the *most* common salutation at meeting and parting, was by a *mere expression* of good-will, equivalent with our "Good morning!" or "How do you do?" or "Farewell." You will please to recollect, also, that I admitted that, in a later period of the empire, an attempt was made by some young bucks at Rome, to introduce salutation with a kiss into ordinary—or at least *fashionable*—practice. But instead of succeeding, they were ridiculed in epigrams, some of which exist to this day.

I should apologize for being betrayed, in addressing you, into any of the regions of scholarship. I think I scarcely should have been so, but that I suspect your ear has been pre-occupied on this subject by some of the systematic opposers of apostolic Christianity; and I am aware of the combined ignorance and dishonesty which *teachers*, especially of that description, manifest; particularly where they conceive that the person whom they mislead, is unable to detect the falsehoods which they put forward. But it is time for me to conclude this long letter; most of which I have written with considerable difficulty, from an attack of gout in my right hand. I have found a copy of another tract, which I shall send you, and am,

Madam,

Your well-wisher and willing servant,

CLV.

TO ———.

———, 1831.

I HAVE long known Mr. Booth as a religious teacher, who held much of the "form of sound words;" and indeed I was many years ago instrumental in putting out a large edition of his work in Dublin. What my faith and hope were at the time, or what his faith and hope were, I feel no interest in inquiring, and have no desire to pronounce. Antichristian doctrine has been not only so widely prevalent, but so insidiously interwoven with a language like that of the truth, that it is hard to say what mixture of the two languages may consist together; nor have I any thing to do with that inquiry. But this I may say, that if a believer of the truth has expressed himself in any way that trenches upon it, whenever this is pointed out to him, it may be expected that he will "abhor the evil and cleave to that which is good;" and that no weight of human authority, or respectability of the names of men, will outweigh in his mind the authority of the divine word. If it be otherwise, if he side with Antichristians against the truth after their opposition has been pointed out to him, a Christian has no scriptural warrant for regarding him as a believer, whatever plausibility of language he may at times employ to disguise his infidelity.

It was so many years since I looked at Mr. B's work that I have now opened it as new, and with some kind of curiosity to see what it is that I formerly assisted to circulate. But I have found no occasion to read beyond the Introduction. As I expected, I immediately found much that is good and important, particularly where he says, in p. xvi. "the ancient gospel is an unceremonious thing. It pays no respect, &c.; no, the virtuous lady and the infamous prostitute stand on the same level in its comprehensive view. Its business is only with the worthless and miserable, whoever they be." Had I not been aware what lengths men go in good words and fair speeches, while they are yet disaffected towards the ancient gospel, I should have been apt to say—surely, the man who penned that sentence must have had a view of it. Yet before I come to the end of the very next page, I find the same man putting forward one of the grossest contradictions of the truth—but one that is certainly embodied in almost all the modern gospels, that are not the gospel of Christ. Speaking of the "sad effects" of the false gospels which have been maintained by those who wished to remove the offence of the cross, he says—"the consciences of *awakened* sinners have been left to grope *in the dark* for that consolation, which nothing but the unadulterated truth could give." Those who are groping in the dark for consolation, or for something to give peace to their consciences, are indeed in darkness and in death: yet Mr. B. more than intimates that such sinners may be at the same time what he calls *awakened*. In this he is countenanced by all the popular divines; and indeed their so-called ministry could not proceed at all, without that classification of unbelievers into *awakened* and *unawakened*. But the idea is fundamentally opposed to the trtuh of God. According to this, there is but a two-fold classification of all to whom the gospel is sent,—namely, into those who *believe* it, and those who *believe it not*. The former are children of the light and of the day: they are not in darkness, as others; and they have given to them everlasting consolation and good hope through grace. 2 Thess. ii. 16. 1 Thess. v. 4, 5. The latter remain under the power of darkness, dead in trespasses and sins: their sleep of death continues alike, whatever dreams may occupy them, whether frightful or pleasurable. But to admit, and honestly to act upon this plain scriptural principle, would be utterly inconsistent with the ministry (so called) of a popular preacher. His meeting-house may be considered as a manufactory of what are termed Christians, but are not. His profane and careless, or unawakened hearers, are the raw material, on which he first labours to get them into a sober and demure mood; then into a state of alarm and perturbation of conscience, which he calls *awakened*; then he is busied in training those who are to seek consolation, and encouraging *them* to *take* the insidious consolation, which he offers them in his gospel: and the various styles of address, which he employs to those different *classes* of hearers, he profanely calls, "rightly dividing the word of truth." I am aware that all this language which I employ upon the subject will appear intolerably harsh, and abominably uncharitable, to those who savour not the things that be of God, but the things that be of men. But whoever regards it so, is really siding with the corrupters of the Gospel of Christ, whatever plausible profession of believing it he may make.

But it may be asked—may not Mr. B have fallen into this language without really perceiving its evil tendency against the truth of the gospel, and without meaning to support it in that opposition to the truth? I can easily admit the general possibility of such a thing: but it does not dispose me at all to lower the tone in which I reprobate the unscriptural sentiment expressed. If Mr. B., or any other who expresses it, be, at bottom, of another mind from what the language appears to convey, that better mind would delight to have the falsehood exposed most plainly; and any mind that would wish to screen the falsehood from exposure (in all its antichristian malignity) on account of the respectability of the names of men, who have held the same language, any such mind is not the mind of Christ.

But I must, in honesty, say, that the lie which I have marked seems to constitute an essential part of Mr. B's system. In the very next page I find this language: "To the *sensible* sinner, therefore, it (the doctrine of reigning grace) must always be a joyful sound." Here we have concentered the quintessence of the popular false gospels. The gospel of Christ *is* glad tidings of great joy to sinners, even the chief, to sinners indiscriminately, and is sent as such to all nations, and all ranks and characters, without distinction, whether they will hear, or whether they will forbear. When Paul in the synagogue at Antioch addressed his hearers, "We declare unto you *glad tidings*," &c., Acts xiii. 32; did he previously inquire whether his hearers were, what Mr. B., and fellow divines call, *sensible* sinners—made somewhat acquainted with the deadly nature of sin—humbled under the conviction of it—panting for deliverance from it—and thus (as is supposed) prepared for the reception of the gospel? No: both there, and wherever he went, he declared the same gospel (or glad tidings) to all whom he met, without distinction; because, preaching God the saviour of sinners, he was certain, not only that they were all sinners, but that they were all sensible sinners, so far as to know that they were sinners—to be charged in their consciences with sin. No doubt, none but those who believed the glad tidings, which he declared, rejoiced in them, or knew the joyful sound: but this was a mind, not which the gospel of God found in those to whom it was sent, but which it produced (as the rod of His power) in those who believed it, having been ordained unto eternal life. When Mr. B. and the divines talk of *sensible* sinners, to whom the gospel "must be a joyful sound," *i.e.* must be a gospel, they plainly intend certain characters, so prepared for the reception of the gospel, that when it is sent to them, they will acknowledge and receive it, as what it is, glad tidings of great joy to sinners. Now, any such preparation in a sinner for the reception of the gospel, while it is a corner-stone doctrine in all the popular systems of theology, is essentially anti-christian, or opposed to the gospel of Christ. Yet, the great object and business of the so-called ministry of the popular teachers is, first, to produce some such preparation in their hearers; and secondly, to apply to their prepared hearers a corrupted gospel accommodated to this idea. "To the *sensible* sinner the gospel *must* always be a joyful sound." I suppose in this it must be at least included, that this *sensible* sinner *must* believe the gospel, when it shall be laid before him. Now, to say that a sinner, not yet acquainted with the gospel, must believe it when he shall hear it, is to say, that darkness must be light, that death must be life, that enmity must be love; it is to attribute to the mind of an ungodly sinner all the characters which belong to the mind of Christ. Mr. B. had learned to say, as in p. xvi.; "the ancient gospel has not the least regard to the devotee for the sake of his zeal or righteousness." But he seems to have been as disaffected as that devotee to the ancient gospel, which has not the least regard to the *sensible* sinner for the sake of his sensibility of sin, the depth of his convictions, and the ardour of his desires for deliverance.

I say, the more confidently, that he seems to have been thus disaffected to the truth, on casting my eye forward to the following page xix. where he says, in plain language; "to have a bare conviction of the truth in the mind, and to experience its *power* on the heart, are very different things." Here we have Mr. B. directly and broadly opposed to the word of God; and this, not on a subordinate and non-essential point of divine truth, but on the very essence of the gospel of Christ. There is no more essential point of the gospel than this; that *whosoever believeth* it *hath* everlasting life and shall be saved eternally. But, according to Mr. B., a man may have a *conviction* of the truth in his mind, or may believe it, and yet may be damned. Nothing more can be necessary to prove to a Christian that Mr. B. was an infidel when he wrote this: and as to all the good words and fair speeches which he employs throughout his work, those who remember what the apostle says about the transformation of ministers of Satan into ministers of Christ, will see nothing inconsistent in them with his infidelity. The man who holds a gospel which may be believed by a sinner, and yet that sinner not be saved, may talk ever so highly about grace, about faith, about the righteousness of God, &c. &c., but all the expressions which he employs, stand in his mind for things essentially different from what they really import in the language of scripture: and to maintain this juggle of deceitful words is, indeed, the grand trade of the so-called ministers or clergy. Mr. B. classes himself with "the faithful *dispensers* of sacred truth." The disciple of Christ taught from the scriptures would expect to find any man a clerical impostor, who makes such a claim; and needs not, therefore, be surprised to find the Baptist minister, Abraham Booth, a wolf in sheep's clothing. I do not think it at all necessary to read or note beyond the introduction of his work.

CLVI.

TO ———

——, 1831.

* * * * * And now let me pass to more important matters. I confess I was considerably startled by the opinions you tell me are broached by some among us on both the first day of the week and on amusements; and I strongly suspect there is a *white devil* at work on these subjects. As you have not told me who the persons are, I know not whom I may hit by any of my remarks: and, perhaps, so much the better, as foolish tenderness might else lead me not to hit hard, 'like a Turk.' I had not been aware that you were acquainted with that phrase.

'Though the Jewish sabbath is no more, it is becoming in Christians, for many reasons, to keep holy the first day of the week.'

If these words mean anything, they seem to me to put forward pretty broadly the common notion, that the first day of the week has succeeded as a *Christian sabbath* to the Jewish. The Jews had strong ground, indeed, for the observance of their sabbath,—the express divine command that they should rest from all the ordinary occupations of life on the seventh day of every week; and thus keep it holy, or set apart from the other six. It would have been very strange language for any one to say, that it was "*becoming*" in the Jews thus to keep holy the seventh day of the week: *becoming* in them not to rebel against the God of Israel! Nay, they were bound on their allegiance to keep holy the sabbath day. Well, we are taught that this Jewish institution was "a shadow of things to come, but the body is of Christ," Col. ii. 17; and this, and the other Jewish shadows, have passed away on the coming of the substance, Heb. ix. 9—12: so that now any adherence to the shadows involves a virtual denial that Christ has come in the flesh. Well, when we are told that it is becoming in Christians to keep holy the first day of the week, is it intended that Christians are bound to sanctify the first day as a sabbath, or rest from the ordinary occupations of life? This, certainly, is the thing intended, though not plainly spoken. Now, where is the scriptural ground for the sentiment? Is there any precept for such an observance in the New Testament scriptures? Let it be adduced. Is there any recorded example of such an observance in the apostolic churches? That would be equivalent with a precept; there is not one: on the contrary, it is easy to collect from what is recorded, that the apostolic Christians pursued the ordinary occupations of life on the first day of the week, just as on any other. For is it not certain that the Jewish Christians, continuing to act as Jews, did continue to observe the seventh day of the week as a sabbath? (It was not till the writing of the epistle to the Hebrews they were taught, that the whole Levitical dispensation "was ready to vanish away.") And is it not as certain that they did not observe the first day of the week as a sabbath? for to have observed two sabbath days in the week would have been as contrary to the fourth precept of the law, as not to have observed one. Well, and what shall we say of the Gentile Christians? That they did not observe the last day of the week as a sabbath is certain, since they were expressly taught their freedom from the law of Moses: and can we suppose that they observed the first? That there were two different sabbath days observed by the two different classes of Christians? That on the day the one class ceased working, the other class worked, and *vice versa*: and that the Christian slaves, for instance, took the first day of every week as a day of idleness, and were allowed to do so even by their heathen masters. The supposition is monstrous. On the contrary, we may see a plain account why the time of Christian assembling was in the *evening* of the first day (as is sufficiently intimated), from their having then done with the ordinary business of the day; which would not have allowed them to meet at the time we usually do. And now, I would ask, is it *becoming* in Christians to adopt as a religious observance, anything that has no foundation whatever in the word of the Lord,—in either a precept or recorded example? This, that you tell me, some urge as becoming in us, I would rather protest against as most unbecoming.

'But the first day of the week was *waited for* by the first Christians?' Yes, indeed, see Acts xx. 6—7. xxi. 4: but what do those passages prove? That Paul and his companions, in their travels, when they wanted to meet with the disciples, waited for the stated period of their assembling as a church on the first day of the week. But does it go a tittle towards proving that day to have been observed as a sabbath? or do any of us deny, that it is not only becoming in us, but our bounden duty, to hold that day distinguished from the other six, as that on which our Lord rose from the dead, and on which we are to "come together to break bread," in remembrance of the great work which He finished in his obedience unto death? This is the blessed observance of the day which has scriptural authority; and no other observance of it can I acknowledge. The divines of the world often tell us gravely, that nature and reason sanction the Christian sabbath, from the great expediency of having a fixed portion of time *peculiarly devoted to religion and religious exercises.* Those with whom that argument carries any weight, or who think that Christians are to be more religious and holy at some seasons than at others, must have gone far, indeed, in imbibing the spirit of false religion. I do not mean to intimate that there are any such among us.

'But a respect is to be paid to the laws of the land.' Yes, indeed: in all things lawful we are to obey them; and, therefore, I would not keep my shop open on Sunday, nor if I were a mason, would I work at building a wall. But, if I were a shoemaker, and had a private room, I should have no scruple about making a pair of shoes in it; nor was the law ever designed to interfere with such private occupations. But, as to the law about Sunday observances, it enjoined every one to go to his parish kirk, and afterwards to amuse himself with *sports and pastimes*, for which they published an authoritative directory. I think we are called to *avow* that we take none of our religion from human law; but would it not be doing so, if we even professed to keep the first day of the week from any respect to acts of parliament.

'As to casting a stumbling-block in the way of the world;' I never could wish to *conceal* from the world, that I do not regard Sunday as a sabbath: but neither should I wish to obtrude that needlessly upon their attention, because this would be putting forward a *subordinate* matter in place of the one grand truth of the gospel.

And now, large as my sheet is, I am obliged to conclude without treating the topic of amusements. Since I began this, I have received a letter from our dear Mrs. P——, communicatiug the double bereavement to which poor Mrs. B—— has been called. May she be abundantly comforted with the remembrance of Him, who has said "I will be with thee in trouble."

CLVII.

TO MR. J——.

April —, 1832.

My dear ——,—Your letter is a painful one, but it describes a state of mind that I have been well acquainted with many a year ago. It is sometimes a sullen dissatisfaction, and at other times a fretful impatience, at finding yourself so very vile. You are out of humour with yourself, and with the Most High: and I am sure I have nothing to say to put you into good humour with yourself. On the contrary, I am sure, that in the blackest view you have of your own vileness, you have never seen the half of it. In fact, amidst all the seemingly strong acknowledgments you make of your wickedness, you altogether suppress or overlook the blackest instance of it, your "making God a liar," by discrediting the plainest declarations of his word. Indeed, it is well for me, and for all the elect of God, that he extends his mercy and salvation to such stubborn, wicked, rebellious, incorrigible infidels. You think not but that he expects some good return from those, to whom he extends what you call mercy, and that, if instead of that, all the returns they make to him are evil, and only evil continually, nothing is to be looked for but that he would cast them off. In short, though you are verbally (I believe) a Calvinist, yet what you call salvation hinges, in your view, upon some conditions to be fulfilled by the sinner. Now, all such imaginations are entertained in direct contradiction to the word of God. He knows what is in man, and tells us plainly of his saved people, that in them dwelleth no good thing. There are manifestations of the evil character, which may come *by surprise* on them; but never upon Him. His design is to "shew the riches of his mercy" on those who need mercy higher than the heavens, and who need it continually—who have nothing else to stand by. Now, that the gospel is such an absolutely *unconditional* declaration of the gracious purpose of God, may appear sufficiently from a reference to Jer. xxxii. 38, 39, 40. There the God of Israel takes the whole upon himself with an "I will," and "they shall:" while, in the preceding verses (30—35), the character of Israel is so marked, that it appears nothing else could meet their case. Nor is there just ground left for any one, while he admits it true that God deals thus with his elect, to put away the joyfulness of it by urging—"Ah! if I knew that I were of the number." He that believeth—he that is convinced that the divine testimony concerning the salvation of God is true—he shall be saved. So the word from heaven declares; and no supplementary revelation is necessary to tell that believer that he is one of the elect. Indeed, if his hope rested on the ground of any such persuasion, as that he is among the elect of God—it would rest on a ground quite different from the hope of the gospel. That hope is derived from the character of God, as He has revealed his glory in the person and work of his anointed, in the combined perfection of righteousness and of mercy, and from the word that brings nigh his salvation to all alike. who read the report of it in the declaration, that he who believeth that report is justified from all things, and has eternal life;—and this on the ground of worthiness too—but the worthiness of Him who died the just for the unjust, and on whose head are many crowns;—and in consequence too, of the fulfilment of conditions—but conditions that have been fulfilled by the mediator of the new covenant—that surety of his people, with whom the covenant has been made, and therefore standeth fast. I know that you have been accustomed to express assent to these things; but if you be now only persuaded of the truth, you would not stop to inquire whether you have heretofore believed, nor would even the certainty that you never had, now keep you back from drawing nigh boldly to the mercy-seat. If you but believed them now, you would come now—you would not hold back in a pet—you would come at once to Him who receiveth sinners—who in no wise casteth out any. Nor can there be any circumstances of malignity of evil, or incorrigibility of wickedness in yourself, that would prevent your drawing near while you are kept in the belief of that word, which shews "heaven *opened*" in setting forth the full prohibition that has been made and accepted, and proclaiming the sure mercies of the beloved throughout a sinful world—sure to all the seed, on account of their being based exclusively on him who is a sure foundation. If you urge, perhaps secretly, that, after all, must we not truly repent, and bring forth fruit, &c. and may not these be justly considered as conditions to be yet fulfilled on our part, I only say that you might as reasonably talk of our being brought to glory, as a *condition* of our being saved. He does give his people repentance unto life; and this in giving his word of truth entrance into their minds. But that is part of the salvation wherewith he saves them; and to talk of one part of his salvation as the condition of another, is nothing but the wicked nonsense of infidel theologians.

CLVIII.

TO D. R. R——, ESQ.

March, 1832.

Your letter has blown off the ashes of forgetfulness, revived all affectionate interest, and stirred me up to bear you in remembrance before the mercy-seat. Much of the intelligence is very interesting. The worst part of it is their being entangled with an ecclesiastic, and him pensioned. In that they have among them one who holds a reasoning fee in the service of Antichrist. Yet, even such—as sinners of every class and description, the Lord does call, as I have to own, to his glory;—but, when called, they will throw up their brief, and fling away the fee that accompanied it with abhorrence. It will rejoice us to hear shortly that ever so few have come out from those who will not follow the Lord fully. Farewell, dear brother. Be strong —yea—be strong.

May, 1832.—Your intelligence about the happy issue of your communications with the ——s is most gratifying. We see in such instances the triumphant power of Zion's king, reigning in the midst of his enemies, and leading captivity captive;—bringing into captivity to the obedience of his word those who were held in willing thraldom by the God of this world. I quite agree with you in considering the second coming of our Lord as very near. All the signs of the times concur in marking its rapid approach. The consumption of the man of sin by the spirit of the Lord's mouth, goes on marvellously; and this we know was to precede his final destruction. 2 Thess. ii. 8. The kings of the earth also are evidently prepared to hate the great whore and her daughters, that have committed fornication with them so long; or at least are beginning to feel that they have tasked themselves with a cumbersome stone, in attempting to combine the concerns of another world with their earthly governments. Then the general *rapidity* with which the wheels of providence are turning—political events more numerous and more important taking place now in a few years, than centuries formerly used to give birth to; this also speaks loudly to us—"behold, I come quickly!" for without attempting to quit our proper province for politics, we know that all things serve *Him*, and are but preparing the way of the Lord. The *general* expectal also, even among those who are most blind to his true character, I do with you think in some degree indicative; though I make not so much of this as of other signs; for I believe history teaches, that a similar expectation was very generally entertained at the time of the *Crusades*. But enough of this.

On the expression—*follow* holiness, (Heb. xii. 14.) little needs to be said, when the true import and nature of scriptural holiness is known. The exhortation is suited only to those who *are* holy, "sanctified in Christ Jesus," "called to be saints:" and when they are exhorted to *follow* holiness, it is simply to *pursue the course* which becomes such a people—a people holy to the Lord, separated to Him and his service—turned from all the gods of the nations that are but idols, and from all the religious ways connected with their worship, and taught to sanctify the Lord God in their hearts as the *only* living and true God; taught this by having their eyes open to the discernment of his revealed glory in the work of his anointed. Others will mistake this, as every part of Scripture; and will imagine they *are following holiness*, when they are striving hard to become something like what they call saints, to become what they are not, or to pretend to be so. The plain import of the expression "*follow after*"—(retained, indeed, in our phrase of *pursuing* a course)—you may see exemplified in 1 Tim. vi. 11. and 2 Tim. ii. 22. The Lord's people are characterized in Is. li. 1. as "following after righteousness," and we know this does not mean *trying to become righteous*—for they *are* righteous, justified from all things, and *have peace* with God: and they are addressed accordingly in the 7th and 8th verses. To us Ps. lxxxv. 13. may stand as a comment on the phrase. But do not unbelieving religionists similarly misinterpret, to their own destruction, the expression of "seeking the Lord," and every other in the Scriptures?

On *churches,* I hope your judgment is cleared from the clouds that ——— raised. If two or three—including certainly one or more brethren—cannot lawfully come together on the first day of the week to break bread, because in the course of time none but the *sisters* may be found adhering to scriptural principles, and they cannot pursue church-discipline against their antiscriptural brother; is it not plain that the same objection might be raised against the lawfulness of a church of two or three and twenty? Are we to anticipate such circumstances, and on account of the possibility of such an occurrence, to abstain from walking together, as long as we can scripturally? Whoever hold *Elders* as necessary to *administer* the ordinances of Christ, or authorize disciples to observe them, hold, under the *name* of elders, the worst of the Antichristian principles of the clerical character and function. And as to preaching sermons—*aptness to teach* is certainly one of the characters, which those called to the eldership ought to have more or less manifested in the church: but it would be hard to say why an elder should teach, the week after his appointment, at greater length than he had taught the week before. In this, as in every thing, he is to be an ensample to the flock. When I deny that either the administration of ordinances, or preaching of sermons is any part of the elder's business, many would think that I leave them nothing to do. They would perhaps think otherwise if they witnessed our dear brother M——'s occupation in the church in D——; or if they entered more into the import of the name, "overseers of the flock." Very high do I hold the importance of having some *specially charged* with that watchful care, *and acknowledged* by the church as called to it, and given them for it by the great Head. Particularly as a church multiplies, I am sure it will be lacking in an important gift, if it remain long without elders; but I am as sure that, in general, the most important service of the elders is rendered not when the church is assembled. But I must have done. My love to all that are with you, though unknown in the flesh. Mercy and peace be multiplied to you.

March, 1833.—Mercy and peace be multiplied to you from Him who is our peace, and from whom abundance of peace flows like a river making glad the city of God; and through whom abounding mercy reigns unto eternal life, where sin had reigned unto death! May you, and all that are with you, one in Christ Jesus, know more and more of the blessedness bestowed on us in Christ; and be led by the great captain, with singing, unto the heavenly Zion, with songs and everlasting joy upon your heads;—glorying in his holy name, and seeing *there* a sufficiency for any sinner upon earth to glory in, and nothing anywhere else for the most blessed saint to glory in. What else have I wherein to glory at this moment? when I am so incurably vile, and bent to backsliding "from the only true God," that, left but to *myself*, I would now turn aside from Him, forget his name, and go on to glory in vanity and lies;—yes, and pretend perhaps at the time that I was offering incense to Him. Truly, "it is not in man that walketh to direct his steps," Jer. x. 23. "Order my steps in thy word," Ps. cxix. 133. is a suitable prayer for us. May we be kept to the end under the abasing conviction of our own character, and the blessed discernment of His as the justifier of the ungodly, through the redemption that is in Christ Jesus.

Should I be living, when our sisters ——— return to Dublin, you may be sure that I shall be ready to give them as much of my time and attention as they may desire, and as circumstances may admit. But it is not very likely that I should ever see their faces in the flesh. Blessed be the mighty God of Jacob, that He is the strength of our hearts and our portion for ever, even when flesh and heart fail. We have had several removals by death for some time past—all of them affording matter of praise;—and some pleasing additions—the body here in general appearing to stand fast in the one faith and hope—and a very pleasing appearance in it of a young growth of promising olive-branches. "One generation *shall* declare thy name unto another." Ps. cxlv. 4. He who has spoken that word makes it good,—in a world where otherwise the fire of his truth would have been long since extinguished. Farewell, my brother.

CLIX.

TO H. M———, ESQ.

May, 1833.

When we recollect the character of the apostolic writings, as differing essentially in the *form* of their instructions from all abstract systems of human composition, we cannot wonder that no passage is to be produced laying down formally the *general* rule that, in all cases where a church is called to remove an offender from their fellowship, the brethren must avoid needless social intercourse with him in matters of this life—all that company-keeping which would indicate complacency in him.

No passage (I say) is to be *expected* formally presenting this abstract rule, even supposing it to be really conveyed in the mind of the Spirit in the scriptures. And, therefore, our inability to produce such a passage forms *no argument at all* against the position, that this principle is really and sufficiently conveyed to us.

I have long conceived that this is obviously to be inferred from *any one* of those passages—1 Cor. v. 11. 2 Thess. iii. 6—14. or Rom. xvi. 17. But within these few days, the consideration of the three combined has struck me with wonder. How very far the Spirit of Truth has gone in condescension to our slowness and hardness of heart, so far as to repeat substantially the same rule in *distinct application to each of the three cases*, which can alone occasion exclusion from the fellowship of a Christian church!

For, while every case of discipline which terminates in that exclusion, must ultimately proceed upon *one* and the same ground—the offender's refusal to hear *the word of the Lord* through his church, —and this, whatever form of evil occasioned the commencement of the discipline, yet it must be admitted that these forms are various. But, however varied, must they not all be reducible to *three* classes? 1st. The evil may consist in some act or conduct violating what is called *morality*—contrary to the dictates of conscience, even in unbelievers. 2dly. It may consist in conduct contrary to the practical injunctions delivered to the churches by the *apostles*, the authority of which rests upon the Apostle's word, and may not be recognized by unbelievers. Or, 3dly, the evil may be something not *immediately* connected with the conduct—either with respect to morality or apostolic ordinance—but some falsehood of *sentiment* opposed to the apostolic doctrine or gospel.

Now, I do think it worthy of most serious remark, and of our thankful admiration, that while this threefold classification comprises every case of evil in which the discipline of a church can originate, we have substantially the same direction *three times repeated, but applied distinctly to such a class of evils*, enjoining much the same course towards the person put away—the avoidance of company-keeping with him.

I repeat it, however, that when we consider the obvious ground of this injunction, as connected either with true love towards the offender, or with godly jealousy over ourselves, we ought to have been forward to draw the *general* conclusion from any one of the particular cases. But now, I really know not what more of detail or explicitness we could reasonably look for.

We surely should think it most unreasonable to maintain, that we are at liberty to hold convivial intercourse with a man removed from our fellowship as a *thief*, and to vindicate such a liberty by urging, that theft is not among the evils mentioned in 1 Cor. v. 11. But would this be more unreasonable than the attempt to confine the direction in 2 Thess. iii. 6. to the idler, as if the only tradition received from the apostle was against idleness?

CLX.

TO THE SAME.

Sept. 18, 1833.

I WRITE immediately to remove a mistake under which I believe you lie as to my meaning. I am informed (whether correctly or not) that you conceived, from my language on Sunday, that I declined hearing you farther on the subject of discussion. Believe me, nothing could be more remote from my real meaning; though I did and do consider it quite unsuitable to continue any debate about it *in our assembly on the first day of the week*. But so far from wishing to withdraw from the discussion impatiently, while any matter of difference remains, I deprecate such a termination; and shall rejoice to resume the subject with you in any other circumstances most convenient to you. Indeed, it would be strange if I were not cut to the heart by the idea of any ultimate difference with a brother, so much and so long endeared, and to whom I am in various ways so deeply indebted; or if I were not anxious to employ every means for averting such a termination.

I have felt, indeed, very desirous to have further communication with you on the subject, from having failed last Sunday to catch the precise meaning of several things that fell from you. For instance, when you expressed yourself as if you considered that the command in 1 Cor. v.—" with such not even to eat," is in all cases to be taken *literally*; and as if you thought I was frittering it away, by interpreting it as forbidding all unnecessary intercourse. Surely, you would not consider a Christian woman warranted in declining to eat at the same table with her husband, because he had been removed from the christian fellowship for *covetousness*. I confess, I should be much afraid of such an apparently strict adherence to the letter of the command; because I think it would go in practice to set it aside altogether, and certainly would set aside its spirit. I should as little think the precept violated by my happening to dine at the same ordinary with such a person, or as a common guest at the table of one, who had never been in Christian fellowship with us. In such cases a disciple, acting under the spirit of the precept (i. e. its real import), will, I conceive, be at no loss to see his way; and I should be very far from desiring to draw *a more distinct line*. Now, if the thing really forbidden in Corinthians be any of that familiarity, which would be at once injurious to the offender and dangerous to myself, as importing complacency in him, and either originating in such complacency or calculated to ensnare me into it; I am quite at a loss to conjecture what difference you design to mark between the course enjoined in Corinthians, in Thessalonians, and in Romans. Do not suppose that, in saying this, I mean to say, that I regard with the same eye all persons removed from the body; or that I would conduct myself towards all of them in precisely the same way. To say the former, would certainly not be true; and the latter (I conceive) would, in some respects, not be consistent with the scriptural principles, which should regulate my estimate of characters—my hopes and my fears about them. But I am fully persuaded, that it does not consist with the principles of either godly fear or christian love, to continue to maintain habits of familiar social intercourse with any who have walked with us in the fellowship of the gospel, but who have been removed from that fellowship, *for whatever evil*—under the authority of our Great Head.

If you agree with this general and broad position (and some of your language would lead me to hope that you do), I know not any ground of variance remaining between us. I certainly do not consider as such our removal of ———; even if we acted in this under an erroneous impression of her sentiments. In the course of any week, that error may be corrected, on finding that her avowed sentiments accord with the truth. But I own that, at present, I am persuaded we did not mistake her, though I should rejoice to discover that we did. How loosely poor S—— must have held his Christian connexion, when he could break off at once on such a ground, and on statements received altogether from herself.

It pains me to occupy so much of your time, my brother. But I trust you will give this note an attentive reading, and that you will suggest some arrangement for a little conference *viva voce*. May our great and gracious Lord " stablish, strengthen, settle you;" and not suffer any weapon formed by the adversary against his church to prosper!

Ever in true affection, &c.

CLXI.

TO THE SAME.

Sept. 23, 1833.

Do not suppose, my dear M——, that I mean to weary you because I write so soon again. But the fact is, I wish you should have before you all I desire to say, before you make any reply. It is not much I am now going to add. Your argument, from the singular form of the word *tradition*, 2 Thes. iii. 6. as confining the direction given us in the 14th verse to the one case of those who will persist in leading idle lives, has always appeared to me so weak, that I did not venture to encounter it. But I noticed, yesterday, a passage that I think must satisfy yourself at once of its inconclusiveness. I refer to Mark vii. 2—13, in reading which I wish you to attend particularly to the 8th and 13th verses. The word *tradition* is there also in the singular number; and yet, is it not obvious that it is employed to denote the whole mass of human *traditions* by which they set at nought the word or commandment of God? Of this, several different *instances* indeed are given, but without limiting the application in the least to those instances. Is it not obvious, that it would be no less unreasonable to infer any such limitation from the singular number of the word *tradition*, than to infer that the expression, "the commandment of God," in the 8th verse, imports but one divine precept?

I have heard also from M—— what I think a very just and important remark. It is this, that your attempt to confine 2 Thess. iii. 14, to *companying* with the *idler*, on account of the singular form of the word *tradition* in the 6th verse, goes immediately to an equal limitation of the command in the 6th verse, which enjoins us to *withdraw* from every brother that walketh disorderly, or contrary to apostolic rule, and therefore goes immediately to unloose the *binding* authority of every apostolic command—even of this, that you acknowledge singularly binding. For what, if any member of a Christian church should persist in *companying* with the obstinate idler? Might he not plead that he was not in this violating the apostolic *tradition*, which enjoins diligence in labour? Other members of the church might indeed say, that he did very wrong in thus companying with the idler; but still as it was not *the* one tradition referred to in the 6th verse that he despised,—they would have no warrant for withdrawing from him; and it would be easy to shew, in the same way, that there is no precept of the Apostles, to which disobedience might not be tolerated in a church—without affording even those who acknowledge the precept any scriptural ground for purging out the evil from among them. Yet it is plain that, in 1 Thess. iv. 1—8. that Apostle reminds the disciples of *all* that he delivered them for regulating their walk as of equal authority, as of "*commandments* he gave them by the Lord Jesus:" just as the same Apostle warns the Corinthians of his being in a readiness to revenge "*all* disobedience, when their obedience should be fulfilled." 2 Cor. x. 6. In fact, the whole question would be decided in your mind, if you were but led to revert in your imagination to the apostolic age; and to suppose any member of an apostolic church associated in familiar intercourse with any one put away from its fellowship as refusing to hear the divine Word. At that day, the awfulness of this wickedness was not disguised by the multitude and respectability of those who walked in it, and yet called themselves Christians. And now, I think, I shall not give you any more last words of Baxter. To the Lord I look; convinced that he alone can effectually command the scales to fall from our eyes at any time—can alone bring us into, and keep us in, that unity in which it is pleasant for brethren to dwell together.

With true affection, yours, &c.

CLXII.

TO J. L———.

Jan. 31, 1833.

My very dear Brother,—It is almost time, you will say, that I should make my appearance to you: but, indeed, I rather expected to have ***disappeared*** before this. Silent as I have been, I have had you daily in my remembrance. Blessed be the father of mercies, that we can say—" now is our salvation nearer than when we believed." Rom. xiii. 11. Yet a little while and we shall see Him in whose presence is the fulness of joy. Oh! the grace that causes ***sinners***—instead of flying from his presence—to draw near to Him now as to their God and Father, and to look forward with well-assured confidence to the approaching period of their being with him for ever: and, alas! for those who are searching about themselves for something to warrant that confidence.

My bodily infirmities and trials continue unabated; but I may well say, in the view of them—" I know, O Lord, that thy judgments are right; and that thou in very faithfulness hast caused me to be troubled." You have, probably, heard that I am likely to leave my bones here. Indeed, since I came over, I have not, at any time, had sufficient strength to return—if I would.

That this paper may not be altogether worthless, I will fill the remainder of it with some brief notes of observation on Ps. v. 8, 9. You will be at no loss to enlarge them. In verse 8, David speaks of his ***enemies***, and in the next verse he gives a ***description*** of them. Now, the apostle, in Rom. iii. 13, quotes this as a description—divinely authentic—of *all* men, " both Jews and Gentiles," as all under sin and enemies of God. And this must satisfy any, who submit to the interpretation of the psalm by the spirit of truth, that David uttered it as a prophet by the spirit of Christ that was in him, and described the enemies of Christ—" For he that hateth me, hateth my Father also." John xv. 23. So, then, we need not look abroad to find owners for the character given in the psalm. The word of Him who knows what is in us points it at each of us with a " thou art the man." 2 Sam. xii. Now this our hostility to God's anointed, and to the true God, is manifested in our aversion to the truth as it is in Jesus, and in our attachment to all the various lies that corrupt and oppose it; so that ***no man*** can say that Jesus is the Lord, but by the Holy Ghost, 1 Cor. xii. 3; and "whosoever believes that Jesus is the Christ, is ***born of God***." Well—but, now that we ***have been*** born of God, 1 John v. 1, surely our character is changed! ***Our own*** not a whit. We are, indeed, new creatures in Christ Jesus: and the mind of the spirit of life in Him is opposite to that of the flesh, or our own mind; and the unchanged character of the latter appears in our continued "*bent* to back-sliding" from God—the true God; and this in our continual readiness to depart from the simplicity and purity of the gospel of Christ,—to let slip the faith, and turn aside to some deceitful hope and false Christ, adapted to the new character in which we view ourselves. And is not this our continued disposition to depart from the faith proved by this—that he who keepeth the feet of his saints keeps them *by his power* through faith unto salvation? Is this any *needless* expenditure of Almighty power? I must have done.

May 6, 1833.—Well, my brother, you find I am still living—groaning in this tabernacle. To depart and be with Christ would be far, far better. But our times are in his hands whose we are. It is very *trying* to live a useless and cumbersome log: but my proud heart may need that lesson. I trust the *fire* burns in this town. How wonderful is it that it remains unextinguished in such a world! It is the wonderful work of God. Lifeless as I am, I shall rejoice to hear good tidings of you, and those with you.

My love be with you all.

Oct. 2, 1833.—In brotherly affection and sincerity I frankly tell you, that I never received a communication from you with less satisfaction than your last; you seem to have written in a fit of *spleen*. The —— church is, indeed, very poor in members, gifts, circumstances, &c., but if you mean the Spirit, by your *animus*, I have every comfortable confidence that *it* has *not* departed from them. Torpid and despicable as the body appears to you, they have witnessed among them, within the last year, some of the wondrous goings of the Lord in his sanctuary: among these I reckon the re-union of one to their fellowship (along with his wife), who manifested his being brought to the mind of the truth at the free sacrifice of two hundred pounds yearly.

What there is to justify you in predicting that the —— body may be expected in the long run to sink, or in apprehending that they unscripturally undervalue *human instruments*, I know not. I confess, I see more reason to apprehend that they overvalued me; and I am sure we are all too ready to forget that divine principle—"man liveth not by *bread* alone, but by every word that proceedeth out of the mouth of God." Mat. iv. 4. If we are warranted to regard a certain *end* as desirable, we cannot be justified in neglecting any instituted means for attaining it; while we, at the same time, recollect that God alone "giveth the increase," &c. But if He see fit to put all ordinary *means* out of our reach, their removal affords no ground at all for shaking our confidence in looking to Him to do his own work. And, to teach us this lesson, does he not often employ instruments the most unlikely? Witness, the widow-woman of Sarepta—the ravens—the reduction of Gideon's men to three hundred, &c. &c. I should consider it quite according to the Lord's ordinary dealings with his people, if he were to make that despised church in ——— distinguished among the churches for the prosperity which he gives. That is a very remarkable word in Jer. xxx. 17, "*because* they called thee," &c.

CLXIII.

TO R. M. B———, ESQ.

Jan. 10, 1833.

Sir,—Whether you will condescend, or can find leisure, to read this letter or any of the printed pieces which I take the liberty of sending you, I am very uncertain. But some passages in three of your publications, which I have lately read—(your letter to the Archbishop of York, and two sermons)—have excited in me an interest which constrains me to make the attempt, if so be it may please God to bless it, for engaging your attention to some points of divine truth, on which you appear at present to be astray; but astray in common with the great mass of religious professors in these countries. You will not be surprised at my writing with all plainness and simplicity, for I write on subjects, on which, if I sought to please men, I should not be a servant of Christ.

You see *something* of the Antichristian character of all *state-religion*, of all attempts to incorporate the kingdom of Christ with the kingdoms of the world. (On this subject I send you a short pamphlet, which I published many years ago.) But you more than once express yourself, as if you conceive that the *soi-disant* church of England may yet become a true church of Christ by an entire disconnection from the state, and some other improvements in her constitution, discipline, liturgy, &c.

This idea arises partly from inattention to the scriptural meaning of the phrase, "a church of Christ;" namely, an assembly of the Christians of any place, coming together on the first day of the week to *break bread*, and walking together in the fellowship of the Gospel as fellow-heirs of the grace of life. In this view it is obviously nonsense to talk of the *church* of *England:* and so far as the phrase has any meaning, it *must* have an unscriptural meaning. Accordingly, we never meet in Scripture with such an expression as, "the *church* of *Judæa*," but, "the *churches* of Christ that were in Judæa," &c. 1 Thess. ii. 14. Now, it has long been one of Satan's devices to give a currency to the words of Scripture in an unscriptural sense: and it is an evil, which a disciple in his right mind will abhor.

But the idea which I have marked is obviously connected in your mind with another deep error: namely, an admiration of the *clerical* character, when the clergyman is devout, zealous, and *evangelical*. Such men you view as ministers of Christ, and almost *semi-apostles*. But stare not, when I assert that the distinction between *clergy* and *laity* is essentially Antichristian, and indeed one of the main pillars supporting the edifice of the man of sin. You are somewhat aware how high the *superior* orders of clergy have carried their pretensions. The blasphemous titles assumed by the pope of Rome go but little beyond the profane arrogance of our English bishops, in styling themselves "*successors of the apostles* in the government of the church." *Successors* of the Apostles! Well do they approve themselves legitimate ministers of *him*, who puts himself forward as having *succeeded* to the throne of the king of Zion. And from the prime ministers of Antichrist all the inferior orders of *clergy* receive their ordination—their appointment to their *sacred* function! But let us forget for a moment the obviously foul source whence they derive it; and consider the *clerical function* itself in the most moderate form of its pretensions. The clergy are a distinct caste, assuming to possess a peculiar or exclusive right to preach sermons, and *administer* Christian ordinances to the *laity*: insomuch that these ordinances are supposed to be deficient in *validity*, unless administered by one of the corps wearing black regimentals. As to the preaching or hearing of *sermons*, I shall only say at present that it forms no part at all of the objects for which a Christian church comes together on the first day of the week: and that, if any member of it should attempt to preach a sermon to the rest, his brethren, holding fast the word, would immediately consider him a subject of reproof and discipline. Then, as to Christian ordinances—for instance, the supper of the Lord —do the words of the divine institution convey the slightest intimation of an administrator of the bread and of the wine? "This do in remembrance of me," saith the Lord. 'No, no!' say the clergy; 'presume not to do it, unless ye have among you one of the clerical caste, to *consecrate the elements*, and administer them to you.'

But some will still urge—had not the Apostolic churches *elders*, or bishops, who were specially charged with the watchful oversight and diligent feeding of the flock? Yes, indeed, they commonly had. These were among the gifts given to his churches by their great head of old, and still given according to his sovereign will. But it is utterly false that these servants of a Christian church were ordinarily coeval with the church; and still more grossly false that they *were any thing like* clergymen, either in their origin or in their office. It appears evident from Acts xiv. that the first churches, as planted by the apostles, were commonly for some time without elders: and indeed, in the nature of the thing, it is evident that a church must ordinarily be going on for some time as a church in Christian fellowship, before it can be proved which of the brethren possess the qualifications needful for the eldership. But in the course of their walking together as churches of the saints, in the observance of all the ordinances delivered to them by the apostles, teaching and admonishing one another, and building up each other in their most holy faith; in the course of such a walk, one and another of the brethren appeared distinguished by "aptness to teach," and the other characters marked in the Epistles to Timothy and Titus. Such persons, according to the apostolic direction, were acknowledged by the church, and recognized as the gifts of the Lord, as raised up for taking the lead of them in the way, and watching over them in it. But the week after one of them was thus called to the elder's office, did he turn aside from the course he had pursued before? Did he cease speaking in the meeting of the brethren *as* he had heretofore spoken, and commenced *preaching a sermon?* or did he attempt to lord it over his brethren, so as not to allow them to keep the ordinances of the Lord, unless he were present to give them *validity* by his administration? But I must hasten to another topic; only adding on this, that they know not the real nature of an elder's office, who suppose that the main exercise of it takes place in the meeting of the church; and that none can comprehend the real nature of a christian church, but those who are given the knowledge of that divine truth, which is the one bond and object of its union.

The subject to which I now pass is of paramount importance, from its immediate connexion with that truth: I mean the notions you have imbibed, concerning the supposed *progressive conversion* of a sinner, through a long course of spiritual exercises and *convictions*, issuing in what is considered as justifying faith. It was in the second of your sermons—(containing just animadversions on Mr. Irving's pretensions)—that I noticed this sentiment; but I cannot quote any of the passages containing it, having returned your publications to the person from whom I borrowed them. It appeared to me from that sermon, that, since your first appearance in print, your ear has been gained by some of the clergy of the high Calvinistic class, and that they have succeeded too well in cramming you with their false theology. (Here I would beg leave to refer to the "*Remarks* corrective," &c. Article xi. on Hebr. ii. 9.) However this may be, nothing is more certain than that all such views of a sinner's conversion to God are utterly opposed to the real conversions we read of in the apostolic word. In these—(see, for instance, Acts xi. 21. xiii. 48. xiv. 1. xvii. 4. xxviii. 24.)—a sinner, dead in sins, heard the glad tidings of the salvation of God, preached to all indiscriminately; he heard and believed the divine report, and was thereby *converted* (or turned from darkness to light, and from the powers of Satan to the living God.) He at once had "wisdom, and righteousness, and sanctification, and redemption." He was complete in Christ, having passed from death unto life; and was led "walking in Christ as he had received him." His conscience was purged from guilt and dead works, by the blood once shed for the forgiveness of sin: it was "purified by faith;" not left for a series of weeks, or months, or years, groaning for deliverance from guilt, and for a participation in Christ. Those who are thus exercised, may be persuaded by their spiritual guides that they are spiritually exercised, and in a hopeful way of attaining to what they pant after. But they are under the power of unbelief, and blindly led by blind guides. No doubt, while life is spared, it may be that the mercy of God, against which they are fighting, may apprehend and overcome them: but, if not, righteous will be their condemnation, for rejecting the counsel of God against themselves, for disbelieving the record which *He* hath given of his son.

According to the Scriptures, there is no ***intermediate*** class between believers and unbelievers. The former are children of the light and of the day: for that divine truth, which they believe, discovers the distinguishing glory of "*the only true God*," as at once just and the justifier of the ***ungodly***, through the redemption that is in Christ Jesus. This is that law of the Lord which has gone forth out of Zion; which "***converteth*** the soul, maketh wise the simple; *rejoiceth* the heart, and enlighteneth the eyes." (Ps. xix.) As to those who disbelieve it, they remain asleep, and under the power of darkness, whatever religious dreams may occupy them, either painfully or joyfully, in that sleep of death.

But this view of conversion obviously strikes at the root of the clerical trade, and the whole of their occupation, and zealous bustling about the *training* of souls for God. No marvel that the clergy are so loud in their outcries against the impious heresy, against the "sect everywhere spoken against." But the temple at Jerusalem "was built of stone, made ready before it was brought thither; so that there was neither hammer, nor axe, nor any tool of iron heard in the house, while it was in building." (1 Kings vi.) And vain is all the hammering of the preachers to build a spiritual house with lifeless stones. (1 Pet. ii. 5.) I the less regret my inability at present to prosecute this all-important subject, because it enters more or less into all the printed pieces, which I *hope* will be forwarded to you with this letter. I shall not extend its unreasonable length by offering any apology. None will be needful, if the Lord bless it. If not, none would be sufficient. Should you have any curiosity to know who it is that addresses you, I just say that I was for many years a fellow of Dublin College, and a clergyman; that many years ago I renounced the clerical character in every shade and modification of it; that I have since had the comfort of walking in the fellowship of the Gospel with several little companies of disciples in Ireland, and a few in Great Britain, among whom, however, I hold not any office of elder or deacon; that, after residing for the last twelve years in London, I now find myself likely to spend the remainder of my days in this my native land; and that, under many infirmities, and that old age, which "*ipsa est morbus*," I am waiting in peaceful expectation of my change, and of the coming glory. Meantime I should receive any lines addressed to me at ———. I can but subscribe myself yours, with every best wish,

CLXIV.

TO A. B——.

——, 1833.

My dear A——,—When you were here, a few evenings ago, you found me rather backward to talk upon some matters into which you and —— were dashing. That arose partly from my being frightened by an appearance of eagerness, that seemed to me like the beginning of a fight, to which I was quite unequal, and every way indisposed—partly from my thinking that the little I did say was not minded—and partly from an inclination for a game of chess with E——. Do you recollect that, on your expressing your judgment that the brotherly admonition enjoined in 2 Thess. iii. 15. could not be any admonition from the church after the idler was removed from their fellowship, I briefly, but distinctly, remarked that in this opinion I decidedly concurred? Yet you seemed to me to go on as if I lent my authority to the interpretation I disclaimed. I well recollect, that I had formerly countenanced it in the "Apostolic Traditions;" but I was as clear in my recollection that, in some of my subsequent publications, I have stated what I could for correcting the error. Unable, however, on the moment, to refer to the place where my recantation might be found, I said no more. I have since found it in the "Letters on Primitive Christianity," (vol. i. 392.) It is couched in language rather needlessly strong, and certainly leaves no room for any one to quote me as supporting the idea of admonition continued after removal from the fellowship. Look also at my language in—(Vol. i. 373, 390.) If you have not a copy of that piece, I have one or more at your service. But I confess to you, that I rather wonder that any should debate the question with much *earnestness;* for I do not see that, in the nature of things, the idea which I have given up as erroneous can affect the practice. If any still adhere to that interpretation, do you find them more engaged than others in renewing their admonition of the person removed? As to the church collectively renewing it, that is obviously impossible; and the epistle is addressed to a church. I am grieved to hear that any among us should take occasion from this matter, to hold a language representing us as at unscriptural variance among ourselves in any matter of faith or practice. It is a language obviously calculated to stumble the weak and rejoice the adversaries. But I do trust that it is not founded in fact; and the faithful Lord will make good his word, that no weapon formed against his church shall prosper. To His blessed keeping I commend you and yours.

Your attached brother,

LETTERS ON VARIOUS SUBJECTS.

CLXV.

TO THE EDITOR OF THE LITERARY GAZETTE.

June 8, 1822.

Sir,—A friend has just pointed out to me an article in your last Number (headed *An Irish Lexicographer*), in which you make yourself and your readers merry at my expense; because, in the Lexicon subjoined to my Selections from Lucian, I interpret διαιτασθαι "to live," while the only passage in the work where the word occurs, is one in which οἱ νεκροι (the *dead*, or the *shades*) are described in the other world as διαιτωμενοι κατα εθνη, "*living* classed according to their tribes," &c. You are pleased to mark the interpretation of "*dead* people *living*," &c. as "a tolerably fair *Hibernicism*."

If it be, sir, give me leave to say that the Hibernicism is not mine, but Lucian's: and that it is Lucian's not only in this passage, but throughout all his *Dialogues of the Dead*; and even embodied in the very title, νεκρικοι διαλογοι. Any one the most moderately acquainted with that author knows, that he describes the *dead*, or those who have done with this life, as possessing a kind of existence in another life, about the nature and reality of which, however, he betrays (as was natural) the most complete scepticism. And although the defence of my *Hibernicism* may afford you additional matter of merriment, I must confess that I see *no blunder* in the idea of the *dead living* in another world.

If your objection be to the accuracy of my interpretation of the word διαιτασθαι, I would invite you to propose your own. In the meantime I assert, that "to live," in that sense which the English expression often bears, of *following a certain course of life*, is the proper meaning of the Greek verb: a meaning which is sufficiently ascertained by the two compounds given in the same *Hibernian* Lexicon, ενδιαιτασθαι and μεταδιαιτασθαι: as well as supported by all the standard lexicographers, not *Irish*, who interpret the word by *vitam degere;* and still more decisively authenticated by the following examples, out of many others which I could adduce:—Thucyd. l. ii. c. 14 and 52. Xen. Memor. l. i. c. 6. l. ii. c. 8. l. iii. extr. Soph. Œd. Col. v. 760.

Yours being the first notice taken by an English journalist of any of my publications, classical or scientific; and this notice being marked (I freely say) with characters of great ignorance, unfairness, and illiberality, I appeal from Philip drunk to Philip sober, and depend on the candour and justice of your second thoughts, for the insertion of this vindication *in your next number;* though I am aware that an *Irish* scholar may think himself flattered, when he is even made the whetstone for sharpening the wit of an English reviewer. However, as I have removed my residence to this country, it is to be hoped that, under the influence of your atmosphere and critical animadversions, I shall gradually be divested of my *Hibernicisms;* and shall also learn that courtesy to strangers, for which your countrymen are distinguished.

I am, Sir,
Your Irish Lexicographer.

CLXVI.

TO THE EDITOR OF THE ECLECTIC REVIEW.

April 21, 1823.

Sir,—A few days ago I met with the passage in the last Number of your Review, in which you do me the honour of introducing me and my religious sentiments to the notice of the public. I met with it accidentally, for I cannot declare myself a constant reader of your work; and how often I may have heretofore figured in your papers I know not. You are pleased to amuse yourself and your readers with my "absurdities," my "almost facetious reasoning," my "Hibernian logic," &c. I confess that I do not consider it altogether fair to let off merely such incidental squibs, against one who has been for so many years publishing his sentiments on scriptural subjects. If you think that my sentiments are false, and that you can refute them, why do you not directly review any of my publications in which they are asserted? I send you copies of two or three of them, that you may not plead ignorance of their existence. Meanwhile, I trust that your feelings, as professedly a gentleman and a man of letters, (to say nothing more) will lead you to give a place to the following brief remarks on the passage, in which you hold me up to the ridicule of your readers. It is rather unfair, either to adduce a quotation from my writings, without referring to the work in which it is to be found, or to mark words as a quotation from my writings, which are no where to be found in them. Yet you have done this, I am sure; though I readily admit that an argument, substantially similar to that which you borrow from me, occurs in some of my theological pieces: I cannot now exactly say in which. Passing this, I come, in the next place, to the reasoning which you mark as so absurd, Hibernian logic, &c. And pardon me—(as a blundering Hibernian)—for avowing my unaltered conviction, that the reasoning is most simple, clear, and conclusive. I have long contended with those that you term Sandemanians, and against the popular divines, that the scriptural meaning of *faith in Christ* is merely *believing the testimony* contained in the scriptures concerning Christ; in that simple sense of the word *believing*, which supersedes all inquiry into the thing to be understood by *faith*, while it leaves open the grand inquiry into the divine testimony which is sent into the world "for the obedience of faith." I have maintained this in opposition to all the views which represent faith as some mysterious work, act, or exercise of the mind, which a sinner, yet unbelieving, is called to perform, instructed to perform, and exhorted to exert himself for its due performance; and I admit, sir, that I have been so absurd as to argue, that those who maintain any such views of faith as the latter, are but deceiving themselves and others, in asserting (as they often do) that a sinner is not *justified by works*, or by something that he does. For the life of me, I cannot distinguish between a work done, and an act done, by the sinner; such is the hebetude of my Hibernian intellect. Indeed, the only difference between you, for instance, and the greatest advocates for justification by works, seems plainly to me to be this—that you conceive the thing to be done for justification in the sight of God is a *mental* act, while others conceive it to be what is called, in common parlance, an outward good life. Now, sir, it is very easy for an anonymous writer in a review to assert, that this reasoning is "almost facetious, meant to turn the whole subject of justification by works into ridicule, that it hardly deserves a serious answer," &c. &c. But let me observe to you, that such assertions are no argument, though perhaps the most successful way of opposing truth. The more absurd my reasoning is, the more easily may it be exposed by fair reasoning. I invite you to the attempt: but I suspect you will find it too hard for you. I am the more confirmed in this suspicion, by observing the little scrap of Eclectic logic which you condescend to employ against my "Hibernian logic." You say—"the reasoner would hardly deny, that *hearing* is an act of the mind." It must amuse you greatly to be told, that I do seriously deny it. In *hearing*, there is an impression made on my bodily organs and conveyed to my mind: but in receiving that impression, I have learned from Mr. Locke—(who, I suppose, was of Irish extraction)—that I am perfectly *passive*—that I cannot help receiving it, and cannot alter or modify it. Your logic may have taught you otherwise. But pardon me for requesting, that you will forbear the exercise of your *active* powers, the next time a pistol is fired off by your ear, and try not to hear it. You seem, indeed, to have had some misgiving about the assertion, that hearing is an *act* of the mind; for you immediately subjoin, *listening*, as if the two things were equivalent. In listening, sir, the mind is active, in so far as we endeavour to dispose our organs so as to catch the sound. Yet even then, in hearing the sound, I do assert that the mind does nothing. As to the Reverend James Carlisle's remarks on my sentiments, it would be very easy to expose the sophistry and misrepresentation on which they proceed: and perhaps I may some time or another take occasion to do so. But I confess I have never yet looked at his book, though I was informed on its first appearance, that he had done me the honour of attacking me.

I am, Sir, yours, &c.

CXLVII.

TO SIR W. C. S———.

March 22, 1827.

Mr. P—— is described in the late debate upon the Irish question as declaring his opinion that a *religious establishment is necessary in every country for the existence of religion.* I cannot think that a man who is of that mind has at heart any religion. He must conceive that all religion is the creature of the state, *i. e.* is a human invention. The religion of such a statesman is the religion of the state, whatever that be;—or, in other words, is no religion, but a political contrivance originating in the wisdom of man, and dependant on his pleasure. Yet, though legislators think this very conducive to the good order and decorous conduct of society, and while they are encouraged to cherish the notion by the priests of all classes whom they employ in such worldly religion, I am satisfied that there is nothing which more effectually in the end propagates irreligion among the people; for they must, sooner or later, see through the inconsistency and hollowness of the contrivance. With the *policy* or *impolicy* of the thing, however, I have nothing to do—except that I cannot view with indifference the national calamities of which it has been—is—and will be, the fruitful source. Is it not one of the striking evidences of the divine origin of scriptural Christianity, that it is utterly incapable of being made a state-religion? and the truth of this position, as a Christian, I must maintain against Mr. P—— and the whole hierarchy of England and Rome. Not only every religion that has been incorporated with the state, but every religion that is capable, under any supposable circumstances, of such incorporation, is essentially distinct from the religion of Him, whose kingdom is not of this world; and however it may pass current under the same name and many of the adopted forms, it is at best a good forgery. There was once, under a really divine revelation, a perfect incorporation (so to speak) of church and state. It was under the Jewish theocracy; and that dispensation is continually spoken of in the New Testament scriptures as earthly—and but a shadow of the heavenly things revealed in the gospel, (Heb. ix. 1. 23. and throughout). That dispensation has passed away, and the declaration of the Messiah is, "Now (νυν δε) is my kingdom not from hence." (John xviii. 36.) Instead of being supported by human power and human legislation, it is continually opposed by them as far as they interfere with the matter at all; and but that the kingdom is his, and that the gates of hell shall not prevail against it, the spurious antichristian systems, which human policy supports, would long since have abolished Christianity from the earth. Thus, the only true religion not only needs not political support, but is absolutely incapable of receiving it: and as to false religion, really, statesmen need not be at the trouble of providing it for the people. There is no danger but that sinful men, under the workings of a guilty conscience, will frame plenty of it for themselves. When will worldly rulers have sufficient common sense to confine themselves to their proper province, the affairs of this life?

CLXVIII.

TO THE EDITOR OF THE TIMES.

——, 1827.

Sir,—Great a quantity of nonsense as I read daily in the newspapers, without ever thinking of vainly interposing my finger to stem the torrent—(you cannot suspect me of intimating that any of the nonsense comes from you)—there is that in an article which appeared in the Times of last Saturday, the wickedness and stupid sophistry of which tempts me to try whether you will admit a brief exposure of it. I allude to the letter from one who assumes that *pye-bald designation*, "another *English Roman Catholic;*" and as I do not think a newspaper the best or most suitable vehicle for theological controversy, I shall confine my remarks to the last sentence of his letter; "With respect to the religion of the primitive Christians, if it was not the Roman Catholic, at any rate it could not be Protestant, for it was only two or three years ago that they themselves were celebrating, in different places, the third centenary of their existence as a religious body, which *proves* that twelve centuries must have elapsed since the close of the Pagan persecutions and the commencement of their religion." This is the old argument newly dished up, of which the papists make so much use, and which has been a thousand times sufficiently answered. But let us look at it a little in its new dress. The religion of the Protestants *cannot* be that of the primitive Christians, because Protestantism is little more than three centuries old. Now, I admit that disease must have existed, before restoration to health is effected: but, it seems a queer inference that, therefore, disease has more of antiquity to recommend it than health. No doubt, the antichristian corrupters of popery preceded all that *protestation* against them, from which Protestants derive their name. But it will require more jesuitical sophistry than your correspondent possesses, to prove that these abominable corruptions therefore formed a part of *primitive* Christianity, or that Protestants have not returned to the latter so far as they departed from the former. The letter-writer seems, indeed, to be in some degree sensible of this, for in the latter part of the sentence he slily shifts his ground from *primitive* Christianity, and the authentic documents of it founded in the apostolic writings, to the period when the Pagan persecutions had ceased; no doubt, in order to involve us in the mist of his traditions, and in many of the corruptions which at that period had confessedly been introduced. I shall not notice that many of the Popish corruptions were long subsequent even to that period. But I protest altogether against that as the period of *primitive* Christianity. The contemptible and absurd dishonesty of the passage is only equalled by its effrontery. Whether the Protestants, at the time of the Reformation, threw off all the corruptions of Popery, is quite a distinct question; upon which this is not the proper occasion for avowing my opinion. But this I say, that those who have but yesterday returned to any point of Christ's truth or practice, from which there has been an antichristian departure, can be at no loss to defend themselves against the Popish argument on the ground of antiquity. I confess, that I have long leaned in my judgment to the opinion, that it would be expedient to grant the Papists all that they at present claim under the absurd name of *Catholic emancipation*. (His majesty has many good Protestant subjects who need *emancipation* more than the papists, and have sounder claims to it.) Not that I have any idea of their being contented with obtaining what they ask at present: but because I have thought it foolish to afford them a specious pretext for their discontent, by withholding what may be much more safely conceded than many things which they have already obtained. But, when I observe the high tone which they begin to assume even in this country, I own that I am almost led to hesitate (perhaps foolishly) about the expediency of any further concessions. I have been long aware, however, of that character of Popery, that she can assume every variety of appearance according to the purpose to be served. Like Virgil's Alecto, she can, one moment, present herself as a pitiable weak old woman, and the next moment disclose her expanding dimensions on the affrighted gaze, in all the terrors of a damning fury.

Yours, &c.

P.S. In using the terms Papist and Popery, I really do not wish to give needless offence to those, whom I rather regard with compassion. I know not why the terms should offend any who acknowledge the Pope of Rome as Christ's vicegerent upon earth. I cannot sacrifice truth by calling them Catholics, nor the common propriety of language by calling them Roman Catholics.

CLXVIII.

TO THE EDITOR OF THE MORNING HERALD.

Sir,—Please to admit into your widely circulated paper a few plain remarks from a plain man, on the strange kind of fracas which occurred a few days ago in the *soi-disant* church of ——. It has always appeared to me a strange inconsistency in those same freethinking Christians (as they term themselves) at once to protest against the marriage ceremony enjoined by the Ecclesiastical Establishment of this country, and to apply to one of its priests to perform that ceremony for them; nor can I, for the life of me, reconcile this with the high pretensions those men commonly make to peculiar *rationality* in their religious principles and practice. But I can as little reconcile it to the plea of conscientiousness on which they ground their protest. Whatever a Christian scruples in his conscience, (*i. e.* considers contrary to the divine will) that thing no human power, and no earthly inducement, can justify him in doing. Let us suppose that the laws of heathen Rome had made it necessary to the legality of marriage, that the contracting parties should offer a sacrifice to Jupiter through the intervention of one of his priests; what would have been thought in the apostolic age of a Christian man and woman who should apply to the priest to make this sacrifice for them, and while they joined in it by throwing incense on the altar, should gravely, at the same time, deliver a written protest against the act? What could, reasonably, be said of them, but that their protest condemned them under their own hands, for doing deliberately, and with their eyes open, that which they knew they ought not to do. Would Christians be authorized to abjure Christianity, if they lived under a government whose laws would not recognize the legal validity of the nuptial relation between Christians, nor the legitimacy of their offspring? But, I must now add, that the plea embodied in the protest delivered by these free-thinking gentlemen is absolutely false, namely, that they cannot in this country have their marriages made legal without employing the antichristian means which they resort to. The parties who desire to have their marriage legalized without religious rites, need only pass into any part of North Britain, and there declare before any competent witnesses that they receive each other as man and wife. This, followed by cohabitation, constitutes a marriage as valid, according to the laws of England, as if it had been celebrated by the Archbishop of Canterbury in *pontificalibus*. And this is so well known that I can scarcely persuade myself that these freethinkers are ignorant of it. If they urge the trouble and expense of going to Scotland on the occasion, it only shews at what a low price they hold their consciences. And now, sir, let me not be misunderstood. I assert, with these men, the essentially civil nature of the marriage contract. Christians, indeed, can have no doubt about that, when they find by the scriptures of the New Testament, that the marriage relation may subsist in binding obligation between a Christian and a heathen (who can have no religious union). I join them, also, in protesting against the usurpation of a priestly character by the clergy, against their altars, &c. &c. I do hope that our legislators will yet see the absurdity and impolicy of imposing any religious ceremonies on his Majesty's subjects, in order to legalize their marriages; and will yet allow us to go before a magistrate on the occasion, after a sufficiently public notification of our intention; and on payment of a certain fee, to be entitled to a certificate and registry of our marriage. I expect that this will yet be allowed, because I look for the progressive emancipation of civil governments throughout Europe from ecclesiastical bondage. However slowly old prejudices are discarded, yet the present course of events is calculated to force corrected principles on the attention of our rulers, while they see priestly domination threatening the overthrow of the Bourbon dynasty both in France and Spain, as well as the dismemberment of Ireland from the British empire. In the mean time, I must say that there are others who have much stronger claims on the legislature for relief in the business of marriage than the so-called Unitarians; and yet they are those who consistently evidence, that it is against their consciences as Christians to employ the clergy for the celebration of their marriages, by quietly submitting to all the inconvenience and hardship of not doing so.

CLXIX.

TO THE SAME.

Sept. 13, 1830.

Mr. Editor,—In your paper of the 8th inst. my attention was attracted by the report of proceedings at a meeting in Cheltenham, of friends of the "Society for Promoting the Religious Principles of the Reformation." Will you afford room in your impartial and very respectable columns for a few grave reflections which the account suggested to me? It was obviously drawn up by one of the gentlemen who made Protestant speeches on the occasion, and who, on that day, had the field to themselves.

But I would remark to them, that the most important principle of the Reformation, as far as I know, was in the manly appeal then made to the Sacred Scriptures, as the only—the sufficient—and the infallible rule of Christian faith and practice; and from this principle, however they may talk of it, there is decisive evidence that Mr. Digby and his coadjutors have departed. If he, for instance, were indeed a hearty friend to that principle, he would not at this day be a priest in the national establishment; that politico-religious system, which its own sons acknowledge to be necessarily and intrinsically a corruption of Christianity. Archdeacon Paley's confession of this, as quoted lately by Mr. Brougham in the House of Commons, must be fresh in the recollection of your readers.

At the time of the Reformation, the light of Scripture broke in upon the foul abominations of the Papal See; and led multitudes to forsake that Antichristian communion. But the Reformers were men —and we cannot, therefore, wonder that they left t e work of reformation imperfect; and retained some sentiments and practices which are opposed to scriptural purity and truth. Among all such instances, there was not one more inconsistent with both, than that unnatural coalition between the *soi-disant* Church and State, which worldly policy led them to adopt and sanction—that coalition, which is plainly stigmatized in the language of prophecy, as fornication committed with the kings of the earth, by "the mother of harlots" and her daughters; which would confound "the things that are Cæsar's," with "the things that are God's;" and pretends to incorporate with the kingdoms of the world that kingdom, which its Divine head declares to be "not of this world."

Those who continue their adherence to such corrupt religious systems, acknowledged by themselves to be corrupt, are not real friends to that which I have marked as the grand principle of the Reformation. If they could, they would arrest the progress of that scriptural light, which exposes the corruptions they wish to screen. But they cannot. The sentence pronounced against "the man of sin," in 2 Thess. ii. 8, shall be fully executed.

Mr. D. had considerable hardihood in mentioning, however slightly and darkly, the "discipline among the members" of a Christian church, "which the New Testament inculcates and requires." Will Mr. D. venture to say that any such discipline either does subsist, or could subsist, in what he calls his church? Nay; he knows well that it would not be "pract cable." He is no stranger to Rosenmüller's admission of this in his Commentary on Matt. xviii. 17.* But is that a Christian church, in which obedience to the express commands of Christ is impracticable? In the Liturgy for that Papistical fast, Ash Wednesday, the framers of it make the priest read to his congregation a grave lament for the non-existence among them of the old godly discipline. Now, if a plain man among his hearers were afterwards to propose this question: "And pray, your reverence, why should we not have among us that discipline of which you lament the want?" What must be the answer but, substantially, this? "O! we could not, without the

* Hæc publica admonitio non poteat habere locum nisi in cœtu minore, ne speciem quidem auctoritatis civilis præ se ferente, seque ipsum e Christi præceptis liberrime gubernante. In statum ecclesiæ externum et civilem, qui apud nos est, hæc disciplinæ Christianæ pars parum convenit.—He might have added, with equal truth, "Nec ulla quidem alia."

leave of the king and parliament." But really the wickedness of waiting for the permission of men to obey the commands of God, is only equalled by the hypocrisy of lamenting that this permission is not afforded. But I ought to recollect that Mr. D. designates his "true Catholic and visible church," as "the widowed spouse of CHRIST;" and that since he considers her former husband as defunct, he naturally considers her at liberty to be married to another. Rom. vii. 2, 3.

Afraid of encroaching unreasonably on your indulgence, I leave, for the present, Mr. D. and the "Society for promoting the Principles of the Reformation:" but would beg leave to add a brief remark or two connected with the subject of state-religion. If it were politic for earthly governments to interfere at all with the concerns of another world, by incorporating any religious system with the state, it would assuredly be their policy to adopt some religious system, as unlike as possible to the Christian. And, in this view, it might be recommended to our statesmen, if it were not too late, to return to Popery, or, what would be substantially the same thing, to form an amicable coalition between the two churches, the mother and the daughter. But, happily for Christians, any such attempt is now too late. Statesmen are therefore finding it their wisdom to loosen the connection between the so-called church and the state; and I doubt not that they will, at length, find it their wisdom to dissolve it. They will find that the things of this world are the proper province of the rulers of this world, and that in attempting to legislate about the concerns of another world, and to provide for the souls of their people, they have cumbered themselves with a burden which they are not called to bear. Is it not, indeed, a "cumbersome stone," the weight of which is obviously pulling down almost all the governments of Europe? What else has dethroned Charles X.? What else is precipitating to their ruin the other branches of the Bourbon dynasty?

And look at the kind of religion which is incorporated with the state? When his Most Christian Majesty, the other day, deliberately perjured himself, and violated the Constitutional Charter which he had solemnly sworn to maintain, who were the prime movers that instigated him to this act of wickedness and infatuation? Priests of the state religion and priest-ridden ministers. It is not long since an Hon. Baronet, in our House of Commons, ludicrously expressed a wish to see a Jesuit, to see some specimen of the breed of animals of which he had heard so much. In the undeniable fact to which I have referred, I would present him with the desired specimen. How does Sir Francis like it?

And is there any essential difference between what was, a few weeks ago, the state-religion of France, and what is now the state-religion of this country? To be satisfied that there is not, we need only look at the celebrated article, on "M. Cottu's Necessity of a Dictatorship," in the late Quarterly Review. There—in a publication professedly the champion of Church and State, and of all the religion that priests put forward as excellent—the hope was avowed, that the King of France might succeed in the measures, which the writer acknowledged to be "a virtual abolition of the Charter;" and a work, which is a kind of recognized organ of our Protestant Hierarchy, urged on his Most Christian Majesty to the same perjury, which his Popish confessor recommended as an acceptable service to God!

One word more, and I have done. After such notorious instances of royal perjury as our day exhibits, can our legislature continue insensible to the utter futility of promissory oaths, as binding men's consciences? And in a country, where one of our legal fictions represents Christianity as a part and parcel of the law of the land, will our legislators—in contempt of Christ's plain command, and without any public advantage—continue to impose and enforce the practice of swearing?

CLXX.

TO ONE OF THE PUBLIC PAPERS.

Sir,—I shall be obliged by your giving the following observations a place in your widely circulated paper, if the signature, under which I write, should not render them inadmissible.

My attention has been a good deal arrested by the course of cross-examination, to which Mr. ——— was subjected on a late trial, and my disgust has not been a little excited by the language, to which it has given occasion, in some of the contemporary prints. I know so much of the latitude allowed to barristers in cross-examination of a witness, that I take it for granted Mr. —— did not transgress the due limits in holding an inquisition upon Mr. ———'s religion. But I should gladly call reflecting minds to think of the reasonableness of the proceeding, and of the system with which it is connected. The testimony of a Jew or of a Gentoo is admissible in our courts of justice, and why the testimony of a native should be impeached, because he has honesty enough to avow himself a deist, is more than I can see. This no doubt is *called* a Christian country; but I am bold to say that perjury is much more common in it, than it was in the old Roman Republic among the worshippers of Jupiter; and that I should think the testimony of Cato, upon a matter of fact, as credible as that of my Lord Primate. But what I wish particularly to notice, is the surprise and horror affected by some of Mr. ———'s opponents at the discovery that he is not a believer in the Christian revelation. The innocent creatures would appear never to have heard before of such a thing as a deist in these countries, or to have heard of it only as a rare monster, against whom all the soi-disant Christians of the country should be up in arms. This hypocritical cant is obviously adopted for the purpose of stage effect, and as a Christian I desire to enter my protest against it. I should be curious indeed to know the result of cross-examination of those pious gentlemen as to their own religious faith, and should not be at all surprised—(supposing them to meet it with as much candour as Mr. ——— manifested, at least upon this point)—if it proved that they are just as sceptical as himself. Is it not notorious that multitudes throughout Christendom, the most respectable for talents, information, and integrity, are deists? very many of the legal profession, for instance, and many of the medical;—and is this a fact, that a real Christian should wish to deny or to conceal? No doubt, most of those would *qualify* (as it is called) for a good place under Government, and most of them perhaps occasionally go to church or to mass: but, though religious establishments are of course contented with such outward compliances, I could not esteem their testimony in a court of justice the more credible, on account of their dishonest inconsistencies. They would all likewise, as well as Mr. ———, be very averse to have their deistical sentiments recorded publicly on their own oaths, however freely they may communicate them in private companies; and this, from a very natural apprehension of some civil disadvantages resulting in a country where all the inhabitants, *by a fiction of law*, are considered Christians. But those who are Christians indeed know how small their number is, and must regret that the name of their divine religion should be profaned, by state policy employing it as an engine for effecting its temporal purposes.

The religion of Christ never was designed by its blessed author for a political engine; and whatever religion is employed as such, though it may bear the name of Christianity, is a thing essentially distinct. I believe the governors of the world will yet find it their interest to cut the connection between religion and the state: but ambitious ecclesiastics of all sorts have long given such currency to the notion of their necessary connexion, that I do not expect the absurd and mischievous prejudice to become extinct in my day. Of its mischievousness, this unhappy country, at least, has long afforded a striking exemplification. For it may be confidently asserted, that the great curse of Ireland has been, and is, Religion. But let not Mr. ——— confound the religion of any of its contending factions with the Christianity of the Bible. To the latter, he is not a whit more opposed than they.

CLXXI.

TO ONE OF THE PUBLIC PAPERS.

Sir,—The more I observe and reflect upon the controversy with the Papists, revived at present by the "Reformation Society," the more am I convinced that the members of the so-called church of England, or of any other politico-religious establishment, are unfit to maintain it; and this, because they cannot effectually expose the corruptions of Popery, without giving themselves a hard slap in the face. For instance, I see they have been lately discussing at Birmingham the question of the "*infallibility of the church;*" and a simple Christian, adhering to the Scriptures, would have no difficulty in refuting all the sophistry and trickeries of argument by which popish priests are trained to perplex the subject, if he only kept clearly in view, and insisted steadily on, the scriptural meaning of the term *church*. But how could this be expected from a clergyman of the establishment? He could not do so without admitting that what he calls his own church, is no church of Christ at all.

It will be admitted that the Greek word, rendered church, literally imports an assembly or congregation. Connected with this literal meaning of the word are the only two acceptations in which it is applied to Christians in the Scriptures of the New Testament. In the first place, it is applied to the whole aggregate of Christ's redeemed people, for whom he gave himself as a ransom, to whom he is the appointed "captain of their salvation" for bringing them unto glory, and who shall be all brought together or *congregated* before the throne of God in the heavenly mansions which he has gone before to prepare for them. This "*general* assembly, or church of the first born which are written in heaven," is evidently to be understood when Christ is said "to have loved the *church*, and given himself for it," as well as in all those passages of the Prophets, in which "the great congregation" is spoken of, in the midst of which he, the Redeemer, declares the name of the Lord to those whom he is not ashamed to call his brethren. (Ps. xxii. 22. Heb. ii. 10—12.) In this application, the phrase—"the church of Christ," imports an assemblage that never yet has been *visible* to the human eye, though all its component members are at once and for ever before the eye of him, to whom all things are alike present from everlasting to everlasting. In this sense of the term, to attribute visibility to the Catholic, or *general* church, is rank absurdity. It amounts to the monstrous assertion that man can discern and distinguish, not only all the real believers scattered over the earth at present, but all that have died in the faith in every antecedent age of the world, and all that are "ordained to eternal life" in the generations yet unborn. I shall by and by mark the only sense in which infallibility can be truly attributed to this church of Christ. But at present I pass on to state the second acceptation, in which the word church is to be understood in Scripture,—namely, as applied to any particular assembly of Christians coming together into one place, on the first day of the week, to "shew forth the Lord's death" in the ordinance of his supper, to "exhort and admonish one another," to maintain the discipline, and observe the other institutions delivered by the apostles to the churches of the saints; and this is obviously the meaning of the term church, when we read of the church at Jerusalem, at Corinth, at Ephesus, &c., or of the church *in the house* of such and such an individual. (Rom. xvi. 5.) Besides these two meanings, distinct indeed, but closely connected, the term church is not employed in any other meaning throughout the Scripture: and however the art of ecclesiastics has misnamed and perverted the phrase, there are few expressions in Scripture of more simple and unambiguous import. And now, when a clergyman of the establishment boasts of his *church* of England, or a Presbyterian clergyman talks of his church of Scotland, is it not manifest that they employ the word church in a way in which it is never employed in Scripture? Do they even profess that there is any assembly, in which all the Christians of England or Scotland come together on the first day of the week? No. Or can they adduce any instance from Scripture of such language as the church of Judea, the church of Galatia, or the *church* of any other *country?* I defy them to do so. Here the language always runs—The *churches* of Judea, churches of Galatia, of Asia, &c.; and, light a thing as those men may regard it, to pervert the language of divine revelation in order to give a currency to scriptural phrases in a sense utterly unscriptural, none who truly reverence the word of God can make light of it. Indeed, it is one of the arts which the father of lies has most successfully employed for overspreading Christendom with every Antichristian corruption. If one of these reformed clergymen adhered in any degree to the scriptural import of the term "a church," he would apply the name —not to the politico-religious system established by acts of Parliament in these countries—but to the *congregation* with which he assembles on Sundays. There is an assembly indeed, an ἐκκλησία— but certainly, in its constitution and its objects, utterly unlike the churches of the saints described in the New Testament; and there might be some danger of directing men's attention to this dissimilarity, if the person should talk of his *congregation* as his church. He professes, therefore, to talk of, as his church, the building of stone and mortar in which the parishioners meet to hear a sermon; a misapplication of scripture language, which is exceeded in its profaneness only by one other perversion of the term—namely, when the word church is employed to designate the clerical order in contradistinction to the so-called laity.

I would, in the next place, desire it to be remarked, that each of the Christian churches, spoken of in the New Testament, was perfectly independent of all the other churches, and subject to no authority in points of Christian faith or practice, but that of Christ himself as the one divine head of his universal church; and that the Apostles were authorized organs of declaring his will. With them Christ declared he would be to the end of the world, sanctioning their word, so that whosoever heard them, hears him, and whoso despises them, despises him. No doubt, among the several churches, while they continued to adhere to the one common rule of the Apostolic word, and so far as they were known to each other, and had opportunities of communication, there would be a brotherly intercourse, and a mutual acknowledgment of each other as sister churches: but as to the idea of any one of those churches exercising the least authority over any others of them, it is utterly contrary to every scriptural principle, and originated in nothing else than the domineering ambition of corrupt ecclesiastics. The first Christian church was that at Jerusalem, and this existed before there was any such a thing as a church of Christ at Rome. But the church at Jerusalem exercised no jurisdiction, as a metropolitan church, over the other churches in Judea, no more than the church that was afterwards planted in Rome exercised any over the other churches in Italy, or in Achaia. Each church of Christ, I repeat it, was in itself competent to every act of discipline or Christian observance directed by the Apostolic word, and this without the interference or control of any other church, and subject to no authority whatsoever but that of Christ himself. The sanction of that authority they had with them for all their course according to that Apostolic word, as really when the Apostles were absent as when they were personally present. And so it is to this very day, wherever there is a church of Christ; and thus the simplicity of scriptural principles strikes at the root of all the Antichristian pretensions of Rome and her pontiffs. But can it be expected that any of the reformed clergy should honestly employ that simplicity of divine truth against the Papists, when it equally exposes the antichristian character of their own ecclesiastical courts and canons.

Again, let it be noted that each of the Christian churches spoken of in the New Testament, was a changeable, transient, and perishable body; and that, however distinguished by the purity of Christian faith and practice at one period, there was no error in faith or corruption in practice that might not be introduced into it. What has become of the church that was at Jerusalem, or that was at Smyrna, or at various other places, where we know that churches of the saints did exist in the Apostolic age? What has become of the church that was then at Rome? It is extinct, and succeeded by something assuming the name of a church of Christ, but really a synagogue of Satan—"a cage of unclean birds"—a mass of idolatrous worshippers of a flour-and-water God, and of a Goddess whom they blasphemously style "the mother of God,"* and "the queen of heaven"—a besotted multitude with their besotted priests, given up

* Let not any theologian pervert this language to represent me as denying the Lord Jesus Christ to be indeed "God over all, blessed for ever." I abhor Socinianism, as much as I abhor Popery. But it was "according to the flesh" that Jesus of Nazareth was made of the seed of David, and conceived in the womb of the Virgin. She was honoured to give birth to his humanity, not to his Godhead.

"to strong delusions that they should believe a lie," because "they received not the love of the truth, that they might be saved."

And now a very few words indeed would be sufficient on the-much-talked of subject, the infallibility of the church. The very language that attributes infallibility to any man or men, or collection of men, or indeed to any creature however exalted, must be revolting to those who have the knowledge and fear of the Most High. To him alone that attribute belongs. All his works are perfect; and all his teaching is infallible. He has declared that all his children shall be taught of the Lord, and is infallibly faithful to his word of promise in accomplishing this, and all the other good things which he has spoken concerning it. So far as they are taught, they are taught infallibly, made wise unto salvation to know the only true God, and Jesus Christ whom he hath sent. It would be utterly false to infer that they are therefore freed from all error, and much more that they are freed from the liability to err. But what has the infallible wisdom and unchangeable faithfulness of God the Saviour to do with the asserted infallibility of either the Pope of Rome, or a general council of ecclesiastics with the Pope at their head? About as much as light has to do with darkness. I believe few will have the hardihood to deny that some, at least, of the individuals who filled the Papal throne were notoriously monsters of iniquity, polluted with every defilement of the flesh, and even the most unnatural crimes. But, according to one of their theological fictions, such a pope, however bad as a man, was as good and valid a pope as any other—(in this, indeed, I agree with them) and gave as much validity and infallibility to acts and decrees of any general council, at the head of which he sat. Now, it cannot be denied that, if such a man had ever been in fellowship with a really Christian church walking by Apostolic rule, he would have been put away from the fellowship as one of the ungodly characters described in 1 Cor. v. Yet that man, who would not have been in even the outward pale of Christian communion, if the divine word had been obeyed, the popish doctors hold to have been the Universal Bishop of the Catholic church, Christ's Vicegerent upon earth, and at the head of a general council of Ecclesiastics like himself to have issued decrees infallible as the oracles of God! But how can any clergyman of the establishment consistently press such a plain remark as this against the Papists, when he himself derives the validity of his clerical character from ordination by a so-called bishop, and that bishop derives his pretended apostolic authority in the government of the church, from a pretended apostolic succession, traced through the very wickedest of the Popes of Rome?

I am, sir, &c.

CLXXII.

TO THE EDITOR OF THE MORNING CHRONICLE.

Sir,—Mr. Locke has long ago noticed how much the world is humbugged by words, when they acquire a currency of use without clear and distinct ideas annexed to them. I think we may see a striking instance of this in the language of which we have heard so much of late, that tithes are the property of the *church;* property which the legislature has no more right to disturb than the property of any private individual. *The church!* What a convenient expression that has been for concealing a world of nonsense and imposture in its womb! and here, I would observe, in general, that men, who professedly acknowledge the divine authority of the scriptures, have no right to give a currency to scriptural phrases in an unscriptural sense, as this tends at once to corrupt the very fountain of divine truth.

Church, or εκκλησια, is one of those phrases statedly employed in the New Testament, in one or other of two very simple meanings, either for the aggregate of all true Christians in all ages and nations (as when Christ is said to have "loved the *church* and given himself for it,") or for the body of Christian disciples in any one place, and at any one time, who come together on the first day of the week to "shew forth the Lord's death till he come;"—as when we read of the church at Rome, at Ephesus, and in the house of such or such an individual. Accordingly, we never find in scripture such a phrase as "the church of Italy,"—but, "the churches of Italy."

But, adherence to the simplicity of scriptural phraseology would not answer the ecclesiastical purposes of the clergy, those great corrupters of the word of God. They have contrived, therefore, to attach to the word church three different senses, distinct from each other, and all of them alike remote from its scriptural meaning. 1st. It is employed to denote an edifice built in imitation of the heathen temples, and commonly dedicated to some of the saints, those modern demigods: as when we read of St. Paul's Church, St. Pancras Church, &c. 2ndly. It is employed to denote a politico-religious system of profession and observances differing in different parts of the British dominions, but receiving from the legislature peculiar favour and support; of which system, as originating in political regulation, the king is the head—as when they talk of the Church of England, the Church of Scotland, &c. (I am no lawyer, but I conceive the king to be not more really the head of the Church of England than he is of the Church of Scotland, in the general synod of which he appears by his high commissioner. The Editor of the New Times, indeed, speaks of "*spiritual* obedience" as due to him, but due only by the members of the Church of England; all which I consider great nonsense. I believe that the constitutional idea of the king's supremacy includes nothing of *spiritual* authority, and, therefore, demands nothing of spiritual obedience. This, by the bye.) 3rdly. The word *church* is employed, and, perhaps, most generally, to denote the *clerical order*—as when a person is said to "enter into the church," *i. e.* to be admitted into a corps, who pretend to have a peculiar sanctity of character, and a peculiar authority for what is called the administration of religious duties. Now, as *property* belongs only to persons, either individuals or bodies corporate, it is plain that, when tithes are said to be the property of the church, the word church must be used in this last sense, for the clergy; and here the clergy are spoken of as a body corporate, which they are not: though I am aware that there are bodies corporate composed of clerical persons. But we are now prepared to examine the truth of the position by the illustration of a similar case.

Let us suppose that the legislature, ever so many centuries ago, had allotted a tenth of the land to the maintenance of the army. While that law continued, military persons undoubtedly would have a legal right to its benefit; and it might be considered unfair to deprive of it any of those who had entered into the army in expectation of this advantage. But suppose that the impolicy of this legal allotment were discovered at any time: who would not laugh if the military or their advocates should question the right of the legislature to alter or abolish it? Who could be imposed on by the outcry, "you are invading the property of the army, and might as well invade the property of any private nobleman?" It would be obvious to reply—no one is injured by the legislature's lessening, commuting, or abolishing, this provision for the maintenance of the army, as long as we guard the interest of those who are already of the military profession: the profession is not hereditary, and no one *has* a right to any of its advantages but those who *are* in the army. It was for the supposed benefit of the country that the legislature formerly decreed that fund for the maintenance of a military force: it is now discovered that such a military force is not beneficial to the country, and (saving the interests of the present officers and soldiers) who is injured by a legislative act applying that military fund to other purposes? All that can be said is, that there will be fewer inducements to men hereafter to take upon them the military profession. It seems to me, Mr. Editor, that all the same reasoning is directly and obviously applicable against the present clamour that tithes are the property of the church. On the question whether it be, or be not beneficial to the country that tithes should be either commuted or abolished, I do not enter. But, that any reasonable man should, for a moment, question the equitable right of the legislature to commute or to abolish them, can be accounted for only from the vulgar errors and prejudices, which are mainly supported by the abuse of language; while that abuse of language, I am aware, originates in man's selfish interests and passions.

CLXXIII.

TO WILLIAM SMITH, ESQ. M.P.

Sir,—We take the liberty of addressing you in behalf of some Christian societies with which we are connected, and in consequence of our learning, through the public papers, that the bill you had intended to introduce on the marriages of Dissenters has been abandoned, and that you designed to frame a new bill upon the subject. Considering you as a warm friend of the most liberal toleration, we doubt not but you will be kindly disposed to frame your bill, as far as possible, so as to afford relief in the matter, to all whose conscientious principles subject them to grievance from the law as it stands at present.

But, from the peculiarity of our sentiments, we apprehend that any new bill which you introduce may fail of meeting our case, as much as that would which you have withdrawn, unless we obtain an opportunity of previous communication with you. We would, therefore, request to be allowed the honour of a personal interview, at any time that you may please to appoint for our waiting on you; and, in the mean time, permit us to submit the following observations to your attention.

In Ireland, where the principal number of our churches is, the law of marriage (as you probably are aware) is much more liberal than here. All dissenting congregations are allowed to solemnize their own marriages by their own ministers, with a full legal validity to the contract. Yet even there we cannot avail ourselves of the act, though it seems to have been studiously drawn up with the view of affording the fullest liberty and indulgence to Dissenters. The framers of the act seem not to have contemplated the possible existence of any churches or congregations, without some persons under the name of ministers or preachers at their head, and exercising something of the clerical character. Now, we neither have nor could allow such persons among us, or the exercise of any such character, however modified. We acknowledge, indeed, the scriptural office of elders, or overseers of a Christian church: but even where any of our churches have those gifts (of which most of them are yet destitute), we consider the office essentially distinct from that of clergymen, ministers, or preachers; and therefore could not think of allowing them to be employed in *solemnizing our marriages:* no more than we could apply to a clergyman of the Establishment for the purpose, even though he should omit all his acts of worship. Yet, considering it our duty to provide things honest in the sight of all men, we feel ourselves called on, as far as possible, to obtain a *legal* validity to our marriage contracts; and we have for some time effected this, though at considerable inconvenience and expense, by going to Scotland, where the declaration of the parties, before any competent witnesses, that they are husband and wife, produces a *civil* obligation of full validity, and afterwards recognized in any part of the British dominions.

We conceive that the marriage contract is binding in the sight of God and the conscience, whenever a man and woman, at present free, seriously and deliberately receive each other in that relation. Yet we own that the state has fairly a right to prescribe certain terms as necessary to civil recognition of this contract. But we think it most unreasonable that the state should prescribe any religious acts for the purpose. This is at once prescribing a religion to the people, and therefore inconsistent with religious toleration. The marriage relation (though so lasting and important) we think essentially a civil and not a religious connexion, else it could not subsist in binding obligation (as we know it may) between a Christian believer and an unbeliever; between whom there can be no religious fellowship. But, waving the discussion of this, we consider it indisputable, that the civil government of the country can have nothing to do with it rightfully but in a *civil* way: while, undoubtedly, so far as the legislature provides a favoured religion for the people, it may quite consistently direct any rites of that religion to accompany the solemnization of marriage in the case of those who choose to conform to it. But to impose those rites on others, or to say that others must employ any religious rites or religious officers for ratifying their marriages, seems as contrary to sound policy as to equitable fairness, and we should hope that the state of the law upon the subject, both in Ireland and in Scotland, might prepare the way for a bill to legalize all marriages declared before a civil magistrate, by parties competent to form the contract, and after a sufficient notice of the intentions of the parties.

The hardship we feel in this matter is very slight indeed, from the resources which the Scottish law affords us, in comparison of the sufferings to which we are exposed from some other principles; as you may perceive, if you condescend to look at the pamphlet which we have the honour of sending to you with this letter. Yet we trust that, if you can, you will be disposed to frame your bill so as to comprehend our societies in its relief.

Hoping to be favoured with a communication from you, and that you will pardon us for occupying so much of your time, we have the honour to be, sir, with much respect,

Your obedient humble servants,

REVIEW

OF

"THE EPISTLES OF PAUL THE APOSTLE,

TRANSLATED;

WITH AN EXPOSITION AND NOTES.

BY THE

REV. THOMAS BELSHAM,

MINISTER OF ESSEX STREET CHAPEL.

4 vols. 8vo. London: Hunter, 1832."

[Published in No. VIII. New Edinburgh Review, April, 1823.]

When we reflect on the history of that version of the Scriptures, which has long been sanctioned by public authority in this country; when we contemplate the multifarious learning and talents which were employed in the work, the caution and sober judgment with which it was conducted, and, above all, the intentional fidelity which it generally manifests;—and, when we turn from this view to consider the ordinary character of those, who have from time to time, in later years, presented their reformed versions to the public; when we mark their ignorance, their rashness, their vanity, but especially their dishonest object of supporting a favourite system:—we cannot but be struck with the contrast, and thankful that the overruling providence of God has given such general currency to a translation, which, with all its imperfections, is so superior to any that could at this day be adopted in its place. In saying this, let us not be supposed either to uphold the received translation as faultless, or to deny as unimportant many of the corrections which are to be picked out of the mass of modern biblical criticism, or to intimate the least dissatisfaction, that ever so many individuals, however various in their sentiments and their qualifications, should bring forward their respective versions: much less should we be disposed to withhold our warmest approbation from *such* a version of any portion of the Scriptures, as Dr. Lowth has given of Isaiah. But we do avow our opinion, that most of the professedly improved translations are such as, in the judgment of a sound and candid scholar, cannot stand a moment in competition, upon the whole, with our public version. We say, *upon the whole*, because, perhaps, in the very worst of them, there are here and there alterations which are undeniable improvements, as might naturally be expected from the quantity of learned labour which has been expended on the original text since the time of James I.

Archbishop Newcome and others have been earnest for obtaining a revision of our English Bible by public authority. We confess, that even his Grace's versions would be sufficient to make us rejoice that our governors have not sanctioned the attempt. And, though we should be very glad to see an edition of the English Scriptures, in which all the *indisputable* corrections should be introduced either into the text or the margin, and a few antiquated phrases exchanged for others more intelligible; yet we cannot wish, that even this object should be taken up by the authority of the state. For we scarcely know any set of men, who would be contented to make *sufficiently little* alteration; and any change in the general texture of our public version, we are persuaded, would be a change for the worse. Many a new translation have we examined; but we have seen very few in which we were not disgusted by the vain and tasteless effort to improve passages, which are not only most faithful to the original, but unrivalled also for excellence as specimens of English composition. One example may perhaps convey and illustrate our meaning.

We read in our English Bible, (Luke ii. 8.) "*And there were in the same country shepherds abiding in the field, keeping watch over their flock by night.*" A writer* of learning and taste has noticed this simple passage as a sentence of exquisite harmony and the most beautiful structure, presenting to attention successively the several circumstances of the scene in the most happy collocation. Let the reader who has an ear, and anything of critical judgment, pause a little on the words, and say whether the praise is undeserved. "And there were—in the same country—shepherds—abiding in the field—keeping watch over their flock—by night." No one also can deny that the English words faithfully convey the meaning of the Greek. Might we not then reasonably expect, that the improvers of our public version would suffer such a passage at least to remain unaltered; a passage in which not a word can be changed or transposed without injury to the sentence? But no: we do not at present recollect one of the new versions, in which even that passage has escaped the prurient vanity of alteration. Curiosity led us to look at the rendering of it given in the last *soi-disant* improved version of the New Testament which has issued from Mr. Belsham's school; and, indeed, we were rather surprised to find so little change. But instead of the fine musical cadence, *keeping watch over their flock by night*, they give us, "keeping night watches over their flock." What an improvement! † Such things, we admit, are comparatively trifles; and we

* We think Dr Thomas Leland, in his Lectures on Eloquence; but we have not the work before us.

† Harwood's *magnificent* version of the passage is really worth exhibiting in a note. "It happened that there were in the adjacent fields a company of shepherds employing the hours of night in guarding their respective flocks!"

may add, *utinam his potius nugis tota isti dedissent tempora!* In noticing such trifles at all, we only mean to justify ourselves for deprecating, even in a *literary* view, the sanctioning by public authority of any new version of the Scriptures, executed by men so vain, and so devoid of the first principles of literary taste. But it were well indeed, if vanity and tastlessness were the worst charges that could be brought against most of them.

We have noticed the intentional *fidelity* of the received version, as one of the important characters which commend it. Mr. Belsham, indeed, denies it this praise; but we defy him to refute our assertion. The translators employed by James, it is well known, were all what are called Trinitarians, and all, probably, what (now at least) are called Calvinists. But who can say that their version is either Trinitarian or Unitarian? that it is either Calvinistic or Arminian? What passage, that is employed by Unitarians or Arminians as a stronghold for maintaining their sentiments, have our translators attempted to alter or disguise? We are bold to say, *not one*. Like honest men and sound scholars, they appear to have examined the original fairly and carefully, and to have aimed at rendering each text faithfully to the best of their judgment, without any regard to its possible bearing on this or that theological system. And we do maintain, that this alone, or, at least, this taken in combination with the very high qualifications of erudition and judgment which they possessed, stamps their version as a whole with characters of inestimable public worth, and characters which strikingly distinguish it from almost every thing that has been offered as a substitute in later days. That they have often left obscure and ambiguous passages which they did not clearly understand, is certain; that, as fallible men, however able and honest, they have erred in their interpretation of several texts, is freely admitted; as well as that the labours of Kennicott and De Rossi, Wetstein and Griesbach, in collating numerous manuscripts of the Scriptures, afford some advantages to a translator at this day, which were not then possessed. Yet, upon this point, we candidly avow our judgment, that the *main* importance of all their laborious collations, and one which indeed amply compensates all the labour bestowed on the object, consists in the resulting evidence of the *general integrity* of the text as it has been transmitted to us, and the *general unimportance* of the various readings which have been collected with so much diligence of research. We are ready also to admit, that in the progress of biblical criticism, so far as it has not been diverted from its legitimate office by theology, several obscure passages of Scripture have been elucidated, and several corrected interpretations proposed since our received version was formed. But we are persuaded, that by far the greater part of what is called *biblical criticism*, in modern times, is a thing utterly unworthy of the name; the vain effort of men, (some of whom have been learned and able men,) to torture the Scriptures into a pretended coincidence with their infidel theories, and to wrest them from that meaning which, to the eye of any candid reader, they obviously present.

For this fact we are no loss to account. From many circumstances, (most of them arising out of the *political establishment* of something under the name of Christianity,) the profession of receiving the Scriptures as a divine revelation has long been general in Europe. Many also, having their attention directed to the external and internal evidences of their authenticity, have had their judgments seriously convinced that they possess more or less of a divine origin. This is by no means wonderful; the evidences are so strong and so numerous. But this is perfectly consistent with their *disbelief* of all the most essential truths which the Scriptures declare from heaven; and, indeed, the belief of these ever has been rare. None were more firmly persuaded of the general divine authority of Moses and the prophets, than the Jews who crucified the Messiah, and of whom it is distinctly testified, that they "believed not Moses," and that they "knew not the voices of the prophets which were read every Sabbath day" in their synagogues, (John v. 46, 47. Acts xiii. 27.) All that remained, therefore, for unbelieving theologians, whose sentiments were not in accordance with the Scriptures, was, to force the Scriptures into a pretended accordance with their sentiments. And, in this vocation, they have indeed laboured diligently, and compiled many a long paraphrase or exposition, as well as published many an *improved* version. Often have we wished, though we are aware that in some views the wish is vain, but often has the wish crossed our minds, that some society, (for the work is too great for any individual,) some society of *Deists*,—(let not our readers be startled,)—possessing the requisite talents and learning, the requisite *kind*, as well as *degree*, of learning, could be induced to bestow the necessary time and labour on giving a critical edition and version of the Bible, as they would of any ancient work in classical literature. But it is certainly a vain wish. Whatever were their talents and learning, they would be found deficient in that sobriety of judgment and candour of mind, which ought to be brought to the task; and, if *avowed* Deists, would want all the needful inducement to undertake and execute it.

But it is time for us to dismiss these general preliminary remarks, and attend to our author. He must excuse us for treating him with very little ceremony; though he informs us in his title-page that he is *The Reverend* Thomas Belsham, *Minister* of Essex Street Chapel. We have not been altogether unacquainted with Mr. Belsham heretofore. Annexed to the present work he gives a list of forty-eight pamphlets, (most of them Sermons or Discourses,) with which he has favoured the public. We have seen one or two of these; and we confess that the little acquaintance which we had with him excited from us an involuntary "*heigh-ho!*" when we found ourselves condemned to wade through four octavo volumes of his composition. But we have long been well acquainted with the school to which he belongs; and we plainly avow our conviction, that it takes the lead of every other in *audacious* corruption of the Scriptures; and that, while its professors put forward the most arrogant pretensions to the character of *rational* divines, they are the most irrational, as well as the most dishonest, that have ever assumed the Christian name. We are aware, that among the *old* Socinians there were many men of considerable talents and learning; and there appeared in them a *comparative* sobriety, which generally attends real talents and sound learning. We acknowledge also, that, in modern days, they may boast of a Priestley,—a man of most acute mind,—a sterling philosopher in all things to which human philosophy is competent. But we plainly assert its utter incompetence to produce the conviction of *divine* truth, even with the Scriptures before us. (For the present we leave that *irrational* assertion, as Mr. Belsham will call it, for his amusement.) Priestley was a curious instance of a man, whose judgment was overcome by the evidences of revelation, while he continued to stumble at the plainest truths revealed, and struggled with—we believe—*intentional* candour to evade their force, through all the shifting varieties of sentiment in which his speculative mind involved him. With this exception, and perhaps a very few others,—(among which we do *not* reckon Mr. Wakefield, saving that we admit him to have been a man of much classical *reading*,)—we really know not any more superficial smatterers in literature, any more self-sufficient pretenders to rational and critical disquisition, than the tribe of modern Socinians. Our language is strong and decisive: and let it be censured as unwarrantably strong, if we do not fully justify it, in the instance of Mr. Belsham, before the termination of this article. Yet how small a portion of our evidence can we bring forward within the limits to which we are necessarily confined!

There is certainly no literary occupation, in which a man may now set up creditably with a smaller stock of his own, than that of biblical criticism: such ample materials are furnished to his hand by lexicographers, commentators, and divines of all sorts and sizes. Accordingly, we have scarcely ever known a half-fledged theologian, who had spent his year or two at a dissenting academy, and learned so much of the Greek (and perhaps Hebrew) grammar as enabled him to consult a dictionary, or to spell the quotations which he found in his expositor,—who did not think himself qualified, when mounted in his wooden eminence, to run a tilt against the learned translators of our Bible, and amaze his audience with the information—how such and such a passage *reads in the original*. But in Mr. Belsham we may expect to find a much larger stock of erudition. He informs us, that he has "officiated as *Divinity Tutor* in the Academical Institutions at Daventry and Hackney"—that he "regards it as an honour to have been one of a committee appointed by the *Unitarian Society* for publishing the *Improved* Version of the New Testament:"—that he was "the party chiefly concerned in *carrying it through* the press;"—that he is "responsible for the whole of the Introduction, and for many, perhaps the major part, of the Notes;"—that his "present work was drawn up above *thirty* years ago," and is now given to the public, with all the improvements of matured age, at the instance of "partial friends, who volunteered a munificent subscription to a quarto edition, the whole of which they took off his hands," &c. &c. We find also immediately, that Mr. Belsham enters the field furnished with all the biblical apparatus of Griesbach's text, (from which, however, he departs *ad libitum*,) Schleusner's Lexicon, Rosenmüller's Commentary; besides the theological productions of the English school, from Locke to Archbishop Newcome, and from his Grace down to Mr. Wakefield. Almost every page also presents to the eye a parade of Greek or Latin quotation. To a theologue making such a formidable display, it might be expected that we should at once doff our bonnets. But we have long known how easily such a display may be made, and what hollowness it often covers.

One of the first things that must strike any judicious reader on opening these volumes, is that it is very hard to say for what class of readers they were designed. The exposition, which forms the more bulky part of them, is obviously calculated for the ladies and gentlemen of the Unitarian society. No one sentence of the text, however plain or unequivocal, is left without its paraphrase, to put what the apostle says—or does *not* say—into genteeler language, to expand or to dilute, to overlay or to distort, its meaning. This, surely, could not be designed for scholars. But for scholars alone, and not for the general mass of readers, the Greek and Latin in the notes must have been intended. Yet, no: we cannot believe this. Every person who is capable of reading the original text, and disposed to such study, must be supposed to possess some of the editions to which various readings are subjoined; at least the elder Wetstein's, or Fell's, or Curcellæus's, even if he be not master of the younger Wetstein, or of Griesbach. And any one who has ever looked at the mass of various readings given by any of these editors, knows that a vast majority of them relate to the omission, insertion, or substitution of words or particles, of which the omission, insertion, or substitution, is absolutely indifferent as to the sense of the passage. Now, Mr. Belsham, though he does not give us the original text, or any regular collection of various readings, every now and then favours his reader with a note of information that such or such a MS. reads so or so; and this in cases where the variety of reading is utterly unimportant *, however suitably preserved by editors who profess to give the various readings. The very smallest collection is vastly more copious than Mr. Belsham's. We are forced, therefore, to ask, why has he introduced such into his notes at all? Or, if at all, why has he not given much more? For what class of readers, we repeat the question, were such notes designed? From his continual references, "see Griesbach," they were ostensibly designed for those who have access to Griesbach, and are capable of consulting him. But against this supposition is the plain fact, that such readers, or indeed those who have access to any of the editions we have mentioned, so far from needing the information which Mr. Belsham gives them, could furnish him with hundreds of various readings *equally* important, of which he has taken no notice. Was it then that his munificent subscribers contracted for a certain quantity of *learning* in his pages? Or was it that he thought it otherwise expedient to give his general readers something that they should admire, because it was unintelligible? We have heard of

* As when he tells us, on 1 Cor. viii. 2. that "the Alexandrine manuscript reads [illegible] for [illegible],"—on the words οὐκ οἴδατε 1 Cor. vi. 2. that "Griesbach prefixes ἢ upon the authority of the Alexandrine, Ephrem, and other copies," &c. &c.

the cross was "the MAN Christ Jesus; and for this end "he humbled himself" to become flesh, that he might "suffer for sins, the just for the unjust." But how absurdly inconsistent with himself is Mr. Belsham, in noticing at all upon this passage the authority of MSS. on one side or the other, when he adduces it in exemplification and confirmation of the rule he has laid down, that mere theological *system* may justify us in adopting one reading or interpretation in preference to another! Does not this involve a plain avowal, that what determines him to adopt the true reading here is—not the decisive authority of MSS.—but that he conceives it more favourable to his system than the other? Let it be well observed, that Mr. Belsham cannot put forward this passage as one in which the text is *ambiguous*, in which the authorities for the two readings are equally or nearly balanced; for he himself indeed distinctly marks the contrary. Yet he does expressly put it forward as an instance, in which *system* is the thing that fairly decides the interpreter; and the whole tenor of his language and argument proves, that he would consider a Trinitarian interpreter *justified* in adopting the spurious reading, if he thought it favourable to his system. Mr. Belsham indeed has plainly said, that he OUGHT to do so. If we did so, it would only prove a secret consciousness that our system was unsupported by the word of God, and a wicked determination to wrest and pervert that word into a seeming support of it. We avow our conviction, that "the *man* Christ Jesus," who redeemed his church by his own blood, was also truly and unequivocally "GOD, blessed for evermore;" while we deprecate the supposition, that we know, or understand, or believe, any thing about the *mode* of that union of the Godhead and manhood in the Messiah; and abhor all human speculations upon it, and all pretences to illustrate or explain it. But the conviction which we avow, rests upon scriptural grounds too strong to need the support of any dishonest arts.

We proceed to the other questions, by which Mr. Belsham attempts to enforce and justify his canon. He asks, "Who can blame a Trinitarian for translating Titus ii. 13. 'the glorious appearance of our great God and Saviour Jesus Christ?'" We reply, in the first place, that we know not who has translated it exactly so. Mr. Belsham tells us that Beza has; but we cannot take Mr. Belsham's word for that, and we do not think it worth while to examine the matter. But, in the next place, we say, that if any man translate the passage, "the glorious appearance," or rather, literally, "the manifestation of the glory of Jesus Christ the great God and our Saviour," he will translate it indubitably right. Every one acquainted with Greek idiom, and unbiassed by system, knows that if the apostle had meant to distinguish "the great God" from "our Saviour," the words should properly have run, *επιφανειαν της δοξης τε μεγαλε Θεε καὶ* TOY *Σωτηρος ημων* I. X. If Mr. Belsham does not know the justice of this simple remark, we cannot help his ignorance; nor can we now stop to read him a lecture on the elementary principles of the Greek language. We may add, that the only various reading of the passage which Griesbach himself exhibits, (but not at all supported so as to commend itself to any critical scholar) is the omission of the copulative και before Σωτηρος, which would unequivocally put the words, "our Saviour Jesus Christ," in what grammarians call *apposition* with the "great God." And although Wetstein has an Arian note upon the verse, in which he asserts that the Scripture nowhere calls Christ *the* great *God*, we assert that in Is. ix. 6. (a passage to which we think it highly probable that the apostle alludes,) he is expressly called אל גבור, "the *mighty* God." We say, the Messiah is there called so; for that the passage is a prophecy of the Messiah, we are distinctly taught by the Scriptures of the New Testament, Matt. iv. 14—16; and we seriously think the Evangelists of more weighty authority in the matter, than the reverend minister of Essex Street chapel. We believe the Scriptures; and care not for any religious principle or practice that has not their support. So *irrational* and *unphilosophic* must we be content to appear in Mr. Belsham's eyes. But whatever he may choose to say of that prophecy, we really know not any thing of two gods, a *great* and a *little*; and therefore think Wetstein's note upon the passage intrinsically nugatory and profane. We leave it to the so-called *Unitarians* to render John i. 1. "the Word was with God, and the Word was *a* God."

And now, after having been led to say so much upon Titus ii. 13. we would only remark to Mr. Belsham, that it is a passage in which we are perfectly content with the public version; and in which, even supposing it *ambiguous*, which we do not think it is, he ought, in consistency with the first part of his own canon, to have retained that version. But it is not upon it, or upon any similar text, our conviction of the true and proper Godhead of the Messiah rests; and we should, therefore, never think of continuing any contest with him upon the translation of that verse. The doctrine, for which we would contend to the uttermost, rests upon scriptural testimonies most numerous, and much more distinct. In our view, indeed, it is so embodied with the whole of divine revelation, that the truth of the one cannot be rejected, and at the same time the authority of the other maintained, without the grossest inconsistency. It cannot be expected that, within the compass of this article, we should discuss at large this or other topics of controversy between us and Mr. Belsham. But the position that we have just now laid down is one, which we shall have occasion by and by briefly to illustrate and confirm.

We now pass to the next question so confidently proposed by Mr. Belsham, "Who can condemn an *Arian* for rendering Heb. i. 4. 'being made so much better than the angels, as he hath by inheritance obtained a more excellent name than they?'" Does the reverend gentleman mean to insinuate, that King James's translators, who give this version, were Arians? He knows the contrary. But he intimates at least, that the passage thus translated, and, as we shall immediately prove, rightly translated, countenances the Arian doctrine rather than what is called the Trinitarian. In this he shows himself as defective in his acquaintance with theological systems, as he is unfair and uncritical in his own version of the text; and though we could not expect fairness or honesty of interpretation from a Socinian divine, we might reasonably expect, from a quondam divinity tutor in two academical institutions, some understanding of the systems which he opposes. The very words of the text, as well as the whole context, prove that in the 4th verse the apostle is not speaking at all of the antecedent glory of him, who *humbled himself*, that he might "put away sin by the sacrifice of himself;" but is speaking of that glory and honour with which he is crowned as Mediator, in recompense of his obedience unto death. And it is well known that every scriptural Trinitarian—(we are compelled for brevity's sake, though reluctantly, to use this and some other *theological* phrases)—not only admits, but asserts, that in the whole of his mediatorial character and work, the Messiah acted as the *servant* of JEHOVAH, as that which he humbled himself to become, "in all things like unto his brethren," truly and literally "the *man* Christ Jesus," trusting in *his Father and his God* (with that perfect faith, of which he is the great exemplar to his people,) for all the promised deliverance from death, and for all that reward of the "travail of his soul" which it was declared that he should see; upheld by the Father in his work, and *receiving* from the Father that kingdom and glory, which he holds as "head over all things to his church." At present we only say, without asserting the truth or falsehood of any system, that every theologian (not to talk of Christians) knows, that this is essentially an integral part of the system called Trinitarian; and most unscriptural indeed are those Trinitarians, in whose system this does not stand forward as a *prominent* principle of divine truth. Now, may we not justly demand of Mr. Belsham, on what grounds, and under what pretext, can he insinuate that the Trinitarian doctrine is discountenanced by Heb. i. 4. as it stands in our present version? discountenanced by the assertion, that He who was "made for a little while lower than the angels, for the suffering of death," has *received by inheritance* a name superior to the highest angels of God, a kingly glory, in which "angels, and authorities, and powers, are made subject unto him." (1 Pet. iii. 22. Eph. i. 21, 22, &c.) On what grounds, we ask, and under what pretext, can he insinuate that this countenances the Arian system, which represents him who became flesh as having been antecedently but a kind of *demi-god*, of a supra-angelic nature indeed, but not properly GOD? The insinuation is as illogical and irrational as it is anti-scriptural.

We press our question the more, because we have been long aware, and long disgusted by observing, that the stronghold both of Arianism and Socinianism, is no other than that silly sophism, which objects against their opponents innumerable passages of Scripture asserting the *proper manhood* of Jesus Christ, and his *subjection* in all things to his heavenly Father; passages which, in their fullest force, are acknowledged and asserted by their scriptural opponents as strongly as by themselves. Take away this line of argument from them, and what in the way of argument have they left? Nothing, but the vain and presumptuous inquiry, "How can it be, that the Word which was *made flesh* was God—God blessed for evermore?" "How can it be, that in the *one* JEHOVAH there should be such a distinction, or plurality, that the Word, which was with God, was God?" How!

a modest question to be proposed about the being of the most high God, by creatures, of whom the most intelligent and reflecting best know their utter incapacity to comprehend the *mode* of their own existence, or to penetrate the How of any fact with which they are most familiar. And what remains for them in the way of scriptural appeal? Nothing but the very grossest perversion, mistranslation, and corruption of the sacred text; such as, in the interpretation of any other book, would stamp with disgrace those who were so absurd as to employ it.

We would once for all tell Mr. Belsham, that we court the most truly *critical* interpretation of the text of Scripture; that we hold it is to be interpreted according to all those rules of sound and fair criticism, which the best scholars employ in the interpretation of the Greek and Latin classics; and that we abhor the profaneness of those popular divines, who make light of the question, "What is the *real meaning* of such or such a passage?" provided they can but give it an *application* suited to their purpose. We think this essentially contrary to real reverence for the word, and therefore to the real fear of that only true God who reveals himself in it. But our grand objection here to those who assume the name of Unitarians, and boast the character of *rational* divines, is that they, above all others, violate every principle of true critical interpretation, in order to torture the Scriptures into an acquiescence with their infidelity. And in the same way in which they treat the Scriptures, we would confidently undertake to misinterpret what is called the Athanasian creed into an Unitarian formulary; though drawn up, as it is, with all the special-pleading precision and metaphysical subtlety which men think needful, but which the word of God disdains. We should only have to set some parts of it in opposition to others; to mistranslate ever so grossly some of the parts which we aimed at putting down; to foist in conjectural emendations of others; and, where any were too stubborn to be got rid of by these means, to assert boldly that they were interpolations, and to expunge them.

We have one more preliminary remark to offer briefly, before we come to the critical examination of Heb. i. 4. Mr. Belsham considers the received version, "being made so much better than the angels," &c. as countenancing the Arian system; and therefore thinks himself quite justified, as a Socinian, in substituting, "being become [very classical English, by the by] so much greater than *these messengers*," &c. *i. e.* than the former prophets. What is the immediate and necessary inference which we must draw? Certainly this: that, according to the principles of modern Socinianism, he, who was made "lower than the angels for the suffering of death," has not even since his ascension to the right hand of the majesty on high, received any glory or authority superior to the angels of God. How old Socinus himself would stare at the minister of Essex Street chapel! The Messiah, since he entered into his glory, has *become* (according to Mr. Belsham) greater than any of the former prophets! How strange is this! We could adduce more than one passage from Mr. Belsham's own exposition, in which he speaks of Christ as having been, in the days of his flesh, *the first of all the prophets*; but then we are aware, that, among all the other features of dishonesty in his book, there is abundance of that vile dishonesty—an *exoteric* language for the weak, and an *esoteric* doctrine for the initiated. Let us treat our readers with a specimen of the latter, which is conveyed but occasionally.

" It cannot, however, be doubted, that God is able to qualify any being for the office to which he may call him out, and he certainly will do it; and Dr. Priestly justly remarks, that they who make this objection," [*i. e.* who object to the idea of a fallible and peccable man being appointed to judge the world,] "do not sufficiently consider *the wonderfully rapid progress in knowledge and in power* which our Lord is necessarily making in the long interval antecedent to the day of judgment."

And these are *rational* divines! But will Mr. Belsham excuse us for suggesting, that, considering *the wonderful rapidity* of these advances, he might perhaps allow, that the Messiah, at the date of the Epistle to the Hebrews, had become greater than even the angels. Truly, the wise of this world are so " taken in their own craftiness," that often their folly becomes manifest to all men except themselves.

And now let us say a few words upon this text, which Mr. Belsham adduces to exemplify his canon of *critical* interpretation. Much will not be necessary. Every schoolboy knows that the Greek word αγγελος properly and literally signifies a *messenger*; and we readily admit, that in some passages of the New Testament it ought to be so rendered, where our translators render it *angels*. But Mr. Belsham himself cannot deny, that in many other passages it does import what we call *angels*; for, though he makes war against the angels as much as he can, and informs us that they are only fictitious beings of the " Hebrew mythology," yet he is obliged not unfrequently to admit them into his version. (1 Cor. iv. 9; vi. 3; xiii. 1. 2 Cor. xi. 14. Gal. i. 8. Col. ii. 18. 2 Thess. i. 7. Heb. ii. 5. 7. 16; xiii. 2.) The only question, therefore, is, or ought to be, which of those interpretations, according to the rules of sound criticism, should be assigned to the word in Heb. i. 4; whether we are there to understand *human* messengers, or supra-human but created intelligences. And this question is to be determined independently of all consideration about its bearing on this or that theological system, though certainly not without due regard to what we are assured of indisputably from all the rest of Scripture. Mr. Belsham, in his note upon the passage, says of his interpretation (which applies the word to those messengers of God, the old prophets,) that it was suggested many years ago by an *ingenious* friend, and " is adopted by Mr. Wakefield in his new translation." He adds, " It is surprising that it was never thought of before." In one view, we are not disposed to contradict this position. For so indefinitely numerous have been the changes of absurdity and wickedness which have long been rung by professed interpreters of the Scripture, that it may be considered surprising that any novelty of absurd falsehood should remain to be excogitated by the moderns. In any other view, we should say that it is surprising how any man, ever so little conversant with the text of Scripture, could think for a moment that the former prophets are there intended. Mr.

Belsham will not, cannot, deny, that the apostle is speaking in that text of the glory which *followed* the sufferings of the Messiah, of his exaltation *subsequent* to his obedience unto death. Now we have the express testimony of Christ concerning John the Baptist, his immediate harbinger, that he was "much more than a prophet;" that among those born of women, there had "not arisen a greater than John the Baptist." (Matth. xi. 9—11.) And we have the testimony of the Baptist equally express concerning Christ: "He that cometh after me is mightier than I, whose shoes I am not worthy to bear." (Matth. iii. 11.) Is it possible then, that Mr. Belsham can deny, that Jesus of Nazareth, even in the days of his flesh, while "made lower than the angels for the suffering of death," was greater than all the prophets, greater even than he who was *much more than a prophet*? And if he admit this, can he possibly maintain that his dignity, when crowned by his Father with glory and honour after his resurrection, consisted merely in his having become, (or, as Mr. Belsham prefers it, being become,) "greater than those messengers?" Do we succeed in making ourselves intelligible to Mr. Belsham? Or does his *rationality* soar above us at a height too great to permit his perception of our argument?

We might adduce other arguments against this version; and, in proof, that *if* the writer had intended to express the idea which Mr. Belsham forces on him, he must have expressed it differently.* But we consider any additional arguments needless; and shall only subjoin the observation, that we might on the present question quote Belsham *against* Belsham. While he renders οἱ αγγελοι by "those messengers," in the 4th, 5th, 6th, 7th, and 13th verses of the first chapter, he yet, in the second chapter, renders the word by "angels," in the 5th, 7th, 9th, and 16th verses. We do not stop to notice some of the extravagancies of his mis-translation, even in these passages. Now, if, according to that version of the second chapter to which Mr. Belsham is driven by considerations that we are at no loss to understand, it be stated, that "unto *angels* God hath *not* committed the world to come," which he has committed to the Messiah; we should be glad to know with what consistency he can pretend, that the 4th verse of the first chapter does not declare the Messiah to be made "greater than the *angels*." The same word, employed on the same subject, in two consecutive chapters so intimately connected, ought surely, according to all the principles of reason and sound criticism, to be interpreted in the same way.

We rather wonder that Mr. Belsham did not add a fourth question to the three which he has proposed in confirmation of his canon. We wonder that he did not ask, "Who can blame a Trinitarian for maintaining the authenticity of the common text in 1 John v. 7?" And, as we have avowed ourselves such sturdy believers of the doc-

* Mr. Belsham is very fond of rendering the Greek article by the English demonstrative pronoun, whenever it can answer his purpose; and often, indeed, from the mere vanity of alteration. We are forward to admit, that there are some connexions in which the article is best and most fairly rendered thus; as, for instance, in Rom. xv. 13. But we assert, that the man who thinks the Greek article may always be so rendered, knows nothing of the Greek language.

trine, which that text was too long brought forward to support, he may probably think us very foolish for avowing our persuasion of its spuriousness. Indeed, the mere indisputable fact, that among all the manuscripts of the Greek Testament in existence, only one can be produced exhibiting it, and that one obviously a manuscript the most modern, this alone ought to be sufficient to decide the judgment of every candid scholar against its authenticity. We only wonder and lament that the contest about it was so long continued, and that any one has attempted to revive it in the nineteenth century.

We have said, that Mr. Belsham's dishonest *theory* of interpretation is abundantly illustrated by his dishonest practice. Under this head, we are obliged, by the necessary limits of our present article, to confine ourselves to a very few examples. But they shall be decisive. In Rom. ix. 4, 5. the apostle, speaking of the Israelites, "his kinsmen, according to the flesh," says of them, "whose is the adoption, &c. whose are the fathers, (ὧν ἡ υἱοθεσια . . . . ὧν οἱ πατερες) and *of whom, as concerning the flesh*, is Christ, who is over all, God blessed for ever," (καὶ ἐξ ὧν ὁ Χριστος, το κατα σαρκα, ὁ ὢν ἐπι παντων Θεος εὐλογητος εἰς τους αἰωνας) This passage has long been a plague to ancient and modern infidels, who have assumed the Christian name, and we have selected it for particular notice, because it is not pretended that any various reading of it appears in any one of the manuscripts, or of the ancient versions, or of the ecclesiastical writings of those who are called *the Fathers*. Let it be observed, that the whole of this constitutes a mass of evidence for the genuineness of the text, such as cannot be adduced in support of any passage in any Greek or Latin classic; the number of existing manuscripts of the Greek Testament being so immensely greater than those of any classic; the old versions being of such various ages and countries, as well as some of them of such very high antiquity; and these same *fathers* forming such an uninterrupted chain of testimony, as we should vainly look for to authenticate any other writings. The words of the original, also, are most plain and unambiguous, and literally rendered by our translators with the strictest fidelity. And, lastly, each of the assertions in the passage, as it stands, is in perfect harmony with other parts of the sacred text, which even Mr. Belsham does not venture to alter or expunge. Can he deny that Christ is elsewhere declared to be *over all?* or that he is elsewhere called God (Θεος)? or that he is elsewhere pronounced *blessed?* Now, we say, that according to every rule of fair critical interpretation, this passage assuredly ought to be left by any translator as he found it, whether he believed the truth declared in it or not. But he found it a passage which (as he says) "must be translated in a sense favourable or unfavourable to his own system;" and, adhering to his canon, he verily thought that he *ought* to force it out of the unfavourable bearing, which he perceived. What then does he do? HE ALTERS THE TEXT! He foists into it, in place of the apostle's words, a *conjectural emendation* of Slichtingius, one of the divines of that German school, which has so conveniently accommodated our modern Socinians with numberless corruptions of the Scriptures. He renders the passage, "of whom is Christ, according to the flesh; WHOSE is the God over all, blessed for evermore." He then treats his readers with the following learned note:

"ὧν ὁ for ὁ ὤν. This, *most probably*, is the true reading, agreeably to the *judicious conjecture* of Slichtingius, Whitby, and Taylor, *though it is not authorized by any manuscript, version, or ecclesiastical authority;* but the connexion *seems* to require it."

We pause here to remark, that Mr. Belsham really seems to us a bungling and inconsistent corrupter of the sacred text. For, as he has not yet decreed that the 1st verse of the Gospel by John is to be expunged, but contents himself with rendering that passage, "the word was *a* God," why should he not have preferred to render the same expression here, "*a* God blessed for evermore?" He might so have avoided the barefaced impudence of manufacturing a text for his own purpose, in defiance of such a weight of uncontradicted evidence for the present reading. But probably he had some secret misgiving, that the mis-translation of even that passage in John was but an awkward evasion of its force, and that the consistent adoption of a similar mis-translation here would still leave the words of the apostle, bearing an ugly complexion in reference to the Socinian system.

However this be, let us hear Mr. Belsham's sagacious reason for pronouncing, that "the connexion *seems* to require" the alteration which he has made.

"It is next to *impossible* that the apostle, when enumerating the distinguishing privileges of his countrymen, should omit the greatest privilege of all: namely, that God was in a peculiar sense their God, the God of Abraham, Isaac, and Jacob. This he has before mentioned as the boast of the Jews, chap. ii. 17; and as the chief glory of believers in Christ, who succeeded to the privileges of God's ancient people, Rom. v. 11; and he *could not avoid repeating it here.*"

Bravo! Mr. Belsham. That is the right way of talking for your purpose. Confidence of assertion will, with most of your readers, pass current for strength of argument. But, disgusting as the task is of combating such imbecility of argument, we must be allowed to examine your assertion. Now, we shall not insist upon the remark, though we could prove it to have considerable force, that the language which Mr. Belsham wishes to force upon the apostle, would appear rather inconsistent with the principle which he asserts in chap. iii. 29, in opposition to that boast of the Jews, which he mentions in ii. 17. We shall not insist upon this, because we are ready to admit, that *if* the apostle had here used the language, "*whose* is the God over all," &c. it might be interpreted in a sense consistent with the declaration, that God is "not the God of the Jews only, but of the Gentiles also." Neither shall we insist upon the obvious verbal criticism, that had he thought it necessary to insert among the privileges of the Jewish nation, "*whose* is the God over all," we might fairly expect it to be inserted in another order, namely, *whose* is the adoption, *whose* are the fathers, *whose* is the God over all, and *of whom*, as concerning the flesh, is Christ; instead of inverting the two last clauses. We shall not press this remark, because Mr. Belsham could easily get over it by saying, that the apostle did not express himself according to the principles of good composition. But we do positively say, what at once overturns all the edifice of Mr. Belsham's reasoning, that it would have been perfect *tautology* to insert the words, which Mr. Belsham asserts it "next to impossible" that the apostle should have omitted; inasmuch, as all the idea of the peculiar relation, in which God had stood to the Jewish people, is intimately included and obviously conveyed in the mention of the other things, which are said to be *theirs;* "the adoption, and the glory, and the covenants, and the giving of the law, and the service, and the promises." Does Mr. Belsham perceive the strength of our position? As he may be unwilling to perceive it, let us force it upon his notice by a brief illustration. The Apostle John (1 John iii. 1.) addressing the disciples of the Lord, and calling them to admire the height of privilege to which they were raised, uses this language: "Behold what manner of love the Father hath bestowed upon us, that we should be called the sons of God!" Who would not laugh at the critic that should gravely assure us, on this passage, that it was *next to impossible* that the apostle, speaking of the privilege of Christians, should not have added, "that God was their father?" Such is the futility of Mr. Belsham's professed reason for altering the apostle's words.

But we must now add a more important remark, which, however, we candidly avow that we do not consider Mr. Belsham competent to understand. We shall be ready to maintain it against any *scholar*, if any such be found to controvert its justice. Many will be *disposed* to controvert it, if they can. We say that the clause, "who is over all, God blessed for ever," is established and confirmed, if it needed any confirmation, by the preceding clause, "of whom, *as concerning the flesh*, Christ came." Mr. Belsham, indeed, with the usual flippancy of ignorance, tells us, that "the phrase, *according to the flesh*, as applied to Christ, no more intimates a superior extraction, different from that of the flesh, than it does when applied (verse 3.) to the Apostle Paul. It is a mere *Jewish idiom*, expressing natural consanguinity." That the phrase κατα σαρκα expresses natural consanguinity, or natural descent, both in the third verse, where it is applied to Paul's kinsmen the Israelites, and in the fifth verse, where it is applied to the man Christ Jesus, we believe no reader needed to be informed by Mr. Belsham. As to his assertion, that it is a *Jewish idiom*, we should have been better pleased if he had adduced the corresponding Hebrew phrase. The unsupported statement, put forward as it is here and elsewhere, reminds us of the artifice by which a professed teacher of Euclid's Elements used to evade the explanation of every difficulty which his pupils proposed: "You cannot understand that at present; that is TRIGONOMETRY." But we assert, that according to the well-known principles of *Greek idiom*, the article το before κατα σαρκα in the fifth verse, indisputably indicates an extraction or descent *different from that of the flesh*. We assert that the words ἐξ ὧν ὁ Χριστος, ΤΟ κατα σαρκα, are learnedly, however inelegantly, rendered by our translators, "of whom, *as concerning* the flesh, Christ came:" where they obviously use the word "*as*" in the restrictive sense of the Latin *quatenus, so far as.* We assert that no competent and *honest* Greek scholar can deny, that the original phrase intimates another view, in which Christ was *not* descended from the Israelites; and that this clause, therefore, is at least in perfect harmony with the following. We have a very similar use of the article in the fifteenth verse of the first chapter: το κατ' εμε, justly rendered by our translators "*as much as* in me is," but sagaciously altered by Mr. Belsham, to, "according to my ability;" with the following *learned* note—"Gr. *that* which is in me!" For any the most moderate Greek scholar, it would be quite superfluous to confirm the justice of our remark by examples: and the attempt would be vain for those, who imagine they understand Greek because they have learned the alphabet, and a little of the grammar, and a little praxis of construction. Mr. Belsham's instance is by no means the first, in which we have seen reason to think it a man's misfortune that he was ever taught the Greek letters.

We must pass more rapidly than we had designed over the remainder of Mr. Belsham's note on this fifth verse. He goes on—"If the *common reading* should be preferred,"—(aye, it is sometimes well to have two strings to our bow,)—" the proper translation would be that of Erasmus, Dr. Clarke, Mr. Locke, Mr. Lindsey," [three Arians and one Socinian,] "and many others, viz. *who is over all, God* be *blessed for evermore;* or, *God who is over all* be *blessed for evermore.*" This would be the *proper* translation! The apostle tacked this benediction to the words, "of whom, as concerning the flesh, Christ came;" much as a Roman Catholic would *cross* himself upon pronouncing them. We shall not condescend to say more upon this outrageous evasion, than that it is every way worthy of those who repel the plain and decisive force of Thomas's acknowledgment, (when convinced by the testimony of his senses that Christ was risen indeed)—"my Lord, and my God," by representing it merely as an exclamation of astonishment, just as a Frenchman with uplifted hands would cry, *O mon Dieu!* Reasoning against such wilful perversions of the Scripture would be quite out of place. But what will the reader say to the effrontery of a short note on the passage last quoted, (John xx. 28,) in the *improved* version of the New Testament, in which the writer *insinuates* that old Beza favoured the Unitarian interpretation of it! We know not whether Mr. Belsham or some of his associates will claim the credit of that note.

We have, however, a parallel instance of dishonesty at the close of Mr. Belsham's note on Rom. ix. 5. from which we have made so many extracts. After the words last cited, he proceeds, "Mr. Lindsey says, (Sequel, p. 204.) that this clause was read so as not to appear to belong to Christ, at least *for the first three centuries.* Origen calls it rashness to suppose that Christ is God over all." If this be not at least an *insinuation* that Origen interpreted this passage, so as not to refer the latter clause to Christ, we know not the meaning of words. And while there is perhaps the same moral turpitude in an insinuated falsehood and in a direct bold lie, we confess that we regard the former as the more *contemptible*. To any smatterer in ecclesiastical history, who is acquainted with Origen's contentions against the Arians of his day, the thing here insinuated must appear, *prima facie*, intrinsically incredible. It was mere curiosity that led us to examine what Origen does say upon the passage. It has come down to us only in the translation of Ruffinus; and we quote the following words from his Commentary on Rom. ix. 4, 5.

"Et miror quidem quomodo quidam, legentes quod idem apostolus in aliis dicit, *Unus Deus Pater, ex quo omnia; et unus Dominus Jesus Christus, per quem omnia*, negent Filium Dei Deum debere profiteri, ne duos deos dicere videantur. ET QUID DE HOC LOCO APOSTOLI FACIENT, IN QUO APERTE CHRISTUS super omnia Deus ESSE PROFITETUR?"* *i. e.* "And I wonder how some, reading that other expression of the same apostle; *There is one God the Father, of whom are all things, and one Lord Jesus Christ, by whom are all things*, infer that they ought not to acknowledge the Son to be God, lest they should seem to speak of two gods. AND WHAT WILL THEY MAKE OF THIS PASSAGE OF THE APOSTLE, IN WHICH CHRIST IS EXPRESSLY DECLARED TO BE *over all God*?"

What an old simpleton was Origen to propose such a question? Little did he imagine what the ingenuity of modern Unitarians can effect. He then goes on to expose the vanity of the argument derived from 2 Cor. viii. 6. remarking with a force of reasoning which Mr. Belsham will find it hard to repel, that they might as reasonably infer from that passage, that the Father is not *Lord*, as they attempt to infer that Christ is not *God*. Yet we are to be gravely told by Messrs. Belsham and Lindsey, that for the first three centuries, Rom. ix. 4. was read so as not to refer the latter clause to Christ!

We could point out a possible source of Mr. Lindsey's blunder, but it would lead us into too long a detail. In Mr. Belsham's case, we find it very hard to account for the assertion altogether from ignorance: and that because we know that he consulted *Rosenmüller* upon the passage; and was he incapable of translating these plain words of that German commentator? "Vulgarius admonet, hoc loco refelli Arianorum impietatem, &c. "*Similia disserit Origines, indicans jam tum fuisse*, qui non audebant Christum appellare Deum, ne plures Deos facere viderentur."

And now, we can honestly assure Mr. Belsham, that, in the highest view, we care not what Origen, or all the so-called fathers of the three first centuries, thought or wrote upon the subject; and that, in the scale of our judgment, their sentiments or practices carry not the weight of a feather as authority. Of Origen, also, we are aware how much he corrupted the doctrine of Scripture upon this subject by his scholastic subtleties and metaphysical refinements; and how hard it would often prove to defend the language of his Trinitarianism from the charge of real Tritheism. The writings of the fathers we value

* *Orig. Op. a C. de la Rue. Par.* tom. iv. p. 612.

chiefly in two views, the latter of which we acknowledge to be of no inconsiderable importance: first, so far as it is a matter of curious historical inquiry to trace the progress of *corrupted* Christianity in the world; and, secondly, so far as they furnish a chain of historic evidence of the genuine authenticity of the Scriptures. But to the Scriptures *alone* we appeal, and acknowledge no *primitive* Christianity but that of which we have an account in the apostolic writings.

Upon the subject on which we have enlarged so much, and indeed upon every other, we find the language of the Old Testament Scriptures in perfect accordance with the New. To prove anything to a modern Socinian *from the Scriptures*, is impossible. But to any one really believing the interpretation given in the New Testament of the things "written in the law of Moses, and in the prophets, and in the Psalms, concerning the Messiah," (Luke xxiv. 44.) it is easy to prove, by numerous quotations, that to the Messiah the incommunicable name of JEHOVAH is expressly applied. See, for instance, Isaiah viii. 13, 14, a passage of which Mr. Belsham himself speaks, but no doubt *exoterically*, as if he admitted its application to the Messiah. (Vol. I. p. 222.) On this point we must add the avowal of our conviction, (however laughably old-fashioned our divinity may appear to Mr. Belsham) that no Hebrew scholar, unless blinded by the most obstinate prejudice of system, could ever have thought of denying the proper plural significancy of the word אלהים, constructed as it is with the singular יהוה; our conviction that all the efforts of theologians to evade the force of that construction, (by adducing a few rare instances in which the plural number is used in Hebrew, as in other languages, where the singular is imported) are in a critical view among the crudest absurdities, by which the wise of this world have endeavoured to support the delusions that they love. And let it be remarked, that the real force of this argument lies, not in any rare and occasional use of that plural designation of the Godhead, as revealing himself in his relations to his redeemed people, but in the *stated* and *continual* use of the construction; while the name יהוה or JEHOVAH, confessedly designating the essential being of God, is never used except in the singular, nor is ever employed *in regimine*, (To this, we are persuaded, the phrase יהוה צבאות forms no real exception.) We avow that we know nothing of the *only true* and living God, but from the *revelation* of his word; and we are persuaded that the testimony of Moses to Israel of old, (Deut. vi. 4.) "Hear, O Israel; JEHOVAH our GOD [יהוה אלהינו] is *one* JEHOVAH," will stand for ever as an impregnable bulwark against the blasphemies of all ancient or modern Socinians, and Arians too. Mr. Belsham may perceive, that we are not afraid of opening to him multiplied points of attack. We court on this subject the assaults of criticism and real learning. But, indeed, much ignorance, and folly the most contemptible, pass current under the name and show of learned criticism, merely because they act as allies to that infidelity which the world loves, and as oppugners of that divine truth which the world hates.

But we must hasten to dismiss this topic with one more observation, to which (as well as to others) the necessary limits of this article forbid us to think of rendering that justice which its importance deserves. The Holy Scriptures never were designed to form scholastic theologians, qualified to discourse philosophically upon every point of their system of divinity. They were designed for making *wise unto salvation*, those, in whose salvation from sin, in all its consequences, the infinite GOD is displaying his own glory; for making them "wise unto salvation through the faith which is in Christ Jesus,"—through the belief of the revealed testimony concerning him. (2 Tim. iii. 15.)* That testimony is one divine and uniform *whole*, from which no part can be separated without destroying the entire texture. It is, therefore, no marvel that those who disbelieve the Scriptural testimony concerning the *work* and *office* of the Redeemer, should stumble at the scriptural testimony that he who was *made flesh*—who became *the man Christ Jesus*—is yet the WORD which "*was with God, and was God*—God blessed for ever"—one with the Father who called him to that work, which he willingly humbled himself to undertake. Nor is it any marvel that those who are led by various circumstances to hold what is called the *orthodox* system, but who really corrupt the doctrine of Scripture on the work and office of the Messiah, should correspondently corrupt the scriptural doctrine concerning his person, and make it the theme of presumptuous metaphysical speculations, and the vain subtleties of the schools. The two things stand in the most intimate and indissoluble connexion; both pervade the whole texture of the Scripture; so that any attempt to disjoin or to corrupt them produces that inconsistency of error, which would turn the truth of God into a lie the most absurd. For instance, we have no hesitation in saying, that even the little which Mr. Belsham professedly allows, concerning the relation in which the Redeemer stands to his people, is so monstrously inconsistent with the rest of his avowed sentiments, that he and his disciples have very little pretensions indeed to the title of rational Christians. In a short note borrowed from Dr. Taylor, on the very first words in the epistle to the Romans,—"Paul, a *servant* of Jesus Christ," he tells us,—and most truly, that "Δυλος is a servant who is the *absolute property* of his master." Correspondently with this, the Redeemer is declared to be ὁ Κυριος, the Lord, the absolute proprietor of his people, *unto whom*

* Innumerable as the matters of reprehension are, which we are obliged to pass over in Mr. Belsham's work, we think it would be unfair to withhold altogether from our readers one that occurs in his *Exposition* of Rom. xv. 4. The apostle having, in the preceding verse, quoted from the Psalms one of those testimonies which he marks as delivered concerning Christ, adds, "For whatsoever things *were written* aforetime, were written for our learning, that we, through patience and comfort of *the Scriptures*, might have hope." This Mr. Belsham chooses to mistranslate as follows:—"For whatsoever things were *formerly written for our instruction*, were written that," &c.; and immediately subjoins this profane exposition: "The examples of patient suffering under reproach and persecution, RECORDED IN ANCIENT HISTORY, and particularly in the Jewish Scriptures, were written for our information and encouragement," &c. It is only a hint, but it is a curious hint, of that *esoteric* doctrine for the initiated, which we noticed as occasionally appearing in the work. And does Mr. Belsham really *believe* that the apostle meant to include in his statement such histories as PLUTARCH'S Lives, and XENOPHON'S account of SOCRATES, as well as the Jewish Scriptures? No; he does not. We must ask another plain question. Is not Mr. CARLILE a more *honest* and a more consistent man, than such professedly Christian *divines*?

they live, and *unto whom* they die: (Rom. xiv. 8, 9.* 2 Cor. v. 15.) —while he himself testifies that plain principle,—that "all live *unto God*;" (Luke xx. 38.) and believers are therefore suitably addressed in this language, "Ye are *not your own*, for ye are bought with a price: therefore, glorify God in your body, and in your spirits, *which are God's*." (1 Cor. vi. 19, 20.) Now, we tell Mr. Belsham, that while he admits anything of the indisputable force of these passages, it is vain for him to struggle against the declared Godhead of the Messiah. He *unto whom* the believer lives, and *unto whom* he dies, is, and must be, the believer's Lord and God. It is vain for him to mis-translate 1 Cor. i. 2. and similar passages,—(as Acts ix. 14. Rom. x. 12, 13. 2 Tim. ii. 22. the last of these Mr. Belsham seems to have forgotten to corrupt,)—in which believers are described as "*calling upon the name* of Jesus Christ their Lord." It is vain for him to bolster up his mis-translation with the parade of learned authorities of men, who try to confound two Hebrew phrases perfectly distinct, and distinctly rendered in the Greek of the New Testament, ἐπικαλεισθαι το ὀνομα, and ἐφ' ὁς ἐπικεκληται το ὀνομα. We tell him that all this unrighteous labour is vain; for that the worship of the lips, or verbal invocation of the name of the Lord, is a small thing, in comparison of that homage of the heart, and that devotedness of the life, which the most high God alone can claim or rightfully receive. And while it is not at all from the exercise of natural reason, that we derive our conviction of the truths for which we contend, we candidly avow, that we consider our views as much more truly *rational* than Mr. Belsham's; nay, that we consider his views as utterly irrational, as they are utterly unscriptural. "The foolishness of God is wiser than men."

Upon the work of the Messiah in *redeeming* his people by his own blood, becoming at once the great high priest over the house of God, and the great sacrifice for sin, "bearing the sins of many in his own body on the cross," and putting them away by dying, "the just for the unjust;" upon this subject our limits forbid us to say much in opposition to Mr. Belsham's perversion of the plain testimony of Scripture. Mr. Belsham, in his exposition of the words "ye have been bought with a price," (1 Cor. vii. 23.) gravely tells us, that "it *is not necessary* to limit the price of redemption to the death of Christ alone;"—that Christians have been *redeemed* not only "by all that he has *taught*, and done, and suffered, by his resurrection and ascension;" but "by the gifts of the holy Spirit and the *labours of his apostles*." We are such tame and unphilosophic readers of the Bible, that we think it of infinitely more importance to inquire what the Scriptures say upon this solemn subject, than what Mr. Belsham or any other reverend gentleman may think it *necessary* to say. And inquiring in that way, we do hold his language to be as impudent an outrage upon the uniform testimony of Scripture, as can be paralleled even from his own writings. The church of Christ has been redeemed

* On the passage, "Whether we live, we live *to the Lord*," &c. Mr. Belsham favours us with the following short note: "Τῳ Κυριῳ —'to this master.' Wakefield, *i. e.* to God. See ver. 6." All the answer we shall make to Messrs. Belsham and Wakefield, but it is decisive, is, *See* verse 9.

"by the labours of his apostles," and no doubt by what they also have *suffered* as well as *done*, in the apostolic character! We need not pursue the profane idea; else we could easily prove that Mr. Belsham considers himself *a redeemer* of the church of Christ. But he must pardon us for giving more weight to the testimony of Christ himself, (Matth. xx. 28.) that he came "to give his own life a ransom for many," λυτρον αντι πολλων· that *his blood* was "shed for many for the remission of sins." According to the Scriptures, we find that HE exclusively is "the Lamb of God, which taketh away the sin of the world;" and that HE "appeared in the last age of the world, to put away sin *by the sacrifice of himself*." (John i. 29. Heb. ix. 26—28.) According to Mr. Belsham, the indignant question which Paul proposed to the Church at Corinth, in rebuke of their classing themselves under human leaders,—"was *Paul* crucified for you?"—might a few years after be repelled by the answer, "No: but Peter was *crucified for us*, and Paul beheaded for us."

But we must forbear to enlarge on this topic; and must abstain even from exposing the dishonest artifice which Mr. Belsham employs in aid of his system;—that stale trick of putting forward the grossest *misrepresentations* of the truth which he opposes. To any one, who wishes to be dishonest here, it is most easy to confound that Scriptural truth with the very unscriptural language, which some professed advocates for the doctrine of atonement have held, about the *blood* of Christ, his *appeasing the wrath* of God, &c. &c. But Mr. Belsham knows right well, that all consistent Christians maintain, that the provision of the Redeemer was the "unspeakable gift" of the love of God; while they maintain that this was the only way in which pardon and eternal life could be given to sinful creatures, consistently with the divine righteousness and holiness and truth. But, passing this point, we think it not inexpedient to illustrate the ignorance of this expositor of Scripture,—his ignorance even of the letter of those Scriptures which he pretends to interpret.

Mr. Belsham finds it convenient for his purpose to assert, that, under the law of Moses, "no sacrifices were appointed for voluntary transgressions," but "only for sins of *ignorance*," by which a Jew contracted *ceremonial* pollution. (Vol. iv. pp. 574-577.) And this assertion he repeats most frequently, and with the utmost confidence. Now, instead of arguing this point with Mr. Belsham, we shall only quote a few verses from Levit. vi.—"If a soul sin, and commit a trespass against the Lord, and lie unto his neighbour in that which was delivered him to keep, or in fellowship, or in a thing taken away by violence, or hath deceived his neighbour, or have found that which was lost, and lieth concerning it, and sweareth falsely," [something more, we think, than sins of ignorance, described here]—"then it shall be, because he hath sinned, and is guilty, that he shall restore, &c. And he shall bring his trespass-offering unto the Lord, a ram without blemish, out of the flock. . . . And the *priest* shall make an *atonement* for him before the Lord," &c. This, we conceive, is quite sufficient for exposing the utter falsehood of Mr. Belsham's assertion. But our *learned* author refers us to the Apostle's words in Hebrews ix. 7, in proof of his position, that "the sacrifices on the day of atonement were expressly appointed for sins of ignorance," and renders the words ὑπερ ἑαυτου και των του λαου αγνοηματων by—"for the sins of ignorance *of himself*, and of the people!" Here, also, he only betrays his ignorance, and that the more inexcusably, because the correction of it lay before his eyes, even in Rosenmüller, upon whom he draws so largely for his learning. We would refer him, also, to Biel's Thesaurus, and Trommius's Concordance, under the words ἀγνοημα, ἀγνοια, ἀγνοεω. Indeed, that the words are used in the same comprehensive sense with ἁμαρτημα ἁμαρτια, and ἁμαρτανω, is obvious even from Hebrews v. 1—3. The biblical student may advantageously trace the analogy between them and the words rendered *fool*, and folly.

But we must dismiss much important matter upon this subject unnoticed, to make a brief remark upon another, and to exemplify the *absurdities* in which Mr. Belsham, and so many others, involve themselves, by their dishonest determination to wrest the Scriptures into a seeming support of their own system, formed altogether independently of the Scriptures. We have now in view the subject of divine influence, or influence of the Spirit of God upon his people, as distinct from those miraculous gifts which were peculiar to the apostolic age, and communicated by the laying on of the Apostles' hands. And, lest our sentiments here should be mistaken, and confounded with those too generally prevalent among religious professors, we wish to premise, that we hold all pretensions to divine influence, except through the medium of the truths revealed from heaven in the written word, to be the delusions of enthusiasm, or the fictions of imposture. But we are as firmly persuaded from the Scriptures, that this word is, "the sword *of the spirit*," which none but the Spirit of God can at any time render effectual, by his own power, for either commencing the work of faith, or maintaining it in his people. We need scarcely observe, also, that, in many passages of the New Testament, the expression "the Holy Spirit" does designate only those extraordinary communications which have ceased with the occasion for which they were made; and which, even while they continued, were essentially distinct from every thing connected with salvation. For example, when we read, in Acts xix. 2. what ought to be rendered as the self-same expression is in John vii. 39.—"We have not so much as heard whether the Holy Spirit be given;"—who can doubt but the gifts of the Spirit are the thing intended?

Mr. Belsham, of course, sets his face against the idea of any work of the Spirit of God, distinct from the communication of *miraculous gifts* in the apostolic age; and these gifts, he repeatedly acknowledges, were not possessed by the Christians at Rome, when the Apostle addressed his letter to them. Well, when he comes to that passage of the letter, (Rom. xv. 13.) where the Apostle thus expresses himself, "Now, the God of hope [of *this* hope] fill you with all joy and peace in believing, that ye may abound in hope [in *this* hope] through the power of the Holy Spirit!" what does Mr. Belsham make of this? The words plainly and unequivocally mark, that while it is only *in believing* the things reported in the Gospel, disciples can be filled with all true joy and peace, it is at the same time only through the divine *power of the Holy Spirit* that this effect can be produced by the gospel. But this would not suit Mr. Belsham's system. He therefore gravely assures us that the meaning is, "Through the promises of the Gospel, *which are confirmed by the powerful operations of the Holy Spirit:*" and adds, "Of these the Roman believers must have had abundant evidence, though, not having been yet visited by an apostle, they had not themselves been the subjects of these powers." Again, on Rom. xiv. 17. he remarks, that "the Roman converts had not indeed yet received the Holy Spirit, but they probably knew and conversed with many who had received it." But, may we not ask Mr. Belsham what a pious humbug, according to his system, was this prayer of the apostle, (and Mr. Belsham himself expounds it very piously as a prayer addressed to God,) that God *might fill them,* &c. if the effect desired was to be produced in a merely natural way, independently of all divine power exerted on their minds? But much more may we not ask him, how it was possible that this effect could have been produced at all by the promises of the Gospel, according to his system? For he elsewhere informs us,—very foolishly indeed,—that, by the gift of his Spirit to the apostolic Christians, God "*announced his acceptance of their services.*" (Vol. ii. p. 60.) So the Roman Christians were to be filled with all peace and joy, by hearing that this gift was communicated to others, while they had themselves no such announcement of the divine acceptance of their own services! Into such absurdities do men plunge themselves, in their zeal for opposing the word of God! We shall only add, that any who were rejoicing in their possession of those miraculous gifts, were filled with a joy essentially different from "joy in the Holy Spirit;" opposed by the express words of Christ himself, Luke x. 20. and inconsistent with the nature and design of those gifts, which were "for a sign not to them that believed, but to them that believed not," 1 Cor. xiv. 22.

At the same time, we are aware that many passages of Scripture, which are commonly otherwise applied by those popular divines who trouble themselves very little about their real meaning, do indeed import nothing but those miraculous gifts of the Spirit, which have ceased with the occasion for them. We are also well aware that Mr. Belsham, in almost the grossest of his perversions and corruptions of the word, is kept in countenance by numbers of the most respectable name; that he may boast the authority, not only of learned philosophers, but also of Most Reverend, Right Reverend, Very Venerable, and Reverend Doctors of Divinity:—high-sounding titles for dying sinners. The believer of the Scriptures can be at no loss to account for this; and sees in the fact only a confirmation of those sacred oracles, which are so generally opposed by those who *profess* to receive them as of divine original. He sees, that in these times *of the Gentiles* just a similar display of human ungodliness and human folly is going on throughout Christendom, as was in the former age exhibited by the mass of the Jewish people under the law of Moses; while the word of God continues in every age to accomplish the purposes for which it has been sent, the grand purposes of his rich mercy and saving power in that remnant left "according to the election of grace;" and shall ultimately confound all the wisdom of the wise, and bring to nought all the understanding of the prudent of his world.

It now only remains that we should justify the opinion which we have pronounced of Mr. Belsham's utter incapacity—in point of *scholarship*—to execute the task which he undertook. Some instances of his *learning* have already incidentally appeared while we were treating of other topics. We subjoin a few more ridiculous specimens, which must prove decisive with every real scholar; though Mr. Belsham so seldom ventures out of the leading-strings of his learned guides, that they may otherwise appear of a very trifling nature. We shall adduce our examples *per lancem saturam*, as they meet our eye in turning over a few of his pages; only avoiding those which might involve us in any prolixity of remark.

1 Cor. vi. 2. "Do ye not know that the saints shall judge the world?"—Mr. Belsham renders it—"What! know ye not," &c. and subjoins the following note:—"What! 'ἢ οὐκ.' Griesbach prefixes ἢ upon the authority of the Alexandrine, Ephrem, and other copies.—*Num ignoratis.* Rosenmuller." Now, is it not most manifest that the writer of this note imagined, that the insertion of the interrogative particle ἢ affected more or less the sense of the passage, so that the translation *num ignoratis*, which he thinks it needful to adduce from Rosenmuller, would not be warranted if ἢ were omitted? And if he conceived that there was some extraordinary force in this particle, which he aimed at retaining by his exclamatory "what!" we beg to know why he did not introduce the same *improvement* into his version of the 9th verse, beginning with the self-same words, ἢ οὐκ οἴδατε.

1 Cor. viii. 2. For—"he knoweth nothing yet as he ought to know,"—Mr. Belsham gives, he knoweth *not yet* as, &c. with the following sagacious note:—

"He knoweth not yet. The received text reads, 'he knoweth nothing,' &c. But the Alexandrine manuscript reads, οὔπω for οὐδέπω, and both that and many other ancient copies drop οὐδέν. See Pearce and Griesbach."

Here it is certain that he imagined some difference of meaning between the two words, οὐδέπω and οὔπω. We suspect also, that we could conjecture the ludicrous mistake upon his mind, which made him dislike the construction, οὐδέπω οὐδέν. But we shall only assure Mr. Belsham that, whether with Griesbach we retain the common text, or adopt that which Mr. Belsham patronizes, in either case, the version of our translators is equally correct.

In a note on 1 Cor. ix. 10. he informs us, that "Griesbach reads, *he who thresheth ought to partake of his hope*." Now Griesbach's reading, and a very good one, is καὶ ὁ ἀλοῶν, ἐπ' ἐλπίδι τοῦ μετέχειν. *i. e.* ὀφείλει ἀλοᾷν. Mr. Belsham will probably stare when we inform him, that this reading—so far from admitting the translation by which he expounds it in his note—is the very reading which he has *unwittingly* introduced into the text, from Bishop Pearce's English version, viz, *he who thresheth* ought to thresh *in hope of partaking*.

1 Cor. x. 33. It has long been remarked by all interpreters, and, indeed, is obvious to an attentive English reader, that the first verse of the following chapter ought to be read in immediate connexion with this verse. But Mr. Belsham, not content with adopting this, and

anxious to add some farther improvement from his own stores, runs the two verses into one sentence, separating them only by a comma; thus, "*And as* I . . . . that they may be saved, *so* be imitators of me," &c. Here, it is evident, that because unfortunately he knew that ἐγω is *I*, and και *and*, he conceived that καθως καγω might signify *and as I*. It would have been much safer for Mr. Belsham not to have been so ambitious, as he commonly is, of improving Griesbach's text. But there is nothing which so infallibly brings its own punishment with it as vanity; and, especially, the vain affectation of learned criticism in an unlettered man.

We believe we might save ourselves the trouble of adducing any farther specimens of Mr. Belsham's learning; but let us open another volume. Rom. v. 20. Mr. Belsham translates, "Now the law *made a little entrance*," with this note "παρεισηλθεν, *subintravit*. Vulg." Is the classical reader curious to know what put this comical idea into the man's head? We shall tell him. Mr. Belsham found *subintravit* as a Latin version of παρεισηλθεν, and again unfortunately happened to know that *sub*, in Latin compounds, often has a *diminutive* significancy. To tell the truth, Dr. Newcome's version, (if Mr. Belsham quote it truly, which we do not stop to examine,) "entered in *privily*," is little less ridiculous. The Greek verb undoubtedly imports, what in common English we express by "to slip in." But in the present passage, it obviously denotes the incidental introduction of the law as an *accessory*; as *subordinate* to that Gospel which was both preached before the law, and continues in force after the law.

In Rom. x. Mr. Belsham transposes the 16th and 17th verses, placing the 17th in connexion with the 15th, and treats us with the following note: "This transposition of the 16th and 17th verses, as suggested by L'Enfant, is so necessary to clearing up the Apostle's reasoning, that the propriety of it can scarcely be doubted, *though it is unsupported by authorities*." So little does he make of the testimony of all MSS. ancient versions, &c. &c. But it is obvious to any one looking at the *original*, that the 17th verse is an inference drawn from the words of Isaiah quoted in the 16th, and, therefore, rightly stands in the most indubitable connexion with these, τις ἐπιστευσε τῃ ἀκοῃ ἡμων; Ἀρα ἡ πιστις ἐξ ἀκοης. Numberless, indeed, are the instances in which Mr. Belsham, from the want of all critical knowledge of his own, adopts the most crude and extravagant *suggestions* of preceding interpreters; and, like a strainer, lets the pure liquor escape, while he faithfully retains the sediment and straws with which it has been blended.

But in the 19th verse of the same chapter, he gives us a really *new* interpretation of the words, "hath not Israel known?" which is properly his own, and for which he seems to take some credit, introducing it with the remark that most of the commentators interpret the text erroneously. It is not worth while to copy the whole of his note: but he tells us, that the Apostle divides some supposed *objection from the unsuccessfulness of the ministry* into two parts: "Ver. 18. Have they not heard? *Answer*. They have. Ver. 19. Have they acknowledged and received the Gospel? *Answer*. No. That the word γινωσκω sometimes bears the sense of ἐπιγινωσκω, is well known. See Schleusner." So, because the simple verb and its compound are sometimes used in the sense of acknowledging, our learned author conceived that the words μη οὐκ ἐγνω Ισραηλ, could mean, *hath Israel acknowledged?* no doubt imagining that μη ουκ were two negatives, and equivalent with an affirmative. It is almost superfluous to remark, that the real meaning of the passage is, *hath not Israel* had notice? *i. e.* of the consequence of their rejection of the gospel. We have a perfectly similar instance of this use of the verb, in Rom. i. 21. διοτι γνοντες τον Θεον, "because that when they *knew God*," *i. e.* had sufficient notification of his "eternal power and Godhead." We might prove Mr. Belsham's ignorance of the common force of the interrogative μη, from his *improved* version of Rom. xi. 1. Λεγω ουν μη ἀπωσατο ὁ Θεος τον λαον αυτου; which our foolish old translators render, "I say then, hath God cast away his people?" but Mr. Belsham so much more accurately, "*Do I say, then,* that God *has* rejected his people?" But really, the task of exposing his ignorance becomes quite disgusting. His ignorance would be blameless, if it were not equalled by the presumption and affectation of learning which accompany it.

Our author often manifests as classical a proficiency in English as in Greek. Rom. viii. 13. "If ye live after the flesh, *you will die.*" xi. 26. "And so all Israel *will* be saved." xi. 34, 35. "For who hath known, &c. Or who *has* first given to him," &c. 1 Cor. viii. 1. "Knowledge puffeth up, but love *edifies*," &c. &c. &c. Such is the improved version of Paul's Epistles with which the Reverend gentleman, after the labour of thirty years, obliges the Unitarian Society and the public.

If we be asked, whether the work does not contain instances of really amended version, we readily reply, several; not one indeed new, but adopted from preceding interpreters: though Mr. Belsham frequently fails of assigning them to their proper authors, and sometimes ludicrously mistakes the meaning of the right translation that he adopts. So much has long since been done in the field of biblical criticism, that it was scarcely possible he should not light upon something good. If we had room, we should gladly quote him with commendation, in Rom. ix. 3. xiv. 23. 1 Cor. i. 26. iii. 9. vi. 4. 2 Cor. v. 3. et al. But we must add, that along with all his wilful corruptions and perversions of the text, and along with all his most puerile and ignorant alterations of the received version, he frequently leaves that version unaltered where it calls for amendment, and where the amendment is most obvious. *E. gr.* in 1 Tim. vi. 10. he retains, "For the love of money is *the* root of all evil," instead of "*a* root." He throughout retains "bishops," for "overseers;" "ministers" and "deacons," for "servants," &c. But we must conclude this article, which we have been obliged to extend to an unusual length; though the criminations of our author, which we have brought forward, form a very small portion indeed, of what we are ready to substantiate. We think it not improbable, that we shall have occasion to return to the subject; and we shall be forward to meet Mr. Belsham again, if he should attempt any defence, even in a sixpenny pamphlet.

REVIEW

OF

"THOUGHTS ON THE ANGLICAN AND ANGLO-AMERICAN CHURCHES.

BY

JOHN BRISTED,

COUNSELLOR AT LAW.

New York, printed: London, reprinted. Holdsworth, 1823."

[This Article was printed for The New Edinburgh Review, but never published.]

We are always well pleased, as reviewers, when an author gives us some account of himself. We understand a work the better for having some acquaintance with the writer; and when he introduces himself to our acquaintance, we sometimes come to know him better than he designed we should,—perhaps better than he knows himself. The auto-biography with which Mr. Bristed favours us, is dispersed through his Introduction, and is interrupted almost as often as the renowned "Story of the King of Bohemia and his Seven Castles." But the following is a summary of it:—

His father was a beneficed clergyman of the Church of England, as his grandfather and great-grandfather had been, and his elder brother is now. He was sent, while yet a child, (as we collect, between eleven and twelve years old,) to Winchester College, of which Dr. Joseph Warton was then head master. (P. 6.) He had been there little more than three years, and was near the head of the senior part of the fifth form, when a rebellion broke out against the authority of Dr. Huntingford, the warden of the college, and now combining with that office the bishopric of Hereford. He describes the rebellion as "headed, and the *oath* of universal conspiracy administered, by Richard Mant, then one of the prefects in the sixth form, and now a Protestant champion of the Popish doctrine of *baptismal* regeneration, and one of the editors of Mant's and Doyley's Family Bible." (P. 10.) We must observe, *en passant*, that this same Right Rev. Dr. Richard Mant seems an object of our author's peculiar spleen and acrimony: whether on grounds exclusively theological, we shall not now inquire. This boyish rebellion issued in the expulsion of the first forty boys, who stood senior on the college rolls; among whom was young Bristed. We hope our author is inaccurate when he charges the Warden and Fellows with a direct *breach of faith* in exercising this severe discipline.

Returning for a few years to his parental roof, he informs us that, until he was seventeen, his " steps were steadily directed towards an *entrance into the vestibule* of the Church of England;" that is, in English, he designed to follow his father's profession of a clergyman in the Establishment. We next find our author at Oxford (p. 15,) where he is dissuaded from taking orders by the Rev. Dr. Septimus Collinson, Provost of Queen's College; the Doctor urging that a man's preferment in the national church is determined, not by his personal merit, but by interest, &c. and that the clerical market is overstocked. He is thus induced to " relinquish all thoughts of *the Church*, and embrace the calling of a physician."—We must pause a little here, to animadvert briefly on our author's inconsistency in the following sentence:—

" My objections to the Church of England *were then*, and are now, confined exclusively to her *political* position; her close alliance with the state; her system of patronage, whether lay or clerical, excluding the *congregations* altogether from any choice of the *clerk* who is to minister to them spiritually; and her provision of tithes. Her liturgy, articles, and homilies, are all strictly *spiritual*," &c. &c.

Fair and softly! Mr. Bristed. Your objections to the Church of England, according to your own showing, *were then*, certainly, neither more nor less than this: that you apprehended she did not afford you a sufficient prospect of preferment adequate to your merit; and we do not say that it was not a very suitable consideration to decide a young man in his choice of a profession for earning his bread. But why should you endeavour to disguise this motive? Whether you *have now* any objection to the Church of England, essentially different from what you *had then*, we shall perhaps be better able to decide, as we proceed in the examination of your work.

Our author tells us, p. 34, that in his eighteenth year he applied himself to the study of medicine; " first in the country, then in London, then in Edinburgh, with the characteristic ardour of a *sanguine* temperament." Whether he ever graduated at Oxford, we are not informed; nor how long he remained at Edinburgh. But on his return to London he soon relinquished all thoughts of the practice of medicine; enrolled himself a member of the Honourable Society of the Inner Temple: and continued for two years in the office of Mr. Chitty, cultivating " the melancholy science of special pleading," p. 37. However, before he was called to the English bar, [Qu. Has he ever been called to it?] he describes himself as bitten with the imagination, that *they order matters better* in America than in Great Britain; and in the spring of 1806, (when, we conceive, he was about the age of twenty-four,) he emigrated to the United States, with sanguine expectations, which appear from his language not to have been realized. At this we are not at all surprised. Many emigrate to America under great mistakes about the country to which they go, and possessing little of the qualifications requisite for succeeding in it.

On his arrival in New York, our author renewed an acquaintance which he had formed in Edinburgh, with the Rev. Dr. Mason, a Presbyterian minister of the Associate Reformed Church, p. 41, and this acquaintance "soon ripened into an intimacy truly fraternal, that lasted about six years, when it was broken up, and for ever scattered to the wild winds, by the systematic sycophancy and incessant intrigue of a very reverend brother." This is very sad: but our readers must receive Mr. Bristed's invectives and panegyrics *cum grano salis*. He lays on both with a trowel. Of Dr. Mason, he tells us, that "if his, &c." he "might have *brightened the remotest recesses of Christendom with the blaze of his intellectual glory*—might have been what Chalmers is"!!! We think we might venture to draw a craniological map of Mr. Bristed's organs. The sentence which immediately follows the words last quoted, and which concludes his personal narrative, affords a curious and awful spectacle of a popular religionist. It runs thus:—

"When the breach between Dr. Mason and myself had been rendered sufficiently deep and *deadly* to admit of *no possible cure on this side of the grave*, I returned into the bosom of that mother church which had nourished me, and my brethren, and my father, and my father's father, for many preceding generations."

It is with a feeling very different from anything hostile towards Mr. Bristed, that we advise him, before he resumes his pen upon such subjects, to *think* what kind of religion it can be, with which the sentiment he has deliberately penned is consistent. A breach between two men, bearing the Christian name, so *deadly*, as to admit of no possible cure on this side of the grave! and this after a truly *fraternal* intimacy of six years! Supposing that *Christian brotherhood* had subsisted between them during that period, whatever might be the trespass of either against the other, (and we have not the least curiosity to inquire into the particulars of the breach,) there was a plain and decisive rule, prescribing, on divine authority, a *healing* course, which, even in the last stage of it, is utterly inconsistent with the sentiment which Mr. Bristed has thought himself warranted to express. We do allude to the precept in Matt. xviii. 15—17. though we are aware that it is commonly considered as antiquated, even by those who make the most ado about evangelical religion; as well as that most of the religious communities called *churches* are so constituted, as to render the observance of the precept *impossible* in them. But we confess that we think little, or think very ill, of any religious system, which sets aside such a divine command. Every thing under the Christian name, which stands opposed to the word of Christ, we regard as *antichristian*.

One more remark we must offer on the passage which we have last quoted from Mr. Bristed. It strikingly exemplifies the light way in which many professors change their religious connexion as they would change a suit of clothes. Our author was bred up a staunch Episcopalian. Settling in America, he formed an intimacy with a Presbyterian minister, and, (as he tells us,) "was *prodigiously struck* with the force, and vigour, and range of intellect, exhibited in his conversation." He also "never heard a *greater preacher*," not excepting "the mighty Horsley himself." He, *therefore*, "during six years, *sat under the ministry*" of this Presbyterian divine. But a deadly breach takes place between them: upon which our author lays aside his Presbyterianism, and returns to the bosom of his mother church. Mr. Bristed has multitudes to keep him in countenance; multitudes who are similarly determined in their selection of a *soi-disant* church, not by any scriptural consideration, not by the slightest regard to divine authority, but by their taste and fancy, and especially by their admiration of one preacher, or their quarrelling with another. A favourite *clergyman* is the factotum of their religious connexion; and to *sit under his ministry* is the phrase constantly employed for expressing their church-fellowship. We only say, at present, that if any thing like this now constitute the fellowship of a Christian church,—if any conduct like this be now allowable to Christians, Christianity must have indeed greatly changed in its nature and principles since the apostolic day. But if "the word of God liveth and abideth for ever," (1 Pet. i. 23. 25.) all such nominal Christianity, as we have exhibited, is but *nominal*.

It may be needful to apprize our readers, that by "The Anglican and Anglo-American Churches," Mr. Bristed means that part only of the religious system in both countries which is termed Episcopalian; and that while he boasts, at the outset of his work, that he has "a kind of hereditary and family claim to be enrolled among the advocates of *the* Protestant Episcopal Church, whether it be that established in England, or its legitimate offspring *located* in these United States;" he at times appears to combine with this attachment to Episcopacy what, we believe, is rarely connected with it, a decided hostility to the close alliance between church and state. We say that he at times appears hostile to this alliance: for he really seems to us to have no fixed principles upon the subject. As to his attachment to Episcopacy, we cannot discover throughout his work any reason that he assigns for it, but his *hereditary* and *family* connexion with that system; and we must submit it to Mr. Bristed's consideration, whether that would not have been fully as cogent a reason why his ancestors should have remained in connexion with the see of Rome. He quotes, indeed, the following from Mr. Granville Sharp, with apparent approbation, p. 22. "If I am prejudiced at all, I am sure it is in favour of Episcopacy; for . . . I am even descended from one of the same *holy function*, . . . and above all, I am thoroughly *convinced by the holy Scriptures*, that the institution of that order in the Christian church is of God." Indeed! convinced of this *from the Scriptures!* Really, we should have thought this impossible, had not Mr. Sharp assured us of it. As far as we know, the other advocates for the divine right of episcopacy bring us, not to the Scriptures, but to the so-called Fathers; whose authority in these matters we utterly deny. But that the Scriptures of the New Testament speak of the ἐπίσκοποι, the *bishops* or *overseers* of a Christian church, as identical with its *elders* or πρεσβύτεροι, we have thought and think indisputably evident. (Acts xx. 17. 28; Phil.

i. 1; Titus i. 5—7.) Would that Mr. Sharp or Mr. Bristed had condescended to point to the Scriptures which teach them otherwise. Till some one does so, we must be allowed to say, in the first place, that the apostles use the expression *Church of Christ* exclusively in one or other of two senses, either for the collective aggregate of those in every age and nation who have been redeemed unto God, and shall be brought unto eternal glory by his Son, or for the assembly of believers in any particular place, who, united together in the profession of the apostolic gospel, walk together as brethren according to the rule of the apostolic word, and meet on the first day of the week, "to show forth the Lord's death;" but that they never use the phrase in any such sense as that in which men now speak of the *Church of England*, the *Church of Scotland*, &c. And, in the second place, we say, that each of these Christian bodies or churches, in any place, is described as having, or designed to have, a plurality of bishops or elders, whose office was very different indeed from that of *clergymen* or *preachers;* persons selected from the brethren as qualified to take the special oversight of the church, and acknowledged by the church as the gifts of Christ to the body for that service; and that this is the only sense in which the *bishops* of a church are spoken of in the New Testament. Without intending to enter into any regular discussion of the question, we throw out these suggestions for Mr. Bristed's consideration; and would only add, that while we allow, within certain limits, the right of every man to use *words* in whatever sense he pleases, if he only make known the meaning in which he employs them, we must yet assert, that the misapplication of *scriptural* terms ought to be dreaded by every one who reverences the word of God; that there has been no more powerful engine for obscuring divine truth, and supporting the most pernicious errors, than the use of the words of Scripture in an unscriptural meaning.

Mr. Bristed, p. 226, speaks of the non-juring bishops of Scotland, to whom Dr. Seabury of America applied for *consecration*, as having "preserved the *succession of their order* by new and regular consecrations." From this language our readers might be led to think, that our author carried his Episcopalianism so far, as to credit the lineal succcession from the apostles transmitted by the *Nags-head* consecration to our Protestant bishops, through all the most profligate and impious of the popes of Rome,—a fiction so monstrously absurd that it might excite laughter, if it were not so monstrously profane that indignation rather must predominate in the Christian who considers it. But in another passage Mr. Bristed himself appears to laugh at the notion. For thus he expresses himself, p. 299.

"Mr. Daubeny denies the *validity* of any *sacrament*, unless it be episcopally administered. Yet two primates of all England, not to mention some simple Anglican prelates, and four supreme, secular, sovereign pontiffs of that church establishment, were never baptized by a bishop, priest, or deacon. What then, according to the Sarum archdeacon's position, is to become of these *un*baptized hierarchs appointed by *un*baptized heads of the church, and consecrated by bishops whose predecessors were excommunicated at Rome by the old lady of

Babylon; from whose hands alone the Anglican Church *derives her unbroken, apostolic, episcopal succession?*"

Indeed, our author, though frequently expressing the most outrageous reverence for the *clerical* order, so that he speaks of them as "priests," "ministers of the sanctuary," "ambassadors of the Lord of hosts," nay, as "waiting upon the stately steppings of Jehovah in the sanctuary," [foh! Mr. Bristed,] yet frequently expresses himself even of bishops in such language as proves that he is not a high churchman, and does not consider them as becoming by mere consecration any successors to the apostles. Thus contemptuously, for instance, he writes about some of that order, whom he dislikes, p. 178.

"No other proof is wanting of the *necessary* tendency to evil engendered by the close connexion of the Anglican Church with a secular empire than the simple fact, that, in the present age, the British government has actually made such clerks as Tomline, Marsh, and Mant, bishops, for the sole merit of having laboured to explain away the essential doctrines of the Church of England, as expressed in her articles, and to fasten the foul stain of *popery* upon a Protestant establishment," &c. &c.

We, who write in a part of the British dominions where Episcopalians are *dissenters*, would scarcely express ourselves with so much scorn, of these right reverend gentlemen. And we do think that the Bishop of Peterborough is treated by our author with very unjustifiable disrespect. Dr. Marsh is a very respectable scholar; whose appointment to the Episcopal bench, considering it only in a political view, (in which alone *we* can consider any such appointments) does credit to our government. If his *eighty-seven questions* have been ever so injudicious, (and we do conceive that it would be the *wisdom* of the English hierarchy to keep matters of that kind as quiet as possible) they were probably designed honestly to promote what his lordship thinks very good, and to put down what he thinks very bad. We might, at least, urge in extenuation of his error, that which Mr. Bristed himself quotes (p. 146.) as a memorable apothegm uttered by Lord Clarendon, in reference to Archbishop Laud, that "of all persons who *can* read and write, the clergy are the most innocent of any practical wisdom or common sense." Far be it from us to say that we agree either with Lord Clarendon or with Mr. Bristed, who would confine the application of the maxim to the *state* clergy. There is no doubt that Laud's bigotry and intolerance contributed much to the loss of Charles's crown and life. But we must be pardoned for thinking that the king, who abandoned himself to the counsels of such an ecclesiastic, and gave full scope to his wildest theological freaks, was just as *innocent* as the prelate of any practical wisdom or common sense. And we do believe that the governments of Europe will yet discover, however slowly, that it is their *practical wisdom* to disentangle the civil polity from the embarrassments of all theological controversy and ecclesiastical rivalship.

On the subject of politico-religious establishments, Mr. Bristed, as we have intimated, seems to us very inconsistent with himself. We think he has not any well-digested views of the question, considering [illegible] "My kingdom is not of this world." [illegible] Mr. Bristed [illegible] to consider this matter calmly.

"My kingdom is not of this world. If my kingdom were of this world, then would my servants fight, that I should not be delivered to the Jews: but now is my kingdom not from hence." John xviii. 36. Do not the latter words, "but now," obviously contrast the character of Christ's kingdom, under the new dispensation, with its character under the old? The things of the former had been earthly: its sanctuary a worldly sanctuary; its ordinances carnal; the sanctions and enforcements of its laws of a worldly and temporal nature; the church and the state really incorporated. See Heb. ix. 1–23. John iii. 12. Even then, indeed, all were patterns of the things in the heavenly kingdom; and the true Israel looked beyond the shadows to the substance, looked to the end or accomplishment, of that dispensation, which was to be abolished: and "confessed that they were strangers and pilgrims upon earth, desiring a better country, that is, an heavenly," Heb. xi. 13—16. But now the shadows have passed away; the earthly kingdom is at an end, and succeeded by an heavenly kingdom, "which cannot be moved." Now, therefore, every attempt to incorporate Christ's kingdom with the kingdoms *of this world*, is an attempt to change its essential nature, a virtual denial "that Christ has come in the flesh."

Accordingly, let us imagine that it had pleased God to convert the Emperor Nero to the faith of Christ. We have reason to know that some of his household were disciples; and there is nothing inconsistent in the *supposition* that he should himself have heard and believed the apostolic testimony concerning Jesus of Nazareth. But let it be observed that the conversion of Nero, which we call Mr. Bristed to *imagine*, is not any such conversion as that of Constantine; but that we suppose him to have become a real convert to real Christianity, to have been made acquainted with the genuine import of the apostolic doctrine, and persuaded of its divine truth. What, we ask, in that case, would have been the consequence? As a Christian, he would have walked with his Christian brethren in the fellowship of the Gospel, observing all the things delivered to them in common by the apostle as the commandments of the Lord, and subject, like any other disciple, to the instruction, admonition, and reproof of the divine word. As the head of the Roman empire, he would have filled the station allotted to him by providence, so as to adorn the gospel which he professed, and to benefit his subjects. He would have certainly put a stop to all outward persecution of the Christians. But would he have proceeded to persecute the pagan idolators, by affixing civil pains and penalties to their disbelief of the gospel? Certainly not, while he hearkened himself to the word of that kingdom which is not of this world; for any such thing would be an attempt immediately to introduce a corrupt Judaizing Christianity. He would undoubtedly be at liberty to select whom he pleased of his subjects to fill the various stations of trust or profit in his empire. But perhaps we may say, that if he acted *wisely*, he would select those, whether Christians or Pagans, who were best qualified and most likely to fill the stations well. But what shall we say to the idea of our *Christian* emperor proposing to grant Paul, and the other brethren, certain great immunities and civil privileges, on condition that they should acknowledge him as *head* of the Christian churches throughout the empire, and allow him to legislate for them in religious matters, to appoint their elders or bishops, &c.? Is it not obvious that, before he could harbour such a thought, he must have altogether forgotten that word of Christ which he professed to believe? Is it not also equally obvious, that the Christians, while they abode in the truth, must have rejected the proposal with indignation; and if they failed of bringing their *brother* Nero to repentance by the admonition and reproof of the word, must have removed him from their fellowship? though still subject to him, as the supreme head of the empire, in all *civil* matters, in all things of *this world*.

The case which we have imagined is a plain one, to any person the most moderately acquainted from the Scriptures with the nature of apostolic Christianity. Whether the nature of the thing be altered by the lapse of so many centuries, we shall not now inquire. Let us rather hear the little which our author says upon the subject:—

" 'My kingdom is not of this world,' emphatically declares the Lord Jesus Christ. But Bishop Warburton urges the position, 'that the church and the state, in England, are, in themselves, two free and independent sovereigns, and, *as such*, form a mutual, equal alliance and league between each other; in the same manner as is, or might be, between any two other earthly potentates.' But, without encountering any detail, we may simply ask, *Who* is the head of this independent, sovereign church? The Lord Jesus Christ himself."

Certainly not, Mr. Bristed; except so far as Christ is *head over* ALL *things* to his church. But the head of that church, which forms a league offensive and defensive with the state, is the King of England.

" And *does He* enter into an equal, mutual alliance, offensive and defensive, with impious, irreligious, profligate, formal sovereigns? For example, with the brutal, bloody Henry, the politic, arbitrary Elizabeth, or the perfidious, persecuting dynasty of the Stuarts? Which will ye believe? The Saviour himself, who says his kingdom is not of this world, or the right reverend William Warburton, who seeks to stamp the secular stain upon its beauty of holiness."

Well, Mr. Bristed, the whole force of this reasoning turns upon the character of the reigning monarch; and suppose it were urged against you, that in the *Jewish* theocracy the individual king was often a very bad man. What would you reply? Again, suppose that the King of England and his ministers were what you consider *evangelical, spiritual* men, would you then see any objection to this alliance between church and state? From many parts of the work before us, we suspect you would not.

Mr. Bristed remarks, pp. 18, 19, that

"The ministerial and lay *patronage* of the Anglican Church . . . almost of necessity insures a constant supply of *formalism*, at least, if not of absolute irreligion to the clerical establishment." "Suppose, what *has* happened in English history, that the British Prime Minister and the Lord High Chancellor of England . . . should be both, or either of them, avowed infidels, or merely irreligious, &c. What sort of bishops would be appointed to fill the vacant sees? What kind of clergy to possess the empty parishes? Evangelical men, think you?"

This is the grand topic on which Mr. Bristed declaims most largely. And it is indeed very obvious, that there is such an opposition between the things that are of *men* and the things that are of *God*, between a human political institution and real religion, that a politico-religious establishment must form a strange and most incongruous mixture; and only the more incongruous, when the religion which it *professes* to establish is truly divine. But it is observable that Mr. Bristed's great objection even to the *ministerial* patronage, in the English establishment, is derived from the way in which that patronage is exercised. And accordingly the grand panacea which he proposes for remedying, not only the *formalism* of the Anglican church, but even all the political evils of Great Britain, is this, that the minister should appoint evangelical bishops, and their lordships give the best benefices to evangelical parsons.

"Let the eleven thousand places of worship in the Anglican Church establishment be filled with evangelical incumbents; let the stalls, and dignities, and *palaces*, be filled with evangelical deans, and bishops, and archbishops, all faithfully discharging, &c. &c. and England will soon be freed from all alarm respecting the infidelity and profligacy which now menace the speedy perdition of all her civil institutions and social order."

"If the British government deem the preservation of the national church of any importance to the state, it ought to know, that the only possible mode of preserving the establishment, is to fill its *palaces* and parishes with an evangelical ministry. Then no apprehension need be entertained of the growth, either of sectaries or of *radicals* . . . they will soon be secure from all alarms of sedition, privy conspiracy, and rebellion—of all false doctrine, heresy and schism,—of hardness of heart, and contempt of God's word and commandment!"

Really, in holding this language, Mr. Bristed pledges himself for a great deal. In short, the whole nation would become what he calls evangelical, if all the clergy of the establishment were so. We might easily expose the inconsistency of his notion with Scripture, and its inconsistency with various passages in his own work, particularly with one, p. 224, in which he states that Mr. Newton, in July 1778, could not hear of one spiritual person in Weston Favel, the scene of Mr. Hervey's evangelical labours. But we rather content ourselves with assuring him, that if he could effect all that change in the patronage of the Anglican church, which would remove his objections, it would be in our view as much a thing of this world as it is now; a *forgery* still, though perhaps a better forgery. We are not, however, disposed to controvert another position of our author's, p. 345. "The most effectual remedy for these, and for *all other* national evils, whether present or prospective, is to be found in the *general conversion of the people to real* evangelical Christianity." No doubt that would be a sovereign remedy for all internal evils in any country, and would form a nation such as never has yet appeared on earth. Mr. Bristed, with many other religionists, thinks the time will come; and yet he elsewhere quotes with approbation the following language from Bishop Burnet's exposition of the 25th article, p. 257. "The greater part, both of the clergy and laity, ever were, and *ever will be*, depraved and corrupted," &c. To much the same effect, but more to the purpose, does Mr. Bristed speak his own mind, p. 155. "Real Christians are always fearfully outnumbered, in every human society, by the formal, the secular, the profane, and the profligate; and should, therefore, keep themselves pure from all contact with a mere worldly religion," &c. We shall leave Mr. Bristed to settle this point with Bishop Burnet and with himself.

While our author would be content with the state-religion of England, if he could get the ecclesiastical *palaces* and parishes filled with ecclesiastics after his own heart, he is so outrageously dissatisfied with the present distribution of the loaves and fishes, that he brings charges the most unfounded against the British government and hierarchy. What must any candid reader think of the following language?

"Indeed, *now*, the British government and its hierarchy unite in their efforts to DESTROY the evangelicals more cordially and more strenuously than has been done before, since the reign of the most execrable of the Stuarts."

"The Anglican Church, ever since its establishment at the Reformation, has generally PERSECUTED pure evangelical religion, whether detected in its own members, or in those of other communions."

"Persecution seems to be a necessary adjunct of an established church; and, at this moment, formal English bishops PERSECUTE, to the utmost extent of their power, the unbeneficed evangelicals within their dioceses."

"The evangelical dissenters . . . must encounter the frowns and opposition of the established hierarchy; which, not contented with generally, as a body, neglecting the spiritual, the immortal interests of the people *committed to their pastoral care*, invariably calumniate and PERSECUTE all who are in earnest about the everlasting safety of their fellow-men."

We must say that we consider these assertions most unfair, and utterly unsupported by fact. We are aware that many religionists are very fond of raising the cry of *persecution* on every the most trivial loss which they suffer, or think they suffer, on account of their religious profession; and at the root of this generally lies the most contemptible and disgusting vanity. But in what consists that *per-*

secution,—that effort to *destroy* the evangelicals which Mr. Bristed imputes to the British government and hierarchy? In this, according to his own statement, p. 145, that, in the dispensation of church *preferments*, "for the most part, effectual care is taken to exclude from the mitre, the stall, and the benefice, those who faithfully preach the evangelical doctrines of the Bible, of the Reformation, of the public formularies of the Anglican Church." Now, we not only think there is much meanness in this, *Et mihi dividuo findetur munere quadra*; but we must beg to put one plain question to Mr. Bristed's conscience. If he, with his present views of those evangelical doctrines, and the present zeal for them which we suppose animates him, were prime minister or Lord Chancellor of England; would he not similarly *persecute* those of opposite sentiments, those whom he terms formalists? Would he not take effectual care, as far as he could, to exclude them from the mitre, the stall, and the benefice? And would he not, perhaps, be forward to expose the absurdity of his being, therefore, charged with a *persecuting* effort to *destroy* them? As to his imputing to the English hierarchy any persecution of the *dissenters* at present, we can only say that we are utterly unable even to conjecture what he alludes to. That they should dislike, and oppose, and frown upon dissenters, is very natural; that they should calumniate them as *schismatics*, for not choosing to join the train of the ecclesiastical *state-coach*, is very comical; and equally comical we consider Mr. Bristed's language, about the people *committed to the* PASTORAL *care* of the English hierarchy. Our author seems unable to disconnect certain ideas, borrowed from the Christian revelation, with a political system which has really nothing to do with it.

While we honestly vindicate the present English hierarchy from the charge of persecution, and while we avow our belief that individuals of that body are men of enlarged and liberal minds, indisposed to persecute even if they had the power; we yet acknowledge that the *tendency* of every religious establishment is to persecute nonconformists: and for the non-persecuting character of our Establishment, we think ourselves indebted, rather to the general prevalence of the principles of *civil* liberty, than to any general change in the character of ecclesiastics. At them *we* must always look, in *this* respect, with a jealous eye. Nor can we be at all surprised, that both they and the government look with a very jealous eye at those whom Mr. Bristed distinguishes as *evangelicals*. He indeed broadly asserts, p. 153, that "the comparatively small portion of evangelical clergy in the Establishment alone preserves that establishment from impending perdition." Unconnected as we are with either of the parties, we must candidly avow our conviction, that the opposite of Mr. Bristed's assertion is true. We are aware that this will bring our *evangelism* with him into discredit. But let him calmly consider what we proceed to offer in vindication of the *reasonableness* of that hostility to the evangelicals, which is generally manifested by the English government and hierarchy.

Mr. Bristed himself truly remarks, p. 179, that "the English established church is a *political machine*." (We might be disposed to extend the remark.) Now, in every political machine, its *quiet* and *regular* operation is obviously important. And this machine being designed for nominally religious objects, every thing which tends to make a stir about religion, to set men a thinking seriously about religion, to institute a comparison of the movements of the machine with a different and higher rule,—every such thing, we say, is evidently to be deprecated. Mr. Bristed frequently notices the tendency of religious establishments to *formalism*. But we beg of him to consider, whether what he calls *formalism* be not necessary to the well-being and safety of every religious establishment. For instance, the system of augury and idol-worship in heathen Rome, so far as it was incorporated with the civil polity, must it not consistently have been hostile to the disturbance of men's minds, which the Christian revelation was calculated to produce? And can Mr. Bristed seriously wonder, that men whom he himself describes as secular and worldly, and proposing only political objects in their religious profession, should regard with a hostile eye the zeal that calls the people to higher principles? Or can he honestly think, that this zeal is not ultimately hostile in its tendency to the merely political machine which they employ? We are not afraid to declare that we think it is.

That the hierarchy, therefore, should generally set their faces against the so-called *evangelicals*, and against the indiscriminate circulation of the Scriptures, we consider perfectly consistent. That the government should make themselves a party in the matter, we deeply lament. However, while they think that the *ecclesiastical* is essentially interwoven with the *civil* constitution of the country, we cannot wonder at this. We are persuaded that the latter might continue to subsist in full vigour if totally disconnected from the former; and that the present connexion is a dead weight upon the state, however it may contribute to "the purpose of swelling the patronage and influence of the crown." But without entering on the discussion of that political question, which we may be very incompetent to treat, we must positively assert that *Protestantism* is not nearly so well adapted as *Popery*, for the politico-ecclesiastical machine. The fundamental principle of Protestantism, (however widely nominal Protestants have departed from it,) that the Bible is the one standard of divine truth and religious practice, must always expose the machine of a Protestant establishment to disturbance, from the agitation of scriptural inquiry, and the progressive elucidation of scriptural principles; whereas the unchangeable stagnation of Popery in its system of darkness and of death, guards against all such danger, as far as the wicked policy of corrupt religion *can* guard against the diffusion of divine truth.

Mr. Bristed, therefore, must excuse us for maintaining against him, that Archbishop Laud formerly, and the Rev. Samuel Wix recently, have been most consistent in pursuing a reunion between the old lady of Babylon and her reformed daughter. If it could be affected, we are persuaded that this would be the *wisest* possible measure next to one other. But in England we see, and are glad to see, great (if not insurmountable) difficulties in the way of the attempt; from the formidable numbers and weight of the Protestant dissenters, and the comparative paucity of the Popish. But perhaps it might not be impracticable in Ireland, where the absurdity of the most expensive of all existing religious establishments, including among its nominal adherents only one-fourteenth part of the entire population, is more and more forcing itself upon general attention; where a vast majority of the inhabitants steadily maintain their attachment to the see of Rome; and their hierarchy (always aspiring at domination, even when they assume the most modest garb and the most lowly language,) must of necessity cherish the hope that they will yet recover the rights, of which they conceive themselves unjustly dispossessed; and must therefore feel it their interest to keep alive the distractions which prevail in that unhappy land. Long has Ireland been presenting to statesmen a lesson, which every year becomes more and more legible. But if our statesmen should ever think of attempting a coalition there with the papal see, they must be prepared to find that the mother-church is too politic to *meet them half way*. She will be glad to receive the advances of her repentant daughter, but she will take care not to give up her own *immutability*; though she might perhaps be induced to concede the cup to the laity, and a liturgy in the vernacular language.

On the whole, we apprehend that the time has gone by, when the reunion might have been effected; and how, therefore, a remedy is to be applied to the evils of unhappy Ireland, assuming that the religious establishment is to be maintained, we confess ourselves utterly unable to conjecture. If any of our readers should think it extraordinary that we have at all admitted the idea of a *Protestant* government establishing *Popery*, we only say to such—look at CANADA. It is sufficiently evinced by existing facts, that, in the political establishment of religion, the truth or falsehood of the religious system is a question altogether out of contemplation. And this certainly is one of the circumstances which render every religious establishment an eminent instrument of promoting *irreligion*. The populace may be very slow to notice this *merely political* character in the state church; but thinking and observing men must perceive it, and will call the attention of others to what they see themselves. Naturally indisposed to view the revelation which the only true God has made in the Scriptures, and willing to draw their puny conclusions against all religion from what they perceive to be the character of *state religion*; they find in this a ready justification to their consciences for laughing at every thing sacred, either openly, or under the profession of ardent zeal for *the church*.

But it is time for us to pass with Mr. Bristed from Great Britain to America. To us by far the most interesting part of his book, is that which describes the state of religious affairs in the New World. We shall here, therefore, extract more copiously for the satisfaction of our readers; premising that Mr. Bristed, throughout his work, employs the barbarous compound *American-Anglo-Church*, to designate that which, in his title-page, he more correctly terms the *Anglo-American*.

"By the fourth article of the constitution of the American-Anglo-Church, it is enacted, that the bishop or bishops, in every state, shall be chosen agreeably to such rules as shall be fixed by the convention, which consists of both laity and clergy of that state. And the second canon ordains, that no diocese or state shall proceed to the election or appointment of a bishop, unless there be at least six officiating presbyters, or priests, residing therein; and who, agreeably to the canons of the church, may be qualified to vote for a bishop—a majority of whom, at least, shall concur in such election. At present there are *nine* in the American-Anglo-Church, to wit, &c. There are two dioceses, the state of Delaware and the State of North Carolina, which have no bishops. Every state in the Union may become a diocese whenever its Protestant Episcopalians are sufficiently numerous, and deem it expedient.

"The whole church is governed by the General Convention, whose power pervades every diocese. It sits regularly once in three years, but may be specially convened in the interval. It consists of an upper house, composed of all the existing bishops, and of a lower house, containing a delegated portion of clergy and laity from each diocese. The state conventions are held, for the most part, annually in each diocese, and consist of clergy and lay delegates from every separate congregation. These bodies *legislate* for their respective dioceses; but their canons must not contradict the constitution of the general church.

"The liturgy, articles, and homilies of the Anglican-Church are adopted, with some few slight local alterations. No particular revenues are attached to the episcopate; and the bishops, generally, are parish priests, in addition to their bishoprics. But efforts are making, in several dioceses, to raise a bishop's fund, in order, &c. Archbishops there are none, nor prebendaries, &c. &c. The senior bishop presides in the House of Bishops during the session of the General Convention.

"The parish priests are elected *according to the charters of the congregations*. Some churches choose their minister by the vestry, consisting of persons elected annually by the *freeholders*. Others by ballot, the whole congregation voting. The bishops have no *direct* patronage—no livings in their gift. The clergy are settled by the choice or call of the people to whom they minister; and the stipend is fixed by the compact between the pastor and the congregation; *and the common law enforces the fulfilment of this contract on both sides*, whence all undue dependence of the clergy upon the people is prevented."

We must pause a little here, to tell Mr. Bristed plainly, that we consider the thing which he describes in his Anglo-American church, as a thing just as carnal, worldly, and utterly unscriptural, as that which he so often reprobates in the political Anglican church—only much more ludicrous. There is something consistently pompous in the Anglican episcopacy, in the mitred fronts of the prelates, their palaces, their lordly endowments, &c. &c. But the republican imitation of this finery in America presents a most heterogeneous compound. We could have wished for more minute information on many points, and are somewhat curious to know how those bishops, who are not parish priests, get their bread, where *no particular revenues are attached to the episcopate?* We know from other passages, that they do not support themselves by honest labour. When Mr. Bristed talks of *the charters of the congregations*, and describes the state conventions as *legislating* for their respective dioceses, he is manifestly little aware that he describes a thing which could not take place in any real churches of Christ. They have nothing to do with *making laws* for their government. They are only called to obey and maintain the laws made by the King of Zion. "The government is upon HIS shoulder." Our author thinks the *patronage* in his Anglo-American church much preferable to that in the Anglican. We think it just as *antichristian*. The congregation, a term which ought to be equivalent with the ἐκκλησία, or assembly of Christian brethren, is composed of the *pew-holders*; and these pew-holders, any persons who choose and can afford to pay rent for one of those pinfolds called pews in the parish kirk, elect, either immediately through a vestry, or immediately by a general ballot, the reverend gentleman called a *minister*, under a legal contract for the regular payment of his stipend on their side, and the due performance of clerical functions on his side, to be enforced, if necessary, by common law. (If we mistake Mr. Bristed's account, we shall be happy to have our mistake corrected.) The bond, and the pleadings on it, must be very comical.

In what light does Mr. Bristed suppose that the whole process would have been regarded by the apostolic church at Philippi? Can he imagine that any man there was admitted to church-membership, and retained in it, by his paying rent for a *pew* in this place of meeting? and that, upon this pecuniary *qualification*, he took part with the Christian body, in the choice of their bishops and deacons; but that the Christian *pauper*, who could not afford to pay for a seat, was either not accommodated equally with the rich, or was excluded from taking any share in the proceedings of the church? Can he imagine that the elders then commenced a legal process against the flocks, of which they were overseers, if they did not regularly pay them a *stipulated salary*? No: little as our author has hitherto attended to the apostolic word, he must be aware that the whole thing which now goes on, in the so-called churches that he describes, is essentially different from the Christianity described in the New Testament: and that while the appointment of his *clergy* is made in a democratic way in America, and in an aristocratic way in England, the one is not a whit less antiscriptural than the other. What we chiefly complain of is, that any such systems should be palmed upon the world as *Christian*. To tell the truth, if we did not believe the Scriptures, if we viewed religion as a matter of human policy and civil regulation, there is no religious profession to which we should be more disposed to conform than to that of the Anglican establishment. It is the most *gentlemanly* and respectable that we know: and whilst it has got rid of some of the glaring absurdities and mummery of the Papal system, it retains a sufficiency of pomp and splendour. As to the objection which Mr. Bristed often urges, that it is too expensive, we think it a pitiful objection against a state-machine in a great kingdom,—if the machine be a useful one.

But in Scotland we can give him his choice of another very decorous establishment, which even the honourable member for Aberdeen must confess to be unobjectionable on the score of economy.

It is very remarkable, that while Mr. Bristed declaims most vehemently against the *formalism* of the Anglican church, and accounts for that formalism from the intimate connexion between church and state, and from the improper exercise of ministerial patronage, he yet repeatedly describes the Anglo-American church as in a state of equal formalism, and equally hostile (in general) to what he speaks of as evangelical, and to the circulation of the Bible.

"The Established Church of England," (that church for which he prays, Amen! *Esto perpetua! αἰὼν ἀριστων*-ΩΝ!) "has always systematically opposed those religious efforts which, &c. &c. All of which, we regret to say, are *too little* regarded by the American-Anglo-Church, while they are hailed, and cherished, and forwarded. by the other denominations, Presbyterian, Congregational, Methodist, Baptist; *all* of which prosper and increase, in proportion as they promote the cause of pure evangelism."—"The American Bible Society is supported almost entirely by non-episcopalians; the American-Anglo-Church generally standing aloof from this labour of love."—"The American-Anglo-Church halts *very far* behind many other denominations, in numbers, and activity, and influence."—"Is in the wake of other Christian denominations, in numbers, talent, influence, and utility."—"The *real* cause why the American-Anglo-Church is so *fearfully* in the wake of other denominations, Presbyterian, Congregational, Baptists, and Methodists, is to be found in the prevalence of *formalism* in her clergy."

We protest, this same *American-Anglo-Church*, at her next general convention, ought to excommunicate her unworthy son, John Bristed, for circulating such evil reports of his mother. But then, Mr. Bristed, you have before accounted for the general formalism of the Anglican church, from "the utter exclusion of the congregations from all part, and lot, and voice, in the selection of the *clerk* who is to *administer to them spiritually*." Now, how do you reconcile this with the existence of the same formalism among the Episcopalians in America, where the congregations elect their bishops and clergy? We are at no loss to account for it. A carnal prime minister is not more likely to appoint a carnal clerk to a benefice than a carnal congregation of *pew-holders* is to elect him; and we think it not worth a moment's controversy *which* is the better system. But we must treat our readers with the following testimony of Mr. Bristed against his favourite Anglo-American-Church, for the sake of the droll prayer with which it concludes.

"It is a deep stain upon the American-Anglo-Church, that she *alone*, of all the compacted religious bodies, has degenerated into extensive formalism. While the Presbyterians, of every various shade in doctrine, discipline, and government, have continued, *as Calvinists, faithfully* preaching the systematic creed contained in their respective confessions; and while the Wesleyan Methodists, *as Arminians*, have preserved the system of *scriptural* instruction, *handed down to them by their great founder and leader*; too many of the Protestant Episcopal clergy have grievously swerved from the high standard of their own evangelical articles, homilies, and liturgy, *to which may the great Head of the church bring them back with all* CONVENIENT *speed!*"

We could not but smile at the drollery of Mr. Bristed's piety. Yet we have really quoted the passage as much with a view to his profit as to the amusement of our readers. We seriously advise him to *think* more when he next resumes his pen.

One of the annoyances we have been plagued with in reading Mr. Bristed's book is this: that while a great part of it consists of quotations from other writers, Mr. Newton, Dr. Chalmers, Dr. Mason, &c. &c. the quotations are seldom marked as such; so that the reader often cannot say who the writer is, whether Mr. Bristed or some other from whom he extracts. The following is among the number of such passages. We give it, as affording some farther view of the religious state of America:—

"Even in the United States themselves, partial legislative enactments, in favour of religion, have been from time to time found necessary: which enactments the civil magistrate is bound to support, and the public purse to carry into effect. From a table, drawn up a few years since, showing the provision for religious instruction, in the states of, &c. it appears, that ten out of fifteen of those states have *no* provision for the maintenance of religious instructors, but the other five have a partial or full provision. Eight have no religious creed; the others use a formal *test:* namely, three require a belief in God; one, faith in the Gospel; two, faith in the Old and New Testaments; four, faith in the *Protestant* religion. To this add, that chaplains are appointed for the army and navy, and paid from the public purse; and strict orders are issued, under severe penalties, for the attendance and decent behaviour of the soldiers at divine worship. Profane cursing and swearing are also punishable," &c.

We believe the preceding passage is extracted by our author from Mr. Wilks, who goes on to remark—

"That there is so little religion throughout the Union is not to be wondered at, when we recollect how scanty and parsimonious are the public means of instruction in almost every state; but that little would probably have been less, had there been no publicly recognized means at all. But America is a new country; and some years must elapse before the general effect of its present system can be fully developed. It is devoutly to be hoped, that *long before* that period shall arrive, the necessity of a church establishment will be sufficiently felt among all classes, to induce the legislature to carry into effect some adequate provision for that purpose; if not on the higher ground of *duty* as Christians, yet, at least, on the principles of political expediency and *civil decorum*."

Upon this Mr. Bristed remarks:—"It would be more difficult than perhaps Mr. Wilks imagines, on such an assumption, to determine *which* should be the dominant state sect. Certainly it would *not* be the American-Anglo-Church; and the political precedency could not easily be settled among the Presbyterians, Congregationalists, Methodists, and Baptists." We are very glad to hear of this difficulty; and, for the sake of America, we hope it will prove insurmountable.

The British Review and Dr. Beecher (a Congregational divine in Connecticut) draw a sad picture of the alarming state of religion in America, from the want of "competent religious teachers." In opposition to this, Mr. Bristed remarks—

"That Dr. Beecher counts only *regular* clergy: all the rest go for nothing with him. By regular clergy, he intends such only as have been *regularly trained* to the ministry* at some academic institution or college; whether at Harvard, Princeton, Yale, or elsewhere. Now, within the limits of this calculation are not included *all*, even of the Independent, Presbyterian, and Episcopal clergy throughout the Union. And they do not comprehend *any* of the three thousand irregular Baptist preachers; the one thousand travelling, and the four thousand local preachers among the Methodists. Deduct the services of all but college-bred ministers in England, and the religion of that country will be *in a very small way*. The clergy *of all arms* in the United States, may be thus counted in round numbers:—

American-Anglo-Church, or Protestant Episcopal	300
Presbyterian, since their late junction - -	1300
Congregational, or Independent - - -	1600
Baptists, chiefly Particular, some general -	3000
Methodists, Travelling Preachers - - -	1000
——— Local Preachers - - -	4000
All other denominations, including Papists -	600
Total of American *Clergy*, in 1822	11,800

"Which gives more than one clergyman to every thousand souls, even computing the population of the United States at ten millions. The established clergy of England and Wales are about eleven thousand. The population of England and Wales is rather more than twelve millions, averaging less than one state clergyman to each thousand souls. Indeed, by adding the dissenting ministers, eleven thousand clergy more may be joined to those in the Establishment. But the formal high-churchmen do not allow any of non-episcopal ministrations to be valid or regular."

"Throughout the United States, pure evangelical religion is much more generally diffused than in the English church establishment, and the standard of morals is higher. We have, in proportion to our population, much less infidelity and profligacy, fewer divorces, robberies, murders, tumults, &c. &c. The American-Anglo-Church herself has at length followed the example of other religious denominations, and established a general theological seminary for the instruction of her divinity students. The Congregationalists have a very flourishing, and munificently endowed, theological seminary at Andover, in Massachusetts; the Methodists, one

* Mr. Bristed's expression is "*the ministry of reconciliation.*"—We really deem such an application, of such a scriptural phrase, little short of profane. Regularly trained to the apostolic office!

in the western part of the State of New York; the Baptists have instituted a divinity college at Washington; the Dutch Church has a *school of the prophets*—(fiddlestick! Mr. Bristed) at Brunswick, in New Jersey; the Presbyterians have a theological hall at Princeton, also in Jersey."

We are sorry to understand that the American colleges are so involved with theology and the manufacture of clergymen. In our view it augurs ill for their literature, and no better for their religion. As to the apprehended scarcity of clergy in the United States, we conceive that the argument drawn from it by the advocates of religious establishments is very idle. We have long understood that there are few parts of the world where the clergy are regarded with more reverence, or drive a more successful trade; and in this, as in every other marketable article, we may be certain that the demand will create a proportionate supply.

Mr. Bristed makes a brief incidental mention of one sect in America, against which, we dare say, all the clergy of all denominations make common cause, p. 448. "The *sine nomine secta* perceives a very clear revelation from heaven, that the New Testament proscribes all clergy, of every order, sort, and kind; and permits none but laymen, who have some secular occupation during the week-days, as tinkers, weavers, cobblers, *et id genus omne*, to be teachers, and preachers, and expounders of the law and gospel, on the sabbath." We confess that we should be glad of some more information about this *sine nomine secta*, of whom our author speaks with such scorn, and we do think it likely that they know much more about Christianity than Mr. Bristed. Does he need to be informed, that the whole distinction between *clergy* and *laity* is confessedly without any foundation in scripture, a mere human invention, unknown for some ages after the apostolic? We say, *is confessedly* so; because Dr. Campbell, himself a regular formal clergyman, owns and proves it, in his "Lectures on Ecclesiastical History;" and we believe none of the clergy have ever attempted a refutation of his statements.

We smile at Mr. Bristed's enumeration of the honest trades by which Christians, who exhort and admonish one another on the first day of the week, may earn their bread in the course of it. But we are struck by its perfect coincidence with the language which he condemns in Lord S., p. 204, when, in the year 1811, he supported his attempted invasion of the Toleration Act by "describing the non-conforming preachers as blacksmiths, cobblers, tailors, pedlars, chimney-sweepers, and *what not?*" Neither the noble British peer, nor the American counsellor at law, seems to have ever thought of what is ascertained to us by the scriptures, that an apostle laboured at his trade, working with his own hands, and urged his own example, in this respect, upon the elders of a Christian church for their imitation. (Acts xx. 34, 35.) But we really do not mean to speak of such elders as an order of men at all like the *clergy;* nor of the churches of which they were overseers, as at all like the congregations to which the clergy minister; nor of that simple "speaking of the truth in love?" which went on in the Christian assem blies, as at all like our modern *sermons*. What a different thing, in the view of Lord S., and of Mr. Bristed too, is Christianity at this day, and Christianity in the days of the apostle! a much *finer* thing certainly now. But, in our view, real Christianity is unaltered and unalterable.

Among all our author's inconsistencies, none strikes us more than his wish for a modified establishment in the American States, and his dissatisfaction that they leave religion so much to itself.

"It is a grave question, which every American statesman, who knows, and feels, *that pure and undefiled religion* is the great *sheet* anchor of *human society*, ought to ask, if there be no safe and effectual *medium* to be found, between making one dominant sect, and the ruling powers completely *disregarding* religion, making no provision for gospel ordinances, &c. &c. Cannot, as in some of the New England States is already done, the American governments generally provide, that in every township throughout their respective jurisdictions, there shall be *SOME religious* ordinances and worship, still leaving to every individual the personal rights of conscience untouched, and *his own choice* of the particular sect, or denomination of Christianity, to which he wishes to be attached, unimpaired?"

But what, Mr. Bristed, if some poor Christian, less liberal than yourself, should be unable to find any one sect or denomination of Christianity in his township, to which he could conscientiously attach himself? What is to become of the rights of his conscience? We fear it might be necessary to teach him more liberality by fine and imprisonment. And when *any* religion *called* Christianity will answer your purpose, we might beg to know why you should not extend your liberality still more widely.

In the following pages Mr. Bristed gives a detailed account of the legislative provisions for religion, in the states of New England and Massachusetts; the whole of which account we should gladly transcribe, if our limits permitted. It proves with sufficient clearness, that the fundamental principle of religious establishments is admitted, and acted upon, in some parts of the United States. We even read of a congregational clergyman (the congregationalists are called *the standing order* in New England) levying his tax from persons of other denominations, by *distraining* and selling their goods. There is, however, an indistinct intimation, that a *considerable modification* of the old law on the subject has recently taken place. But the citizens must by law be nominal *Christians* and *Protestants*; while they may pick and choose among all the assortments of protestantism, which the public warehouse of religion furnishes, for that denomination which they wish to support. And our author wishes something like this to take place throughout the rest of the Union; while he is comically perplexed to know how it shall be equitably effected.

For our parts, if the state is to interfere at all with the *religion* of the people, we think it much more consistent to fix on some one religious system,—no matter what, which shall be legally patronized and supported, to the exclusion or discountenance of every other. We do not say this would be more *wise*; but it would be more consistent. In a Christian view, indeed, there is something grossly profane in the extended liberality of the New England and Massachusetts establishment. The legislature says in effect to the people, "Good citizens, we care not a fig what religion you have; but you must have, or pretend to have, some. We care not what your faith is; but you must call it Christian and Protestant. We care not what God you worship, or whether you worship any; but you must appear at church once in three months, if it even be a church composed of Johanna Southcott's followers." And this is the political and religious wisdom which Mr. Bristed has learned in America! He assures us, indeed, p. 345, that a *pious* man "could not possibly disapprove of the care taken in New England to *keep the Sabbath holy*;" and that "it is self-evident that there can be no stability for the American, or for any other political institutions, if once a majority, or even a considerable portion of the population become *infidels*, whether baptized or unbaptized. So, after all that Mr. Bristed has elsewhere said about the paucity of real Christians in every age and country, he conceives that a great majority of the American population are indeed believers of the Gospel of Christ; and that legislative provisions for religion have effected this, and are necessary to secure its continuance. On his idea of a national "keeping of the Sabbath holy," we would only say at present, that there is one observance of the first day of the week, which is of indisputable obligation from the Scriptures to disciples of Christ; their coming together into one place to break bread, in commemoration of that sacrifice for sin by which they have been redeemed unto God. But we have never found any more regardless of this scriptural observance of the day, than those who are most zealous for what they call the observance of the *Sabbath*.

If Mr. Bristed, when he speaks of the great mass of the American population as not being infidels, merely mean that they assume the Christian name, and profess something which they *call* Christianity; we must beg to know, in the first place, why the poor papists should not pass muster along with all the various sects of nominal protestants: and, in the second place, what there is in the mere *name* and *profession* of Christianity, which is essential to the well-being and security of a state. We could point to some parts of the British dominions, in which there would be much less distraction and outrage, much less of all that is to be deprecated in a well-ordered polity, if the present *Christian* population were exchanged for an equal number of *Gentoos*.

But elsewhere Mr. Bristed seems to restrict his position to something more than the mere name and form of Christianity, p. 58. "Those who have learned from the study of their Bible, and from acquaintance with the history of the world, that human communities and nations *invariably flourish or fade in proportion* to the prevalence or absence of *pure vital religion* in the hearts and actions of the people, will readily acknowledge, &c." P. 167. "The periods of national history are prosperous or calamitous, in proportion as *piety* prevails or languishes." Will our author be shocked, when we plainly protest against the sentiment which he so confidently advances, and avow our persuasion that it is wholly unsupported either by history or the Bible. The idea seems altogether Jewish, and connected with a misunderstanding of that dispensation which has passed away, and in which national prosperity was annexed to the observance of the law given by Moses. That the flourishing and decay of empires is closely connected with the *manners* of the people, we readily admit. But the character of popular *manners*, as far as they affect civil society, is commonly determined by things very different from popular *religion*. Will Mr. Bristed maintain, that it was the prevalence of *pure vital religion* among the people, which occasioned the flourishing of the Roman republic during so many centuries? He does, indeed, assure us, p. 167, that the reason why England was so "terrible to all her foes abroad, as well as secure at home, during the protectorate of Cromwell," was, that "a great portion of her people were *seriously inclined*, and *religion* was encouraged." But we must tell him, that the plain account of the fact is to be found in the talents, energy, and firmness of that military usurper; just as, a few years after, the opposite character of the executive produced the opposite effect. Certainly the prevalence of this same "pure vital religion" is a very precarious thing, and altogether dependent on the excitement of court-favour, if, in so few years as elapsed between the death of Cromwell, and Charles's acting as "a hireling pensioner of the French court," the religion of the people became extinct.

We can no longer wonder at Mr. Bristed's lamentation, p. 390, that in the Anglo-American church, there is "no *bounty* for *piety*, because formalists proscribe every thing in the shape of evangelism," &c. &c. But does it not become more and more manifest, that he would be quite content with the English establishment, in spite of all the hard things he says against it, if he could persuade the minister and the hierarchy to such an exercise of their church-patronage, as would give a sufficient *bounty* to piety and evangelism? Yet with extraordinary inconsistency, Mr. Bristed writes as follows: P. 363.

"Persons who have never lived out of England have no adequate opportunity of knowing how religion is to subsist, when left to find her own level, without the interference, and free from the close embrace, of the civil magistrate. The English people never see Christianity, but as embodied in one dominant state sect, clothed with power, rioting in wealth, and proscribing, and discountenancing all other denominations; which, nevertheless, are compelled to contribute to the support of the national priesthood, as well as to maintain their own clergy. In recompense for which, they are put under the ban of the empire, the brand of religious disability is stamped upon them, &c. &c. Under such circumstances, and always seeing religion inseparably blended with state policy, what can the English people know about the progress of Christianity, when left entirely to the guidance of its Almighty Author? It is quite childish to suppose, that the arm, whether civil or military, of the British, or of any other government, is necessary to *preserve alive* the church of Christ. Its divine Master has promised to be always with her to the end of the world. And he *has* always hitherto protected her, alike against," &c. &c.

Again,

"Immediately after the Ascension of its Almighty Founder, Christianity experienced, according to his own predictions and warnings, the increasing enmity of a corrupt and idolatrous world. During the three first centuries of its progress, it was called upon to struggle with, &c. Yet, under all the persecutions, general and local, imperial and popular, Christianity increased daily, and spread itself over every corner of the then discovered world. By the time, says Bishop Porteus, the *empire* became Christian, there is every reason to believe, that the Christians were more numerous and more powerful than the Pagans. Which consideration induced Constantine to make the first established national Christian church; a measure that injured Christianity infinitely more, than all the ten bloody persecutions of his Pagan predecessors."

In the preceding extracts, along with much truth there are various points on which we should wish to animadvert. But we must content ourselves with a brief remark on the assertion in the last sentence. Previous to the time of Constantine, Christianity (understanding by this word the prevalent *profession* of Christianity) had become so corrupted, as to be quite prepared for his political establishment of it; otherwise, indeed, the Roman emperor could not have found it an engine fitted to his purposes. That his nominal conversion, and his political patronage of the thing, opened the floodgates of corruption wider, and developed the existing corruption in a grossness of form, which perhaps it could not otherwise have assumed, we freely admit. But all the while, Christianity, real Christianity, remained, and has since remained uninjured. IT is that kingdom of heaven, the interests of which are always effectually cared for, and secured by divine power.

But we do apprehend, that our main difference with Mr. Bristed, and indeed the main source of all his perplexity and inconsistency, lies in the erroneous view which he takes of the nature and design of that kingdom. He seems to have an idea, with multitudes of religionists, that Christianity has been designed for that which certainly it has *never yet* accomplished; for effectually communicating to whole *nations* upon earth what he calls "pure vital religion." We are sure that it has effected, and will effect, to the end, all that it was designed for. This certainly indeed is embodied in our persuasion of its really *divine* origin and nature. But we learn from the Scriptures, that they were designed to make sinners, who believe their testimony, "wise unto salvation;" to set *their* feet in the way of righteousness and peace. As to those who, under the profession of Christianity, believe a lie, (and few there are who do not,) we do not wonder at all that they should not be benefitted by that gospel, which they discredit just as much as those who avowedly reject it. Our author does sometimes speak a language, in a degree, corresponding with this view; and expresses his *fear*, that "the *real* Christians, in these national ecclesiastical establishments, are, comparatively, a very little flock." P. 353. But he is enamoured of the dream, that it will be otherwise: and meanwhile he clings to the common notion, that Christianity has introduced a higher tone of *public morals*, even among those whom he would not own as real Christians. For ourselves, we would be glad that the tone of public morals, (or *manners* rather,) were as high in Christianized England, as it was in the republic of heathen Rome. We are sure that it is not; that adultery, perjury, murder, drunkenness, fraud of every form, and all other vices most injurious to the well-being of a state, are unspeakably more common in the former than they were in the latter. Some of them, indeed, were for centuries almost unknown in the latter. Yet we are by no means among those who are fond of amusing themselves with invectives against the manners of the age. But we would appeal to Mr. Bristed's knowledge of history, whether the general history of Christendom present not just the same scene of human folly and wickedness, of bloodshed and cruelty, with that which the history of the world exhibits before the introduction of Christianity. And if so, what reason has he to suppose, that the gospel ever was designed by its divine Author to alter the character of that world?

It is not easy to say precisely what Mr. Bristed means by the gospel, or by evangelical religion; but it is plain to us, that his sentiments on this subject are derived more from preachers and commentators, than from the Scriptures. Divine TRUTH holds a very subordinate place in his system, in comparison of the excitement of strong *religious feelings*, "yearnings" after this and that, (Pp. 33. 43. 464. &c.) especially after the due performance of that indeed arduous task, to "*obtain a personal interest in the all-sufficient sacrifice.*" P. 40. Calvinism and Arminianism are all one with him. He even quotes with approbation, (.P 436.) John Wesley's infidel language—"I will not quarrel with you about ANY *opinion*, only see that your heart be right towards God," &c. Yet he certainly does demur, in the same page, to John's view of Marcus Antoninus as a *spiritual* person, because this emperor unfortunately was "a horrible persecutor of the Christians." To the same effect, however, is all that language, in which Mr. Bristed employs the phrases, *seriousness, piety, religion*, &c. as equivalent with the *Christian* mind. This so called *charity* is so extended, that he seems to view all who are very *serious, pious*, and *religious*, as right in the main; and urges on them the excellence of "that *mysterious union*, in which men *agree to differ*." P. 293. The central point of union, in which such liberal divines meet, has been well characterized by one, as consisting in PIETY TOWARDS THE GODS. We must appear sad bigots to Mr. Bristed, when we assure him that the greatest fervour of piety, where a false god is the object of religion, appears to us not a whit better than irreligion; and that we consider the only true God as known and worshipped, feared and loved, only by those who believe the one unadulterated testimony of his character in the Scriptures.

Our author, in his last chapter, is very vehement against Dr. Mant's doctrine of *baptismal regeneration*, or the efficacy of water baptism, when *regularly* administered, to communicate to the infant some inward spiritual change. He quotes the Docter as asserting, that "the Spirit moveth upon the face of the baptismal waters, imparting to them a quickening power!" From such blasphemous nonsense, certainly, a Christian can only turn away with disgust and abhorrence: though we may remark, that his lordship's sentiments on the subject, or rather, perhaps, the sentiments which he *advocates*, seem to be in obvious harmony with the language of the catechism and baptismal service of the Anglican church. But we do conceive that Mr. Bristed himself needs to have his attention directed to the simple account of regeneration, which the Scripture gives, 1 John v. 1. "Whosoever *believeth* that Jesus is the Christ, is born of God." Here it is obvious that the apostle states a divine *truth*, in the words, "Jesus is the Christ," the *belief of which* he declares to be always accompanied with the change called *regeneration*. But what Mr. Bristed means by *faith*, or *believing*, it is very hard to say: for he tells us, (p. 433.) that it is "unscriptural, unprotestant, unchurchmanlike, and dangerous to say, that *infants* are justified without *faith*." Now, it is evident that the *infant*, whether baptized or unbaptized, neither believes nor disbelieves any thing about a truth, of which it has never heard, and the import of which it is utterly incapable of understanding.

Yet we have the highest authority for maintaining, that *of such*, of objects so helpless, ignorant, and utterly incapable of doing aught to forward their own interests, "of *such* is the kingdom of God." We are aware that the expression which we have just quoted is commonly interpreted in a very different way, as if it described characters as *innocent*, *simple*, and *teachable* as little children. It might easily be shown, that this popular comment is in direct opposition to the whole context of the passage, as well, indeed, as to the whole analogy of scriptural truth. But we must abstain, and hasten to conclude an article, from the length of which Mr. Bristed may perceive that we consider his book, with all its faults, as containing much interesting matter. The hints which we have suggested to his consideration, and a few more which we are about to subjoin, we hope he will receive with the same friendly feelings which have prompted them.

In his future publications, we strongly recommend that he should aim at more *sobriety*; sobriety of thought, and sobriety of language. No doubt it is much easier to prescribe this to an ardent, desultory, and head-long writer, than to administer the remedy. But let us ask him, whether the following position be not most unwarrantably strong. (P. 397.) "The chief objects of *every native* American, after bettering his own condition, are to aggrandize his country; *to drive all Europeans out of this western world*; to federate the two Americas, north and south, &c. and, eventually, to dictate the law to Europe, and to the world?" These the chief objects of *every native* American! even of the *Christian* natives! Alas! alas! for America, if this be true. Setting aside the influence of Christian principles altogether, we really had attributed a much greater share of *good sense* to the Americans than this passage would intimate; though we never doubted that there are foolish and hot-headed politicians among them who may conceive that such objects are desirable. Those who pursue them will be found among the worst enemies to the real interests of America.

Let us submit it also to Mr. Bristed's good taste whether such *language* as the following be really energetic, or do not rather throw a ludicrous and disgusting air upon his sentiments? (P. 410.) "He (Rev. Mr. Polwhele) dips his pen in *the doubly-distilled venom of the damned*, when he raves against the evangelical clergy." (P. 188.)

"Formal high churchmen . . . generally have about as much mercy, as there is *milk in a male tiger*."

We would especially advise Mr. Bristed to abstain from *cant*. Ought not either a Christian, or any educated man, to blush for penning such sentences as the following? (P. 42.) "It is my wish not to be understood as in any way designing to reflect upon the study or the practice of the law, by *occasionally escaping* from the toil and dust, and litigation of the forum, *into the city of refuge*." (P. 56.) "The unction of humility, which flowed from the silvered temples of Beveridge, down to the skirts of his garment."

As we are anxious for the preservation of the English language in the new world, we could have wished (though it is certainly a very subordinate matter), that our author had studied more purity of English style: and we might have reasonably expected, that a gentleman, who has received a literary education in these countries, should abstain from such barbarisms, or perhaps Americanisms, as the following: "to *locate*," "to *eventuate*," "*procinct* to drive," "*intermediate the complaints*," "one of our *largest* divines," &c. &c.

But, to use Mr. Bristed's language, p. 413, the *limits* of the present article are, *waning to their close*. We therefore only add our advice, that when he next writes on theological subjects, he would adhere more closely to the good principle expressed in the Greek motto of his title-page: ἐκ των θειων γραφων θεολογουμεν καν θελωσιν οἱ ἐχθροι, καν μη. Hitherto certainly we may complain, that, in adopting that motto, he has hung out false colours.

REVIEW

OF

"A GREEK AND ENGLISH LEXICON;

IN WHICH ARE EXPLAINED ALL THE WORDS USED BY THE BEST GREEK WRITERS OF PROSE AND VERSE, &c.

BY

JOHN JONES, LL.D.

AUTHOR OF *the* GREEK GRAMMAR.

Longman and Co. 8vo. pp. 870."

[Published in No. II. of The Westminster Review, April, 1824.]

When we consider the numerous and ample endowments which the liberality of former ages has provided in this country for the support of learning, and especially classical learning, it seems extraordinary that our schools have remained so long almost wholly destitute of books properly adapted for facilitating its acquisition. In numerous instances is this want observable; but in none is it more strikingly apparent, or more injurious in its effects, than in the instance of *Lexicons*. Every competent judge, acquainted with the state of scholastic education in England, is aware that the Lexicons generally used in our schools, for teaching both the Greek and Latin languages, are grossly and scandalously defective, utterly inadequate to afford that critical aid to the learner which a Lexicon ought to supply.

We have sometimes been inclined to think that it would be a fair and expedient object of legislative enactment, to apply some of the literary funds which exist in the country to the purpose of providing for our classical schools—what may be called—suitable *classical furniture*. In this we include Grammars, Exercise-books, Lexicons, and editions of the classic authors.

The most elementary works ought always to be drawn up by the most advanced scholars. But other qualifications, besides profound scholarship, would be essentially requisite in the persons engaged to undertake the task which we point out. It would be requisite especially that they should have *good sense*; that they should have the faculty of taking a clear view of the end to be proposed, and of the means by which it is to be attained. They should be well acquainted with the kind of aid which a school-boy needs and ought to be furnished with; and they should aim at supplying that aid with all the brevity that is consistent with clearness, and not suffer themselves to be diverted from the singleness of this object by any of the literary vanity, which prompts to a display of erudition.

Such men, though they are not met with every day, yet surely might be found, and engaged in the work: nor do we see how the work is likely to be effected without some national interference, such as we suggest. It is vain to look to our Universities for stirring in it. They seem to think, with the bishops, that things go on very well *as they are*. Yet, even if this were admitted, it might be worth considering *how long* they are likely to go on as they are. All who know what passes in the world, know that the tide of public opinion has for some time been setting most strongly against classical learning. We are persuaded that it will be decried only by those who possess it not. We therefore consider the prevailing disesteem in which it is held as one of the indications, that our numerous public seminaries founded for its advancement are sadly inefficient; and we confess that, in the present unsettled state of Europe, we apprehend that all institutions ineffective, but costly, are of a very precarious duration.

It is, however; with great caution that the legislature ought to be desired to take a part in providingfor the wants of the literary consumer (in this case the schoolmaster, tutor, &c.) who is generally the best judge of them, and who will sooner or later procure the object of his wishes. We have never seen the co-operation of literary bodies patronized by the state, attended with such advantages as to make us much lament the absence of that kind of assistance. The Delphin Classics may serve as a warning against empowering a government to appoint and pay individuals for remedying deficiencies in books designed for the purposes of instruction; the fact is, that had even a society for such a purpose been formed, we should have had nothing better than a revisiou of the old books, or perhaps more cumbrous and inefficient new ones upon the old bad plan. Neither literary individuals, competent to the duty of composing really good books, have been wanting, nor yet have *the trade* been backward in adopting the suggestions of such men. The backwardness has been on the part of the bodies who have hitherto monopolized the public education, and has arisen from the general mass of ignorance and prejudice in which the whole subject has for centuries been immersed, and which that monopoly was calculated to perpetuate. In the instances in which good books have been proposed to *them*, they have not been adopted: and it is *now* only, when these prejudices are beginning to disperse, that such good books are coming into favour, and many more into being; now that there is some chance of *sale* to the trade—and some hope of reward to the scholar. It never could be expected that the *trade* would produce books to rot in their warehouses, or that competent individuals would expend their labour on works which were met with no other reception than that of neglect—or if not neglect, ridicule.

If in any case national funds are appropriated for the advancement of either literature or science, it ought to be especially provided, that they should be distributed in the way of compensation; and not after the manner too generally established. To give a man a place or sum of money to induce him to perform any given task, is to take away the principal motive to accomplish it; and, generally, to change an active and vigorous promoter of knowledge, into a lazy, and often dissatisfied, spectator of improvement.

But the more we lament the want which we have noticed in our schools, the more must any of the attempts to supply it, which are occasionally made by literary individuals, be commended to our favourable acceptance; and the more disposed are we to extend to such attempts all the encouragement that we can *honestly* afford. In the work which now claims our attention, Dr. Jones has made a commendable exertion, to furnish our schools with a Greek Lexicon of a moderate size and critical character. He states that it has cost him "three years' hard labour in composing and printing." We can readily believe it: and we know not many—may we say—*operative* scholars. οἷοι νῦν βροτοί εἰσι, who could labour so hard. In former ages, indeed, one scholar would bring out as many learned works, well executed, as we should think sufficient to employ the lives, and task the powers, of many.

Dr. Jones describes himself as engaged in preparing a larger and more general Lexicon of the Greek language, to finish which, he calculates, will cost him "the labour of five or six years more." Would that we could infuse the doctor's active industry into a dozen of the crack scholars of Oxford or Cambridge! And, as we are wishing, we may as well add—would that we could infuse all their knowledge of Greek into Dr. Jones! and then—would that he might *live a thousand years!*

We cannot, however, flatter Dr. J. with having succeeded in producing such a work as is wanted in our schools. The plan of giving the interpretations in English instead of Latin, we decidedly approve; and we think it likely that this circumstance alone will give his Lexicon a considerable currency, in a certain class of academies in this country. We expect, therefore, that a new edition will be called for; and as he promises to spare no pains in the revisal, and to give attention to "the suggestions of enlightened and candid criticism," we shall proceed the more freely to offer some strictures on the general plan, and on the execution of the work. Our author tells us, that he is "sufficiently sensible of its errors and imperfections." We hope it will not be between him and us, as it was with the facetious Rowland Hill, and the woman who came to him complaining that she was a *great sinner*. "Indeed, I know you are," said his reverence drily, "a very great sinner." "What!" exclaimed the humble complainant, breaking out into a rage, "what bad have you ever known of me, or can any one say of me, with truth?" Seriously, we assure the doctor, that it is with no hostile feelings we have examined his publication; and that we should much rather have found occasion to speak of it in the language of strong commendation, than of critical animadversion.

We must remark, in the first place, that the Lexicon might have been much more useful, if, in forming the plan, Dr. Jones had fixed upon one class of students, to whose use it should be adapted; and if he had not extended his view beyond schoolboys. That they principally were in his view in this publication is evident, even from its size and form; as well as from the fact, that our author is actually preparing a more extensive work, in a large quarto volume, for more advanced scholars. But he tells us in the title-page, and repeats it in his preface, that the present work is "intended, not only for the use of learners in private and in the public schools, but also for those, who, after the usual periods of education, seek to acquire a more accurate and extensive acquaintance with the language," &c. From his aiming at the two objects at once, we may in some degree account for his missing both.

In a School-Lexicon, of such confined limits, why should Dr. Jones admit words for which he could adduce no authority but that of the obscurest writers, of whose works a few fragments alone have come down to us, and whose names are scarcely known even to many advanced scholars? In two consecutive pages,* beginning with the word εὐρύπεδος, and ending with the word εὐτάκτως, we are referred for authority, four times, to "Leon. Tar.;" three times to "Antip. Sid.;" once to "Theodorid.;" to "*Anyte;*" to "Jul. Aeg.;" and to "Crinag." Perhaps, unless the reader has the Greek Anthology at hand, he may be at a loss to guess what names the learned doctor intends by some of his abbreviations. Most of them certainly might be in vain searched for in Harles's copious Introduction to the History of the Greek Language.

But may we not ask, of what use to school-boys is the great mass of Dr. Jones's references even to the best-known Greek writers? He refers, for instance, but without *quoting the passages*, to the book, section, and line of Schweighæuser's Polybius, in nine volumes, or to the volume and page of Reiske's Plutarch, in twelve volumes, or of Hemsterhuis's Lucian, in four volumes, &c. &c. where a passage may be found containing the word, and in the sense, which he supports by this authority. Now, are we to suppose a schoolboy possessed of a Greek library, affording not only these authors, but these particular editions of them? Or, if we should suppose any thing so improbable, are we to suppose that the schoolboy will verify the doctor's reference and interpretation, by turning to the passage?

If our author reply, that this part of his work was intended not for boys, but for men; we must say, that to the man, as much as to the boy, it is useless, unless he possess the authors and editions referred to; and is it to be supposed that the adult scholar, who has any such collection of Greek classics, is unprovided with even that knave Scapula's compilation, or with some Greek Lexicon, which

* Before we close the two pages to which we refer, we would incidentally suggest to Dr. Jones, that although εὐρυχανὴς might be formed from χαίνω, εὐρυχαδὴς cannot. This must be considered as formed from χάζω, *to contain*.

must supersede the use of Dr. Jones's? In a Lexicon otherwise adapted to the use of advanced scholars, we should by no means undervalue the bare reference to the pages of specified editions, even though unaccompanied with any quotation of the passages. For ourselves, we should rather that Stephens, for instance, had given such precise references without the quotations, than the quotations without such precise references. But we confess, that the latter alone seem to us very useless in such a work as that now before us.

But there is no volume to which Dr. Jones makes such numerous references, as to the sacred Scriptures, the version of the Seventy, and the writers of the New Testament: and in citing from the latter, he is too frequently tempted to enlarge in the way of comment. Now, for what class of readers was this part of the work designed? Biblical scholars have Biel, Schleusner, and a tribe of subordinate lexicographers in this department. In our schools, we believe, the New Testament is made a kind of *first* Greek book; and perhaps to some of them, Dr. Jones's copiousness here may commend his work. But, for our parts, we have too great a reverence for the Scriptures, not to reprobate any such use of them; and we should have considered Dr. Jones as acting much more judiciously, if he had not admitted into his work a single reference to either the Septuagint or the New Testament.

This would have been quite consistent with his professed object, of explaining "all the words used by the *best* Greek writers." To say nothing at present of the Seventy, it surely is not a matter of controversy at this day, that the writers of the New Testament do not write in classical Greek; but, as might be expected, in a style abounding with Hebraisms and Latinisms, as well as variously affected by the peculiar nature of the subject which they treat. Are such writings fit to be employed for teaching boys Greek?

The shortness, indeed, of many sentences in the narratives of the Evangelists, and the simplicity of their structure, seem to have induced teachers to mis-employ that volume so grossly, as if it were not easy to select from the classic writers plenty of sentences as short and as simple. But we are bold to affirm, that the New Testament, so far from being a book suited to the youngest learners of the Greek language, is one which cannot, with any advantage, be studied in the original but by those who have otherwise attained a manly acquaintance with the language. The smattering, upon which many set up to spell, and parse, and criticise, the text of the Evangelists and Apostles, by the aid of some of the numerous lexicons manufactured for the purpose of assisting them, is commonly but the occasion of making them dupes to their own vanity, and to the ignorance or the dishonesty of others.

But allowing that Dr. Jones, from whatever cause, might have thought it necessary not to exclude altogether the sacred writers from the number of the Greek classics, we must still urge the question—why should he be so extraordinarily copious in his comments on them? And why should he so needlessly multiply references to them in cases where numerous classical authorities were at hand? Did he think that there is any dearth of lexicographers and commentators on the New Testament? *Above all, why should he make such references the occasion of bringing forward, we might say of smuggling in, his own theological sentiments and favourite interpretations?* It may be needful to adduce some examples to vindicate the justice of our censure.

"ΜΟΡΦΗ', ης, ἡ, a form, shape, figure, beauty, ἐν μορφῇ Θεῦ ὑπάρχων, being in the form of God, in a splendid form, alluding, seemingly, to our Lord's transfiguration, Matth. 17.*

"Χρηστολογία, ας, ἡ, flattery, or gentleness of language, opposed to guile in the heart. *This word occurs only in* Rom. 16, 18, *and, in truth, the composition of it is* Χρηστὸς λόγια, *i. e.* λόγια περὶ τῦ Χρηστῦ, oracles concerning Chrestus; that is, oracles which certain impostors in the church at Rome propagated concerning Christ, Χριστὸς being changed by them into Χρηστὸς, the usual name given him by the Gnostics, and even by unbelievers.

"'Ανάθεμα, ατος, τὸ, that which is set apart for holy purposes, a victim—ηὐχόμην αὐτὸς ἐγὼ ἀνάθεμα εἶναι ἀπὸ (rather ὑπὸ) τοῦ Χριστοῦ, Rom ix. 3. I too (*i. e.* I too, as well as Peter) would have gloried in being separated, *i. e.* appointed by Christ, for converting my brethren, and to be sacrificed as a victim in their cause.

"'Ιλασμὸς, οῦ, ὁ, atonement, sacrifice for sin—the means of expiating sin, or of forsaking a sinful life, and thus reconciling man to God; and this is said of Christ, who is the author of salvation to mankind, and said of him in reference to the sacrifices of the law, with a view to withdraw the attention of the Jewish believers from the Levitical code, to which they were prone, and fix it on repentance and reformation through Christ, as the only means of acceptance with God. 1 John ii. 2; iv. 10."

Now, if these theological interpretations were as indisputably excellent as the author conceives, may we not ask, what business have they in such a lexicon as the present? Was Dr. Jones at a loss for classical examples of the words μορφὴ and ἱλασμὸς, that he turned aside to those passages of theological controversy in the New Testament? No such thing: but he wished to take the opportunity of throwing the weight of his authority into one of the controversial scales, against the divinity or pre-existence of Christ, and against his atonement. The doctor ought not to be allowed to compile a Greek lexicon for the use of schools without being *bound over to keep the peace* theologically.

But are his comments of such value as might apologize for his stepping out of the way to introduce them? He must excuse us for holding them very cheap. Whatever any one may suppose to be the precise meaning of the words ἐν μορφῇ Θεῦ ὑπάρχων in Phil. ii, 6, no candid and competent reader of the passage can deny, that they evidently denote a state of the person spoken of *antecedent* to that in which it is said that ἑαυτὸν ἐκένωσε, μορφὴν δύλυ λαβὼν, ἐν ὁμοιώματι ἀνθρώπυ γενόμενος. And will Dr. Jones pretend to say that Christ took not on him the form of a servant, nor was made in the likeness

* Dr. Jones's book is printed without accents. He will pardon us for disfiguring his Greek with those vain marks.

of men, till after his *transfiguration* on the mount? It would be amusing to follow our author into his *chaotic* interpretation of ἱλασμὸς: but the subject would lead us further into theological disquisition than the nature and limits of the present article allow.

As to Dr. Jones's whim about χρηστολογία, one can but smile at the oracular confidence with which it is put forward, in opposition (we believe we may say) to all lexicographers, commentators, and translators, ancient and modern. Dr. J. remarks that "the word occurs only in Rom. xvi. 18;" and we believe the remark was designed to convey a justification of himself for departing so strangely from the received interpretation. We wonder how he could venture to pen that article without even looking at Henry Stephens, who would have furnished him with a passage from Chrysostom, in which the word occurs; as well as with the word χρηστόλογος from Julius Capitolinus. Wetstein, on the passage, would have furnished him with other examples of the word, as well as with citations which decide its meaning, if there were any doubt about it. *E. gr.* Anthol. 71. 4. χρηστὸν λόγοισι, πολέμιον δὲ τοῖς τρόποις. Herodian, viii. 3, 10. χρηστοῖς λόγοις δελεασθέντας. But, in truth, a Greek scholar can be at no loss or uncertainty about the formation of the word; the analogy is so obvious between it and εὐλογία (which occurs in immediate juxta-position with it in the passage), as well as a numerous tribe of similar compounds, βραχυλογία, παλιλογία, πολυλογία, ψευδολογία, ψυχρολογία, &c. &c. And how Dr. Jones could dream that the word was formed from λόγια, *oracles* (a neuter-plural), would be unaccountable, but that it made part of a dream about the Gnostics, and Chrestus, and oracles concerning Chrestus.

With respect to our author's interpretation of Rom. ix. 3, it is needless to state the objections to it, since an interpretation altogether different has been assigned, which we conceive at once commends itself as unquestionably true. Dr. Jones may see what we allude to in Mr. Belsham's late work on the Epistles of Paul; though Mr. B. is quite mistaken in assigning the interpretation to Mr. Wakefield as its author.

When the doctor interprets μὴ μετεωρίζεσθε (Luke xii. 29) "do not, through anxiety about the future, *imitate those who go to the stars for the knowledge of future events*," he ought to have been guarded against this idle fancy, by attending to one of the significations which he himself has just before assigned to μετέωρος, "anxious, suspended, Nub. 263." Demosthenes and Thucydides employ the word in the same sense; which seems borrowed from the agitation of a ship riding at anchor.

We thought that the meaning and origin of the name of *Pharisee* had been perfectly ascertained and generally known; but Dr. Jones informs us, that the Pharisees were "a sect among the Jews, who professed to explain the law of Moses from פרש, to expound, or unfold!"*

* On examination, we find that Joh. Drusius long ago offered the same account, in which, however, we believe he has not been followed by any scholar since. The proposed etymology, and the misinterpretation on which it proceeds, obviously confound the Pharisees with the scribes and lawyers, from whom they were altogether distinct.

This leads us to notice another circumstance. in which we think Dr. Jones's Lexicon, in its present state, ill-adapted to boys, and nothing the more adapted to men—we mean his eastern etymologies. He informs us, that "whenever the primary sense of a simple term has been overlooked, or mistaken, the origin of that term is pointed out in one of the oriental tongues;" and in this part of his work our author seems to take peculiar pride. It must be inferred that Dr. Jones could with equal certainty assign the oriental origin of every simple term in the Greek tongue, and we really think that he could. But while some may regret that he has not done so, we confess that this profession in his title-page and preface did not raise in us any high expectations. We have known a good deal of the vagaries of etymologists, and of their empty parade of oriental learning. We formerly knew one of them whose works abound so with etymologies from the Hebrew, Syriac, Arabic, Persic, &c. &c. and with words exhibited in every variety of oriental character, that many admired him as a prodigy of eastern learning. But he was more honest than most; for he has frequently acknowledged to his confidential friends, that of all these languages with which he made so fine a show, he knew nothing beyond their alphabets, and what he learned from indexes and glossaries. In short, nothing is more easy, or requires a smaller stock of philological knowledge, than either to collect or to invent etymologies from the oriental tongues.

We are very far from undervaluing etymological researches, in their proper place, and soberly conducted: but, unfortunately, the subject affords so many allurements to the indulgence of the imagination, and such easy means for indulging it, that it is more rare to find *sobriety* in etymologists than in any other class of writers. We were not, therefore, much surprised at finding Dr. Jones very extravagant and fanciful in many of his eastern etymologies: as well as very ignorant, not only of the eastern languages in general, but even of Hebrew.

Into the evidence of this ignorance we shall not at present go, inviting as the field is which the subject opens to us; because our immediate business is with the doctor's knowledge of Greek, and competence for compiling a lexicon of that language for the use of schools. And to schoolboys we do think it very useless to trace Greek words to oriental roots, and very likely to mislead them from the real etymology to which their attention ought to be directed, as well as from the real meaning also of the word, whenever the etymologist ventures to deduce its meaning from its supposed oriental derivation.

Few etymologies bear a more plausible aspect at first view than that which Parkhurst (and Dr. J. after him) assigns for the Greek word *μυστήριον*, viz. from the Hebrew root סתר *to conceal*, with a formative מ; or, as the doctor says, "from the Hebrew מסתר *mustar*." Suppose the schoolboy attends to this. He is not much the wiser for it if it were true: but we say that he is misled from the real etymology. When we observe the words *μύω*, *μύστης*, *μυστήριον*, can there be any reasonable doubt that the two latter are

means—*in fact, indeed, truly, then?* Or, will any Greek scholars credit his assertion, that the primary sense of φιλέω is *to marry?* an assertion, for which he offers no other proof, but his fancy that the word is derived from the Hebrew בעל. We fear that we must have Dr. Jones bound over to keep the peace etymologically, as well as theologically.

We have remarked that Dr. J. needlessly multiplies the significations of γὰρ; and we could adduce many instances of the same fault. One, that immediately presents itself to us, is rather amusing. Among the other significations of πίπτω or πίτω, he assigns the following:—"fall *into the world*, am born," Il. τ. 110. Our classical readers no doubt recollect the passage:—Ὅς κεν ἐπ' ἤματι τῷδε πέσῃ μετὰ ποσσὶ γυναικός. The doctor must look for another example to justify his interpretation: for we can assure him, that in the passage to which he refers, the verb imports literally and simply—to *fall* or *drop*.

Our author is very ambitious, to "preserve the same original idea through the several ramifications" of meaning annexed to a word; and he carries to an extravagant length this plausible, but often impracticable, notion. In assigning the original idea, also, he has often no ground to support him, but some whimsical conjecture that strikes his fancy. Thus, "the particle ἄρα," he says, "seems to have the same common origin with ὁράω:" and from this seeming, he concludes, that "its primary signification is that of LO BEHOLD;" and he then proceeds to dance this idea through two columns for the edification of the student.

"It is," he tells us, "a common notion, that many words in all languages convey a variety of significations. But, in strict propriety, a term has but one sense, or at most but two, a literal and analogical sense. Every word, on every occasion, presents the same idea; and it conveys different ideas only, because it stands in different connexions."—After all, then, although the same word "on every occasion *presents* the same idea," yet it does not on every occasion *convey* the same idea. We are rather bewildered.—"Thus, in one connexion, ἀκτὴ may mean *bread;* in another, a *shore;* and with an accidental change of termination (ἀκτὶς) it denotes *a ray of the sun*. But in every place the word still means the same thing. For ἀκτὴ is ἀγετὴ, *broken;* from ἄγω, *to break; corn broken* is *meal; broken ground* or *rock*, is *a shore;* and *the broken, scattered light of the sun* is its *rays*. So λέγω, *to speak;* and λέγομαι, *to lie down*, are still the self-same word. For it is the Hebrew לחק, *to assemble* or *gather: to gather letters*, or *words*, is to utter them; *to gather myself for repose*, is to lie down."

We acknowledge that we hold such fancies very cheap. It is nothing new certainly to derive ἀκτὴ and ἀκτὶς, from ἄγω, *frango;* and we are not disposed to dispute it, though we confess that we know not what is meant by calling a sunbeam, the *broken* light of the sun. But if Dr. Jones holds ἀκτὴ and ἀκτὶς (or ἀκτὶν) for the same word, notwithstanding "the *accidental* change of termination," we beg to know why he considers ἄγω and ἄγω as different words, on account of the accidental change of quantity; why he does not trace the two ideas of *breaking* and *leading* to some one common stock? We think it would not be difficult to a writer of the doctor's lively imagination. But what if we find the doctor assigning to the self-same word two senses, not only different, but directly *contrary* to each other; and this, in opposition (as far as we know) to all Greek lexicographers, ancient and modern? *E. gr.*

"Ἀπαρτίζω, *f.* ἴσω (ἀπὸ ἄρτιος) I make a thing even with a design or model, *i. e.* complete—make uneven or unequal, σπουδὴ καὶ τοῦδε οὐκ ἀπαρτίζει πόδα, Septem 376, haste makes his step not uneven with that man, i. e. an urgent business makes him come with speed equal to this man.—*Eteocles and the scout hastily come on the stage the same moment.*"

Here our author forgets the canon he laid down in his preface; and after assigning to the word the sense of *making even*, he coins for it the contrary sense of *making uneven*, in order to bring forward a pet interpretation of a line in Æschylus. The expression of the poet, we conceive, evidently denotes the hurried and irregular movement of each. A man walking leisurely plants his foot steadily, so as to make a *perfect* step; but this their hurry did not allow.

We seriously, and with the most friendly intention, advise Dr. Jones to withdraw all the *original* matter from his Lexicon, and to be content with the humbler office of a mere compiler. The existing materials for a useful Greek Lexicon are ample, but widely scattered. To select judiciously, to collect, and to abridge, would task the powers and employ many years of the life of the ablest scholar; and the ablest scholar need not be ashamed of the employment, even under the restriction which we should think it necessary to impose on our author.

We are disposed to account for his doing so imperfectly and incorrectly, that which we must suppose to be within his powers, from his attention being so much occupied by the seductions of other, and, as he conceives, higher objects. Dr. Jones almost entirely neglects that needful labour, which, in his title-page and preface, he professes to have employed—the marking of the quantity of doubtful vowels. Of the few instances in which he has marked it, a majority are of that kind in which we should be disposed to omit it; *e. gr.* the penultimate of the verbs in ινω—of the future of verbs in ζω, &c. where the youngest scholar ought to be familiar with the common rule of prosody, which determines the quantity. But the student will in vain seek in this Lexicon the quantity of such words as ἀκριβὴς, κίνδυνος, κριθὴ, μάλα, θύμος, and a whole tribe of its derivatives and compounds, ζάθεος and all the words compounded with the particle ζὰ, &c. &c. And we complain of the omission only in those cases, in which Dr. Jones could have found no difficulty in supplying it, at least with the aid of Dr. Maltby's edition of Morell.

Useless also to schoolboys as we think his mere references to this and that passage in the Greek classics without citing the words, yet, for ourselves, we could wish that he had better fulfilled his engagement of authenticating each word, and the senses assigned, even by such references. For instance, we are somewhat curious to know on what authority Dr. J. assigns to ἄπαξ the meaning of, *as soon as.*

We believe he is singular in that interpretation of the word: and we confess that, until we see a decisive classical example of such an application of it, we must remain incredulous, notwithstanding the weight of the doctor's authority. There must have been some passage under his view, in which he thought the word had this meaning; and had he referred to it, we should probably be able to trace the origin of his mistake, as in other instances.

Thus, on the verb γνωρίζω, our author assigns to the passive γνωρίζομαι the meaning, *I am reconciled;* and refers to a passage in Demosthenes, p. 1390. ed. Reisk. We were very certain that the verb never had this meaning; and accordingly, on examining the page referred to, we found the words τὰς προσηγορίας ἔχοντες, αἷς ὑπὸ τῶν ἐν γένει γνωρίζονται—"titles by which they are distinguished by those belonging to the family." As no blundering of translation could introduce the idea of *being reconciled* here, we were still at a loss to account for Dr. J.'s interpretation and reference; till at length we examined "Reiske's Index Gr. Demosth." under the word γνωρίζειν, which immediately cleared up our author's mistake. There, immediately before the passage to which Dr. J. referred, Reiske cites (from p. 925), the words ὁπόθεν δήποθεν ἐγνωρισμένοι, and adds the following interpretation: "quacunque tandem ratione *cum eo conciliati.*" Now, it becomes evident that our author hastily consulted this Index alone, without examining the text of Demosthenes; accidentally referred to the words in p. 1390, instead of to those in p. 925, and mistook the meaning of Reiske's Latin, *cum eo conciliati.* The words ὁπόθεν δήποθεν ἐγνωρισμένοι τούτῳ simply mean "from whatever circumstance they had *become acquainted* with this man,"—without the slightest intimation of any previous enmity between the parties, or any *reconciliation.* To justify our assertion, it way be well to quote the context:—

"Ἐγὼ γὰρ, ὦ ἄνδρες δικασταὶ, αὐτὸς μὲν οὐδ᾽ ὁπωστιοῦν ἐγνώριζον τοὺς ἀνθρώπους τούτους. Θρασυμήδης δὲ . . . καὶ Μελανωπὸς, ὁ ἀδελφὸς αὐτοῦ, ἐπιτήδειοί μοί εἰσι, καὶ χρώμεθα ἀλλήλοις, ὡς οἷόντε μάλιστα. οὗτοι προσῆλθόν μοι μετὰ Λακρίτου τουτουΐ, ὁπόθεν δήποθεν ἐγνωρισμένοι τούτῳ· οὐ γὰρ οἶδα· καὶ ἐδέοντό μου κ. τ. λ.—We have insisted the more at large on this example, in order to press upon our author the importance of examining the original of each passage which he cites.

It must surely be to haste and inattention, that we should attribute Dr. Jones's gross mistranslation of a very simple passage, which he adduces from Xenophon (K. Π. i. 6.) under the particle ἄν.—φρόνιμος δὲ περὶ τοῦ συνοίσειν μέλλοντος πῶς ἄν τις τῷ ὄντι γένοιτο; δηλονότι, ὦ παῖ, ἔφη, ὅσα μὲν ἐστι μαθόντα εἰδέναι, μαθὼν ἄν; *i. e.* "plainly he may by being taught, as far as matters can be known by teaching." Instead of which the doctor renders the words—"whatever things *it is lawful* to know *after having* learnt them." If he had read on to the end of the sentence, he must have seen that ἃ ἐστι μαθόντα εἰδέναι is equivalent with μαθητά.—We may remark also, that when Dr. J. on the same particle informs us, that ἐπισχὼν ἄν, in the beginning of the first Philippic, "means ἐπίσχοιμι ἄν," (the Dr. means ἐπίσχον ἄν) his language is calculated to lead a schoolboy into a great mistake. Taking the words in connexion with the following, they may, indeed, advantageously be translated as if they ran—ἐπίσχον ἂν ἕως . . . καὶ, εἰ μὲν . . . ἡσυχίαν ἂν ἦγον. But when we so resolve the sentence, the necessity of inserting a copulative particle shows, that ἐπισχὼν retains its proper participial meaning. We almost blush, while we are obliged to pen an observation so puerile.

Our author, indeed, often seems more anxious about teaching a boy to *translate* a phrase into English, than about explaining the construction. Thus, after interpreting μέλω—" I am a subject of concern, a matter of care or attention to," he adds, " But this verb is used impersonally with the person in the dative, which requires to be in the nom. in English, οἷς ἔτι μέλει πολεμήϊα ἔργα, Il. B. 338." Used *impersonally!* Not a whit more so in such a construction, than in the expression ἀνθρώποισι μέλω. Indeed, the construction in both expressions is identically the same. We have to complain of the same *negligence* in Dr. Jones on the cognate word ἐάν. Among the other significations, which he assigns to this conjunction, we stared at finding, " except, unless;" our author carelessly giving to ἐὰν the meaning of ἐὰν μή.

But what shall we say of such remarks as the following? That they originate in oscitancy? or in what else? On the neuter participle ἐξόν, put absolutely, our author says—" ἐστι with this participle seems understood, ἐξὸν αὐτοῖς, scil. ἐστι. it is lawful to them, it is in their power." Thuc. 4. 65. It is almost superfluous to quote the historian's words; but here they are, ὡς, ἐξὸν αὐτοῖς τὰ ἐν Σικελίᾳ καταστρέψασθαι, δώροις πεισθέντες ἀναχωρήσαν. Is it possible, that Dr. J. really conceives ἐξὸν there to be put for ἐξὸν ἐστι, or ἔξεστι? Does he think that the sentence would be commonly grammatical or intelligible, if the latter were substituted for ἐξόν? Curiosity led us to turn to δέον; but the Doctor takes no notice of the similar and equally frequent use of that participle.

In all the editions of Hederic which we have examined, (except the edition of 1766), after the interpretation of ἐξὸν—*cum liceat*,—the following words are subjoined in a parenthesis. " Tota dictio hæc est, ἐκποδὼν ἐστι, via plana, aperta est, obstantibus amotis, *Ern.*" This remark of Ernesti, in its present connexion, appears to us utterly unintelligible. It has been misplaced, we conceive, by the blunder of a printer originally: though we have searched in vain for the passage to which it ought to be transferred. But we are not without suspicion, that with this blunder Dr. Jones's has some ludicrous connexion.

Frequently, as we have already intimated, his errors can be accounted for only from his eagerness to establish a favourite fancy, which seems so to engross his mind, that he has no eyes for things the most plain before him. Thus, in a long diatribe on the participle ὤν, he is anxious to prove that it has commonly a greater emphasis than merely *being*,—that it includes in its signification the idea of ὄντως *in reality*. (We turned to the verb εἰμί, to try whether he said the same of it: but we were disappointed; for he dismisses the word, without any interpretation, with " see Sturz. in εἶναι, Damm. 832." (Very instructive to a schoolboy.) So much is he occupied with this fancy, that he grossly mistranslates at least four passages, which he adduces to establish it. "When ὢν is joined with τυγχάνω, as is often the case, its real force is best expressed in English by really, true: φίλος τυγχάνει ὤν, he is really a friend. ὅσοι αὐτῶν φυγάδες τότε ὄντες ἐτύγχανον, Ἀγ. 2, 2. as many of them as were then real slaves." To do our author justice, we must add that he immediately subjoins, "or happened to be slaves," [exiles], as if the two interpretations were equivalent. But again:—

"Εἰ μὲν ἐλάττους ἐποίησα τὰς δυνάμεις, παρ' ἐμοὶ τἀδίκημ' ἂν ἐδείκνυεν ὄν, Dem. 305, 11,—if I diminished the resources of the state, wrong being on my side, he would have proved so—he would have proved that wrong actually existed on my part." Instead of, *he would have proved that the wrong was with me—lay at my door.*

Again,—

"Εἰ μὲν γὰρ μὴ ἐχρῆν, ἀλλὰ τὴν Μυσῶν λείαν καλουμένην τὴν Ἑλλάδα οὖσαν ὀφθῆναι, ζώντων Ἀθηναίων καὶ ὄντων, περιειργασμαι μὲν ἐγὼ περὶ τῶν τοιούτων εἰπών, Dem. 248, 25, if indeed it was not fit that Greece, while really *Greece*, should appear what is called a Mysian prey, (*i.e.* an easy unresisting prey to Philip) while the Athenians lived and were really so (and were really worthy of that name), I have trifled in speaking of these things."

Here, along with every thing else that is extraordinary, our author makes the orator say exactly the contrary of what he really says. He had proposed the indignant question—"Ought there, or ought there not, to have appeared some of the Greeks, to oppose him in these proceedings?" He immediately adds, *If there ought not, but Greece ought to have been seen the prey (as is said) of Mysians ... then indeed I have been over-busy in speaking about such matters; and you, &c.*

As to the words ζώντων Ἀθ. καὶ ὄντων, Dr. Jones is more excusable for assigning some emphasis to ὄντων there. Yet we confess that we are disposed to think it one of those pleonastic expressions which occur in all languages: as we say, *while I live and breathe*. Perhaps, however, the words may import, *while Athenians lived, and the Athenian state subsisted;* the city and commonwealth undestroyed.

Demosthenes is one of those prose writers whom Dr. Jones professes to explain in this Lexicon; and strongly should we recommend that classic to his most assiduous study, before he brings out another edition of the work. At present, certainly, the student, who should sit down to read Demosthenes with the aid of this Lexicon, would not only be absolutely led astray upon many passages, but would continually find himself left in the lurch, without any of that assistance and information which a young student must need; and this, even in cases in which the commonest lexicons afford it. A few examples will explain and illustrate our meaning.

The Greek Orator contiuually uses the expression οἱ παριόντες, for those who *come forward* to address the people. But Dr. Jones furnishes the student with no other meanings for the verb, but to "pass by, withdraw, neglect:" assigning, in fact, to πάρειμι the significations of παρίημι, as well as its two participles παρεὶς and παρεθείς. The verb παρελθεῖν is employed in the same sense (Dem, 169, 559, and Luc. Menipp.) But of this also no notice is taken by our author: though in both instances, even Hederic's Lexicon would supply his deficiency.

As totally would Dr. Jones's guidance fail the student upon the orator's expression (pp. 36, 174) ἀλλ' ὅσης ἅπαντες ὁρᾶτε ἐρημίας ἐπειλημμένοι—where ἐρημία is used for "an open field, in which there are no antagonists to oppose us." And upon that passage (p. 90) ἡ μὲν ὤν σπουδὴ περὶ τῶν ἐν χεῤῥονήσῳ πραγμάτων ἐστὶ . . . τῶν δὲ λόγων οἱ πλεῖστοι, περὶ κ. τ. λ., where σπουδὴ is used for the real business, and proper subject of deliberation, in opposition to the talk of the orators. And upon the force of δύνασθαι in all such passages as the following (p. 95) ὅ, τι τοίνυν δύναται ταῦτα ποιεῖν, ἐνίους ὑμῶν μαθεῖν δεῖ (p. 103) τοῦτ' αὐτοῖς δύναται τὸ λέγειν ὡς κ. τ. λ., where δύνασθαι imports the *real tendency* of a thing, what it is really adapted to effect.

Almost all the instances, which we have hitherto adduced, of defect or error in Dr. Jones's Lexicon, are of such a nature, that we must suppose he could have easily avoided them, had he but carefully availed himself of the labours of his predecessors. There are other instances, in which he has been led astray by preceding interpreters. Thus, when Minerva (E. 831) calls Mars τυκτὸν κακὸν, the Latin version renders it, "*preter-naturam-ascitum malum*;" and Dr. Jones therefore interprets τυκτὸς—"made, *and not natural*, artificial." Now, we conceive that τυκτὸν κακὸν imports—"*constitutionally* evil, evil in the constitution of his nature." And the epithet may be illustrated by the expression in v. 901—οὐ μὲν γάρ τι καταθνητός γ' ἐτέτυκτο—"in the constitution of his nature he was not mortal."

Thus, again, under φθάνω, our author quotes the following passage from Lucian's Dialogue between Menippus and Tantalus: Οὐ φθάνω βρέξας ἄκρον τὸ χεῖλος, καὶ διὰ τῶν δακτύλων διεῤῥύειν, ἀπολείπει ξηρὰν τὴν χεῖρά μου—and thus interprets the words, "I no sooner wet the top of my lips, than escaping through my fingers it left [leaves] my hand dry." This would import that Tantalus succeeded in wetting the top of his lips; which certainly is contrary to Lucian's meaning. The proper import of the Greek words is, "I do not succeed in wetting the top of my lips, before it runs through my fingers," &c. The Latin interpreter, however, renders the words, "simul ac rigavi extrema labia, statim per digitos dilapsa," &c. And we freely acknowledge, that in many instances the phrase may very justly be rendered as Dr. Jones proposes. Thus, the other example of it, which he quotes—οὐκ ἔφθη ἐλθὼν, καὶ τὴν φιλοτιμίαν ἐνεδείξατο, may fairly be translated, "he no sooner came than he shewed his ambition." Yet the strict and proper import of it is, "he had not arrived before he shewed his ambition." And the quotation from Lucian proves, that the two expressions are not always equivalent.

But for all inaccuracies, into which he has been led by former lexicographers and interpreters, we hold our author perfectly excusable. For the others, which are truly and properly his own, and of which we have given but a very small specimen, we have been as lenient in our censure, as justice and honesty to the public would allow. We are willing, as far as possible, to impute some of them to haste; others to a vain pursuit of novelty of interpretation; and many of them to a fondness for hobbyhorsical etymologies.

Some of them are of a description, for which it is hard to account, but from a supposition, which we are reluctant to admit; because it would be conclusive against Dr. Jones's capacity for the task which he has undertaken. Whatever may be thought upon this point, we should hope he must now be sensible that he published much too soon; and that his Lexicon needs to be re-composed, in order to be useful either to boys or men.

In preparing it anew for the press, we should strongly advise him to arrange the words either alphabetically or radically. The former arrangement, though not the most useful, is the least troublesome to schoolboys. The latter alone is adapted to the scholar. But the *disarrangement*, which our author has at present adopted, forfeits alike the advantages of both.

Before we close this article, we wish briefly to justify some opinions which we expressed in the beginning of it. We have unequivocally avowed our approbation of Dr. Jones's giving his interpretations in English, rather than in Latin; and we have also strongly declared our conviction, that a new Greek Lexicon for the use of schools is deeply wanted; that those at present in use in this country are scandalously bad;—and that Dr. Jones's attempt to supply their deficiency is therefore in itself commendable.

Upon the first of these topics it is the less necessary to enlarge, because the remarks in our last number, on the absurdity of teaching boys the rules of Latin grammar in the Latin language, are mostly applicable to the Latin interpretations in a Greek Lexicon for schools. If any, after having had their attention called to the subject, continue to maintain the expediency of such Latino-Latin grammars, we conceive, that with them, reasoning can be of little avail to remove the *veteres avias** which have possession of their minds. And we shall only recommend to these gentlemen one improvement on their system; and that is, to teach boys the rules of the *Greek* grammar in the *Greek* language.

But some, who give up as indefensible the idea of conveying the rules of Latin grammar in Latin, may yet be disposed to vindicate the propriety of making that language the medium of teaching schoolboys the Greek grammar, and the meaning of Greek words;—inasmuch as their acquaintance with a language, in which they are supposed to have made some progress, is thus increased, while they learn another language. But may we not ask, in the first place, why it should be made necessary to learn Latin before we learn Greek? The inverse order would seem the more natural of the two; though we conceive that the two languages may be most advantageously studied together.

But, waving this, we would ask in the next place, whether *clearness* and *intelligibility* be not the most essential requisite in all explanations afforded to a learner? whether the object of the interpretations given in a Lexicon ought not to be, to *explain* the meaning of the words or phrases with as much clearness and precision as *possible*? and, whether this object can be as effectually attained by Latin interpretations, as by English, in the period of their progress at which boys commence the study of Greek?

* Persius.

We believe this will not be asserted by any. It will be admitted that the boy commonly finds a difficulty in understanding the assigned interpretations in a Greek and Latin Lexicon, which he would not find if they were given in his native tongue. Why, then, should we sacrifice *clearness* of explanation to another object? Is it because the latter object cannot otherwise be attained? Assuredly not. Nay, it may be more effectually attained otherwise; namely, by exercising the schoolboy in translating his Greek lessons into Latin. Indeed, it ought to be sufficient to remark, that the time which he now loses in surmounting needless difficulties—in finding out an *explanation of the explanations* in his Greek Lexicon—might be much more advantageously employed in studying *classical* latinity.

In short, if it be admitted, that the interpretation of a Greek word is less *clear* and *intelligible* to a schoolboy, when proposed in Latin, we think it decided that the interpretation ought to be afforded him in English: and we conceive that common sense and sound reason must allow the inevitable force of the conclusion. On the other hand, *we* are ready to allow, that if—to the boy or to the man—Latin interpretations be as clearly intelligible as English, it must be a matter of great indifference which language is employed: though we are of opinion that the English language is in some respects better adapted than Latin to the interpretation of Greek.

But is the information conveyed to boys, in our School Lexicons and Grammar, so correct, and suited to the occasions of the student, as to redeem the absurdity of the form in which it is conveyed? Certainly, those who preside over the literature of the country, seem to think so. Their utter indifference about providing any better literary aids for our youth would appear to argue that they are quite satisfied with the present. And yet, we can scarcely reconcile this with the high estimate which we are bound to form of their critical knowledge.

Is it possible, for instance, that the head of Eton College, in the 19th century, conceives that the relative in Latin has any different rule of concord from the adjective? or, that in such a construction as *fratris mei est hicce liber*, the genitive *fratris* is governed by the verb substantive *est*?

But we must refrain at present from exposing the crude absurdities, with which the Eton Grammars are filled; and confine our attention to the Greek Lexicons in common use. It is very seldom, we believe, that any other is used in our schools, than Schrevelius's or Hederic's. Upon the former we need say little. It is a very unpretending work: a meagre vocabulary, professedly designed by the compiler for the interpretation only of Isocrates and Æsop among the prose classics; Homer, Hesiod, and a few of the minor writers, among the poets, along with the New Testament, and Septuagint version of the Old.

It would be a waste of criticism, to show proof that any such compilation must be utterly inadequate to the interpretation of Greek; and it is the less necessary, because (if we mistake not) the work is generally considered to be decisively inferior to Hederic's; and because every instance of deficiency, or error, which we shall proceed to notice in the latter, is to be understood by our readers as common to the former.

The work of Hederic has come to us with the improvements of

Patrick, Ernesti, Morell, and Larcher. But it was bad in the first concoction. Ernesti, in his Preface, justly expresses himself thus, of the original compiler:—" Non libenter dico, quod præsens institutum dicere cogit: Hedericum illum, virum bonum cetera et laboriosum, at Græce doctum, et ad tale Lexicon rite conficiendum satis a lectione Græcorum scriptorum instructum non fuisse. Totus ille, id quod per totum opus observare licuit, e Scapula, aliisque vulgaribus Lexicis, pendebat; tot præclaras doctorum hominum de verbis plurimis, post Stephanum et Scapulam, observationes ignorabat, nec ipse e lectione ipsorum scriptorum meliora didicerat." Now, we say, that a Greek Lexicon, compiled by such a man, must have that radical unsoundness in all its frame, which no sanative process can remove.

To the booksellers of this city we seem to be indebted for the last —and not the least—improvement of it: the insertion of numerous additions and corrections from the papers of the learned Larcher; which they purchased at the sale of his library in Paris, and submitted for revisal to an eminent scholar of this country. We could wish that the editor had distinguished Larcher's additions by the first letter of his name, or some other mark. They can now be ascertained only by comparison with the former editions; though they may often be *conjectured* from the verdure of certain spots, amidst surrounding sterility. But after all the attempts that have been made to supply the deficiencies, and correct the errors, of the work, it still remains so erroneous, defective, and utterly unscholarlike, that we do consider the continued use of it in our schools disgraceful to the literature of this country. Let us adduce a few examples to justify our opinions.

Longinus (§ 24), marking the beauty of that expression in Herodotus, *ἐς δάκρυα ἔπεσε τὸ θέητρον*, says, *τὸ γὰρ ἐκ τῶν διηρημένων εἰς τὰ ἡνωμένα ἐπισυστρέψαι τὸν ἀριθμὸν, σωματοειδέστερον.* Here it is plain, that *ἐπισυστρέψαι* means *conglobare*, to collect, or incorporate into one; according to the common import of the verb *συστρέφω*. But let the student consult Hederic on the word, and what does he find for the interpretation of *ἐπισυστρέφω*? "*Una converto ad aliquid suscipiendum contra aliquem!*"

Now, this stuff passed from Stephens to Scapula, from Scapula to Schrevelius, and so on to Hederic; in whose Lexicon it is carefully retained to this day, for the instruction of our English youth in the Greek language. We beg pardon of Stephens's memory, for having mentioned him in such company. Longinus is not among the classics to whose authority he refers, or with whom he appears to have been familiar (Pseudo-Longinus is frequently cited by Stephens.) On this word he evidently was at a loss for classical authority; endeavoured to conjecture its meaning from its composition; and ultimately wavered in his judgment. For, after giving the interpretation which alone Hederic has retained, he adds—" vel, Colligo, seu cogo ad aliquid, &c. [*i. e.* suscipiendum contra aliquem] ea nimirum signif. qua aliquis dicitur factiosam catervam cogere. Sed affertur ex Maccab. l. i. c. 14 *ἐπισυστρέψαι συστροφὴν* pro *convocare conventum*." Here it is plain that Stephens was led astray by wanting a classical example of the word, and by endeavouring to give some peculiar force to the preposition *ἐπὶ* in its composition. There is none; no more than in ἐπισυναγόμενα* at the beginning of the same section. But Hederic omits all that *approached* towards the right meaning in Stephens; and retains only the interpretation, in which he furthest departed from the true.

Lucian, in his treatise on the composition of history (§ 45), says, δεήσει γὰρ τότε ποιητικοῦ τινὸς ἀνέμου ἐπουρίσαντος τὰ ἀκάτια, καὶ συνδιοίσοντος ὑψηλὴν . . . τὴν ναῦν, where it is evident that ἀκάτια means the *sails*. (See Xen. Hell. 6. 2, 27. Ed. Schneider.) But the only interpretation of the word which the student will find in Hederic, is, "*parvi navigii genus, genus naviculæ piscatoriæ, cymba*:" in which sense certainly the word occurs in Thuc. l. 4, c. 67, and elsewhere. Stephens, though he complains of wanting a classical example of the word, supplies the other meaning; but Scapula, upon whom Hederic depended, deserted him.

A few lines after the passage we have last quoted from Lucian, that writer urges the importance of the historian's examining most carefully what he relates as facts, and adds καὶ μάλιστα μὲν παρόντα καὶ ἐφορῶντα, εἰ δὲ μὴ κ. τ. λ. "if possible, from his own personal presence and inspection: but if that cannot be," &c. This use of μάλιστα μὲν . . . εἰ δὲ μὴ is common in the Greek classics, and perfectly analogous to a corresponding use of *maxime* in Latin. Sall. B. Jug. c. 46.—*maxume vivum, sin id parum procedat, necatum*. We observe that Stephens largely illustrates the phrase; but in vain would the student look for any notice of it in Hederic.

Upon another equally common use of μάλιστα, and noticed by Stephens, Hederic is equally silent; ἐν τοῖς μάλιστα εὐδόκιμος (Luc. Som. § 2.) which Hemsterhuis illustrates with his usual copiousness of learning. We need scarcely add, that Hederic appears to have been equally a stranger to the similar use of ἐν ὀλίγοις, as ποταμὸν ἐν ὀλίγοισι μέγαν (Her. iv. 52.) But why should we proceed in the disgusting task of collecting particular instances of error and defect in Hederic? When the general texture of his work is, as we have said, utterly unscholarlike. An example will illustrate our meaning.

"Σαθρὸς, ρὰ ρὸν, putris, flaccidus, marcidus, vietus; (2) debilis, fragilis, quassus, futilis, frivolus; (3) vitio aliquo occulto laborans, et *in neutro* vitium ipsum. A σήπω."

We shall not pause to examine the accuracy of these several interpretations. He seems just to have collected together, without any examination, all the Latin expressions which he could find for σαθρὸς, in the former Lexicons: and he flings them in a mass before the student, to take his choice from among them, in whatever connexion or application the epithet may occur. We would ask any scholar, is this the way in which the meaning of σαθρὸς should be illustrated for our youth? In the same compass it would have been easy to mark distinctly the literal meaning of the word *decayed, unsound;* and then to enumerate various substantives, to which it is figuratively applied, with brief references to classical authorities.

* We are far from meaning that Longinus had *no reason* for employing, in this passage, the compounds, ἐπισυναγόμενα and ἐπισυστρέψαι, rather than the simpler forms συναγόμενα and συστρέψαι. We think the construction εἰς τὰ ἔσω ἐπισυναγόμενα, and εἰς τὰ ἀνάμεσα ἐπισυστρέψαι is very parallel with ἐπάγειν, ἐπιβαίνειν, ἐπιβάλλειν, ἐπιτιθέναι – ἐπί, &c.

The reader, who wishes more examples of such interpretation, may examine Hederic's ten meanings for ἀνάστασις, ten for ἐπίστασις, eleven for κατάστασις, nine for παράστασις, ten for περίστασις, ten for σύστασις, &c. thrown out without any quoted authorities or examples, except one from Larcher's papers at the close of the article on ἐπίστασις. And when we mention so many different meanings, it is to be observed that he is commonly very liberal under each. For instance, the second meaning assigned to σύστασις is expressed by six different Latin words: *coagmentatio, compositio, coagmentum, concrementum, crassitudo, concretio.* Surely, the student must be fastidious, who cannot please himself, and find something suitable to his wants, in such a copious assortment of explanations as is spread before him.

Some may have imagined that the necessary limits of size and price, within which a School-Lexicon must be confined, are inconsistent with the critical character, which we contend it ought to possess. But is it not evident, even from the examples which we have adduced, that the most vague and indistinct interpretations are the most diffuse and wordy? Those which are accurate and critical, may commonly be proposed in the briefest form. Again, let it be observed that a considerable portion of Hederic's pages is occupied with the merely grammatical analysis of words, which ought to present no difficulty to a boy, even moderately disciplined in his grammar. We have opened the volume at random; and in the first column which has presented itself to our eye, we find ten lines occupied with the analysis of the following forms: θολοῦντα, θόρε, θορυβοῦσιν, θορυβήσω, θορύνεσθαι, θούρμαιον. And perhaps there is scarcely one of these words in which any such assistance ought to be afforded to the student.

But again, we remark that many thousands of words have place in Hederic, which might, without any loss, be omitted in a Greek Lexicon compiled for the use of schools; words, of which many are of no classical authority, and many others are found only in writers the most obscure, or most out of the line of a schoolboy's reading. We must add, and we wish Dr. Jones particularly to attend to the remark, that there is a class of words, which not only may well be omitted, but which ought never to appear in the pages of a School Lexicon. Begging pardon of the *reverend* gentlemen, to whose care the education of our youth has been for ages almost exclusively committed in this country, we must confess that we know not what legitimate business a schoolboy can have with studying the filthiest obscenities of Aristophanes; and we know not why a Greek Lexicon, compiled for the use of schools, should afford him any interpretation of them.

The considerations which we have suggested, convince us, that in a volume not much larger than Dr. Jones's, and nothing more costly, all the Greek words which a young student will meet with, in an extended course of school-reading, might be critically interpreted, classically authenticated, and by brief quotations illustrated in their several connexions and applications. At the same time we are aware, that to execute such a work, however humble some may think it, would require several years of laborious application, sound judgment, and good sense, extensive reading, and a critical acquaintance with the Greek language.

OBSERVATIONS

ON

"AN ANSWER TO A PSEUDO-CRITICISM

OF THE

GREEK AND ENGLISH LEXICON,

WHICH APPEARED IN THE SECOND NUMBER OF THE WESTMINSTER REVIEW."

1824.

We are cordial friends to the right of appeal from our critical decisions to the tribunal of the public; and are equally disposed to pay all due attention to any motion for a re-hearing in our own court. But the extreme scurrility of this pamphlet has caused us to hesitate considerably whether we should take any notice of it. We shall handle the foul object as delicately as possible, and hasten to wipe our fingers, and dismiss it and the author for ever. If self-partiality and passion had not blinded Dr. Jones, he might easily perceive that, in our last number, we laboured to be as gentle in our censures on his work as possible. We went quite as far as was consistent with the honest discharge of our duty to the public, in attributing his blunders, absurdities, and defects, to haste—to inattention—to every thing rather than to ignorance and incapacity. Our feelings of tenderness to him led us to hold a language of encouragement and hope, that a future edition of his work might be so altered and amended as to merit praise. We confess, that in this we held a language not warranted by the inward conviction of our own judgment; but we must add, that we then had not any adequate conception of the depth of Dr. Jones's ignorance. If we had any of these hostile feelings towards him, which he so profusely attributes to us, they might be abundantly gratified by his present production. But, indeed, we sincerely regret that any one who has devoted so much time to literary pursuits, should make such a melancholy exposure of himself both as a man and as a scholar. He shows himself even incapable of understanding the plainest corrections which we offered of his grossest errors. For instance, on that passage of Xenophon, ὁσα μεν ἐςι μαθοντα εἰδεναι, which he translated "whatever things it is *lawful* to know *after having* learnt them," p. 608, we briefly remarked, that if he had read on to the end of the sentence he must have seen, that ἁ ἐςι μαθοντα εἰδεναι is equivalent with μαθητα, things which may be known by teaching. (These Xenophon contrasts with things discoverable only by *divination*.) But it now appears that we judged quite too favourably of Dr. Jones's attainments, in conceiving that he must have seen this if he had read the whole passage. He gravely maintains that his version—"whatever things it *is lawful* to know *after having learnt* them"—is "an exact representation of the original"—twice alleges that we accuse him of mistranslating the passage, *because he has given to* μανθανω *the meaning of to learn*—and exclaims against our assertion, that ἁ ἐςι μαθοντα εἰδεναι is equivalent with μαθητα, as an assertion that "things which *are known after being learnt* are the same with things to be learnt." Certainly, this man "cannot teach and will not learn." The same obstinacy of error appears throughout his strictures on our article; and is carried so far, that he even employs two pages in maintaining the justice of his version of οὐκουν βασιλευς εἰ συ; "Thou art not, then, a king?" in place of the common version, "Art thou a king, then?" We had asked, "Is it possible that Dr. Jones is ignorant that οὐκουν has not a negative signification?" It now appears that he not only was, but is. He gravely tells us, that οὐκουν "is an *interrogative*"! and that "it depends upon the views of the person who puts the question—whether the question which it was intended *to elicit*, (what can the man mean?) is to be understood as negative or affirmative"!

There is but one instance in which Dr. Jones defends himself successfully; and of that instance we wish to give him the full benefit. We noticed the extraordinary meaning assigned to the verb γνωριζομαι, *I am reconciled*, and offered an account of the error, which struck us as bearing internal characters of being indubitably the true one. But Dr. J. gives us a different account. He says—"The word reconciled, is a typographical mistake for *recognised*, which escaped me when correcting the press, but which, soon after the publication of the book, I discovered and corrected."—(He must mean corrected in his private copy of the work.) Very well, let all we have written on that passage be considered as expunged. But could he not state the fact of this typographical error without charging us as having been aware of the fact? "The inserting of *recognise*, as I have done, under the active form γνωριζω, must lead every reader, however superficial, to perceive that by—*I am reconciled*—under the passive γνωριζομαι, I must have meant, *I am recognised*. Common candour, therefore, would lead the critic to point it out as a typographical mistake." Rude and foolish man! The very circumstance which he marks as sufficient to convince us of the typographical error has exactly the opposite tendency.

He sets up a similar defence, but altogether ineffectually, in another instance. We animadverted on his mistranslation of the sentence in Demosthenes, beginning, Ἐι μεν γαρ μη ἐχρην, ἀλλα την Μ. λ. κ. την Ἑ. ἐασαν ὀφθηναι, κ. τ. λ. Here, also, Dr. J. tells us, "there is an error of the press, which unfortunately escaped detection—the omission of *but*;—My manuscript was thus—If indeed it was not fit, *but* that Greece, &c.: my reviewer *perceived the typographical error*, but instead of pointing it out, he, with his characteristic candour, leaves the reader to infer it to be the consequence of incapacity in me." Rude and foolish man! we must say again. Let the passage be read as he says it stood in his manuscript, and the sentence is still altogether mistranslated. But he cannot understand that the construction is ὀφθηναι ὀυσαν την M. λ.; he will persist in making it την 'E. ὀυσαν, "Greece while really Greece;" and talks of "the participle ὀυσαν qualifying Ελ. and standing opposed to ὀφθηναι."

Lest we should omit any concession to Dr. J. which he does or ought to claim, we must observe, that among the instances which we gave of words whose quantity Dr. J. had neglected to mark, ἀκριβης ought to be expunged, as the remark (pen. long.) does occur after the word. It is no wonder that this escaped our notice, as it is so very rarely that Dr. J. thus designates the quantity. The place of ἀκριβης may be supplied by ἀγκυρα, or by examples afforded in almost every page of the Lexicon.

Dr. J. goes out of his way to furnish multiplied additional evidences of his ignorance of Greek by playing the critic upon others. He tells us, that ἡ ὀθονη παρακεκρουσται (in the beginning of Lucian's Καταπ.) means, "the sail *is beating itself* in the wind." The same hardy defiance of all distinction of tenses he employs in his spirited version of the words ἠπου στρατοπεδον ου κεφαλην ἐληλυθεις ἐχων! "Zounds, sir, you *seem not to know that you have* a camp, and not a head on your shoulders."

Defending the common reading in that passage of Lucian's Νεκ. και μαλιστα τους Αιγυπτιων ἀυτους, he interprets it, "and especially those of the Egyptians we *have* found *to be themselves, i. e.* such as they were when alive," and he assures us that "Lucian alludes to the beginning of the Iliad, ἀυτους δ' ἑλωρια τευχε κυνεσσιν"! He tells us that "ειλον is for ειλον αν," in that verse of the Iliad, (Π. 698.) Ενθα KEN ὑψιπυλον Τροιην ἑλον ὑιες Αχαιων.

But we must abstain from adducing any further specimens of Dr. J.'s *learning*, amusing as many others are. He gravely informs us, that the principle on which a great portion of his Lexicon is founded, has been "unknown to all lexicographers, ancient and modern." We think it very probable, and here dismiss JOHN JONES, LL.D. without exhibiting any of the flowers of Billingsgate rhetoric with which his pamphlet is decorated; and without gratifying his inquisitiveness by either affirming or denying the truth of his conjecture about the writer of that article which has excited in him so much causeless rage.

REVIEW

OF

"LUCIAN OF SAMOSATA;

FROM THE GREEK, WITH THE COMMENTS AND ILLUSTRATIONS OF WIELAND, AND OTHERS.

BY WILLIAM TOOKE, F.R.S.

MEMBER OF THE IMPERIAL ACADEMY OF SCIENCES, AND OF THE FREE ECONOMICAL SOCIETY OF ST. PETERSBURG:

2 Vols. 4to. pp. 790 and 793, 1820."

[Published in The Monthly Literary Register, No. II.]

The character of Lucian as a writer has been so well and so long established, that it would be superfluous for us to detain our readers by any panegyric on his excellencies or censure of his faults. Erasmus, who, in many respects, resembled the Grecian, expresses but our own opinion of his happier pieces, when he says,*—"He possesses so much gentlemanly ease in his style, so much felicity of invention, such elegance of humour and poignant raillery; he is so delicately playful in his allusions, so blends the serious with the trifling, and the trifling with the serious; tells the gravest truths so sportively, and, in his sportiveness, tells so much truth; he depicts in such lively colours the manners, passions, and pursuits of men, and so brings them before the reader's eye in all the reality of life; that, whether we regard amusement or utility, no satire nor comedy can be compared with Lucian's dialogues."

Such a classic it was natural that many should be ambitious of presenting to the public in an English dress. Accordingly, besides two old translations by *Hickes* and by *Spence*, we have had in modern times (previous to the appearance of the present work,) an English translation of the works of Lucian (of all that ought to be translated, and of *some more*,) by Thomas Franklin, D.D. some time *Greek*

* Tantum obtinet in dicendo gratiæ, tantum in inveniendo felicitatis, tantum in jocando leporis, in mordendo aceti; sic titillat allusionibus, sic seria nugis, nugas seriis miscet; sic ridens vera dicit, vera dicendo ridet; sic hominum mores, affectus, studia, quasi penicillo depingit, neque legenda, sed plane spectanda oculis exponit; ut nulla comœdia, nulla satyra cum hujus dialogis conferri debeat, seu voluptatem spectes, seu spectes utilitatem. *Erasm. l.* 29, *Epist.* 5.

Professor in the University of Cambridge; and another by Mr. J. Carr. The former lies before us, and some extracts from the latter, which would lead us to conjecture that Mr. Carr was a somewhat better Greek scholar than Dr. Franklin, and not so good an English scholar. On Franklin's version, which, we believe, has been the more popular, we shall say little. We hope that the University of Cambridge has acquired much more knowledge of Greek than it appears to have possessed when he was *Professor* in it of that language. His blunders are such as would disgrace a schoolboy.* However, his translation has in general an air of gentlemanly scholarship, is *readable*, and perhaps sufficient to convey to the English student some idea of Lucian's manner.

This is much more than we can say for the work which now comes under our review. The author is the late *Rev.* William Tooke, about forty years ago (if we mistake not) Chaplain to the English Factory at Petersburg; and since known to the world (with how much credit to himself, or benefit to the public, we shall not stop to enquire,) by his translation of Mr. Zolikoffer's sermons, a freethinking divine of the German school; by his life of the Empress Catherine II. made up of extracts from the Annual Register incorporated with a translation from the French; and by his View and History of the Russian Empire.

Less than two years have elapsed since the publication of the present work; and within that short interval the author has died. We received this intelligence accidentally, after we had nearly prepared a long article on his translation of Lucian, in terms of the severest castigation, but not more severe than merited. The greater part of that article we now consign to oblivion in his grave. And were it not that the *author* often survives the *man*, and that in the present case we owe a paramount duty to the public, from the honest discharge of which we dare not shrink; we should gladly decline all notice of this publication, under the feelings which at present predominate in our minds. It is marked with some characters, which, we are persuaded, had they been known to the very respectable publishers whose names appear in the title-page, would have prevented them from having any concern with its sale. On this point we shall say no more; for it fortunately happens, that, considering it only in a *literary* view, we can say with truth, and shall prove incontrovertibly, that it is one of the grossest impositions which have for some time been attempted on the public; that the author was utterly destitute of every qualification for such a task; destitute of taste, of judgment, and of scholarship; destitute of all real acquaintance either with the Greek language or

* If any of our classical readers should wish for some examples to justify this expression, let them compare with the original his version of that passage in Lucian's dream, αγαλματια τινα μικρα κατασκευαζειν (ed. Bipt. i. p. 5.) of the words το του Σινωπεως εκεινο in the treatise on writing History, (ib. t. 4. p. 161.) where by one stroke of his pen he transfers the Κρανειον from the Isthmus of Corinth to the shores of the Euxine sea; of the passage in the same piece οιδα μεν ως ου πανυ πολλους αυτων επιτρεψων κ.τ.λ. (pp. 163, 164.) and of the sentence (in p. 665,) beginning Ἁ μεν εν κοινα παντων λογων. In a very sligbt inspection of his work, to which the present occasion has led us, we have observed a multitude of blunders equally ridiculous.

even with his own; if we except that use of words which Mr. Locke speaks of, by a curious association, as sufficient for the purposes of "merchants and lovers, cooks and tailors:"* while it is not more strongly characterized by the ignorance which it throughout displays, than it is by those most disgusting forms of ponderous stupidity, which spring from the unsuccessful effort to appear witty, wise, and learned.

To pronounce a judgment so decisive and so unfavourable would be idle, if we did not adduce a body of evidence to confirm its justice; and to do this effectually will require us to go into some detail. As we shall not often trespass in the same way on the patience of our general readers, we hope for their indulgence on the present occasion, though our critique must be much less *amusing* than we think it would have been if Mr. Tooke were still alive. It shall also be much shorter and less severe.

When a man writes for the public, and especially when he professes to compose a work of taste and polite literature, the first qualification he should be expected to possess is, a scholarlike acquaintance with the language in which he writes. We are ready to admit that there are cases in which the importance of an author's matter may atone for many deficiencies and inaccuracies in his manner of conveying it. We do not, therefore, say that no man ought to write for the public who cannot write with elegance and classic purity of style; though in a translation of Lucian we should consider even this an essential requisite. But we mean to charge Mr. T. with ignorance of the first principles of general grammar. We mean to say and prove that he is nearly as unable as the most uneducated dregs of the populace to express himself with ordinary correctness and propriety. And when Lucian had been before translated *decently*, we do conceive it great effrontery for such a man to impose upon the public a new version of that elegant author in two massy quarto volumes. Let our readers observe a few specimens of his English composition, which we take almost at random, as we turn over his pages.

V. i. pp. 80 and 81. "Whence we may in some degree form a judgment how this astonishing Colossus, which, with its throne and appertaining figures, composed a mass that filled the whole recess of the temple, from the ground to the ceiling, which rendered necessary, all that framework of timber, with all the pitch and mortar that Lucian speaks of, in order to keep it properly together, and enable it to bid defiance to the attacks of time."

P. 254. "I could not restrain my indignation, and it appeared to me exactly as if an actor, who, though in person a soft and effeminate little fellow, should play the part of Achilles, or Theseus, perhaps even Hercules, though he had neither the voice nor the looks of a hero, but disgraced the part of those great men by an effeminacy, which even in Helena or Polyxena would be found insupportable; whereas Hercules, if he saw himself so basely represented, would scarce be

* Essay on the Human Understanding, B. 3. Ch. 11. Merchants in his day must have been a very different class of persons from our merchants, or he would not have placed them in such company.

able to refrain from crushing with his club the masked head of such a mimic."

P. 130. "On another side I beheld how Arsaces, raging with jealousy, fell upon his concubine with a drawn sword; and how Arbaces, her chamberlain, coming to her assistance, attacked Arsaces with a naked sabre, while the handsome Mede, Spartinus, who being wounded on the forehead with a golden cup, was dragged out by the heels by some of the satellites. The like was to be seen in Africa," &c. &c.

Pp. 353, 354. "That is easily to be accounted for; her brother is a youth who has strength and fortitude to endure such a trip; whereas the girl, alarmed at the first thought of her perilous adventure; and giddy with the dart-like velocity of the flight, when casting a sudden glance of the eye upon the horrid abyss beneath her, no more was wanting to complete the dizziness so as for an instant to let the horn of the ram by which she had held slip out of her hand, and thus was precipitated into the sea."

P. 628. "It is with you precisely as with him, who, mounted on a vicious and unruly horse, which, having set off at once and run away with him, could not dismount, but must resign himself to the caprice of his horse."

P. 522. "And after Mercury officially as herald has duly called together those who think they have a right to assist in the divine councils, they shall, each bringing along with him his sworn witnesses, and producing his regular testimonials and records, one after the other, before the said committee, and then, strict examination having been first made of their validity, the postulants shall either be declared true gods, or sent back to their appropriate graves or to their family vault."

V. ii. p. 320. "An allusion to the amnesty which, in the second year of the 94th Olympiad, immediately after the expulsion of the famous thirty tyrants, and the restoration of the old form of government, it was proclaimed, for the confirmation of the internal peace of Athens, under the archon Euclides, by an edict, in pursuance whereof it was prohibited, under the severest penalties, to dispute or converse concerning any thing that had been done under the usurped administration of the thirty tyrants."

But—*ohe! jam satis.* Enough, at least, of *this class* of sentences, —if sentences they can be called. For it may be observed that, as we have turned over the leaves of this work for collecting examples, we have confined our selection to sentences of a particular species;—in which the latter end of the period runs away from the beginning, and the disjointed members lie sprawling and looking in vain for something to support them. If our object had only been to quote instances of bad English, we might have taken any twelve consecutive pages of the work, and found abundance of examples. But the extracts which we have made—(and we can honestly assert that we have copied them most faithfully in every word and letter and point)—are of that peculiar kind, which most decisively stamps the publication with the character of *illiterate*, in the view of every English scholar. We should not be surprised, indeed, if our readers, in wading through those few specimens, should at first suspect—as we did ourselves, for a time—that they must be disfigured by some most extraordinary blunders of the compositor. But a very slight examination of the work will soon remove that suspicion.

We had intended to exemplify our author's barbarous ignorance of the English language by other sentences, of a great variety of species. But we are really afraid of wearying the patience of our readers by any more lengthened extracts: and we believe it is unnecessary. None can now wonder at such barbarisms, as the following, meeting us in almost every page:

"It is them from whom I promise myself the most candour."—"Exactly so does the lives of men appear to me"—"the mask was tore off"—"she had took me up"—"if it had been shook"—"had fell in love"—"all that had befell him"—"it was broke to shatters"—"it must have been writ"—"let you and I"—"the like of which"—&c. &c.

Equally numerous are such instances, as the following, of vulgarism and vile *slang*:—

"A wipe at the philosophers"—"a wipe at the affected subtlety"—"a good-humoured fellow, and an arch dainty-chops"—"that I may no longer keep your beak watering"—"hatched a plot against his life"—"they are gone, every mother's son"—"they worry the quality with their importunities"—"this oracle was dispensed only to the quality"—"you should have given the fellow something to wet his whistle"—"he began to smell a rat"—"he had a month's mind to her"—"my worthy"—"the worthies are very enlightened on that point"—"he swung himself by his talents into the favour of King Lysimachus"—"it can hardly be believed that Lucian sucked the circumstance out of his fingers"—&c. &c.

And this is the man, who gravely assures us, at the close of his Introductory Essay—"My principal endeavour has been to do him (Lucian) no injury; and that the beauties which are so much admired in him by the adepts in the Greek language, might suffer as little as possible under my hands, I have strove to acquire his spirit, his humour, his *geniality*, and, as far as the nature of our language, so different from his, perspicuity, and *other regards* would allow, to imitate even his turns and the colouring of his diction:" modestly adding—"but how can I dare to hope, that I have *always* and *every where* actually accomplished it?"—"I may *occasionally* have missed somewhat of his elegance." This is the man who talks, in one of his notes, of introducing his "old friend of Samosata into the *genteel* societies" of his countrymen; nay—incredible as it might appear in some views—intimates, in another note, his expectation that he shall have female readers! i. 736.

But we would not wish it to be understood that Mr. T. is incapable of rising to the finery and grandeur of English composition. We think he excels in that as much as in the free and easy style. A few short examples may not be unamusing.

Introd. Essay, p. xviii. "We will not presume to pry into the innermost replications of the heart."

Ib. p. xxi. "Deducting a few effusions of a too careless joviality, and ocasionally a prevention trespassing on the Aristotelian line of demarcation between the too much and too little, against the founders of sects and their votaries."

V. i. p. 69. " A sort of facetious characters, who were hired by agitating the midriff to promote the digestion of the company by all kinds of buffoonery and harlequinades."

P. 131. " To go articulately through the whole of it, my friend, would be impracticable."

V. ii. p. 329. " The words—strew genuine lucianic salt on this sarcastic prosopopœia"—(Note on a passage, in which the reader will look in vain for anything like that figure.)

P. 573. " Contained nothing but reiterated *loci communes*, amplifications, digressions, and opportunities to fabricate a superficial omniscience."

P. 635. " Only it amounts to an impossibility, for them not to lose in any translation a portion of those diminutive beauties, to which the Greeks were so particularly sensible, and which consist not so much in thoughts as in the dress and collocation of them, in the various metaphors, and in the elegant absorption of these propositions in ornamental periods, and the like, and can rarely without detriment be rendered in a foreign tongue."

This certainly is what may be called *fine* writing, and its admirers may be assured that Mr. T.'s pages will enrich their vocabulary with a numerous supply of elegancies; such as—" ornature—parentation—demagogy—domesticity—teratologers—autonomy—clarity—eudæmony—epistolation—hereticizing—autorculus," besides—" homerican, homerical, and homerian:" for by no chance does Mr. T. ever light upon *homeric*.

We have introduced our readers to Mr. T. as a writer of English prose. He shines equally as a poet. Lucian has left us a mock-heroic drama on the Gout: the opening of which runs thus in Dr. Franklin's version:

" O name for ever sad abhorr'd of heaven,
Parent of groans, from dark Cocytus sprung,
Immortal GOUT! in gloomy Erebus,
Whom erst Megæra, dreadful fury, bore;
And from her poison'd breasts Alecto fed," &c. &c.

Let us now observe how gallantly Mr. Tooke acquits himself in breaking a lance with Dr. Franklin:

" Ah! cursed name! abhorred by gods and men,
Pitiless Podagra, Cocytus born,
That in the darkest depths of Tartarus
From her womb Megæra Erinnys dropt,
And Alecto from her empoisoned drugs
Distilled into thy lips," &c. &c.

Our translator, with equal modesty and elegance, expresses his hope, that " through this imperfect attempt, enough of the spirit of the original will be *transparent*, for discerning," &c. &c.

He favours us with the following version of the opening of Pindar's first Olympiac. v. i. p. 67.

" Water is the chiefest thing,
But gold is far more bright
Than any riches else beside,
And gives a fairer light
Than doth the clear and flaming fire
Within the darksome night."

Nay, so ambitious is he of the bays, that he fears not to challenge Mr. Pope himself to the contest. Observe the following elegant anapæstic in which he renders a verse of Homer;

" No league can subsist between lions and men."

And, in the same page, (v. i. p. 239.) the *novel* metre, in which he translates two other verses of the same poet:

" Reviler, brass nor gold shall blind our sight!
Thou'rt my captive, hope not to purchase flight."

But we beg pardon for having designated this metre as *novel*. We penned that epithet, before we had appealed to our FINGERS. But as we transcribed the lines, a suspicion occurred that Mr. T. might have framed them according to that unerring standard: which we find on trial, to be actually the case. No doubt therefore can be raised, but that the lines belong to the class of English heroics: much as—*Urbem fortem super cepit fortior hostis*—is a Latin hexameter.

But we might be charged with injustice to Mr. T. as a poet, if we did not treat our readers with one more specimen, of which he appears to have been particularly proud. In that elegant little dialogue between Venus and Cupid, where the mischievous urchin accounts to his mother for his not venturing to attack the muses; our learned translator has the following note:—" This REMINDS ME of a pretty epigram in the Anthologia, a translation of which I throw *en passant* as a flowret on the altar of the Muses." Then follows the original epigram in good Greek, (excepting of course the errors of the press) succeeded by this spirited translation:

" Court Aphrodite maids! Thus Cypris spoke;
If not, against you I will Cupid arm;
To her the Muses: spare for Mars that joke;
Thy Cupid's wings can't reach to do us harm."

Well; but ridiculous as Mr. T.'s poetry appears, must he not have been a man of some classical attainments, when a passage in Lucian *reminded* him of an epigram in the Greek Anthologia? Unfortunately, Hemsterhuis, in his note on the same passage, adduces verbatim the same Greek epigram. However, we own that there is no reason why the same thought should not have occurred to two great scholars; and that it is very extraordinary, if Mr. T. employed a contemptible untruth in throwing his delicate flowret on the altar of the Muses. But alas! we have long remarked that there is nothing which makes such fools of men, as VANITY.

Wishing to keep our English readers in our company as long as we can, we shall here offer a few miscellaneous remarks; before we proceed to establish by evidence Mr. T.'s utter ignorance of the Greek tongue.

We own ourselves indebted to him for some most extraordinary information on ancient manners and ancient history. For instance, in a long note on the piece entitled "Διονυσος," he assures us—"The antients did not drink as we do, by lifting the cup, or goblet up to the lips, but by *pouring the liquor from on high into the open mouth*, so that it required address to empty a goblet with promptitude and precision." No doubt of that; and the greater address, because in their compotations they certainly employed *brimmers*—κρητηρας επιστεφεας οινοιο. Mr. T. having omitted to quote his authority for the assertion, we own that we were at first a little sceptical about the fact. But finding that he repeated the same statement *verbatim* in a note, v. ii. p. 626, we were put upon a laborious search, and at length discovered authentic evidence of his accuracy, in that most scarce and erudite work—M. SCRIBLERI *Antiquitatis reconditioris janua reserata*, tom. xvii. p. 598. "*Non eadem, qua apud nos, methodo compotationes apud antiquos fiebant,*" *&c.* (It is in the same chapter, in which the profound author proves that the ancients did not walk, as we do, on their feet; but on their hands, and with their feet elevated, as he expresses it, *supra nates*. These antients were certainly queer fellows.) The point being now established, we would humbly suggest to our learned universities that some obvious advantages might arise from reviving the ancient method of drinking; that it would conduce particularly to the virtue of sobriety: and that a new statute, therefore, should be framed, enforcing this as the only mode of academic compotation after commons; and appointing a professor to instruct the members in the classical method of emptying a goblet "with promptitude and precision." We beg, however, (as we are too old to learn the new trick) that a clause may be introduced in favour of occasional visitors, who have taken any of the higher degrees; so that they may be allowed to empty their glasses in the *modern* way.

Ou author is as deeply read in ancient history as in ancient customs. He informs us, in a note, vol. i. p. 67, that Demosthenes, (the Athenian general) "was *surrendered to Nicias*, as commander of the troops by which the Athenians expected to conquer Sicily." And, in p. 59, he gives the following translation of a passage in Lucian's Treatise on the Composition of History: "Since now Thucydides, *as all the world knows*, was *the first who delivered a sort of funeral oration* on those who fell in the Peloponnesian war:" with the following short and learned note upon the words "funeral oration"—"*On Pericles.*" But we must treat our classical readers to the original of that passage. Ειτα επειδη Θουκυδιδης επιταφιον τινα ειπε τοις πρωτοις τῳ πολεμῳ εκεινῳ νεκροις. Literally—*Then since Thucydides has introduced a funeral oration on* the first who fell *in that war.*

The same page presenting to our eye two other instances of the author's critical wisdom and sagacity, we may as well introduce them here. Lucian is laughing at the absurd imitators of Thucydides in his day, one of whom introduced a soldier making a ridiculous oration over the grave of Severianus, and stabbing himself with his sword at the conclusion of his speech. He drily adds, swearing by the god of war, that "the man deserved to have died long before, if he were accustomed to make such harangues:" και παλαι, μα τον Ενυαλιον, προ πολλου αποθανειν, ει τοιαυτα ερρητορευε. Upon these words Mr. T. has the following annotation.

"I here give rather a different turn to the words of Lucian, because, by a more faithful translation, I must have made him say what the reader would think very *dull* and *insipid*. I hope, in behalf of this kind of liberty, by which Lucian *rather gains than loses*, &c. &c."

Now, what is the turn for which Lucian is so much indebted to Mr. William Tooke, and by which he becomes so much less dull and insipid? "He drew his sword, and slew himself before the eyes of all the assembly; *which I had rather he had done much sooner, before he began his deplorable speech*."

In the beginning of the next paragraph, Lucian says:

"Many, my friend, are the similar instances which I could enumerate: however, *after mentioning only a few*, ολιγων ὁμως επιμνησθεις, I shall then pass to the second topic I have proposed," &c.

And accordingly, he adduces a few more examples of similar absurdities, before he enters on the second part of his treatise. But Mr. T. thus translates the preceding sentence:

"I could, my dear friend, cite to you numerous other examples of this sort; *but these few may suffice at present*, that I may pass on to the second part of my promise," &c.

And then, grounding a censure of his author upon his own mistranslation, he gives Lucian the following castigation in his next note, p. 60.

"*Method is not the bright side of this tract, as it appears.* Lucian *has hardly begun* the didactic part, but he forgets his words in the same breath, and runs on a good while in making merry upon the wretched scribbler who had *created Parthian wars in such quantities*."

Lucian had not yet entered on the didactic part, nor intimated that he was commencing it. And if Mr. T. had combined a little more modesty with his ignorance, he might have suspected that he did not understand his author, when LUCIAN appeared to him to write absurdly.

As we have been accidentally led to this topic, we shall offer a few more specimens of the incredible *platitude*, (to use one of Mr. T.'s favourite phrases) with which he occasionally animadverts on his "old friend Samosata." In the *council of the Gods*, vol. i. p. 521, the decree, which Momus brings forward against the spurious divinities, is prefaced with the customary formula, αγαθη τυχη. This Mr. T. elegantly renders, "with good luck!" and subjoins the following note:—"Lucian here allows his Momus to forget that he is wishing good luck *to those whom he had just before declared monsters*." The same charge certainly lay, with equal force, against the Athenian people, in every damnatory decree which they passed against any culprits.

In that pleasant and truly Lucianic piece, the *Menippus*, when the Cynic informs his friend of the occasion which led him to descend to the shades in order to consult Tiresias, Mr. T. makes the following admirably wise remark :—

V. i. p. 466. "What Ulysses wisely did, Menippus does *foolishly*. The former wants to know somewhat future, and asks a prophet: what the latter would know is a moral problem, which reason alone can solve, and to which a soothsayer can avail him nothing."

We wonder much how the foolish Horace escaped the critical lash of our translator, l. ii. Sat. 5.

In the *Panegyric on Demosthenes*, falsely attributed to Lucian, the author introduces Demosthenes as holding this language :—

"The friends, whose sons or relations I have freed from captivity, or the fathers whose daughters I have portioned out." V. ii. p. 592.

Upon which Mr. T. makes this remark :—

"*Of such a tirade* any eloquent orator, and even Lucian himself, who could not always forget his old trade, might *applaud himself*: but to put into the mouth of Demosthenes, *who always expressed himself with so much modesty*, even when compelled to speak of his own merits, without object or necessity, such a boasting declamation, is *unpardonable*."

Yet it happens, unfortunately, (as any man might know who possessed even much less classical erudition than Mr. T. pretends to) that Demosthenes actually uses this identical "boasting declamation" in his oration on the Crown. ed. Reisk. t. i. p. 316. *ουτ' ει τινας εκ των πολεμιων ελυσαμην, ουτ' ει τισι θυγατερας απορουσι συνεξεδωκα.*

We cannot now wonder that Mr. T. ventures at times to play the critic on the other translators of Lucian. Dr. Franklin and the Abbe Massieu, he repeatedly charges with translating from the Latin: and we think it very likely that the charge is well founded. There is an old and homely proverb, *set a thief to catch a thief*. We shall now prove to demonstration, that Mr. T. in general does not even attempt to translate from the Greek; that he frequently translates, or strives to translate, from the Latin; but more commonly, we believe, from the German. Not having Wieland's version before us, we speak doubtfully there. Call the evidence. (In quoting the Greek, we shall refer to the Bipontine edition.)

Pro. laps. int. sal. t. iii. p. 294. *Και Πτολεμαιος δε ὁ Λαγου, Σελευκῳ επιστελλων.* Lat. *Et Ptolemæus Lagi, scribens ad Seleucum.* Mr. T. v. ii. p. 405. "Ptolemy LAGI, writing once to Seleucus." Yet we acknowledge that in p. 624 we have "Ptolemy the son of Lagus." But why? There (t. i. p. 21.) the Latin version is, "Ptolemæus igitur Lagi filius." We hear the classical jurors calling on us to close the case for the prosecution, and to allow them now to bring in their verdict without leaving the box. But there are considerations which oblige us to proceed, till we shall have fully redeemed our pledge, and proved the guilt of this writer on every count in the indictment.

T. i. p. 88. *οἱ δε, καθαπερ ὁ Φινευς, απο της φαρυγγος την τροφην ὑπο των ἁρπυιων αφαιρουμενοι. αλλ' απιθι ηδη κ. τ. λ.* Mr. T. v. i. p. 41. "the others, like Phineus, have their meat snatched out of their mouths by harpies, just when on the point of swallowing it. *But of what use is all this chattering?* Get you gone, I say." &c.

With this note upon the question, which we have marked in italics, and of which there is not one tittle in the original :—

"Lucian seems to snatch this question out of the mouth of his reader; for truly this dialogue abounds more than the rest in the verbose babble of the rhetors and sophists of his time."

Here our translator must surely have been ignorant that the words on which he makes this wise remark, were not at all in the original: and must, therefore, have been translating from something else than the Greek Or, will the counsel for the defendant choose to say, that Mr. T. did know they were not in the Greek, but wittingly foisted them into the text, in order to hang upon them his own *impertinence of annotation*?

Passing two other ridiculous blunders in the same page, we offer Mr. T. the benefit of the same dilemma, in his note, v. i. p. 394. on the words, "should call for a *full flowing* cup;" and in his note, p. 520, on the words, "big words, *the abstract notions of which militate against one another*." If the reader turn to the Greek text, t. ii. p. 148, and t. ix. p. 189, he will see that in each of these passages Mr. T. is sagaciously commenting on his own insertions. In the same page in which the former passage stands, our eye catches another tolerably decisive evidence that Mr. T. is not translating from the Greek. The original says—"*ειτα ὁ μεν επιεν*"—which runs thus in our elegant version:—"so that the old man *voided* his (cup) without receiving any injury." Who can doubt but that some of the other translators rendered the words—*the old man* emptied *his cup*; and that Mr. T. ingeniously mistook this for *voiding* it?

T. i. p. 124. *παπαι, χρονιος ἡμιν Θρασυκλης*; Mr. T. v. i. p. 59. "Ey, here comes Thrasycles, *as if called*."

We are almost ashamed to acknowledge that we have taken some pains, but ineffectually, to *trace* our translator in these words. Every smatterer in Greek must be certain, that he is quite innocent of meddling with the original. But how did he come by the nonsense which he has substituted? Instead of offering a reward for the solution of that question, we shall hazard our own conjecture. We suspect, then, that he found some foolish editor or commentator, who—ignorant of the stated use of the phrase *χρονιος ελθειν*, see Arist. Θεσμ. 912.—gave some such note upon the passage as this; "*quasi vocatus χρονιος*"—"as if called, Thracycles *the Tardy*;" from which Mr. T. naturally concluded that *χρονιος* means *as if called*. We give ourselves some credit for this conjectural criticism.

T. iv. p. 207. *κινδυνος γαρ αυτος τοτε μεγιστος παραμειναι*. Lat. *Tum enim maximum periculum est ne* extra numeros *moveatur*. Mr. T. v. ii. p. 72. "otherwise he is in imminent danger of *getting out of the metre*."

Here it is evident that Mr. T. was at the Latin version, and unable to interpret it. The reader will observe, that Lucian is speaking of the *prose* style of historic composition: and of the danger to be guarded against, peculiarly when the subject calls for some extraordinary elevation in the diction. We had begun to transcribe a passage from the preceding page—"*επει τοις κατηρτυμενοις των ζωμων εοικοτας απο φαινουσι τους λογους*"—as another evidence of Mr. T.'s translating from the Latin. But we forbear, as he there succeeds in expressing Gesner's interpretation. But we must add that Gesner altogether mistakes the meaning of the Greek.

As to Mr. T.'s utter ignorance of Greek, there is not a page of his translation which does not evince it. We shall therefore confine ourselves to a few instances of such a kind, as may afford a little *amusement* to our classical readers. And we have only to turn over the leaf, after the passage which we last adduced, in order to find a specimen of this description.

Lucian remarks, that the historian may sometimes commence without any formal prooemium; as the mere declaration of his subject may be a sufficient introduction. 'But,' he adds—alluding to the three objects of an exordium which rhetoricians lay down, viz. 1. That the *good-will* of the hearers is to be conciliated; 2. Their *attention* excited; and, 3. Their minds prepared to *understand* what is to follow—'But the historian, even when he employs a prooemium, should commence with two topics alone, not with three, like the rhetoricians: he should omit the topic of conciliating good-will, and confine himself to such observations as shall engage the attention and inform the understanding of his hearers.' T. iv. p. 211. Οποταν δε και φροιμιαζηται, απο δυοιν μονον αρξεται, ουχ' ώσπερ οἱ ρητορες απο τριων, αλλα το της ευνοιας παρεις, προσοχην η ευμαθειαν ευπορισει τοις ακουουσι. Now let us hear the learned and sagacious Mr. Tooke. Nor shall we quote the preceding sentence from his version, though full of blunders.

V. ii. p. 74. "If, however, the historian shall think proper to make an introduction, *he has only occasion to use two or three common-place sentences of the orators,* without soliciting the benevolence of his audience, it is enough for him," &c. &c.

Shades of THUCYDIDES and LIVY! learn how uselessly ye were employed in composing the introductions to your histories. Ye had only occasion to have used *two or three common-place sentences* of the orators.

Ib. p. 202. Γυλιππον...αποτειχιζοντα, και αποταφρευοντα τας ὁδους. Mr. T. p. 68. "*Gysippus*"—(so it stands twice in the page, and *Clesias*, for Ctesias; as well as the *Pœzile* continually for Pœcile—mount *Pelios*, &c. &c., but these are trifles—"who blocked up against the poor Athenians every *avenue to the city*, by his fortifications and ditches." There is a fine intermixture here of critical skill in the Greek tongue with deep historical information.

Ib. p. 203, οὓς παλαι ἡ ἱστορια εξ αρχης ευθυς απεστραπτο, ου μειον η (κομμωτικην) κομμωτικην ἡ γυμναστικη. Mr. T. p. 69, "whose manufacture of history has ever been as disgusting as *the cosmetic of gymnastics.*"

With a learned note upon the words, beginning thus:—

"Du Soul and Gesner observe here a very plain allusion to a passage in Plato's Gorgias, where Socrates *contrasts* the κομμωτικην *of* the γυμναστικη."

The reader perceives that the note and the text are quite of a piece.

But it occurs to us, that our specimens latterly are taken from Mr. Tooke's second volume, because it is the one that happened to lie open before us. Perhaps it may be suspected that he flagged there; and ought to have some benefit from the plea—*opere in longo*, &c. Let us, therefore, lay that volume aside, and open the first:—no matter where. We have opened *the Cobbler and the Cock.*

T. vi. p. 289. ην γουν πριν ανατειλαι ἡλιον μιαν κρηπιδα εργασαιο, πρoσθεν εση τουτο ες τα αλφιτα πεπονηκως. i. e. *For if you should finish but one slipper before sunrise, you shall have made so much way towards earning your dinner.*"

Now let us hear Mr. Tooke—

V. i. p. 63. "For if you go out before sunrise with only one slipper on, you have earnt so much for your next day's support."

As we turn over the leaves, why should we withhold from our readers the following short note on the cestus of Venus?

P. 73. "The girdle that Juno borrowed of Venus, for *inducing somnolency* on the father of the gods."

Ib. p. 318. εγυναικιζε ες το εταιρικον. Mr. T. i. p. 76, "and kept a gynæceum of lovely lasses."

Poor Aspasia! The elegant Aspasia is turned into a bawd. But to do Mr. T. justice, he found *gynæceum* in the Latin.

T. i. p. 73. ὡστε τηλικαυτη εν ακαρει χρονω ναυαγια επι του Δευκαλιωνος εγενετο, ὡς κ. τ. λ, i. e. *so that in the time of Deucalion such a general wreck took place in an instant, that*, &c. Mr. T. i. p. 34. "Witness the great deluge in Deucalion's time, when, ere a man could turn him round, such a horrid inundation ensued, that all the ships, on which mankind had cursed and swore, went to the bottom."

But there, also, our poor translator was wrecked on Gesner's absurd Latin.

Ib. p. 80. μηδε απαλλαττεσθωσαν ουτω ραδιως, και ὁτι μαλιστα ὑπο χρηστοτητος αυθις εκδιωκη αυτους της οικιας. Mr. T. p. 38. "and not lightly depart from him, UNLESS he, by means of his old acquaintance, Goodnature, turns them out of doors again."

Ib. p. 82. μονον ουχι δικρανοις με εξεωθει της οικιας, καθαπερ οἱ το πυρ εκ των χειρων αποῤῥιπτουντες. i. e. *He drove me out of doors almost with main force, as hastily as a man would fling a coal of fire out of his hand.* Mr. T. p. 38. "he drove me out of doors; not indeed with a pitchfork, nor by suddenly throwing at me something that burnt his hand, but in perfect cold blood," &c.

We were going on to quote from the next page his translation of the simple words—απωδυρου προς με—"you complained bitterly of me;" but we believe it would be superfluous to adduce any further evidence in proof of Mr. T.'s absolute ignorance of Greek.

We are sorry to be here obliged to quote the last sentence from his introductory essay:—

"So much the seldomer on the contrary I believe I have mistaken the meaning of his words and thoughts, and can the more confidently hope this, but therefore with less merit on my part, since I could not only avail myself of the labours of my predecessors in various languages, but also of *the celebrated editor* of *Æschylus*, whose ingenuity and taste are no less conspicuous than his knowledge of the Greek language and literature, who has such a friendship both for Lucian and for me as to *revise the greater part of this translation in manuscript*, and to employ some of the few moments left him by the multitude of his other affairs, in *correcting* it."

We confess that this statement at present appears to us incredible; and we do heartily hope—*on more accounts than one*—that it may prove to be one of those groundless boasts into which Mr. T.'s egregious vanity has in numberless instances betrayed him. But as there are in this country three editors of Æschylus now living,—Messrs. BLOMFIELD, BURGESS, and BUTLER,—we think it but justice to at least two of them to afford them an opportunity of publicly disavowing the imputation. Our pages shall be open to them for the purpose. They shall be open also to any defence of Mr. Tooke's publication, which any *scholar* may unfortunately think fit to offer. And we add, that—should we thus be called upon to take up the subject again—we shall be content to confine ourselves to the first short piece of Lucian, his humourous imitation of Prodicus's Choice of Hercules,—occupying with the notes not quite eleven pages,—or to any equal number of consecutive pages which Mr. T.'s advocate may select; for the purpose of establishing every charge which we have brought against the work.

We cannot close this article, though already protracted to too great length, without offering a remark in vindication of the severity of chastisement which we have inflicted. Some perhaps may ask—Is *ignorance*, however gross, the just object of such keen reprehension? We reply, that when gross ignorance and dull inanity assume the mask of learning and critical sagacity; when they appear in the walks of literature in the form of two large and costly volumes; we hold it the duty of an honest literary journal plainly and promptly to expose the fraud. But when such a writer supports his pretensions to extraordinary erudition with unblushing effrontery, by a contemptible system of the vilest plagiarism and dishonest artifice; the duty is the more incumbent of tearing off the lion's skin, and sending the animal—whipped—to rejoin the company of his long-eared brethren. The application of the lash is always a more ungrateful task, than to confer the wreath: but it is often more useful to the public. Did we not still maintain the silence, which we have prescribed to ourselves, upon other characters of Mr. T.'s work, we could easily prove that—instead of being severe—we have been very unwarrantably lenient.

None but those who have examined Mr. T.'s volumes, as we have, can conceive the ridiculousness of dishonest vanity, which pervades his notes and dissertations. Had he even been really possessed of any learning, it would have argued bad taste to display it in critical disquisitions on the text—not only of Lucian—but of various other classics; to make a parade of Greek quotations in an English version of the author; and that, when he thinks it needful to explain most copiously the commonest allusions to Greek mythology, with which every school-boy is familiar. But what shall we say of this vanity, when it appears that the whole garb of erudition in which he attires himself is stolen from the commentators, to whom every scholar has access?—except perhaps when it becomes his *own* (according to Mr. Locke's theory of the origin of property) by being *blended*, soiled, and disfigured with his own absurdities and impertinence. We re-open the book once more; and find in one page (v. ii. p. 492.) two examples sufficiently illustrative of this charge.

In the beginning of the piece, Διαλ. προς Ἡσιοδον (t. viii. Ed. Bip.) Lycinus says, addressing Hesiod—ὁπως κλειοις και ὑμνοιης τα παραληλυθοτα, και θεσπιζοις τα εσομενα. Upon these words Solanus (Du Soul) and Gesner very properly remark—properly in a critical edition of the Greek classic—that Lucian appears to have found a different reading from the common, in the passage of Hesiod to which he refers: the poet giving ὡςτε κλυοιμι τα τ' εσσομενα κ. τ. λ. and Gesner adds that the metre requires κλυοιμι. Here was a bit of learning which Mr. T. *thought* he found within his reach; and thus bedecks himself with it, to astonish his English readers.

"Lucian, it must be owned, has here allowed himself a legerdemain trick, by changing the κλειοιμι *of Hesiod* into κλειοις, which gives rather a *different meaning*. . .However, to give him fair play, we will here insert the poet's own words, Θεογ. lin. 30, et seq."

And then he *attempts* to transcribe the same lines which Gesner had quoted; but unfortunately in the third line gives κλειοιμ τα τ' εσσομενα, which, as Gesner has noticed, the verse would not admit. —Let us be allowed to remark—(though we feel how much out of place any thing of critical learning would be in reviewing such a work as the present)—that we think Lucian's text immediately leads to the emendation of Hesiod's. We would read κλειοιμι. See Hom. Od. ν. 299. The words ενεπνευσαν αυδην seem to require this alteration.

In another note, in the same page, Mr. T. favours the reader with the following display of his emendatorial sagacity:—

"'Whoever heard,' exclaims here M. Du Soul, 'that Telephus was among the prophets? This word is therefore corrupt, *or* what other is to be put in its room might not prove so easy to divine.'— —(*Sed quid reponendum sit*, &c.)—If it were allowable, notwithstanding this, to guess (*without, however, positively asserting that I have guessed it*,) I would say that Lucian perhaps casually *miswrote* it himself, intending to write Telemus; or the transcriber, from inattention, or the rapidity of his pen, metamorphosed the less known Telemus into the better known Telephus."

Then, after quoting a passage from the Odyssey, and from Ovid's Metam., he concludes—

"*I should think*, however, that we ought to adhere to the Homerican Telemus: since it is only to put in an ν and μ for ε and φ."

Ingenious critic! But, alas! all that is good in the note is stolen from the commentator following Solanus, on the passage: (t. viii. p. 491.) "Pro Τηλεφον Valkenarius ad Herod. &c. rescripsit Τηλεμον, assentiente Cl. Bel. de Ball. [Belin de Ballu.] De Telemo vid. præter Homer. in Od.—Ovid. Metam. xiii. v. 771."

We here close the case for the prosecution; and close Mr. T.'s volumes: handing them up, however, to the Bench, with some passages marked for his Lordship's inspection.

The Counsel for the Prisoner has thrown up his brief—the Jury have protested against the Judge's troubling them or himself with any charge or any summing up of evidence,—they have brought in their verdict, finding the prisoner Guilty on every count. The Judge flings the book from him with a frown, and pronounces the sentence of the Court: That the Prisoner at the bar, falsely styling himself "Lucian of Samosata, from the Greek, by William Tooke," &c. &c. be twice publicly whipped through the pages of The Weekly Register, and then transported for life *in vicum vendentem thus et odores*—the Botany Bay of Literature.

PLAIN TRUTHS:

OR,

A SPEECH

WHICH MAY BE DELIVERED IN THE APPROACHING SESSION, BY ANY MEMBER WHO LIKES IT,

ON A MOTION FOR

GOING INTO A COMMITTEE OF THE WHOLE HOUSE

UPON

THE STATE OF IRELAND.

Αισχρον εστιν, ὦ ανδρες Αθηναιοι, φενακιζειν ἑαυτους.

[Translated for the benefit of the Country Gentlemen.]

"It is shameful, Gentlemen, that we should humbug OURSELVES."

[Published 1825.]

A SPEECH, &c.

SIR,—I rise to oppose the motion that this House should go into a Committee on the state of IRELAND. I oppose it, because I think it unfair to mock that unhappy country by holding out hopes, which we are not prepared to realize.

If the disorders of Ireland could be healed by any measures, which the British Legislature is likely to adopt, I would gladly go into the Committee. But I am persuaded that they cannot: and thinking it important that the House should itself be undeceived, and cease to encourage delusive expectations, I beg leave to state, with all plainness, the grounds upon which I regard the case of IRELAND as at present hopeless.

In offering my sentiments to the attention of the House, I feel that I am likely to displease all parties; because I cannot agree with the views of any. Yet I may, in some measure, also avail myself of the support of all; because, even those who have advanced opinions the most opposite to each other, appear to me to speak some important truths.

There are certain topics, upon which honourable Members are accustomed to enlarge very eloquently, but which, I think, have nothing to do with the question that properly comes under the consideration of this House; because they concern matters that come not within the limits of legislative interference. If the IRISH peasantry be oppressed by rack-rents, if they be in a state of squalid poverty and wretchedness, an overgrown population of ragged paupers, can we gravely think of passing an Act of Parliament for remedying these evils? an Act of Parliament for regulating the amount of rent which the landlord may demand, or the tenant pay? an Act of Parliament for prohibiting the use of potatoes as food, or the marriages of those who cannot afford to use wheaten bread? an Act of Parliament for preventing the peasant's pig from occupying the same hovel with his family?—No, Sir; there is no use in declaiming here upon such topics as these. They are either matters of private regulation; or evils which bring with them their own correction: or mere indications of a state of rude society.

But as one honourable Member has insisted largely on the *distresses* of the IRISH peasantry, as at once the cause and palliation of their outrages, I cannot forbear making two brief remarks. The first is, that the persons most actively engaged in those deeds of outrage and plans of lawless combination, are notoriously—not the lowest and most distressed of the peasantry—but men who are comparatively in easy circumstances, and who might possess every comfort of life, if their habits were industrious and peaceful. My second remark is, that gentlemen of this country, who talk of the extreme *wretchedness* of the lower orders in Ireland, really do not know Ireland. They have, perhaps, made a six-weeks' tour in the country, and imagine that this has made them acquainted with it. They have observed the peasant living in a mud-built cabin, surrounded with smoke, and dirt, and naked children, and pigs, and poultry; and have concluded that he must be *wretched*, because they would be so in such circumstances. But let me tell such gentlemen, that these circumstances produce not the slightest discomfort to the object of their sympathy. And let me not be charged with speaking paradoxically, when I say—and I say it (upon a long and intimate acquaintance with the people)—that, except when a rare failure of the potatoe-crop occasions real famine in the country, I do believe that the IRISH peasantry have more pleasurable enjoyment of existence than the ENGLISH; and that for one who has not a sufficiency of wholesome food in that island, scores die of starvation in this metropolis of the British empire.

But I dismiss such questions, as really unconnected with the proper subject of our debate. And I have observed, that whatever other topics were introduced by the speakers who have preceded me, they appear all to agree in marking what is called the CATHOLIC QUESTION as of primary importance on the present occasion; that to this they all ultimately reverted, from whatever point their arguments set out; and that apart from this they seem aware that the state of IRELAND cannot be discussed. In this, sir, they are right.

But, in other respects, I maintain that both the advocates and the opponents of the Catholic claims are equally wrong; the opponents in maintaining that these claims may safely be resisted; and the advocates in maintaining—not only that they may safely be conceded—but that the concession will satisfy the claimants, and tranquillize IRELAND. Sir, it will not; and in the nature of things i cannot.

Yet do I agree with those who say, that the concession ought to be made. It ought to be made, in order to remove the stalking-horse of disaffection. It ought to be made, in order to detach from the ranks of the disaffected a few of the Popish nobility and gentry, who are safe subjects of the British Empire. It ought to be made, in order to expose the further objects of those, who are essentially hostile to British connexion. It ought to be made, even for the sake of vindicating the legislature from the imputation of absurd inconsistency;—the inconsistency of granting to thousands of semi-barbarous peasants the right of electing Members of Parliament, and withholding from a few respectable gentlemen of the same faith the right of being eligible to a seat in Parliament. But it is idle to think, that any concessions which can be made, consistently with the existence of a Protestant Establishment in IRELAND, will satisfy the Popish aspirants, and tranquillize the country. No, sir; it is impossible: and the expectation of it is founded in utter ignorance of the genius of Popery, and inattention indeed to the nature of man.

It has for some time been fashionable to talk of the genius of Popery as considerably altered from what it was in former days. The encaged tiger is supposed to havethrown off its pristine ferocity, and to have become as gentle as a lamb. While I protest against the notion, let me not be misunderstood. I distinguish between the character of individuals professing the Romish faith, and the genius of the faith itself, particularly as maintained by its hierarchy. That there are individuals of that communion, as amiable as any Protestants in private life, and as safe and useful members of civil society, I gladly acknowledge. But they constitute not what is called THE CHURCH, to whose decrees even *their* private sentiments and wishes must bend. That CHURCH boasts of her *immutability*: and simple indeed are they who dispute the immutability which she claims, and who refuse to estimate what she *is* at this day by the undisputed records of what she *has been* in days of old.

Well indeed does she know how to assume every variety of form and appearance, according to her varying occasions. For the thunders, in which she was once accustomed to speak, she can employ the feeble timid accents of helplessness. Concealing her snakes and her scourges,* she can present herself in all the pitiable decrepitude of anility. But even then she only waits the fit moment for re-assuming her proper form; for repelling the man who scorns or opposes her; and bursting on his confounded sight in all the terrors and expanding dimensions of the fury.

Many were surprised lately at finding that the Popish priests revived their pretensions to miraculous powers. But every one who knew their system knew that these powers were reserved *in petto*. In these heretical countries, indeed, the exercise of them has been,

* Alecto torvam faciem et furialia membra
Exuit: in vultus sese transformat aniles, &c.
At . . . . tot Erinnys sibilat hydris
Tantaque se facies aperit.—VIRG. l. vii. ÆN.

for good reasons, very rare. But who has not heard of the annual liquefaction of the blood of St. JANUARIUS at Naples? though it has been so fashionable to forget all the lying legends of the Church of Rome, that many may not have heard of the flight of the *Holy House* from Judea to Loretto.

Great certainly is the impudence of the Reverend and Right Reverend Knaves, who, in the nineteenth century, and in these countries, put forward their grossest claims upon the public credulity; but great also is their cunning. They seem to have rightly estimated the temper of the times. When Prince HOHENLOHE falls a praying to one of the innumerable gods or goddesses, with which they have peopled their heaven; and his confederates assure us, that on the invoked interference of St. JOHN NEPOMUSCENE, a miraculous cure has been effected;—the protestants of these countries,—instead of laughing at the imposture, and simply remarking the long-established character of the shop from which it issues,—gape with wonder at the prodigy, and proceed gravely to canvass its authenticity in pamphlets without number.

And shall I be told that the men, who still practise these *pious frauds* for the good of the Church, would not still also consider every other means sanctified by that end?—that they would not still also, if they had the power, enforce submission to the Church's dictates even by the tortures of the inquisition, and impose her iron yoke (as formerly) upon the necks of kings?

I may be told, that—however willing—they have not the power, and are not likely to recover it; that the world is now too enlightened, the rights of conscience too well understood. And I admit it to a certain degree; though I do think that the age boasts of much more light, and much more liberality, than it really possesses. But I aim at present only at asserting the unchangeable character of the Church of ROME, as it influences the *wishes* and the *aims* of her priesthood; the domination which they seek to establish over the consciences of men; and their ambitious aspirings after worldly power, in order to advance the interests of their ecclesiastical system. And knowing that such is the essential character of Popery, can I rationally expect tranquillity in Ireland, while there is a Protestant establishment and a Popish populace? No: there will, and must be, a continued struggle, on the one hand, to obtain Popish ascendancy, and, on the other, to maintain Protestant ascendancy;—a struggle, which in various forms must spread barbarism and distraction throughout the land;—a struggle, in the course of which every advance of the Popish multitude in numbers, wealth, and political privilege, will be employed as a stepping-block to further elevation.

I am old enough to remember the first relaxations of the penal code in Ireland, during the last reign. The Papists had long been patient sufferers, and were then humble petitioners for relief. They have since become loud claimants for privilege and power; and their claims have proceeded from one object to another, till they now avow, that they require a new modelling of the Established Church, and an admission of their professors to every office in the state most intimately connected with our Religious Establishment,—even to that of the Lord High Chancellor of England. And if all this were conceded, think ye that they would be content, while their religion was excluded from the throne itself, and while any other religion than theirs was established in Ireland? No, Sir; it were idle to expect it.

And I must add, that the ultimate object of their priesthood, to become the Establishment in Ireland, is as fair, and their claims for that as reasonable, as any which they now avow. You have one form of religion established in England, the religion of the majority: you have another established in Scotland, the form that best pleases the major part of our Northern fellow-subjects. And why—may an Irish Papist well demand—why should not Popery be established in Ireland? Is it, that the principles of the British constitution are inconsistent with the political support of *Popery* in any part of his Majesty's dominions? Assuredly not so. Look at CANADA; and there you will see Popery established by British law. I know that a distinction has been set up between its establishment, and the political support and endowment of tithes, which it there receives. But it is a distinction without a difference.

That there are in Ireland some of the Popish communion, men of property, and of cultivated minds, who do not propose to themselves the overthrow of the present Establishment, I believe. They naturally dread the violent convulsion, which would, probably, accompany such a change: and though abundantly dissatisfied with the existing order of things, they yet would rather bear its evils, than seek a remedy for them by a civil war. To lessen the causes of that dissatisfaction, which such men feel,—(to lessen them as much as possible, for, under a Protestant Establishment, they cannot be wholly removed) is, I am persuaded, among the important objects of legislation for IRELAND.

But the great mass of its Popish population have nothing to lose, but the blood of which they are prodigal: and are little accustomed in any case to the cool calculation of consequences: while the priests —cut off by their celibacy from the ordinary connexions and engagements of civil society—have but one paramount object perpetually in view, the advancement of the interests of their *Church*; an object, which their system teaches them to pursue *per fas et nefas*. In the pursuit of this, they do generally lay themselves out with insidious industry, to keep alive in the minds of their people a feeling of hostility to BRITISH connexion; and to attach to the name of *Sassenach* the combined ideas of one of English blood, a heretic, an oppressor of the country, and usurper of the rights of IRISHMEN.

Some of those men I have known to be distinguished by the title of *loyal* priests: and I remember one of these, in a very disturbed district, who invited his Protestant neighbours to hear a *pacific* harangue, which he was to deliver from the altar, for the express purpose of quieting the minds of his people, and persuading them to give up their insurrectionary schemes. Yet Mark Antony's speech to the Roman populace, over the body of Cæsar, was not more insidiously inflammatory, than the pacific harangue of that *loyal* priest on that occasion—while it must be admitted that he did strongly impress upon the people the hopelessness of their being then able to avenge the wrongs of ages, which he detailed, and the prudential necessity of their forbearing to break out into rebellion then. The priests of IRELAND I do not hesitate to denounce as, generally, the great agitators of that country; and if, in the rebellion of 1798, a ship had been freighted for Port Jackson, with all the officiating priests, I am persuaded that there would not have been expatriated six persons guiltless of misprision of treason. It would have been a measure not more illegal than others, which were then adopted; but much more effectual for restoring quiet to IRELAND.

I am aware, that in speaking of the Popish population of IRELAND as generally disaffected, I hold a language likely to offend both the advocates and opponents of their claims. Their long and general *loyalty* is a favourite theme: and even the ebullitions of joyous revelry, which the novel pageantry of a Royal visit lately excited in the metropolis, have been adduced as evidence that they are very good subjects of King George the Fourth. Some who talk in this manner, must undoubtedly know better: but they are afraid to avow the truth. For my part, I think it quite time that this House, and the British public, should be disabused; and informed that the deeply-rooted feeling of the great mass of Irish papists is hostile to GREAT BRITAIN; that the hope which lies nearest to their hearts is that of recovering their country at some future period, out of the hands of the English invaders. It is time that this House should know the real characters of the distemper for which we seek a remedy.

Yet let me not be understood as partaking in the fears of those, who apprehend an immediate or speedy rebellion in IRELAND. No, Sir: the leaders of disaffection there have learned more prudence. And however well pleased that there should be a continuance of that kind of smothered and harrassing warfare, which has distracted many parts of the island, yet, I am sure they would be forward to restrain the people from openly taking the field against the overwhelming power of GREAT BRITAIN. But let EUROPE be again involved in war, and let the military resources of GREAT BRITAIN be occupied as they have been in former wars of EUROPE, then I do avow my apprehension, that IRELAND will be lost to this country, lost probably after an internal struggle the most bloody.

Sir, I am not an *Orange-man*; and I am decidedly of opinion that, in a well-regulated state, no secret political association ought to be tolerated. But I must add, that the principles of a well-regulated state are not applicable to IRELAND: and that, combined as the numerical majority of its populace is against the existing laws and constitution, I cannot wonder that the minority should combine for their own preservation and the maintenance of the existing order. Nor do I think that the latter combination can be either safely or effectually put down, while the former continues: and I repeat it, that the former must continue, as long as the religious Establishment of the country is *Protestant*, and the great mass of its population *Popish*.

What then is to be done? what can be done for that unhappy country! You are moved to go into a Committee upon its state. But is this House prepared to go to the root of the evil? And if not, what use in deceiving yourselves and the nation, by employing temporary palliatives? You can but keep military possession of IRELAND, while she is a hostile country, and the ground of her hostility continues unremoved. This is undoubtedly a very precarious tenure; much more so than many flatter themselves; and every year it will become more and more precarious. But if this must be the course adopted, abandon the inconsistent notion of applying British law and British liberty to that country. These are in fact little suited to a people combined against established law and order. That they will cease to be so combined, if what is absurdly called *Catholic emancipation* be conceded, the advocates of that measure are fond of representing. But the expectation is vain: and one of the reasons for which I am favourable to that concession is, that its inefficacy for the quieting of IRELAND may be the sooner discovered. Already the claims of the Irish papists, (I say, their *claims*—for they have long ceased to hold the language of petitioners) go far beyond any of the civil privileges formerly demanded, and obviously beyond what can be granted them consistently with the maintenance of the Protestant Establishment. But let every concession be made, which can be made consistently with that; let it be made without further opposition or delay; and then it will be seen, whether there be not ulterior objects in view of the agitators of IRELAND.

I would particularly urge the prompt removal of the existing disqualifications, which prevent Papists from sitting in Parliament; because I am persuaded that this concession may be made most safely. It is not in this house that factious demagogues are formidable to the state. The —— and the —— would dwindle into harmless insignificance within these walls. But if you apprehend that too many of such firebrands might be imported, let the concession, which I advocate, be accompanied by an Act, abolishing the elective franchise of *forty-shilling* freeholders. To the rabble, who at present exercise that privilege, the privilege is not worth a straw; and it were nonsense to talk of its abolition as any deprivation to *them*. They are mere machines, worked either by the land-owner or the priest; and are certainly too much under the controlling influence of the latter, to be safely trusted with such civil power. But our legislation for IRELAND has hitherto proceeded with an absurdity of inconsistence, at once laughable and melancholy.

I have spoken, as persuaded that the House is not prepared to go to the root of the evils in that country, or to look them fairly in the face. But perhaps some are disposed to say—"While you speak of the tranquillity of IRELAND as hopeless under any regimen which you think likely to be applied, what is that course which you conceive would tranquillize her, if adopted?" I feel some difficulty in replying to such a question; not from any dubiousness in my own judgment, but from uncertainty whether a plain answer be quite consistent with prudence. This much, however, I may say:—If I have rightly traced the disorders of IRELAND to her Popish population and her Protestant establishment, is it not plain that the only effectual remedy must be—either to make Popery the religious establishment there,—or altogether to remove the object of contention, by having *no religious establishment* in that country, but leaving the Protestants to support their own clergy, as the Papists support theirs?

In mentioning this remedy, let me be understood—not as recommending it,—not as saying that it would be our wisdom and our duty to employ it. I simply mark it as, in my view, the only remedy which would meet the nature of the disease. But it *may* perhaps be wiser to allow the disease to take its course, or even to let the patient die, than employ such a remedy. It *may* perhaps be our duty, rather to lose IRELAND ultimately, than to cease providing and supporting a RELIGION for her, which her people will not accept. This *may* be political wisdom, for reasons which I am too shallow a politician to penetrate. And if this be so, I can only say that I admire the *religious* zeal of our legislature, and the high cost at which they are ready to promote—(shall I say?)—the *good of souls*. I admire their *religious* zeal for others the more, because I observe how little many of them care about the matter for themselves. Sir, the honourable members who laugh, sufficiently betray their conviction, that RELIGION—in its real import as connected with the conscience—has nothing in the world to do with the affair; that the kingdom of the *Clergy* and the kingdom of GOD are altogether distinct.

However this may be, there are some who think that the period will yet arrive, when human governments shall discover that they have stepped quite aside from their proper province, in providing *religion* for their subjects, in pretending to take care of their *souls*, and to interfere with the concerns of another world. There are some, I say, so simple as to imagine, that the rulers of this world have properly nothing to do—in their official capacity—but with the things of *this* world; and that their whole province is the *civil* conduct and *temporal* concerns of the people. They imagine that the connexion of CHURCH and STATE is as impolitic as it is unnatural; that it is the crafty device of ecclesiastics, seeking their own aggrandizement by imposing the incumbrance of their alliance on kings and legislators. Men of these sentiments I know: and I have perceived that it is more difficult to refute them, than to put them down by that outcry of the churchmen of old—"GREAT IS DIANA OF THE EPHESIANS."

But whatever may be said for or against the policy of employing *state-religion*, as an engine of government,—(and I would not strenuously contest that point with any)—I must, as a CHRISTIAN, avow my decided conviction that CHRISTIANITY *is incapable of being so employed;* and that no politically-established religion either is or *can* be CHRISTIANITY: I mean the Christianity of the New Testament. I am well aware, Sir, of the legal principle, that Christianity is a part and parcel of the law of this country: and—in the legal sense—I by no means wish to controvert it. But I am aware also, that this is one of the many *fictions* of law; and that the thing called Christianity, and embodied with the law of England, is most *unchristian*. Upon this topic I can hold no measured or ambiguous language.

The attempt to embody Christianity with the political constitution of any state, is an attempt to *falsify the word of* CHRIST, when he uttered that memorable saying—"*My kingdom is not of this world.*" In this spiritual "fornication with the kings of the earth," the clergy have been the great panders, and the church of Rome has been "the *great* whore:" but she is also "the *mother* of harlots," and has many daughters, who have left her house, to prosecute on their own account the same unclean trade. The high-church party in this country acknowledge and boast of their *relationship* to the papal see: for to support their profane pretension to the character of *successors of the Apostles*, they are content to trace their succession through the most impious and profligate of the Roman pontiffs, who have blasphemously arrogated to themselves the title of CHRIST'S *Vicegerents* upon earth.

No marvel that such men are afraid of the circulation of the Scriptures: for it has been clearly proved even by a clergyman,* that the whole distinction between *clergy* and *laity* is without a shadow of foundation in the Scriptures of the New Testament; and this comes to be progressively known to those who have any ear for the word of God. But neither is it any marvel, that among the most zealous partisans of the established church, among the loudest vociferators for the happy union of church and state, are found the men who care not a straw for any religion, but as they think the profession of it connected with their interests. And these indeed are the churchmen most bitterly exasperated against conscientious Dissenters from the establishment; and most disposed to reclaim them, if it were allowed, by the infliction of pains and penalties, as in days of old. This is all quite consistent with a so-called church, of which the avowed head may be such a bloody and libidinous tyrant as our 8th HENRY. It is only marvellous how—in a country where the Scriptures have been circulated so long—any reader of them can confound with CHRISTIANITY such a mongrel, monstrous production of the unnatural connexion between Church and State.

Many think, or pretend to think, that this connexion ought to be maintained, in order to prevent the prevalence of irreligion and consequent immorality in the nation. But the fact is, that it—more than anything else—promotes irreligion and impiety. The discovery is quickly made by acute and reflecting individuals, that the *state-religion* is a humbug, the device of worldly politicians for their political ends. And the same discovery sooner or later forces itself on the mass of the community; few of whom have any inclination to examine the higher and only true standard of pure religion, or to distinguish between genuine CHRISTIANITY and that which is put forward by public authority under the name.

But those who urge the hackneyed argument, that *religion* is the great basis of civil society, and that we therefore ought to provide some state-religion for the people, pretty plainly avow that they are not nice about the characters of the religion which they would establish. They are only anxious to enforce and regulate the external worship of *some* god or gods, lest the people should worship none. Now I need not go beyond IRELAND for a proof, that rulers may save themselves all trouble and expense upon this object. There we see a people, not only rejecting the religion provided for them by their

* DR. CAMPBELL in his Lectures on Ecclesiastical History.

rulers, but maintaining a religion for themselves independently of their rulers; and not only so, but maintaining it for centuries in spite of all the efforts of government to put it down. How far their *manners* are the better for their religion, is another question. For my own part, I am persuaded, that in these so-called *Christian* countries there is in any one year more of fraud, in various forms, more of perjury, murder, adultery, and every crime most hostile to the well-being of society, than occurred in the course of a century in the ancient republic of *heathen* Rome. And I believe that more than 99 in a 100 of those who expiate their crimes on the gallows, die *unworthy members* of the churches either of England or of Rome. However this be, our governors need not apprehend that the people will be without Religion, unless the state supply them.

It is not uncommon for the zealous advocates of our religious establishments, to speak of all who dissent from them as necessarily ill-affected to the State.—"The *Church* and *State*," say they, "form one Constitution in these realms: and to that constitution those who dislike the church must be hostile." If this be so, nothing can more clearly show the impolicy and absurdity of the connexion. If this be so, the British constitution has indeed a host of irreconcilable foes, not only in IRELAND, but in ENGLAND, SCOTLAND, and WALES; and that host yearly increasing; for I believe it will not be denied, that the number of Dissenters from the Establishment is decisively on the increase. If this be so, it was most pernicious to introduce the Reformation into these countries: for the appeal then made to the Scriptures must necessarily produce dissenters from any political establishment of religion which could be adopted: whereas the continued domination of Popery, keeping down the spirit of inquiry, might have united the people in blind submission to the dictates of their priests.

But I must add, Sir, that—if this be so—then the Lord Chancellor himself, and all our Most Reverend Archbishops, and Right Reverend Bishops, and Very Reverend Deans, and Venerable Archdeacons, are disaffected subjects on the northern side of the TWEED: and all the sincere members of the Established Church of Scotland are disaffected subjects on the southern side of that stream. The Orthodox Hierarchy of the English Church deny the *validity* of Presbyterian ordination, and look down upon the people of that communion as destitute of the so-called Sacraments. But let me tell them, that the stiff Presbyterian looks down upon them, and all the Episcopalian system, as but a relic of Papal corruption.

But his MAJESTY himself—God bless him!—what should we say of him, upon the supposition against which I argue? He has in his dominions at least two ecclesiastical systems, of which he is the common head. For though our northern neighbours do not like to hear of him as the *head* of the Scottish Church, I believe he undoubtedly is, and accordingly presides by his representative in their general synod. Now, those who maintain that a man cannot be well affected to the State, unless he be attached to *the Church*, would do well to say, *which* of his churches the King himself must be attached to? They would do well to pause, and consider the disloyal imputation which they cast upon his Majesty, if he be considered as cordially attached to either.

I have pointed, sir, at some of the absurd and mischievous consequences, which would flow from the admission of the charge brought by some against the loyalty of dissenters. But the ground of their assertion is utterly untenable. Our civil constitution might subsist in full vigour, though the so-called church were sent adrift: and to that constitution, as consisting in the well-balanced powers of King, Lords, and Commons, a man may be cordially attached, who yet thinks that the Church is a dead incumbrance on the State,—a morbid tumour, which it would be desirable to eradicate, if it might be done without danger from hæmorrhage.

Whatever opinion may be formed on the latter question, I think it demonstrable that, if there were no Ecclesiastical Establishment, the utmost demands of our Popish countrymen might be conceded with perfect safety; and that it would then be politically indifferent, whether the King himself were a Papist or a Protestant. On the other hand, I think it as demonstrable that, while there is a Protestant Establishment in Ireland, that island must remain a distracted country, and a most vulnerable part of the British empire,—whether you concede, or whether you withhold what is now included under the name of Catholic Emancipation.

Let me be allowed, sir, before I sit down, to meet another objection, to which I am aware I shall be exposed from the mere *mention* of the abolition of all religious Establishments, though I have not ventured to recommend the measure. The very suggestion of the idea is likely to excite that common outcry about the *sacrilegious invasion of* CHURCH-PROPERTY. And then will be vociferated in various forms that contemptible sophism, which infers—because such property was violently invaded in France during the wildness of democratic anarchy—that therefore the man who suggests any legislative interference with it must be a wild anarchist at bottom. How utterly unfounded such an imputation is with respect to myself, those who are best acquainted with my views, and principles, and conduct, best can testify.

But waving this; I would remark that, in this current phrase of CHURCH-PROPERTY, the church is represented as a body corporate, endowed with certain civil privileges and rights: while the various orders of clergy, from the archbishop to the curate, are considered as the members of the corporation. What an abuse this is of the term CHURCH, it would be easy to demonstrate; and what an utter departure from its primitive and scriptural meaning, as importing in general an assembly of persons convened for any purpose, and peculiarly a congregation of Christians coming together into one place for Christian purposes. I briefly notice this, because the perception of it will relieve any man from the dread of SACRILEGE in touching the *soi-disant* CHURCH.

And as to the alleged *injustice* of diverting church-property from the present purposes for which it is employed, I must say that, *if* these purposes were found inconsistent with the peace and welfare of the nation, it would be more unjust to sacrifice the peace and welfare of the nation to the abstract conception of the clergy as a *body corporate*, however countenanced that abstract conception may be by the technicalities of legal language. The interest in this church property, which any existing individuals actually possess, ought assuredly to be preserved inviolate: for I have no idea of promoting even public benefit by private wrong. But I deny that any principles of *justice* bind the legislature to continue a system for providing a continued succession of claimants to that property.

Let me suppose a case, which will at once illustrate my meaning, and establish the truth of my opinion. Let me suppose, that by the common law of England, for time immemorial, the tenth part of the produce of the soil had been allotted to the maintenance of a favourite corps of military officers; each of whom should have but a life interest in his portion of these military tithes; but, on his death or promotion, should be succeeded by one educated for the profession, and appointed by some public functionary to hold the vacant commission. Supposing this, we may easily imagine that, in a course of years, other corps of officers would feel a strong desire to participate in those pecuniary advantages, as well as much jealousy and irritation at being precluded from them. We may easily imagine, also, that the military *tithe-proctors* would become very obnoxious to the people; and that the land-owners and land-holders would at length murmur loudly at this disposal of the tenth part of the produce of the soil. Yet I am ready to admit, that it might fairly be replied against such murmurs, that the land-owners held their lands for time immemorial subject to this defalcation, or, in other words, were legally owners of but nine-tenths of the produce; and that, if the military tenth were abolished, it would benefit not the tenants of the land, but the proprietors, as they would certainly demand and receive a proportionally greater rent.

But let us suppose that the public should at length become convinced, that this old allotment of the tenth of the soil, and the tenth of the labour and expense of its cultivation, had been exceedingly absurd and impolitic; that its effects were to the highest degree injurious to the community, and endangered the peace and well-being of the nation. In such a case, shall I be told that the legislature would act *unjustly*, if they dissolved that corps of officers, set up to auction these military tithes, and applied the public fund thus formed to purposes beneficial to the state? In such a case, if the officers raised a loud clamour, and held a high language about their being a *corporate body*, whose property could no more be legally invaded than the property of an individual, should we not laugh at the sophism? Should we be at any loss to say—

"Gentlemen, whom do we injure? You have but a personal and life interest in these military tithes, which some foolish monarch of old allotted to the maintenance of your corps. Your vested interests we shall not invade. We shall take care that you shall not be losers; that you shall have an income fully equivalent to what you have received. But we think it for the good of the State, that your corps, as a favoured military body, should become extinct. And whom, again we ask, do we injure? Your successors? And who are they?

Non-entities at present; and we think it expedient that they should remain so,—that you should have *no successors*. That there are many, who would be very glad of the appointment to succeed to your commissions, we have no doubt. But is there an individual who can say that he has a legal right to the appointment? And no man can reasonably complain that he is *deprived* of what he has never had, either in possession or in right. That many may have had it in prospect and expectation, that many may have indulged the *hope* of being appointed to your commissions, we do not deny. Such may be disappointed, but will not be injured. And perhaps even they will ultimately have no cause to regret, that they are obliged to turn their exertions into another channel?"

Common sense, I think, would dictate such a reply in such a case: and, for my part, I can see no essential difference between this imaginary case, and that which I brought it to illustrate.

I am aware, sir, that the clerical system has struck its roots most deeply, and spread its ramifications most widely, throughout Christendom. I am aware, that even in this country it overlays the State, which it professes to support. I am aware, that it is employed as an engine of every administration; because no ministers yet dare to risk their political existence by dissolving their alliance with *the church*. But, sir, there is a train of causes in progressive operation, which will yet make every state sick of that alliance, and convince all that the views which I have proposed to your attention are just and important. Perhaps no force of reasoning can anticipate the operation of those causes. My object in addressing you on the present occasion has been to mark the real alternative, which offers itself to our selection. We have to choose between two courses: on the one hand—the military maintenance of a Protestant religious establishment in Ireland, accompanied with the continuance and increase of all the distractions of that unhappy country, and issuing probably in its ultimate separation from Great Britain:—on the other hand, the discontinuance of our legislative interference with the *religion* of the people, followed by the tranquillity and increasing prosperity of Ireland, as an attached, vigorous, and progressively useful member of the British empire. There is no third or middle course between these two, which can rationally be adopted.

Persuaded, sir, that this is the only light in which the subject can be rightly viewed, but apprehending that the House is not yet able to bear the steady contemplation of it in this light; I shall vote against the motion for our going into a Committee on the state of Ireland.

AN

ESSAY

ON THE FOLLOWING

PRIZE QUESTION,

PROPOSED BY THE

ROYAL IRISH ACADEMY,

"WHETHER AND HOW FAR THE CULTIVATION OF SCIENCE AND THAT OF POLITE LITERATURE ASSIST OR OBSTRUCT EACH OTHER?"

Etenim omnes artes, quæ ad humanitatem pertinent, habent quoddam commune vinculum, et quasi cognatione quadam inter se continentur.—Cic. pro Arch.

[First Published, 1812.]

TO HIS EXCELLENCY

CHARLES, DUKE OF RICHMOND,

LORD LIEUTENANT GENERAL AND GENERAL GOVERNOR OF IRELAND, KNIGHT OF THE MOST NOBLE ORDER OF THE GARTER, &c. &c. &c.

My Lord,—Deterred, by the consciousness of my obscurity as an individual, from soliciting permission to inscribe the following pages to your Excellency, I have yet been induced to risk the charge of presumption by doing so without permission.

Your Excellency's known condescension encourages me to hope for pardon; and to conceive that the subject of this short Essay may perhaps appear not uninteresting to a nobleman of cultivated mind. Happy should I be, if it proved so fortunate as to engage your Excellency's attention to the state of *Classical Literature* in Ireland, and to the easy means suggested for its advancement.

While so many Dissenters from the religious Establishment of this country are evidencing, by their conduct as political agitators, that their religion is not that of genuine Christianity, I would entreat permission, as a conscientious Dissenter from all religious establishments, to express my deep thankfulness for the blessings which I enjoy under your EXCELLENCY'S administration of his MAJESTY'S Government in this island;—the invaluable blessings of civil protection, of equal law, and of liberty of conscience. Bound by the principles, which I have learned from Scripture, to conduct myself as a quiet and peaceable citizen of any state, I have a lively feeling of the further claims, which the Government of this country possesses on my grateful attachment.

I have the honour to be, my Lord,
With the highest respect,
Your EXCELLENCY'S most devoted, obedient,
And very humble Servant,
JOHN WALKER.

ADVERTISEMENT.

THE occasion of my writing the following Essay is sufficiently indicated by the title-page. In now submitting it to the public, I have only to declare that I have not the remotest idea of appealing from the decision, which allotted to another composition the prize proposed by the Academy. I have no doubt that this decision was founded on the most correct and impartial judgment; can readily believe that the successful Essay possesses merit ever so much superior to mine; and am too dead to the rivalry of authorship to have any feeling, but that of satisfaction, at finding that polite literature has a more able advocate than myself.

If it be asked—*Why then publish?*—I reply,—from the same motive, which chiefly induced me to write; a desire of calling the public attention to the state of *classical learning* in this country, and of exciting those, who possess the means, to remove some of the greatest hindrances to its successful cultivation.

If this production of my pen have any tendency to promote that very important object,—(and to this, I conceive, its very brevity may somewhat contribute)—I shall indulge the hope that, in the eye of the candid critic, its practical usefulness may cover its literary defects.

No. 73, *Lower Dorset Street,*
August 24, 1812.

AN ESSAY, &c.

It is owing to the littleness and vanity of the human mind, that we are all so prone to depreciate the studies of others, while we extol the usefulness and dignity of our own. The man of science, the naturalist, the experimental philosopher, and the polite scholar, are apt each to represent his own department in literature as the only one worthy of cultivation; while, in fact, none of them could be cultivated with success, if any one of them were cultivated exclusively.

And this indeed is one of the many benefits of a truly liberal education, that it tends to correct that narrowness of view; discovers the general connexion between the multifarious objects of human intellect; lays a broad and solid foundation for the further prosecution of any one among them, which may recommend itself most to the taste of the individual; and, while it furnishes him with peculiar advantages for the successful pursuit of his own favourite study, guards him against a contemptuous indifference to the literary engagements of others.

It is in the literary, as in the natural world. Presumptuous ignorance is forward to pronounce the uselessness of some parts in the works of nature. But an intimate acquaintance with what appears most minute and unimportant establishes the maxim, that *Nature does nothing in vain:* and to the most extended survey such a concatenation appears subsisting between her least and greatest productions, that we may doubt whether the least of them could be annihilated, without disturbing the harmony and destroying the well-being of the whole.

But, although there be a similarly common interest and mutual subserviency amongst all the branches of literature, some of them are from time to time liable to pass into neglect, while others engross more than due attention. And it is one of the most important duties of those enlightened few, to whom the general superintendence of learning belongs, to check such an evil on its first appearance, and to guard against a retrograde movement in any part of human knowledge, under a conviction that it must be unfavourable in its consequences to the real progress of every other.

I have long apprehended a danger of this kind, with respect to *classical learning;* and think I perceive many alarming symptoms, which threaten its extinction. In one great empire, which now possesses the dominion or controul over the larger part of Europe, classical learning is declared by authority to be unnecessary for—what are called the learned professions. For several years also the convulsed state of the civilized world—unfavourable to literature universally—has been peculiarly so to the elegances of polite literature: and the general temper of the times is marked by a growing contempt for all that is ancient.

In these countries, no doubt, there are old and valuable institutions, which insure—while they continue—a continued attention to the forms at least of classical learning. But it would be folly to deny or conceal the fact, that it has lost its hold upon the public mind. From having been once over-rated,—and perhaps partly on that very account,—it is rapidly passing into disesteem: and to a cultivated taste the vitiated style of modern composition must appear at once one of the consequences, and one of the evidences, of its neglect.

On these accounts, and from the intimate connexion between classical learning and all polite literature, I hope I shall be excused for somewhat narrowing the question proposed by the Academy, and confining myself in this Essay to the inquiry—*How far the cultivation of* SCIENCE *and that of* CLASSICAL LEARNING *assist or obstruct each other.*

In speaking of *Science*, I shall use the word in that extended signification, which I conceive was designed to be attached to it by the terms of the question; as comprehending all those departments in learning, which are commonly distinguished from *polite* literature:—though it may be remarked, that the name perhaps strictly belongs only to *mathematics* and the *mathematical* branches of natural philosophy; and that in mathematics the ancients are confessedly our masters. To the geometrical science of the Greek school,—unrivalled in the beauty, clearness, and accuracy of its method,—NEWTON himself was indebted for the principles, which his genius extended and applied;—applied, as to other subjects, so to the demonstration of that very system of the universe, which had been asserted by one of such remote antiquity as PYTHAGORAS.

In another respect also we stand indebted to the ancient classics for all our modern improvements in science. What was it, that awakened Europe from a long sleep of ignorance, in which the powers of the human mind had lain unexercised and torpid? What was the light that first broke in upon the dark ages, and roused an unlettered world to literary exertion? We were awakened, enlightened, and refined by the Greek and Latin classics, circulated through the introduction of the art of printing. Nor is it any wonder, that for some time a critical acquaintance with their writings usurped almost exclusively the name of learning; or that scholars, in their admiration of the beauties of classical antiquity, conceived at first that the whole of human knowledge was comprehended in their works. But hence certainly proceeded the original stimulus, which has issued in the present advanced state of the sciences and arts.

There might appear therefore some degree of ingratitude in our now consigning to neglect those classics, to whom our literary obligations are so great. And perhaps there is an equal degree of presumption in the supposition, that we have nothing more to learn from them.

I know that the ancients are commonly decried as children in science; because, charmed with the attractions of *abstract* science, they certainly did neglect experiment, and undervalued the practical applications of scientific principle. Yet—even here—such various instances stand on record of their skill in mechanics and other arts, which promote the conveniences of polished life, as prove they were not such children, as many represent them. And it might abate the pride of modern knowledge, to observe how much we are indebted to *accident*, for the discovery of many of those instruments, which have made us superior to the ancients in some branches of knowledge.

But I shall yield to the adversaries of classical learning every advantage, in the argument, which they can desire. I shall suppose, that every thing valuable in the writers of Greece and Rome has been either transfused into the works of the moderns, or is accessible to the mere English reader in translations: that we are in full and permanent possession of all the information they contain in mathematics, logic, and astronomy,—in history, geography, and criticism. I shall suppose, that no more treasures of antiquity remain, to be brought to light, in all those inedited manuscripts, which—to the disgrace of literary Europe—still continue unexplored. Nay, I shall suppose that our orators and poets are as successful rivals of the ancients, as the worst of them in his ignorance and vanity can imagine.

Nor shall I insist upon that consideration, which must ever stamp classical learning with paramount importance, in the view of all the friends of Revelation;—upon the connexion between sound theology and a critical interpretation of the dead languages;—or upon the degree, in which their extinction must shake all historic evidence, and in this affect the very foundation of revealed truth.

Let that consequence also be supposed as desirable, as it may secretly appear to some. Let every thing, which they can demand, be conceded to those who think that the classics ought to fall into oblivion and neglect. Yet I hope to prove, that the cultivation of classical learning, as a constituent part of liberal education,—so far from obstructing science,—is most importantly conducive to its advancement; that they have common interests, and common adversaries; and that the progress of scientific learning is materially impeded by the declining state of classical.

There is no argument more frequently employed by the declaimers against classical learning, than that it is absurd to devote so many years, in the spring-time of life, to the study of *words*;—words, which the wise man uses but as counters, while the fool alone values them as money. But this argument, with all the changes that are rung upon it, proceeds upon multiplied mistakes; and exemplifies the abuse of words, which it professes to decry. The argument might have conclusive force, if languages were but vocabularies of unmeaning sounds. But, in learning languages, does not the youthful mind learn ideas too? Is not its stock of these materials of knowledge progressively enlarged? Are not its powers exercised in comparing, discriminating, and combining ideas? And ought not this to be the first object of liberal education?

I speak not now of the knowledge of *things*, acquired in the perusal of the Greek and Roman classics. I speak not of the acquaintance, to which it introduces us, with the facts, the manners, the characters, the sentiments of ancient times. I speak of the initiatory exercises of grammar and of syntax: and, at the early age which ought to be allotted to these, I maintain that there is no intellectual exercise better calculated to furnish the elements of thought, to fix the attention, to call forth the latent powers of the understanding, and to employ—without overstraining—its most important energies.

Indeed, the connexion between language and thought is much more intimate, than superficial inquirers imagine. Language is allowed by all to be the great vehicle, by which thoughts are communicated: and in this view alone, the importance of an accurate acquaintance with language is incalculable. But many are not aware, that it is also the great *instrument*—if I may be allowed the expression—of thought; that every man thinks in language, even when he thinks in privacy and utters not a word.

If there be any subject of human reason, in which the mind can exercise its powers independently of language, it may be supposed to be geometry. But let any man, most familiar with a geometrical demonstration, endeavour to present it, in all its steps, to his own mind divested of words; and he will find himself baffled in the attempt. Nor is it unreasonable to suppose, that—if words alone could be totally effaced from the recollection—the mind, though retaining all its other acquisitions, would retain them to no effectual purpose, but would be reduced to a state of infantile imbecility. With so much is it of philosophic justice, that in the Greek tongue the same term, which expresses a *word*, expresses also the *reasoning* faculty.—But alas! though we cannot think without employing words, we may employ words without thinking. Were it not so, many would be tongue-tied, who are now most voluble in decrying the wisdom of our forefathers.

In scientific pursuits, no mental habit is of more importance, than a readiness in examining the closeness of our own reasoning, and a quickness in detecting any latent vagueness or inaccuracy of conception. And nothing promotes this habit, more than an early acquaintance with the accurate analysis of language. Any defect of correctness in thinking is betrayed most immediately by the perplexity, or want of clearness and precision, in the expressions which embody our thoughts. And hence it is, that—as all real scholars, who have been engaged in *teaching*, must have experienced—many a man has conceived himself to possess a perfect knowledge of scientific principles, till he came to express himself on the subject to others: but then has discovered that his conceptions have been erroneous, inaccurate, or obscure. By the person unacquainted with the structure of language, and unaccustomed to examine it strictly, this evidence of defective reasoning is commonly overlooked; and he rests at once in thoughts without precision, and expressions without distinct meaning.

Let me not be understood as saying, that the skilful *linguist* must also be of course a sound reasoner. He may possess inferior powers of natural understanding: and if a mere linguist, whatever be his intellectual powers, he has neglected to exercise and invigorate them by scientific studies. But I do say, that the highest genius labours under the most considerable disadvantage in science, if not skilled in language: and that the intellect of a BACON or a NEWTON could not be supposed—under such a disadvantage—to have produced the works which immortalize their names.

Yet let not the mere linguist be despised, as a useless trifler in the field of literature. That field is so spacious, that all parts of it cannot be occupied by the same person; and to be cultivated with general advantage, some spots must receive the undivided attention of certain individuals. The objects of human knowledge are so numerous, and there subsists such a mutual subserviency of each to all, that literary labour must be divided: and none but the superficial observer will lament the minuteness of the portion, which engrosses the attention of some; or laugh at the ardour, with which they prosecute the investigation of apparently unimportant objects. That very ardour of individual research, however disproportionate—even really disproportionate—to the objects which excite it, contributes to the increase and perfection of the common stock; and often gives employment to a mind, which would otherwise be idle.

I wish also the friends of science to give their special attention to this fact:—that the same men, who decry the study of the dead languages as a useless waste of mental exertion,—as the unprofitable study of words instead of things,—are also the most forward to point their shafts of ridicule against such *scientific* pursuits, as present no obvious utility to the optics of these arbiters of literature. The same flippancy of presumptuous ignorance, that laughs at a learned disquisition upon Greek accents, is equally prompt to deride the ardour of the naturalist in hunting butterflies, in exploring the varieties of a moss, or collecting specimens of rude stones. Nay, a Newton, examining the colours of a bubble, or demonstrating the properties of a crooked line, would be screened—if screened—from their sneers, only by the celebrity of his name.

It certainly is not peculiar to this age, that the ignorant vulgar should despise what they do not understand. But the magisterial arrogance of the ignorant vulgar does seem to me a characteristic feature of the present times. Such are now writers, orators, philosophers, correctors of old prejudices, discoverers of new systems, enlightening and instructing the world. Such, with the brazen front of self-satisfied folly, put themselves forward as wiser than the wisest of the ancient: and by the very boldness of their pretensions are often too successful, in imposing their crudest absurdities on the public. But such are the common enemies of literature; whom all its friends should combine together to repress.

Nor let any of its friends imagine, that they have no cause to be alarmed, because it is not *their* province which is immediately invaded, but one perhaps of which they—from unacquaintance with it—have overlooked the importance. We have already remarked, that between the several departments in the great commonwealth of literature there is such a community of interest, such a reciprocal dependence and mutual connexion, that even the smallest cannot be destroyed without danger to every other. In time of peace from foreign foes, the competitions of its different members may but contribute to that activity of diversified pursuit, which shall prove conducive to the general good:—provided such a sovereign control be maintained over their petty emulations, that no individuals shall be allowed to aggrandize themselves by the depression of their neighbours. But when any part of the state is invaded by a barbarous enemy, the danger is common to all; and all ought to forget their mutual differences in the common interest of repelling it.

There is a sentiment, which I am sorry to observe obtains increasing currency even among men of cultivated minds,—that knowledge is to be valued only as far as it is practically useful; and that its practical utility is to be measured by its subserviency to the common purposes of life. This sentiment—in the form and extent in which it is frequently maintained—appears to me derogatory to the dignity of the human mind; and to degrade man from the rank of an intellectual being, to that of a creature merely corporeal, and capable only of animal enjoyments. Nay, as held by many, it seems little different from the sordid feeling—that nothing is worth more than the *money* which it will bring. To this commercial principle a commercial nation perhaps has a natural tendency: but it is a principle most unfavourable to all sciences and arts, however it may seem for a time to cherish some of them.

I would be far from undervaluing the beneficial results of science, in improving the arts, and increasing the conveniencies—or even the luxuries,—of civil life. I can smile at the excess of philosophic dignity in Archimedes,* who felt as if he degraded mathematics in condescending to fabricate machines for his royal relative. I view with admiration the advancement of navigation by the perfection of the lunar tables; the economizing of human labour by the invention of the steam-engine; and the various other instances, in which the triumphant discoveries of science have been extended, from the study of the philosopher to the palace of the king and the cottage of the peasant. But I confess that I retain so much of the feelings of the old school, as to conceive that knowledge possesses still stronger claims on our estimation; that the improvement of our fortunes, our habitations, our clothing, and our food, is not its highest recommendation; and that the enlargement of our views, the rectification of our judgment, and the refinement of our intellectual taste, constitute its chief value; a value—not cognizable, indeed, except by its possessors—yet as much superior to the former, as the rational and imperishable mind is pre-eminent above the body. The man who pursues science only, or chiefly, for the sake of those beneficial results, which she occasionally affords, is not among her real votaries. He may be an artist, but is not a philosopher: and for the highest improvements of the arts themselves he must still be indebted to those —her more disinterested admirers,—whose ardour is excited by the abstract charms, which he disesteems.

Nor let me be charged with digressing in these observations from

* — *πᾶσαν ὅλως τέχνην χρείας ἐφαπτομένην ἀγεννῆ καὶ βάναυσον ἡγησάμενος.* Plut. in Marcell.

the question which I have proposed to discuss. The intimate connexion between the interests of science and of polite literature may be more clearly discerned, when we observe, that not only the same characters are hostile to both, but that the same principles of argument, by which they attempt to decry the one, are equally pointed against the other. No topic of declamation is more frequently employed against classical learning, than the question—*cui bono!* *What is the use*, say they, *of spending so much time and pains in learning dead languages? To what practical purpose can the knowledge afterwards be turned?* The narrow view which these men take of practical utility, is confined within the circle of pecuniary advantages and corporeal enjoyments: and their objection equally tends to overturn the very foundation of science, and to bring back a dark night of unlettered barbarism. For, let it be once established, that science is to be prosecuted no further, than as it is applicable to the purposes of common life; and the very first principles of science will be soon forgotten.

The man, who would despise the demonstrative calculation of the velocity of light from the aberration of the fixed stars, unless he were assured that it might be turned to some practical use;—the man, who would suspend his admiration of the splendid discoveries in modern chemistry, till he should see that they afford some profitable results;—the man, who would prefer the discovery of a dye for improving the colour of cloth, to that noble stretch of ingenious speculation, which connects the phenomena of the solar spectrum with voltaic electricity;—that man has a servile and sordid mind: and it would be a degradation of literature to admit the justice of his principles, by telling him that benefits, the most important, have accrued to society from scientific sources apparently the most remote. This reply, however confessedly true, would seem to abandon the intrinsic excellence of knowledge; would seem to surrender the strong vantage ground, on which her claims to our regard must ever stand,—as distinguishing men from the rest of the animal creation, and raising him in the scale of intellectual being. On that impregnable ground we may always maintain the unvaried dignity and importance of universal literature and science.

The keenest adversaries of the dead languages are often, with strange inconsistency, warm advocates for learning the living languages of foreign countries. A knowledge of French and Italian is reckoned a necessary part even of female education. Yet few comparatively in these countries have actual occasion, in future life, either to speak or write in French or in Italian: and still fewer, after jabbering them in their youth for years, are able to speak or to write in these languages with accuracy and elegance. It must be supposed therefore that the main advantage, which recommends them to these patrons of *useful* education, is this;—that they introduce us to an acquaintance with the writers and literary productions of foreign countries. And I readily admit that this is an important object; while I lament that the class of continental writers, most generally obtruded on our acquaintance, is of a description either worthless or pernicious. But what judge of literary excellence will compare the productions of modern Europe with those standards of composition, which the poets, orators, philosophers, and historians of ancient Greece and Rome afford us? Their works are the great storehouse from which every thing of correct taste in the beautiful and sublime has been derived: and among the writers of modern times, they have made the nearest approaches to perfection, who have formed themselves most studiously upon the unrivalled models of antiquity. What modern language, indeed, on a comparison with the Greek—or even with the Latin tongue, must not yield the palm! Which of them must not be owned inferior, in the combined characters of brevity and copiousness of expression, in elegance, and force, and harmony of varied structure? Let it also be observed, that Latin is the common basis of most European languages; and that the classical scholar can find no difficulty in mastering any of these, at any time, by the application of a few months: while it is rare to find, and hard indeed to conceive, any one ignorant of the classics, and at the same time critically acquainted with his mother-tongue.

In short, if the knowledge of French, Italian, &c. extend our literary citizenship to other countries than our own; an acquaintance with the languages of ancient Greece and Rome at once infinitely facilitates the former acquirement,—opens to us the original and richer sources of literature,—and connects us by a kind of co-existence with past ages. Let classical learning become extinct, and we become inhabitants of a younger world, to which the experience, the wisdom, and the wit of ancient times are effectually lost. Let the popular objection be admitted against classical learning, as a thing of little practical benefit; and the very citadel—not only of polite literature—but of science, is surrendered to a barbarous foe.

But some may say—"We are not enemies to polite literature; nor do we desire that classical learning should become extinct. But is it not put out of place, in being made the chief, or sole, object of liberal education in our schools?" My design is not to defend, in all respects, the present system of school education; and I shall hereafter point out some particulars, in which it appears to me defective, injurious, and absurd. But I confess that I prefer it, with all its present defects, to any pretended reformation, which would displace classical learning from the rank of a constituent—and principal—part of all liberal education.

If education be conducted aright, it must commence at a very early age. And if, at a still earlier age, that preparatory control has been maintained over the child, which is needful for subjecting it to discipline and habits of attention; the subsequent course of instruction may proceed—not only without trenching at all upon youthful enjoyments—but so as to promote them considerably. Far, indeed, would I be from abridging the exercise or amusements of childhood. But no mistake can be greater, than the supposition that absolute idleness promotes, or is consistent with the true enjoyment of life, either in man or child. Few states are more wretched, than the void of listless satiety, in which the mind—wearied of pleasure—preys upon itself, and knows not where to turn for employment. If you would bring up a child for the sole object of *pleasurable* existaence, form in that child early habits of submission to control, and of application to business.

It is not then unreasonable to suppose, that the child at eight years of age is so far acquainted with his mother tongue, as to be able to read it with correctness and facility, and to know some of the principles of general grammar. Now I ask, in what branch of study can he be employed more profitably, from that period till the age of fourteen, than in the study of the Greek and Latin tongues? Childhood is peculiarly the age for learning the elements of languages. The elements of languages can at that time be effectually taught; and in acquiring the knowledge of them, the youthful mind is exercised, and cultivated, and stored with ideas, and trained to skill in using an instrument the most extensively important, whatever be the future objects to which the attention may be directed;—the most important in its connexion both with accurate thinking, and with the clear and elegant communication of our thoughts. The moderate, but regular application of two hours a day, under a proper method of instruction, would be sufficient—I am bold to assert—for conveying to the child, during the period which I have specified, such a knowledge of the languages of Greece and Rome, as would render the further study of their writers a matter of elegant enjoyment to his ripening taste, and delightful improvement to his maturer judgment.

But if we exclude the classics from the general system of liberal education, what can we effect during the same period in the cultivation of science? Shall we proceed to make the child of eight years old a philosopher? Yes; I am aware that some of our modern reformers conceive the notion, of teaching children *geometry*, and *astronomy*, and *chemistry*, and *geology*, and I know not what.* But it is a preposterous and cruel notion, founded in ignorance—both of the human mind—and of the sciences, which these smatterers in literature profess to patronize. We must wait for the progress of nature to develope and strengthen the intellectual powers; and if we attempt by injudicious culture to force the fruit of science, we can at most obtain a production crude and noxious; and we bid fair to destroy the mental faculties by overstraining them.

Others there are, who would avoid this error by letting the child *run wild* to the age of puberty: and the eloquent, but visionary, Rousseau has employed all the fascinations of language and fancy, to recommend this system—of *leaving the intellectual faculties inactive as long as possible*, that they may at length be called to the most effectual exercise. According to this theory, "if we could but bring up our pupil healthy and robust to the age of twelve years, without his being able to distinguish his right hand from his left, the eyes of his understanding would be open to reason at our first lesson; and he would become under proper instructions the wisest of men." If this were so, what a rare philosopher might have been formed out of the savage of AVEYRON!

I formerly knew a gentleman, who followed Rousseau's plan in bringing up his son. I very early warned him of the probable result;

* See Note A. at the end.

and had afterwards abundant opportunities of seeing my predictions verified. The youth,—who seemed to labour under no inferiority of natural understanding, and had grown up to the age of twelve or thirteen without knowing even his letters,—when an attempt was afterwards made to educate him, proved wholly unequal to the attention and mental exercise requisite in abstract reasoning. I saw him once brought, by great exertion, to perceive the inference—that two lines, of which one was neither greater nor less than the other, must be equal. I believe it was the first rational inference, the force of which he ever discerned; and I believe it was the last. Having succeeded in producing any motion in the wheels of the intellectual machine, I entertained a hope that they might receive a continued progressive impulse. But I soon perceived, that his mind—as if exhausted by the effort—sunk back to its former state of motionless inactivity.

Indeed it is hard to say, which is most injurious to the intellect of children, the total neglect of early culture, or a culture excessive in degree, and ill-adapted in its kind to the tenderness of early life. As the latter exhausts the soil, and produces a growth as unhealthy and ill-formed, as it is premature; so the general consequence of the former is a rigidness of texture, which defies future cultivation. And it is worthy of observation, that the study of *languages* is that to which the mind in very early childhood appears most competent; which—in its first elements—exercises the attention and the memory, while—in the progress of interpretation—it employs thought, calls forth the ingenuity of research, multiplies the ideas, enlarges the views, informs the judgment, and refines the taste.

But let it also be observed, that the time, which I propose allotting to the acquisition of the learned languages, can by no means interfere with any other objects, which may be supposed suited to the age of childhood. For the prosecution of other studies, one or two hours more in each day, during the same period, would be found amply sufficient: and during childhood, I would never extend the time of application to business beyond four hours in the day. Writing, English reading, History, Geography, and Chronology (as far as connected with the two latter)—one or more of these I suppose to form part of the daily employment: while some of them may be taught in such a form, as will contribute to the amusement and relaxation of the pupil. In the course also of English reading, a considerable acquaintance with facts in Natural History may be formed: and I am aware, that under proper masters a child may—in his walks—be usefully led to distinguish various objects in the vegetable and mineral kingdoms; so far, at least, as to be familiar with the leading characters of the principal classes. Yet I confess that I value these acquirements, at the early period of which I speak, rather as calculated to awaken a spirit of accurate and attentive observation, than for the immediate information which they convey.

But there is one branch of science,—science strictly so called—the elements of which I am persuaded are level to the capacity of a child; and I consider the neglect of it as a great and lamentable defect, in our system of liberal education. I mean ARITHMETIC :—not that art of technical calculation, which commonly goes under the name:—but the science of numbers, considered as a branch of Mathematics. I know not any class of ideas, with which the mind may be sooner made familiar, than those of *number:* nor any, about which it may sooner be engaged, with much advantage, in close reasoning. The thing taught as Arithmetic, in mercantile schools, is unworthy of the name of SCIENCE; and even to this, in classical schools, little or no attention is paid: which, I am convinced, is the reason, why so many students in the University find insuperable difficulties in Geometry and Analytics. If I might presume to suggest a hint to the heads of that learned body, I would say that the remedy of this evil might well deserve their consideration; and that it might be remedied, by their introducing into the schools a system of scientific Arithmetic, which should combine familiarity of illustration with a method strictly demonstrative. The use of such a treatise might easily be enforced in the classical schools, by their including it in the course of examination requisite for admission into College.

The mention of this leads me to not the most grateful part of my subject;—to point out some other particulars, in which the present system of classical education does seem to me to impede the progress of science and of general literature. This is an ungrateful task; in which nothing but the paramount consideration of public utility could induce me to engage. But most of the particulars, which I shall notice, are such as admit an easy remedy; and are but the accidental imperfections of a system, which I value as radically good, and would lament to see displaced by any of the visionary theories of modern reformers.

The first evil I would mark is—the extravagant length of time in each day, for which children are kept in school. I leave it to the medical profession to determine, how far so much confinement is consistent with the health and vigour of their bodies. The objections which I advance against it are two: 1st. that it tends to give them a distaste to study,—a relish for which it ought to be one great object of liberal education to form: 2dly. that it promotes a habit of mental indolence and inattention during the periods of study,—than which no habit is more unfavourable to literary progress. The child cannot, in the nature of things, have his mind actively engaged for so many hours, as he is obliged to have his books and papers before him. But he must in general *seem* to be engaged; and he therefore lounges, and dreams over his books and papers. Half the time, or less, would be sufficient to finish his assigned task; but, from this very circumstance, he is often led to give no real application to it from first to last. It may perhaps be more easy to point out this evil, than to find a remedy for it, as long as that observation of the Roman Satyrist shall remain true—*res nulla minoris constabit patri, quam filius.* But parents may be assured, that their children might make much greater progress in literature, if the time they nominally spend in study were much less.

Another evil, connected with the former, though apparently of an opposite nature, is—the number of holidays, so called, and the length of vacations, which boys are allowed in most schools. This contributes to impress on their minds the sentiment, that absolute idleness is enjoyment;—a sentiment as unfounded in truth, as it is pernicious in its influence on the future habits. It besides accustoms them to that kind of desultory application, by fits and starts, which never can supply the place of regular diligence. A course of uniform—daily study, attentively pursued, and therefore moderately continued,—is that which alone can insure effectual progress; and that which—so far from impeding—promotes enjoyment.

I have now to notice the comparative inefficiency of our school-education, for communicating a real and manly acquaintance with the languages of Greece and Rome. And in stating this, and proceeding to assign one of the obvious causes of it, I do not really depart from the subject of this Essay. The imperfectness of school-education is most unfavourable to the success of Collegiate; and too much diverts the latter from that which ought to be its principal object—science, to that which cannot be taught effectually in College—the learned languages. I by no means intend that they should not, as they do, form a considerable part of Collegiate exercises. But I conceive that the student, passing from school to College, ought to possess such a radical acquaintance with Greek and Latin, as would render his further prosecution of the Classics rather a literary relaxation, than a laborious and ungrateful task. Now, on the contrary, it commonly happens, that he is so occupied with the drudgery of classical preparation throughout his collegiate course, that he has little attention to spare for the sciences; and looks forward with impatience to the close of his Academic studies, as the period when he shall be released from the irksome necessity of studying at all.

For the defectiveness of our present system of school-education various causes might be assigned; and among them, some general errors in the methods of teaching employed. But I shall confine myself to one cause, which I believe is little noticed; while its existence is certain, and its influence most injurious. I mean the total want of proper books, for teaching the learned languages. I speak not now of the absurdities of the common Grammars and Dictionaries. I speak of the editions of the Classics used in our schools: and I denounce them, with very few exceptions, as scandalous to a country professing literature.

In the first place, they are printed with so much typographical inaccuracy, as to be in many passages unintelligible even to a scholar; while they often present, in almost every page, difficulties utterly insuperable to a schoolboy. The last edition published in this city of the selection of Lucian's Dialogues, which is read in schools, and the only edition now to be obtained in this country, exhibits in the first Dialogue (containing about one duodecimo page of Greek) no fewer than nine gross errors of the press: and a similar imputation, though not in equal degree, lies against almost every other schoolbook, printed either in this country or in Great Britain. This indeed is but the natural effect of their being left, as a matter of trade, to illiterate printers. Each subsequent edition retains all the errors of the former; and creates at least an equal number of its own.

I remember once asking an old schoolmaster, how he managed with such copies. "I will tell you," said he, "how we manage. When the poor boy comes to one of these errors of the press, he spends half an hour puzzling his brains, and searching his dictionary for a word which is no where to be found. When all has failed, he comes blubbering to me, with a declaration of his inability to make out the passage: and then I send him away with—*Pugh, you blockhead! it is an error of the press; and ought to be so or so.*"—Is it thus, that the time and mental energy of an ingenuous youth ought to be employed? In fact, there are few books, in which typographical accuracy of execution is of so much importance, as in those designed for the use of schools; and there are none, in which it so much neglected.

But besides this objection to them, most of them are intrinsically unfit for their professed purpose. Among these I must reckon all, in which the notes are written in the language to be learned; instead of being written in that, which is most intelligible to the scholar. I know, that—in saying this—I have to combat with a considerable force of old prejudice. Many still insist upon the usefulness of obliging schoolboys to read Latin notes. "It familiarizes them with the language: and the very difficulty, with which they obtain the information in the note, imprints the information more deeply."—Now the fact is, that not one schoolboy in ten thinks of taking the trouble to read any length of Latin annotation. But if they did, —and if the notes were written in purer Latinity than they often are, —might not the time thus spent be more profitably employed, in reading a greater quantity of original Latin writers? And does not common sense dictate, that the explanation, or illustration, or remark, which the note is intended to convey, ought to be made easily accessible, and conveyed in the clearest form to the learner? It is quite time for the friends of classical learning, to abandon some of the absurdities, with which the study of it has been embarrassed.

But I have objections as decisive against the matter, as against the form of the annotations, in most of the Classics read in schools. They are defective, and redundant, and grossly erroneous. As to the Latin classics, those published *in usum Delphini* are almost exclusively employed: and I venture to assert, that the editors of these—with few exceptions—were fitter to be at school themselves, than to publish books for the use of schools. As this assertion may be thought to require proof, I shall adduce in a note* a few instances of their ignorance, from *De La Rue's* edition of Virgil,—the first of the Latin poets to which the schoolboy is introduced,—and from *Crispin's* edition of Sallust, the only prose writer in the language, which he is required to read previous to his entrance into College. The number of instances it would be more easy to enlarge, than to exhaust. But I conceive the specimens I have noted are quite sufficient, to mark the character of these editions as beneath criticism; and to mark also the low state and lamentable neglect of classical learning in a country, where such books continue to be employed—year after year—for teaching boys to misinterpret Latin. It is a

* See Note B. at the end.

great mistake to suppose, that any largeness of pecuniary endowments, allotted to the advancement of literature,—(and they are in this island liberal)—is sufficient for the object; unless their application be actively superintended by literary men.

As to the Greek Classics read in schools, the character of their editions is not quite so contemptible: for it happened fortunately that *Greek* Classics were not published *in usum Delphini*. Yet even of these, I know not one fitted for the purpose. The selection from Lucian, to which I have already referred, has the notes indeed in English: but the editor possessed no critical acquaintance with the language, has adopted a text the most vicious, and has fallen into perplexities and mistakes the most ridiculous;*—while the vulgarity of his attempts at humour must disgust any reader of taste.

Of HOMER—venerable, wonderful, HOMER!—the only edition used is Doctor Clarke's; a man who deserved well of literature. But it is well known, that this is a posthumous work of that editor, left by him incomplete, and never designed by him for the use of schools. This edition has gone through perhaps more than twenty reimpressions; while it is every time republished with all its imperfections and all its errors;† and this, although it would be just as easy, and just as cheap, to reprint ERNESTI'S revision of the work, in which many of these errors are corrected. Many others indeed remain, as must be well known to those, who are acquainted with the invaluable Lexicon of the laborious DAMM, and the edition of the book-making, but literary HEYNE. And why—let me be allowed to ask—why should mistakes be perpetuated in our schools, which have been for half a century exposed and rectified in the learned world? Do not such facts evince, beyond contradiction, the neglect of classical learning? And does not such neglect account for the general deficiency of progress in it among our youth, notwithstanding the length of time which is devoted to the study?

Nor is this to be remedied, by attempting to make them all *Latin poets*,—to enforce the composition of verses in a dead language. The attempt, though such a favourite one in the sister island, has always appeared to me a ridiculous waste of time. There really are not so many, who can write *poetry* even in their mother tongue;—though all now write *verses*. It is very well, that encouragement should be held out to any, whose taste leads them to cultivate this exercise. But the structure of classic verse, and an accurate acquaintance with quantity, may be attained, as efficiently, with much less trouble.

To promote the great object, a sound and critical interpretation of the Greek and Latin Classics,—completely new editions of them all are wanted; and these, furnished with critical *Indices Græcitatis et Latinitatis*,‡ in order to supply the defects of the common Lexicons.

* See Note C. at the end. † See Note D.

‡ These are the more needful in the Greek Classics, because at least three-fourths of the Students, who enter College, possess no Lexicon but *Schrevelius's*;—a bad Lexicon for Homer and the Greek Testament, but not designed for any other book. Such *indices* also, accompanying the Greek Classics, would more than any thing else facilitate, what is so much wanted,—a new and improved Edition of STEPHENS'S THESAURUS.

Never also should they be destitute of that class of annotation, which is calculated to form the taste of the youthful student, to regulate his judgment, and to excite his attention to the elegances of classic structure, and his admiration of the beauties of classic composition.

In such a well-directed and regular application to classical studies, let the age of boyhood be passed; and in other such pursuits, as are adapted to a boy. And at the age of sixteen,—the very earliest, assuredly, at which any ought to enter the University,—the youth will come to his collegiate studies with a mind so furnished,—with faculties so invigorated and enlarged,—with powers of combining and discriminating his ideas so exercised,—that his literary progress shall be insured; and multiplied experience shall satisfactorily decide the question—*Whether the cultivation of science and that of polite literature assist or obstruct each other*.

NOTES.

(A.) page 658.

The curious reader may find this absurdity notably exemplified, in the Monthly Review for August, 1796, pp. 456 and 457. The article is a review of—*An Essay on an Analytical Course of Studies, containing a complete System of Human Knowledge*. By J. B. Florian; A. M.—It announces a new system of general education, which the Reviewers tell us "may deservedly claim the attention of the public, as well adapted to furnish a regular series of instruction in the principal branches of natural knowledge, in the room of that NARROW plan of education which has devoted eight or ten precious years of early life to the mere acquisition of *dead languages*."

"Mr. Florian," they proceed, "lays down precisely the business of each year, from the 7th to the 17th, as follows."—The whole is a choice *morceau*, which will amply repay the trouble of turning to the passage. But the *sciences* of the 4th and 7th years may serve as a specimen to those, who have not the work at hand.

"Fourth year. *Astronomy. Mechanics. Dialing.*

"Seventh year. *Anatomy. Theory of Surgery, of Medicine, and Pharmacy. Pneumatology. Physiognomy.*"—*Augur, schœnobates, medicus, magus: omna novit.*—But Juvenal's Grecian was a fool to Mr. Florian's schoolboy.

Latin is mentioned, as part of the business in the three *last* years. But as to Greek—*Græcum est: non legitur*. In place of it, however,

"*Politics* and *Political Economy*" are introduced: and an ample share of attention is given to *Music, Dancing*, &c. Now which of the good citizens of Bath, (where Mr. F. was about to open an Academy, for "carrying this plan into execution") would not rather see his boy a fiddling, capering statesman, with the combined accomplishments of a Surgeon, Physician, Apothecary, Physiognomist, &c. &c. &c. than cramp his genius by the *narrow plan* of studying the *dead languages*? Accordingly, the Reviewers—(blessed guardians of literature)—conclude the article with observing, "that the undertaking seems to promise *considerable utility* to the public." Who can doubt it?

(B.) page 662.

Virg. l. 7. Æn. v. 154.—*ramis* velatos *Palladis omnes.*—Interpreted—*omnes* coronatos *ramis Minervæ.*

v. 236.—*ne temne, quod* ultro *Præferimus manibus vittas*, &c.—Interpreted—*quia* sponte *portamus*, &c.

v. 413.—*et nunc magnum manet Ardea nomen. Sed* fortuna fuit. —Interpreted—*Sed* casus ita tulit—with the following critical note. *Vel ad superiora refertur;* Fortuna casusque fuit, ut nomen urbi tamdiu remanserit, &c. *Vel ad subsequentia;* Fortuna casusque fuit, quod Turnus tum dormiebat, &c.

v. 634.—*alii thoracas ahenos, Aut leves ocreas lento* ducunt argento. —Interpreted—*alii* excudunt *loricas æreas, vel politas ocreas argento flexili.* It is well that Ruæus is not an *Irish* name.

Let one more instance suffice of this Editor's learning. That passage in the 8th book, v. 408. *cum femina primum, Cui tolerare colo vitam tenuique Minervâ Impositum, cinerem et sopitos suscitat ignes*, &c. is thus exhibited—*ad usum Serenissimi Delphini*—

> —*cum femina, primum*
> *Cui tolerare colo vitam tenuique Minervâ,*
> *Impositum cinerem et sopitos suscitat ignes*, &c.

—And thus interpreted—*quando mulier, cui* præcipuum *est sustentare vitam colo et exiguâ arte, excitat ignem coopertum et cinerem* superadditum igni.

Now for Crispin—

Sall. Bell. Cat. c. 18.—*prohibitus erat consulatum petere, quod intra legitimos dies* profiteri *nequiverit.* Note—*Profiteri*] *Defensionem suam et expurgationem, scilicet.*

Bell. Jug. c. 4.—*At contra, quis est omnium* his moribus, *quin divitiis et sumptibus, non probitate neque industriâ, cum majoribus suis contendat?*—Interpreted—*Quis omnium ita vivit?*

c. v.—*Bello Punico secundo, quo dux Carthaginiensum Hannibal,* post magnitudinem nominis Romani, *Italiæ opes maxume attriverat:* &c. Note—*Post magnitudinem*] *Id est,* non contentus Romanorum gloriam proculcasse.

c. 35.—*Huic Sp. Albinus . . . persuadet, quoniam ex stirpe Masinissæ sit,* Jugurtham ob scelera invidiâ [invidia] cum metu urgeat; *regnum Numidiæ ab senatu petat.* Note—*Metu*] *Id est,* invidiâ et metu.

Arbitror verò intelligendum esse de metu Romanæ plebis, ut aliquando etiam contra se ipsa auxurum Jugurtham credat scelera sua convertere.

Ecce iterum Crispinus—once more, and I have done. Sallust (Bell. Jug. c. 45.) describing the strictness of discipline, which Metellus restored in the Roman army, says—*ceteris* arte *modum statuisse*: upon which we have the following sagacious note. Arte] *Eá opus est omnino, eâque maximè in ejusmodi occasionibus. Quá verò in re sita sit, vix ullus dixerit: ita sunt, aut certè videntur, exigui momenti innumera quæ ad id concurrunt.*

Although this be the edition most commonly used, yet it must be confessed that the two other editions of Sallust are accessible to boys in this country. One of these, however, might rank with the Dauphin's: and the other, (by *Mair*) though of a more respectable character, is accompanied with a literal English translation, by the side of the text.

(C.) page 663.

If the classical reader will turn to any of the following passages, he may satisfy himself by reading Mr. Murphy's notes upon them, that I have not underrated this edition. *Necyomantia*.§. 12. ἐπεψήφισαν μὲν αἱ ἀρχαὶ.—*Charon*.§. 4. Ὡς ὁ Ποσειδῶν συνήγαγε, &c.—ib. ἐκ τοσούτου ἱματίου ὀλίγα γοῦν διαφυλάττειν.—*Somnium Luciani*. §. 6. ὧδε γὰρ ὁ Ξενοφῶν, &c.—*Concio Deorum*, §. 2 ὅτι τὴν μίτραν.—*Timon*. §. 5. Τοῦ τε γὰρ Τίμωνος.—ib. §. 9. Μὴ κέκραχθι.

(D.) page 663.

The following are a few specimens of the errors of interpretation, which occur in the first twelve books of the Iliad.

Il. Α. v. 284. αὐτὰρ ἔγωγε Λίσσομ' Ἀχιλλῆϊ μεθέμεν χόλον. *verum ego* Precabor Achillem *deponere iram*.

Β. 99. ἐρήτυθεν δὲ καθ᾽ ἕδρας. [καθ' ἕδρας.] *tenebantque sedes*; and again in v. 211.

Δ. v. 472. ἀνὴρ δ' ἄνδρ' ἐδνοπάλιζεν. *virque virum manu occidebat.*

Ε. v. 150. Τοῖς οὐκ ἐρχομένοις ὁ γέρων ἐκρίνατ' ὀνείρους. *Quibus non, ad bellum proficiscentibus, senex interpretatus est somnia.*

Ib. v. 844. Τὸν μὲν Ἄρης ἐνάριζε. *Hunc utique Mars occidebat.* (See vv. 843. 847. and 848.)

Μ. v. 139. Ἄσιον ἀμφὶ ἄνακτα, &c. *Asium circa regem*, &c.

Ib. v. 152. Ἄντην βαλλομένων. *Hinc illinc percussorum.*

Ib. v. 172. πρίν γ' ἠὲ κατακτάμεν, ἠὲ ἁλῶναι. *antequam vel* interficiantur, *vel* capiantur. (See Γ. v. 379. This mistake is the more extraordinary, because Wetstein's version, which Clarke quotes and condemns in a note, is perfectly right; except that ἁλῶναι should be rendered by *interficiantur*, not *capiantur*.)

Ib. v. 446. λᾶαν φέρεν ὅς . . . πρυμνὸς, παχὺς, [πρυμνὸς παχὺς,] αὐτὰρ ὕπερθεν Ὀξὺς ἔην. *extremus, crassus.*

It may be remarked that the Latin translation in Heyne's edition also abounds with inaccuracies; and this, even in passages, which he has rightly interpreted in his notes.

HYMNS.

HYMN

COMPOSED FOR THE OPENING

OF

BETHESDA CHAPEL, DUBLIN.

June 22, 1794.

I.

Thou God of pow'r, and God of love!
Whose glory fills the realms above,
  Whose praise archangels sing,
And veil their faces, while they cry
"Thrice holy!" to their God most high,
  "Thrice holy!" to their king.

II.

We too, poor worms of earth, would join
In work and worship so divine;
  O! deign to bow thine ear,
And send a ray of heavenly light
To scatter all our nature's night,
  And in our midst appear.

III.

Thee as our God we too would claim,
And bless the Saviour's precious name,
  Thro' whom this grace is giv'n,
Who bore the curse to sinners due,
And forms their ruin'd souls anew,
  And makes them heirs of heav'n.

IV.

The veil that hides thy glory rend,
And here in saving pow'r descend,
Here fix thy bless'd abode;
Here to each heart thyself reveal,
And all who enter cause to feel
The presence of our God.

V.

Here let thy Spirit's voice proclaim
The glories of IMMANUEL'S name—
The LORD in whom we live;
"GOD the REDEEMER!" strong to save
From sin, from Satan, and the grave,
And waiting to forgive.

VI.

The dead shall hear thy quick'ning voice,
And mourners in the sound rejoice,
And learn celestial strains;
Hell shrink appall'd, and yield his prey,
His captives hail the Gospel day,
And spring to burst their chains.

VII.

Touch with a living coal, O LORD!
Their lips, who shall proclaim thy word;
Fill them with zeal divine:
Give them to glory in thy cross,
To meet with joy, reproach, and loss,
And seek no praise but thine.

VIII.

While earth and hell shall rage in vain,
Here let thy gospel firm remain,
Thro' time's remotest days.
Thine is the pow'r, the work is thine;
And O! let all to thee assign
The glory and the praise.

HYMN.

I.

Dear Saviour! at thy feet we bow,
  Thy servants poor, thy flock behold;
Our only Lord, our shepherd thou,
  Govern and keep us in thy fold:
Keep us, O keep us near thy feet—
That peaceful—that secure retreat.

II.

More of thyself—still more reveal;
  Nor let us after idols stray:
But still thy nearer presence feel,
  Still walk in thee, our living way:
With fixed eye, attentive ear,
To catch thy looks, thy voice to hear.

III.

Weary, distress'd, assaulted, poor,
  Where, but to thee, should such apply?
Thou art for them a boundless store
  Of blessings in variety:
Their joy, their shelter, strength, and rest;
Be thou but ours, and we are bless'd.

IV.

We thank thee for thy love, thy pow'r,
  We thank thee for thy won'drous grace:
Bring us, in thine appointed hour,
  To see unveil'd thy glorious face.
Then, then, from sin, from sorrow free,
More loudly shall we sing to thee.

END OF VOL. II.

G. H. Davidson, Printer,
Tudor Street, New Bridge Street, Blackfriars.

[The following articles did not come under my observation in time to be inserted in their suitable places—I add them here, as every way worthy of preservation.—Ed.]

TO THE EDITOR

OF

THE HIBERNIAN EVANGELICAL MAGAZINE,

1803.

Mr. Editor,—I have never before willingly allowed my name (insignificant as it is) to appear in any publication such as yours; because I would not wish to be thought answerable for the sentiments of a production so miscellaneous, and conducted by such a variety of hands. But a particular circumstance leads me, at present, to beg a place for the following in your pages.

Some days ago I got—and have this evening read a pamphlet, entitled, "Human Nature Vindicated, with a Short View of the Conduct of Providence towards Mankind," &c. I beg leave to announce, through the medium of your Magazine, my intention of examining, at a future day, that publication. And I do so, because from my engagement with another antagonist (Mr. Knox), it is possible that so long time may elapse before I reply to it, as might lead the Author to suppose I had no intention of giving it an answer.

I differ from some who have spoken to me concerning that pamphlet. The writer seems to me to be a sensible thinking man, who comes forward with tolerable plainness to tell what he believes. That, to be sure, is very opposite to what the Bible declares; and various parts of it are very inconsistent with each other. But I really think he has made as much of his side of the question as any man else. And after having read various doctrinal productions of Arminians, and Pelagians, and Arians, and Socinians, I seriously declare that I think his pamphlet as good as any of them; and, as comprising in a small compass the leading errors of most of them, I consider it deserving of a reply—which, in one form or another, I mean to give it, if my life be spared. Meanwhile your readers may take the essence of his system (as far as he has any) in the words of Cowper, the poet: and it is a system very generally adopted, but contrary alike to the divine justice and the divine mercy, as those attributes are revealed in the Scriptures:

I plant my foot upon this ground of trust,
And silence every fear with—God is just;
But if perchance, on some dull drizzling day,
A thought intrude that says, or seems to say,
If thus th' important cause is to be tried,
Suppose the beam should dip on the wrong side;
I soon recover from those needless frights,
And, God is merciful—sets all to rights.
Thus, between justice, as my prime support,
And mercy fled to as the last resort,
I glide and steal along with heaven in view,
And—pardon me—the bottle stands with you.

COWPER'S HOPE.

If the vindicator of human nature should happen to see this letter, I would recommend to his serious consideration a question, which has occurred to me upon a passage in his work. He says (p. 20,) that Paul, "when a blasphemer and a persecutor, was not *a bad man*." Well, but—good a kind of thing as human nature is—I suppose the writer will acknowledge that there are *some bad men* in the world. Now, I wish him to consider whether there is any hope for *such*; and if there be, what it is. *I* am sure the Gospel which Paul preached, held out a blessed hope to the worst of men, in the testimony—that "Jesus Christ came into the world to save sinners," and that "whosoever believeth in Him shall be saved." Indeed, *I* have been long accustomed to consider the Apostle himself as an *instance* of the greatness of that salvation. But no matter for the present: let the writer *suppose* some *bad men*, in whose case this blessed hope should be realized; and let him consider how he will state "the conduct of Providence,"— in such an instance.

I wish him in the first place to examine this question, in its various bearings, for himself; and if he afterwards take up his pen upon the subject, I shall be well pleased to see his thoughts on it given to the public, as an Appendix to his—"Views of the Conduct of Providence"—towards sinners that are—*not bad men*.

I am, Sir,

Yours, &c.

"*The light of the body is the eye; if therefore thine eye be single, thy whole body shall be full of light.* But if thine eye be evil, *thy whole body shall be full of darkness.*"—Mat. vi. 22, 23.

These words are closely connected with the preceding admonition against laying up for ourselves treasures upon earth, and with the following declaration of the impossibility of serving both God and Mammon.

The expression "an evil eye" occurs frequently in Scripture; and commonly imports a *grudging* mind, opposed to *bountiful* kindness. See Matt. xx. 15. Deut. xv. 9. Prov. xxii. 6. And so the lust of the *eyes*, in 1 John ii. 16, appears specially to mean the love of riches, or covetousness. But in the present passage, I think the Lord uses the figurative term *eye* in a more extended sense, for that which the mind *looks at as good and desirable*. And in this sense, if our *eye* be *evil*—if that which we view as good be emptiness and vanity—we are full of darkness. But if we be given to see, and be kept in the discernment of the "One thing" that is good indeed—substantially and completely good—so as to include in it *all the blessedness* that a sinner ever can need, thus our whole body shall be full of light. And whenever it is otherwise with a disciple, it is because he has so imperfectly *in view* that one glorious object; and is therefore lusting after *other* things, (often of a very religious kind) and not *satisfied* with the revealed *goodness* of the Lord to the evil and unthankful.

THE END.

London: G. H. Davidson, Printer,
Tudor Street, New Bridge Street, Blackfriars.

CPSIA information can be obtained at www.ICGtesting.com
Printed in the USA
LVOW131613130312

272907LV00005B/119/P

9 781144 725240